Cloud Computing Security

The book provides a fundamental exploration of cloud security, addressing the growing risks associated with modern cloud environments. It combines foundational theory with hands-on applications, equipping readers with the knowledge and tools needed to secure cloud platforms. Topics include cloud attack vectors, defense mechanisms, implementation challenges, and real-world case studies of major cloud service providers. Practical exercises and end-of-chapter questions reinforce key concepts, making this an essential resource. Designed for undergraduate and postgraduate students in computer science and cybersecurity, this book serves as a vital guide to securing cloud infrastructures and ensuring data integrity in a rapidly evolving technological landscape.

- Covers cloud security concepts, attack types, and defense mechanisms
- Includes cloud security tools, real-world case studies, and hands-on projects
- Discusses risk mitigation techniques and security best practices for cloud environments
- Examines real-world obstacles and solutions in cloud security adoption
- Analyzes major cloud service providers and their security models

Cloud Computing Security

Strategies and Best Practices

Neha Agrawal
Rohit Kumar
Shashikala Tapaswi

CRC Press
Taylor & Francis Group
Boca Raton London New York

CRC Press is an imprint of the
Taylor & Francis Group, an **informa** business
A CHAPMAN & HALL BOOK

First edition published 2026
by CRC Press
2385 NW Executive Center Drive, Suite 320, Boca Raton FL 33431

and by CRC Press
4 Park Square, Milton Park, Abingdon, Oxon, OX14 4RN

CRC Press is an imprint of Taylor & Francis Group, LLC

Access the Support Material (Resource Centre): \\EUW1FS01\bks_digipub\COMPANION_WEBSITE_HANDOVERS\EDITORIAL\

ISBN: 978-1-032-83415-3 (hbk)
ISBN: 978-1-032-84009-3 (pbk)
ISBN: 978-1-003-51077-2 (ebk)

DOI: 10.1201/9781003510772

Typeset in Times
by SPi Technologies India Pvt Ltd (Straive)

Contents

Preface

Cloud computing is a prominent enabling technology offering its support for varieties of services. Numerous companies have started to offer cloud services and are defining their way of functioning. A cloud deployment may be of a particular type, ideally suited for specific needs. However, the design and deployment of any cloud environment tries to serve its intended purpose with minimum possible chances of any security breach. Nonetheless, the possibilities and presence of the security concerns can't be denied. Thus, it becomes a prominent requirement to understand the concepts of security, possible loopholes, their countermeasures, etc. In this textbook, the basic concepts of cloud computing are discussed followed by their security aspects. The security issues at each layer of cloud computing are explored. Then the different types of attacks with their defense mechanisms are presented. The discussion of various tools such as attack tools, traffic monitoring, analysis tools, and defense tools is also provided. The advanced related topics and the current research challenges are also given in this textbook.

Additionally, the role of cloud computing in other domains has also become prevalent over the period of time. Its invaluable benefits urge for the usage of cloud services offering hassle-free operational and functional management. Hence, cloud and associated technologies have also become an active domain of research. Numerous researchers are exploring the fine aspects of cloud-related solutions and respective security issues.

To cope up with the latest practical issues of any technology, it's very important to test and verify its performance in a real-time environment. Nonetheless, it's not practically feasible to deploy a real environment for each technology. Huge infrastructure-based technologies such as public clouds need to be understood and evaluated using some simulated and/or emulated environments. In addition to this, the discussion of some real-time case studies helps to develop a deeper understanding of the subject matter.

AIM AND SCOPE OF THE BOOK

The aim of this textbook is to provide a comprehensive and up-to-date resource that delves into the critical aspects of security within the context of cloud computing. The textbook aims to equip readers with the knowledge and understanding needed to address the unique security challenges and opportunities presented by cloud-based technologies. By presenting a holistic view of cloud computing security, the textbook intends to empower professionals, researchers, students, and decision-makers to make informed choices and implement robust security measures to protect data, applications, and infrastructure in cloud environments.

Scope: The textbook's scope covers a wide range of topics related to cloud computing security, including but not limited to:

- Fundamentals of Cloud Computing
- Cloud Security Architecture

- Threats and Vulnerabilities
- Security Best Practices
- Cloud Security Management
- Emerging Trends and Technologies
- Future Challenges and Opportunities

Throughout the textbook, practical examples, case studies, and hands-on exercises are included to reinforce the concepts and enable readers to apply the knowledge gained. The scope of the textbook aims to be accessible to both beginners and experienced professionals interested in enhancing their expertise in cloud computing security.

Author Biography

Neha Agrawal is currently working as an Assistant Professor in the Department of Computer Science and Engineering at the Indian Institute of Information Technology (IIIT) Sri City, Chittoor, AP, India. She received her Ph.D. degree from Atal Bihari Vajpayee – Indian Institute of Information Technology and Management (ABV-IIITM), Gwalior, Madhya Pradesh, India. She completed her M.Tech. in Computer Science and Engineering with a specialization in Information Security from ABV-IIITM, Gwalior and her B.E. in Information Technology from Madhav Institute of Technology and Science, Gwalior. She is a Senior Member of IEEE and Life Member of the International Association of Engineers (IAENG) and the Internet Society (ISOC). She was a Visiting Research Scholar at Anglia Ruskin University, Chelmsford, United Kingdom. She has published many research papers in reputed journals/conferences including *IEEE Communications Surveys and Tutorials*. She is also an active reviewer of many SCI-indexed journals. Her primary research interests are Cloud Computing Security, Software-Defined Networking, Cyber Security, Fog/Edge Computing, and Industry 4.0. She has been teaching various subjects across Institute Core, Institute Elective, Program Core, and Specialization Elective categories including C Programming, Design and Analysis of Algorithms, Computer Architecture, Cloud Computing, Network and Data Security, Introduction to Cyber Security, Software Defined Networks, etc. Her publications can be accessed using the link below.

https://scholar.google.com/citations?user=EqJapj4AAAAJ&hl=en

Rohit Kumar is currently working as an Assistant Professor in the Department of Engineering Sciences at the Atal Bihari Vajpayee – Indian Institute of Information Technology and Management (ABV-IIITM), Gwalior, Madhya Pradesh, India. He completed his Ph.D. in Computer Science and Engineering from Dr. Shyama Prasad Mukherjee International Institute of Information Technology, Naya Raipur (DSPM-IIITNR), India, and his M.Tech. from ABV-IIITM, Gwalior, India. He is a Senior Member of IEEE, and Life Member of the Computer Society of India (CSI-INDIA) and the Indian Society for Technical Education (ISTE). His current research interests include Cyber Physical Systems, Software Defined Networking, Internet of Things, and Cloud Computing networks. He has published some of his research works in reputed international conferences and SCI/SCIE-indexed journals including IEEE International Conference on Advanced Networks and Telecommunications Systems (IEEE ANTS), International Conference on COMmunication Systems & NETworkS (COMSNETS), *IEEE Transactions on Network and Service Management*, *IEEE Systems Journal*, *Computer Science Review*, *Computer Networks*, etc., respectively. In addition to this, he has been the best paper recipient for his work in IEEE ANTS-2019. He has been teaching many subjects such as Network Security, System Security and Management, Software and Programming in IoT, Industrial IoT, etc.

Shashikala Tapaswi is a Professor (HAG) in Atal Bihari Vajpayee – Indian Institute of Information Technology and Management, Gwalior, Madhya Pradesh, India. She received her Ph.D. degree from Indian Institute of Technology (IIT) Roorkee. She has 30+ years of professional experience. Her primary research areas are Computer Networks, Network Security, Mobile Adhoc Networks, Artificial Intelligence, Neural Network, Fuzzy Logic, Digital Image Processing, and Cloud Computing. She has been teaching many subjects such as Cloud Computing, Malware Analysis, Computer Networks, Operating System, etc.

1 Introduction to Cloud Computing

1.1 WHAT IS CLOUD COMPUTING?

Few years back, significant research efforts were put into transforming computing into a model where services can be commoditized and delivered similar to utilities such as electricity, water, gas, etc. Such a model allows the users to use the services anytime, anywhere without human intervention. This model was introduced as Cloud Computing which is the most emerging computing paradigm and turns the computing utilities into reality [1].

There are numerous factors working as a motivational force to shift from the traditional working environment to the cloud environment. Some of the major reasons are as follows:

- A cloud solution is supposed to be flexible in nature. Thus, it should allow ease of scalability in terms of users, services, communication technologies, etc.
- The off-site storage of personal and professional data may raise the issues of security and privacy. However, the inherent complex sophisticated design and highly secure access mechanisms assure the users.
- The large degree of redundant information nodes denies the possibilities of any information loss. In this way, the cloud system becomes a reliable place to store and access the information.
- The increasingly popular virtualization platforms help to develop low-cost working environments. Thus, the cloud solutions and their support to various virtualization technologies make it really easy to set up new IT ventures without needing any large IT infrastructure.
- Additionally, the utility computing-based model of cloud computing helps it to evolve like a very affordable technology. The pay-per-use mechanism-based model allows almost every IT user to have the latest IT solutions at a very reasonable and bearable service cost.
- Other than the above-mentioned reasons, multiple other reasons such as wide support to various IT devices, ease of management, access from anywhere, assured service-level agreements, etc., do exist. All these factors make it a very easy choice to prefer cloud-based services and solutions over other traditional alternatives.

DOI: 10.1201/9781003510772-1

1.1.1 Cloud Computing and Its Definitions

Cloud computing represents a burgeoning technological domain aimed at mitigating maintenance and management expenses through the migration of robust computing infrastructures to the Internet. By leveraging cloud computing, users gain seamless access to resources and applications via the Internet, thereby transforming traditional desktop computing into utility-oriented computing. This paradigm shift involves the centralization of vast data repositories across geographically dispersed data centers.

Organizations and industries increasingly favor cloud computing for its on-demand self-service capabilities and adaptable pay-as-you-go business models, diverging from traditional deployment-centric approaches. Figure 1.1 illustrates the foundational components of the cloud environment. Various authoritative definitions of cloud computing underscore its multifaceted nature and strategic significance in contemporary IT landscapes.

Peter Mell and Tim Grance of the National Institute of Standards and Technology (NIST) [2] defined cloud computing as: *Cloud computing is a model for enabling convenient, on-demand network access to a shared pool of configurable and reliable computing resources (e.g., networks, servers, storage, applications, services) that can be rapidly provisioned and released with minimal consumer management effort or service provider interaction.*

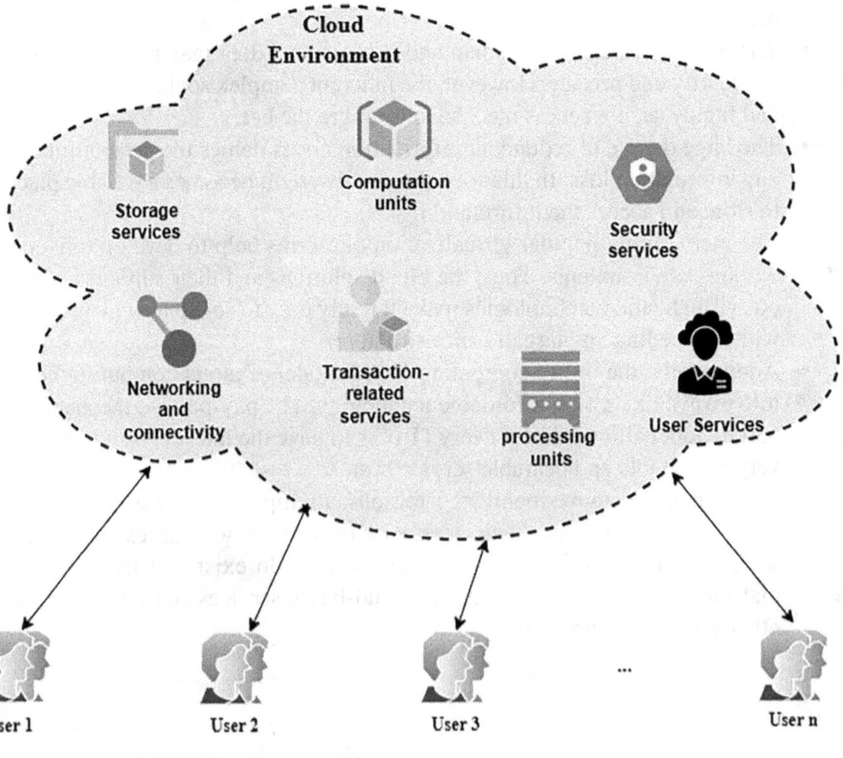

FIGURE 1.1 The basic cloud environment.

TABLE 1.1
Different Layers of Cloud Computing Architecture

Layer	Description
Front-End	The client-side application that interacts with the cloud (e.g., web browser, mobile app) to access cloud services.
Back-End	The cloud infrastructure, including servers, storage, and network resources, that manages and delivers the cloud services.
Cloud Service Layer	A layer that includes the service models (IaaS, PaaS, SaaS, etc.) and APIs enabling developers to interact with the cloud infrastructure.
Network	The communication and connectivity between the front-end and back-end, ensuring the transfer of data and requests.

Khorshed et al. [3] defined cloud computing as: *Cloud computing is defined as a system where the resources of large data centers are shared among the users using the virtualization technology*. Cloud computing defined by Armbrust et al. [4] as: *Cloud computing refers to both the applications delivered as services over the Internet, and the hardware and system software in the data centers that provide those services*. The definition of cloud computing given by Buyya et al. [5] is: *A cloud is a type of parallel and distributed system consisting of a collection of interconnected and virtualized computers that are dynamically provisioned and presented as one or more unified computing resources based on service-level agreements established through negotiation between the service provider and consumers*.

A general cloud computing architecture has different layers, as discussed in Table 1.1.

1.2 HISTORY AND ORIGIN OF CLOUD COMPUTING

In early 1993, the term "Cloud" emerged to describe platforms for distributed computing, initially employed by Apple spin-off General Magic and AT&T in reference to their Telescript and PersonaLink technologies [6]. The timeline detailing significant events in the evolution of cloud computing is presented in Figure 1.2.

The phrase "Cloud Computing" first appeared in 1996, notably documented in an internal Compaq memorandum [7]. The term "Cloud" was chosen metaphorically to symbolize the Internet, evoking its expansive and interconnected nature. As early as 1977 in ARPANET [8] and 1981 in CSNET [9], the cloud icon visually represented networks of interconnected computing devices.

The advent of "Cloud Computing" gained significant prominence in 2006 with Amazon.com's launch of Elastic Compute Cloud (EC2) [10]. Subsequently, pivotal advancements over the past two decades have shaped the landscape of this technology.

- In April 2008, Google introduced the beta version of Google App Engine [11]. Concurrently, NASA's OpenNebula emerged as the inaugural open-source software for deploying private and hybrid clouds, and facilitating cloud federation, marking a milestone in early 2008 [12].

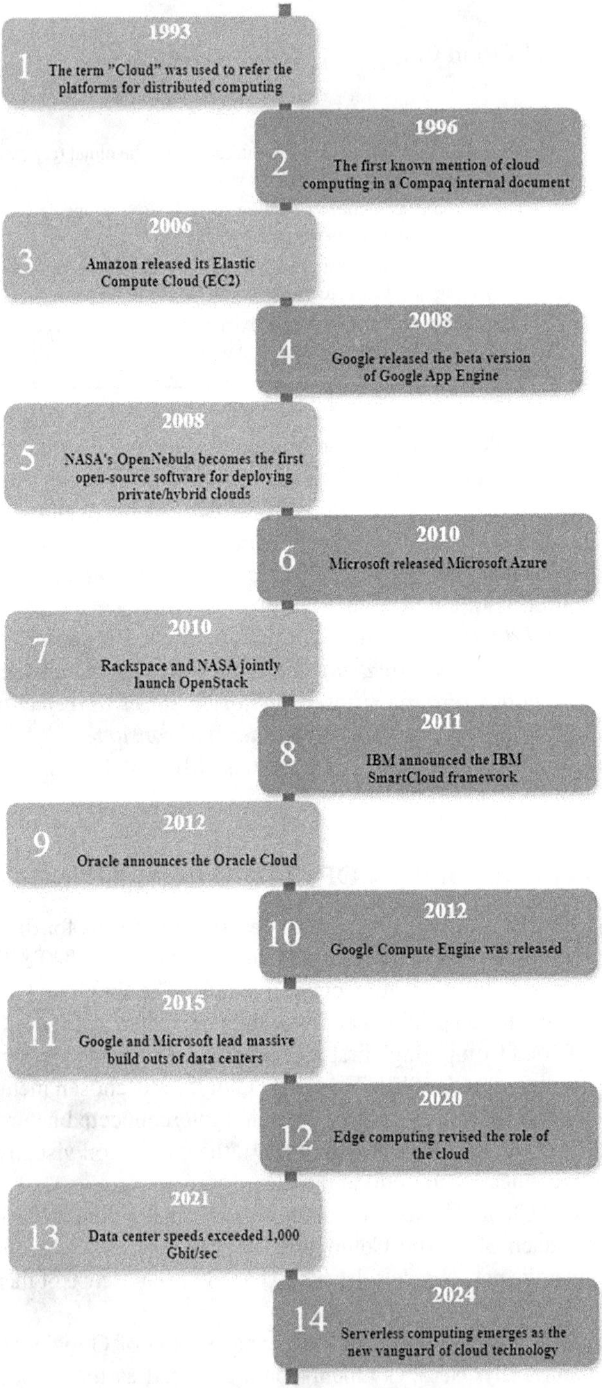

FIGURE 1.2 The timeline of major cloud computing related events.

- The U.S. National Science Foundation initiated the Cluster Exploratory program in 2008 to facilitate academic research utilizing Google-IBM cluster technology for large-scale data analysis [13,14].
- Microsoft unveiled Microsoft Azure in February 2010, following its announcement in October 2008 [15]. In July 2010, Rackspace Hosting and NASA collaborated on OpenStack, an open-source cloud platform, which alongside Ganeti, CloudStack, and OpenNebula garnered significant community interest [16].
- IBM introduced the IBM SmartCloud framework on March 1, 2011, to bolster the Smarter Planet initiative [17], while Oracle announced its comprehensive Oracle Cloud offering on June 7, 2012, encompassing SaaS, PaaS, and IaaS solutions [18,19].
- Google Compute Engine debuted in May 2012 and attained general availability in December 2013 [20]. Docker's introduction of open-source container software in 2013 revolutionized application deployment practices.
- Major investments in data center infrastructure by Google, Microsoft, Huawei, Tencent, and Alibaba in subsequent years underscored the burgeoning scale of cloud operations globally [21,22].
- Technological advancements such as the adoption of 400 Gbps data speeds and Silicon photonics in data center networking architectures, commencing in 2018, reflect ongoing efforts to enhance performance and efficiency [21].
- By 2024, forecasts by Global Data project cloud services (SaaS, PaaS, and IaaS) expenditure to surpass $429 billion, underscoring the pivotal role of cloud computing in modern economies [21].

1.3 CORE TECHNOLOGIES

Cloud computing amalgamates various technological advantages with the primary objective of minimizing maintenance costs and enabling users to concentrate on their core business activities. At its core, cloud computing leverages virtualization, a pivotal technology that partitions a physical machine into multiple virtual machines, each independently operable and manageable to execute diverse computing tasks. This book will delve into the foundational elements of cloud computing comprehensively, with Table 1.2 summarizing key technologies, while Figure 1.3 delineates the core technologies underpinning cloud computing.

1.4 CLOUD COMPUTING CHARACTERISTICS

In 2009, a consortium of organizations including IBM, Intel, and Google collaborated to formulate the Open Cloud Manifesto, which aimed to propose guidelines for the deployment of cloud computing services. The "Open Cloud Manifesto" [23] delineates cloud computing as possessing distinct characteristics and offering various value propositions. Specifically, the manifesto defines:

1. The capability to dynamically scale and provision computing resources in a cost-effective manner.

TABLE 1.2
Summary of the Core Technologies of Cloud Computing

Technology	Description	Key Benefits	Use Cases	Key Technologies	Challenges
Distributed Computing	Distributed computing involves multiple computers working together to form a unified system, improving performance and efficiency.	• Enhanced performance and scalability • Fault tolerance • Efficient resource utilization	• Large-scale data processing • Cloud computing • Big Data analysis	Cloud platforms, Distributed file systems	• Managing data consistency • Security concerns • Complex system management
Client-Server Computing	A framework where clients request services from servers, which provide resources and data in response.	• Improved resource management • Centralized control • Scalability	• Web applications • Database access • Enterprise applications	HTTP, TCP/IP, REST APIs, Web servers	• Server overload • Single point of failure • Network latency
Cluster Computing	A collection of homogeneous computers that work together to perform computational tasks, typically connected within a single location.	• High performance • Fault tolerance • Parallel task execution	• Scientific simulations • Rendering farms • High-performance computing (HPC)	HPC systems, Interconnects, Parallel computing	• Scalability limitations • Hardware failure risks • Complex cluster management
Grid Computing	Multiple geographically dispersed clusters interconnected to share resources, providing a collective computing power for complex tasks.	• Efficient resource utilization • Large-scale computing power • Scalability across locations	• Large-scale scientific research • Weather forecasting • Computational chemistry • Distributed storage	Grid middleware (e.g., Globus), Virtualization	• Security risks across networks • Data synchronization • Bandwidth and latency issues
Utility Computing	On-demand access to computing resources, billed like utilities, allowing flexible scaling without maintaining dedicated infrastructure.	• Cost-effective • Scalability • Pay-as-you-go model • Flexibility	• Cloud services (e.g., AWS, Azure) • Hosting services • Backup and disaster recovery systems	Virtualization, Cloud services, On-demand billing	• Dependence on service providers • Data privacy concerns • Vendor lock-in

Autonomic Computing	Self-managing systems that automatically adjust to changing conditions, reducing the need for human intervention.	• Reduced manual intervention • Proactive resource management • Increased reliability and efficiency	• Data center management • Cloud resource optimization • Network traffic management	AI, Machine learning, Monitoring tools, Feedback systems	• Implementation complexity • Ensuring adaptability • Balancing automation with control
Service-oriented Architecture (SOA)	A design where services interact to deliver specific functionalities, promoting interoperability and reusability.	• Improved agility • Reusability of components • Interoperability between platforms • Easier integration with existing systems	• Web services • Business process automation • Cross-platform data sharing	SOAP, REST, WSDL, Web services frameworks	• Service orchestration complexity • Dependency management • Performance overhead due to service communication overhead

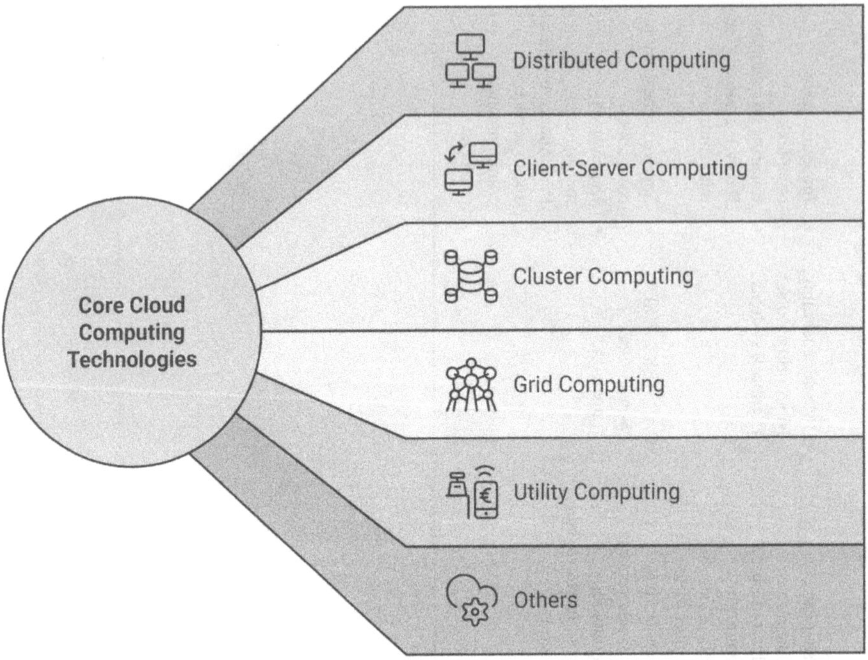

FIGURE 1.3 Core cloud computing technologies.

2. The empowerment of consumers (whether end users, organizations, or IT personnel) to leverage these resources without necessitating management of the underlying technological intricacies.
3. The architecture of the cloud can be categorized as private (operating within an organization's internal network) or public (accessible via the Internet).

Broadly, the cloud computing characteristics can be divided into two groups, namely Essential and Common. The major cloud computing characteristics are detailed in Figure 1.4.

1.4.1 Essential Characteristics

According to the National Institute of Standards and Technology (NIST) [2], the cloud model encompasses five fundamental characteristics as follows:

1. **On-demand self-service**: This feature empowers cloud users to independently provision computing resources such as server time and network storage, without requiring human interaction with the cloud service provider.
2. **Broad network access**: Cloud computing resources are accessible over the network and can be accessed from a variety of devices including PCs, tablets, smartphones, and other devices capable of connecting to the Internet.

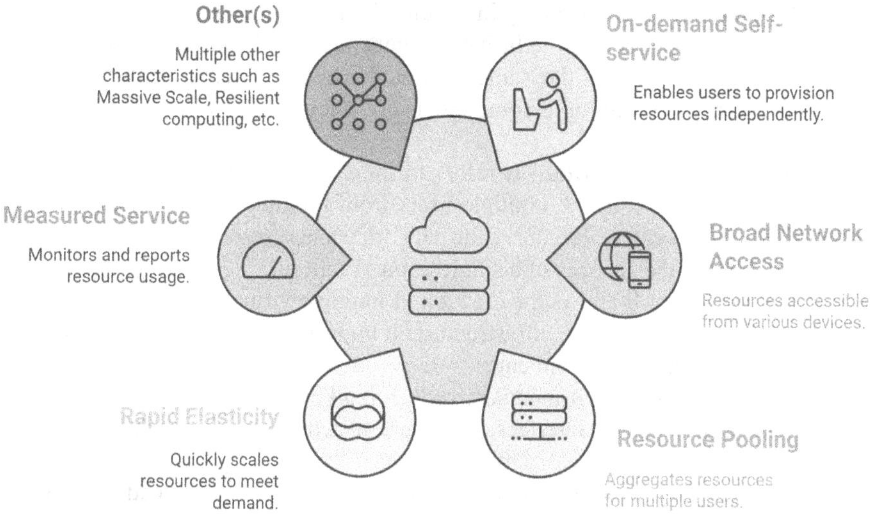

FIGURE 1.4 Cloud computing characteristics.

3. **Resource pooling**: Cloud providers aggregate computing resources to serve multiple consumers in a multi-tenant model. This pooling allows resources to be dynamically assigned and reassigned according to consumer demand, achieving economies of scale and meeting varying workloads.
4. **Rapid elasticity**: The cloud's capability to rapidly and elastically expand or reduce resources allows it to quickly scale up or down provisioning to meet the consumer's requirements. This scaling is often automatic, presenting users with an illusion of unlimited resources available on-demand and with a pay-as-you-go model.
5. **Measured service**: Cloud systems efficiently manage resource utilization by employing metering capabilities tailored to different service types such as storage, processing, bandwidth, and user accounts. This allows for monitoring, control, and transparent reporting of resource usage, benefiting both service providers and consumers.

1.4.2 Common Characteristics

Besides the essential characteristics, cloud computing also provides other common characteristics which are as follows:

1. **Massive scale**: Cloud computing involves massive scale of geographically distributed data centers implemented using commodity hardware. These massive-scale data centers are capable of satisfying varying users' demands. The real-time processing of big-data is the major requirement.
2. **Resilient computing**: Due to the massive scale feature, the redundant implementation of IT resources is performed across multiple locations. This feature allows the cloud to rebuild its infrastructure quickly in case of failure. Thus, the overall service downtime is reduced.

3. **Homogeneity**: Homogeneity in the cloud refers to the fact that everything is from the same vendor. In a homogeneous cloud, the entire software stack is provided by the same vendor. However, heterogeneous clouds also exist where multiple components are integrated from more than one vendor.
4. **Geographic distribution**: It refers to the cloud computing services and resources offered to the multiple users from multiple geographically distributed data centers. It reduces the network latency, response time, etc., and also reduces the chances of a single point of failure.
5. **Virtualization**: It allows the creation of multiple virtual instances over the same physical hardware infrastructure. It improves resource utilization in a cloud computing environment.
6. **Service orientation**: It modularizes the cloud business services and establishes well-designed interfaces to assure that these services will work in different situations.
7. **Advanced security**: Cloud computing offers several advanced security features such as intrusion detection systems with event logging, advanced perimeter firewall, data-at-rest encryption, etc.

1.5 CLOUD SERVICE DELIVERY MODELS

Cloud service providers deliver their services under the following models as highlighted in Figure 1.5.

1.5.1 Infrastructure-as-a-Service (IaaS)

Cloud Infrastructure-as-a-Service (IaaS) delivers essential computing resources including processing power, network capabilities, storage solutions, and other fundamental components to users via the Internet. These resources are provisioned using virtualization technology, enabling users to deploy and manage their operating systems and software applications on top of the cloud infrastructure. Leading IaaS providers such as Google Compute Engine (GCE), Amazon Web Services (AWS), Microsoft Azure, and Rackspace offer scalable and flexible solutions tailored to meet diverse computing needs across various industries.

1.5.2 Platform-as-a-Service (PaaS)

Platform-as-a-Service (PaaS) furnishes users with computing platforms such as operating systems and integrated development environments (IDEs) where they can manage and execute their applications. Unlike IaaS, PaaS users do not have direct control over the underlying infrastructure but retain control over the applications they deploy. Major PaaS providers, including Microsoft Azure, AWS Elastic Beanstalk, Force.com, and Google App Engine, offer robust platforms tailored for application development and deployment.

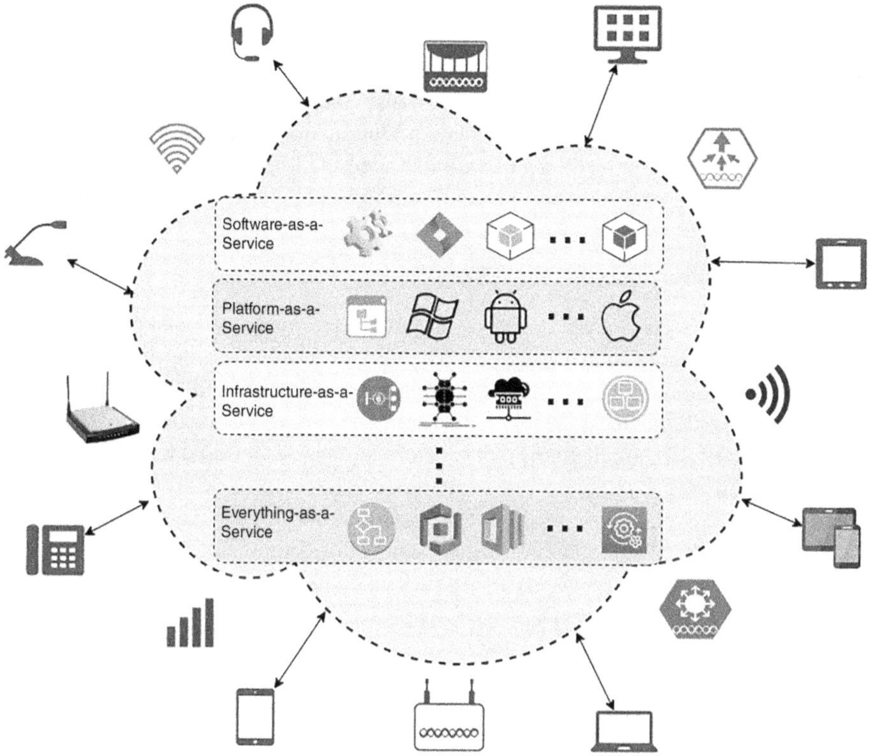

FIGURE 1.5 Cloud computing service delivery models.

1.5.3 Software-as-a-Service (SaaS)

Software-as-a-Service (SaaS) allows users to access applications hosted by a cloud service provider (CSP) via a thin client interface like a web browser. Users lack control over both the underlying cloud infrastructure and the applications themselves, focusing instead on utilizing the applications and paying based on usage. Leading SaaS vendors, such as Google Apps, Salesforce.com, DropBox, and Microsoft Office 365, offer a wide array of applications from productivity tools to enterprise software solutions.

1.5.4 Network-as-a-Service (NaaS)

Network-as-a-Service (NaaS) provides secure, direct access to network infrastructure through virtualized network services. Management and maintenance of network services are handled by the network service providers, allowing clients to leverage scalable network solutions without the burden of infrastructure management.

1.5.5 Security-as-a-Service (SECaaS)

Security-as-a-Service (SECaaS) delivers cybersecurity services through a subscription model, relieving organizations of in-house security responsibilities. SECaaS scales security measures according to demand fluctuations and reduces maintenance costs. Services encompassed by SECaaS include email security, web security, continuous monitoring, and intrusion prevention, offered by various cloud providers.

1.5.6 Everything-as-a-Service (XaaS)

Everything-as-a-Service (XaaS) defines the extensive range of tools, products, and technologies delivered to end-users via the Internet, encompassing the entire spectrum of cloud computing services. XaaS represents a flexible and scalable approach to meeting diverse business needs, with examples ranging from infrastructure and platforms to software applications and specialized services tailored to specific industries and functions.

The comparative analysis of the different Cloud Service Delivery Models (IaaS, PaaS, SaaS, NaaS, SECaaS, and XaaS) is provided in Table 1.3.

1.6 CLOUD DEPLOYMENT MODELS

Cloud computing infrastructure deployment models are categorized into private, public, hybrid, or community cloud models based on specific requirements, as illustrated in Figure 1.6. Each model is described as follows.

1.6.1 Public Cloud

The physical infrastructure of the public cloud is owned and managed by the Cloud Service Provider (CSP) and is accessible to the general public or a broad group of organizations. This type of cloud is situated off-site from the users' premises. Resources in the public cloud are shared among multiple users, who compensate the CSP based on their usage of the services.

1.6.2 Private Cloud

The private cloud infrastructure is exclusively operated and managed for a single private organization. Access to services within the private cloud is restricted solely to this organization and not extended to external users. Ownership of the physical infrastructure may or may not lie with the organization and could be situated either on-site or off-site. Management of the private cloud may be undertaken internally by the organization or outsourced to a third party.

1.6.3 Community Cloud

The community cloud infrastructure is shared among multiple organizations and users within a specific community. This community typically shares common interests such as mission objectives, security requirements, policies, or jurisdictional

TABLE 1.3
Common Service Models of Cloud Computing

Model	Control	Target Users	Customization	Examples	Scalability	Cost Model
IaaS	Full control over resources	IT teams, developers, businesses	Highly customizable	AWS, Google Cloud, Azure	Highly scalable	Pay-as-you-go.
PaaS	Control over applications only	Developers and businesses	Moderate customization	AWS Elastic Beanstalk, Azure, GAE	Scalable within platform	Usage-based
SaaS	No control over infrastructure or apps	End-users for productivity, collaboration	Limited customization	Google Apps, Microsoft Office 365	Limited scaling per app	Subscription-based
NaaS	Control over network usage	Organizations needing network services	Moderate customization.	AWS Direct Connect, Google Interconnect	Scalable network solutions	Pay-as-you-go or subscription
SECaaS	Minimal control, managed by provider	Organizations needing cybersecurity	Customizable security features.	McAfee, Cloudflare, Zscaler	Scalable security services	Subscription-based
XaaS	Limited control, flexible services	Businesses with varied needs	Highly customizable.	AWS, Microsoft Azure, Salesforce	Scalable across services	Flexible, usage-based

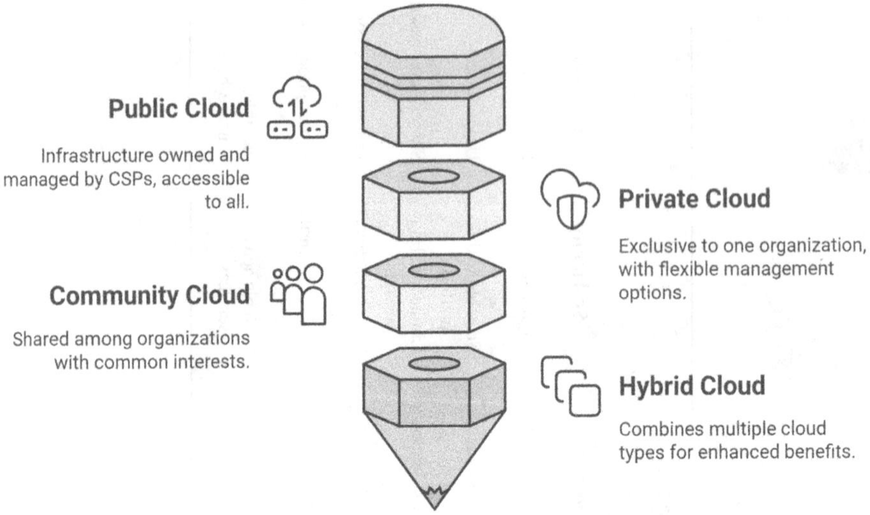

FIGURE 1.6 Cloud computing deployment models.

considerations. The management of a community cloud can be administered by any participating organization or entrusted to a third-party provider. The physical infrastructure of the community cloud may be located either on-premises or off-premises.

1.6.4 Hybrid Cloud

A hybrid cloud environment integrates two or more types of clouds, such as private, community, or public clouds. This configuration leverages the strengths of each cloud type, offering significant advantages including scalability, flexibility, cost efficiency, and enhanced security. Organizations utilizing a hybrid cloud can allocate sensitive workloads to dedicated hardware within the private or community cloud, while less-sensitive workloads can be hosted on public cloud infrastructure.

These models vary in terms of ownership, accessibility, and management responsibilities, etc. The comparative analysis of each model is provided in the form of Table 1.4.

1.7 KEY TECHNOLOGIES

In the operational framework of the cloud environment, several pivotal technologies synergistically drive the comprehensive suite of services. Notably elucidated in Figure 1.7, a selection of these instrumental technologies is expounded upon below.

1.7.1 Virtualization Technology

Central to the architecture of cloud computing is virtualization, representing the foundational technology that underpins its infrastructure. Virtualization achieves the abstraction of essential computing components, encompassing hardware, storage,

TABLE 1.4
Comparative Analysis of Different Cloud Deployment Models

Feature	Public Cloud	Private Cloud	Community Cloud	Hybrid Cloud
Ownership	Cloud Service Provider (CSP)	Single organization	Multiple organizations	Combination of multiple clouds
Management	Managed by CSP	Managed by organization or third-party	Managed by community or third-party	Managed internally and externally
Access	Open to public or broad organizations	Exclusive to one organization	Shared by specific community	Flexible, with dynamic workload allocation
Security	Lower (shared resources)	High (dedicated resources)	Moderate (shared but controlled)	Flexible (based on workload sensitivity)
Cost	Pay-per-use, low upfront cost	High initial investment, ongoing costs	Shared cost among community members	Variable, based on resource usage
Scalability	High (on-demand)	Limited by internal resources	Moderate (depends on community size)	Very high (leverages multiple clouds)

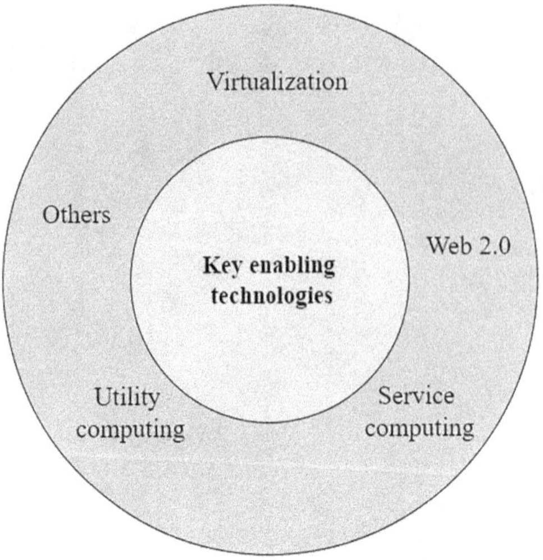

FIGURE 1.7 Cloud computing key enabling technologies.

networking, and runtime environments. This transformative technology facilitates the creation of distinct computing environments known as virtual machines (VMs), each simulating interfaces tailored to guest requirements. The predominant manifestation of virtualization is encapsulated in "Hardware Virtualization," wherein the hardware interface is simulated to conform to the expectations of the operating system. This capability enables disparate software stacks to coexist on shared hardware infrastructure, segregating their operations into discrete VM instances that operate independently of one another.

1.7.2 Web 2.0

Fundamentally rooted in cloud computing, the delivery of services is intrinsically intertwined with the Web, a multifaceted amalgamation of technologies and services facilitating interactive information sharing, collaborative application composition, and user-centered design. This evolutionary paradigm shift has propelled the Web into the dynamic platform recognized as Web 2.0. At its core, Web 2.0 integrates an array of technologies including Extensible Markup Language (XML), Asynchronous JavaScript and XML (AJAX), and others, thereby enriching user experiences through heightened flexibility and interactivity within web pages. Prominent examples of applications harnessing Web 2.0 capabilities include Google Maps, Facebook, Twitter, Flickr, YouTube, among others.

1.7.3 Service-oriented Computing

Integral to the landscape of cloud computing, Service-oriented Computing (SOC) embodies a pivotal technology that facilitates the agile development of cost-effective, interoperable, and flexible systems and applications. At its essence, SOC revolves around services as the primary building blocks for system and application development. Each service functions as a self-describing component capable of executing specific tasks, leveraging network-accessible protocols to expose its functionalities.

SOC introduces two seminal concepts: Quality of Service (QoS) and Software-as-a-Service (SaaS). QoS serves as a metric to gauge system performance and behavior across functional and non-functional attributes such as availability, reliability, scalability, and response time. This metric is formalized through Service Level Agreements (SLAs), which stipulate minimum quality benchmarks that must be upheld during service interactions.

On the other hand, Software-as-a-Service (SaaS) empowers Application Service Providers (ASPs) to deliver applications to users over the Internet on a rental or subscription basis. ASPs shoulder the responsibility of maintaining and updating applications, thereby alleviating maintenance and upgrade costs for clients.

1.7.4 Utility-Oriented Computing

Utility computing epitomizes a service-oriented model wherein computing resources ranging from storage and network capacities to CPU processing power are provisioned to clients on a pay-per-use basis. This paradigm shift, realized through cloud computing, parallels the provisioning of traditional utilities such as water, natural gas, and electricity.

A concise comparative analysis of the key cloud computing technologies is given in Table 1.5.

1.8 CLOUD COMPUTING PLATFORMS

The discussion of the major cloud computing platforms is provided in this section. Some of the major cloud service providers and/or related platforms are depicted in Figure 1.8.

TABLE 1.5
A comparative Analysis of Key Cloud Computing Technologies

Technology	Description	Key Features	Examples
Virtualization	Creates virtual machines on shared hardware for efficient resource use.	• Hardware abstraction • Multiple VMs on one server	VMware, Hyper-V, KVM
Web 2.0	Enables interactive, user-driven web experiences.	• Dynamic content • Rich Internet apps	Google Maps, Facebook, YouTube
Service-oriented Computing	Builds systems through network-accessible services.	• Services as building blocks • SaaS, QoS	Salesforce, AWS
Utility Computing	Provides computing resources on a pay-per-use basis.	• On-demand resources • Scalable, flexible	Amazon EC2, Azure

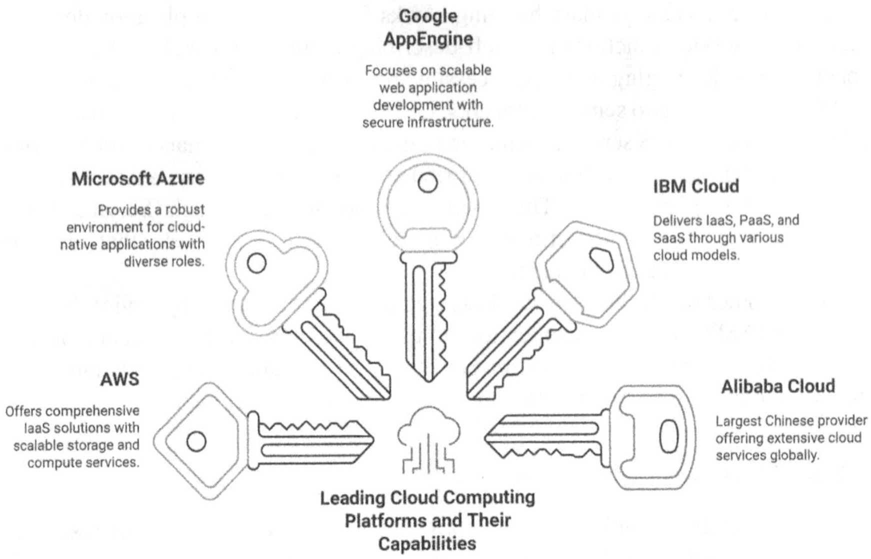
Google AppEngine
Focuses on scalable web application development with secure infrastructure.
Microsoft Azure
Provides a robust environment for cloud-native applications with diverse roles.
IBM Cloud
Delivers IaaS, PaaS, and SaaS through various cloud models.
AWS
Offers comprehensive IaaS solutions with scalable storage and compute services.
Alibaba Cloud
Largest Chinese provider offering extensive cloud services globally.
Leading Cloud Computing Platforms and Their Capabilities

FIGURE 1.8 Major cloud service providers and/or related platforms.

1.8.1 Amazon Web Services (AWS)

Amazon Web Services (AWS) [24] represents a cornerstone in cloud computing infrastructure, offering a comprehensive suite of Infrastructure-as-a-Service (IaaS) solutions. AWS's repertoire spans virtual networking, compute capabilities and storage, extending to full-fledged computing stacks. Noteworthy among its offerings are Simple Storage Service (S3) and Elastic Compute Cloud (EC2), heralded for their on-demand scalability and customization options. S3 facilitates the organization of data into containers known as buckets, wherein objects ranging from simple files to entire disk images are stored in binary format, accessible globally at any time.

1.8.2 Microsoft Azure

Microsoft Azure [25] stands as a robust platform and cloud operating system tailored for the development of cloud-native applications. Azure furnishes a scalable run-time environment optimized for distributed and web-centric applications. Central to Azure's architecture are three pivotal roles: Worker roles, designated for processing workloads; Web roles, tailored for hosting web applications; and Virtual Machine roles, which provide virtualized computing environments. Beyond these roles, Azure augments its service catalog with additional offerings encompassing networking, storage, content delivery, caching, and myriad other functionalities, thereby catering comprehensively to diverse enterprise needs.

1.8.3 Google AppEngine

Google AppEngine [26] provides a scalable run-time environment for the execution of Web applications. Google infrastructure can be scaled-up and -down based on the user's requirement. The high-performance and scalable Web applications can be easily developed using AppEngine and can be executed in a secure environment. The applications provided by the AppEngine are scalable data store, in-memory caching, messaging, job queues, etc. AppEngine Software Development Kit (SDK), which replicates the production run-time environment, enables the developers to build and test applications on their own machines. Once the application development is done, it can be easily migrated to the AppEngine by the developers.

1.8.4 IBM Cloud Services

IBM cloud [27] offers IaaS, PaaS, and SaaS via public, private, and hybrid cloud delivery models. IBM provides three cloud computing hardware platforms, such as SmartCloud Foundation, SmartCloud Services, and SmartCloud Solutions. IBM Cloud provides the freedom to select and integrate the desired tools, delivery models, and data models for designing the applications or services. The agility and speed of IBM Cloud fulfill the users' requirements and make them feel satisfied. This cloud offers the best services in a cost-effective manner.

1.8.5 Alibaba Cloud

Alibaba Cloud [28], also known as Aliyun, is the largest Chinese cloud-based company. Alibaba Cloud offers several IaaS, PaaS, and SaaS services, namely data storage, elastic compute, big-data processing, relational databases, content delivery network, etc. Around the globe, this cloud works in 56 availability zones where 19 data centers have been globally deployed around the world. This cloud backup stores user's data and provides quick results.

1.8.6 OpenStack

OpenStack [29] is an open-source IaaS-supported cloud computing platform which provides virtual machines and other resources to the users via public and private cloud delivery models. OpenStack has a modular architecture and mainly consists of three components such as compute, networking, and storage. The compute node, also known as Nova, written in Python, offers various computing services. Nova supports the creation of bare metal servers and virtual machines. The network node, also called Neutron, provides network connectivity between the interface devices. The storage node, Cinder, provides volumes to the bare metal hosts, Nova virtual machines, containers, etc. Cinder volumes provide persistent storage to the guest VM instances which are managed by the compute software. OpenStack storage system handles the creation, deletion, attaching, detaching the volumes to the servers. The storage services offered by the Cinder are fault tolerant, highly available, and recoverable.

1.8.7 Force.com and SalesForce.com

Force.com stands prominently as a specialized cloud computing platform dedicated to the creation and deployment of social enterprise applications. This platform serves as the foundational bedrock for SalesForce.com [30], renowned as a premier

Software-as-a-Service (SaaS) solution specifically designed for customer relationship management (CRM). Within the Force.com ecosystem, developers harness a robust toolkit to craft applications seamlessly by integrating pre-built, modular components. Force.com distinguishes itself by offering a streamlined development environment where developers can swiftly assemble applications without the overhead of traditional software development cycles. By leveraging ready-to-use components, developers can focus their efforts on innovation and functionality, accelerating the time-to-market for enterprise-grade applications.

1.8.8 OpenNebula

OpenNebula [31] is a free and open-source cloud platform that manages the infrastructure of heterogeneous distributed data centers. The virtual infrastructure of data centers is managed to offer IaaS services using private, public, and hybrid cloud deployment models. Cloud infrastructure virtualization and data center virtualization are the two primary functions of OpenNebula. The basic components of OpenNebula are host, template, cluster, image, virtual machine, and virtual network. Host represents the physical machine running on the hypervisor, and cluster is the set of hosts that shares the virtual networks and the data stores. Template defines the virtual machine while image specifies the disk image of virtual image. Virtual machine represents the instantiated template and the group of virtual machines IPs represents the virtual network.

1.8.9 Manjrasoft Aneka

Manjrasoft Aneka [32] is a cloud application platform that allows the rapid creation of distributed applications which can be deployed on various types of cloud. For developing applications, this platform supports a set of programming abstractions and a distributed runtime environment. For designing applications such as distributed threads, tasks, and map reduce, developers can choose any abstraction. These applications are then executed on a runtime environment which dynamically scales the resources based on the user's requirements. Aneka cloud is a collection of virtualized and physical resources connected through the private Intranet or the Internet. Aneka provides the flexibility to express the applications using different programming models.

A tabular comparative analysis of the major cloud computing platforms is provided in the form of Table 1.6.

1.9 SUMMARY

The objective of this chapter is to provide the basic understanding of cloud computing architecture. This chapter starts with the introduction to cloud computing and some of its noteworthy definitions. Then the discussions of related key technologies and its characteristics are given. The chapter further describes the various cloud deployment models and service delivery models. At last, major cloud computing providers and platforms are discussed. This chapter helps the reader to summarize the cloud computing concepts that will be helpful in the subsequent chapters (focused on cloud computing security).

TABLE 1.6
A Comparative Analysis of Major Cloud Computing Platforms

Cloud Platform	Primary Service Model	Key Features	Deployment Models	Target Users	Notable Services
Amazon Web Services (AWS)	IaaS	Scalable virtual computing, storage, networking, and compute; S3 and EC2 services	Public Cloud	Enterprises, developers, startups	EC2, S3, Lambda, RDS
Microsoft Azure	IaaS, PaaS, SaaS	Web app hosting, virtual machine roles, distributed apps, networking, and storage	Public, Private, Hybrid Cloud	Large enterprises, developers	Virtual Machines, Azure Active Directory, App Services
Google AppEngine	PaaS	Scalable runtime for web apps, integrated SDK for app development	Public Cloud	Developers, startups, web developers	Data Store, Caching, Job Queues, SDK
IBM Cloud Services	IaaS, PaaS, SaaS	Public, private, hybrid clouds, custom solutions for applications	Public, Private, Hybrid Cloud	Enterprises, businesses	Cloud Foundry, AI, Blockchain
Alibaba Cloud	IaaS, PaaS, SaaS	Global reach, big data services, storage, compute, CDN, elastic compute	Public Cloud	Enterprises, developers, global users	ECS, OSS, RDS, Elastic MapReduce
OpenStack	IaaS	Open-source, modular architecture with compute (Nova), networking (Neutron), storage (Cinder)	Public, Private Cloud	Developers, businesses, cloud providers	Nova (Compute), Neutron (Networking), Cinder (Storage)
Force.com and Salesforce.com	SaaS	Social enterprise app development, CRM solutions, integration of pre-built components	Public Cloud	Enterprises, businesses	Sales Cloud, Service Cloud, Force.com
OpenNebula	IaaS	Open-source, heterogeneous data center management, infrastructure virtualization	Public, Private, Hybrid Cloud	Developers, businesses, cloud providers	VM Management, Cluster Virtualization, Cloud Management
Manjrasoft Aneka	PaaS	Distributed app development, flexible programming models (threads, tasks, map-reduce)	Private, Public Cloud	Developers, researchers, enterprises	Distributed Runtime, Map-Reduce, Task Execution

1.10 PRACTICE QUESTIONS/SOLUTIONS

MULTIPLE OBJECTIVE QUESTIONS

1 **What is cloud computing?**
A) Traditional computing model
B) A decentralized computing model
C) A model for enabling ubiquitous, convenient, on-demand network access to a shared pool of configurable computing resources
D) A model that relies on physical servers only

Answer: C) A model for enabling ubiquitous, convenient, on-demand network access to a shared pool of configurable computing resources

2 **Which of the following is not a characteristic of cloud computing?**
A) On-demand self-service
B) Network access
C) High initial setup cost
D) Resource pooling

Answer: C) High initial setup cost

3 **Which service model provides users with the highest level of control over their computing resources?**
A) Infrastructure as a Service (IaaS)
B) Platform as a Service (PaaS)
C) Software as a Service (SaaS)
D) Function as a Service (FaaS)

Answer: A) Infrastructure as a Service (IaaS)

4 **What is the main benefit of elasticity in cloud computing?**
A) Ability to dynamically provision and deprovision resources to match workload demands
B) Static allocation of resources
C) Increased security
D) Higher initial setup costs

Answer: A) Ability to dynamically provision and deprovision resources to match workload demands

5 **Which cloud deployment model offers the highest level of privacy and control?**
A) Public cloud
B) Private cloud
C) Hybrid cloud
D) Community cloud

Answer: B) Private cloud

6 Which of the following is an example of a public cloud provider?
A) Amazon Web Services (AWS)
B) Microsoft Azure
C) Google Cloud Platform (GCP)
D) All of the above

Answer: D) All of the above

7 Which cloud computing characteristic refers to the ability to rapidly and elastically provision and release resources?
A) On-demand self-service
B) Broad network access
C) Rapid elasticity
D) Measured service

Answer: C) Rapid elasticity

8 Which cloud service model offers ready-to-use applications over the Internet?
A) Infrastructure as a Service (IaaS)
B) Platform as a Service (PaaS)
C) Software as a Service (SaaS)
D) Function as a Service (FaaS)

Answer: C) Software as a Service (SaaS)

9 What does the term "multi-tenancy" refer to in cloud computing?
A) Each user has dedicated physical resources
B) Multiple users share the same physical resources
C) Users cannot access resources simultaneously
D) All of the above

Answer: B) Multiple users share the same physical resources

10 Which cloud computing characteristic ensures that users pay only for the resources they use?
A) On-demand self-service
B) Broad network access
C) Rapid elasticity
D) Measured service

Answer: D) Measured service

DESCRIPTIVE QUESTIONS

1 What do you understand about cloud computing?

Answer: Cloud computing refers to the delivery of computing services including servers, storage, databases, networking, software, analytics, and more, over the Internet, commonly referred to as "the cloud." These services are typically offered on a pay-as-you-go basis, allowing organizations to scale resources up or down as needed without investing in physical infrastructure.

2 What are the key characteristics of cloud computing?

Answer: The key characteristics of cloud computing include on-demand self-service, broad network access, resource pooling, rapid elasticity, and measured service. On-demand self-service allows users to provision and manage resources without human intervention from the service provider. Broad network access ensures services are accessible over the Internet or through standard platforms. Resource pooling refers to the provider's computing resources being pooled to serve multiple consumers. Rapid elasticity enables users to scale resources up or down quickly to meet demands. Measured service allows for resource usage to be monitored, controlled, and reported, providing transparency and accountability.

3 What are the different deployment models in cloud computing?

Answer: The different deployment models in cloud computing are:

- Public Cloud: Services are offered over the public Internet and are available to anyone who wants to purchase them.
- Private Cloud: Services are maintained on a private network and are dedicated solely to one organization.
- Hybrid Cloud: Combines both public and private cloud models, allowing data and applications to be shared between them.
- Community Cloud: Infrastructure is shared among several organizations with similar concerns, such as security, compliance, or jurisdiction requirements.

4 Explain the service models in cloud computing.

Answer: Service models in cloud computing are categorized into:

- Infrastructure as a Service (IaaS): Provides virtualized computing resources over the Internet, such as virtual machines, storage, and networking.
- Platform as a Service (PaaS): Offers a platform allowing customers to develop, run, and manage applications without worrying about underlying infrastructure.
- Software as a Service (SaaS): Delivers software applications over the Internet on a subscription basis, eliminating the need for users to install, maintain, or upgrade software locally.

5 What are the advantages of cloud computing?

Answer: The advantages of cloud computing are as follows:

- Cost Efficiency: Cloud computing typically operates on a pay-as-you-go model, reducing upfront costs associated with physical infrastructure.
- Scalability: Cloud resources can be scaled up or down quickly in response to changing demand.
- Flexibility: Users can access cloud services from anywhere with an Internet connection and on any device.
- Reliability: Cloud providers often offer robust infrastructure with built-in redundancy, ensuring high availability of services.
- Security: Cloud providers invest heavily in security measures, often providing greater security than individual organizations can achieve on their own.

6 What is virtualization in the context of cloud computing?

Answer: Virtualization in cloud computing refers to the technique of creating virtual versions of computing resources, such as virtual machines (VMs) or virtual networks, which allows multiple users to share physical hardware resources efficiently.

7 How does load balancing work in cloud computing?

Answer: Load balancing in cloud computing involves distributing incoming network traffic or workload across multiple servers or resources to ensure optimal resource utilization, maximize throughput, minimize response time, and avoid overloading any single resource.

8 Explain the concept of auto-scaling in cloud environments.

Answer: Auto-scaling is a feature in cloud computing that automatically adjusts the number of compute resources (e.g., virtual machines) allocated to an application based on its current demand. It ensures that the application can handle varying levels of traffic or workload efficiently without manual intervention.

9 Explain the concept of network virtualization in cloud computing.

Answer: Network virtualization abstracts the physical network infrastructure, enabling multiple virtual networks (VLANs) to coexist on the same physical network. It allows for flexible and efficient allocation of network resources, isolation of traffic, and secure communication between virtual machines and applications in cloud environments.

10 What is Service-oriented Architecture (SOA) and why is it important?

Answer: Service-oriented Architecture (SOA) is an architectural approach that structures software applications as modular services. These services are loosely coupled, reusable, and interoperable, enabling flexibility, scalability, and integration across different systems and platforms. SOA is important because it allows organizations to align IT infrastructure closely with business needs, promote reusability of services, and support agile development and deployment of applications.

REFERENCES

1. Buyya, R., Vecchiola, C., & Selvi, S. T. *Mastering cloud computing: foundations and applications programming*. Newnes, 2013.
2. Mell, P. and Grance, T. "*The NIST Definition of Cloud Computing*," National Institute of Standards and Technology Publication, vol. 145, pp. 1–7, 2011.
3. Khorshed, M.T., Ali, A.S., and Wasimi, S.A. "A survey on gaps, threat remediation challenges and some thoughts for proactive attack detection in cloud computing." *Future Generation Computer Systems*, vol. 28, no. 6, pp. 833–851, 2012.
4. Armbrust, M., Fox, A., Griffith, R., Joseph, A., Katz, R., Konwinski, A., et al. *Technical Report No. UCB/ EECS-2009-28 Above the Clouds: a Berkeley View of Cloud Computing*. USA: University of California at Berkeley, 2009.
5. Buyya, R., Yeo, C.S., and Venugopal, S. Market oriented cloud computing: vision, hype, and reality for delivering IT services as computing utilities. *Proceedings of the tenth conference on high performance computing and communications* (HPCC 2008, IEEE Press, Los Alamitos, CA). Dalian, China, 2008.
6. AT&T. "What Is The Cloud?," 1993. https://www.youtube.com/watch?v=_a7hK6kWttE
7. Antonio Regalado. "Who Coined 'Cloud Computing'"?. *Technology Review*. MIT. 31 October 2011. Retrieved from http://www.technologyreview.com/news/425970/who-coined-cloud-computing on 31 July 2013.
8. https://www.computerhistory.org/internethistory/1970s
9. National Science Foundation, "Diagram of CSNET," 1981. http://gu.friends-partners.org/Bookwriting/PART_I/Chapter_I/Total/Insertions/NSF/CSNET/CSNET.html
10. Announcing Amazon Elastic Compute Cloud (Amazon EC2) – beta. 24 August 2006. Retrieved from https://aws.amazon.com/about-aws/whats-new/2006/08/24/announcing-amazon-elastic-compute-cloud-amazon-ec2---beta on 31 May 2014.
11. "Introducing Google App Engine + our new blog." Google Developer Blog. 4 April 2008. Retrieved from http://googleappengine.blogspot.nl/2008/04/introducing-google-app-engine-our-new.html on 7 March 2017.
12. Rochwerger, B.; Breitgand, D.; Levy, E.; Galis, A.; Nagin, K.; Llorente, I. M.; Montero, R.; Wolfsthal, Y.; Elmroth, E.; Caceres, J.; Ben-Yehuda, M.; Emmerich, W.; Galan, F. "The Reservoir model and architecture for open federated cloud computing". *IBM Journal of Research and Development*, vol. 53, no. (4), pp. 4:1–4:11, 2009. http://doi.org/10.1147/JRD.2009.5429058
13. https://www.networkworld.com/article/808528/data-center-keep-an-eye-on-cloud-computing.html
14. Program Solicitation NSF 08-560. https://www.nsf.gov/pubs/2008/nsf08560/nsf08560.htm

15. Windows Azure General Availability. *The Official Microsoft Blog*. Microsoft. 1 February 2010. Archived from the original on 11 May 2014. Retrieved from http://blogs.technet.com/b/microsoft_blog/archive/2010/02/01/windows-azure-general-availability.aspx on 3 May 2015.
16. Milita, Datta. "Apache CloudStack vs. OpenStack: Which Is the Best?". *DZone Cloud Zone*. 9 August 2016. https://dzone.com/articles/apache-cloudstack-vs-openstack-which-is-the-best
17. "Launch of IBM Smarter Computing". Archived from the original on 20 April 2013. Retrieved from https://web.archive.org/web/20130420162543/https://www-304.ibm.com/connections/blogs/IBMSmarterSystems/date/201102?lang=en_us on 1 March 2011.
18. "Launch of Oracle Cloud". Retrieved from https://www.theregister.co.uk/2012/06/07/oracle_cloud_rehash_platinum_services on 28 February 2014.
19. "Oracle Cloud, Enterprise-Grade Cloud Solutions: SaaS, PaaS, and IaaS". Retrieved from https://cloud.oracle.com/home on 12 October 2014.
20. "Google Compute Engine is now Generally Available with expanded OS support, transparent maintenance, and lower prices". Google Developers Blog. 2 December 2013. Retrieved from http://googledevelopers.blogspot.nl/2013/12/google-compute-engine-is-now-generally.html on 7 March 2017.
21. https://www.verdict.co.uk/cloud-computing-timeline/
22. Vaughan-Nichols, Steven J. "Microsoft developer reveals Linux is now more used on Azure than Windows Server". *ZDNet*. Retrieved on 2 July 2019.
23. www.opencloudmanifesto.org
24. https://aws.amazon.com/
25. https://azure.microsoft.com/
26. https://cloud.google.com/appengine
27. https://www.ibm.cloud
28. https://www.alibabacloud.com/
29. https://www.openstack.org/
30. https://www.salesforce.com/
31. https://opennebula.io/
32. https://www.manjrasoft.com/aneka_architecture.html

2 Cloud Computing Security

2.1 INTRODUCTION TO CLOUD SECURITY

Cloud computing has emerged as a predominant paradigm in contemporary technology, leveraging virtualization techniques to offer on-demand services via the Internet. This integration has captivated academia, compelling scholars to explore its intersections with various disciplines and industries. The allure lies in cloud computing's inherent benefits such as enhanced service availability and the scalable allocation of computational resources, prompting both consumers and enterprises to migrate their operations and data to remote cloud servers. The scalability, cost efficiency, and operational flexibility exemplify the manifold advantages that cloud computing affords.

However, this transition from localized to remote computing environments has not been without its challenges, particularly concerning security. The migration introduces a spectrum of security threats and complexities, affecting both cloud providers and their clients. It is imperative, therefore, to address these security concerns comprehensively as data and applications migrate to cloud infrastructures. A typical cloud security environment is shown in Figure 2.1.

Cloud security encompasses a layered approach aimed at safeguarding cloud resources, including the underlying infrastructure, platforms, and applications. This entails protecting data at rest and in transit, implementing robust authentication mechanisms, ensuring secure access controls, and adhering to pertinent legal and regulatory frameworks [1, 2]. Collectively, these practices, technologies, and policies constitute the domain of cloud security, essential for fortifying data, applications, and infrastructure against unauthorized access, breaches, and other cyber threats.

The key aspects of cloud security are detailed below:

- *Data Protection*: Data protection in cloud environments poses significant challenges centered around ensuring the confidentiality, integrity, and accessibility of stored data. To mitigate risks such as unauthorized access, data breaches, and data loss, robust encryption methods, access controls, and comprehensive data backup procedures are imperative safeguards.
- *Identity and Access Management (IAM)*: IAM assumes a critical role in cloud security by governing user access to resources. IAM frameworks encompass authentication, authorization, and user management protocols,

DOI: 10.1201/9781003510772-2

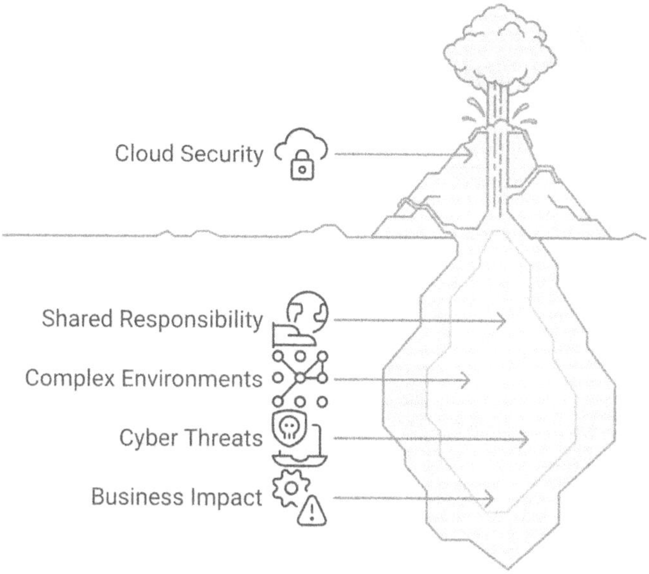

FIGURE 2.1 A general cloud security environment.

ensuring that only authorized entities can access and modify data and applications within the cloud environment.

- *Network Security*: Network security measures are indispensable for safeguarding the infrastructure that facilitates communication between cloud resources and users, as well as among various components within the cloud itself. Technologies such as firewalls, intrusion detection and prevention systems (IDPS), and virtual private networks (VPNs) are employed to secure communication routes and protect against unauthorized access and malicious activities.
- *Vulnerability Management*: Vulnerability management is essential for maintaining a secure cloud environment. Regular security audits, vulnerability scanning, and proactive patch management are critical practices aimed at identifying and remedying vulnerabilities in cloud infrastructure and applications promptly.
- *Compliance and Regulatory Considerations*: Compliance with regulatory requirements is paramount in cloud security, necessitating adherence to relevant legal and industry standards such as the General Data Protection Regulation (GDPR), Payment Card Industry Data Security Standard (PCI DSS), or Health Insurance Portability and Accountability Act (HIPAA). Compliance ensures that data privacy and protection obligations are met, tailored to the specific data types and industry contexts involved.

TABLE 2.1
Comparative Analysis of Different Key Aspects of Cloud Security

Cloud Security Aspect	Focus	Challenges	Mitigation
Data Protection	Data confidentiality and integrity	Unauthorized access, data breaches	Encryption, access controls, backups
IAM (Identity and Access Management)	Governing user access	Unauthorized access, access management	MFA, role-based access, user management
Network Security	Protecting communication and infrastructure	Malicious activity, unauthorized access	Firewalls, VPNs, IDPS, encryption
Vulnerability Management	Identifying and fixing security risks	Unpatched vulnerabilities	Regular audits, scanning, patching
Compliance and Regulations	Adhering to legal standards	Evolving laws and regulations	Compliance checks, automated tools

A concise comparative analysis of different cloud security aspects is highlighted in Table 2.1 with respect to key areas, challenges, and mitigation strategies in cloud security.

The benefits of cloud security are shown in Figure 2.2.

2.2 CLOUD SECURITY VS TRADITIONAL ON-PREMISE SECURITY

Cloud security is different from traditional on-premises security due to the following key factors.

- *Shared Responsibility*: In conventional on-premises systems, businesses are completely in charge of their IT infrastructure, which includes all hardware, software, and security measures. However, in the cloud, both the cloud user and the Cloud Service Provider (CSP) are accountable for security. The platform's security in some areas as well as the physical security of the foundation are under the purview of the CSP. The user of the cloud, on the other hand, is in charge of protecting its settings, data, applications, and user access within the cloud environment. This shared responsibility paradigm necessitates communication and cooperation between the cloud user and the CSP.
- *Scalability and Elasticity*: Cloud systems provide quick resource scaling up or down in response to demand. Although this scalability is beneficial, it also makes it more difficult to ensure uniform security across constantly changing resources. Due to the dynamic nature of cloud settings, traditional security procedures and controls cannot be easily scalable or flexible, necessitating the adoption of new security techniques.
- *Multi-tenancy*: A multi-tenant environment is one in which cloud infrastructure is often shared by numerous users or organizations. The possibility of

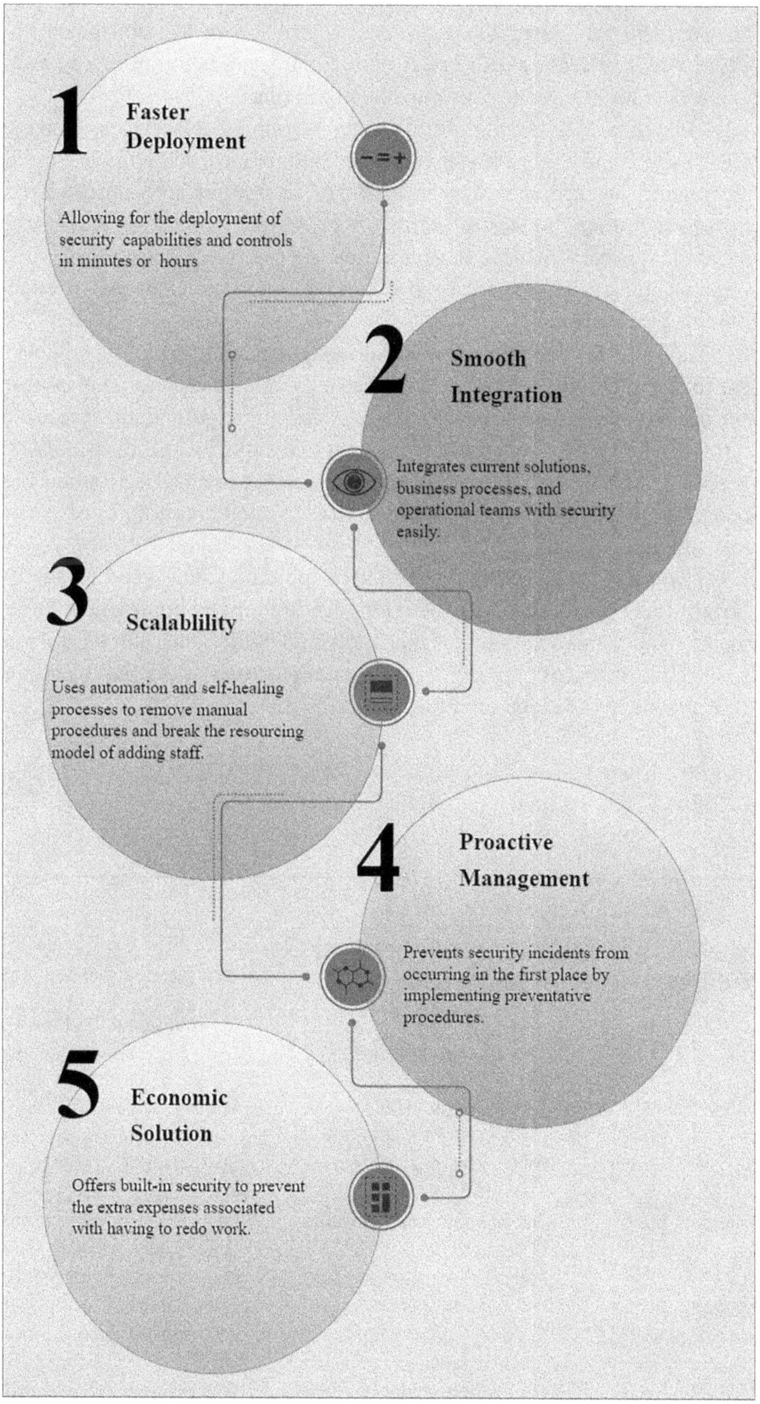

1
Faster
Deployment
Allowing for the deployment of security capabilities and controls in minutes or hours
2
Smooth
Integration
Integrates current solutions, business processes, and operational teams with security easily.
3
Scalablility
Uses automation and self-healing processes to remove manual procedures and break the resourcing model of adding staff.
4
Proactive
Management
Prevents security incidents from occurring in the first place by implementing preventative procedures.
5
Economic
Solution
Offers built-in security to prevent the extra expenses associated with having to redo work.

FIGURE 2.2 Cloud security benefits.

unauthorized access or data leakage between tenants is raised by this shared environment. To guarantee security and privacy in a multi-tenant cloud environment, effective resource isolation and segregation must be ensured, and robust access restrictions must be put in place.

- *Virtualization and Abstraction*: To offer resources as services, cloud systems significantly rely on virtualization and abstraction technologies. This abstraction layer makes it more difficult to comprehend the underlying infrastructure and creates difficulties for security monitoring and management. To properly handle the particular security requirements of virtualized systems, traditional security technologies and practices may need to be modified or replaced.
- *Expanded Attack Surface*: By making resources and services available via the Internet, cloud environments increase the attack surface. This increased surface area increases the number of risks that might potentially access cloud infrastructure, apps, and data. Since external risks including unauthorized access, data breaches, Distributed Denial-of-Service (DDoS) attacks, and other malicious Internet activity are a concern, cloud security must incorporate safeguards against these.
- *Compliance and Legal Issues*: Users of the cloud may need to abide by certain industry rules, data protection legislation, and contractual commitments. Understanding the rules that apply and putting the right security controls and procedures in place to comply with them are essential for ensuring compliance in the cloud environment.

A comparative analysis of cloud security with traditional on-premises security is given in Table 2.2 based on the mentioned key factors.

TABLE 2.2
Key Differences in Security Models between Cloud and Traditional On-premises Systems

Factor	Cloud Security	Traditional On-Premises Security
Shared Responsibility	Shared between CSP and user (platform vs. data security).	Entirely managed by the organization.
Scalability and Elasticity	Dynamic scaling, harder to secure consistently.	Static resources, easier to secure.
Multi-tenancy	Shared infrastructure requires strong isolation.	Dedicated to a single organization, no tenant overlap.
Virtualization & Abstraction	Relies on virtualization, complicates monitoring.	Direct control over physical infrastructure.
Expanded Attack Surface	More exposed to external threats via the Internet.	Less exposed, internal network.
Compliance & Legal	Users ensure compliance with support from CSP.	Full responsibility for compliance and legal matters.

Overall, the shared responsibility paradigm, scalability issues, multi-tenancy considerations, virtualization and abstraction, larger attack surface, and compliance difficulties distinguish cloud security from traditional on-premises security. Organizations utilizing cloud services must be aware of these variances and implement appropriate security measures if they want to properly safeguard their data, apps, and infrastructure.

2.3 CLOUD SECURITY RESPONSIBILITIES

It is easier to understand the separation of security activities and assures a thorough approach to safeguarding the cloud environment by dividing cloud security obligations between the Cloud Service Provider (CSP) and the cloud user. Depending on the cloud service type (Infrastructure as a Service, Platform as a Service, or Software as a Service) and deployment strategy (public, private, or hybrid cloud), the precise duties may change. The overall breakdown of duties is depicted in Figure 2.3 and described as follows.

2.3.1 Cloud Service Provider Responsibilities

- *Physical Security*: The CSP is in charge of protecting the physical data centers from risks by implementing access restrictions, surveillance systems, and environmental controls.
- *Architecture Security*: The CSP is in charge of protecting the virtualization layers, servers, storage, networking, and other elements of the cloud

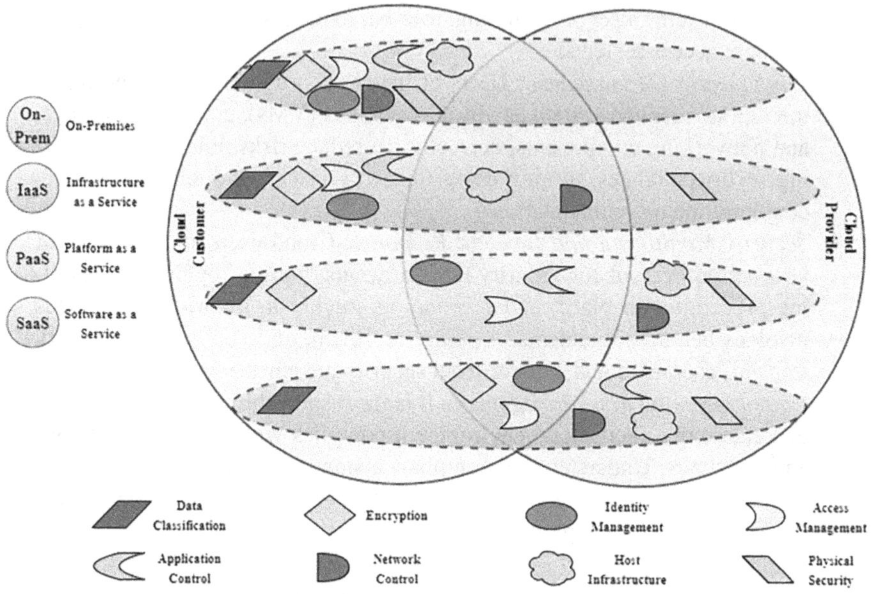

FIGURE 2.3 Cloud security responsibilities.

architecture. This entails ensuring correct configuration, patching, and defense against assaults on the infrastructure.

- *Network Security*: To guard against unauthorized access and network-based threats, the CSP is in charge of designing and maintaining network security measures inside the cloud environment, such as firewalls, intrusion detection and prevention systems, and network segmentation.
- *Hypervisor Security*: In virtualized settings, the CSP is in charge of protecting the hypervisor and related management systems against intrusions and ensuring the isolation and integrity of virtual machines (VMs).
- *Data Center Operations*: To guarantee data availability and continuity, the CSP oversees all aspects of the data centers' operations, including backup and disaster recovery systems, data replication, and high availability solutions.

2.3.2 Cloud User Responsibilities

- *Data Security*: Users of the cloud are in charge of protecting their data inside the cloud environment. To prevent unauthorized access, data breaches, and data leaking, this comprises data categorization, encryption, access restrictions, and data lifecycle management.
- *Application Security*: Cloud users are in charge of protecting their applications deployed in the cloud against application-level assaults and vulnerabilities. This includes safe coding practices, vulnerability management, and application-level access restrictions.
- *Identity and Access Management (IAM)*: Users of the cloud are in charge of controlling who has access to their resources. To maintain proper access rights and prevent unauthorized access, this entails installing robust authentication systems, user provisioning, role-based access controls (RBAC), and frequent access reviews.
- *Configuration Management*: Users of the cloud are in charge of setting up their cloud resources, such as virtual machines (VMs), containers, storage, and networking components, correctly. To reduce risks, this entails installing security updates, turning down unused services, and adhering to safe configuration recommendations.
- *Security Monitoring and Incident Response*: Cloud users are in charge of keeping an eye out for security-related events, putting logging and auditing procedures in place, and responding quickly to security issues. This involves detecting incidents, looking into them, and taking the necessary steps to respond to and recover from security breaches.
- *Compliance and Risk Management*: It is the responsibility of cloud users to make sure that their cloud environment complies with all applicable laws and standards. Understanding compliance standards, putting relevant controls in place, and regularly conducting risk assessments to find and reduce security threats are all part of this.

Table 2.3 highlights the clear distinction between the roles and responsibilities of the CSP (focused primarily on infrastructure, physical security, and foundational

TABLE 2.3
Cloud Service Provider vs. Cloud User Responsibilities

Responsibility Area	Cloud Service Provider (CSP)	Cloud User
Physical Security	Ensures physical security of data centers (access control, surveillance).	Relies on CSP's physical security; doesn't manage it directly.
Architecture Security	Secures infrastructure (virtualization, networking, servers).	Secures applications and data using CSP's infrastructure.
Network Security	Maintains firewalls, intrusion detection, and network segmentation.	Secures network at the application/resource level (APIs, encryption).
Hypervisor Security	Secures hypervisor and VM isolation.	Ensures VM configurations and security within the cloud.
Data Center Operations	Manages backup, disaster recovery, and high availability solutions.	Manages disaster recovery and data protection within the cloud.
Data Security	Ensures basic data protection (encryption at rest).	Encrypts, classifies, and controls access to their own data.
Application Security	Secures cloud platform but not user applications.	Secures their applications, coding practices, and access controls.
Identity and Access Management	Provides IAM tools at the platform level.	Manages IAM for cloud resources (authentication, roles, permissions).
Configuration Management	Ensures secure platform configurations.	Configures cloud resources securely (updates, settings).
Security Monitoring and Response	Monitors infrastructure security, logs, and responds to threats.	Monitors and responds to incidents at the application/resource level.
Compliance and Risk Management	Ensures platform compliance with regulations.	Ensures their environment meets legal and regulatory requirements.

architecture) and the cloud user (focused on securing data, applications, identity management, and configuration within the cloud).

The specific allocation of tasks may vary depending on the cloud service model, deployment methodology, and the parameters established in the service-level agreement (SLA) between the CSP and the cloud user. It is crucial to note that this breakdown of duties is just intended to serve as a basic guideline. To guarantee effective security protection, it is advised that organizations fully comprehend the precise obligations and arrangements with their CSP.

2.4 CLOUD SECURITY ISSUES

The broad-level view of the security issues [3, 4] associated with cloud computing is shown in Figure 2.4. However, the security issues at application, network, platform, and infrastructure levels are given in Figure 2.5 and described as follows.

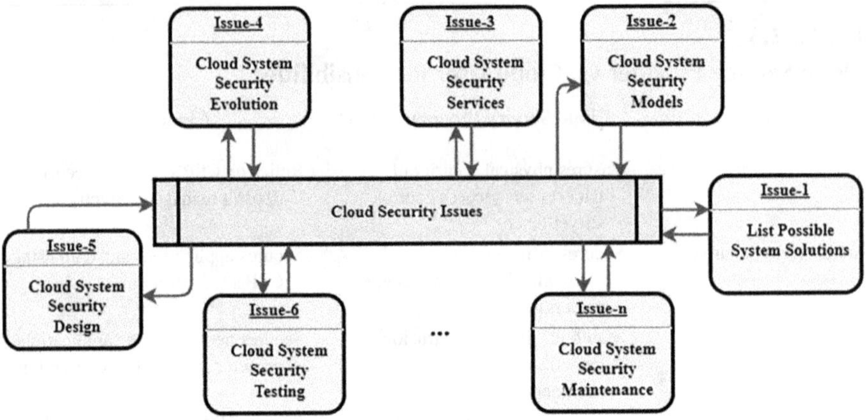

FIGURE 2.4 Cloud security issues.

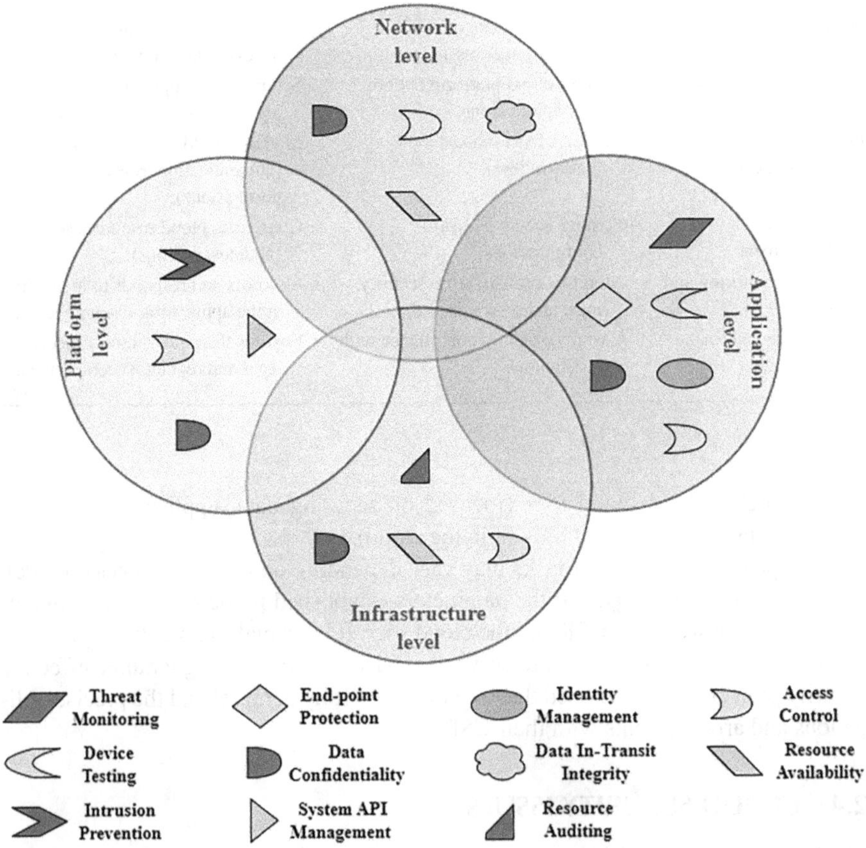

FIGURE 2.5 Security issues at various levels of cloud computing.

2.4.1 Application-level Security

Application-level security refers to the procedures, policies, and safeguards put in place to defend applications against security risks and weaknesses. Here are a few typical application-level security problems that businesses need to fix.

- *Input Validation*: Improper input validation can result in security flaws including command injection, SQL injection, and cross-site scripting (XSS). In order to stop malicious code execution and data manipulation, applications should verify and sanitize user inputs.
- *Authentication and Authorization*: Improper or ineffective authentication and authorization procedures may allow unauthorized access to critical information or functionality. To guarantee that only authorized users may access certain resources, applications should enforce strict password requirements, implement secure authentication methods (such as multi-factor authentication), and employ proper permission controls.
- *Session Hijacking*: Poor session management might result in attacks such as session hijacking or session fixation. Applications should provide secure session IDs, deal with session timeouts appropriately, and safeguard session data while it is in use and at rest.
- *Cross-Site Scripting (XSS)*: XSS flaws let attackers insert harmful scripts into web pages that users are viewing, which can result in session hijacking, data theft, or page defacement. To stop XSS attacks, applications should include input validation, output encoding, and appropriate context-aware output sanitization.
- *Cross-Site Request Forgery (CSRF) attacks*: These types of attacks persuade authorized users to take unexpected activities on a website without their awareness. To minimize CSRF vulnerabilities, applications should utilize CSRF tokens, check the source of requests, and make sure the right user actions are taken.
- *Security Misconfigurations*: Application servers, web servers, databases, and other components may have security flaws due to incorrect configuration. These risks may be reduced by regular security assessments, appropriate configuration hardening, and adherence to security best practices.
- *Insecure Direct Object References (IDOR)*: When an application exposes internal object references, it creates an IDOR vulnerability that enables attackers to change or access private data. To avoid IDOR vulnerabilities, applications should enforce data segregation, sufficient authorization checks, and access constraints.
- *Secure File and Resource Management*: Improper management of files and resources might result in arbitrary code execution, file inclusion flaws, or unapproved access to private data. Applications need to verify and clean up file uploads, limit user access to private information, and define secure file permissions.
- *Secure Coding Techniques*: Bad coding techniques might result in flaws like buffer overflows, code injection, or improper usage of cryptographic

functions. To find and address security issues, developers should use safe development frameworks, adhere to secure coding standards, and do routine code reviews.

- *Third-Party Components and Libraries*: Using outdated or vulnerable versions of third-party components and libraries pose a risk. Risks related to third-party dependencies can be reduced by frequently upgrading and patching these components, performing vulnerability assessments, and monitoring security advisories.

These are only a few instances of the application-level security problems that businesses must solve. Building and maintaining safe applications require using secure coding practices, doing extensive security testing, and keeping up with the most recent security threats and best practices.

2.4.2 Network-level Security

Vulnerabilities and threats that target the network infrastructure and communication channels are referred to as network-level security concerns. The availability, confidentiality, and integrity of data and resources may all be jeopardized by these problems. The following are some typical network-level security problems that businesses need to address.

- *Unauthorized Access*: It happens when an attacker enters a network, system, or device without authorization. Weak or default passwords, unprotected network services, or hacked user accounts can all lead to this. Unauthorized access can be avoided by putting in place reliable authentication systems, access controls, and consistent password management procedures.
- *Malware and Viruses*: Malicious software has been created to take advantage of holes in networks and computer systems. They have the ability to corrupt data, infect devices, and impede network performance. Malware and virus risk may be reduced by implementing and frequently updating antivirus software, running malware scans, and teaching users on safe surfing practices.
- *Distributed Denial-of-Service (DDoS) Attacks*: DDoS attacks [6] try to overload network resources or services so that authorized users cannot access them. This may be accomplished by using excessive bandwidth, exhausting available resources, or abusing weaknesses in network protocols. DDoS assaults can be lessened by putting in place DDoS defense measures such firewalls, intrusion prevention systems, and traffic filtering.
- *Man-in-the-Middle (MITM) Attacks*: MITM attacks [7] entail intercepting and changing two parties' communication without either party being aware of it. Attackers can use this to modify data, intercept sensitive information, or pass themselves off as trustworthy organizations. MITM attacks may be recognized and avoided by using secure communication protocols (such as Transport Layer Security – TLS), employing encryption, and routinely monitoring network traffic.

- *Network Infrastructure Vulnerabilities*: These include holes in routers, switches, and firewalls that may be used to break into networks, alter traffic, or otherwise cause havoc. Vulnerabilities in the network infrastructure may be found and fixed by completing security audits and vulnerability assessments, updating firmware often, and setting devices securely.
- *Wireless Network Security*: Security threats associated with wireless networks include unauthorized access, eavesdropping, and rogue access points [8]. Strong encryption (such as WPA2 or WPA3), secure authentication techniques (such as EAP-TLS), and routine network activity monitoring can all improve wireless network security.
- *Data Interception and Sniffing*: This technique involves recording and examining network traffic in order to get private information such as usernames and passwords or secret data. Using secure methods for transmitting sensitive data and implementing encryption protocols (such VPNs, SSL/TLS, etc.) can assist prevent data interception and sniffing.
- *Insider Threats*: Those with authorized access to a network within an organization who commit malevolent acts or inadvertent blunders are referred to as insider threats. Insider dangers can lead to sabotage, unauthorized access, or data breaches. Insider risks may be reduced with the use of strict access controls, user activity monitoring, and frequent security awareness training.
- *Network Segmentation and Access Controls*: Inadequate network segmentation and access controls can provide unauthorized users access to critical resources, let them move laterally inside a network, or let them advance in rank. Implementing firewall rules, least privilege access restrictions, and network segmentation can limit unauthorized access and stop possible security breaches.
- *Insecure Remote Access*: Attackers may gain unauthorized access to networks and systems via insecure remote access techniques, such as weak passwords, unprotected protocols, or unpatched remote access software. Remote access security may be improved by using secure remote access methods (such VPNs), multi-factor authentication, and routine software updates.

Combining technological restrictions, security best practices, and user awareness is necessary to address network-level security challenges.

2.4.3 Platform-level Security

Platform-level security describes the security policies and procedures put in place to safeguard the operating system or platform that serves as the foundation for all other apps and services. This covers safeguarding the databases, application frameworks, server operating systems, and other platform elements. Considerations for platform-level security are listed below.

- *Operating System Security*: Servers and other platforms' operating systems (OS) need to be fortified and maintained up to date with security patches and upgrades. In order to do this, security settings must be configured, superfluous services must be disabled, access restrictions must be put in place, and secure authentication methods must be used.

- *Database Security*: Because databases manage and hold important data, they are a top target for attackers. Databases may be protected against unauthorized access and data breaches by implementing robust access restrictions, encrypting critical data, deploying security updates on a regular basis, and performing security audits [9].
- *Patch Management*: To fix vulnerabilities and defend against known attacks, platform components must be updated and patched on a regular basis. The timely installation of patches and updates throughout the platform is ensured by establishing a patch management mechanism.
- *Secure Configuration*: To reduce risks, platform components should be set up securely. This entails turning off or deleting unneeded services and protocols, requiring strong passwords, allowing logging and auditing, and adhering to security best practices recommended by the platform vendor, among other things.
- *Secure Application Development Frameworks*: A lot of platforms offer application development frameworks, which come with libraries, APIs, and tools for creating apps. To lower the danger of common vulnerabilities, developers should make use of safe coding practices and secure features and services offered by these frameworks.
- *Access Controls and Privilege Management*: In order to restrict user access rights to the platform, it is essential to implement access controls and privilege management techniques. The application of role-based access controls (RBAC), the least privilege principle, and routinely assessing and removing unused rights are some examples of this.
- *Logging and Monitoring*: Putting in place logging and monitoring methods makes it possible to spot shady goings-on and potential security lapses. Monitoring platform logs, network activity, and system activities may aid with early identification and response to security issues as well as providing insights into security concerns.
- *Authentication and Authorization*: To make sure that only users who have been given permission may access the platform, secure authentication measures should be put in place. This might involve integration with identity and access management (IAM) systems, multi-factor authentication, and strict password regulations.
- *Secure Deployment and Configuration Management*: Securing the platform during initial setup and ongoing configuration management can be accomplished by implementing secure deployment procedures such as using secure communication channels, securely storing sensitive configuration data, and using secure deployment scripts.
- *Incident Response and Recovery*: Setting up backup and recovery processes as well as an incident response plan is essential for minimizing the effects of security issues. This entails verifying the platform's restoration from backups, establishing a written incident response strategy, and routinely backing up the data on the platform.

To safeguard the underlying infrastructure and give operating applications and services a secure basis, platform-level security solutions are crucial. Organizations may reduce risks and guarantee the integrity, availability, and confidentiality of their systems and data by taking platform-level security issues into account.

2.4.4 Infrastructure-level Security

Infrastructure-level security refers to the security policies and procedures put in place to safeguard the structural underpinnings and visible parts of an IT system. This comprises servers, storage units, network hardware, data centers, and other infrastructure parts. Aspects of infrastructure-level security include the following.

- *Physical Security*: Physical security measures are intended to prevent theft, unauthorized access, and other forms of harm to the physical infrastructure components. Access controls, video surveillance, alarm systems, and secure perimeter controls for data centers and server rooms are implemented as part of this.
- *Network Security*: The goal of network security is to protect the routers, switches, firewalls, and intrusion detection/prevention systems that make up the network infrastructure. In order to guard against unauthorized access and network-based risks, network segmentation, firewalls, VPNs, network monitoring tools, and regular security audits can be implemented.
- *Server and Endpoint Security*: Securing individual servers, workstations, and devices inside the infrastructure is known as server and endpoint security. Implementing safe settings, routine patch management, endpoint protection software (antivirus/anti-malware), host-based intrusion detection/prevention systems, and secure remote access tools are all part of this.
- *Data Centre Security*: The security measures put in place inside the actual data center facilities are referred to as data center security. To protect the availability and integrity of the infrastructure, this includes limited access controls, environmental monitoring (such as temperature and humidity), fire suppression systems, power redundancy, and backup power generators.
- *Storage Security*: SAN (Storage Area Network) and NAS (Network-Attached Storage) are examples of data storage systems that are the focus of storage security. Access restrictions, data at rest encryption, routine backups, and safe data disposal procedures can all be implemented to prevent unauthorized access and data breaches.
- *Virtualization Security*: In settings that use virtualization, virtualization security [10] measures are meant to keep hypervisors and virtual machines (VMs) safe. This covers isolated VMs, routine patch management, safe hypervisor setups, and monitoring of VMs for security flaws and unauthorized activity.
- *Backup and Disaster Recovery*: To maintain business continuity and data resilience, it is essential to implement frequent data backups and disaster recovery procedures. Offsite backups, redundant systems, data replication, thorough disaster recovery planning, and testing all fall under this category.

TABLE 2.4
Summary of the Key Security Concerns and Solutions

Level	Concerns	Solutions
Application	Input validation, authentication, XSS, CSRF, misconfigurations, file management	Sanitize inputs, multi-factor authentication, secure sessions, CSRF tokens, audits, secure file handling
Network	Unauthorized access, malware, DDoS, MITM, insider threats	Strong authentication, antivirus, DDoS protection, TLS encryption, network monitoring
Platform	OS vulnerabilities, database security, misconfigurations, access controls	Patching, encryption, RBAC, secure setup, privilege management
Infrastructure	Physical access, server security, data center, storage, monitoring	Access control, backup, redundancy, SIEM tools, environmental monitoring

- *Access Controls and Authentication*: To guarantee that only authorized users may access the infrastructure components, strong access controls and authentication procedures should be put in place. Role-based access controls (RBAC), strong password restrictions, multi-factor authentication, and frequent access reviews are a few examples of this.
- *Security Monitoring and Incident Reaction*: The use of security monitoring technologies and procedures enables the early identification and quick reaction to security incidents. This comprises tools for security information and event management (SIEM), intrusion detection/prevention systems, log monitoring, and incident response protocols.
- *Security Audits and Assessments*: To find security flaws and vulnerabilities, infrastructure components must undergo regular security audits, vulnerability assessments, and penetration tests. This assists in proactively resolving security holes and guaranteeing ongoing security posture improvement for the infrastructure.

Organizations may secure their physical and underlying components, preserve sensitive data, and uphold the overall security and integrity of their IT infrastructure by addressing infrastructure-level security issues.

A summary of the four levels of security (Application, Network, Platform, and Infrastructure) with respective key security concerns and suggested solutions are provided in Table 2.4.

2.5 CLOUD SECURITY CHALLENGES

Cloud computing offers numerous benefits, and it also presents unique security challenges that organizations must address. The common cloud security challenges are offered in Figure 2.6 and described below.

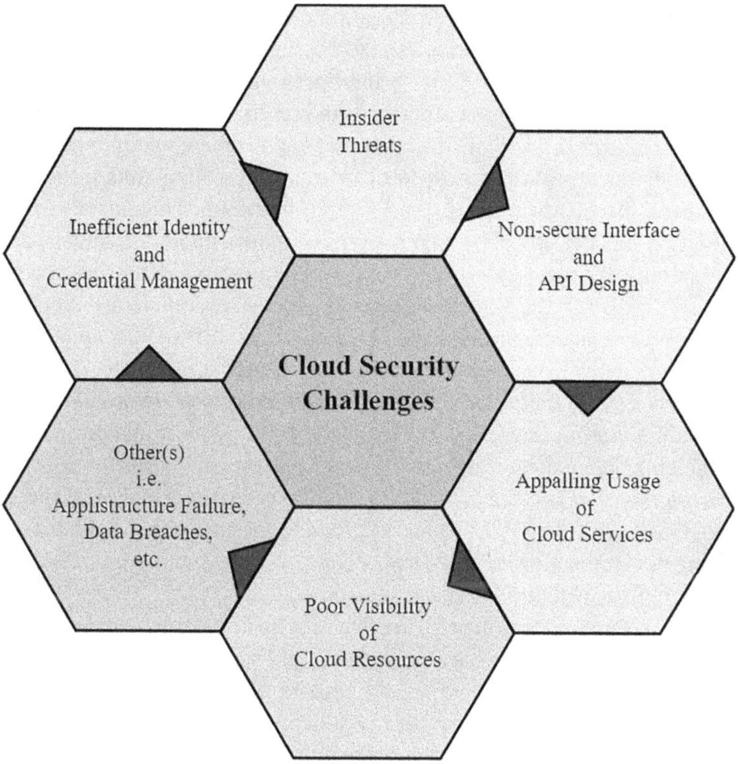

FIGURE 2.6 Cloud security challenges.

- *Data Breach*: In the cloud, data breaches are still a major worry. Weak access restrictions, improperly set permissions, or flaws in the cloud provider's infrastructure can all lead to unauthorized access to critical data. To safeguard data from unauthorized access, it is essential to incorporate strong authentication, encryption, and tight access restrictions.
- *Data Loss*: Data loss can happen as a result of hardware malfunction, natural calamities, or unintentional deletion. Usually, cloud service providers have backups and replication of data in place as protection against data loss. To guarantee data availability and resilience, organizations must comprehend the provider's data protection rules and put supplementary data backup and recovery methods into place.
- *Deduplication*: It refers to the process of identifying and eliminating duplicate copies of data stored in the cloud. While deduplication can offer several benefits such as reduced storage costs and improved efficiency, it also raises certain security concerns such as data leakage, side-channel attacks [11], etc. To address this, secure deduplication schemes should be developed for the cloud computing environment [12].
- *Insecure APIs and Interfaces*: Cloud services frequently make APIs and Interfaces available for users to interact and govern the cloud environment.

Unauthorized access or data leakage may result from attacks against insecure interfaces and APIs. To minimize possible dangers, it is crucial to protect and correctly configure these interfaces and APIs, put in place robust authentication and access restrictions, and often update and fix them.

- *Insider Threats*: A worry in any computer environment, including the cloud, is insider threats. With access to cloud resources, malicious insiders may purposefully misuse or divulge critical information. To reduce the dangers posed by insider threats, organizations should establish stringent access restrictions, frequent user monitoring, and security awareness programs.
- *Shared Infrastructure Vulnerabilities*: To service several clients, cloud companies rely on shared infrastructure. Unauthorized access to or compromise of data might result from exploiting flaws in the shared infrastructure or underlying resources. To guarantee the integrity and security of their data, organizations should evaluate the security measures used by the cloud provider, such as isolation techniques, vulnerability management, and intrusion detection.
- *Compliance and Legal Issues*: Using cloud services may make it difficult for organizations to comply with legal and regulatory standards. Regulations governing data protection, privacy, and security vary by industry. Understanding the compliance environment and selecting cloud service providers who provide the necessary compliance certifications and guarantees are critical.
- *Reliability of Cloud Service Providers*: Cloud service providers might have service interruptions or outages, which would impact the accessibility of cloud resources and services. To make sure that the cloud services satisfy their needs for availability and performance, organizations should carefully assess the dependability and service-level agreements (SLAs) provided by cloud providers.
- *Lack of Visibility and Control*: Using the cloud frequently entails giving up some level of control over the infrastructure and security measures. Having total access to the underlying infrastructure, data processing procedures, and security measures put in place by the cloud provider might be difficult. To ensure visibility and keep control over their data, organizations should negotiate contracts that offer transparency, carry out frequent audits, and put extra security controls in place.
- *Multi-tenancy Risks*: In a cloud environment, numerous clients often use the same infrastructure. As a result of the acts of other tenants, there is a danger of unauthorized access, data leakage, or resource depletion. To minimize the risks related to multi-tenancy, it is crucial to implement strong isolation mechanisms, access controls, and monitoring.
- *Security Incident Response*: Organizations must modify their incident response strategies to take into account potential security incidents in cloud environments. The effect of security issues may be lessened and downtime reduced by coordinating incident response with the cloud provider, comprehending their incident response procedures, and having a well-defined strategy.

The common cloud security challenges and respective mitigations are discussed in Table 2.5.

TABLE 2.5
Cloud Security Challenges

Challenge	Description	Mitigation
Data Breach	Unauthorized access due to weak controls.	Use strong authentication and encryption.
Data Loss	Loss from hardware failure or disasters.	Implement backups and recovery methods.
Deduplication	Data leakage risks from duplicate removal.	Use secure deduplication methods.
Insecure APIs	Exploits in APIs and interfaces.	Secure and update APIs.
Insider Threats	Malicious insiders misusing data.	Set access limits and monitor users.
Shared Infrastructure	Risks in shared cloud resources.	Ensure proper isolation and security.
Compliance Issues	Struggling to meet legal requirements.	Choose compliant providers.
Provider Reliability	Service outages affecting availability.	Assess provider reliability and SLAs.
Visibility and Control	Limited control over cloud security.	Negotiate transparency and audits.
Multi-tenancy Risks	Risks from shared resources.	Use isolation and access controls.
Incident Response	Slow response to cloud security incidents.	Coordinate and establish response plans.

Careful planning, strong security measures, regular monitoring, and cooperation with the cloud provider are all necessary to meet these obstacles. To ensure the security of their data in the cloud, organizations should evaluate their unique security requirements, choose reputable cloud providers with robust security measures, and implement additional security controls.

2.6 CLOUD SECURITY SOLUTIONS

There are several cloud security options available to handle the particular difficulties in protecting cloud systems. These solutions offer a variety of capabilities to safeguard cloud infrastructure, applications, and data. Following are a few popular cloud security options.

- *Identity and Access Management (IAM)*: IAM solutions assist with managing user identities, authentication, and access controls in the cloud [5]. To guarantee that only authorized users may access cloud resources, they provide features such as user provisioning, single sign-on (SSO), role-based access control (RBAC), and multi-factor authentication (MFA).
- *Data Encryption*: Cloud-based data encryption solutions help safeguard data while it is in motion and at rest. Data is encrypted using algorithms to prevent unauthorized parties from accessing it or decrypting it without the encryption keys.
- *Cloud Security Gateways (CSGs)*: CSGs serve as a bridge between consumers and suppliers of cloud services. They oversee traffic, enact security

regulations, and check information moving between users and the cloud environment. To improve the security of cloud communications, CSGs include features including data loss prevention (DLP), malware detection, and encryption.

- *Security Information and Event Management (SIEM)*: SIEM tools gather and examine log data from multiple cloud services in order to identify and address security events. They enable organizations to recognize and address potential threats in their cloud environments through real-time monitoring, event correlation, and alerting capabilities.
- *Cloud Access Security Brokers (CASBs)*: CASBs are security platforms that stand in between customers of cloud services and the companies that offer those services, giving customers visibility and control over how the cloud is being used. They let businesses to safeguard data stored in cloud applications and services, monitor cloud activities, and enforce security regulations.
- *Threat Intelligence Services*: Threat intelligence services offer up-to-date details on new dangers, security holes, and attack patterns. They assist businesses in maintaining awareness of emerging security vulnerabilities in their cloud systems and taking preventative action against them.
- *Cloud Workload Protection (CWPP) Platforms*: These solutions concentrate on protecting virtual machines (VMs) and workloads in the cloud. To defend against threats aimed at cloud-based applications and services, they offer capabilities like vulnerability assessment, intrusion detection/prevention, and workload firewalling.
- *Cloud Data Loss Prevention (DLP)*: Cloud DLP solutions aid in preventing the unauthorized disclosure of sensitive data in the cloud. They recognize and keep track of sensitive data, uphold data protection regulations, and recognize and stop efforts at data exfiltration.
- *Container Security*: Technologies for containerization, including Docker and Kubernetes, demand particular security precautions. Container security solutions provide vulnerability detection, image integrity verification, and runtime protection for containers, ensuring that containerized applications stay safe in the cloud.
- *Cloud Security Assessments and Audits*: Ongoing security assessments and audits assist businesses in assessing the level of security in their cloud environments. Penetration testing, vulnerability analyses, and compliance audits are a few of the assessments that might be used to find holes and make sure that security best practice and legal requirements are being followed.

The Table 2.6 summarizes the key cloud security solutions, their functions, and features to help address the challenges of securing cloud environments.

To create a strong and complete security framework for their cloud environments, it is crucial for organizations to assess their unique security requirements, take into account the cloud deployment model (such as public, private, or hybrid), and select the right combination of cloud security solutions [13].

TABLE 2.6
Analysis of Cloud Security Solutions

Cloud Security Solution	Description	Key Features
Identity and Access Management (IAM)	Manages user identities, authentication, and access control in the cloud.	• User provisioning • Single Sign-On (SSO) • Role-Based Access Control (RBAC) • Multi-Factor Authentication (MFA)
Data Encryption	Protects data while it is in transit and at rest by encrypting it with algorithms.	• Encryption for data in transit and at rest • Key management
Cloud Security Gateways (CSGs)	Serves as a bridge between cloud service providers and users, overseeing traffic and enforcing security.	• Data Loss Prevention (DLP) • Malware detection • Encryption • Traffic monitoring and regulation
Security Information and Event Management (SIEM)	Collects and analyzes logs from cloud services to detect and respond to security events.	• Real-time monitoring • Event correlation • Alerting • Threat detection
Cloud Access Security Brokers (CASBs)	Provides visibility and control over cloud usage between customers and service providers.	• Data protection in cloud apps • Activity monitoring • Enforcement of security policies
Threat Intelligence Services	Provides up-to-date information on emerging threats, vulnerabilities, and attack patterns.	• Threat feeds • Vulnerability alerts • Attack pattern detection
Cloud Workload Protection (CWPP)	Protects virtual machines (VMs) and workloads in the cloud.	• Vulnerability assessment • Intrusion detection/prevention • Workload firewalling
Cloud Data Loss Prevention (DLP)	Prevents unauthorized disclosure of sensitive data in the cloud.	• Sensitive data tracking • Data exfiltration detection • Data protection regulations compliance
Container Security	Secures containerized applications, such as Docker and Kubernetes, in the cloud.	• Vulnerability detection • Image integrity verification • Runtime protection for containers
Cloud Security Assessments and Audits	Provides ongoing evaluations of cloud security through assessments and audits.	• Penetration testing • Vulnerability assessments • Compliance audits • Security gap identification

2.7 IMPORTANCE OF CLOUD SECURITY

Cloud security is of utmost importance due to the following reasons.

- *Data Protection*: Cloud environments store and process vast amounts of sensitive data belonging to individuals and organizations. It is crucial to safeguard this data from unauthorized access, security breaches, and theft. Cloud security mechanisms, such as encryption, access restrictions, and data loss prevention, protect the confidentiality, integrity, and availability of data.
- *Regulatory Compliance*: A lot of industries must abide by legal frameworks that impose privacy and data protection requirements. Compliance with standards such as the General Data Protection Regulation (GDPR), Health Insurance Portability and Accountability Act (HIPAA), or Payment Card Industry Data Security Standard (PCI DSS) demand establishing sophisticated cloud security solutions. These regulations carry serious legal and financial repercussions for noncompliance.
- *Business Continuity*: Organizations may store data and apps on the cloud and access them from any location at any time. However, if cloud environments are not adequately secured, the risk of service disruptions, data loss, or unauthorized access increases. Business continuity and disruption minimization are ensured by putting cloud security measures in place, such as data backups, disaster recovery plans, and resilience mechanisms.
- *Defense against Cyber Threats*: Because cloud environments house important data and resources, hackers target them as the danger landscape is always changing. Protection from viruses, ransomware, DDoS assaults, and unauthorized access attempts is provided by cloud security. To lessen the effects of these threats, it offers mechanisms for detection, prevention, and response.
- *Trust and Customer Confidence*: Cloud service providers and companies that employ cloud services need to create trust with their customers. Demonstrating a commitment to cloud security reassures clients that their data is treated with greatest care and preserves the reputation and integrity of the firm. Strong security measures can be a competitive advantage in attracting and retaining customers.
- *Shared Responsibility Model*: In the cloud, there is a shared responsibility model between the cloud service provider and the customer. Customers are responsible for protecting their data and applications within the cloud, while the provider is in charge of protecting the underlying infrastructure. Implementing cloud security measures ensures that customers fulfill their part of the shared responsibility and adequately protect their assets
- *Vendor Selection and Due Diligence*: Organizations must evaluate the security practices and capabilities of potential vendors before selecting a cloud service provider. Organizations may choose suppliers who meet their security needs by assessing their security certifications, compliance observance, data protection measures, and incident response procedures.
- *Insider Threats*: Authorized persons who purposefully or accidentally abuse or disclose sensitive data can still occur in cloud systems. Implementing access

controls, monitoring user activities, and enforcing strong authentication measures helps mitigate the risks associated with insider threats in the cloud.

- *Scalability and Flexibility*: Cloud infrastructures offer scalability and flexibility, allowing enterprises to adapt to changing business demands. However, cloud scalability may expose businesses to risks and vulnerabilities if sufficient security precautions aren't taken. Scalability and flexibility are achieved without compromising the security of the infrastructure and data thanks to the use of cloud security.
- *Risk Mitigation*: Security measures for cloud environments are created to recognize, evaluate, and reduce risks. Organizations may proactively address possible vulnerabilities, lower the probability of security events, and lessen the effects of any security breaches by putting these procedures in place.

Table 2.7 offers the key reasons for cloud security and the related security measures.

Some of the other reasons for cloud security importance are shown in Figure 2.7. In general, cloud security is essential to safeguard data, ensure legal compliance, maintain business continuity, fend off cyberattacks, and win over customers' trust. In today's cloud-driven digital environment, it is a crucial part of a complete strategy to information security.

TABLE 2.7
Key Reasons for Cloud Security

Reason	Description	Security Measures
Data Protection	Safeguards sensitive data from breaches and theft.	• Encryption • Access restrictions
Regulatory Compliance	Ensures compliance with laws like GDPR, HIPAA, PCI DSS.	• Compliance audits • Security certifications
Business Continuity	Maintains access and prevents disruptions in cloud services.	• Backups • Disaster recovery plans
Defense against Cyber Threats	Protects against evolving threats like malware and DDoS attacks.	• Threat detection • Intrusion prevention
Trust and Customer Confidence	Builds customer trust by ensuring data protection.	• Transparency • Strong security protocols
Shared Responsibility Model	Divides security responsibilities between provider and customer.	• Clear role definitions • Shared security efforts
Vendor Selection and Due Diligence	Evaluates potential vendors' security measures.	• Security certifications • Compliance checks
Insider Threats	Mitigates risks from authorized personnel misusing data.	• Access controls • Monitoring • Authentication
Scalability and Flexibility	Enables growth without compromising security.	• Secure scaling • Vulnerability monitoring
Risk Mitigation	Identifies and reduces potential security risks.	• Risk assessments • Incident response plans

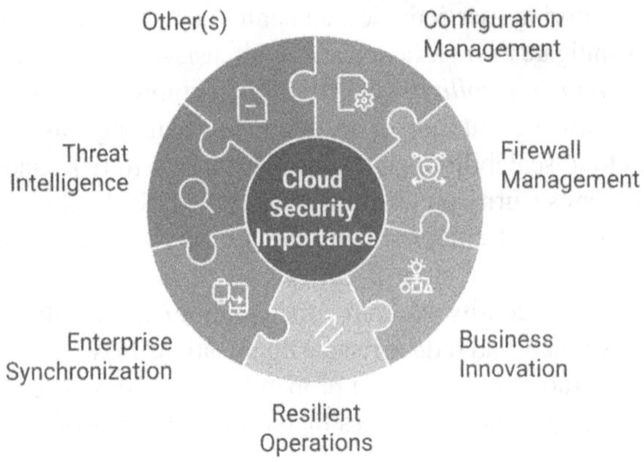

FIGURE 2.7 Cloud security importance.

2.8 SUMMARY

Modern IT infrastructure must include cloud security. Businesses must take a comprehensive approach to cloud security in order to protect their data, applications, and infrastructure. Businesses can maximize the advantages of cloud computing while reducing the associated security risks by implementing strong security measures, performing frequent risk assessments, and staying informed about emerging threats.

This chapter aims to provide the readers an understanding of the cloud computing security concepts, its challenges, issues, and the related solutions. Cloud computing security is a challenging topic that demands careful consideration and preparation. Although storing and accessing data in the cloud comes with certain inherent dangers and difficulties, there are also several practical steps that can be taken to reduce these risks and guarantee the privacy, integrity, and accessibility of cloud-based systems and data. This chapter helps to adopt a proactive and thorough approach to cloud security, which includes the use of effective access restrictions, encryption, monitoring, and incident response tools, as well as routine testing and assessment of security policies. This chapter will help the researchers to understand the highest standards of data protection and privacy, a properly designed and implemented cloud security strategy, which can offer significant advantages in terms of cost savings, flexibility, and scalability.

2.9 PRACTICE QUESTIONS/SOLUTIONS

MULTIPLE OBJECTIVE QUESTIONS

1 **What is the primary concern in cloud computing security?**
A) Data privacy
B) Network latency
C) Scalability
D) Cost efficiency

Answer: A) Data privacy

2 Which of the following is NOT a common cloud deployment model?

A) Public cloud
B) Private cloud
C) Hybrid cloud
D) Standalone cloud

Answer: D) Standalone cloud

3 What is the term for a security attack that involves overwhelming a system with traffic in order to make it unavailable to users?

A) Phishing
B) Spoofing
C) Denial of Service (DoS)
D) Man-in-the-Middle (MitM) attack

Answer: C) Denial of Service (DoS)

4 Which encryption method is commonly used to secure data in transit within a cloud environment?

A) RSA
B) AES
C) DES
D) MD5

Answer: C) DES

5 What is the concept of least privilege in cloud security?

A) Granting users the maximum possible access permissions
B) Granting users the least amount of access permissions necessary to perform their tasks
C) Granting access permissions based solely on user seniority
D) Granting access permissions based solely on user request

Answer: B) Granting users the least amount of access permissions necessary to perform their tasks

6 What is the purpose of multi-factor authentication (MFA) in cloud security?

A) To authenticate users using a single factor such as a password
B) To authenticate users using multiple factors such as a password and a fingerprint
C) To prevent users from accessing cloud resources
D) To allow unlimited access to cloud resources

Answer: B) To authenticate users using multiple factors such as a password and a fingerprint

7 **Which of the following is NOT typically considered a best practice for securing cloud environments?**
A) Regularly updating security patches
B) Implementing network segmentation
C) Storing sensitive data in plaintext
D) Enforcing strong password policies

Answer: C) Storing sensitive data in plaintext

8 **What is the term for a security breach caused by exploiting vulnerabilities in third-party software used by an organization?**
A) Insider threat
B) Supply chain attack
C) Zero-day attack
D) Phishing attack

Answer: B) Supply chain attack

9 **Which regulatory compliance framework is often relevant for cloud security, especially concerning personal data protection?**
A) HIPAA
B) GDPR
C) SOX
D) FISMA

Answer: B) GDPR

10 **Which cloud service model provides the highest level of control and responsibility for security to the cloud consumer?**
A) Infrastructure as a Service (IaaS)
B) Platform as a Service (PaaS)
C) Software as a Service (SaaS)
D) Function as a Service (FaaS)

Answer: A) Infrastructure as a Service (IaaS)

11 **What is the primary concern in cloud computing security?**
A) Data availability
B) Data confidentiality
C) Data integrity
D) Data scalability

Answer: B) Data confidentiality

12 Which of the following authentication methods is commonly used in cloud computing?

A) Biometric authentication
B) Single-factor authentication
C) Multi-factor authentication
D) Password authentication

Answer: C) Multi-factor authentication

13 Which encryption technique is commonly used to protect data in transit in cloud computing?

A) DES (Data Encryption Standard)
B) RSA (Rivest-Shamir-Adleman)
C) AES (Advanced Encryption Standard)
D) SHA (Secure Hash Algorithm)

Answer: C) AES (Advanced Encryption Standard)

14 What is a DDoS attack?

A) Distributed Detection of Service attack
B) Denial of Distributed Service attack
C) Distributed Denial of Service attack
D) Distributed Data on Storage attack

Answer: C) Distributed Denial of Service attack

15 Which of the following is not a cloud deployment model

A) Public
B) Private
C) Hybrid
D) Encrypted

Answer: D) Encrypted cloud

16 What is the term used for the process of managing and controlling access to resources in the cloud?

A) Resource management
B) Access control
C) Cloud governance
D) Identity management

Answer: B) Access control

17 Which of the following is not a potential security threat in cloud computing?

A) Insider threats
B) Data loss
C) Physical security breaches
D) Uninterrupted service

Answer: D) Uninterrupted service

18 Which compliance standard is commonly associated with cloud computing security?

A) HIPAA
B) GDPR
C) PCI DSS
D) All of the above

Answer: D) All of the above

19 What is the purpose of penetration testing in cloud security?

A) To monitor network traffic
B) To simulate cyberattacks
C) To manage encryption keys
D) To perform data backups

Answer: B) To simulate cyberattacks

20 What is the term for a security mechanism that monitors and manages traffic coming into and out of a cloud environment?

A) IDS
B) DDoS protection
C) Firewall
D) Antivirus software

Answer: C) Firewall

DESCRIPTIVE QUESTIONS

1 What are the primary security concerns associated with cloud computing?

Answer: The primary security concerns in cloud computing include data breaches, loss of control over data, insecure APIs, data loss, account hijacking, and inadequate security controls. Ensuring compliance with regulatory requirements and managing the shared responsibility model are also critical concerns.

2 How does the shared responsibility model impact cloud security?

Answer: The shared responsibility model divides security responsibilities between the cloud provider and the customer. The provider typically manages the security of the cloud infrastructure (hardware, software, networking), while the customer is responsible for securing their data, applications, and access controls. Understanding this model is crucial for effective security management.

3 What is data encryption, and why is it important in cloud computing?

Answer: Data encryption involves converting data into a coded format to prevent unauthorized access. It is essential in cloud computing because it protects data both at rest (stored data) and in transit (data being transferred). Encryption helps ensure confidentiality and integrity, safeguarding sensitive information from breaches.

4 What are the best practices for securing cloud data?

Answer: Best practices for securing cloud data include:

- Implementing strong encryption for data at rest and in transit.
- Regularly updating and patching software.
- Using multi-factor authentication (MFA).
- Regularly backing up data.
- Employing robust access controls and monitoring systems.
- Conducting regular security audits and vulnerability assessments.

5 What role does identity and access management (IAM) play in cloud security?

Answer: IAM is crucial in cloud security as it controls who can access cloud resources and what actions they can perform. Effective IAM involves creating and managing user identities, assigning roles and permissions, and monitoring access patterns. It helps in ensuring that only authorized users have access to sensitive resources.

6 How can organizations protect against data breaches in the cloud?

Answer: Organizations can protect against data breaches by:

- Implementing strong encryption practices.
- Using firewalls and intrusion detection/prevention systems.
- Enforcing strict access controls and user authentication mechanisms.
- Regularly monitoring and auditing access logs.
- Educating employees about phishing and other security threats.

7 What is a cloud security posture management (CSPM) tool, and how does it enhance security?

Answer: CSPM tools continuously monitor and assess cloud configurations to ensure they meet security best practices and compliance standards. They help identify and remediate misconfigurations, vulnerabilities, and compliance violations, enhancing overall cloud security by proactively addressing potential issues.

8 How can organizations ensure compliance with data protection regulations in the cloud?

Answer: Organizations can ensure compliance by:

- Understanding relevant regulations (e.g., GDPR, HIPAA).
- Implementing appropriate data protection measures (e.g., encryption, access controls).
- Regularly auditing and assessing cloud configurations.
- Collaborating with cloud providers to ensure their services meet compliance requirements.
- Keeping detailed records of data handling practices and policies.

9 What is the importance of secure APIs in cloud computing?

Answer: Secure APIs are crucial because they allow applications to interact with cloud services. If APIs are not properly secured, they can be vulnerable to attacks such as injection or unauthorized access. Ensuring APIs are protected with proper authentication, encryption, and rate limiting is essential for maintaining overall cloud security.

10 What strategies can be used to manage security in a multi-cloud environment?

Answer: Strategies for managing security in a multi-cloud environment include:

- Implementing consistent security policies and controls across all cloud platforms.
- Using centralized monitoring and management tools.
- Ensuring interoperability and integration of security solutions.
- Regularly assessing and auditing each cloud provider's security measures.
- Establishing clear communication and protocols for incident response.

11 How does data sovereignty affect cloud security?

Answer: Data sovereignty refers to the legal implications of data being subject to the laws and regulations of the country where it is stored. It affects cloud security by dictating how data must be handled and protected based on regional laws. Organizations must ensure their cloud providers comply with relevant data sovereignty requirements.

12 What is a cloud access security broker (CASB), and how does it contribute to security?

Answer: A CASB is a security tool that sits between an organization's on-premises infrastructure and cloud services. It provides visibility into cloud usage, enforces security policies, and helps detect and respond to threats. CASBs can enforce data protection measures, monitor user activities, and ensure compliance with security policies.

13 What are some common types of cloud security threats?

Answer: Common cloud security threats include:

- Data breaches
- Insider threats
- Denial-of-Service (DoS) attacks
- Account hijacking
- Insecure interfaces and APIs
- Misconfiguration of cloud resources

14 How can organizations prevent unauthorized access to cloud resources?

Answer: Organizations can prevent unauthorized access by:

- Implementing strong password policies and multi-factor authentication (MFA).
- Restricting access based on roles and responsibilities.
- Regularly reviewing and updating access permissions.
- Monitoring and logging access attempts and activities.
- Using network segmentation and firewall rules to limit access.

15 What is the significance of regular security audits in cloud computing?

Answer: Regular security audits are significant because they help identify vulnerabilities, misconfigurations, and compliance issues. They provide insights into the effectiveness of security controls and help organizations address potential risks before they are exploited. Audits also ensure that security policies and practices are up to date.

16 How does cloud service provider (CSP) transparency affect security?

Answer: CSP transparency affects security by providing insight into the provider's security practices, incident response protocols, and compliance certifications. A transparent CSP helps organizations assess risks, understand the security measures in place, and make informed decisions about cloud service adoption.

17 What is the role of data backup and recovery in cloud security?

Answer: Data backup and recovery are crucial components of cloud security as they ensure that data can be restored in case of loss, corruption, or attack (e.g., ransomware). Regular backups and well-defined recovery procedures help maintain business continuity and mitigate the impact of data breaches or system failures.

18 How can organizations protect against insider threats in the cloud?

Answer: Organizations can protect against insider threats by:

- Implementing least privilege access controls.
- Monitoring user activities and behavior.
- Conducting background checks and security training for employees.
- Using data loss prevention (DLP) tools.
- Establishing clear policies and procedures for reporting suspicious activities.

19 What are the key components of a cloud incident response plan?

Answer: Key components of a cloud incident response plan include:

- Incident detection and identification procedures.
- Roles and responsibilities for response teams.
- Communication plans for internal and external stakeholders.
- Procedures for containment, eradication, and recovery.
- Documentation and analysis of the incident for future prevention.

20 How can encryption be implemented in a cloud environment?

Answer: Encryption in a cloud environment can be implemented by:

Encrypting data at rest using cloud provider's encryption services or third-party tools.
Encrypting data in transit using secure protocols such as TLS/SSL.
Managing and securing encryption keys with a key management service (KMS).
Ensuring end-to-end encryption for sensitive data exchanges between cloud services and applications.

REFERENCES

1. Singh, A., & Chatterjee, K. (2017). Cloud security issues and challenges: A survey. *Journal of Network and Computer Applications*, *79*, 88–115.
2. Khalil, I. M., Khreishah, A., & Azeem, M. (2014). Cloud computing security: A survey. *Computers*, *3*(1), 1–35.
3. Khan, M. A. (2016). A survey of security issues for cloud computing. *Journal of Network and Computer Applications*, *71*, 11–29.
4. Liu, W. (2012, April). Research on cloud computing security problem and strategy. In *2012 2nd International Conference on Consumer Electronics, Communications and Networks (CECNet)* (pp. 1216–1219). IEEE.
5. Indu, I., Anand, P. R., & Bhaskar, V. (2018). Identity and access management in cloud environment: Mechanisms and challenges. *Engineering Science and Technology, An International Journal*, *21*(4), 574–588.
6. Agrawal, N., & Tapaswi, S. (2019). Defense mechanisms against DDoS attacks in a cloud computing environment: State-of-the-art and research challenges. *IEEE Communications Surveys & Tutorials*, *21*(4), 3769–3795.
7. Chowdary, P. R., Challa, Y., & Jitendra, M. S. N. V. (2019, May). Identification of MITM attack by utilizing artificial intelligence mechanism in cloud environments. In *Journal of Physics: Conference Series* (Vol. *1228*, No. 1, p. 012044). IOP Publishing.
8. Kavianpour, A., & Anderson, M. C. (2017, June). An overview of wireless network security. In *2017 IEEE 4th International Conference on Cyber Security and Cloud Computing (CSCloud)* (pp. 306–309). IEEE.
9. Denning, D. E., & Denning, P. J. (1979). Data security. *ACM Computing Surveys (CSUR)*, *11*(3), 227–249.
10. Lombardi, F., & Di Pietro, R. (2011). Secure virtualization for cloud computing. *Journal of Network and Computer Applications*, *34*(4), 1113–1122.
11. Harnik, D., Pinkas, B., & Shulman-Peleg, A. (2010). Side channels in cloud services: Deduplication in cloud storage. *IEEE Security & Privacy*, *8*(6), 40–47.
12. Kaaniche, N., & Laurent, M. (2014, March). A secure client side deduplication scheme in cloud storage environments. In *2014 6th International Conference on New Technologies, Mobility and Security (NTMS)* (pp. 1–7). IEEE.
13. Sengupta, S., Kaulgud, V., & Sharma, V. S. (2011, July). Cloud computing security--trends and research directions. In *2011 IEEE World Congress on Services* (pp. 524–531). IEEE.

3 Attacks in Cloud Computing

3.1 ATTACK DEFINITION

A set of harmful actions conducted by an attacker with the goal to interfere with a system or network constitutes an attack. It refers to any malicious attempt to breach the security of a system or a network with the aim to gain unauthorized access. Such attacks can be carried out by an individual or a group of technical skills. Security breaches provide a genuine and constant threat. In the realm of cloud computing, an "attack" refers to any malicious activity or attempt to compromise the security, integrity, or availability of cloud-based resources, services, or data. These attacks can take various forms and can target different layers of the cloud computing stack, including infrastructure, platform, and software layers. One common type of attack in cloud computing is a Distributed Denial of Service (DDoS) attack, where a large volume of traffic is directed at a cloud service or infrastructure with the intention of overwhelming it, rendering it unavailable to legitimate users. This can result in downtime, loss of revenue, and reputational damage for the affected organization.

Another significant threat is data breaches, where unauthorized parties gain access to sensitive or confidential information stored in the cloud. This can occur due to vulnerabilities in the cloud provider's infrastructure, misconfigured security settings, weak authentication mechanisms, or insider threats. Data breaches can lead to severe consequences, including financial losses, regulatory penalties, and damage to customer trust. Furthermore, cloud computing environments are susceptible to malware and other forms of malicious software. Attackers may deploy malware to compromise cloud instances, steal data, or launch further attacks within the cloud environment. This can lead to data loss, system downtime, and compromise of sensitive information. Additionally, insider threats pose a significant risk in cloud computing, where authorized users with malicious intent or compromised credentials may abuse their privileges to access, modify, or exfiltrate data. Insider threats can be particularly challenging to detect and mitigate, as the attackers may already have legitimate access to the cloud environment.

To address these threats, organizations must implement robust security measures, including encryption, access controls, intrusion detection systems, and regular security audits. It is also essential to stay informed about emerging threats and vulnerabilities in the cloud computing ecosystem and to continuously update security

DOI: 10.1201/9781003510772-3

policies and procedures to mitigate evolving risks. Collaboration with cloud service providers is also crucial to ensure that security best practices are implemented effectively across the cloud infrastructure. By taking proactive steps to enhance security posture and resilience, organizations can better protect their assets and mitigate the risk of attacks in the cloud computing environment.

3.2 ATTACK SCENARIO IN CLOUD COMPUTING

The market for cloud computing is enormous. The cloud services market is expected to reach *$287 billion* in value by *2025* after enjoying recent growth in popularity. However, many new risks have also been discovered as a result of this surge in popularity. For example, in one attack scenario, an attacker compromises a Cloud Service Provider (CSP) before leveraging their privileged access to steal data from the company's other clients. The DDoS attack scenario in a cloud computing environment is depicted in Figure 3.1. The DDoS attacks can be broadly classified into two types: High-Rate and Low-Rate. In a High-Rate DDoS attack (HR-DDoS), the attacker sends a high volume of attack traffic toward the victim server. The visibility of such an attack is high. Thus, the attackers are fascinated toward sophisticated attack launching strategies such as Low-Rate DDoS attacks (LR-DDoS). LR-DDoS attacks also known as the vulnerability attack or the semantic attack which exploit the protocols weaknesses rather than exhausting the network bandwidth or cloud computing resources [1]. The LR-DDoS attack traffic looks similar to the legitimate traffic. Thus, it is hard to identify such an attack as compared to the HR-DDoS attack [2]. In Figure 3.1, to mimic the real environment, both benign and attack traffic are considered. The DDoS attacks in the cloud may affect the economic budget of the CSP or guarantee quality services that are being offered to legitimate users or make the services unavailable.

Access to virtualized computer resources is made available through on-demand services provided by cloud infrastructure. The services are provided via an online connection that is normally secure. Businesses now frequently choose cloud computing because it is seen to be more economical and effective than conventional on-premises alternatives. Organizations may profit from the cloud services in a number of ways, including enhanced flexibility, scalability, and cost savings. It does, however, also introduce fresh security vulnerabilities that do not exist in conventional IT systems.

Insider attacks and external assaults are the two broad categories into which cloud computing attack scenarios may be divided. When compared to outsider attacks, which are conducted by malevolent users outside of the cloud infrastructure, insider attacks are initiated by trusted internal users of the organization and are more harmful and difficult to detect. A detailed sample DDoS attack scenario is explained below in formal mathematical terms, to offer the conceptual understanding in a cloud environment modelling. It captures various aspects, such as traffic dynamics, mitigation, resource allocation, and system resilience.

A Sample Mathematical Model for DDoS Attack in Cloud Computing

1) **System Parameters**

We define the following parameters for the model:

- C: Total computational capacity of the cloud (e.g., in requests per second).

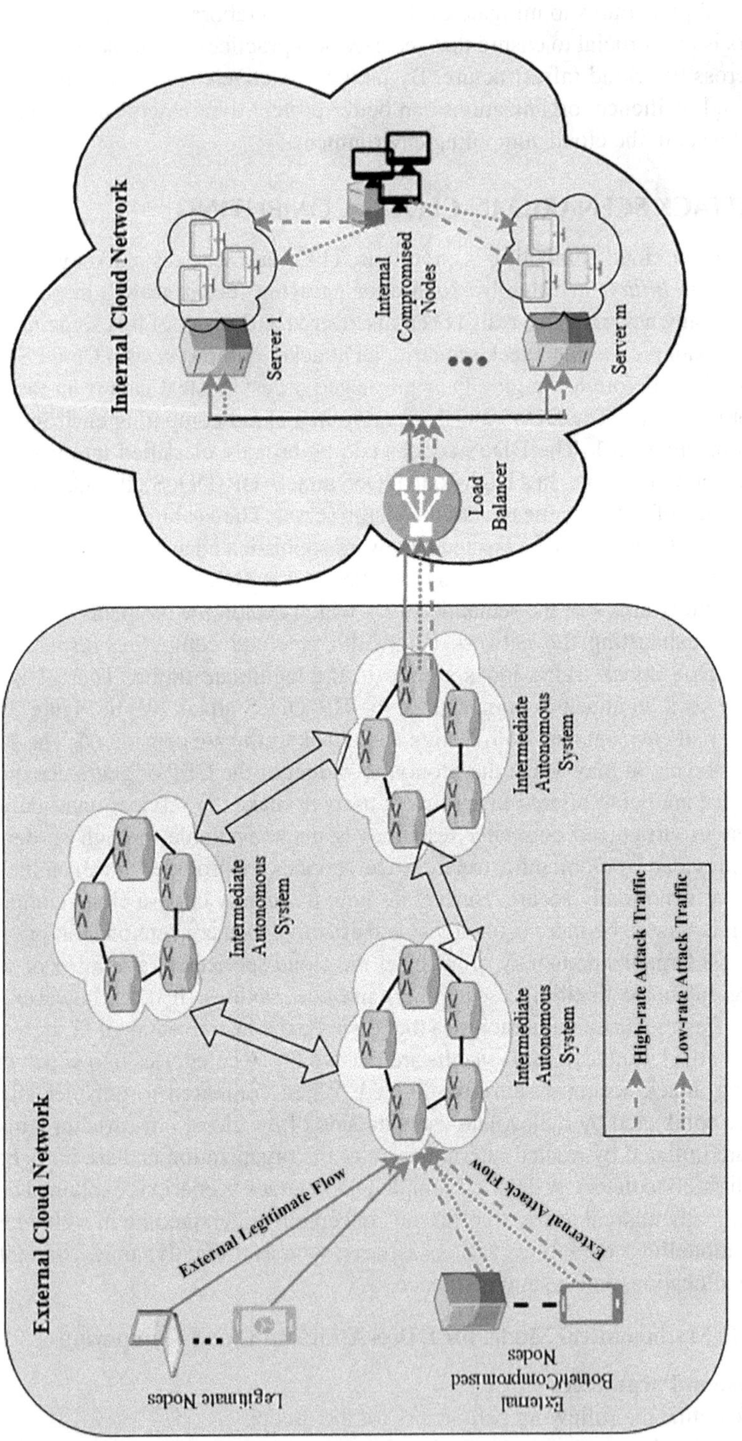

FIGURE 3.1 DDoS attack scenario in cloud computing [1].

- R: Rate of legitimate traffic (in requests per second).
- $A_i(t)$: Attack traffic rate from the i-th attacking source at time t.
- N: Total number of attacking sources.
- D(t): Mitigation efficiency of the system at time t, where $0 \leq D(t) \leq 1$.
- U(t): Resource utilization of the system at time t.
- M(t): Mitigation resources allocated by the system at time t.
- P(t): Probability of successful attack detection at time t.
- Δt: Detection delay (time taken to start mitigating the attack).
- λ: Growth rate of attack traffic.
- ρ: Depletion rate of attacker resources.
- M_{max}: Maximum mitigation resources available.
- β: Effectiveness of mitigation per unit resource.
- α: Detection efficiency constant.
- δ: Delay constant for detection.
- γ: Scaling factor for resource allocation.
- T_{attack}: Time at which the attack starts.
- M_{budget}: Total mitigation budget.

2) Traffic Dynamics

a) Total Incoming Traffic:

$$T(t) = R + \Sigma_{i=1}{}^{N} A_i(t) \tag{3.1}$$

The total traffic entering the system, combining legitimate traffic R and attack traffic from N sources.

b) Attack Traffic:

$$A(t) = \Sigma_{i=1}{}^{N} A_i(t) \tag{3.2}$$

The total traffic generated by all attack sources.

c) Mitigated Attack Traffic:

$$A_{eff}(t) = (1 - D(t))A(t) \tag{3.3}$$

The attack traffic that remains after applying mitigation.

d) Effective Total Traffic:

$$T_{eff}(t) = R + A_{eff}(t) \tag{3.4}$$

The traffic that must be processed by the system, including mitigated attack traffic and legitimate traffic.

3) Resource Utilization

a) Utilization Rate:

$$U(t) = T_{eff}(t) / C \tag{3.5}$$

The proportion of system resources utilized by incoming traffic.

b) Overload Condition:

$$U(t) > 1 \tag{3.6}$$

The condition indicates that the system is overloaded.

c) Service Availability:

$$S(t) = \max(0, 1 - U(t)) \tag{3.7}$$

The probability of maintaining service availability based on resource usage.

4) **Mitigation Efficiency**

a) Detection Probability:

$$P(t) = 1 - e^{-\alpha M(t)} \tag{3.8}$$

The probability of detecting an attack, which depends on the resources allocated for detection.

b) Mitigation Function:

$$D(t) = \beta M(t) \tag{3.9}$$

The efficiency of mitigation as a function of the resources allocated.

c) Dynamic Resource Allocation:

$$M(t) = \min(M_{max}, \gamma \cdot A(t)) \tag{3.10}$$

The allocation of resources for mitigation, proportional to attack intensity.

5) **Attack Dynamics**

a) Attack Traffic Growth:

$$A(t) = A(0)e^{\lambda t} \tag{3.11}$$

Exponential growth of attack traffic over time.

b) Cumulative Attack Traffic:

$$A_{cumulative}(t) = \int_0^t A(t')dt' \tag{3.12}$$

The total attack traffic over a given period.

c) Resource Depletion:

$$A_{depletion}(t) = A(t)/(1+\rho t) \quad (3.13)$$

Describes the gradual depletion of attacker resources over time.

6) **System Resilience**

a) Maximum Sustainable Traffic:

$$T_{max} = C + M_{max}\beta \quad (3.14)$$

The maximum traffic the system can handle, considering mitigation.

b) Resilience Threshold:

$$T_{threshold} = T_{max} - R \quad (3.15)$$

The maximum attack traffic the system can sustain without failure.

c) Failure Condition:

$$A(t) > T_{threshold} \quad (3.16)$$

The condition where attack traffic exceeds the system's resilience.

7) **Detection and Response Delay**

a) Detection Delay:

$$\Delta t = \delta / P(t) \quad (3.17)$$

The time delay in detecting an attack, inversely related to the detection probability.

b) Response Time:

$$T_{response} = T_{attack} + \Delta t \quad (3.18)$$

The total time required to detect and respond to an attack.

8) **System Load Analysis**

a) Legitimate Traffic Utilization:

$$U_{legit}(t) = R / C \quad (3.19)$$

The proportion of system resources used by legitimate traffic.

b) Attack Traffic Utilization:

$$U_{attack}(t) = A_{eff}(t)/C \quad (3.20)$$

The proportion of system resources consumed by attack traffic after mitigation.

c) Total Utilization:

$$U(t) = U_{legit}(t) + U_{attack}(t) \quad (3.21)$$

The combined resource utilization of legitimate and attack traffic.

9) **Long-Term Stability**

a) Resource Stability:

$$\int_0^{\infty} M(t)dt \le M_{budget} \quad (3.22)$$

Ensures that the total resources allocated for mitigation remain within budget.

b) Traffic Stabilization:

$$\text{Lim} \to \infty A_{eff}(t)/T_{eff}(t) = 0 \quad (3.23)$$

Ensures that attack traffic becomes negligible relative to total traffic over time.

This detailed mathematical model provides a comprehensive framework for analyzing DDoS attacks and mitigation strategies in cloud computing environments. The description of various attacks in a cloud computing environment is illustrated in Table 3.1.

TABLE 3.1
Various Attacks in a Cloud Computing Environment

Attack	Description	Potential Impact
Data Breach	Unauthorized access or theft of sensitive data stored in the cloud.	Compromise of sensitive information, financial loss, reputation damage.
Denial of Service (DoS)	Overwhelming cloud resources or infrastructure to disrupt service availability.	Service unavailability, loss of productivity, financial losses.
Man-in-the-Middle (MITM)	Intercepting communication between cloud users and services to eavesdrop or manipulate data.	Data interception, unauthorized access, data manipulation, information disclosure.

TABLE 3.1
(Continued)

Attack	Description	Potential Impact
Account Hijacking	Unauthorized access to user accounts or administrative privileges.	Unauthorized data access, data manipulation, service disruption, identity theft.
Malware Injection	Introduction of malicious software into the cloud environment.	Data corruption, unauthorized access, system compromise, disruption of services.
Insider Threat	Unauthorized activities or malicious actions by individuals with authorized access to the cloud environment.	Data breaches, unauthorized access, data manipulation, service disruption.
Virtual Machine (VM) Escape	Exploiting vulnerabilities to escape from a virtual machine and access the underlying host system.	Unauthorized access to other VMs, data exposure, compromise of cloud infrastructure.
Data Loss	Accidental or intentional deletion or corruption of data stored in the cloud.	Data loss, unrecoverable data, financial and operational impact.
API Vulnerabilities	Exploiting weaknesses in cloud application programming interfaces (APIs).	\Unauthorized access, data exposure, service disruption, privilege escalation.
Crypto-currency Mining	Unauthorized utilization of cloud resources for crypto-currency mining.	Increased resource usage, reduced performance, financial losses.

Although it is not comprehensive, Table 3.1 gives a basic summary of different attacks in cloud computing. Depending on the particular conditions and security mechanisms in place, the possible impact may change.

3.3 TYPES OF ATTACK

Both insider and outsider attacks can be classified into four categories based on the cloud components, namely network, virtual machines, storage, and applications which are elaborated as follows [3–7]. The related taxonomy is provided in Figure 3.2.

3.3.1 Network-based Attacks

A network that connects the cloud machines inside the cloud architecture and connects them to other external cloud computers. An attacker may target the cloud services and resources by taking advantage of network flaws. It might compromise the services' promised level of quality and jeopardize the security and privacy of user data. Below is a discussion of the network-based assaults.

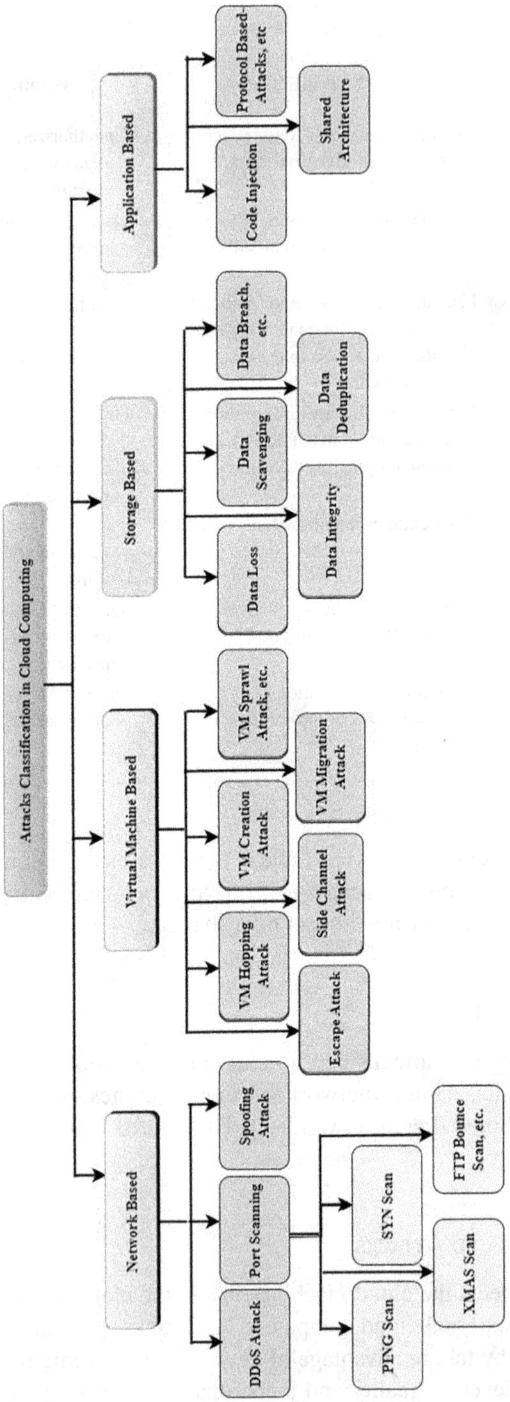

FIGURE 3.2 Classification of attacks in cloud computing.

a. *Port Scanning*: The attacker uses the port scan approach to find the network's openings or weak spots. Cybercriminals use port scanning attacks to locate open ports and determine whether they are transmitting or receiving data. Additionally, if any active security devices such as firewalls are present in the network, it offers information about them. Additionally, it provides information on the services that are active, the people who control them, whether anonymous logins are permitted or not, whether services need user authentication, etc. Any of the following port scanning methods can be used by an attacker, depending on their objectives.
   1) Ping Scan: It is one of the most straightforward scanning techniques used to determine the condition of any host. Ping scan delivers ICMP queries to several servers using the Internet Control Message Protocol (ICMP). The IT administrators can utilize this strategy for troubleshooting. A firewall may also be used to deactivate the ping scan, which prevents attackers from utilizing it to scan the network.
   2) SYN Scan or Half-open Scan: Synchronize scan, often known as SYN, checks a port's condition without creating a complete connection. SYN scans leave the target waiting while sending the SYN message. It is an efficient method for finding networks' open ports.
   3) XMAS Scan: The firewalls are less alerted by the quieter XMAS scan. For instance, a successful data transmission results in the termination of a TCP connection using a FIN packet, which the firewall misses. Since no response is anticipated and the port is open, XMAS scan transmits packets with all flags set, including FIN.
b. *Botnet*: A botnet is a collection of hacked or hijacked computers (sometimes referred to as zombies) that the attacker may remotely manipulate to carry out different cyberattacks. A botnet may be used by an attacker to perform DDoS assaults while being controlled by a command and control server. In DDoS assaults, botnets overwhelm the target server with attack flows, rendering the services inaccessible to authorized users. Blacklisting, packet filtering, reverse engineering, port blocking, and other defenses are available to combat botnets.
c. *Spoofing Attack*: When engaging in a spoofing attack, a fraudster hides his own identity and attempts to pass for someone else. Spoofing attacks come in a variety of forms, including IP spoofing, ARP spoofing, DNS spoofing, MAC spoofing, etc. To make the IP traceback challenging, attackers use the IP spoofing method. In IP spoofing, the source IP address is used by the attacker to target the victim computer or get access to the authorized data. Similar to IP spoofing, DNS spoofing involves the DNS server returning a fictitious IP address and diverting network traffic to the attacker's machine. Filtering, route fingerprinting, the ratio of TCP SYN and FIN packets, and other techniques can be used to detect spoofing attempts.
d. Man-in-the-Middle (MITM) Attack: In this attack, an attacker secretly intercepts, alters, or relays communication between two parties without their knowledge. The attacker essentially "sits" between the two parties, impersonating each one to the other, and can read, modify, or inject malicious

content into the communication. MITM attacks can be active or passive. In active MITM, the attacker aims to target the integrity of the message, whereas in passive attack, the attacker aims to listen to the communication.

e. Distributed Denial of Service (DDoS) Attack: It is a malicious attempt to disrupt the normal traffic of a targeted server, service, or network by overwhelming it with a flood of malicious traffic. The goal is to make the targeted system unavailable to its intended users, often causing a service outage or slowdown. Based on the literature, DDoS attacks can be categorized into two types: high rate and low rate. In high-rate DDoS attacks, an attacker sends a flood of malevolent packets toward the target server to make its services/resources unavailable to the benign users. Since the high-rate DDoS attacks are easy to detect, the attackers are fascinated toward the low-rate DDoS attacks. Low-rate DDoS attacks exploit the protocol vulnerabilities and aim to target the guaranteed quality of service.
f. Phishing Attack: In this attack, an attacker attempts to deceive individuals into providing sensitive information, such as login credentials, personal details, or financial data, by pretending to be a trustworthy entity or person. The attackers often use email, text messages, or fake websites to mislead victims.

Table 3.2 summarizes the different attack types, their methods, impacts, and potential mitigation strategies in a precise and concise format.

The general progression of network-based attacks in cloud computing is shown in Figure 3.3.

Figure 3.4 represents the distribution of various network-based attacks targeting cloud environments in 2023. DDoS attacks remain the most prevalent, followed by ransomware attacks and credential theft [8,9].

Additionally, the data discussed in [10] effectively summarizes the landscape of network-based attacks targeting cloud computing infrastructures, emphasizing the need for robust security measures to mitigate these threats. The data indicates that DDoS attacks account for 40% of the identified incidents, highlighting their prominence as a threat in cloud environments. This is supported by findings from a study that analyzed over 200 TB of NetFlow records, which categorized attacks based on significant traffic volume and abnormal communication patterns. SQL injection attacks make up 25%, with attackers exploiting vulnerabilities in applications hosted on cloud platforms. Port Scanning and Brute Force attacks represent 15% and 10%, respectively, showcasing common tactics used by attackers to probe for vulnerabilities within cloud services. Lastly, Malicious Web Activity, including interactions with known malicious hosts, also constitutes 10% of the attack types observed.

3.3.2 VM-based Attacks

In the cloud, virtual machine (VM)-based attacks often include taking advantage of holes in the virtualization layer to obtain unauthorized access to other virtual machines or the host system below. Here are several typical virtual machine-based assaults in the cloud.

TABLE 3.2
Comparative Analysis of Network-Based Attacks

Attack Type	Description	Method	Impact	Mitigation
Port Scanning	Identifying open ports and network vulnerabilities.	Ping, SYN, or XMAS scans.	Exposes open ports, services, and attack vectors.	Firewalls, port filtering, IDS.
Botnet	Remote control of hijacked machines for attacks.	DDoS via botnets controlled by C&C servers.	Service disruption, resource exhaustion.	Traffic filtering, anti-bot tools, network monitoring.
Spoofing Attack	Impersonating trusted entities.	IP, ARP, DNS spoofing.	Unauthorized access, data manipulation.	IP traceback, DNS filtering, anomaly detection.
MITM Attack	Intercepting and altering communications.	Active (modifying) or passive (eavesdropping).	Data theft, confidentiality breach.	Encryption (SSL/TLS), VPNs, mutual authentication.
DDoS Attack	Overloading servers with malicious traffic.	Distributed traffic floods (botnets).	Service downtime, slowdowns.	Anti-DDoS services, traffic scrubbing, rate limiting.
Phishing Attack	Deceptive attempts to steal sensitive info.	Fake emails/websites to steal data.	Identity theft, unauthorized access.	Email filtering, MFA, user training.

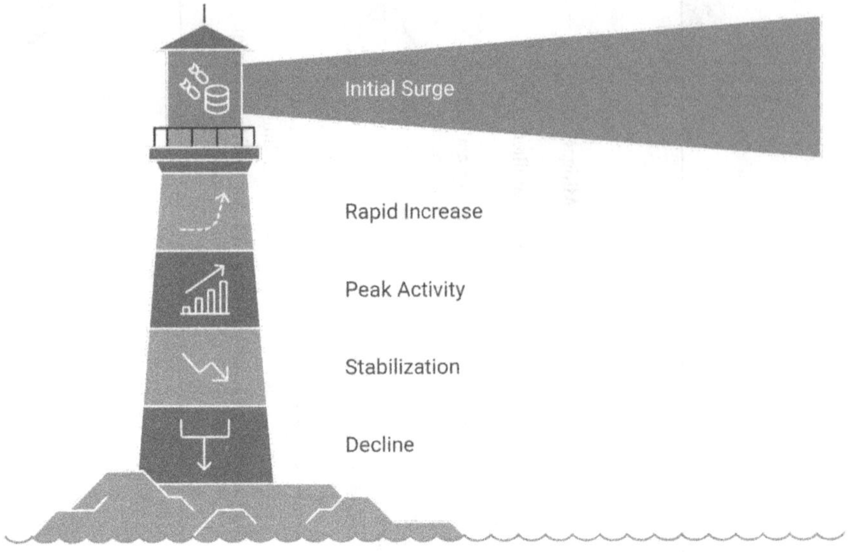

FIGURE 3.3 Progression of network-based attacks.

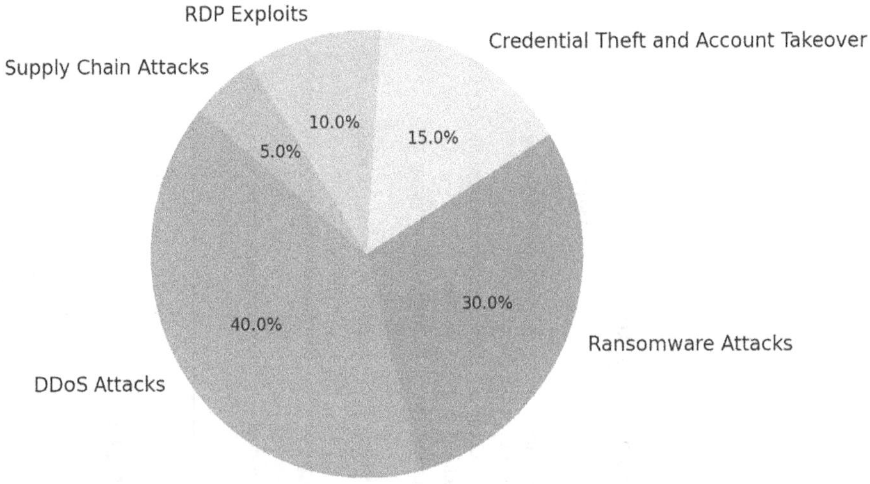

FIGURE 3.4 Distribution of network-based attacks in cloud computing.

a. *Escape Attempt*: An attacker may try to leave a virtual machine and access the host system below. This can be accomplished by taking advantage of flaws in the hypervisor or other virtualization layer components.
b. *VM Hopping Attack*: In a multi-tenant cloud system, an attacker may try to hop laterally from one virtual machine to another by taking advantage of holes in the virtualization layer. Accessing private information or resources on other virtual computers is possible using this method.

c. *Side Channel Attack*: Attacks that take advantage of information leaking from the virtualization layer are known as side channel attacks. For instance, a hacker may utilize timing data to guess what other virtual machines on the same host are doing. Authentication mechanisms and cryptographic methods can be used to handle these attacks.
d. *VM Sprawl Attack*: This involves an attacker creating a large number of virtual machines in the cloud, which can consume resources and cause performance issues for legitimate users. This can be used as a distraction or as part of a larger attack.
e. *VM Creation Attack*: A VM can be replicated by placing a malicious code inside the VM image and further used for the malicious intents. Such VMs can be identified using the VM management system with filters and scanners.
f. *VM Migration and Roll Back Attack*: During active VM migration from host physical machine to other physical machine, the content of the VM (such as log of execution state) becomes accessible to unauthorized users and vulnerable to various attacks. Such attacks can be prevented by configuring effective security policies.

Table 3.3 highlights the key types of VM-based attacks in cloud environments, their potential risks, and some strategies to mitigate such attacks effectively.

To protect against these types of attacks, cloud providers and users should ensure that their virtualization layer is properly configured and kept up-to-date with security patches. Additionally, users should implement strong access controls and network segmentation to limit the impact of any potential attacks.

Figure 3.5 represents the Distribution of VM-Based Attacks in Cloud Computing. The data is based on [11,12] and summarizes the prevalence of various types of VM attacks, highlighting their significance in cloud security. According to recent analyses, VM Escape attacks account for 30%, allowing attackers to breach the isolation of a guest VM and access the hypervisor, potentially compromising all VMs on the host. VM Hopping follows at 25%, where attackers exploit vulnerabilities to move between VMs on the same physical host, risking unauthorized access to sensitive data. Hyperjacking, representing 20%, involves taking control of the hypervisor itself, granting attackers management over all VMs. Additionally, VM Migration Attacks constitute 15%, targeting vulnerabilities during the migration process between hosts, which can jeopardize data integrity. Finally, Administrative VM Attacks make up 10%, involving malicious insiders who misuse their administrative privileges to manipulate or compromise VMs. This distribution underscores the diverse and evolving nature of threats facing virtualized environments in cloud computing.

3.3.3 Storage-based Attacks

Storage-based attacks exploit the vulnerabilities of cloud storage infrastructure. These attacks target the storage repositories or system where the user data is stored and managed. A malicious user from outside or inside may steal sensitive data stored

TABLE 3.3
Analysis of VM-based Attacks in the Cloud

Attack Type	Description	Impact	Mitigation
Escape Attempt	Attacker tries to break out of the VM and access the host system.	Full compromise of the host system.	Patch hypervisor vulnerabilities, ensure strong isolation.
VM Hopping Attack	Attacker moves between VMs, exploiting virtualization flaws.	Unauthorized access to other VMs.	Enhance VM isolation and monitoring.
Side Channel Attack	Attacker uses indirect info (e.g., timing) from VMs on the same host.	Data leakage from other VMs.	Apply cryptographic protection and timing defenses.
VM Sprawl Attack	Attackers create excessive VMs to drain resources or distract.	Resource exhaustion and potential DoS.	Limit VM creation and monitor resource usage.
VM Creation Attack	Malicious VM with harmful code is created and spread.	Malware spread and system damage.	Scan VM images and enforce creation policies.
VM Migration Attack	Sensitive data exposed during VM migration.	Data leakage or exposure of system state.	Encrypt VM migration and control access.

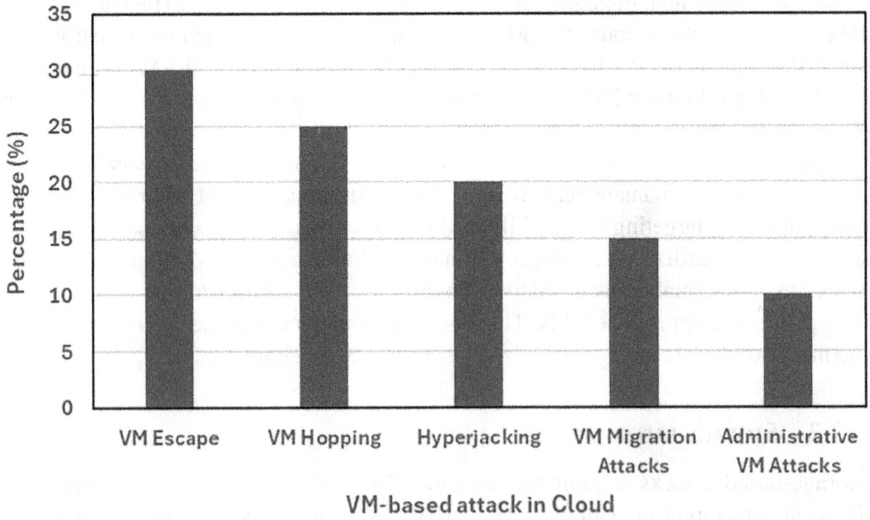

FIGURE 3.5 Distribution of VM-based attacks in cloud computing.

on the storage devices. With access, the attacker may perform data manipulation or alteration. Some of the major storage-based attacks are elaborated below.

a. *Data Breach*: It refers to the unauthorized access to the sensitive data stored on cloud storage infrastructure. Attackers may exploit weak authentication mechanisms, misconfigured access control, or vulnerabilities on cloud storage to gain unauthorized access.
b. *Data Loss*: Data loss may occur because of software bugs, hardware failures, or malicious activities. Attackers may intentionally corrupt or delete cloud data and make it inaccessible to the legitimate users.
c. *Data Integrity Attack*: The aim of such attacks is to compromise the veracity of the cloud data. Attackers may temper or modify the data which leads to unauthorized changes or malicious manipulations.
d. *Data Scavenging*: When data is erased from a storage device, it may not be removed completely from the file system. Consequently, the erased data may be recovered by the attacker which is known as the data scavenging.
e. *Data Deduplication*: It is a technique to eliminate the redundant data and reduce the storage requirements. An attacker may exploit data deduplication to inject the malicious data into the storage system or to recreate the sensitive data.

Table 3.4 summarizes the nature, attack mechanisms, impacts, and potential examples/methods for each of the listed storage-based attacks.

TABLE 3.4
Analysis of Storage-Based Attacks

Attack Type	Description	Attack Mechanism	Impact	Examples
Data Breach	Unauthorized access to sensitive data.	Exploiting weak authentication or misconfigured access.	Data exposure, privacy violations.	Phishing, weak passwords, access control flaws.
Data Loss	Loss of data due to bugs, failure, or attacks.	Corrupting or deleting data intentionally.	Data loss, operational disruption.	Data corruption, DoS attacks.
Data Integrity Attack	Compromising the accuracy of cloud data.	Tampering with or modifying data.	Data corruption, loss of trust.	Changing records or logs.
Data Scavenging	Recovering deleted data that was not fully erased.	Using tools to recover erased data.	Exposure of sensitive information.	Data recovery tools to retrieve deleted files.
Data Deduplication	Exploiting data deduplication to inject malicious data or recover erased data.	Manipulating deduplication processes.	Malicious content injection, data exposure.	Inserting malicious data through deduplication.

Figure 3.6 outlines the prevalence of various types of storage-based attacks that pose significant risks to cloud environments [13,14]. Data breaches, representing 35%, are the most common type of attack, where unauthorized access to sensitive data occurs, often resulting from vulnerabilities in cloud storage systems or misconfigurations. Following this, Insider Threats account for 25%, highlighting risks posed by employees or contractors who may intentionally or unintentionally expose sensitive information. Ransomware attacks, which encrypt data and demand payment for decryption, comprise 20% of incidents, reflecting the growing trend of cybercriminals targeting cloud-stored data for financial gain. Additionally, Data Loss, attributed to accidental deletion or corruption, accounts for 10%, emphasizing the need for robust backup solutions. Lastly, Insecure APIs also represent 10% of attacks, where vulnerabilities in application programming interfaces can be exploited to gain unauthorized access to cloud storage services. This distribution underscores the critical need for enhanced security measures and vigilance in managing cloud storage environments to protect sensitive data from these diverse threats.

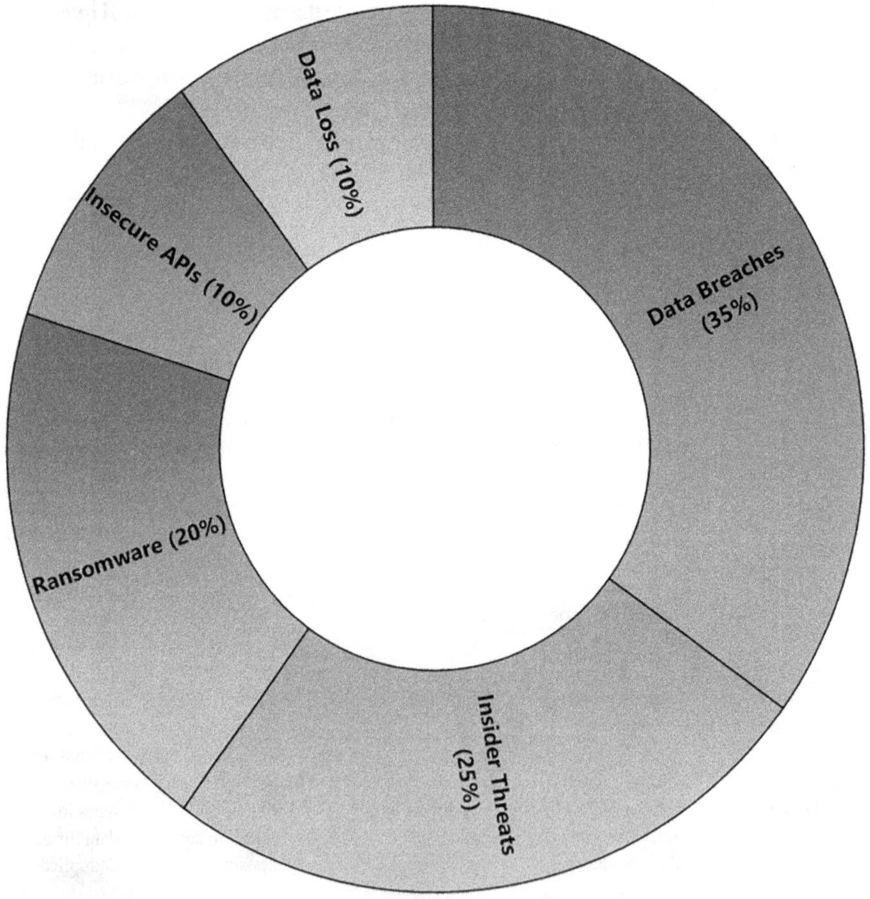

FIGURE 3.6 Distribution of storage-based attacks in cloud computing.

3.3.4 Application-based Attacks

The applications running on the cloud are vulnerable to various attacks by exploiting the protocols used to provide cloud services. The cloud architectural components that are being shared may also be exploited by the applications to perform malicious activities. The application-based attacks can be categorized into three types as described below.

a. *Code Injection*: By exploiting the insecure application interface, an attacker may inject the malicious code in the application. This malicious code is then executed and allows the attacker to perform malicious activities.
b. *Shared Architecture*: The execution path of a target application can be traced back on a shared architecture. This may be used to monitor the victim's activities or hijack the account. The application binary code analysis may be done to detect such a possibility.
c. *Web Services and Protocol-Based Attacks*: The message header of web service protocols such as SOAP may be manipulated with invalid requests. Application firewalls may be used to identify and block such attacks.

Table 3.5 summarizes the types of application-based attacks, their methods of execution, and potential countermeasures to mitigate such risks in cloud environments.

Figure 3.7 presents the prevalence of various types of application-based attacks that threaten cloud environments [15,16]. SQL injection attacks are the most common, accounting for 30% of incidents; these attacks exploit vulnerabilities in database queries to manipulate or access sensitive data. Following closely, Cross-Site Scripting (XSS) represents 25% of attacks, where attackers inject malicious scripts into web applications, allowing them to steal session tokens or redirect users to harmful sites. Denial-of-Service (DoS) attacks, which aim to overwhelm applications and render them inaccessible, comprise 20%, highlighting the significant risk they pose to service availability. Account Hijacking, making up 15%, involves unauthorized access to user accounts, often through stolen credentials or social engineering tactics. Lastly, Malware Injection attacks account for 10%, where malicious software is

TABLE 3.5
Analysis of the Application-Based Attacks in Cloud Environment

Attack Type	Description	Method of Attack	Countermeasures
Code Injection	Malicious code injected into insecure app interfaces.	Injecting code via vulnerable APIs.	Input validation, secure coding, Web Application Firewalls (WAF).
Shared Architecture Exploits	Exploiting shared cloud resources to trace or hijack applications.	Tracing execution paths, binary analysis.	Resource isolation, encryption, regular security audits.
Web Services and Protocol-Based	Manipulating web service protocol headers (e.g., SOAP).	Manipulating message headers or payloads.	Input validation, API security, message integrity checks, firewalls.

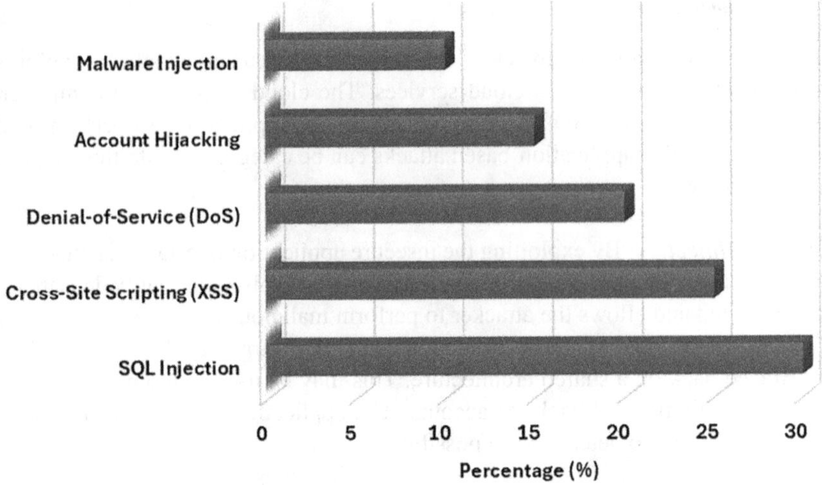

FIGURE 3.7 Distribution of application-based attacks in cloud computing.

introduced into cloud applications, potentially compromising data integrity and security. This distribution underscores the critical need for robust security measures and proactive monitoring to safeguard cloud applications against these diverse threats.

3.4 ATTACK LEVELS IN CLOUD

In terms of cloud security, attack levels relate to the numerous cloud infrastructure layers that might be the target of online assaults [17–20]. The various cloud infrastructure layers include application layer, platform layer, and infrastructure layer. The attacks on each of these levels are discussed below.

3.4.1 Application Layer

Attacks at the application layer in a cloud environment target the software applications and services that run on cloud infrastructure. These attacks exploit vulnerabilities in applications, often bypassing network-level defenses. Here are some common types of application layer attacks in the cloud.

1. **SQL Injection**: Attackers inject malicious SQL queries into input fields, potentially gaining unauthorized access to a database, modifying data, or even executing administrative operations.
2. **Cross-Site Scripting (XSS)**: Malicious scripts are injected into web pages viewed by other users. These scripts can steal cookies, session tokens, or other sensitive information.
3. **Cross-Site Request Forgery (CSRF)**: Attackers trick users into performing actions on a web application where they are authenticated, potentially leading to unauthorized actions on the user's behalf.

4. **Command Injection**: Malicious input is executed as commands on the server, leading to unauthorized actions or access to the underlying system.
5. **File Inclusion Attacks**: Attackers include files on the server to execute code or access sensitive data. This can be local file inclusion (LFI) or remote file inclusion (RFI).
6. **Session Hijacking**: Attackers steal or predict session tokens to gain unauthorized access to a user's session and perform actions as if they were the legitimate user.
7. **Denial of Service (DoS)**: Overloading an application with excessive requests, which can disrupt service availability. In cloud environments, attackers can leverage distributed denial of service (DDoS) tactics.
8. **Man-in-the-Middle (MitM) Attacks**: Attackers intercept and potentially alter communication between users and applications, which can lead to data breaches or unauthorized actions.
9. **Insecure Direct Object References (IDOR)**: Attackers exploit improper access controls to access objects or resources that they should not be able to access, such as user profiles or files.
10. **Security Misconfiguration**: Incorrect configuration of cloud resources or application settings that exposes the system to attacks. Examples include exposing sensitive data or allowing excessive permissions.
11. **API Vulnerabilities**: Exploiting weaknesses in application programming interfaces (APIs) that can lead to unauthorized access or manipulation of data. Common issues include inadequate authentication, insufficient rate limiting, and exposure of sensitive data.
12. **Business Logic Flaws**: Exploiting logical errors in application design or implementation to perform actions that should not be permitted, such as manipulating workflows or data.

An analysis of the different application layer attacks in a cloud environment is presented in the form of Table 3.6.

TABLE 3.6
Analysis of Application Layer Attacks in Cloud

Attack Type	Description	Impact	Targets
SQL Injection	Malicious SQL queries in input fields.	Unauthorized access, data loss	Database-driven web apps
XSS	Malicious scripts in web pages.	Stealing session data, cookies	Websites, forms
CSRF	Tricking users into unauthorized actions.	Actions on behalf of user	Authenticated web apps
Command Injection	Malicious input executed as commands.	System compromise	Web apps with user input
File Inclusion	Including malicious files on the server.	Code execution, data leaks	Web apps handling files

TABLE 3.6
(Continued)

Attack Type	Description	Impact	Targets
Session Hijacking	Stealing session tokens to impersonate users.	Unauthorized access	Web apps with sessions
DoS	Overloading an app with requests.	Service disruption	Web apps
MitM	Intercepting and altering communications.	Data breaches, tampering	Communication channels
IDOR	Accessing unauthorized resources.	Data exposure	Web apps with weak access control
Misconfiguration	Incorrect cloud or app setup.	Data exposure, access issues	Misconfigured cloud apps
API Vulnerabilities	Exploiting weak APIs (e.g., bad authentication).	Unauthorized access, data changes	APIs
Business Logic Flaws	Exploiting design flaws for unauthorized actions.	Data or workflow manipulation	Apps with flawed logic

3.4.2 Platform Layer

Attacks at the platform layer of cloud computing target the underlying cloud infrastructure and platform services that provide the foundational resources for applications. The platform layer includes the operating systems, virtual machines, container orchestration systems, and other platform services. Here are some common attacks at this layer:

1. **Hypervisor Attacks**
    - **Hypervisor Escape**: Attackers exploit vulnerabilities in the hypervisor to escape from a virtual machine (VM) and gain access to the host system or other VMs. This can lead to unauthorized access or control over the underlying infrastructure.
    - **VM Escape**: Similar to hypervisor escape but specifically targets the virtual environment to move from one VM to another, potentially compromising other VMs on the same host.
2. **Container Attacks**
    - **Container Breakout**: Exploiting vulnerabilities in containerization technologies (like Docker) to escape the container and gain access to the host operating system or other containers.
    - **Image Vulnerabilities**: Using compromised or vulnerable container images that could be exploited to execute malicious code or gain unauthorized access.
3. **Resource Exhaustion**
    - **Denial of Service (DoS)**: Overloading platform resources such as CPU, memory, or storage to disrupt service availability. This can affect

not only the targeted application but also other tenants sharing the same resources.
- **Resource Starvation**: Exploiting platform resource allocation to deplete shared resources, causing performance degradation or outages.

4. **Privilege Escalation**
   - **Unauthorized Access**: Exploiting misconfigurations or vulnerabilities to gain higher privileges than intended within the platform layer, which can lead to unauthorized access to critical resources or services.
5. **Platform Service Exploitation**
   - **Service Misconfigurations**: Exploiting misconfigured platform services (such as managed databases or storage) to gain unauthorized access or manipulate data. This could involve insecure storage settings, overly permissive access controls, or unpatched vulnerabilities.
   - **API Exploits**: Targeting platform APIs that control infrastructure and services to perform unauthorized actions or extract sensitive information.
6. **Side-Channel Attacks**
   - **Spectre and Meltdown**: Exploiting hardware vulnerabilities to extract sensitive information from other VMs or containers running on the same physical hardware. These attacks leverage flaws in CPU architectures to gain access to privileged information.
7. **Insider Threats**
   - **Malicious Insiders**: Individuals with legitimate access to the platform who misuse their privileges to compromise data or disrupt services. This could be through deliberate actions or by exploiting weak security policies.
8. **Data Leakage**
   - **Unintended Data Exposure**: Improperly configured storage or platform services leading to exposure of sensitive data. For instance, misconfigured cloud storage buckets or databases may be accessible to unauthorized users.
9. **Configuration and Deployment Issues**
   - **Improper Configuration**: Misconfigurations in platform settings (e.g., network settings, access controls) that can lead to vulnerabilities or expose services to attacks.
   - **Deployment Flaws**: Errors in deploying or updating platform services that introduce vulnerabilities or disrupt normal operations.
10. **Supply Chain Attacks**
    - **Compromised Components**: Attacks targeting components or services in the supply chain of the platform layer, such as third-party software or updates, which could introduce vulnerabilities or malicious code.

A comprehensive analysis of the attacks at the platform layer of cloud computing, detailing various attack types, their targets, techniques, and possible consequences, is presented in Table 3.7.

TABLE 3.7
Analysis of the Platform Layer Attacks in Cloud

Attack Type	Description	Targets	Techniques	Consequences
Hypervisor Attacks	Exploiting hypervisor flaws to access host or other VMs.	Hypervisor, Host System	- Exploit hypervisor vulnerabilities.	- Unauthorized control over host/VMs.
VM Escape	Moving between VMs on the same host via hypervisor flaws.	VMs, Host System	- Exploiting VM isolation flaws.	- Unauthorized access to VMs, data breaches.
Container Breakout	Escaping containers to the host OS or other containers.	Containers, Host OS	- Container isolation weaknesses.	- Host compromise, data access.
Image Vulnerabilities	Using compromised container images to run malicious code.	Containers, Images	- Malicious payloads in images.	- Unauthorized access, resource compromise.
Resource Exhaustion	Overloading platform resources to disrupt services.	Platform Resources (CPU, Memory, Storage)	- Flooding resources.	- Service downtime, degraded performance.
Denial of Service (DoS)	Overloading platform resources to cause service unavailability.	Platform Resources, Apps	- Resource flooding or misallocation.	- Service disruption, degraded performance.
Privilege Escalation	Gaining higher privileges to access sensitive resources.	Platform Services, VMs, Containers	- Exploiting misconfigurations or vulnerabilities.	- Unauthorized access to critical resources.
Unauthorized Access	Gaining access through misconfigurations or weak access controls.	Platform Services, APIs, Databases	- Exploiting weak controls.	- Data theft, service manipulation.
Platform Service Exploitation	Attacking misconfigured platform services or APIs.	Platform APIs, Managed Services, Databases	- Exploiting misconfigured services or weak APIs.	- Data breaches, service disruptions.
Side-Channel Attacks	Exploiting hardware flaws (e.g., Spectre, Meltdown) to extract data.	CPUs, VMs, Containers	- Exploiting CPU vulnerabilities.	- Data leakage across VMs/containers.
Insider Threats	Malicious insiders abusing access to compromise services/data.	Platform Services, Data	- Abuse of legitimate privileges.	- Data theft, service sabotage.
Data Leakage	Exposing sensitive data due to misconfigurations or weak controls.	Cloud Storage, Databases	- Misconfigured storage, weak encryption.	- Data exposure, unauthorized access.
Configuration Issues	Misconfigurations or deployment flaws creating vulnerabilities.	Platform Services, Network, Databases	- Poor network security or settings.	- Increased attack surface, unauthorized access.
Supply Chain Attacks	Targeting third-party components or updates to inject malicious code.	Platform Components, Third-Party Services	- Compromising third-party software.	- Malicious code execution, system-wide compromise.

3.4.3 Infrastructure Layer

Attacks at the infrastructure layer of cloud computing focus on the fundamental hardware and low-level virtualized resources that support the cloud environment. This layer includes physical servers, storage systems, network components, and hypervisors. The discussion of common types of attacks at this layer is as follows.

1. **Physical Attacks**
   - **Physical Theft**: Stealing physical hardware (e.g., servers, storage devices) to access or tamper with data.
   - **Tampering**: Physical tampering with hardware components to compromise data integrity or access.
   - **Environmental Attacks**: Disrupting the physical environment (e.g., power outages, environmental control failures) to impact data center operations.
2. **Hypervisor Attacks**
   - **Hypervisor Exploits**: Exploiting vulnerabilities in the hypervisor software to gain unauthorized access to the host or other virtual machines (VMs) running on the same hardware.
   - **VM Escape**: Attacking from a VM to gain access to the hypervisor and potentially other VMs or the host system.
3. **Side-Channel Attacks**
   - **Spectre and Meltdown**: Exploiting hardware vulnerabilities in modern CPUs to access sensitive information from other VMs or processes running on the same physical hardware.
   - **Cache Attacks**: Using CPU cache timing to infer sensitive information from other VMs sharing the same CPU cache.
4. **Resource Exhaustion**
   - **Denial of Service (DoS)**: Overloading infrastructure resources (e.g., network bandwidth, storage IOPS) to disrupt availability or degrade performance.
   - **Resource Starvation**: Depleting resources such as CPU, memory, or storage to impact the performance of other services sharing the same infrastructure.
5. **Network Attacks**
   - **Network Eavesdropping**: Intercepting and analyzing network traffic to gain unauthorized access to sensitive data.
   - **Man-in-the-Middle (MitM)**: Intercepting or altering communications between systems to compromise data integrity or confidentiality.
   - **Network Spoofing**: Impersonating legitimate network devices or services to gain unauthorized access or disrupt network operations.
6. **Data Center Attacks**
   - **Cooling and Power Failures**: Exploiting weaknesses in data center cooling or power systems to cause disruptions or damage.
   - **Data Center Access**: Unauthorized physical or remote access to data centers to tamper with or steal data.

7. **Firmware and Hardware Attacks**
   - **Firmware Exploits**: Exploiting vulnerabilities in firmware (e.g., BIOS, firmware updates) to compromise the hardware or gain unauthorized access.
   - **Hardware Backdoors**: Installing or exploiting hardware-based backdoors to gain persistent access or control over infrastructure.
8. **Supply Chain Attacks**
   - **Compromised Hardware**: Infiltrating the supply chain to insert malicious components into hardware before it is deployed.
   - **Malicious Updates**: Compromising firmware or software updates provided by hardware vendors to introduce vulnerabilities or backdoors.
9. **Cloud Service Provider (CSP) Attacks**
   - **Provider Compromise**: Targeting the cloud service provider itself to gain unauthorized access to the infrastructure, potentially affecting all tenants on that provider.
   - **Misconfiguration**: Exploiting misconfigurations in CSP infrastructure or management tools that expose sensitive resources or allow unauthorized access.

A tabular analysis of the attacks at the infrastructure layer of cloud computing, detailing various attack types, descriptions, targets, and respective consequences, is shown in Table 3.8.

TABLE 3.8
Analysis of Infrastructure Layer Attacks in Cloud

Attack Type	Description	Targets	Consequences
Physical Attacks	Attacks on physical hardware.	Servers, Storage	• Data theft, hardware damage, service disruption
Hypervisor Attacks	Exploiting hypervisor vulnerabilities.	Hypervisor, VMs, Host	• Unauthorized access to host/VMs, data breach
Side-Channel Attacks	Exploiting CPU vulnerabilities to leak data.	CPUs, VMs	• Data leakage across VMs, system compromise
Resource Exhaustion	Overloading infrastructure to disrupt services.	Network, Storage, CPU	• Service disruption, degraded performance
Network Attacks	Intercepting or altering network traffic.	Network Infrastructure	• Data theft, service disruption, communication compromise
Data Center Attacks	Attacks targeting data center infrastructure.	Data Centers, Power, Cooling	• Data loss, service downtime
Firmware/ Hardware Attacks	Exploiting vulnerabilities in firmware and hardware.	Firmware, Hardware	• Persistent access, control over infrastructure, hardware damage
Supply Chain Attacks	Attacking hardware or updates in the supply chain.	Hardware, Firmware	• System compromise, backdoors
CSP Attacks	Targeting cloud providers or misconfigurations.	Cloud Providers, Infrastructure	• Unauthorized access, provider-wide compromise

3.5 RESEARCH DIRECTIONS

Cloud security is a significant and active research area. Below are some potential study areas for cloud computing security [21–25].

- *Secure resource management and allocation*: Cloud computing requires the sharing of resources among many users, which might pose security risks. The development of methods for secure resource allocation and management, such as access control, isolation, and multi-tenancy, can be the subject of research.
- *Data security and privacy*: Concerns about data privacy and protection might arise when sensitive data is processed and stored on the cloud. The development of safe data processing and storage methods, such as data anonymization, secure data exchange, and encryption, can be the subject of research.
- *Threat identification and response*: A variety of security risks, such as malware, denial-of-service assaults, and insider threats, can affect cloud computing infrastructures. The development of efficient methods for spotting and combating security risks in the cloud, such as real-time monitoring, intrusion detection, and incident response, might be the subject of research.
- *Trust Management*: For consumers and service providers in particular, trust and reputation are important aspects of cloud computing. Techniques for measuring and maintaining trust and reputation in the cloud, such as identity and access management, authentication, and auditing, might be the subject of research.
- *Compliance and regulatory concerns*: Cloud computing is governed by a variety of compliance and regulatory norms, including those pertaining to data protection, privacy, and security. The development of methods for handling compliance and regulatory challenges in the cloud, such as frameworks for regulatory compliance, risk assessment, and compliance monitoring, can be the subject of research.
- *Security based on blockchain*: Blockchain technology may be able to address a number of security concerns in cloud computing, including safe data sharing and access management. Blockchain-based security methods for cloud computing environments might be the subject of research.

These are just a few potential research directions for security in cloud computing. Other areas of research could include secure cloud migration, secure DevOps practices, and cloud security economics. Furthermore, Table 3.9 provides the research directions for cloud computing security, along with a general description and future options. The table summarizes key research directions in cloud security, outlining the main focus areas and potential future developments. These areas address critical challenges such as data privacy, threat detection, resource management, and compliance within cloud environments. Future research options highlight emerging technologies and methods, including artificial intelligence, blockchain, and advanced encryption techniques, aimed at enhancing security, efficiency, and trust in cloud computing.

TABLE 3.9
Research Directions in Cloud Computing Security

Research Direction	Description	Future Options
Data Privacy and Confidentiality	Ensuring privacy through encryption, access control, and secure sharing.	Explore homomorphic encryption and differential privacy.
Threat Detection and Intrusion Prevention	Developing threat detection and mitigation systems.	Use AI and machine learning for improved detection.
Secure Data Outsourcing	Securing data transfer, deletion, and integrity when outsourcing to the cloud.	Investigate verifiable computation and secure data provenance.
Identity and Access Management	Enhancing authentication and access controls.	Integrate biometrics and blockchain for identity management.
Cloud Resource Management	Optimizing resource allocation and load balancing.	Explore machine learning for resource allocation.
Cloud Security Governance	Ensuring compliance with security standards and regulations.	Develop automated compliance tools and multi-cloud governance.
Secure Cloud Service Composition	Securing integration of multiple cloud services.	Focus on secure service orchestration and interoperability.
Cloud Forensics and Incident Response	Developing cloud-specific forensics and attack response methods.	Create forensic tools and standardized procedures.
Secure Cloud Monitoring and Auditing	Designing systems for monitoring, breach detection, and compliance.	Use AI and big data for real-time monitoring.
Secure DevOps in the Cloud	Integrating security into the DevOps lifecycle.	Automate security testing and compliance in DevOps pipelines.

3.6 SUMMARY

This chapter focuses on various attacks and attack levels in cloud computing. Attacks in cloud computing pose significant threats to organizations relying on cloud services for data storage, processing, and networking. Because cloud computing environments are open and dispersed, they might harbor flaws that hackers can use to enter systems without authorization, steal data, or interfere with services. These attacks encompass a range of techniques, including data breaches, DDoS (Distributed Denial of Service) attacks, and unauthorized access to cloud infrastructure. Malicious actors exploit vulnerabilities in cloud platforms, applications, or misconfigurations to compromise sensitive information, disrupt services, or gain unauthorized control. Moreover, insider threats and supply chain vulnerabilities further exacerbate security risks in cloud environments. Cloud providers and users must put in place a number of security controls, such as secure access restrictions, network segmentation, encryption, threat detection and response, and compliance monitoring, to combat these dangers. To remain ahead of changing threats and guarantee the ongoing security and resilience of cloud computing systems, ongoing research and development in cloud security is also provided along with future research directions.

3.7 PRACTICE QUESTIONS/SOLUTIONS

MULTIPLE OBJECTIVE QUESTIONS

1 **What is a Distributed Denial of Service (DDoS) attack?**

A) A type of attack where attackers gain unauthorized access to cloud servers.
B) An attack that floods a server with traffic, making it unavailable to legitimate users.
C) A method used by hackers to intercept data transmitted between cloud servers.
D) A form of social engineering attack targeting cloud users.

Answer: B) An attack that floods a server with traffic, making it unavailable to legitimate users.

2 **Which of the following is a characteristic of a Man-in-the-Middle (MitM) attack in cloud computing?**

A) Attackers exploit vulnerabilities in cloud server software.
B) Attackers intercept and manipulate communication between cloud users and servers.
C) Attackers flood a cloud server with fake requests.
D) Attackers steal user credentials by tricking them into providing sensitive information.

Answer: B) Attackers intercept and manipulate communication between cloud users and servers.

3 **What does SQL injection refer to in the context of cloud security?**

A) Exploiting vulnerabilities in SQL databases hosted on cloud servers.
B) Injecting malicious code into a cloud application to gain unauthorized access.
C) Manipulating SQL queries to retrieve sensitive information from a cloud database.
D) Overloading a cloud server with SQL requests to disrupt its operation.

Answer: C) Manipulating SQL queries to retrieve sensitive information from a cloud database.

4 **Which type of attack involves exploiting weaknesses in cloud infrastructure to gain unauthorized access?**

A) Insider attack
B) Cross-site scripting (XSS) attack
C) Zero-day exploit
D) Infrastructure as a Service (IaaS) attack

Answer: D) Infrastructure as a Service (IaaS) attack

5 What security measure can help mitigate the risk of data breaches due to insider threats in cloud computing?

A) Implementing multi-factor authentication for cloud users.
B) Encrypting sensitive data stored in the cloud.
C) Regularly monitoring and auditing user activities in the cloud environment.
D) Using strong firewall protection for cloud servers.

Answer: C) Regularly monitoring and auditing user activities in the cloud environment.

6 Which of the following is a common type of attack targeting cloud computing environments?

A) Phishing Attack
B) SQL Injection
C) Distributed Denial of Service (DDoS)
D) Man-in-the-Middle Attack

Answer: C) Distributed Denial of Service (DDoS)

7 In cloud computing, what is the primary goal of a data breach attack?

A) To increase network traffic
B) To alter the functionality of the cloud service
C) To gain unauthorized access to sensitive data
D) To shut down cloud infrastructure

Answer: C) To gain unauthorized access to sensitive data

8 Which attack involves an attacker gaining control of a cloud instance and using it to attack other systems?

A) Cross-Site Scripting (XSS)
B) Insider Threat
C) Cloud Service Misconfiguration
D) Cloud Instance Hijacking

Answer: D) Cloud Instance Hijacking

9 Which of the following is a typical method used to mitigate the risk of a DDoS attack in a cloud environment?

A) Implementing strong passwords
B) Using multi-factor authentication
C) Utilizing DDoS protection services
D) Regularly updating software

Answer: C) Utilizing DDoS protection services

10 What type of attack takes advantage of vulnerabilities in cloud storage configurations?

A) SQL Injection
B) Misconfigured Cloud Storage
C) Phishing
D) Ransomware

Answer: B) Misconfigured Cloud Storage

11 In the context of cloud computing, what does "data exfiltration" refer to?

A) Encrypting data for security
B) Unauthorized transfer of data from the cloud
C) Regularly backing up data
D) Increasing the amount of stored data

Answer: B) Unauthorized transfer of data from the cloud

12 Which security measure helps protect against unauthorized access to cloud resources by validating users' identities?

A) Firewall
B) Encryption
C) Identity and Access Management (IAM)
D) Backup Solutions

Answer: C) Identity and Access Management (IAM)

13 Which attack exploits weak or default passwords to gain access to cloud systems?

A) Credential Stuffing
B) Cross-Site Scripting (XSS)
C) SQL Injection
D) Malware Injection

Answer: A) Credential Stuffing

14 What is the main purpose of a Cloud Security Posture Management (CSPM) tool?

A) To create backups of cloud data
B) To monitor and manage cloud security configurations
C) To encrypt cloud data
D) To perform penetration testing

Answer: B) To monitor and manage cloud security configurations

15 What is a "drive-by download" attack in the context of cloud computing?

A) Downloading malicious software via compromised cloud services
B) Using a cloud service to store and distribute malware
C) Automatically installing malware when a user visits a compromised website
D) Downloading software updates from untrusted sources

Answer: C) Automatically installing malware when a user visits a compromised website

DESCRIPTIVE QUESTIONS

1 What is a DDoS attack in cloud computing?

Answer: A Distributed Denial of Service (DDoS) attack in cloud computing is a malicious attempt to disrupt the normal traffic of a targeted server, service, or network by overwhelming it with a flood of Internet traffic. This renders the service inaccessible to legitimate users.

2 How does a DDoS attack impact cloud services?

Answer: A DDoS attack can severely impact cloud services by causing downtime, slowing down performance, or even making the service completely unavailable. This can result in financial losses, damage to reputation, and potential breaches of Service Level Agreements (SLAs).

3 What is a man-in-the-middle (MITM) attack in cloud computing?

Answer: A man-in-the-middle (MITM) attack in cloud computing occurs when a malicious actor intercepts communication between two parties in a cloud environment. This can allow the attacker to eavesdrop on sensitive data, manipulate the communication, or impersonate one of the parties involved.

4 How can encryption help mitigate MITM attacks in cloud computing?

Answer: Encryption can help mitigate MITM attacks in cloud computing by securing the data transmitted between parties. With encryption, even if an attacker intercepts the communication, they would be unable to decipher the encrypted data without the encryption key, thus protecting the confidentiality and integrity of the data.

5 What is a data breach in cloud computing?

Answer: A data breach in cloud computing refers to unauthorized access to sensitive or confidential information stored in cloud-based systems. This can occur due to various factors such as weak security measures, insider threats, or external attacks, leading to the exposure of sensitive data to unauthorized parties.

6 How can multi-factor authentication (MFA) help prevent data breaches in cloud computing?

Answer: Multi-factor authentication (MFA) adds an extra layer of security by requiring users to provide multiple forms of verification before accessing cloud services. This can help prevent unauthorized access in case one of the authentication factors, such as a password, is compromised, thus reducing the risk of data breaches.

7 What is a ransomware attack in cloud computing?

Answer: A ransomware attack in cloud computing involves malware that encrypts files or systems hosted on cloud infrastructure, demanding payment from the victim in exchange for decryption keys. These attacks can disrupt operations, cause data loss, and result in financial losses for affected organizations.

8 How can regular data backups help mitigate the impact of ransomware attacks in cloud computing?

Answer: Regular data backups can mitigate the impact of ransomware attacks in cloud computing by enabling organizations to restore their data from backup copies without having to pay the ransom. This ensures business continuity and reduces the leverage of attackers, as organizations can recover their data without succumbing to extortion demands.

9 How does a man-in-the-middle attack manifest in cloud computing?

Answer: A man-in-the-middle attack intercepts communication between cloud users and services, allowing the attacker to eavesdrop, modify, or steal data transmitted between them.

10 What characterizes a SQL injection attack in cloud computing?

Answer: A SQL injection attack exploits vulnerabilities in an application's input validation process to inject malicious SQL queries, potentially gaining unauthorized access to the cloud database.

11 What is a cross-site scripting (XSS) attack in the context of cloud computing?

Answer: In a cross-site scripting attack, malicious scripts are injected into web applications hosted on the cloud, allowing attackers to hijack user sessions, steal cookies, or deface websites.

12 How does a data breach occur in cloud computing?

Answer: A data breach in cloud computing involves unauthorized access to sensitive data stored in cloud services, often due to weak authentication mechanisms, misconfigurations, or insider threats.

13 What distinguishes a malware attack in cloud computing?

Answer: In a malware attack, malicious software is deployed within the cloud environment, infecting virtual machines or compromising cloud infrastructure to steal data, disrupt operations, or propagate further.

14 What vulnerabilities can be exploited in an API attack targeting cloud services?

Answer: API (Application Programming Interface) attacks exploit vulnerabilities in the interfaces of cloud services, allowing attackers to gain unauthorized access, execute unauthorized actions, or exfiltrate data.

15 What is a privilege escalation attack in cloud computing?

Answer: A privilege escalation attack involves exploiting vulnerabilities to gain higher levels of access privileges within the cloud environment, potentially allowing attackers to compromise sensitive data or resources.

16 How does a container escape attack impact cloud computing environments?

Answer: A container escape attack targets vulnerabilities in containerization technologies within cloud environments, allowing attackers to break out of containers and gain unauthorized access to host systems or other containers.

17 What role does social engineering play in cloud computing attacks?

Answer: Social engineering techniques are used to manipulate individuals within organizations or cloud service providers, tricking them into divulging sensitive information or granting unauthorized access to cloud resources.

18 What are the characteristics of an insider threat in cloud computing?

Answer: An insider threat involves individuals with legitimate access to cloud resources exploiting their privileges for malicious purposes, such as stealing data, disrupting services, or sabotaging infrastructure.

19 How do zero-day exploits impact cloud computing security?

Answer: Zero-day exploits target previously unknown vulnerabilities in cloud services or software, posing significant security risks as attackers can exploit them before patches or mitigations are developed.

20 What distinguishes a DNS poisoning attack in the context of cloud computing?

Answer: DNS poisoning attacks manipulate domain name resolution processes within the cloud infrastructure, redirecting users to malicious websites or intercepting their communication with legitimate services.

REFERENCES

1. Agrawal, N., & Tapaswi, S. (2019). Defense mechanisms against DDoS attacks in a cloud computing environment: State-of-the-art and research challenges. *IEEE Communications Surveys & Tutorials*, *21*(4), 3769–3795.
2. Agrawal, N., & Tapaswi, S. (2017, November). A lightweight approach to detect the low/high rate IP spoofed cloud DDoS attacks. In *2017 IEEE 7th International Symposium on Cloud and Service Computing (SC2)*. (pp. 118–123). IEEE.
3. Singh, A., & Chatterjee, K. (2017). Cloud security issues and challenges: A survey. *Journal of Network and Computer Applications*, *79*, 88–115.
4. Somani, G., Gaur, M. S., Sanghi, D., Conti, M., & Buyya, R. (2017). DDoS attacks in cloud computing: Issues, taxonomy, and future directions. *Computer Communications*, 107, 30–48.
5. Duncan, A. J., Creese, S., & Goldsmith, M. (2012, June). Insider attacks in cloud computing. In *2012 IEEE 11th International Conference on Trust, Security and Privacy in Computing and Communications* (pp. 857–862). IEEE.
6. Masdari, M., & Jalali, M. (2016). A survey and taxonomy of DoS attacks in cloud computing. *Security and Communication Networks*, *9*(16), 3724–3751.
7. Somani, G., Gaur, M. S., Sanghi, D., & Conti, M. (2016). DDoS attacks in cloud computing: Collateral damage to non-targets. *Computer Networks*, *109*, 157–171.
8. https://cloudsecurityalliance.org/blog/2023/09/21/2023-global-cloud-threat-report-cloud-attacks-are-lightning-fast
9. https://www.sentinelone.com/blog/endpoint-identity-and-cloud-top-cyber-attacks-of-2023-so-far/
10. https://minlanyu.seas.harvard.edu/writeup/imc15.pdf
11. https://www.scirp.org/journal/paperinformation?paperid=72584https://www.scirp.org/journal/paperinformation?paperid=72584
12. https://www.techtarget.com/searchsecurity/tip/VM-security-in-cloud-computing-explained
13. https://www.technoarete.org/common_abstract/pdf/IJERCSE/v10/i9/Ext_53041.pdf
14. https://www.scirp.org/journal/paperinformation?paperid=72584
15. https://www.computer.org/publications/tech-news/trends/prevent-cloud-computing-attacks/
16. https://www.apriorit.com/dev-blog/523-cloud-computing-cyber-attacks
17. Khalil, I. M., Khreishah, A., & Azeem, M. (2014). Cloud computing security: A survey. *Computers*, *3*(1), 1–35.

18. Wang, K., Hu, C., & Shan, C. (2024). Evaluation of Application Layer DDoS Attack Effect in Cloud Native Applications. *IEEE Transactions on Cloud Computing*, *12*(2), 522–538.
19. Nautiyal, A., Saklani, S., Mishra, P., Kumar, S., & Bisht, H. (2024). A State-of-the Art Survey on Various Attacks and Security Tools at the Virtualization Layer of Cloud Computing: A Virtual Network Security Perspective. In *Integration of Cloud Computing with Emerging Technologies* (pp. 65–79). CRC Press.
20. Goswami, P., Faujdar, N., Debnath, S., Khan, A. K., & Singh, G. (2024). Investigation on storage level data integrity strategies in cloud computing: classification, security obstructions, challenges and vulnerability. *Journal of Cloud Computing*, *13*(1), 45.
21. Singh, S., Jeong, Y. S., & Park, J. H. (2016). A survey on cloud computing security: Issues, threats, and solutions. *Journal of Network and Computer Applications*, *75*, 200–222.
22. Shahzad, F. (2014). State-of-the-art survey on cloud computing security challenges, approaches and solutions. *Procedia Computer Science*, *37*, 357–362.
23. Srinivasamurthy, S., & Liu, D. Q. (2010, November). Survey on cloud computing security. In *Proceedings Conference on Cloud Computing*, CloudCom (Vol. *10*).
24. Zhang, Y. Q., Wang, X. F., Liu, X. F., & Liu, L. (2016). Survey on cloud computing security. *Journal of Software*, *27*(6), 1328–1348.
25. Rani, P., Singh, S., & Singh, K. (2024). Cloud computing security: a taxonomy, threat detection and mitigation techniques. *International Journal of Computers and Applications*, *46*(5), 348–361.

4 Defense Techniques in Cloud

4.1 INTRODUCTION TO DEFENSE TECHNIQUES

Without the ability to remotely store, process, and manage data, made possible by cloud computing, modern enterprises cannot function. But as cloud computing has become more widespread, so has the need for effective defense measures to protect systems and data from Internet dangers [1–3]. The relevance of defense tactics in cloud computing is supported by the following.

- Cyberattack defense: Data and systems based in the cloud are extremely vulnerable to cyberattacks. Attackers may gain unauthorized access to cloud resources, steal information, or obstruct business procedures. Examples of defensive tactics that can halt these attacks and mitigate their impact include firewalls, intrusion detection systems, and access controls.
- Compliance standards: Many different firms have specific compliance requirements for data security. Consider the Health Insurance Portability and Accountability Act (HIPAA) in the healthcare industry and the Payment Card Industry Data Security Standard (PCI DSS) in the financial services industry. By utilizing defending tactics, organizations can abide by these requirements and avoid paying astronomical fines.
- Data privacy: It is the responsibility of cloud service providers to protect customer data from unauthorized access or disclosure. Defense tactics like tokenization and encryption can help ensure that data is protected even if it is breached.
- Business continuity: Cloud computing can be vulnerable to natural disasters, power outages, and other disturbances. Backup and disaster recovery solutions can help ensure that data and systems are still accessible and functional in the event of an outage or disaster.

In conclusion, defense strategies are essential in cloud computing to safeguard against cyberattacks, satisfy regulatory requirements, guarantee data privacy, and keep operations running smoothly.

DOI: 10.1201/9781003510772-4

4.2 CATEGORIES OF DEFENSE APPROACHES

To increase security in the cloud, there are a number of defense strategies that can be used, as shown in Figure 4.1.

1) Prevention: The control measures to stop attacks from happening in the first place, like firewalls, access controls, and encryption.
2) Detection: The control measures to find attacks after they have already happened, like intrusion detection systems, log analysis, and monitoring tools.
3) Mitigation: It refers to the strategies and actions taken to reduce the severity, impact, or likelihood of a negative event, such as a cyberattack.
4) Traceback: It refers to techniques used to trace the origins of a cyberattack or malicious activity. This process helps in identifying the source of an attack, understanding its nature, and taking appropriate measures to mitigate the threat. Traceback mechanisms are crucial for improving security measures, preventing future attacks, and recovering from incidents.
5) Corrective: Corrective control measures to correct any errors that may have occurred.
6) Deterrent: Deterrent control measures intended to deter potential attackers from attempting to breach a system, such as security awareness training, warning banners, and security audits.
7) Compensating: Compensating control measures intended to provide an alternate method of achieving the same level of security in circumstances where other controls are not practical or cost-effective, such as compensating controls for compliance requirements, such as PCI-DSS, HIPAA, or ISO/IEC 27001.
8) Hybrid: Organizations may create a thorough and efficient cloud security plan by combining these defense strategies.
9) Others: The description of other different defense approach categories is provided in Table 4.1.

The defense strategy categories listed below are generalizations, and different defense tactics may fall under more than one category or overlap. Additionally, a successful cloud security plan often combines these techniques to offer complete protection against constantly emerging threats.

4.2.1 Prevention Techniques

The goal of prevention strategies is to stop assaults before they start. The following are some typical preventative measures for cloud security.

- Access control and authentication: Reliable processes to guarantee that only users with the appropriate authorization can access cloud resources.
- Sensitive data may be protected using data encryption both during transmission and while it is at rest in the cloud.

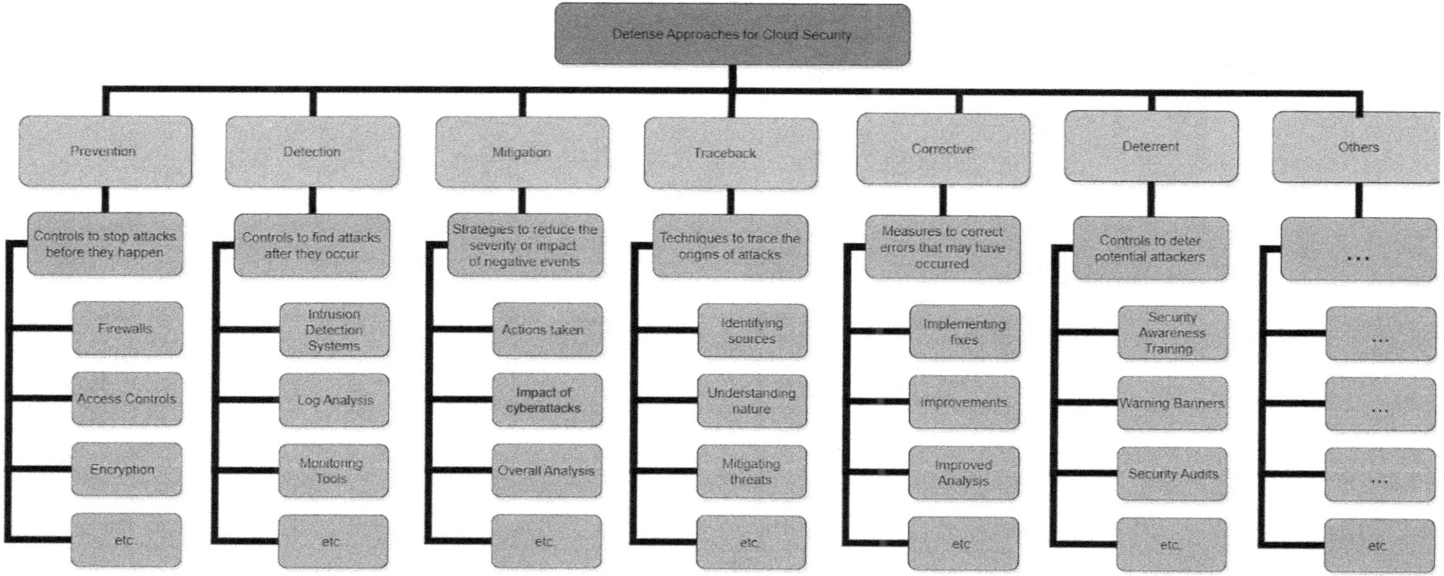

FIGURE 4.1 Categories of defense approaches for cloud security.

TABLE 4.1
Summary of the Defense Approaches

Defense Approach Category	Description
Prevention-Based Approaches [4,5]	Defense strategies focused on preventing attacks and vulnerabilities from being exploited in the first place. This includes implementing access controls, encryption, firewalls, intrusion detection systems, and proactive security measures to mitigate risks.
Detection and Response Approaches [6–13]	Defense strategies centered around the detection of potential security incidents and timely response to mitigate the impact. This involves the use of security monitoring tools, log analysis, anomaly detection, security incident and event management (SIEM) systems, and incident response procedures to detect and respond to threats effectively.
Identity and Access Management Approaches [14]	Defense strategies aimed at ensuring the proper management of user identities, authentication, and authorization processes. This includes implementing strong authentication mechanisms, identity federation, role-based access control (RBAC), and privileged access management (PAM) to control and monitor user access to cloud resources.
Data Protection and Privacy Approaches [15–22]	Defense strategies focused on safeguarding data confidentiality, integrity, and privacy within the cloud environment. This involves employing data encryption techniques, data loss prevention (DLP) mechanisms, secure data backups, and complying with data protection regulations to protect sensitive information stored and transmitted in the cloud.
Cloud Security Governance Approaches [23]	Defense strategies that revolve around establishing robust governance frameworks, policies, and procedures to ensure compliance with security standards, regulations, and industry best practices. This includes conducting regular security audits, risk assessments, establishing security controls, and enforcing security policies across the cloud infrastructure.
Resilience and Recovery Approaches [24]	Defense strategies designed to enhance the resilience and recovery capabilities of cloud systems in the event of a security incident or disruption. This involves implementing disaster recovery plans, backup and restoration mechanisms, fault tolerance, and redundancy to ensure business continuity and minimize the impact of security breaches or service interruptions.

- Network security: Unauthorized access may be avoided and threats like Distributed Denial of Service (DDoS) attacks [25,26] repelled by a secure network design.
- Patch management, which involves applying frequent software updates and patches, can help to address known vulnerabilities and reduce the risk of exploitation.
- In order to control and filter incoming and outgoing network traffic and help stop invasions and other unwanted actions, firewalls can be deployed.
- Application security: Strict testing protocols and secure coding guidelines can aid in protecting cloud apps from problems.
- Solutions for data loss prevention can help to stop unauthorized use of, access to, or movement of sensitive data on the cloud.

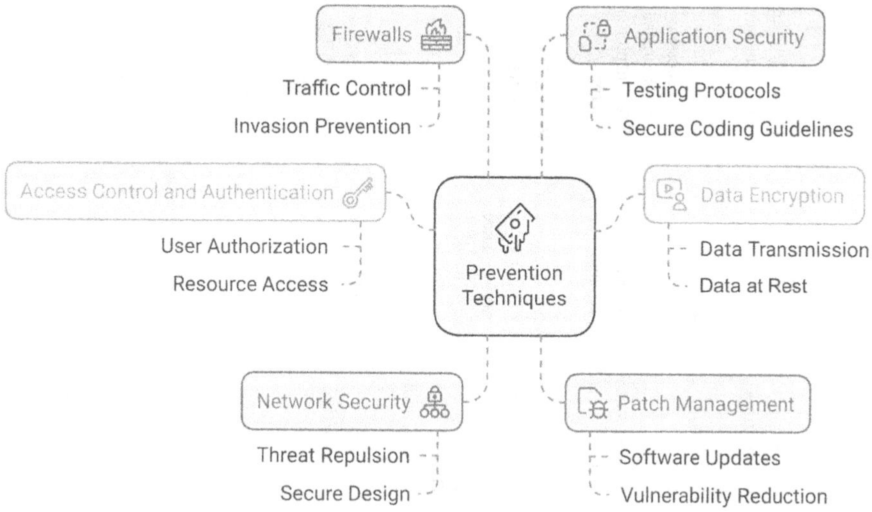

FIGURE 4.2 Different prevention techniques.

Organizations may aid in defending their cloud environments from numerous security risks and assaults by putting these preventative measures into practice. An overview of different prevention techniques is given in Figure 4.2.

Furthermore, a more in-detail discussion of different prevention approaches is provided in Table 4.2.

4.2.2 Detection Techniques

In order to discover and notify organizations of possible security events or breaches, detection techniques are used. Some of the typical detection methods for cloud security include the following:

- Network traffic may be monitored by IDS, which can alert security staff to any potential hazards such as malware infections or unauthorized access attempts.
- Security professionals may be alerted to any suspicious conduct by gathering and analyzing log data from multiple cloud services using Security Information and Event Management (SIEM) technologies.
- Tools for analyzing network traffic can spot patterns and irregularities that can indicate a security incident or compromise.
- By providing real-time information on emerging threats, threat intelligence feeds can assist enterprises in identifying and responding to potential security incidents.
- UEBA (User and Entity Behavior Analytics) systems may monitor user and object behavior in the cloud to look for questionable conduct, such as peculiar login tendencies or data access patterns.
- By regularly doing vulnerability scanning, you may help identify potential security gaps in cloud services that criminals might try to exploit.

TABLE 4.2
Analysis of Cloud Security Prevention Techniques

Prevention Technique	Description	Benefits	Implementation Strategies	Key Features	Challenges	Monitoring and Maintenance
Access Control and Authentication	Ensures that only authorized users can access cloud resources using methods such as MFA and RBAC.	Reduces unauthorized access risk; helps maintain regulatory compliance; enhances user accountability.	Implement MFA, create strong password policies, perform regular role audits, and ensure access logs are reviewed.	User activity logging, session management, periodic reviews.	User resistance to MFA; complexity in role management.	Regular audits of access logs; automated alerts for suspicious activity.
Data Encryption	Encrypts sensitive data both in transit (using SSL/TLS) and at rest (using encryption standards like AES).	Protects data integrity and confidentiality; enhances trust among users; mitigates risks associated with data breaches.	Employ encryption protocols for data in transit and at rest; manage encryption keys with a secure key management system; ensure encryption standards are up to date.	Key management, compliance support (GDPR, HIPAA), audit trails.	Key management complexity; performance overhead.	Regularly review encryption protocols; monitor key access and usage.
Network Security	Secures the network infrastructure using firewalls, IDS/IPS, and secure configurations to prevent unauthorized access and mitigate DDoS attacks.	Enhances security posture; prevents data exfiltration; protects against external threats and intrusions.	Design a secure network architecture, segment networks, implement VPNs, and regularly update firewall rules and network configurations.	Network segmentation, anomaly detection, traffic filtering.	Complexity in configuration; evolving threat landscape.	Continuous monitoring of network traffic; regular vulnerability assessments.
Patch Management	Involves applying regular updates and patches to cloud applications and infrastructure to address vulnerabilities.	Reduces the risk of exploitation; ensures systems are up-to-date with security improvements; enhances overall system performance.	Develop a patch management policy; automate patch deployment where possible; prioritize patches based on criticality and compliance requirements.	Automated patch scanning, reporting dashboards, prioritization.	Resource allocation for updates; potential downtime during updates.	Regular reviews of patch status; automated alerts for critical updates.

Firewalls	Deploys firewalls to control and monitor traffic entering and exiting the cloud environment, blocking unauthorized access and malicious activities.	Provides a barrier against threats; helps manage network traffic effectively; allows for custom security policies.	Configure firewalls according to best practices; use next-generation firewalls (NGFW) for deep packet inspection; conduct regular firewall rule reviews.	Stateful and stateless filtering, VPN support, threat intelligence integration.	Complexity in configuration; managing rules can be challenging.	Regular audits of firewall rules; real-time alerts for policy violations.
Application Security	Implements secure coding practices and rigorous testing (static and dynamic analysis) to protect applications from vulnerabilities.	Protects applications from common threats (e.g., SQL injection, XSS); enhances application reliability; fosters user trust.	Conduct regular code reviews, penetration testing, and vulnerability assessments; adopt secure coding frameworks (like OWASP); integrate security into DevOps (DevSecOps).	Security testing tools, code quality analysis, compliance checks.	Balancing security with development speed; ensuring team training.	Continuous monitoring for vulnerabilities; integrate security checks into CI/CD pipelines.
Data Loss Prevention (DLP)	Enforces policies to prevent unauthorized access, use, or transfer of sensitive data within cloud environments.	Protects against data breaches; ensures compliance with data protection regulations; enhances visibility into data movements.	Implement DLP solutions, classify data, create policies for data handling, and provide employee training on data security.	Content inspection, user activity monitoring, policy enforcement.	False positives; user education on data handling.	Regularly review DLP policies; conduct audits of data handling practices.

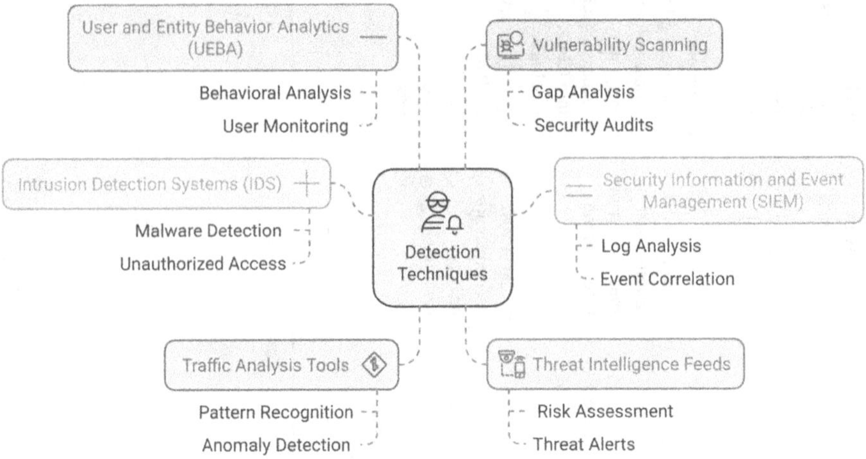

FIGURE 4.3 Different detection techniques.

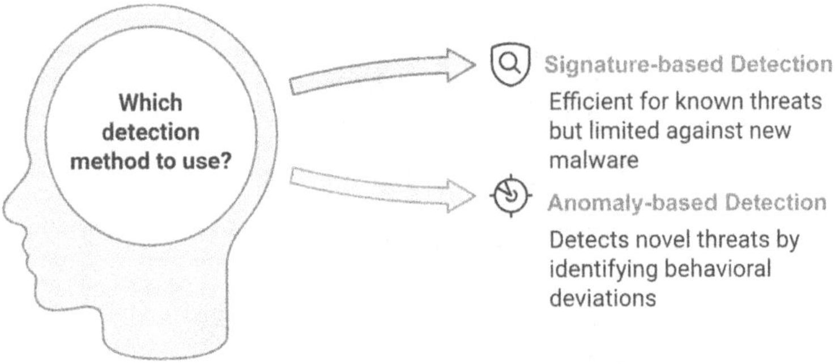

FIGURE 4.4 General types of detection methods.

Employing these detection strategies enables businesses to swiftly spot and address possible security events or breaches in their cloud systems, hence reducing the severity of any security risks. An overview of different detection techniques is given in Figure 4.3.

The detection techniques can be broadly classified into two categories: signature-based and anomaly-based, as shown in Figure 4.4.

The in-detail discussion of these categories is as follows.

4.2.2.1 Signature-based Techniques

Signature-based detection is a method used in cybersecurity to identify and prevent known threats, such as viruses, malware, or other malicious activities. This technique relies on comparing the characteristics of files or network traffic against a database of known signatures, which are essentially patterns or specific sequences associated with known threats.

The steps involved in signature-based detection techniques are as follows.

1. Signature Creation: Security experts analyze malicious code or behavior to identify unique patterns, file attributes, or sequences of commands that are characteristics of specific types of threats.
2. Signature Database: These identified signatures are then compiled into a database. This database contains the signatures of various known threats, such as viruses, worms, Trojans, and other types of malware.
3. Detection Process: When a file or network traffic is scanned, the security system checks for matches against the signatures stored in the database. If there's a match, the system identifies the file or traffic as malicious and takes appropriate action, such as quarantining the file or blocking the network traffic.
4. Updates: Regular updates are essential to keep the signature database current. New threats emerge constantly, so security vendors continuously analyze and create signatures for newly discovered malware to ensure effective protection.

While signature-based detection is efficient at identifying known threats, it has limitations. It cannot detect new or previously unseen threats for which signatures haven't been created yet. Additionally, attackers can attempt to evade signature-based detection by modifying their malware to change its signature or by using techniques such as polymorphism to generate unique variants of the same malware. As a result, signature-based detection is often used in conjunction with other security measures, such as behavior-based analysis and heuristic methods, to provide comprehensive protection against cyber threats.

4.2.2.2 Anomaly-based Techniques

Anomaly-based detection is a technique used in various fields, including cybersecurity, fraud detection, and system monitoring. It involves identifying patterns or behaviors that deviate from what is considered normal or expected within a given context. Instead of relying on predefined signatures of known threats (as in signature-based detection), anomaly detection focuses on detecting unusual activities or data points that may indicate malicious behavior, system faults, or other abnormalities.

The processes involved in anomaly-based detection techniques are given below.

1. Data Collection: The first step involves collecting data from the system or environment being monitored. This data could include network traffic, system logs, user behavior, financial transactions, or any other relevant information.
2. Profile Creation: Next, a profile of normal behavior is established based on historical data or known good patterns. This profile represents what is considered typical or expected within the system.
3. Anomaly Detection: Once the normal behavior profile is established, the system continuously compares new data points or activities against this profile. Any deviations or anomalies from the expected behavior are flagged for further investigation.

4. Alerting or Response: When an anomaly is detected, the system can trigger alerts to notify administrators or automated responses to mitigate potential threats. Depending on the severity and nature of the anomaly, actions may include blocking suspicious network traffic, quarantining affected systems, or escalating the incident for further analysis.
5. Feedback Loop: Anomaly detection systems often incorporate feedback mechanisms to adapt and improve over time. This may involve updating the normal behavior profile based on new data, refining detection algorithms, or adjusting thresholds for triggering alerts.

Anomaly-based detection techniques leverage various statistical, machine learning, and data mining algorithms to identify patterns and outliers within the data. Common approaches include clustering, classification, time series analysis, and neural networks. These techniques can be applied across a wide range of domains, from detecting intrusions in computer networks to identifying fraudulent transactions in financial systems. A more in-detail discussion of detection approaches is provided in Table 4.3.

4.2.3 Mitigation Techniques

The purpose of mitigation measures is to lessen the effects of security events or breaches. The following are a few typical mitigating strategies for cloud security:

- Planning for incident response may help firms respond to security incidents or breaches quickly and effectively, hence lessening their impact.
- Planning for disaster recovery can help businesses recover from serious security failures or breaches while maintaining company continuity.
- Regular data backup and recovery procedures can help firms recover from data loss or corruption caused by security incidents or breaches.
- Redundancy and failover solutions can help ensure high availability of cloud services while reducing the impact of security incidents or breaches.
- Isolation and segmentation of cloud resources can assist lessen the impact of these occurrences by limiting security incidents or breaches to certain areas of the cloud environment.
- Network segmentation can help stop the spread of malware or other security issues in the setting of the cloud.
- By quickly fixing software defects, patch management helps to decrease the impact of security events or breaches.

Organizations may lessen the effects of security events or breaches in their cloud systems and guarantee business continuity by implementing these mitigating strategies. Some common Mitigation Techniques are shown in Figure 4.5.

Additionally, a more in-detail discussion of mitigation approaches is provided in Table 4.4.

TABLE 4.3
Analysis of Cloud Security Detection Techniques

Detection Approach	Description	Benefits	Implementation Strategies	Key Features	Challenges	Monitoring and Maintenance
Intrusion Detection Systems (IDS)	Monitors network traffic for suspicious activity and known threats, generating alerts for potential security breaches.	Enhances threat visibility; enables rapid response to intrusions; assists in forensic analysis.	Deploy network-based and host-based IDS; regularly update detection signatures; integrate with security information and event management (SIEM) systems.	Signature-based detection, anomaly detection, alerting mechanisms.	High false positive rates; potential performance impact.	Continuous tuning of detection rules; regular review of alerts.
Security Information and Event Management (SIEM)	Aggregates and analyzes security data from multiple sources in real time to identify and respond to potential threats.	Provides a centralized view of security incidents; enhances threat correlation; improves incident response times.	Implement log aggregation from various sources; establish correlation rules; conduct regular security audits and compliance checks.	Real-time alerting, dashboard visualizations, automated reporting.	Complexity in implementation; resource-intensive.	Regular updates to correlation rules; continuous monitoring of system performance.
Anomaly Detection	Uses machine learning and statistical analysis to identify deviations from normal behavior in user activities or network traffic.	Helps detect unknown threats; reduces reliance on predefined signatures; improves detection of insider threats.	Train models on baseline behavior; continuously update models with new data; use supervised and unsupervised learning techniques.	Behavioral analytics, real-time alerts, adaptive learning.	Requires large amounts of data; potential for false positives.	Ongoing retraining of models; regular evaluation of effectiveness.

(Continued)

TABLE 4.3 (Continued)

Detection Approach	Description	Benefits	Implementation Strategies	Key Features	Challenges	Monitoring and Maintenance
Log Management and Analysis	Involves collecting, storing, and analyzing log data from various systems to identify suspicious activities and compliance issues.	Provides insights into user activities; aids in forensic investigations; helps in compliance reporting.	Implement centralized log management solutions; establish log retention policies; perform regular log reviews and audits.	Centralized logging, real-time analysis, compliance reporting.	Volume of log data can be overwhelming; difficulty in identifying relevant events.	Regular log analysis; continuous improvement of log management processes.
Endpoint Detection and Response (EDR)	Monitors and responds to security threats on endpoints, providing detailed visibility into endpoint activity.	Enhances endpoint security; provides forensic capabilities; allows for quick incident response and remediation.	Deploy EDR solutions across all endpoints; configure alerts for suspicious behavior; conduct regular endpoint assessments and threat hunting exercises.	Real-time monitoring, threat intelligence integration, incident response capabilities.	Resource-intensive; potential for performance degradation.	Continuous monitoring of endpoint activity; regular updates to detection rules.
User and Entity Behavior Analytics (UEBA)	Analyzes user and entity behavior to detect anomalies that may indicate compromised accounts or insider threats.	Improves detection of advanced threats; reduces false positives by focusing on behavioral changes; enhances overall security posture.	Implement UEBA tools; establish baseline behavior profiles for users and entities; continuously monitor and adjust profiles as necessary.	Machine learning algorithms, risk scoring, real-time alerts.	Complexity in establishing baselines; data privacy concerns.	Ongoing monitoring and adjustments of behavior profiles; regular evaluation of effectiveness.
Vulnerability Scanning	Regularly scans systems and applications for known vulnerabilities that could be exploited by attackers.	Identifies weaknesses before they can be exploited; helps prioritize remediation efforts based on risk.	Implement automated vulnerability scanning tools; establish a scanning schedule; integrate findings into a patch management process.	Automated scanning, reporting dashboards, prioritization of vulnerabilities.	High volume of findings can lead to alert fatigue; prioritizing remediation efforts can be challenging.	Regular updates to scanning tools; continuous monitoring of vulnerability landscape.

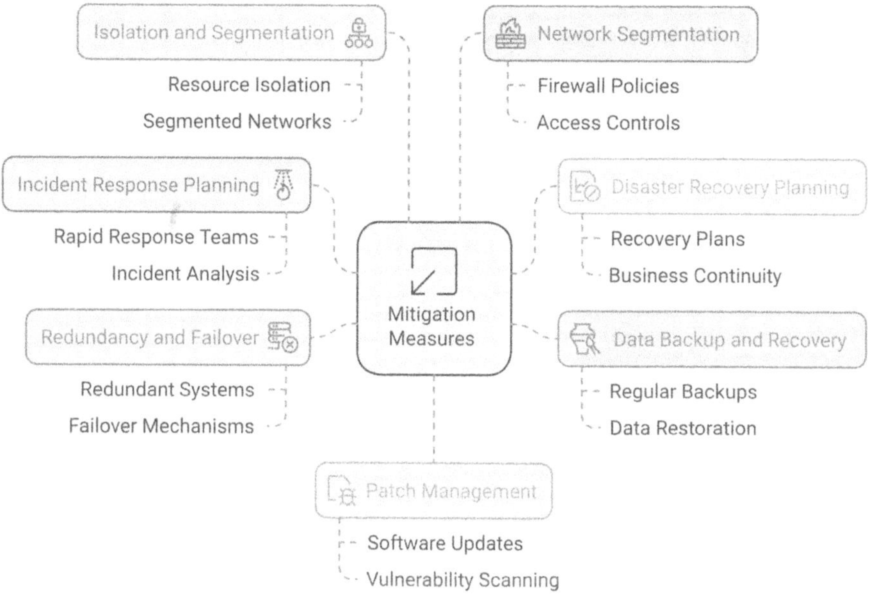

FIGURE 4.5 Different mitigation techniques.

4.2.4 Traceback Techniques

The term "traceback" typically refers to the process of identifying the origin or the source of a security breach or attack. It involves tracing the path that an attacker took through a network or system to gain unauthorized access, launch an attack, or exfiltrate data. Traceback techniques are crucial for understanding the scope of a security incident, identifying vulnerabilities, and implementing measures to prevent future attacks.

Traceback techniques can include:

1. Log Analysis: Analyzing logs from various network devices, servers, and applications to trace the activities of an attacker. This may involve examining timestamps, IP addresses, user accounts, and commands executed.
2. Packet Analysis: Examining network traffic to identify patterns or anomalies that indicate malicious activity. Packet analysis can reveal the communication pathways used by attackers and help trace their actions back to the source.
3. Forensic Analysis: Conducting forensic investigations to gather evidence from compromised systems. This may involve analyzing disk images, memory dumps, and other artifacts to reconstruct the sequence of events leading up to a security breach.
4. IP Tracing: Tracing the IP addresses associated with suspicious network traffic or malicious activities back to their origin. This can involve using tools such as traceroute or conducting WHOIS queries to identify the responsible parties.

TABLE 4.4
Analysis of Cloud Security Mitigation Techniques

Mitigation Approach	Description	Benefits	Implementation Strategies	Key Features	Challenges	Monitoring and Maintenance
Incident Response Planning	Develops a structured approach for responding to security incidents, including roles, responsibilities, and procedures for containment and recovery.	Enhances readiness to respond to incidents; minimizes impact and recovery time; ensures effective communication during incidents.	Create an incident response team; develop and document an incident response plan; conduct regular training and simulations to test the plan.	Defined roles and responsibilities, communication protocols, playbooks for response.	Difficulty in coordination during actual incidents; keeping the plan updated.	Regular drills and tabletop exercises; ongoing reviews and updates to the plan.
Data Backup and Recovery	Regularly backs up data to ensure recovery in case of data loss due to incidents like ransomware attacks or system failures.	Ensures data availability and integrity; reduces downtime during recovery; enhances business continuity.	Implement automated backup solutions; establish a backup schedule; regularly test backup restorations to ensure data integrity.	Incremental backups, off-site storage options, recovery point objectives (RPOs).	Potentially high storage costs; managing backup versions can be complex.	Regular testing of backup and recovery processes; continuous monitoring of backup integrity.
Network Segmentation	Divides the network into segments to limit access and contain potential breaches, minimizing the impact of attacks.	Enhances security by limiting lateral movement; simplifies compliance; improves performance by reducing congestion.	Identify critical assets; implement VLANs or micro-segmentation; enforce strict access controls between segments.	Access control policies for each segment, traffic monitoring, isolation strategies.	Complexity in configuration; potential for misconfigurations.	Continuous monitoring of segment activity; regular audits of access controls.

Threat Intelligence	Utilizes external and internal threat intelligence to anticipate and mitigate potential attacks based on known tactics, techniques, and procedures (TTPs).	Improves proactive defense; enhances incident response by providing context; helps prioritize security efforts based on emerging threats.	Subscribe to threat intelligence feeds; integrate threat intelligence into security operations; conduct regular reviews to update intelligence sources.	Real-time updates, threat correlation, actionable insights.	Difficulty in distinguishing relevant intelligence; potential information overload.	Regular review of threat intelligence sources; ongoing evaluation of relevance.
Access Management Policies	Establishes strict policies governing user access to cloud resources, including least privilege and role-based access controls.	Reduces risk of unauthorized access; improves compliance; enhances overall security posture.	Define access roles and permissions; implement identity and access management (IAM) solutions; regularly review access logs and user permissions.	Automated access provisioning, policy enforcement, audit trails.	Complexity in managing access controls for large teams; user resistance to change.	Continuous monitoring of access patterns; periodic reviews of access policies.
Application Security Measures	Implements security practices and tools throughout the application development lifecycle to mitigate vulnerabilities.	Reduces the risk of exploitation; ensures applications are secure from the ground up; enhances user trust in applications.	Adopt DevSecOps practices; integrate security testing tools into the CI/CD pipeline; conduct regular security training for developers.	Security testing tools (SAST/DAST), code reviews, vulnerability assessments.	Balancing security with development speed; ensuring comprehensive coverage.	Continuous monitoring for application vulnerabilities; regular updates to security tools.
User Training and Awareness	Provides ongoing training and awareness programs for employees about security best practices and emerging threats.	Reduces the risk of human error; empowers employees to recognize and respond to security threats; enhances organizational security culture.	Develop a comprehensive training program; conduct regular security awareness sessions; simulate phishing attacks to assess employee readiness.	Interactive training modules, assessment tools, phishing simulations.	Variability in employee engagement; keeping content current with evolving threats.	Regular feedback on training effectiveness; ongoing updates to training materials.

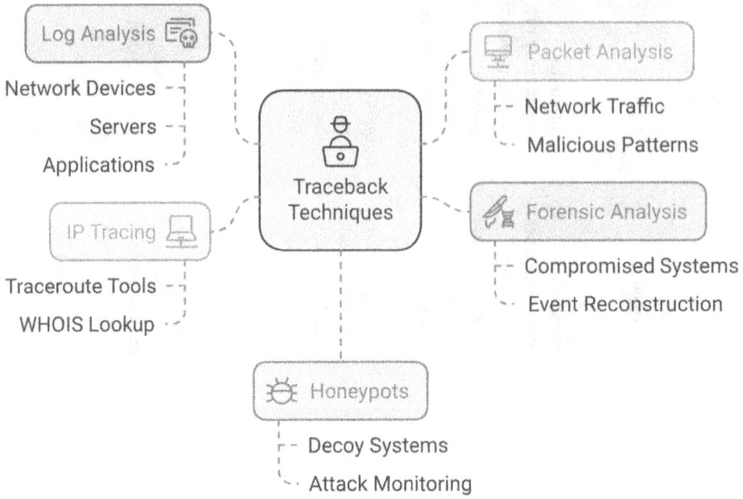

FIGURE 4.6 Different traceback techniques.

5. Honeypots and Deception: Deploying decoy systems or honeypots to lure attackers and gather information about their tactics and techniques. By monitoring interactions with these deceptive assets, security teams can gain insights into the methods used by attackers and trace their activities back to their origins.

Overall, traceback techniques play a crucial role in incident response and cybersecurity investigations by helping organizations understand how security breaches occurred and take appropriate remedial actions to mitigate future risks. Different traceback techniques are shown in Figure 4.6.

In addition to the above, a more in-detail discussion of traceback approaches is provided in Table 4.5.

4.2.5 Hybrid Techniques

Hybrid detection techniques refer to the combination of multiple methods or approaches for detecting and identifying certain phenomena, such as security threats, anomalies, or patterns. In the context of cybersecurity, for instance, hybrid detection techniques might involve using a combination of signature-based detection, anomaly detection, and behavioral analysis to identify and mitigate various types of cyber threats.

By combining these techniques in a hybrid approach, organizations can leverage the strengths of each method while compensating for their individual limitations. For example, combining signature-based detection with anomaly detection can provide both broad coverage for known threats and the ability to detect new and evolving threats. Similarly, integrating machine learning algorithms with behavioral analysis can improve the accuracy and efficiency of threat detection by learning from historical data and adapting to new attack vectors. A detailed discussion of hybrid approaches is provided in Table 4.6.

TABLE 4.5
Analysis of Cloud Security Traceback Techniques

Traceback Approach	Description	Benefits	Implementation Strategies	Key Features	Challenges	Monitoring and Maintenance
Network Forensics	Involves capturing and analyzing network traffic to trace the source of security incidents and malicious activities.	Provides detailed insights into attack vectors; aids in identifying perpetrators; enhances incident response capabilities.	Deploy packet capture tools; establish monitoring policies; analyze captured data for anomalies and malicious patterns.	Real-time traffic analysis, data correlation, detailed logs.	High volume of data can be overwhelming; requires skilled personnel for analysis.	Regular updates to forensic tools; continuous training for analysts.
Log Analysis and Correlation	Analyzes logs from various sources (servers, applications, network devices) to identify patterns and trace unauthorized access or anomalies.	Helps in identifying the timeline of an attack; facilitates incident investigations; assists in compliance reporting.	Implement centralized log management solutions; establish correlation rules; conduct regular log reviews and audits.	Centralized logging, real-time correlation, anomaly detection.	Volume of logs can complicate analysis; distinguishing relevant logs from noise.	Continuous monitoring of log data; regular updates to correlation rules.
Attribution Techniques	Methods used to identify the source or perpetrator of an attack based on digital fingerprints, IP addresses, or behavioral patterns.	Enables targeted responses to threats; aids in understanding attacker motivations; improves overall security posture.	Use threat intelligence sources to validate IP addresses; analyze patterns of behavior; maintain databases of known malicious actors.	Behavioral profiling, IP reputation databases, context-based analysis.	Difficulty in confirming identities; potential for false attribution.	Regular updates to attribution databases; continuous monitoring of threat intelligence.
Incident Replay	Reconstructs the sequence of events leading to a security incident to understand the attack and improve defenses.	Provides clarity on attack methods; aids in developing more effective security measures; enhances training for response teams.	Capture session data and logs; use forensic tools to recreate incidents; conduct post-incident reviews with stakeholders.	Visualization of attack paths, comprehensive reports, interactive analysis.	Complexity in accurately reconstructing events; time-consuming process.	Regular reviews of incident replay findings; updates to incident response strategies.

(Continued)

TABLE 4.5
(Continued)

Traceback Approach	Description	Benefits	Implementation Strategies	Key Features	Challenges	Monitoring and Maintenance
Data Provenance Tracking	Monitors and records the history of data movement and changes to trace unauthorized access or alterations.	Helps ensure data integrity; provides insights into data usage; assists in compliance with data protection regulations.	Implement data tracking tools; establish data access policies; regularly audit data access and modifications.	Data lineage visualization, access history, compliance reporting.	Complexity in implementation; potential performance impacts on data access.	Continuous monitoring of data access patterns; regular audits of data provenance records.
Anomaly Detection Systems	Employs machine learning algorithms to identify unusual patterns in network traffic or user behavior that may indicate a security incident.	Detects threats that traditional methods may miss; reduces reliance on signature-based detection; improves response time to anomalies.	Train machine learning models on historical data; continuously update models with new data; implement real-time monitoring and alerting systems.	Machine learning algorithms, real-time alerts, adaptive thresholds.	Requires large datasets for training; potential for false positives.	Ongoing model evaluation and retraining; continuous monitoring for effectiveness.
Digital Signature Verification	Uses cryptographic methods to verify the authenticity and integrity of data or communications, helping to trace the origin of information.	Ensures data authenticity; aids in tracing data back to its source; enhances trust in data integrity.	Implement digital signature protocols; regularly audit key management practices; educate users on the importance of digital signatures.	Cryptographic protocols, non-repudiation, tamper detection.	Key management complexity; potential performance impacts.	Continuous monitoring of signature verification processes; regular updates to cryptographic methods.

TABLE 4.6
Analysis of Cloud Security Hybrid Techniques

Hybrid Approach	Description	Benefits	Implementation Strategies	Key Features	Challenges	Monitoring and Maintenance
Security Information and Event Management (SIEM) + Threat Intelligence	Combines real-time log analysis and monitoring with external threat intelligence to enhance detection and response capabilities.	Improves threat visibility; enables proactive defense; enhances incident response through contextual information.	Integrate threat intelligence feeds with SIEM solutions; configure correlation rules based on threat intelligence; conduct regular updates to threat databases.	Real-time alerts, contextual insights, threat correlation.	Complexity in integration; data overload can hinder effective response.	Continuous updates to threat intelligence sources; regular tuning of SIEM rules.
Intrusion Detection and Prevention Systems (IDPS) + Behavioral Analytics	Utilizes both signature-based and anomaly detection methods to identify and respond to security incidents.	Enhances detection capabilities by combining known attack patterns with behavior analysis; reduces false positives.	Deploy both signature-based IDS/IPS and anomaly detection systems; regularly update detection signatures; establish baseline behaviors for normal operations.	Dual detection methods, automated responses, comprehensive reporting.	Resource-intensive; balancing performance with comprehensive monitoring.	Continuous monitoring of detection effectiveness; periodic reviews of behavior baselines.
Cloud Access Security Broker (CASB) + Data Loss Prevention (DLP)	Integrates CASB solutions with DLP technologies to monitor and control cloud service usage while protecting sensitive data.	Ensures secure cloud usage; prevents unauthorized data access and exfiltration; enhances compliance with data protection regulations.	Deploy CASB solutions to monitor cloud applications; implement DLP policies to enforce data handling practices; regularly review user access and data movement.	Real-time visibility, policy enforcement, risk assessment.	Complexity in managing policies across multiple services; potential performance impacts.	Ongoing monitoring of user activity; regular audits of DLP policies.
Endpoint Detection and Response (EDR) + Threat Hunting	Combines automated endpoint monitoring and response capabilities with proactive threat hunting to identify advanced threats.	Enhances endpoint security by proactively searching for threats; improves response times; enables detailed analysis of potential incidents.	Deploy EDR tools across endpoints; establish a threat hunting team; conduct regular threat hunting exercises based on the latest threat intelligence.	Advanced endpoint monitoring, proactive threat discovery, incident response capabilities.	Requires skilled personnel for effective threat hunting; resource-intensive.	Continuous monitoring of endpoint activity; ongoing training for threat hunters.

(Continued)

TABLE 4.6
(Continued)

Hybrid Approach	Description	Benefits	Implementation Strategies	Key Features	Challenges	Monitoring and Maintenance
Identity and Access Management (IAM) + Zero Trust Architecture	Integrates IAM solutions with a Zero Trust framework to enforce strict access controls based on user identity and device verification.	Reduces the risk of unauthorized access; enhances security posture; improves compliance with data protection regulations.	Implement IAM tools with strong authentication mechanisms; define access policies based on least privilege; regularly review user access and permissions.	Granular access controls, continuous verification, identity context.	Complexity in policy management; potential user resistance to strict controls.	Continuous monitoring of access logs; regular reviews of IAM policies.
Multi-Factor Authentication (MFA) + Risk-Based Authentication (RBA)	Combines MFA with adaptive authentication methods that assess risk based on user behavior and context.	Enhances security for sensitive operations; reduces the risk of unauthorized access; provides a balance between security and user experience.	Implement MFA solutions; integrate RBA tools that assess risk factors (e.g., location, device); regularly review and update authentication policies.	Adaptive security measures, user behavior analysis, risk scoring.	Complexity in implementation; potential for user frustration with multiple checks.	Ongoing evaluation of authentication effectiveness; regular updates to risk assessment criteria.
Data Encryption + Blockchain Technology	Uses encryption alongside blockchain to secure data integrity and traceability within cloud environments.	Enhances data security; provides a tamper-proof record of data access and modifications; improves compliance with regulations.	Implement encryption protocols for data at rest and in transit; use blockchain for maintaining data integrity and access logs; regularly audit blockchain transactions.	Immutable records, enhanced transparency, strong data integrity.	Complexity in blockchain integration; scalability issues.	Continuous monitoring of blockchain transactions; regular reviews of encryption practices.

4.3 RESEARCH CHALLENGES

In order to improve defense strategies for cloud security, a number of research difficulties must be resolved as cloud computing's popularity grows. The following are some of the main research obstacles:

- Scalability: As cloud systems become more complex, it becomes increasingly difficult to increase security defenses to ward off new and emerging threats.
- Automation: In order to fully protect the cloud, attack detection, response, and recovery must all be automated.
- Integration: Several security technologies and solutions must be coupled for cloud security to be successful. Integration can be challenging, though, given the large range of cloud platforms and technologies.
- As more sensitive data is being stored in the cloud, better data privacy and protection policies are needed to prevent unauthorized access and breaches.
- Compliance is necessary for cloud security but may be challenging due to industry and regulatory standards' constant change.
- Innovative threats: Cyber attackers are increasingly using cunning and inventive methods to get past cloud security protections. Research is necessary to develop advanced threat detection and prevention systems to counter these hazards.
- Human variables, such as user behavior, insider threats, and security expertise and education, can impact cloud security. Research is necessary to address these problems and offer practical answers.

We can enhance cloud security defense tactics and assure the continuing use of cloud computing by solving these research problems. Figure 4.7 highlights these research challenges.

Furthermore, research challenges for defense techniques in cloud computing is given in Table 4.7. The research issues described below are not all-inclusive, and as technology develops, new issues will inevitably arise in the realm of cloud computing security. Researchers and professionals are working hard to solve these issues and provide strong defense strategies for protecting cloud systems. Table 4.7 highlights the main research challenges and potential solutions in cloud security.

4.4 SUMMARY

Cloud environments must be protected from a range of security threats and incursions using defensive tactics for cloud security. This chapter provides an in-depth knowledge of the defense techniques for cloud computing environments. Preventative methods can help thwart attacks before they ever begin. These include strong authentication and access control, encryption, network security, patch management, firewalls, application security, and data loss prevention. Utilizing detection techniques such as intrusion detection systems (IDS), security information and

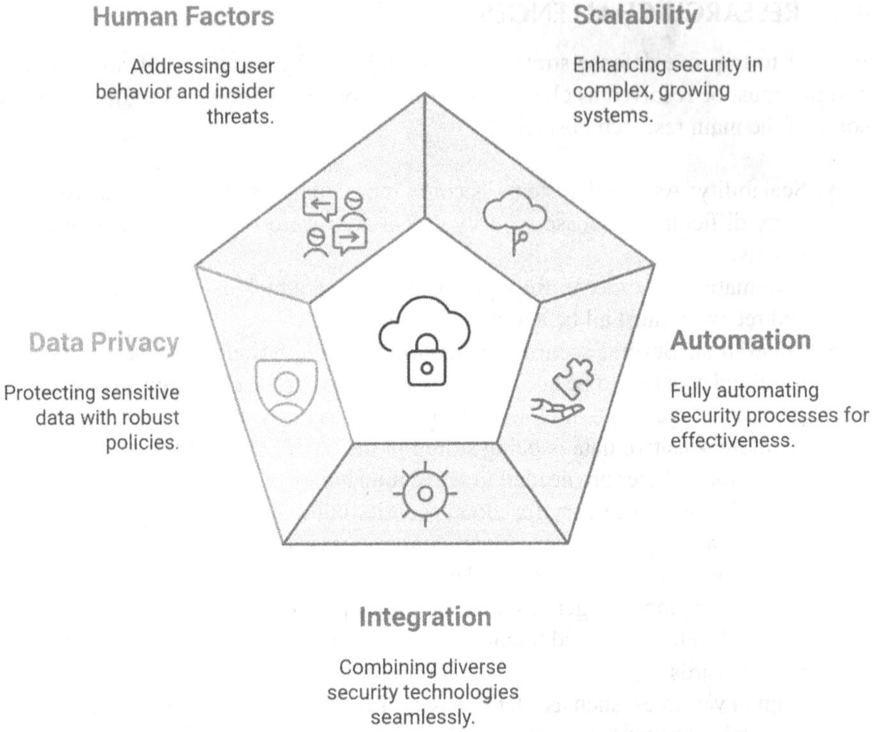
Human Factors
Addressing user behavior and insider threats.
Scalability
Enhancing security in complex, growing systems.
Data Privacy
Protecting sensitive data with robust policies.
Automation
Fully automating security processes for effectiveness.
Integration
Combining diverse security technologies seamlessly.

FIGURE 4.7 Different research challenges.

TABLE 4.7
Summary of the Research Challenges

Challenge	Description	Potential Solutions
Scalability and Performance	Ensuring defense techniques scale without impacting performance.	Use decentralized defenses, lightweight encryption, and dynamic performance tuning.
Adaptability and Flexibility	Designing security measures that adapt to dynamic cloud environments.	Context-aware security, flexible protocols, and cross-platform integration.
Resilience to Advanced Attacks	Defending against sophisticated, evolving attacks.	Machine learning-based detection, behavioral analysis, and advanced encryption.
Privacy and Compliance	Protecting privacy and ensuring compliance in multi-tenant clouds.	Privacy-preserving techniques, automated compliance auditing, and data segmentation.
Interoperability and Standardization	Developing standardized security protocols across platforms.	Adopt open standards, inter-cloud protocols, and common security frameworks.

TABLE 4.7
(Continued)

Challenge	Description	Potential Solutions
Trust and Assurance	Establishing trust and verifying the security of cloud services.	Third-party audits, transparent security metrics, and blockchain for trust.
Cloud-specific Threats	Addressing unique threats in cloud environments (e.g., multi-tenancy, virtualization).	Container security, shared resource monitoring, and VM hardening.
Cost-effectiveness and Optimization	Ensuring cost-effective security measures in cloud environments.	Security-as-a-service, resource-efficient encryption, and automated orchestration.
User Awareness and Education	Promoting cloud security awareness and best practices among users.	Security awareness campaigns, user-friendly interfaces, and behavioral nudges.

event management (SIEM), network traffic analysis, threat intelligence, user and entity behavior analytics (UEBA), and vulnerability scanning, potential security incidents or breaches in the cloud environment can be found. With the aid of mitigation strategies such as incident response planning, disaster recovery planning, data backup and recovery, redundancy and failover mechanisms, isolation and segmentation, network segmentation, and prompt patch management, the effects of security incidents or breaches in the cloud environment can be lessened. To strengthen defensive methods in cloud security, however, a variety of research challenges, including scalability, automation, integration, data privacy and protection, compliance, advanced threats, and human elements, must be addressed. By addressing these problems and putting in place strong defensive mechanisms, organizations can protect their cloud environments from a variety of security threats and attacks, ensuring the continued growth and usage of cloud computing. The research challenges while implementing these defense mechanisms in a cloud environment are also highlighted in this chapter.

4.5 PRACTICE QUESTIONS/SOLUTIONS

MULTIPLE CHOICE QUESTIONS

1 **What is the purpose of defense techniques in cloud computing?**
A) To prevent unauthorized access
B) To enhance network speed
C) To increase server storage
D) To reduce software licensing costs

Answer: A) To prevent unauthorized access

2 **Which of the following is NOT a common defense technique used in cloud security?**
A) Encryption
B) Firewalls
C) Cloud Bursting
D) Intrusion Detection Systems (IDS)

Answer: C) Cloud Bursting

3 **What does the term "Multi-factor Authentication (MFA)" refer to in cloud security?**
A) A security measure that requires only one form of authentication
B) A security measure that requires multiple forms of authentication
C) A method to boost server performance
D) A technique to reduce cloud storage costs

Answer: B) A security measure that requires multiple forms of authentication

4 **Which of the following is an example of a physical security measure in cloud computing?**
A) SSL Certificates
B) Two-factor Authentication
C) Biometric Authentication
D) Security Tokens

Answer: C) Biometric Authentication

5 **What is the primary purpose of Data Loss Prevention (DLP) in cloud security?**
A) To maximize data storage
B) To minimize network latency
C) To prevent unauthorized access to sensitive data
D) To optimize cloud resource allocation

Answer: C) To prevent unauthorized access to sensitive data

6 **What role do Virtual Private Networks (VPNs) play in cloud security?**
A) They provide secure access to cloud resources over the Internet
B) They improve cloud performance
C) They enhance server storage capacity
D) They reduce encryption overhead

Answer: A) They provide secure access to cloud resources over the Internet

7 Which of the following is an example of an Intrusion Detection System (IDS) in cloud security?

A) Antivirus software
B) Network-based IDS (NIDS)
C) Data encryption
D) Single sign-on (SSO)

Answer: B) Network-based IDS (NIDS)

8 What is the purpose of regularly updating security patches in cloud computing?

A) To enhance cloud performance
B) To reduce data storage costs
C) To fix vulnerabilities and prevent cyberattacks
D) To increase network bandwidth

Answer: C) To fix vulnerabilities and prevent cyberattacks

9 Which security technique involves monitoring and analyzing user behavior to identify anomalies?

A) Intrusion Detection Systems (IDS)
B) Data Loss Prevention (DLP)
C) Security Information and Event Management (SIEM)
D) Encryption

Answer: C) Security Information and Event Management (SIEM)

10 What is the purpose of Disaster Recovery (DR) in cloud security?

A) To maximize cloud storage capacity
B) To prevent data breaches
C) To ensure business continuity in case of disasters
D) To optimize network performance

Answer: C) To ensure business continuity in case of disasters

DESCRIPTIVE QUESTIONS

1 What is multi-factor authentication in cloud defense?

Answer: Multi-factor authentication in cloud defense is a security technique that requires users to provide two or more authentication factors to gain access to cloud resources, such as passwords, biometric verification, or one-time passcodes.

2 How does encryption contribute to cloud defense?

Answer: Encryption in cloud defense involves encoding data before it's transferred to the cloud, making it unreadable to unauthorized users. This ensures that even if data is intercepted, it remains protected.

3 What is network segmentation in cloud defense?

Answer: Network segmentation in cloud defense involves dividing a network into smaller, isolated segments to prevent unauthorized access to sensitive data and limit the impact of potential breaches.

4 How does intrusion detection and prevention work in cloud defense?

Answer: Intrusion detection and prevention systems monitor network traffic and identify potential threats or security breaches in real time. They can automatically block or mitigate these threats to protect cloud resources.

5 What role does security monitoring play in cloud defense?

Answer: Security monitoring involves continuously monitoring cloud environments for suspicious activities or unauthorized access attempts. It helps detect and respond to security incidents promptly.

6 How does identity and access management enhance cloud defense?

Answer: Identity and access management systems control user access to cloud resources based on their roles and permissions. This ensures that only authorized users can access sensitive data or perform specific actions.

7 What is the principle of least privilege in cloud defense?

Answer: The principle of least privilege dictates that users should only be granted the minimum level of access or permissions necessary to perform their job functions in the cloud environment. This reduces the risk of unauthorized access or misuse of resources.

8 How does data loss prevention contribute to cloud defense?

Answer: Data loss prevention systems monitor and control the transfer of sensitive data within the cloud environment, preventing unauthorized disclosure or leakage of confidential information.

9 What is cloud sandboxing and its role in defense?

Answer: Cloud sandboxing involves running untrusted applications or files in a controlled environment to analyze their behavior and identify potential threats. It helps protect against malware and other malicious activities in the cloud.

10 How does cloud access security brokers enhance cloud defense?

Answer: Cloud access security brokers (CASBs) act as intermediaries between cloud users and cloud service providers, providing visibility and control over cloud applications and enforcing security policies to protect data.

11 What role does threat intelligence play in cloud defense?

Answer: Threat intelligence involves gathering and analyzing information about potential cybersecurity threats and vulnerabilities. It helps cloud defenders stay informed about emerging risks and take proactive measures to mitigate them.

12 How does vulnerability management contribute to cloud defense?

Answer: Vulnerability management involves identifying, prioritizing, and remedying security vulnerabilities in cloud environments to prevent exploitation by attackers and reduce the risk of breaches.

13 What are the benefits of employing cloud-native security solutions?

Answer: Cloud-native security solutions are specifically designed to protect cloud environments, offering advantages such as scalability, agility, and integration with cloud platforms, making them well-suited for defending modern cloud infrastructures.

14 How does threat hunting enhance cloud defense?

Answer: Threat hunting involves proactively searching for signs of malicious activity or potential security threats within cloud environments. It helps identify and neutralize threats before they can cause significant damage.

15 What is containerization, and how does it improve cloud defense?

Answer: Containerization involves encapsulating applications and their dependencies into lightweight, portable containers. It enhances cloud defense by isolating applications and reducing the attack surface, making it harder for attackers to compromise cloud resources.

16 How does distributed denial of service (DDoS) protection work in cloud defense?

Answer: DDoS protection in cloud defense involves deploying specialized tools and techniques to mitigate the impact of DDoS attacks by filtering malicious traffic and ensuring the availability of cloud services.

17 What role does security automation play in cloud defense?

Answer: Security automation involves using automated tools and processes to streamline security tasks such as threat detection, incident response, and compliance management in cloud environments, improving efficiency and reducing the risk of human error.

18 How does cloud workload protection improve cloud defense?

Answer: Cloud workload protection involves implementing security controls and policies to safeguard the workloads running in cloud environments, including virtual machines, containers, and serverless functions, against threats and vulnerabilities.

19 What is the importance of regular security audits in cloud defense?

Answer: Regular security audits in cloud defense help assess the effectiveness of security measures, identify weaknesses or compliance issues, and ensure that cloud environments adhere to security best practices and regulatory requirements.

20 How does continuous security monitoring contribute to cloud defense?

Answer: Continuous security monitoring involves real-time monitoring of cloud environments for security threats and vulnerabilities, enabling rapid detection and response to security incidents to minimize their impact on cloud operations.

REFERENCES

1. Agrawal, N., & Tapaswi, S. (2019). Defense mechanisms against DDoS attacks in a cloud computing environment: State-of-the-art and research challenges. *IEEE Communications Surveys & Tutorials*, *21*(4), 3769–3795.
2. Khalil, I. M., Khreishah, A., & Azeem, M. (2014). Cloud computing security: A survey. *Computers*, *3*(1), 1–35.
3. El Kafhali, S., El Mir, I., & Hanini, M. (2022). Security threats, defense mechanisms, challenges, and future directions in cloud computing. *Archives of Computational Methods in Engineering*, *29*(1), 223–246.

4. Eddermoug, N., Mansour, A., Azmi, M., Sadik, M., Sabir, E., & Bahassi, H. (2023). A Literature Review on Attacks Prevention and Profiling in Cloud Computing. *Procedia Computer Science*, *220*, 970–977.
5. Parwani, D. A. L. I. M. A., Dutta, A., Shukla, P. K., & Tahiliyani, M. (2015). Various techniques of DDoS attacks detection & prevention at cloud: A survey. *Oriental Journal of Computer Science and Technology*, *8*(2), 110–120.
6. Patel, A., Taghavi, M., Bakhtiyari, K., & Júnior, J. C. (2013). An intrusion detection and prevention system in cloud computing: A systematic review. *Journal of network and computer applications*, *36*(1), 25–41.
7. Liu, Z., Xu, B., Cheng, B., Hu, X., & Darbandi, M. (2022). Intrusion detection systems in the cloud computing: A comprehensive and deep literature review. *Concurrency and Computation: Practice and Experience*, *34*(4), e6646.
8. Inayat, Z., Gani, A., Anuar, N. B., Anwar, S., & Khan, M. K. (2017). Cloud-based intrusion detection and response system: open research issues, and solutions. *Arabian Journal for Science and Engineering*, *42*, 399–423.
9. Lo, C. C., Huang, C. C., & Ku, J. (2010, September). A cooperative intrusion detection system framework for cloud computing networks. In *2010 39th International Conference on Parallel Processing Workshops* (pp. 280–284). IEEE.
10. Khorshed, M. T., Ali, A. S., & Wasimi, S. A. (2012). A survey on gaps, threat remediation challenges and some thoughts for proactive attack detection in cloud computing. *Future Generation computer systems*, *28*(6), 833–851.
11. Hatef, M. A., Shaker, V., Jabbarpour, M. R., Jung, J., & Zarrabi, H. (2018). HIDCC: A hybrid intrusion detection approach in cloud computing. *Concurrency and Computation: Practice and Experience*, *30*(3), e4171.
12. Chang, V., Golightly, L., Modesti, P., Xu, Q. A., Doan, L. M. T., Hall, K., ... & Kobusińska, A. (2022). A survey on intrusion detection systems for fog and cloud computing. *Future Internet*, *14*(3), 89.
13. Chiba, Z., Abghour, N., Moussaid, K., El Omri, A., & Rida, M. (2016, September). A survey of intrusion detection systems for cloud computing environment. In *2016 international conference on engineering & MIS (ICEMIS)* (pp. 1–13). IEEE.
14. Ahmed, K. E. U., & Alexandrov, V. (2011). Identity and Access Management in Cloud Computing. In *Cloud Computing for Enterprise Architectures* (pp. 115–133). London: Springer London.
15. Yang, P., Xiong, N., & Ren, J. (2020). Data security and privacy protection for cloud storage: A survey. *IEEE Access*, *8*, 131723–131740.
16. Sun, Y., Zhang, J., Xiong, Y., & Zhu, G. (2014). Data security and privacy in cloud computing. *International Journal of Distributed Sensor Networks*, *10*(7), 190903.
17. Domingo-Ferrer, J., Farras, O., Ribes-González, J., & Sánchez, D. (2019). Privacy-preserving cloud computing on sensitive data: A survey of methods, products and challenges. *Computer Communications*, *140*, 38–60.
18. Diallo, M. H., Hore, B., Chang, E. C., Mehrotra, S., & Venkatasubramanian, N. (2012, June). Cloudprotect: managing data privacy in cloud applications. In *2012 IEEE Fifth International Conference on Cloud Computing* (pp. 303–310). IEEE.
19. Sood, S. K. (2012). A combined approach to ensure data security in cloud computing. *Journal of Network and Computer Applications*, *35*(6), 1831–1838.
20. Schwartz, P. M. (2012). Information privacy in the cloud. *University of Pennsylvania Law Review*, *161*, 1623.
21. Kaaniche, N., & Laurent, M. (2017). Data security and privacy preservation in cloud storage environments based on cryptographic mechanisms. *Computer Communications*, *111*, 120–141.

22. Xiao, Z., & Xiao, Y. (2012). Security and privacy in cloud computing. *IEEE Communications Surveys & Tutorials*, *15*(2), 843–859.
23. Alassafi, M. O., Hussain, R. K., Ghashgari, G., Walters, R. J., & Wills, G. B. (2017). Security in organisations: governance, risks and vulnerabilities in moving to the cloud. In *Enterprise Security: Second International Workshop, ES 2015*, Vancouver, BC, Canada, November 30–December 3, 2015, Revised Selected Papers (pp. 241–258). Springer International Publishing.
24. Colman-Meixner, C., Develder, C., Tornatore, M., & Mukherjee, B. (2016). A survey on resiliency techniques in cloud computing infrastructures and applications. *IEEE Communications Surveys & Tutorials*, *18*(3), 2244–2281.
25. Agrawal, N., & Tapaswi, S. (2017). Defense schemes for variants of distributed denial-of-service (DDoS) attacks in cloud computing: A survey. *Information Security Journal: A Global Perspective*, *26*(2), 61–73.
26. Somani, G., Gaur, M. S., Sanghi, D., Conti, M., & Buyya, R. (2017). DDoS attacks in cloud computing: Issues, taxonomy, and future directions. *Computer Communications*, *107*, 30–48.

5 Cloud Computing Tools

5.1 CYBERATTACK SIMULATION TOOLS

Cyberattack simulation tools are essential for organizations to test and improve their cybersecurity defenses. These tools simulate real-world cyberattacks to identify vulnerabilities and weaknesses in a system or network. Some popular cyberattack simulation tools are discussed below:

1. Cobalt Strike: This widely used penetration testing tool allows security professionals to simulate various types of attacks, including spear phishing and social engineering. It also provides advanced post-exploitation capabilities [1].
2. Metasploit: Metasploit is an open-source penetration testing framework offering a vast array of tools for simulating cyberattacks. It includes exploits, payloads, and auxiliary modules for testing vulnerabilities [2].
3. OWASP ZAP (Zed Attack Proxy): ZAP is an open-source web application security testing tool that helps identify security vulnerabilities in web applications during development and testing [3].
4. Nmap (Network Mapper): Nmap is a powerful network scanning tool used to discover hosts and services on a computer network, often employed as a preliminary step in assessing network security [4].
5. BeEF (The Browser Exploitation Framework): BeEF focuses on exploiting web browser vulnerabilities to assess the security of web applications through client-side attacks [5].
6. SQLMap: SQLMap is an open-source tool automating detection and exploitation of SQL injection flaws in web applications during penetration testing [6].
7. Wireshark: Wireshark is a network protocol analyzer used to capture and analyze data flowing through a network, aiding in the identification of suspicious activity and security threats [7].
8. Burp Suite: A popular web vulnerability scanner offering tools for automated scans, manual testing, and more to identify security issues in web applications [8].
9. Empire: Empire is a post-exploitation framework enabling simulation of advanced cyberattacks such as lateral movement and data exfiltration within a network [9].

DOI: 10.1201/9781003510772-5

10. Mimikatz: Mimikatz focuses on post-exploitation scenarios, particularly extracting credentials from Windows systems' memory for lateral movement.
11. Infection Monkey: Infection Monkey is designed to test network security by simulating cyberattacks such as lateral movement and privilege escalation to assess vulnerability [10].
12. Threatcare: Threatcare validates controls, identifies risks, and provides insights quickly by mimicking hacker attacks on infrastructure to pinpoint security gaps [11].
13. NeSSi2 (Network Security Simulator 2): NeSSi2 is an open-source network simulation tool for evaluating security protocols and techniques in various scenarios, aiding in testing and validating network security solutions [12].
14. Caldera: Caldera is an open-source framework for simulating real-world attacks, enabling organizations to test cybersecurity defenses and incident response procedures.
15. Foreseeti: Foreseeti provides attack simulation tools such as securiCAD to simulate cyberattacks on IT infrastructure, helping organizations understand vulnerabilities and prioritize security measures [13].

Figure 5.1 depicts different common cyberattack simulation tools in cloud environment. Table 5.1 highlights the main function and features of each tool. The table provides a summary of popular cyberattack simulation tools, outlining their primary use cases, key features, and licensing information.

These tools help organizations identify vulnerabilities and strengthen their cybersecurity defenses by simulating real-world attacks across various domains, including penetration testing, web application security, network analysis, and post-exploitation scenarios.

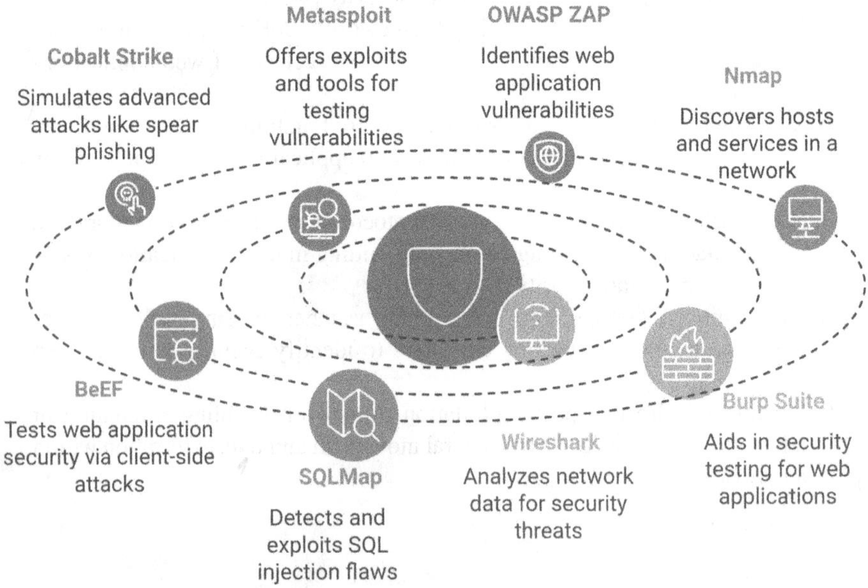

FIGURE 5.1 Common cyberattack simulation tools.

TABLE 5.1
Analysis of Popular Cyberattack Simulation Tools

Tool Name	Type	Use	Key Features	License
Cobalt Strike	Penetration Testing	Simulates spear phishing and social engineering	Post-exploitation, lateral movement	Commercial (Paid)
Metasploit	Penetration Testing	Tests vulnerabilities with exploits and payloads	Exploits, payloads, modules	Open Source (Free)
OWASP ZAP	Web Testing	Identifies web app vulnerabilities	Automated scanning, passive/active scanning	Open Source (Free)
Nmap	Network Scanning	Discovers hosts and services	Port scanning, service enumeration	Open Source (Free)
BeEF	Web Testing	Exploits browser vulnerabilities	Client-side attacks, browser exploits	Open Source (Free)
SQLMap	Web Testing	Automates SQL injection detection	Detects and exploits SQL injection flaws	Open Source (Free)
Wireshark	Network Analysis	Captures and analyzes network traffic	Real-time packet capture, protocol analysis	Open Source (Free)
Burp Suite	Web Testing	Scans web apps for vulnerabilities	Vulnerability scanning, proxy, manual testing	Commercial (Paid)
Empire	Post-Exploitation	Simulates advanced attacks (e.g., lateral movement)	PowerShell-based, post-exploitation	Open Source (Free)
Mimikatz	Post-Exploitation	Extracts credentials from memory	Credential extraction, password dumping	Open Source (Free)
Infection Monkey	Network Testing	Simulates lateral movement and privilege escalation	Automated attack simulation	Commercial (Paid)
Threatcare	Infrastructure	Mimics hacker behavior to identify risks	Infrastructure attack simulations	Commercial (Paid)
NeSSi2	Network Simulation	Simulates network environments and security protocols	Topology simulation, security validation	Open Source (Free)
Caldera	Attack Simulation	Simulates real-world cyberattacks	Automated attack simulations, adversary emulation	Open Source (Free)
Foreseeti	IT Testing	Simulates attacks on IT infrastructure	Risk management, attack simulations	Commercial (Paid)

These tools are invaluable for testing and improving cybersecurity defenses, but they should only be used in authorized and controlled environments to avoid unintended harm. Organizations must ensure they have the necessary permissions and legal agreements in place before conducting any cyberattack simulations.

5.2 CLOUD MONITORING AND ANALYSIS TOOLS

A different cloud service provider offers a diverse array of services and tools tailored for cloud operation and management. These technologies are indispensable for organizations looking to integrate, procure, oversee, optimize, and track cloud services across private, public, or hybrid cloud environments. The complexity of each tool typically corresponds to its placement within the service model architecture – Infrastructure as a Service (IaaS), Platform as a Service (PaaS), or Software as a Service (SaaS). For instance, IaaS tools generally focus on foundational infrastructure components and are often more straightforward to use compared to PaaS tools, which require familiarity with specific interfaces and development environments. Meanwhile, SaaS tools are typically user-friendly applications accessible via the Internet, minimizing the need for infrastructure management. These tools also vary in classification as either open-source or proprietary, influencing factors such as customization options, community support, and licensing considerations. Open-source tools offer flexibility and community-driven development, whereas proprietary tools often provide robust support and integration capabilities tailored to specific business needs. To ensure comprehensive transparency into cloud operations, these technologies must be supplied by reliable cloud service providers. For example, in managing and safeguarding a moderate size city, a diverse toolkit would be essential. This toolkit would encompass tools for infrastructure provisioning, application development and deployment platforms, software for monitoring and optimizing cloud resources, as well as security solutions to protect against cyber threats and ensure data integrity. Figure 5.2 highlights the different cloud monitoring and analysis tool categories.

In essence, these tools not only facilitate efficient cloud management but also play a critical role in enhancing operational transparency and security, ensuring smooth and secure operations crucial for the well-being and safety of urban environments.

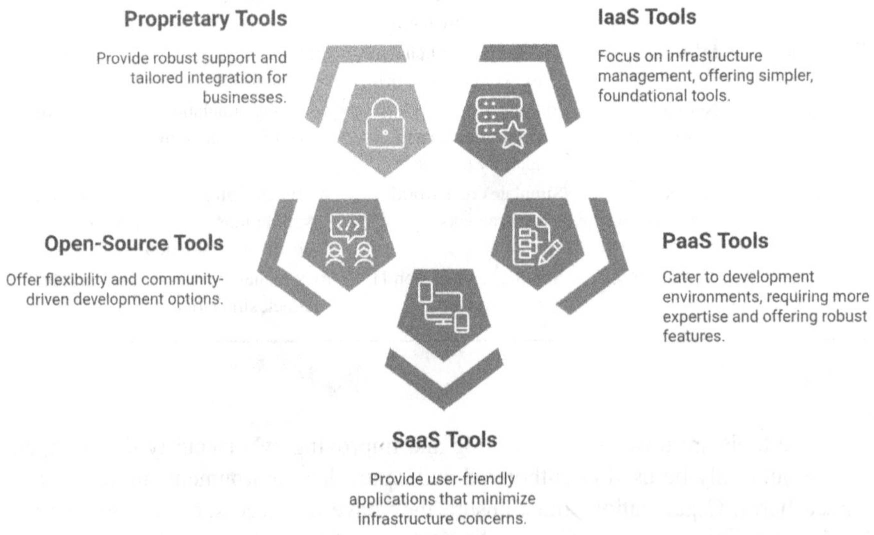
Proprietary Tools
Provide robust support and tailored integration for businesses.
IaaS Tools
Focus on infrastructure management, offering simpler, foundational tools.
Open-Source Tools
Offer flexibility and community-driven development options.
PaaS Tools
Cater to development environments, requiring more expertise and offering robust features.
SaaS Tools
Provide user-friendly applications that minimize infrastructure concerns.

FIGURE 5.2 Generalized categories of cloud monitoring and analysis tools.

The primary uses of cloud computing tools serve businesses in a variety of ways, resulting in verifiable benefits in their operations.

5.2.1 Assist Enterprise Integration

- These tools assist organizations with any data integration challenges as well as integration deployment. These tools also create the path for IT governance and control to be followed.
- Analogous Situation: Having a governing body to help unify disparate parts of Gotham City to maintain the city's seamless operation.
- Examples include ServiceMesh's Agility Platform, MuleSoft's CloudHub (Open Source), Informatica's cloud, and Dell Boomi's AtomSphere.
  - **ServiceMesh's Agility Platform**: ServiceMesh's Agility Platform constitutes a comprehensive cloud management solution engineered to streamline and automate the administration of cloud services across diverse providers. It incorporates functionalities such as governance, compliance, security, and cost management, empowering enterprises to effectively oversee their cloud resources and applications.
  - **MuleSoft's CloudHub (Open Source)**: MuleSoft's CloudHub stands as an open-source integration platform as a service (iPaaS) designed to facilitate seamless application integration and connectivity across a variety of systems, services, and APIs. It equips organizations with tools for constructing, deploying, managing, and monitoring integrations within cloud environments, enabling the creation of smooth connections between applications and data sources.
  - **Informatica's Cloud**: Informatica's cloud platform offers a spectrum of cloud-based services focused on data management and integration. These services encompass data integration, data quality, master data management, and data governance, providing tools and capabilities to securely manage and integrate data across hybrid and multi-cloud environments. This aids organizations in upholding data quality, consistency, and reliability throughout their IT infrastructure.
  - **Dell Boomi's AtomSphere**: Dell Boomi's AtomSphere [14] represents an integration platform as a service (iPaaS) enabling organizations to interconnect applications, data, and devices across both on-premises and cloud environments. It features a visual interface for designing, deploying, managing, and monitoring integrations, enabling users to efficiently construct intricate integration workflows without necessitating extensive coding or development proficiency.

5.2.2 Assist Enterprise Management

These tools facilitate a range of functions within cloud service management, encompassing infrastructure management, configuration management, automation of management services, and adherence to regulatory frameworks governing infrastructure and cloud computing applications. The tools provide compliance and security of cloud services through a single integrated control point for governance.

- Analogous Situation: Managing Gotham City to ensure that the regulations are obeyed and to manage various sections of the city such as city planning, employment planning, and so on.
- RightScale Cloud Management, Puppet (Open Source), Chef (Open Source), and Enstratius are a few examples (acquired by Dell and is currently support-only).
  - ***RightScale Cloud Management*:** RightScale provides a cloud management platform that helps organizations manage and optimize their cloud infrastructure across multiple providers such as AWS, Azure, and Google Cloud Platform. It offers features like automated scaling, cost management, and governance to streamline cloud operations.
  - ***Puppet (Open Source) [15]*:** Puppet is an open-source configuration management tool designed to automate the deployment and administration of software and infrastructure configurations. It utilizes a declarative language for defining system configurations, enabling administrators to specify the desired state of their infrastructure and automate its enforcement.
  - ***Chef (Open Source)*:** Chef is an open-source configuration management tool similar to Puppet, focusing on automating the deployment and management of infrastructure. It employs a domain-specific language (DSL) to define system configurations, allowing administrators to create "recipes" that detail system configurations. Chef adopts a "model-driven" approach, aligning the actual state of systems with the desired state specified in the recipes.
  - ***Enstratius (Dell Cloud Manager)*:** Enstratius, rebranded as Dell Cloud Manager, serves as a cloud management platform aiding organizations in the governance and management of their cloud resources across multiple providers. It offers features such as multi-cloud orchestration, governance, and security management, simplifying the administration of complex cloud environments.

5.2.3 Assist Enterprise Monitor

These applications facilitate the monitoring of cloud computing architecture, infrastructure, and services. They enable administrators to detect potential system issues either proactively or reactively, helping to prevent minor glitches from escalating into critical problems.

- Analogous Situation: The monitoring of Gotham City will keep any problems in the city from escalating into pandemonium.
- Amazon CloudWatch (Proprietary), Microsoft Cloud Monitoring (Proprietary), and Nagios are a few examples (Open source).
  - ***Amazon CloudWatch [16]*:** It is a comprehensive monitoring and observability service provided by Amazon Web Services (AWS). It offers real-time insights into the performance and health of applications, infrastructure, and services deployed on AWS. The service includes customizable dashboards, alarms, and logs designed to monitor resource utilization, application performance, and operational efficiency. These features assist in proactive troubleshooting and optimization of AWS resources.

- ***Microsoft Cloud Monitoring*:** It is an integral component of the Azure suite, offering comparable capabilities for monitoring the performance, availability, and usage of applications and infrastructure hosted on Microsoft Azure. Features such as Application Insights and Azure Monitor provide detailed insights into application health, performance trends, and operational telemetry. This functionality supports effective management and optimization of Azure resources.
- ***Nagios [17]*:** It is an open-source monitoring solution known for its robustness and flexibility. It is widely used for monitoring IT infrastructure, network services, and applications, offering extensive support for plugins and customizable alerting capabilities. Nagios enables organizations to monitor diverse environments and systems, ensuring continuous availability and performance optimization through proactive monitoring and alerting mechanisms.

5.2.4 Assist Enterprise in Tweaking/Optimizing

These techniques assist the company in over-purchasing resources. These assist them in tweaking by providing insights into inefficiencies in the service and also recommending an approach to eliminate the inefficiencies. Reservations, Rightsizing, Automation, and other approaches are used by these programs to optimize/tweak.

- Analogous Situation: Gotham City requires structure so that all resources can perform at their peak.
- S3 Life-Cycle Tracker (Proprietary), EC2 Reservation Detector (Proprietary), and RDS Reservation Detector are some examples (Proprietary).

5.2.5 Assist Enterprise Tracking/Auditing

These tools assist businesses in tracking and analyzing the use of cloud computing services. For example, there are technologies that assist in analyzing the cost of the services being utilized and identifying cost-cutting opportunities/alerts/recommendations.

- Similar Situation: Having a regulatory agency in Gotham to analyze and track the economy/activities will help the city grow.
- Cloudability (proprietary) and Apache CloudStack AMFC are two examples (Open source).

In the age of cloud computing, it is unavoidable to overlook asset and application performance monitoring in addition to physical servers. A proper fit for an enterprise's services depends on elements such as needs, budget, and type of necessity. Some of these tools have a "do-it-all" tagline, while others have certain specialized functions; again, depending on the parameters listed above, the company has the ability to choose from a wide range of options.

A summary of the cloud monitoring and analysis tools, along with their descriptions and examples, is provided in Table 5.2.

TABLE 5.2
Summary of the Cloud Monitoring and Analysis Tools

Category	Description	Examples
Assist Enterprise Integration	Tools for data integration, deployment, IT governance, and control.	ServiceMesh Agility Platform, MuleSoft CloudHub (Open Source), Informatica Cloud, Dell Boomi AtomSphere
Assist Enterprise Management	Tools for infrastructure management, automation, compliance, and governance of cloud services.	RightScale Cloud Management, Puppet (Open Source), Chef (Open Source), Enstratius (Dell Cloud Manager)
Assist Enterprise Monitor	Tools for monitoring cloud infrastructure, services, and applications to detect and prevent issues.	Amazon CloudWatch (Proprietary), Microsoft Cloud Monitoring (Proprietary), Nagios (Open Source)
Assist Enterprise Tweaking/ Optimizing	Tools for optimizing cloud resources, reducing inefficiencies, and making adjustments for cost savings.	S3 Life-Cycle Tracker (Proprietary), EC2 Reservation Detector (Proprietary), RDS Reservation Detector
Assist Enterprise Tracking/Auditing	Tools for tracking and analyzing cloud usage, costs, and identifying opportunities for optimization.	Cloudability (Proprietary), Apache CloudStack AMFC (Open Source)

5.3 ATTACK DEFENSE TOOLS

Detecting attacks in cloud computing environments requires a combination of tools and techniques to ensure comprehensive security coverage. Some common attack detection tools used in cloud computing are as follows.

1. Intrusion Detection Systems (IDS):
   - Host-based IDS (HIDS): Monitors activities on individual cloud instances, looking for suspicious behavior or known attack patterns.
   - Network-based IDS (NIDS): Analyzes network traffic within the cloud environment to identify potential threats or malicious activities.
2. Security Information and Event Management (SIEM):
   - Collects and analyzes log data from various cloud services and infrastructure components to identify security incidents or anomalies.
   - Correlates events across different sources to provide a holistic view of the security posture.
3. Endpoint Detection and Response (EDR):
   - Monitors activities on endpoints (virtual machines, containers, etc.) within the cloud environment.
   - Detects and responds to suspicious behavior or signs of compromise on individual endpoints.
4. Vulnerability Scanners:
   - Identifies security weaknesses and misconfigurations within cloud infrastructure and applications.

- Helps in proactively addressing vulnerabilities before they are exploited by attackers.

5. Web Application Firewalls (WAF):
   - Web Application Firewalls safeguard cloud-based web applications through meticulous inspection and filtering of HTTP traffic.
   - They are adept at identifying and thwarting prevalent web application threats such as SQL injection and cross-site scripting (XSS).
6. Behavioral Analysis Tools:
   - These tools meticulously scrutinize user and application behavior within the cloud ecosystem to pinpoint deviations from established norms.
   - Their functionality extends to identifying internal threats, compromised accounts, and any potentially malicious activities.
7. Threat Intelligence Platforms:
   - These platforms aggregate and meticulously analyze threat data from diverse sources to furnish actionable insights into emerging threats and prevailing attack patterns.
   - They empower proactive measures such as threat hunting and swift incident response.
8. Cloud Access Security Brokers (CASB):
   - CASBs furnish comprehensive oversight and administrative control over cloud services leveraged within the enterprise.
   - They continuously monitor data access and operations across cloud applications to preclude unauthorized or malevolent activities.
9. Packet Capture and Analysis Tools:
   - These tools seize and dissect network traffic within the cloud milieu, enabling exhaustive scrutiny and interpretation of packet contents.
   - They prove invaluable in identifying malicious payloads, communication patterns, and other discernible signs of compromise.
10. Anomaly Detection Systems:
    - These systems harness advanced machine learning algorithms to detect aberrant or suspicious activities occurring within the cloud infrastructure.
    - Their adaptive capability, honed through continuous learning from historical data, enhances their efficacy in detecting novel threats over time.

Some common categories of attack defense tools are depicted in Figure 5.3. In addition to this, Table 5.3 summarizes various attack detection tools commonly used in cloud computing environments.

These tools help ensure comprehensive security by monitoring, analyzing, and responding to potential threats. Each tool serves a specific purpose, such as detecting suspicious activities, identifying vulnerabilities, or protecting against web-based attacks, to safeguard cloud infrastructure and applications.

By amalgamating a suite of these sophisticated tools and seamlessly integrating them into a unified security framework, organizations can significantly fortify their ability to preemptively identify and swiftly counteract threats within cloud computing environments.

FIGURE 5.3 Common categories of attack defense tools.

TABLE 5.3
Analysis of the Attack Detection Tools in Cloud Environments

Tool/Technique	Description	Examples
Intrusion Detection Systems (IDS)	Monitors for suspicious activities or attack patterns in cloud instances/networks.	Host-based IDS (HIDS), Network-based IDS (NIDS)
Security Information and Event Management (SIEM)	Collects and analyzes log data to detect security incidents and anomalies.	Splunk, IBM QRadar, AlienVault
Endpoint Detection and Response (EDR)	Monitors and responds to suspicious activity on cloud endpoints (VMs, containers).	CrowdStrike Falcon, Carbon Black
Vulnerability Scanners	Identifies security weaknesses and misconfigurations in cloud infrastructure.	Nessus, Qualys, OpenVAS
Web Application Firewalls (WAF)	Protects cloud apps from web threats like SQL injection and XSS.	AWS WAF, Imperva WAF, Cloudflare WAF
Behavioral Analysis Tools	Detects unusual behavior in users and apps to identify potential threats.	Exabeam, Varonis, Sumo Logic
Threat Intelligence Platforms	Aggregates and analyzes data to provide actionable threat insights.	ThreatConnect, Anomali, Recorded Future
Cloud Access Security Brokers (CASB)	Monitors and controls cloud service usage and data access.	McAfee MVISION, Netskope, Symantec CASB
Packet Capture Tools	Captures and analyzes network traffic to detect malicious activity.	Wireshark, tcpdump, SolarWinds
Anomaly Detection Systems	Uses machine learning to detect abnormal activities and potential threats.	Darktrace, Vectra AI, Sift

5.4 SIMULATORS

Cloud computing simulators serve as indispensable tools for modeling, testing, and analyzing cloud computing environments, obviating the necessity for physical infrastructure deployment. These simulators enable users to replicate various facets of cloud computing, encompassing resource provisioning, network configurations, workload distribution, and application deployment. Some common simulators are shown in Figure 5.4 with respective key features. Additionally, several prominent cloud computing simulators are discussed below.

5.4.1 CloudSim

CloudSim [18] stands out as one of the most extensively utilized cloud computing simulators. It furnishes a robust simulation framework that supports the modeling and simulation of cloud computing infrastructures and services. CloudSim empowers users to simulate diverse elements of cloud environments, including data centers, virtual machines, scheduling policies, and application workflows.

Key features of the CloudSim simulator include:

1. Modularity: CloudSim adopts a modular architecture, facilitating users to extend and tailor its functionalities to meet specific research requirements. This modular design enhances flexibility and promotes seamless integration of new features.
2. Cloud Infrastructure Simulation: CloudSim enables the simulation of various types of cloud data centers, encompassing private, public, and hybrid clouds. Users can model critical aspects of data center infrastructure such as hosts, virtual machines (VMs), data centers, and networking components.

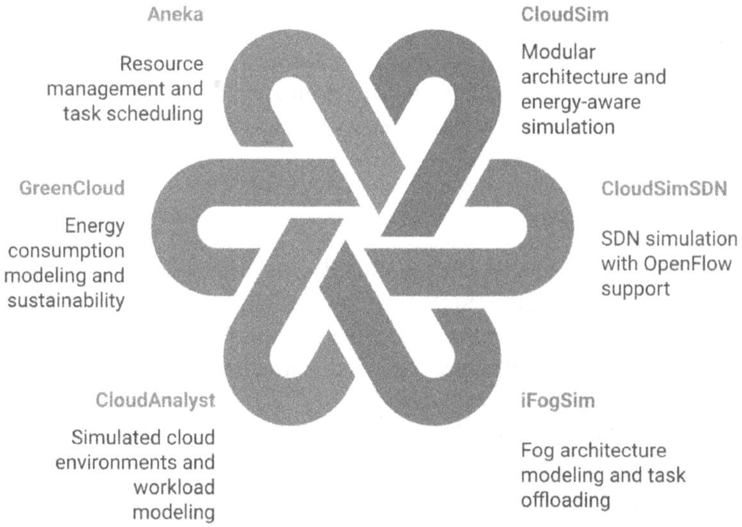

FIGURE 5.4 Common cloud simulators and key features.

3. Workload Modeling: It supports the simulation of diverse workload patterns, including bursty, periodic, and stochastic workloads. Researchers can assess the performance of cloud systems under varied workload conditions to comprehend their behavior and scalability.
4. Resource Provisioning Strategies: CloudSim facilitates the implementation and evaluation of resource provisioning algorithms and policies. Users can experiment with dynamic provisioning strategies such as VM allocation, migration, and scheduling to optimize resource utilization, energy efficiency, and performance.
5. Energy-Aware Simulation: CloudSim addresses energy efficiency concerns in cloud computing environments by simulating energy consumption and exploring energy-aware resource management techniques. This approach aims to minimize operational costs and environmental impact.
6. Networking Simulation: The simulator includes capabilities for simulating network characteristics and behaviors within cloud data centers. This feature enables researchers to analyze the impact of network configurations on application performance and quality of service (QoS).
7. Scalability and Performance Evaluation: Researchers leverage CloudSim to evaluate the scalability and performance of cloud applications and services under diverse conditions, such as varying workload intensities, resource capacities, and system configurations.
8. Experimentation and Analysis: CloudSim facilitates rigorous experimentation and in-depth analysis of simulation results through built-in tools and utilities. Users can derive insights into system behavior, evaluate algorithm effectiveness, and compare different cloud deployment strategies.
9. Integration with Other Tools: CloudSim supports integration with external tools and frameworks, promoting interoperability and expanding its capabilities. This integration fosters collaboration and enables leveraging existing resources and expertise within the cloud computing community.

In summary, CloudSim serves as a pivotal platform for both academia and industry, facilitating exploration, innovation, and advancement in the realm of cloud computing through simulation-based research and experimentation.

5.4.2 CloudSimSDN

CloudSimSDN is an extension of CloudSim designed to facilitate the simulation of Software-Defined Networking (SDN) within cloud environments [19]. This specialized framework offers a comprehensive suite of features tailored for modeling and evaluating SDN-based architectures, network virtualization strategies, and traffic management techniques.

Key Features of CloudSimSDN:

1. **SDN Simulation**: CloudSimSDN provides a robust framework for simulating various SDN architectures, enabling researchers and developers to explore and analyze different aspects of SDN networks.

2. **OpenFlow Support**: Integral to its functionality is support for the OpenFlow protocol, a fundamental technology in SDN environments. OpenFlow facilitates centralized control of network devices, allowing for dynamic and programmable network management.
3. **Network Topology Creation**: Users benefit from the ability to create customized network topologies, defining switches, routers, hosts, and interconnecting links to simulate diverse network configurations.
4. **Traffic Generation and Management**: The simulator facilitates the generation and management of network traffic patterns, crucial for assessing network performance under different conditions.
5. **Resource Management**: CloudSimSDN supports the simulation of resource allocation strategies within SDN environments. This includes bandwidth allocation, routing decisions, and Quality of Service (QoS) management.
6. **Virtualization Support**: It incorporates capabilities for network function virtualization (NFV) and the simulation of virtual network functions (VNFs), enabling evaluation of performance for virtualized network services in SDN contexts.
7. **Energy Efficiency**: The simulator includes features to model the energy consumption of network devices and evaluate energy-efficient SDN strategies, addressing sustainability concerns in network operations.
8. **Visualization**: CloudSimSDN provides visualization tools essential for comprehending and analyzing simulated SDN networks. This includes graphical representations of network topologies, traffic flows, and performance metrics.
9. **Customizability**: Researchers and practitioners can extend and customize CloudSimSDN to meet specific research or application requirements. This flexibility encompasses the integration of new network protocols, algorithms, or modules.

In summary, CloudSimSDN stands as a versatile simulation tool empowering researchers and practitioners alike to study, refine, and optimize SDN architectures, protocols, and applications within a controlled and reproducible environment. Its comprehensive feature set makes it an invaluable asset for advancing SDN research and development efforts.

5.4.3 iFogSim

iFogSim [20] is a prominent toolkit tailored for modeling and simulating fog computing environments, offering researchers and developers a robust platform to explore the deployment of applications within complex fog computing architectures. This simulation framework allows for comprehensive evaluation of application performance, scalability, and energy efficiency in realistic fog computing scenarios, obviating the need for physical deployment.

Key Features of iFogSim:

1. **Architecture Modeling**: iFogSim enables users to model intricate fog computing architectures encompassing fog nodes, IoT devices, and cloud data centers. Users can define the structural layout of the fog network and establish communication links between nodes.

2. **Task Offloading**: It supports various task offloading strategies, empowering users to simulate diverse policies for distributing computation tasks among fog nodes and cloud data centers. This includes dynamic offloading based on real-time resource availability and network conditions.
3. **Resource Management**: The toolkit facilitates comprehensive resource management within the fog network, encompassing allocation of CPU, memory, and bandwidth resources. Users can define and simulate resource constraints for fog nodes, assessing scenarios involving resource contention.
4. **Network Simulation**: iFogSim incorporates robust network simulation capabilities to model crucial parameters such as communication latency, bandwidth availability, and reliability between fog nodes and IoT devices. This capability aids in evaluating application performance under varying network conditions.
5. **Energy Consumption Modeling**: It includes features for modeling energy consumption across different levels of the fog architecture, from IoT devices to fog nodes and cloud data centers. Users can analyze and optimize energy efficiency within fog computing deployments based on simulation results.
6. **Scalability Analysis**: iFogSim supports scalability analysis to evaluate how fog computing applications perform as the number of IoT devices and fog nodes scales up. This analysis helps in identifying potential scalability bottlenecks and optimizing architecture for large-scale deployments.
7. **Visualization**: The toolkit provides visualization tools for intuitively interpreting simulation outcomes, including task execution times, resource utilization patterns, and network traffic flows. These visual aids facilitate deeper insights into the behavior and performance of fog computing applications.
8. **Extensibility**: Designed with extensibility in mind, iFogSim allows users to integrate custom algorithms, policies, and modules tailored for tasks such as task scheduling and resource management. This flexibility supports adaptation to specific research or application requirements within fog computing simulations.

In summary, iFogSim serves as a comprehensive simulation platform enabling researchers and practitioners to simulate, evaluate, and optimize fog computing architectures and applications in a controlled environment. By leveraging its diverse feature set, users can gain insights into performance metrics, scalability factors, and energy efficiency considerations crucial for advancing fog computing technologies.

5.4.4 CloudAnalyst

CloudAnalyst stands as a pivotal tool in the realm of cloud simulation, dedicated to the evaluation and optimization of cloud computing environments. It provides robust capabilities for simulating diverse scenarios and meticulously analyzing performance across critical metrics such as response time, cost efficiency, and resource utilization. This tool is indispensable for researchers, developers, and enterprises aiming to gain profound insights into the behavior of cloud-based applications under varying conditions, thereby empowering them to enhance deployment strategies for optimal performance and economical operation.

Key Features of CloudAnalyst

1. **Simulation Environment**: CloudAnalyst facilitates the creation of simulated cloud environments where users can deploy applications and conduct comprehensive behavioral analyses.
2. **Resource Provisioning**: Users can dynamically allocate virtual machines, storage resources, and other critical components to simulate various configurations and assess their impact on performance and cost.
3. **Workload Modeling**: The tool supports the modeling and simulation of diverse workloads, including web traffic, batch processing, and database transactions, enabling precise performance predictions under different operational loads.
4. **Performance Metrics**: CloudAnalyst quantifies essential performance metrics such as response time, throughput, and resource utilization throughout the simulation process, offering actionable insights for performance optimization.
5. **Cost Analysis**: Users can conduct detailed cost analyses to evaluate the financial implications of different cloud configurations, taking into account factors such as resource usage and pricing models.
6. **Visualization**: The tool enriches user experience through intuitive visualizations and comprehensive reports, facilitating easier interpretation and decision-making based on simulation outcomes.

CloudAnalyst serves as an invaluable asset for researchers investigating cloud computing algorithms, developers refining cloud-based applications, and businesses strategizing cloud infrastructure deployments. By leveraging simulation capabilities, users can explore diverse scenarios without the financial commitments associated with live environments, thereby fostering innovation and efficiency in cloud computing endeavors.

5.4.5 GreenCloud

GreenCloud [21] emerges as a sophisticated simulator tailored specifically for modeling and analyzing energy-efficient computing and networking environments, with a primary focus on optimizing cloud computing infrastructures. It provides a versatile platform for researchers and practitioners alike to meticulously evaluate energy consumption patterns, performance dynamics, and environmental impacts across a spectrum of cloud computing scenarios.

Key Features of GreenCloud:

1. **Simulation Environment**: GreenCloud offers a virtualized environment conducive to simulating intricate cloud computing scenarios, encompassing data centers, virtual machines (VMs), and networking components.
2. **Energy Consumption Modeling**: A cornerstone feature involves precise modeling and analysis of energy consumption within cloud infrastructures, encompassing servers, networking devices, and cooling systems, crucial for assessing operational efficiency.

3. **Resource Allocation Strategies**: The simulator empowers users to implement and assess diverse resource allocation strategies aimed at optimizing energy efficiency. This includes dynamic VM consolidation, workload scheduling, and advanced power management techniques.
4. **Networking Models**: GreenCloud integrates comprehensive models for networking elements such as switches, routers, and communication protocols, enabling users to evaluate energy consumption and performance implications under varied configurations.
5. **Green Metrics**: Critical metrics provided include assessments of environmental impact through metrics such as carbon emissions, energy efficiency ratios, and utilization of renewable energy sources.
6. **Integration with Cloud Platforms**: The tool may feature integration capabilities with leading cloud platforms and APIs, facilitating realistic simulations of cloud deployments and validation of energy-efficient strategies in practical settings.
7. **Scalability Analysis**: Users can leverage GreenCloud to evaluate the scalability of their cloud infrastructures, analyzing energy implications associated with scaling operations based on fluctuating workload demands.
8. **Visualization Tools**: Enhanced with visualization tools such as graphs, charts, and interactive dashboards, GreenCloud empowers users to intuitively interpret simulation results and derive actionable insights.
9. **Customization and Extensibility**: Offering flexibility, GreenCloud supports customization of simulation parameters, algorithms, and models to align with specific research objectives. It may also accommodate extensions and plugins for integrating additional functionalities or modules.

GreenCloud represents an indispensable tool for researchers, engineers, and policymakers committed to advancing energy-efficient solutions within cloud computing, thereby fostering sustainability and resilience in digital infrastructure developments.

5.4.6 Aneka

Aneka [22], developed by the Distributed Systems Group at the University of Messina in Italy, stands as a robust cloud platform designed to simplify the development and deployment of distributed applications across various cloud infrastructures. By abstracting the complexities inherent in distributed computing, Aneka empowers developers to focus squarely on application logic, facilitating the creation of scalable and efficient cloud-based solutions.

Key Features of Aneka:

1. **Resource Management**: Aneka provides comprehensive tools for efficient management of computational resources in cloud environments, encompassing virtual machines, containers, and physical servers.
2. **Task Scheduling**: Equipped with advanced scheduling algorithms, Aneka optimizes task allocation across available resources, enhancing efficiency and minimizing execution time.

3. **Scalability**: A core capability of Aneka lies in its ability to dynamically scale applications in response to demand fluctuations, seamlessly provisioning and releasing resources as needed.
4. **Fault Tolerance**: The platform integrates mechanisms for graceful handling of failures, including task migration and fault recovery, ensuring robustness and reliability in distributed applications.
5. **Programming Models**: Supporting diverse programming paradigms such as task parallelism, data parallelism, and workflow-based models, Aneka accommodates varied application needs with flexibility.
6. **Monitoring and Logging**: Aneka features robust monitoring and logging functionalities to track the performance and behavior of distributed applications, facilitating rapid issue identification and resolution.
7. **Security**: Security is paramount with Aneka, incorporating robust measures such as authentication, authorization, and encryption to safeguard sensitive data and prevent unauthorized access.
8. **Integration**: Offering seamless integration with other cloud services and technologies, Aneka enables developers to leverage existing infrastructure and tools effectively.
9. **Multi-tenancy**: Aneka supports multi-tenancy, ensuring secure coexistence of multiple users or organizations on shared infrastructure while maintaining strict isolation between resources and applications.
10. **Customization and Extensibility**: Developers can extend and customize Aneka through plugins, extensions, or custom components tailored to specific requirements, thereby enhancing platform adaptability.

Aneka emerges as a comprehensive platform for building and deploying distributed applications in cloud environments, prioritizing scalability, reliability, performance, and security. Its robust feature set caters to the diverse needs of developers and organizations seeking efficient cloud-based solutions, underscoring its significance in advancing distributed computing technologies.

Some other cloud simulators which are currently available, each catering to distinct aspects of cloud computing simulation, are illustrated below.

1. **iCanCloud [23]**: Known for its flexibility and scalability, iCanCloud empowers users to model intricate cloud infrastructures and applications. It accommodates diverse cloud deployment models – public, private, and hybrid – while offering comprehensive performance analysis tools.
2. **DISSECT-CF [24]**: Specifically tailored for simulating cloud federations, DISSECT-CF facilitates the modeling of collaborative scenarios among multiple cloud providers. It enables dynamic simulation of federation behaviors, resource allocation strategies, and service-level agreements (SLAs).
3. **GridSim [25]**: Originally designed for grid computing simulations, GridSim extends its utility to certain aspects of cloud computing environments. It supports the modeling of distributed resource management, scheduling algorithms, and workload characteristics.

4. **SimGrid [26]**: It is a versatile simulation toolkit catering to various distributed computing scenarios, including cloud computing. SimGrid features a high-level API that simplifies the modeling of complex distributed systems, accommodating diverse cloud architectures and applications.

Table 5.4 provides a summary of some of the prominent cloud computing simulators, their key features, and their primary focus areas. Each simulator is designed to address different aspects of cloud computing, from infrastructure modeling to energy efficiency and SDN research, providing valuable tools for both academic and industry-related cloud computing research.

TABLE 5.4
Summary of the Major Cloud Computing Simulators

Simulator	Key Features	Primary Focus
CloudSim	• Modular architecture • Supports various cloud infrastructures (private, public, hybrid) • Energy-aware simulation • Resource provisioning strategies • Scalability and performance evaluation	Cloud infrastructure modeling, resource provisioning, and performance analysis
CloudSimSDN	• SDN simulation with OpenFlow support • Network topology creation • Traffic generation and management • Resource management • Energy efficiency modeling	Software-Defined Networking (SDN) simulation and network management
iFogSim	• Fog architecture modeling • Task offloading strategies • Resource management • Energy consumption modeling • Scalability analysis	Fog computing, task offloading, and energy efficiency in fog environments
CloudAnalyst	• Simulated cloud environments • Workload modeling and resource provisioning • Performance and cost analysis • Visualization tools	Cloud application performance, cost efficiency, and resource utilization
GreenCloud	• Energy consumption modeling • Resource allocation strategies • Networking models • Green metrics (e.g., carbon emissions) • Scalability analysis	Energy-efficient cloud computing, focusing on sustainability
Aneka	• Resource management • Task scheduling • Scalability and fault tolerance • Security features • Multi-tenancy support	Distributed application development and deployment in cloud environments
iCanCloud	• Flexible and scalable cloud modeling • Supports public, private, and hybrid clouds • Performance analysis tools	Cloud infrastructure and application simulation

TABLE 5.4
(Continued)

Simulator	Key Features	Primary Focus
DISSECT-CF	• Simulates cloud federations • Dynamic modeling of resource allocation and SLAs	Cloud federation and collaborative scenarios among cloud providers
GridSim	• Distributed resource management • Scheduling algorithms • Workload modeling	Grid and cloud computing simulation, focusing on distributed resources
SimGrid	• High-level API for distributed systems • Flexible for various cloud architectures	General-purpose distributed computing, including cloud environments

These simulators offer a range of features, capabilities, and abstraction levels. Users can select the most appropriate tool based on their specific simulation requirements and objectives. Each simulator contributes uniquely to the understanding and analysis of cloud computing dynamics, from infrastructure modeling to performance evaluation and beyond.

5.5 TOOLS FOR CLOUD INFRASTRUCTURE AUTOMATION

Effective management and scalability of cloud-based resources hinge upon cloud infrastructure automation. Various tools are prevalent in this domain, each offering diverse features and functionalities. Some of the prominent and well-known cloud infrastructure and automation tools are shown in Figure 5.5. Furthermore, presented below is a detailed discussion of prominent tools tailored for cloud infrastructure automation:

1. Terraform: Developed by HashiCorp, Terraform serves as a widely adopted infrastructure as code (IaC) tool. It facilitates the definition and provisioning of cloud infrastructure through a declarative configuration language. Terraform supports multiple cloud providers, including AWS, Azure, Google Cloud, and others.
2. AWS CloudFormation: AWS CloudFormation is an AWS-specific service designed for defining and deploying AWS infrastructure using JSON or YAML templates. It boasts extensive resource coverage and seamless integration with other AWS services.
3. Azure Resource Manager (ARM) Templates: Analogous to AWS CloudFormation, ARM Templates enable the specification and deployment of Azure infrastructure resources via JSON templates. They offer a comprehensive array of resources tailored to Azure services.
4. Google Cloud Deployment Manager: Google Cloud Deployment Manager functions as Google's infrastructure as code solution, facilitating the definition and deployment of Google Cloud Platform (GCP) resources using YAML or Jinja2 templates. It supports the creation of intricate infrastructure configurations.

5. Ansible: Recognized for its robust automation capabilities, Ansible is adept at both cloud infrastructure automation and configuration management. It employs straightforward YAML-based playbooks for defining infrastructure configurations and interfaces with cloud APIs to provision resources.
6. Pulumi: Pulumi represents an infrastructure as code tool that allows the definition of cloud infrastructure using familiar programming languages such as Python, JavaScript, TypeScript, and Go. It offers elevated abstraction levels and greater flexibility compared to conventional tools.
7. Chef: Initially established as a configuration management tool, Chef extends its utility to infrastructure automation. It facilitates the definition of infrastructure configurations through reusable cookbooks and integrates seamlessly with various cloud platforms.
8. Jenkins: Jenkins serves as a widely utilized automation server, pivotal in orchestrating continuous integration and continuous delivery (CI/CD) pipelines. It automates the provisioning and management of cloud infrastructure as an integral component of the deployment process.
9. Packer: Packer specializes in generating machine images for diverse platforms, including cloud providers. It enables the definition of machine configurations via JSON templates and automates the image building process, facilitating subsequent provisioning of cloud instances.
10. Cloud-specific SDKs and APIs: Many cloud providers furnish software development kits (SDKs) and APIs, enabling programmable interactions with their services. While these tools do not offer the same level of abstraction as infrastructure as code tools, they deliver considerable flexibility for automation tasks.

Figure 5.5 highlights some common IaC and cloud automation tools. Furthermore, Table 5.5 offers the analysis of prominent tools for cloud infrastructure automation.

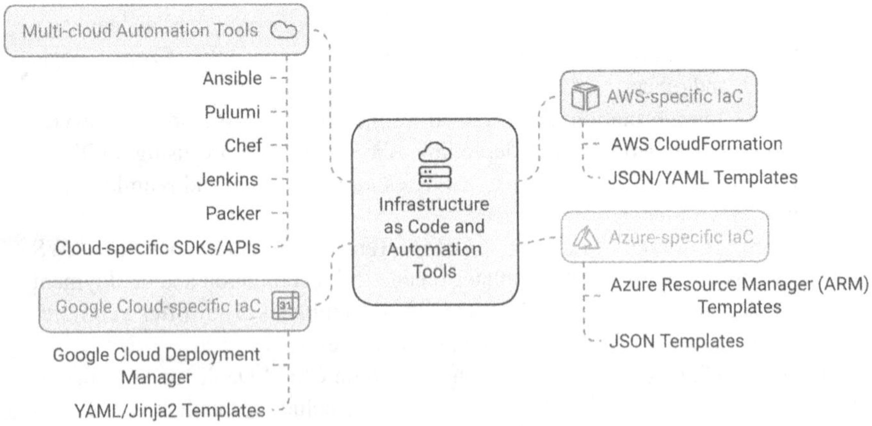

FIGURE 5.5 Common cloud IaC and automation tools.

TABLE 5.5
Tools for Cloud Infrastructure Automation

Tool	Primary Function	Supported Platforms	Key Features
Terraform	Infrastructure as Code (IaC)	AWS, Azure, Google Cloud, and others	Declarative configuration, multi-cloud support, modularity, state management
AWS CloudFormation	AWS-specific IaC	AWS	JSON/YAML templates, extensive AWS integration, automated resource provisioning
Azure Resource Manager (ARM) Templates	Azure-specific IaC	Azure	JSON templates, tight integration with Azure services, rich resource support
Google Cloud Deployment Manager	IaC for Google Cloud Platform	Google Cloud	YAML/Jinja2 templates, Google Cloud integration, complex infrastructure setups
Ansible	Cloud automation and configuration management	Multi-cloud (AWS, Azure, Google Cloud, etc.)	YAML-based playbooks, cloud API integration, agentless automation
Pulumi	IaC with programming languages	AWS, Azure, Google Cloud, others	Supports Python, JavaScript, TypeScript, Go; higher flexibility and abstraction
Chef	Infrastructure automation and configuration management	AWS, Azure, Google Cloud, others	Reusable cookbooks, cloud platform integration, configuration management
Jenkins	Automation server for CI/CD and infrastructure provisioning	Multi-cloud (via plugins)	CI/CD orchestration, cloud provisioning integration, extensibility via plugins
Packer	Automated machine image creation	AWS, Azure, Google Cloud, others	JSON templates, machine image generation, support for multiple platforms
Cloud-specific SDKs/APIs	Programmable interaction with cloud services	AWS, Azure, Google Cloud, others	SDKs/APIs for custom automation, flexibility, lower abstraction compared to IaC

This table summarizes each tool's core functionality, supported platforms, and key features, offering a quick comparison for selecting the appropriate tool for cloud infrastructure automation.

These tools exemplify a fraction of the available options for cloud infrastructure automation. The selection of an appropriate tool hinges on factors such as the chosen cloud provider, specific operational requirements, and the team's proficiency with the toolset.

5.6 SUMMARY

This chapter delves into the various cloud computing tools. It begins by outlining the significance of cyberattack simulation tools followed by the discussion of the popular cyberattack simulation tools. The chapter then proceeds to discuss different cloud monitoring and analysis tools by categorizing them into four categories. Each category is explained in detail, highlighting its features, benefits, and some examples. Furthermore, the chapter explores various attack defense tools and the major cloud simulators. This chapter also discusses the best tools for cloud infrastructure automation and highlights their features.

5.7 PRACTICE QUESTIONS/SOLUTIONS

MULTIPLE OBJECTIVE QUESTIONS

1 Which of the following is NOT an attack simulation tool?

A) Metasploit
B) Wireshark
C) Cobalt Strike
D) Atomic Red Team

Answer: B) Wireshark

2 What is the primary purpose of attack simulation tools?

A) Monitoring network traffic
B) Penetration testing
C) Network visualization
D) Data encryption

Answer: B) Penetration testing

3 Which attack simulation tool is commonly used for red team operations?

A) Nessus
B) Nmap
C) Cobalt Strike
D) Snort

Answer: C) Cobalt Strike

4 Which attack simulation tool focuses on endpoint security testing?

A) Wireshark
B) BloodHound
C) Atomic Red Team
D) John the Ripper

Answer: C) Atomic Red Team

5 Which attack simulation tool is widely used for vulnerability scanning?

A) Metasploit
B) Nessus
C) Cobalt Strike
D) Mimikatz

Answer: B) Nessus

6 Which attack simulation tool is primarily used for password cracking?

A) Wireshark
B) John the Ripper
C) Nmap
D) Snort

Answer: B) John the Ripper

7 Which attack simulation tool focuses on Active Directory reconnaissance?

A) Wireshark
B) BloodHound
C) Cobalt Strike
D) Nmap

Answer: B) BloodHound

8 Which attack simulation tool allows for automated exploit generation and execution?

A) Wireshark
B) Nmap
C) Metasploit
D) Nessus

Answer: C) Metasploit

9 Which attack simulation tool is designed for network intrusion detection?

A) John the Ripper
B) Snort
C) BloodHound
D) Mimikatz

Answer: B) Snort

10 Which attack simulation tool is commonly used for privilege escalation?

A) Cobalt Strike
B) Atomic Red Team
C) BloodHound
D) Mimikatz

Answer: D) Mimikatz

11 **Which of the following is NOT a commonly used cloud monitoring and analysis tool?**
A) Prometheus
B) Nagios
C) Google Docs
D) Datadog

Answer: C) Google Docs

12 **Which cloud monitoring tool is known for its ability to monitor infrastructure, applications, and logs in real time?**
A) New Relic
B) Splunk
C) Amazon CloudWatch
D) Azure Monitor

Answer: A) New Relic

13 **Which of the following is an open-source cloud monitoring tool often used for metrics collection and visualization?**
A) Grafana
B) Dynatrace
C) AppDynamics
D) Azure Monitor

Answer: A) Grafana

14 **Which cloud monitoring tool is specifically designed for monitoring Amazon Web Services (AWS) resources and applications?**
A) Datadog
B) Prometheus
C) AWS CloudWatch
D) Nagios

Answer: C) AWS CloudWatch

15 **Which cloud monitoring tool provides advanced analytics and AI-driven insights for application performance management?**
A) Nagios
B) Datadog
C) AppDynamics
D) Prometheus

Answer: C) AppDynamics

16 Which cloud monitoring tool is known for its capabilities in monitoring Kubernetes clusters and containerized applications?

A) New Relic
B) Prometheus
C) Dynatrace
D) Grafana

Answer: B) Prometheus

17 Which cloud monitoring tool offers a unified platform for monitoring multi-cloud environments and on-premises infrastructure?

A) Azure Monitor
B) Datadog
C) Splunk
D) Google Cloud Monitoring

Answer: B) Datadog

18 Which cloud monitoring tool provides features such as anomaly detection, log management, and customizable dashboards?

A) Google Cloud Monitoring
B) Nagios
C) Splunk
D) Grafana

Answer: C) Splunk

19 Which cloud monitoring tool offers integration with popular collaboration tools like Slack and PagerDuty for alerting and incident management?

A) Dynatrace
B) Prometheus
C) Datadog
D) New Relic

Answer: C) Datadog

20 Which cloud monitoring tool is known for its scalability and support for monitoring hybrid cloud environments?

A) Azure Monitor
B) Google Cloud Monitoring
C) Prometheus
D) Dynatrace

Answer: A) Azure Monitor

DESCRIPTIVE QUESTIONS

1 What are attack simulation tools?

Answer: Attack simulation tools are software applications designed to mimic the behavior of real-world cyber threats and simulate various cyberattacks on a network, system, or application.

2 How do attack simulation tools work?

Answer: Attack simulation tools work by using predefined attack scenarios and techniques to emulate the behavior of hackers or malicious actors. They assess the security posture of an organization by attempting to exploit vulnerabilities and weaknesses in systems, networks, and applications.

3 What types of attacks can be simulated using these tools?

Answer: Attack simulation tools can simulate a wide range of cyberattacks, including but not limited to phishing attacks, malware infections, ransomware attacks, DDoS (Distributed Denial of Service) attacks, SQL injection, cross-site scripting (XSS), privilege escalation, and insider threats.

4 What are the benefits of using attack simulation tools?

Answer: Using attack simulation tools provides organizations with several benefits, including identifying vulnerabilities and weaknesses in their security defenses, testing the effectiveness of security controls and incident response procedures, raising awareness among employees about potential cyber threats, and improving overall cybersecurity readiness.

5 Can attack simulation tools be customized for specific environments?

Answer: Yes, many attack simulation tools offer customization options to tailor the simulated attacks according to the specific environment, industry, or compliance requirements of an organization. This customization ensures that the simulated attacks closely resemble real-world threats that the organization may face.

6 Are attack simulation tools only used for offensive purposes?

Answer: While attack simulation tools are primarily used to test and assess the security posture of an organization from an offensive perspective, they can also be used defensively. By identifying weaknesses and vulnerabilities proactively, organizations can strengthen their security defenses and better protect against real cyber threats.

7 How frequently should organizations conduct attack simulations?

Answer: The frequency of conducting attack simulations depends on various factors, including the organization's risk profile, industry regulations, and evolving cyber threats. However, it's generally recommended to perform attack simulations regularly, such as quarterly or semi-annually, to stay ahead of emerging threats and ensure continuous improvement of cybersecurity defenses.

8 What are some popular attack simulation tools available in the market?

Answer: Some popular attack simulation tools include Cobalt Strike, Metasploit, Core Impact, Immunity CANVAS, AttackIQ, SafeBreach, and Verodin. These tools offer a range of features for simulating different types of cyberattacks and assessing security posture.

9 What is cloud monitoring?

Answer: Cloud monitoring refers to the process of overseeing and managing the performance, availability, and security of cloud infrastructure and applications. It involves collecting data from various cloud resources, analyzing it, and taking appropriate actions to ensure optimal performance and security.

10 What are some key features of cloud monitoring and analysis tools?

Answer: Cloud monitoring and analysis tools typically offer features such as real-time performance monitoring, automated alerts and notifications, customizable dashboards and reports, scalability, integration with various cloud platforms and services, and advanced analytics for trend analysis and predictive insights.

11 How do cloud monitoring tools collect data?

Answer: Cloud monitoring tools collect data from various sources including cloud infrastructure components (e.g., virtual machines, containers, storage), application logs and metrics, network traffic, user interactions, and external monitoring services. They use APIs, agents, log collectors, and other data collection mechanisms to gather information from these sources.

12 What is the importance of real-time monitoring in cloud environments?

Answer: Real-time monitoring in cloud environments is crucial for detecting and responding to performance issues, security threats, and other operational anomalies as they occur. It enables rapid incident response, minimizes downtime, and helps maintain a high level of service availability and reliability.

13 How do cloud monitoring tools help optimize resource utilization?

Answer: Cloud monitoring tools provide insights into resource utilization metrics such as CPU, memory, storage, and network usage. By analyzing these metrics, organizations can identify under-utilized resources, right-size their infrastructure, and optimize resource allocation to reduce costs and improve efficiency.

14 What role do analytics play in cloud monitoring and analysis?

Answer: Analytics in cloud monitoring and analysis tools help organizations gain deeper insights into their cloud environments by identifying patterns, trends, and correlations in the collected data. This enables proactive problem detection, predictive resource planning, and optimization of performance, security, and cost efficiency.

15 How do cloud monitoring tools enhance security?

Answer: Cloud monitoring tools enhance security by continuously monitoring for suspicious activities, unauthorized access attempts, compliance violations, and other security threats in cloud environments. They provide visibility into security events, facilitate threat detection and response, and help enforce security policies and compliance regulations.

16 What are some popular cloud monitoring and analysis tools in the market?

Answer: Some popular cloud monitoring and analysis tools include Amazon CloudWatch, Google Cloud Monitoring, Microsoft Azure Monitor, Datadog, New Relic, Dynatrace, Splunk, and Sumo Logic. These tools offer a wide range of features and integrations to meet the diverse monitoring needs of organizations operating in the cloud.

17 What are attack defense tools?

Answer: Attack defense tools are software or hardware solutions designed to protect computer networks, systems, and data from cyberattacks by identifying, preventing, or mitigating security threats.

18 How do attack defense tools work?

Answer: Attack defense tools typically employ various techniques such as firewalls, intrusion detection systems (IDS), intrusion prevention systems (IPS), antivirus software, sandboxing, encryption, and vulnerability scanners to detect, block, or mitigate malicious activities on networks or systems.

19 What are some common examples of attack defense tools?

Answer:

- Firewalls: Firewalls monitor and control incoming and outgoing network traffic based on predetermined security rules.
- Intrusion Detection Systems (IDS): IDS monitor network or system activities for malicious behavior or policy violations.
- Intrusion Prevention Systems (IPS): IPS can detect and block suspicious network traffic or activities in real time.
- Antivirus Software: Antivirus programs detect, prevent, and remove malware, including viruses, worms, and Trojans.
- Sandbox: A sandbox provides a controlled environment to execute suspicious files or programs to analyze their behavior without risking harm to the host system.
- Encryption Tools: Encryption tools secure data by converting it into unreadable ciphertext, which can only be decrypted with the appropriate key.
- Vulnerability Scanners: Vulnerability scanners identify weaknesses or vulnerabilities in software, systems, or networks that attackers could exploit.

20 How do organizations benefit from using attack defense tools?

Answer: Organizations benefit from attack defense tools by:

- Enhancing security posture: Attack defense tools help organizations strengthen their defenses against a wide range of cyber threats.
- Mitigating risks: By proactively identifying and addressing security vulnerabilities, organizations can reduce the likelihood and impact of successful cyberattacks.
- Ensuring compliance: Many attack defense tools help organizations comply with industry regulations and standards regarding data protection and cybersecurity.
- Safeguarding sensitive data: Attack defense tools protect sensitive data from unauthorized access, modification, or theft.
- Preserving business continuity: By preventing or minimizing the impact of cyberattacks, organizations can maintain continuous operations and avoid costly downtime.

REFERENCES

1. https://www.cobaltstrike.com/
2. https://www.metasploit.com/
3. https://owasp.org/
4. https://nmap.org/
5. https://beefproject.com/
6. https://sqlmap.org/

7. https://www.wireshark.org/
8. https://portswigger.net/burp
9. https://www.alpinesecurity.com/blog/empire-a-powershell-post-exploitation-tool/
10. https://www.akamai.com/infectionmonkey
11. https://threatcare.com/
12. https://www.nessi2.de/
13. https://www.bitcyber.com.sg/foreseeti-securicad/
14. https://boomi.com/platform/
15. https://www.puppet.com/
16. https://aws.amazon.com/cloudwatch/
17. https://www.nagios.org/
18. Goyal, T., Singh, A., & Agrawal, A. (2012). Cloudsim: simulator for cloud computing infrastructure and modeling. *Procedia Engineering*, *38*, 3566–3572.
19. Son, J., Dastjerdi, A. V., Calheiros, R. N., Ji, X., Yoon, Y., & Buyya, R. (2015, May). Cloudsimsdn: Modeling and simulation of software-defined cloud data centers. In *2015 15th IEEE/ACM International Symposium on Cluster, Cloud and Grid Computing* (pp. 475–484). IEEE.
20. Khan, E. U. Y., Soomro, T. R., & Brohi, M. N. (2022, October). iFogSim: a tool for simulating cloud and fog applications. In *2022 International Conference on Cyber Resilience (ICCR)* (pp. 01–05). IEEE.
21. https://greencloud.gforge.uni.lu/
22. https://www.manjrasoft.com/aneka_architecture.html
23. Castane, G. G., Nunez, A., & Carretero, J. (2012, July). iCanCloud: A brief architecture overview. In *2012 IEEE 10th International Symposium on Parallel and Distributed Processing with Applications* (pp. 853–854). IEEE.
24. Kecskemeti, G. (2015). DISSECT-CF: a simulator to foster energy-aware scheduling in infrastructure clouds. *Simulation Modelling Practice and Theory*, 58, 188–218.
25. https://gridsim.hevs.ch/
26. https://simgrid.org/usages.html

6 Secure Cloud Computing Implementation Challenges

6.1 INTRODUCTION

Cloud computing presents security concerns even though it has numerous advantages, including scalability, flexibility, and cost savings. For businesses that keep sensitive data on the cloud, data security is of utmost importance. Financial losses, legal responsibilities, and reputational harm can all be brought on by data breaches. These hazards can be reduced with the aid of monitoring, access limits, and encryption. Similar to this, cloud computing frequently entails several users and devices accessing resources from various places. In order to guarantee that only authorized users may access sensitive data and applications, identity and access management (IAM) is crucial [1–3].

Organizations must also adhere to a number of laws and industry standards, including HIPAA, PCI DSS, and GDPR. Although cloud service providers may issue compliance certifications, organizations must still make sure that their usage of the cloud complies with all relevant rules and laws. In a cloud context, security is a shared responsibility between the cloud provider and the client. Because of this shared responsibility paradigm, it may be unclear who is in charge of what security-related duties. Additionally, it might be difficult to select a cloud provider that satisfies the organization's security requirements. It is important to assess variables such as the provider's security policies, data center locations, and incident response procedures. However, data loss can happen for a number of reasons, including inadvertent deletion, technology malfunction, or hacking. To prevent data loss and guarantee business continuity, organizations need to establish a data backup and recovery strategy. Additionally, defining policies, processes, and standards for the usage of cloud services is a component of cloud governance. Organizations may guarantee that cloud resources are utilized safely and in line with organizational goals by implementing effective cloud governance [4–7].

Some common cloud security implementation challenges and respective features are depicted in Figure. 6.1. Furthermore, the general security issues in cloud computing are highlighted in Table 6.1 in detail.

According to the requirements of the organization and the particular cloud computing environment, the implementation issues listed in the table may change. Organizations may also have other difficulties that are particular to their requirements for cloud deployment and security.

DOI: 10.1201/9781003510772-6

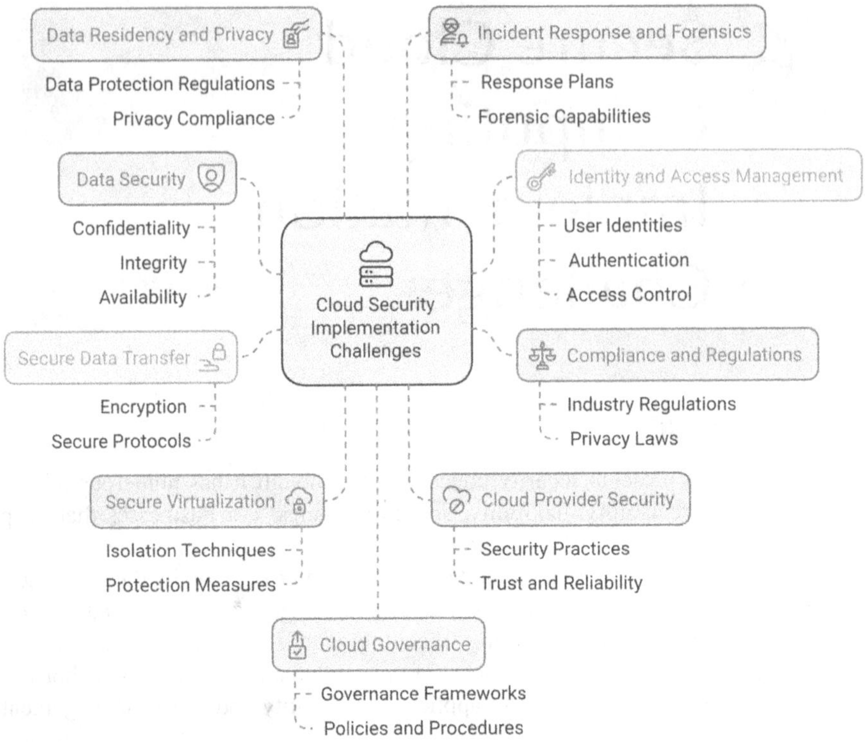

FIGURE 6.1 Some common cloud security implementation challenges and features.

TABLE 6.1
Security Issues Cloud Computing

Implementation Challenge	Description
Data Security [7]	Ensuring the confidentiality, integrity, and availability of data stored and processed in the cloud environment.
Identity and Access Management [8]	Managing user identities, authentication, and access control to prevent unauthorized access to cloud resources.
Compliance and Regulations [9,10]	Adhering to industry-specific regulations, privacy laws, and compliance requirements in the cloud environment.
Secure Data Transfer [11,12]	Protecting data during transmission between the client and the cloud service provider to prevent interception or tampering.
Secure Virtualization [13]	Implementing secure virtualization techniques to ensure isolation and protection of virtual machines in a shared cloud infrastructure.
Cloud Provider Security [14]	Assessing the security practices and measures implemented by the cloud service provider to ensure trust and reliability.
Data Residency and Privacy [15–17]	Addressing concerns related to data residency, data privacy, and ensuring compliance with data protection regulations.

TABLE 6.1
(Continued)

Implementation Challenge	Description
Incident Response and Forensics [18,19]	Developing effective incident response plans and forensic capabilities to handle security breaches and investigate incidents in the cloud environment.
Cloud Governance [20]	Establishing governance frameworks, policies, and procedures to ensure proper oversight, risk management, and compliance in the cloud.
Vendor Lock-in [21]	Mitigating the risk of vendor lock-in by implementing standards-based approaches and ensuring data portability and interoperability.

An all-encompassing strategy that includes risk assessment, security controls, compliance management, and continuing monitoring and improvement is needed to adopt safe cloud computing. The following subsections detail some major challenges that businesses could experience while deploying safe cloud computing.

6.2 LACK OF VISIBILITY AND CONTROL

One of the significant challenges of cloud computing is the lack of visibility and control that organizations may experience. Here are some of the reasons why this can be a problem.

- Shared security responsibilities: Cloud security is a shared duty between clients and cloud service providers. Customers are in charge of protecting their data and applications, while cloud providers are in charge of protecting the infrastructure. This separation of responsibilities may result in a lack of visibility and control as well as misunderstanding about who is in charge of what.
- Multi-tenancy: To distribute resources across several clients, cloud companies frequently utilize multi-tenancy. Although this strategy may result in cost savings, if the provider does not effectively separate consumer data, it may also raise the danger of data breaches. Customers might not be able to see how their data is protected or how other customers are accessing it.
- Shadow IT: Employees using unauthorized cloud services are referred to as shadow IT. Employees who utilize cloud services that have not been authorized by the IT department of the company may experience this, which leaves them without insight into and control over the data and apps they are using.
- Limited control over infrastructure: In a conventional IT setting, businesses have complete control over the infrastructure, which includes the hardware, software, and network. The infrastructure is owned and controlled by the cloud provider in a cloud environment, which restricts the customer's access to and control over the infrastructure.

To address the lack of visibility and control in cloud computing, following approaches are proposed.

- Encryption [22]: Utilize encryption for data both in transit and at rest. This ensures that even if data is intercepted or accessed without authorization, it remains unintelligible without the encryption key.
- Access Control and Identity Management [23]: Implement strong access control mechanisms to regulate who can access what resources within the cloud environment. Utilize identity management solutions to authenticate and authorize users, devices, and applications.
- Auditing and Logging [24]: Maintain comprehensive auditing and logging mechanisms to track user activities, system events, and data access within the cloud environment. This enables visibility into actions taken and helps detect any unauthorized or suspicious behavior.
- Multi-factor Authentication (MFA) [25]: Enforce multi-factor authentication for accessing sensitive resources or performing critical operations within the cloud environment. This adds an extra layer of security beyond just passwords, enhancing control over access.
- Network Segmentation and Virtual Private Clouds (VPCs): Employ network segmentation techniques to isolate different parts of the cloud infrastructure and create virtual private clouds (VPCs) with dedicated network boundaries. This helps control the flow of traffic and restricts access to specific components.
- Third-party Security Solutions: Consider utilizing third-party security solutions such as cloud access security brokers (CASBs) or cloud security posture management (CSPM) tools. These solutions offer additional visibility and control over cloud resources, including the ability to enforce security policies and monitor compliance.
- Regular Security Assessments and Penetration Testing: Conduct regular security assessments and penetration testing to identify vulnerabilities and weaknesses within the cloud environment. This proactive approach helps ensure that security controls are effective and provides opportunities for remediation before any potential breaches occur.
- Vendor Due Diligence: Perform thorough due diligence when selecting cloud service providers, ensuring they adhere to industry best practices and compliance standards. Review their security policies, practices, and certifications to ensure they provide adequate visibility and control over your data and resources.

By taking these steps, organizations can mitigate the risks associated with the lack of visibility and control in cloud computing and ensure that their data and applications are secure. The root causes for lack of visibility and control in the cloud are highlighted in Figure 6.2.

Additionally, a comprehensive analysis of the factors contributing to a lack of visibility and control in cloud computing, along with strategies to mitigate these challenges, is presented in Table 6.2.

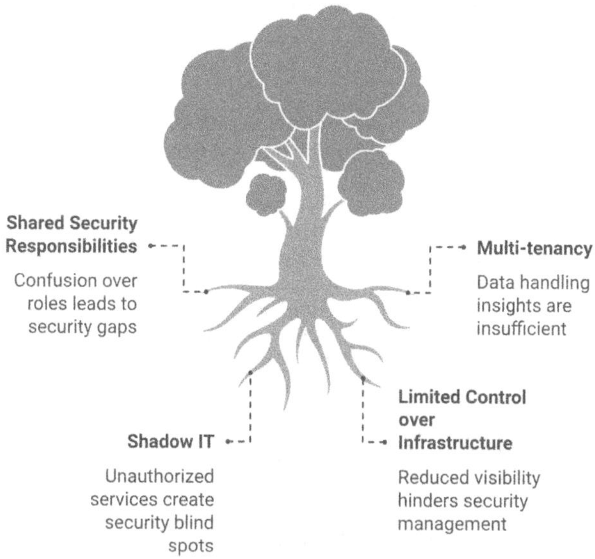

FIGURE 6.2 Root causes for lack of visibility and control in cloud.

TABLE 6.2
Analysis of the Lack of Visibility and Control in Cloud and Related Mitigation Strategies

Factor	Description	Impact of Lack of Visibility and Control	Strategies to Mitigate
Shared Security Responsibilities	Cloud security is a shared responsibility between clients and providers, which can lead to confusion over roles.	Misunderstanding of who is responsible for what can lead to gaps in security and control over data and applications.	• Clearly define roles and responsibilities for security between the provider and the client. • Regularly review security responsibilities to ensure alignment.
Multi-tenancy	Cloud providers often use multi-tenancy, where multiple customers share the same infrastructure and resources.	Customers may lack insight into how their data is being handled, and security vulnerabilities in one tenant can impact others.	• Ensure proper data isolation through strong segmentation. • Choose cloud providers who implement strict separation of tenant data and resources.
Shadow IT	Employees using unauthorized cloud services create blind spots in security and control.	Lack of oversight into unauthorized services may lead to data leaks, security breaches, or compliance violations.	• Implement policies to prevent the use of unauthorized cloud services. • Use monitoring tools to detect and control Shadow IT activities.

TABLE 6.2 (Continued)

Factor	Description	Impact of Lack of Visibility and Control	Strategies to Mitigate
Limited Control Over Infrastructure	Customers have limited access to or control over the cloud infrastructure, owned by the cloud provider.	Reduced visibility and control can result in a lack of understanding of how the infrastructure is managed and secured.	• Use cloud service providers who offer transparent management and monitoring tools. • Enforce strict access controls and audit logs for any available infrastructure management.

6.3 DATA BREACHES AND DOWNTIME

Data breaches and downtime are two significant risks associated with cloud computing. Figure 6.3 offers a depiction of data breaches and downtime-based cloud security and downtime risks. The discussion of each of these risks and how organizations can mitigate them are as follows.

a) Data breaches: Cloud computing involves storing and accessing data over the Internet rather than on local servers or personal devices. While cloud providers implement robust security measures, data breaches [26] can still occur due to various reasons such as:
   - Weak Authentication: Breaches can happen if user authentication mechanisms are compromised, allowing unauthorized access to sensitive data.
   - Insecure APIs: Application Programming Interfaces (APIs) are essential for cloud services to communicate with each other. However, if these APIs are not properly secured, they can be exploited by attackers.
   - Insider Threats: Employees or insiders with access to sensitive data may misuse their privileges intentionally or unintentionally.
   - Data Leakage: Misconfigured storage settings or inadequate encryption can lead to unintentional exposure of data to unauthorized parties.
   - Third-party Vulnerabilities: Cloud environments often rely on third-party services or integrations, which can introduce vulnerabilities if not thoroughly vetted.

Businesses can take the following measures to reduce the risk of data breaches:

- Encrypt sensitive data while it is in transit and at rest.
- Implement strong identity and access management controls to ensure that only authorized users can access data.

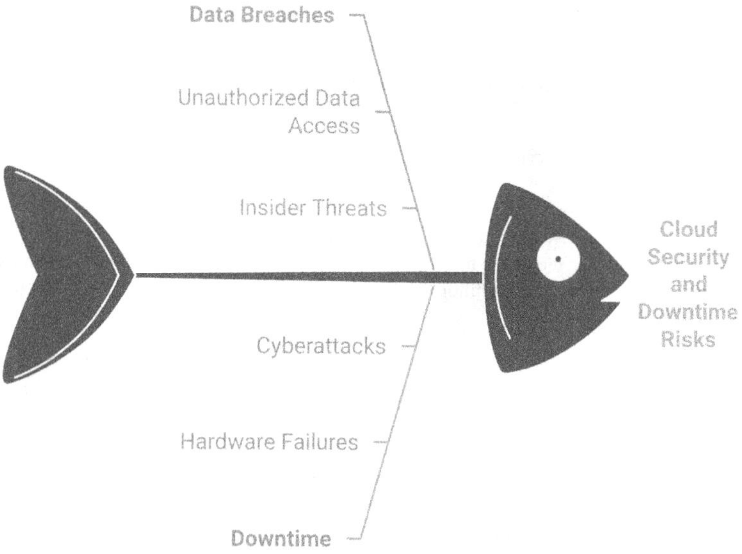

FIGURE 6.3 Role of data breaches and downtime in cloud security and downtime risks.

- Use multi-factor authentication to further enhance security.
- Regularly monitor network activity to detect potential threats.

b) Downtime: Hardware failure, software flaws, and cyberattacks are a few of the causes of downtime [27]. Customer happiness, productivity, and income can all be negatively impacted by downtime. The organizations can take the following actions to reduce the risk of downtime:
   - Establish a disaster recovery strategy to maintain company continuity in the case of interruption by selecting a cloud provider with a track record of uptime and dependability.
   - To lessen the effects of downtime, utilize numerous data centers and backup and recovery services.
   - Test the disaster recovery strategy on a regular basis to make sure it works.

Overall, there are big hazards with cloud computing, such unavailability and data breaches. However, organizations may reduce these risks and guarantee the security and availability of their data and applications in the cloud by putting in place strong security measures and disaster recovery strategies. An analysis summarizing the risks of data breaches and downtime in cloud computing and the corresponding mitigation strategies are summarized in Table 6.3.

In summary, while cloud computing poses significant risks such as data breaches and downtime, these can be mitigated through robust security measures, proactive monitoring, and solid disaster recovery plans.

TABLE 6.3
Analysis of Data Breaches and Downtime in Cloud and Related Mitigation Strategies

Risk	Description	Mitigation Strategies
Data Breaches	Unauthorized access to sensitive data stored in the cloud due to various vulnerabilities.	1. Encryption: Encrypt sensitive data both in transit and at rest. 2. Strong Authentication: Use strong identity and access management with multi-factor authentication. 3. Secure APIs: Ensure APIs are properly secured and monitored. 4. Insider Threat Management: Monitor and control access privileges to prevent misuse by employees or insiders. 5. Regular Monitoring: Continuously monitor network activity for suspicious behaviors.
Downtime	Periods of unavailability of cloud services due to hardware failures, software bugs, or cyberattacks.	1. Disaster Recovery Strategy: Develop a comprehensive disaster recovery plan and select reliable cloud providers with high uptime. 2. Redundancy: Use multiple data centers and backup/recovery services to reduce the impact of downtime. 3. Regular Testing: Regularly test the disaster recovery plan to ensure it is effective

6.4 VENDOR LOCK-IN

Organizations may have a problem with vendor lock-in while using cloud computing. It is the circumstance in which a company gets dependent on a certain cloud service provider and is unable to quickly transfer providers without incurring considerable expenses and interruption [28]. Some common cloud vendor lock-in properties are depicted in Figure 6.4. Following are some elements that might lead to vendor lock-in in cloud computing.

- Proprietary APIs: Some cloud service providers may employ proprietary APIs that are exclusive to their platform, making it challenging to move apps to another cloud platform.
- Data formats: Cloud service providers may employ exclusive data formats that are difficult to convert to other platforms.
- Integration with other services: It may be difficult to transfer providers since organizations have connected their cloud services with other on-premises or cloud services.
- Cost of migration: Switching to a different cloud provider may be time-consuming and expensive, requiring a lot of resources and knowledge.

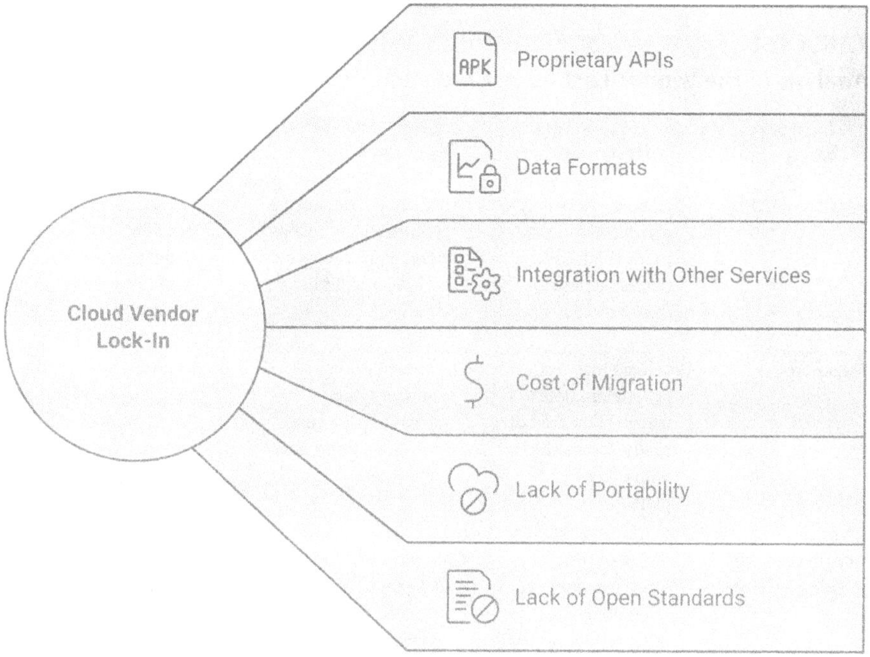

FIGURE 6.4 Common cloud vendor lock-in properties.

Because it may diminish their flexibility, raise their expenses, and hinder their capacity to innovate, vendor lock-in poses a serious risk to organizations. Several approaches have been proposed to address this issue [29,30]. Companies can take the following actions to lessen the danger of vendor lock-in.

- Pick cloud service providers who adhere to open standards for data formats and APIs.
- Steer clear of proprietary services that could tie them to a specific cloud platform.
- Create programs in a way that makes it simple for users to switch platforms if necessary.
- Establish precise policies and practices for managing and choosing vendors.
- Assess the cloud environment on a regular basis to look for issues related to vendor lock-in.

By following these actions, businesses may lower their risk of cloud computing vendor lock-in and make sure they have the flexibility and agility to adjust to shifting business demands. A comparative analysis of the factors contributing to vendor lock-in in cloud computing, along with strategies to mitigate these risks, is provided in Table 6.4.

TABLE 6.4
Analysis of the Vendor Lock-in in Cloud and Related Mitigation Strategies

Factor	Description	Impact of Vendor Lock-In	Strategies to Mitigate
Proprietary APIs	Cloud providers may use exclusive, proprietary APIs that are unique to their platform.	Difficulty in transferring applications to other cloud platforms due to API incompatibilities.	• Select providers that adhere to open, standardized APIs. • Avoid proprietary APIs and use industry-standard interfaces.
Data Formats	Providers may use proprietary data formats that are not easily compatible with other platforms.	Conversion of data to a new provider's format may be costly, time-consuming, and error-prone.	• Choose providers that use open data formats. • Avoid reliance on provider-specific data formats; prioritize common data standards.
Integration with Other Services	Cloud services may be deeply integrated with other on-premises or cloud-based services.	Tight integration makes migration difficult, as it may require reconfiguring or re-architecting systems.	• Design systems with modularity and interoperability in mind. • Avoid deeply embedding cloud-specific integrations into core business processes.
Cost of Migration	Migrating to a different cloud provider may incur significant costs, both in time and resources.	High switching costs, both in terms of financial investment and resource allocation.	• Plan and budget for potential future migrations. • Consider cloud-agnostic tools and platforms to reduce long-term migration costs.
Lack of Portability	Lack of portability between cloud environments due to proprietary solutions.	Hinders the ability to move to alternative cloud platforms quickly and easily.	• Use cloud-agnostic technologies (e.g., Kubernetes) for application deployment. • Invest in cloud services that offer easy portability or multi-cloud compatibility.
Lack of Open Standards	Cloud providers may not support open standards, making it harder to migrate workloads.	Increases the dependency on a specific provider's ecosystem and infrastructure.	• Prioritize cloud providers that support industry-wide open standards (e.g., OpenStack, Terraform). • Advocate for open-source cloud solutions to promote flexibility.

TABLE 6.4
(Continued)

Factor	Description	Impact of Vendor Lock-In	Strategies to Mitigate
Customization/ Optimization	Providers may offer customized services that are highly optimized for their own platforms.	Customized solutions could be incompatible or difficult to replicate on another platform.	• Build applications using general-purpose services that work across multiple clouds. • Limit customizations to avoid being tied to specific platform features.
Contractual Commitments	Long-term contracts and SLAs (Service-Level Agreements) may lock the organization into a provider.	Restricts flexibility and creates financial penalties for switching vendors.	• Negotiate contracts with exit clauses and flexibility for changes. • Evaluate cloud vendors based on the flexibility of their contractual terms.
Data Transfer and Exit Fees	Some providers may charge high fees for transferring data out of their platform.	High exit fees can make migration cost-prohibitive, especially for large datasets.	• Understand data transfer and exit terms before committing. • Prioritize vendors with transparent and reasonable data transfer policies.
Security and Compliance Issues	Security and compliance requirements may be specific to the cloud provider's environment.	Differences in security protocols or compliance certifications can impede migration.	• Ensure that the cloud service provider follows industry-standard security practices. • Regularly review security and compliance certifications to remain flexible.

6.5 COMPLIANCE COMPLEXITY

Organizations may struggle with compliance complexities while using cloud computing [31]. Because cloud computing entails storing and processing data elsewhere, adhering to rules and standards may become increasingly difficult. Figure 6.5 discusses some common cloud compliance challenges.

Here are some of the elements of cloud computing compliance difficulty.

- In a cloud system where data can be dispersed over different locations, it might be difficult to comply with regulations that demand that data be stored in particular geographical regions.

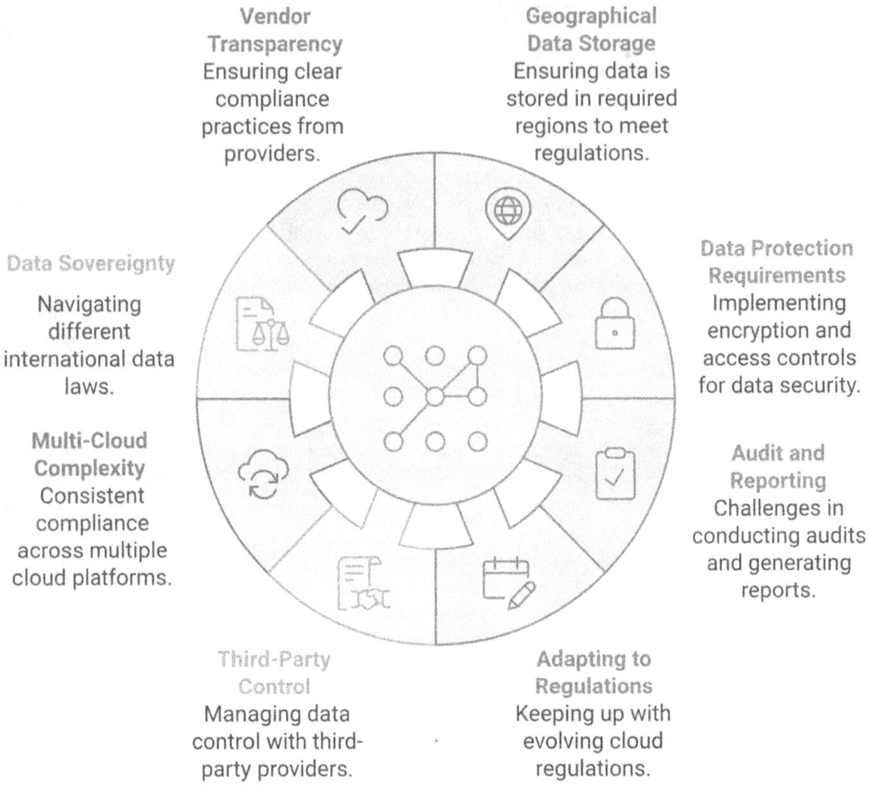
Vendor Transparency
Ensuring clear compliance practices from providers.
Geographical Data Storage
Ensuring data is stored in required regions to meet regulations.
Data Sovereignty
Navigating different international data laws.
Data Protection Requirements
Implementing encryption and access controls for data security.
Multi-Cloud Complexity
Consistent compliance across multiple cloud platforms.
Audit and Reporting
Challenges in conducting audits and generating reports.
Third-Party Control
Managing data control with third-party providers.
Adapting to Regulations
Keeping up with evolving cloud regulations.

FIGURE 6.5 Common cloud compliance challenges.

- Regulations may call for certain data protection measures, such as encryption or access controls, which might be difficult to put into practice in a cloud setting when data is handled by a third-party provider.
- In a cloud environment where data is dispersed across many locations and controlled by a third-party provider, it can be difficult to conduct extensive audits and reports of the cloud environment, which may be required by regulations.
- Adapting to changing regulations: Rules and standards are continuously changing, making it difficult for organizations to keep up and make sure they stay compliant.

To mitigate the risk of compliance complexity in cloud computing, organizations can take the following steps:

- Recognize the legal specifications that concern their data and applications.
- Pick cloud service providers who are open about their compliance procedures and have strong security and compliance standards in place.
- To safeguard information in the cloud, use encryption and access controls.

- Establish precise policies and practices for the access to and management of data.
- Assess the cloud environment on a regular basis to make sure it complies with rules and specifications.

Organizations may lower the risk of compliance complexity in cloud computing by implementing these measures, which will also guarantee that they continue to adhere to the rules and standards that concern their data and applications. An analysis of the factors contributing to compliance complexities in cloud computing, along with strategies to mitigate these challenges, is presented in Table 6.5.

TABLE 6.5
Analysis of the Compliance Complexities in Cloud and Related Mitigation Strategies

Factor	Description	Impact of Compliance Complexity	Strategies to Mitigate
Geographical Data Storage	Data in cloud systems can be stored in various locations, making it difficult to meet regulations on data locality.	Organizations may fail to comply with regulations that mandate data to be stored in specific geographical regions.	• Choose cloud providers with data centers in the required regions. • Ensure that the cloud provider offers location-specific data storage options.
Data Protection Requirements	Regulations may require specific data protection measures, like encryption or access control.	Implementing these requirements in a cloud environment may be challenging due to third-party control of the data.	• Implement end-to-end encryption. • Use access controls and identity management tools provided by the cloud vendor. • Ensure provider offers robust security features.
Audit and Reporting Difficulties	Cloud environments may make it difficult to conduct comprehensive audits or produce required compliance reports.	Difficulty in ensuring full visibility and control over cloud infrastructure can hinder audit and compliance reporting.	• Choose a cloud provider that offers extensive audit logs and compliance tools. • Use third-party audit and reporting tools compatible with the cloud environment.
Adapting to Changing Regulations	Cloud regulations and standards are evolving, making it difficult to stay compliant over time.	Constantly changing regulations increase the burden on organizations to stay updated and compliant.	• Establish a regular process for monitoring regulatory changes. • Work with legal and compliance experts to ensure up-to-date compliance. • Choose adaptable cloud providers.

TABLE 6.5
(Continued)

Factor	Description	Impact of Compliance Complexity	Strategies to Mitigate
Third-Party Data Control	Data is often handled and controlled by a third-party provider in cloud environments.	Lack of direct control over the data can create challenges in maintaining compliance with data protection regulations.	• Negotiate clear data control terms in cloud service contracts. • Implement strong governance and control over data access.
Complexity of Multi-Cloud Environments	Using multiple cloud services may lead to challenges in compliance across various platforms and regions.	Increased difficulty in managing compliance standards consistently across multiple providers and systems.	• Standardize policies and procedures across multiple cloud platforms. • Use multi-cloud management tools to streamline compliance enforcement.
Data Sovereignty Issues	Different countries have different rules for data storage, access, and processing.	Compliance with local and international laws may be more complicated if the data is stored or processed in multiple regions.	• Conduct a thorough analysis of the legal requirements for each region where data is stored. • Work with providers who offer data sovereignty guarantees.
Vendor Transparency	Lack of transparency in a cloud provider's compliance practices can increase uncertainty.	Organizations may not have full visibility into how the provider meets regulatory requirements.	• Select cloud providers with clear compliance documentation and transparency about their practices. • Perform regular compliance audits of the provider's operations

6.6 LACK OF TRANSPARENCY

Lack of transparency is a challenge that organizations may face in cloud computing. Transparency refers to the ability of organizations to have visibility into the cloud environment and understand how their data and applications are being managed [32]. Some of the common transparency challenges and respective countermeasures are highlighted in Figure 6.6.

Here are some of the factors that contribute to lack of transparency in cloud computing:

- Shared responsibility: It can be difficult for organizations to determine who is in charge of what when cloud providers and their clients share responsibilities for maintaining the cloud environment.

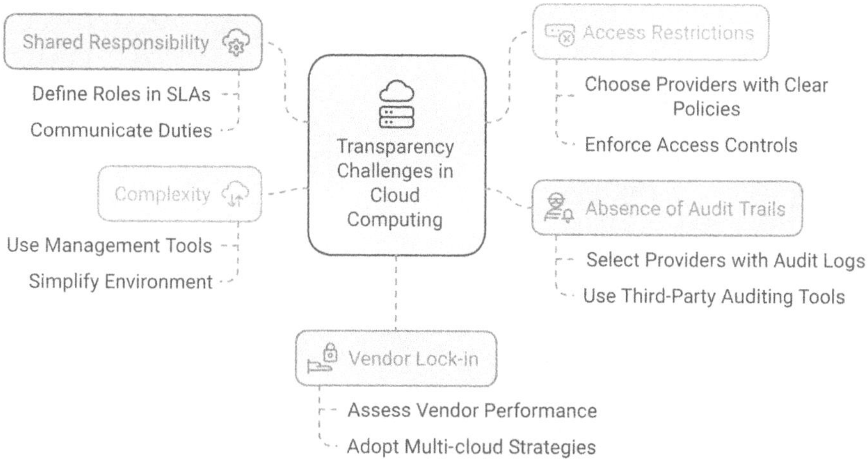

FIGURE 6.6 Common Transparency Challenges in Cloud.

- Access restrictions: Cloud providers may place restrictions on who has access to their infrastructure and systems, making it difficult for businesses to comprehend how their data and applications are handled.
- Absence of audit trails: Organizations may not be able to trace who has accessed their data and when, due to cloud providers occasionally failing to offer thorough audit trails.
- Complexity: Organizations may find it difficult to comprehend the full ecosystem in cloud settings because of the complicated interactions between various systems and apps.

To mitigate the risk of lack of transparency in cloud computing, organizations can take the following steps.

- Pick cloud service providers who are open about their security and compliance procedures and who give thorough details about their infrastructure and systems.
- Establish precise policies and practices for access to and management of data.
- Use monitoring systems and other tools and technology that offer visibility into the cloud environment.
- Assess the cloud environment on a frequent basis to make sure it is safe and legal.

Organizations may increase their cloud environment's openness, lower their risk of data breaches and other security issues, and make sure they are complying with compliance standards by adopting these actions. Other solutions to tackle this issue are presented in [33–35]. A comprehensive tabular analysis of the factors contributing to lack of transparency in cloud computing, along with strategies to mitigate these challenges, is highlighted in Table 6.6.

TABLE 6.6
Analysis of the Transparency Challenges in Cloud Related Mitigation Strategies

Factor	Description	Impact of Lack of Transparency	Strategies to Mitigate
Shared Responsibility	Cloud providers and clients share responsibility for managing the cloud environment, making it unclear who is accountable for what.	Difficulty in understanding the division of responsibilities can lead to gaps in security and management.	• Clearly define roles and responsibilities in service-level agreements (SLAs). • Ensure clear communication of shared duties with the cloud provider.
Access Restrictions	Cloud providers may impose limitations on who can access their infrastructure and systems.	Limited visibility into how data and applications are being managed and handled.	• Choose providers with clear access control policies. • Define and enforce access controls and permissions within the organization.
Absence of Audit Trails	Some cloud providers fail to provide complete audit trails, hindering the ability to track data access and changes.	Lack of audit logs reduces accountability and makes it difficult to trace unauthorized access.	• Select cloud providers that offer detailed and comprehensive audit logs. • Implement third-party auditing tools for additional transparency.
Complexity	The cloud environment may be complex, with interactions between various systems and applications that are hard to understand.	Complexity reduces the ability to have full visibility and oversight of the entire ecosystem.	• Use cloud management and monitoring tools to gain visibility. • Simplify the cloud environment where possible and provide training to internal teams for better understanding.
Vendor Lock-in	Some providers may lock organizations into specific services, making it difficult to assess or switch providers.	Restricts the ability to compare cloud providers and understand their systems' full operation.	• Regularly assess cloud vendor performance and policies. • Work with multi-cloud or hybrid cloud strategies to reduce dependence on a single provider.

6.7 INSECURE INTERFACES AND APIs

Organizations may have difficulty with insecure interfaces and APIs in cloud computing. Different applications and services in the cloud environment are connected through APIs (Application Programming Interfaces). They are a target for cyberattacks because they may grant access to sensitive data and systems. Here are several elements that cloud computing's unsafe interfaces and APIs may be attributed to:

- Weak authentication and authorization: APIs could not have robust controls for authentication and authorization, making it simple for attackers to access sensitive data.
- Inadequate encryption: Some APIs broadcast data in plain sight or employ shoddy encryption, which makes it simple for hackers to intercept and steal information.
- APIs that are badly developed: APIs may be poorly designed and include vulnerabilities that attackers can take advantage of.
- Lack of testing: APIs might not undergo extensive testing for security flaws before being put into use, making it simple for attackers to exploit holes.

Figure 6.7 highlights the process of mitigating API security risks. Each of the elements that contribute to the cloud's unsafe interfaces and/or APIs may be countered in a funnel-based approach.

To reduce the risk of insecure interfaces and APIs in cloud computing, organizations can take the following steps:

- Using two-factor authentication and role-based access restrictions are examples of robust authentication and authorization mechanisms for APIs.

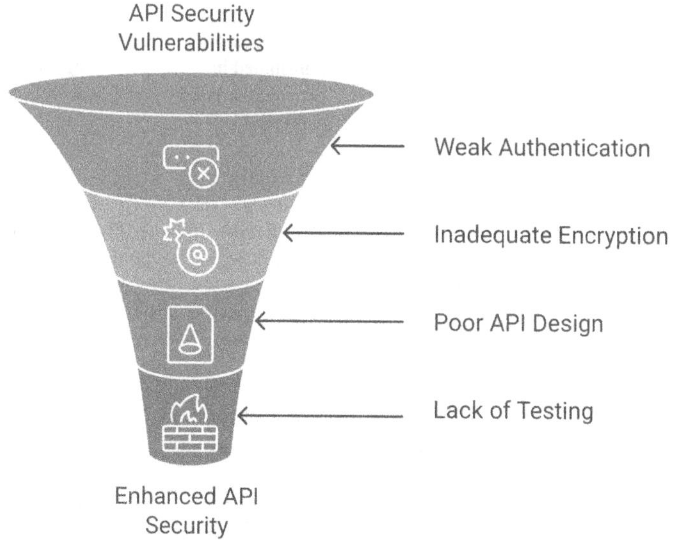

FIGURE 6.7 General process of API security risks mitigation.

- Use robust encryption for data sent over APIs, such as Secure Sockets Layer (SSL) or Transport Layer Security (TLS).
- Use APIs that are well-designed, adhere to industry best practices, and have had their security vulnerabilities evaluated.
- Regularly examine APIs for vulnerabilities and perform penetration tests to find and fix security flaws.

By taking these steps, organizations can reduce the risk of insecure interfaces and APIs in cloud computing and ensure that their data and systems are protected from cyberattacks. A comprehensive analysis of the factors contributing to insecure interfaces and APIs in cloud computing, along with strategies to mitigate these risks, is presented in Table 6.7.

TABLE 6.7
Analysis of the Insecure Interfaces and APIs in Cloud and Related Mitigation Strategies

Factor	Description	Impact of Insecure Interfaces and APIs	Strategies to Mitigate
Weak Authentication and Authorization	APIs may lack strong authentication and authorization mechanisms, allowing unauthorized access.	Attackers can easily access sensitive data and systems if authentication and authorization are weak.	• Implement two-factor authentication (2FA) for APIs. • Use role-based access control (RBAC) to restrict access based on user roles and permissions.
Inadequate Encryption	APIs may not use proper encryption, leaving data vulnerable to interception and theft.	Data can be intercepted and compromised if transmitted in plain text or poorly encrypted.	• Ensure APIs use strong encryption protocols like SSL/TLS. • Regularly update encryption methods to align with industry best practices.
Poorly Designed APIs	Some APIs may be badly developed, with design flaws and security vulnerabilities.	Vulnerabilities in API design can be exploited by attackers, leading to data breaches or system compromise.	• Adopt industry standards and best practices for API design. • Conduct security reviews and audits of API designs before deployment.
Lack of Testing	APIs may not undergo sufficient testing for security flaws before deployment, leaving them open to exploitation.	Unidentified vulnerabilities could be exploited by attackers, compromising the security of the system.	• Perform regular penetration testing and vulnerability assessments on APIs. • Implement continuous integration/continuous deployment (CI/CD) with security testing.

6.8 INSUFFICIENT DUE DILIGENCE

Organizations may experience difficulties with inadequate due diligence while using cloud computing. The term "due diligence" refers to the procedure of investigating and assessing potential cloud service providers before choosing one in order to make sure they satisfy the organization's security and compliance needs. Here are some of the elements that cloud computing's inadequate due diligence is influenced by:

- Lack of knowledge: Businesses might not be able to assess cloud providers or comprehend the security and compliance issues connected to employing cloud services.
- Limited resources: Businesses might not have the means to thoroughly assess cloud providers' security and compliance procedures.
- Lack of transparency: It may be difficult for cloud providers to be honest about their security and compliance procedures, which makes it difficult for organizations to assess their appropriateness.
- The cloud computing market is continuously evolving, making it difficult for businesses to stay on top of new providers and technology.

Figure 6.8 depicts the process of mitigating common due diligence challenges. To mitigate the risk of insufficient due diligence in cloud computing, organizations can take the following steps:

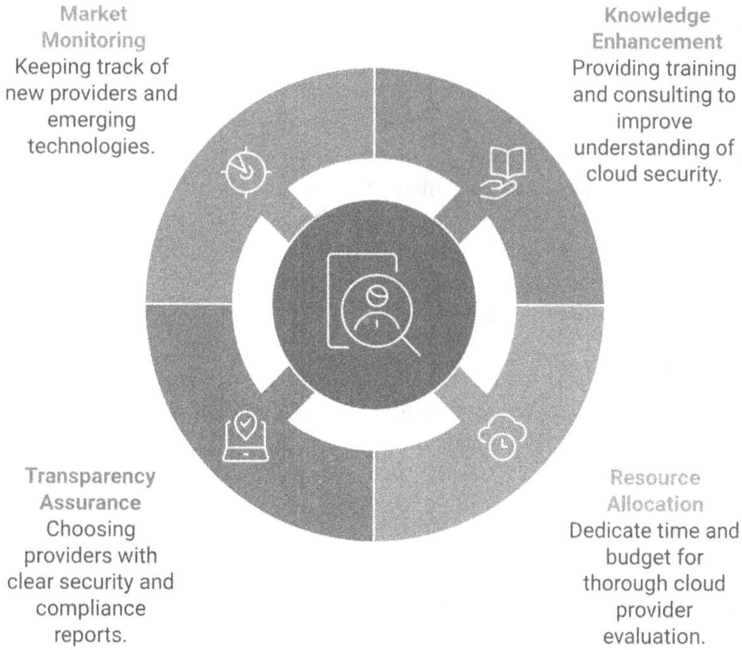
Market Monitoring
Keeping track of new providers and emerging technologies.
Knowledge Enhancement
Providing training and consulting to improve understanding of cloud security.
Transparency Assurance
Choosing providers with clear security and compliance reports.
Resource Allocation
Dedicate time and budget for thorough cloud provider evaluation.

FIGURE 6.8 Mitigating due diligence challenges.

- Establish precise standards for comparing cloud service providers according to security and compliance specifications.
- Thoroughly assess possible cloud service providers, checking references and learning about their security and compliance procedures.
- Assess cloud service providers and confirm their security and compliance procedures using impartial third parties.
- Keep an eye on the functioning of the cloud environment and the cloud provider to make sure they continue to adhere to the organization's security and compliance standards.

By following these measures, businesses may lessen the risk of using cloud computing without doing adequate due diligence and guarantee that the cloud provider they choose complies with security and compliance standards. A comprehensive analysis of the factors contributing to inadequate due diligence in cloud computing, along with strategies to mitigate these challenges, is provided in Table 6.8.

6.9 SHARED TECHNOLOGY VULNERABILITIES

Organizations may struggle with shared technological risks in the cloud. Because cloud providers make use of common infrastructure and services, many clients can utilize the same technological stack. This raises the possibility of shared technology vulnerabilities, where a weakness in one customer's system or application might have an impact on other customers' systems or applications. Figure 6.9 navigates the shared technological risks in cloud environments.

Here are some of the elements that cloud computing's shared technology vulnerabilities are caused by:

- The utilization of common infrastructure by cloud providers, including servers, storage, and networks, raises the possibility that a vulnerability in one customer's application or system can impact other customers.
- Shared services: Cloud providers provide shared services including load balancers, messaging systems, and databases, which raises the possibility that a flaw in how one client uses the service might impact other users.
- Complex architectures: Because cloud systems may include many different levels of infrastructure and services, it might be difficult to find and fix vulnerabilities.
- Lack of visibility: It may be difficult to discover and fix vulnerabilities when customers do not have complete insight into the shared infrastructure and services offered by the cloud provider.

To mitigate the risk of shared technology vulnerabilities in cloud computing, organizations can take the following steps:

- To prevent unauthorized access to shared infrastructure and services, implement strict access restrictions.

TABLE 6.8
Analysis of the Inadequate Due Diligence in Cloud and Related Mitigation Strategies

Factor	Description	Impact of Inadequate Due Diligence	Strategies to Mitigate
Lack of Knowledge	Organizations may lack the expertise to evaluate cloud service providers and understand related security and compliance issues.	Without the necessary knowledge, organizations may fail to assess the risks and requirements of cloud services effectively.	• Provide training for staff to enhance understanding of cloud security and compliance needs. • Collaborate with experts or consultants who specialize in cloud security and compliance.
Limited Resources	Organizations may not have sufficient resources (time, personnel, budget) to thoroughly evaluate cloud providers.	Inadequate resources can result in rushed decisions or overlooking critical security and compliance issues.	• Allocate dedicated resources for evaluating cloud providers. • Use automated tools to assess security and compliance aspects more efficiently.
Lack of Transparency	Cloud providers may not be fully transparent about their security, compliance practices, or data handling.	Without transparency, organizations cannot fully assess whether a provider meets their security and compliance needs.	• Choose cloud providers that offer detailed, transparent reports on security and compliance procedures. • Demand clear visibility into the provider's security and audit logs.
Evolving Cloud Market	The cloud computing market is rapidly evolving, making it hard for businesses to keep track of new providers, technologies, and standards.	Rapid changes in the market can lead to outdated decisions or missed opportunities for selecting more secure or compliant providers.	• Continuously monitor the cloud market for new providers and emerging technologies. • Stay updated on industry trends and regulatory changes.

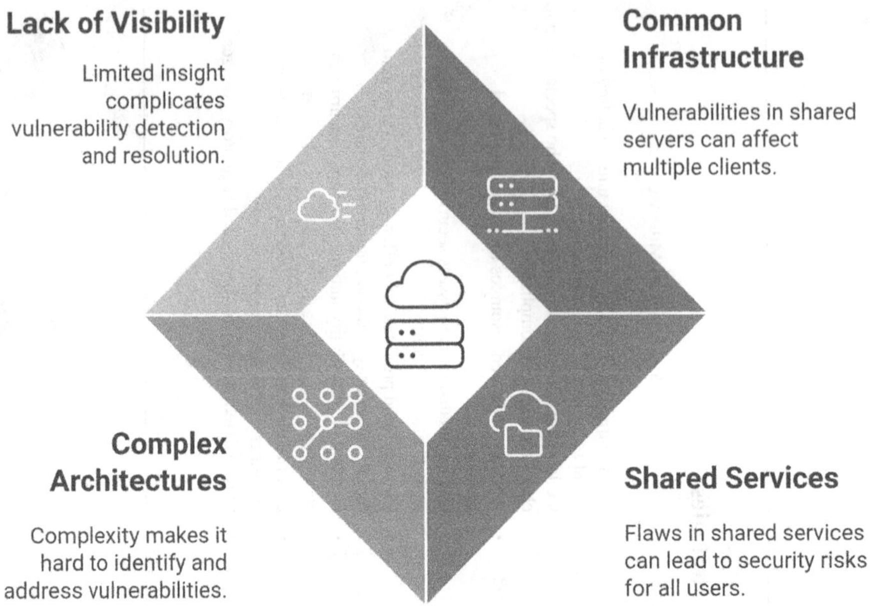
Lack of Visibility
Limited insight complicates vulnerability detection and resolution.
Common Infrastructure
Vulnerabilities in shared servers can affect multiple clients.
Complex Architectures
Complexity makes it hard to identify and address vulnerabilities.
Shared Services
Flaws in shared services can lead to security risks for all users.

FIGURE 6.9 Navigating shared technological risks in cloud environments.

- To find and fix vulnerabilities in applications and systems, use secure coding techniques and vulnerability management procedures.
- To reduce the impact of a vulnerability in one customer's application or system on other customers, use segmentation and isolation.
- Assist the cloud service provider in putting strong security and compliance procedures in place to guard against and fix shared technology vulnerabilities.

A tabular analysis of the factors contributing to shared technological risks in cloud computing, along with strategies to mitigate these risks, is presented in Table 6.9.

By adopting these actions, businesses may lower the danger of cloud computing's shared technology vulnerabilities and guarantee that their data and systems are secure from intrusions. Table 6.10 highlights the above-mentioned challenges of different attributes. The table is just intended as an example and not all of the features for each challenge are included. Additionally, organizations may give particular traits a higher priority based on their own needs and concerns. The columns point to different types of risks or issues that an organization might encounter when using cloud computing services. Each column represents a specific area of concern or risk that could impact the organization in some way. The rows represent specific types of challenges or situations where these risks may manifest. Each row describes a particular situation, action, or concern in the context of cloud services.

TABLE 6.9
Analysis of the Shared Technological Risks in Cloud and Mitigation Strategies

Factor	Description	Impact of Shared Technological Risks	Strategies to Mitigate
Common Infrastructure	Cloud providers use shared infrastructure (e.g., servers, storage, networks) for multiple clients.	A vulnerability in one customer's application or system may affect other clients using the same infrastructure.	• Implement strong access control mechanisms to limit exposure to shared resources. • Regularly patch and update infrastructure components to fix vulnerabilities.
Shared Services	Cloud providers offer shared services (e.g., load balancers, messaging systems, databases) to multiple clients.	A flaw in how one client uses a shared service can lead to security risks or disruptions for other users.	• Implement secure configurations for shared services. • Use dedicated or isolated services when possible. • Regularly test services for vulnerabilities.
Complex Architectures	Cloud systems have complex architectures with many layers of infrastructure and services.	Complexity makes it difficult to identify and address vulnerabilities in a timely manner.	• Simplify the architecture where possible. • Use automated vulnerability scanning and monitoring tools to identify issues in complex environments.
Lack of Visibility	Organizations may lack full visibility into the shared infrastructure and services provided by cloud providers.	Limited insight into shared infrastructure increases the difficulty of detecting and resolving vulnerabilities.	• Request transparency from cloud providers about the infrastructure and services in use. • Use monitoring tools to gain visibility into the cloud environment.

TABLE 6.10
Relation of Different Security Challenges with Probable Issues

Challenge	Description	Data Security	Vendor Lock-In	Compliance Complexity	Lack of Transparency	Insecure Interfaces and APIs	Insufficient Due Diligence	Shared Technology Vulnerabilities
Lack of Visibility and Control	Limited visibility and control over the underlying cloud infrastructure and security measures.	×	×	×	✓	×	×	×
Data Breaches and Downtime	The risk of data breaches and system downtime in the cloud environment.	✓	×	×	×	×	×	×
Vendor Lock-In	Difficulty in switching cloud service providers due to proprietary technologies and lack of data portability.	×	✓	×	×	×	×	×
Compliance Complexity	The complexity of ensuring compliance with regulatory requirements in the cloud environment.	×	×	✓	×	×	×	×
Lack of Transparency	Limited transparency into the internal operations, security controls, and processes of the cloud service provider.	×	×	×	✓	×	×	×
Insecure Interfaces and APIs	Vulnerabilities in interfaces and APIs used for accessing and interacting with cloud services.	×	×	×	×	✓	×	×
Insufficient Due Diligence	Failure to conduct thorough due diligence when selecting and evaluating cloud service providers.	×	×	×	×	×	✓	×
Shared Technology Vulnerabilities	Security vulnerabilities stemming from the shared technology and resources in the cloud environment.	×	×	×	×	×	×	✓

6.10 SUMMARY

This chapter discusses the implementation challenges in secure cloud computing. Organizations must overcome a number of obstacles in order to deploy secure cloud computing and guarantee the security and privacy of their data. Uncertainty and lack of control, data breaches and downtime, vendor lock-in, compliance complexity, a lack of due diligence, a lack of transparency, unsafe interfaces and APIs, shared technological vulnerabilities, etc. are a few of these issues. Strong access controls, secure coding techniques, thorough evaluations of cloud providers, and collaboration with the cloud provider to ensure that they have strong security and compliance practices in place are just a few measures that organizations can take to mitigate these challenges. Organizations may make sure that their cloud installations are safe, legal, and robust by addressing these issues. This chapter provides a comprehensive analysis of these challenges along with the related mitigation strategies.

6.11 PRACTICE QUESTIONS/SOLUTIONS

MULTIPLE CHOICE QUESTIONS

1 **Which of the following is a primary challenge in securing cloud computing environments?**
A) Managing hardware resources
B) Securing the physical data center
C) Data privacy and compliance
D) Providing sufficient storage capacity

Answer: C) Data privacy and compliance

2 **Which of the following best describes the concept of "data encryption at rest" in cloud computing?**
A) Encrypting data while it's being transmitted over the network
B) Encrypting data that is stored on physical storage media
C) Encrypting data only when it is accessed by users
D) Encrypting data during processing in the cloud

Answer: B) Encrypting data that is stored on physical storage media

3 **What is a major security concern when dealing with multi-tenant environments in cloud computing?**
A) Lack of computational power
B) Data leakage between different users
C) Increased energy consumption
D) Limited scalability of services

Answer: B) Data leakage between different users

4 Which of the following is a significant challenge in maintaining access control in cloud environments?

A) Ensuring constant network connectivity
B) Defining and enforcing appropriate permissions
C) Managing physical server locations
D) Reducing the cost of data storage

Answer: B) Defining and enforcing appropriate permissions

5 Which of the following security measures helps to mitigate risks associated with unauthorized access in a cloud environment?

A) Multi-factor authentication (MFA)
B) Virtual private cloud (VPC)
C) Data deduplication
D) Serverless computing

Answer: A) Multi-factor authentication (MFA)

6 What is the main risk of relying on a single-cloud service provider for hosting critical applications and data?

A) Data redundancy
B) Vendor lock-in and limited flexibility
C) High latency
D) Increased system throughput

Answer: B) Vendor lock-in and limited flexibility

7 Which of the following is a key challenge related to cloud data storage security?

A) Ensuring high availability of cloud services
B) Securing data during processing in the cloud
C) Managing data encryption keys effectively
D) Reducing the cost of cloud storage

Answer: C) Managing data encryption keys effectively

8 What is the purpose of a Service-Level Agreement (SLA) in cloud security?

A) To define the cost structure for cloud services
B) To ensure compliance with industry regulations
C) To outline the security measures and performance guarantees provided by the cloud service provider
D) To specify the physical locations of the cloud infrastructure

Answer: C) To outline the security measures and performance guarantees provided by the cloud service provider

9 Which of the following is a challenge when migrating sensitive data to a cloud environment?

A) Ensuring that the cloud provider offers sufficient compute resources
B) Maintaining compliance with data protection regulations (e.g., GDPR, HIPAA)
C) Reducing cloud provider costs
D) Managing network bandwidth for data migration

Answer: B) Maintaining compliance with data protection regulations (e.g., GDPR, HIPAA)

10 What type of cloud deployment model is most likely to have the highest level of control over security configurations?

A) Public cloud
B) Private cloud
C) Hybrid cloud
D) Community cloud

Answer: B) Private cloud

11 Which of the following is a critical factor to consider when ensuring the security of cloud applications?

A) Cloud service provider's physical security measures
B) Ensuring applications are built with secure coding practices
C) Maximizing resource utilization
D) Reducing energy consumption of cloud infrastructure

Answer: B) Ensuring applications are built with secure coding practices

12 What is "cloud sprawl" in the context of cloud computing, and how does it pose a security risk?

A) The inability to scale cloud infrastructure
B) The uncontrolled growth of cloud services across multiple providers, leading to a lack of visibility and security risks
C) The over-provisioning of cloud storage
D) The rapid depreciation of cloud services over time

Answer: B) The uncontrolled growth of cloud services across multiple providers, leading to a lack of visibility and security risks

13 Which of the following is the most important factor in ensuring secure data transfer in cloud environments?

A) Use of secure APIs
B) Application of strong encryption protocols
C) Ensuring high network throughput
D) Optimizing cloud storage configurations

Answer: B) Application of strong encryption protocols

14 Which of the following is a challenge associated with ensuring cloud infrastructure security from external cyber threats?

A) Limited cloud storage capacity
B) Increased complexity of security patches and updates
C) Ensuring adequate bandwidth for data transfer
D) Cloud vendor reliance for monitoring network traffic

Answer: B) Increased complexity of security patches and updates

15 What is the primary function of a cloud access security broker (CASB)?

A) To monitor user traffic and enforce security policies between the cloud provider and the user
B) To provide additional storage capacity for cloud services
C) To optimize the performance of cloud applications
D) To facilitate the migration of data to a cloud environment

Answer: A) To monitor user traffic and enforce security policies between the cloud provider and the user

16 Which of the following is the primary concern when cloud service providers share resources among multiple customers?

A) Redundancy of data
B) Insecure API integrations
C) Lack of resource allocation for each customer
D) Data isolation and privacy between tenants

Answer: D) Data isolation and privacy between tenants

17 What is the concept of "shared responsibility model" in cloud security?

A) The cloud provider is responsible for securing the entire cloud infrastructure
B) The customer is responsible for securing the entire infrastructure
C) Both the cloud provider and customer share security responsibilities, depending on the service model
D) No security is required, as the cloud provider takes care of everything

Answer: C) Both the cloud provider and customer share security responsibilities, depending on the service model

18 Which cloud service model (IaaS, PaaS, or SaaS) places the most security responsibility on the customer?

A) SaaS (Software as a Service)
B) PaaS (Platform as a Service)
C) IaaS (Infrastructure as a Service)
D) All models have the same level of security responsibility

Answer: C) IaaS (Infrastructure as a Service)

19 What is a common security issue faced during cloud service integration with on-premise IT infrastructure?

A) Limited cloud storage capacity
B) Compatibility of APIs between cloud and on-premise systems
C) Reduced network throughput
D) Lack of scalability of on-premise infrastructure

Answer: B) Compatibility of APIs between cloud and on-premise systems

20 Which is one of the biggest challenges of ensuring data integrity in cloud computing?

A) Lack of available data backup services
B) Preventing unauthorized access to cloud data
C) Ensuring that data is not altered or corrupted during storage or transfer
D) High cost of securing cloud applications

Answer: C) Ensuring that data is not altered or corrupted during storage or transfer

DESCRIPTIVE QUESTIONS

1 What is the "shared responsibility model" in cloud computing?

Answer: The shared responsibility model outlines the division of security responsibilities between the cloud service provider and the customer. In IaaS, the provider secures the infrastructure, while the customer manages security for the applications and data. In SaaS, the provider handles most of the security aspects, and the customer is responsible for user access and data integrity.

2 What are the main security concerns in multi-tenant cloud environments?

Answer: The main concerns include data isolation, unauthorized access, and data leakage between tenants. Since multiple customers share the same infrastructure, improper isolation can result in one tenant accessing another's data.

3 How can organizations mitigate risks to data storage in the cloud?

Answer: Organizations can mitigate risks by implementing strong encryption (both at rest and in transit), access control policies, regular backups, and using a robust encryption key management system to prevent unauthorized access and data breaches.

4 What are the compliance challenges when migrating sensitive data to the cloud?

Answer: The challenges include ensuring adherence to regulations such as GDPR, HIPAA, or PCI-DSS. Organizations must ensure that cloud providers are compliant and implement security measures such as encryption, audit trails, and data localization to meet these regulations.

5 How can organizations manage secure access control in cloud environments?

Answer: Organizations can use Identity and Access Management (IAM) systems, implement multi-factor authentication (MFA), and apply role-based access control (RBAC) to ensure that only authorized users can access cloud resources.

6 What are the risks of integrating legacy systems with cloud infrastructure?

Answer: Risks include compatibility issues, inadequate security for legacy systems, and potential vulnerabilitiesw when connecting on-premise systems to the cloud. Organizations need to ensure secure API integrations, network security, and a phased migration plan.

7 What is a Zero Trust security model in the cloud?

Answer: The Zero Trust model assumes no user or device is trusted by default. It requires continuous authentication and strict access controls, ensuring that only verified users can access resources, regardless of whether they are inside or outside the network.

8 Why are cloud APIs considered a security risk?

Answer: Cloud APIs are a potential target for cyberattacks because they are often exposed to the Internet and can provide unauthorized access if not properly secured. Securing APIs involves using encryption, authentication, and regular vulnerability testing.

9 How does data encryption help in securing cloud environments?

Answer: Data encryption helps protect sensitive information by making it unreadable to unauthorized users, both when it is stored (at rest) and during transmission (in transit). It ensures confidentiality and prevents data breaches.

10 What is vendor lock-in, and how does it affect cloud security?

Answer: Vendor lock-in occurs when an organization becomes overly dependent on a single-cloud provider, making it difficult and costly to switch to another provider. This can affect security by limiting flexibility and the ability to implement tailored security measures across different platforms.

11 What are the primary security challenges related to cloud application development?

Answer: Cloud application development faces challenges such as ensuring secure coding practices, protecting against vulnerabilities such as SQL injection and cross-site scripting (XSS), securing application interfaces (APIs), and ensuring proper access control and user authentication within the app.

12 How does a Distributed Denial of Service (DDoS) attack impact cloud computing environments?

Answer: A DDoS attack overwhelms cloud infrastructure with excessive traffic, making services unavailable and causing disruption to normal operations. Cloud providers often implement DDoS protection services, but organizations must also take measures to mitigate such attacks at the application and network levels.

13 What is the significance of encryption key management in securing cloud data?

Answer: Encryption key management is critical in ensuring that encryption keys are stored, accessed, and rotated securely. Poor key management can lead to unauthorized access to encrypted data, undermining the security of sensitive information in the cloud.

14 What role does multi-factor authentication (MFA) play in cloud security?

Answer: MFA enhances cloud security by requiring users to provide multiple forms of verification (e.g., a password and a one-time code sent to a phone) before accessing cloud resources, reducing the likelihood of unauthorized access due to compromised credentials.

15 How can organizations address cloud security concerns related to third-party vendors and service providers?

Answer: Organizations should conduct thorough security assessments of third-party vendors, ensure clear contractual agreements regarding data protection and security, and enforce strict monitoring and audit practices to ensure third-party services comply with security standards.

16 What is the role of a Cloud Access Security Broker (CASB) in securing cloud environments?

Answer: A CASB provides visibility and control over cloud service usage by enforcing security policies, such as data encryption, access control, and threat protection, for cloud services that are not directly under the organization's control, helping to secure shadow IT and unsanctioned cloud use.

17 What are the security risks associated with cloud data migration, and how can they be mitigated?

Answer: Cloud data migration risks include data loss, unauthorized access, and data integrity issues. These can be mitigated by using encryption during transit, ensuring proper backup procedures, and conducting thorough testing and validation before and after migration.

18 Why is securing cloud APIs crucial for cloud computing security?

Answer: Securing cloud APIs is crucial because they are often exposed to external users and can be vulnerable to attacks like injection or man-in-the-middle (MITM). APIs must be secured with authentication, encryption, and proper input validation to prevent unauthorized access and data breaches.

19 What are the risks of using public cloud services for storing sensitive data, and how can these risks be reduced?

Answer: Risks include potential unauthorized access, data breaches, and lack of control over the physical security of data centers. These risks can be reduced by encrypting data, implementing strict access control measures, and ensuring the cloud provider complies with relevant security standards and regulations.

20 What steps should an organization take to ensure business continuity in the cloud?

Answer: Organizations should implement disaster recovery plans, regularly backup cloud data, ensure geographical redundancy across cloud regions, and use cloud-native tools to monitor and respond to service disruptions, ensuring minimal downtime and business continuity.

REFERENCES

1. Bamiah, M., Brohi, S., Chuprat, S., & Brohi, M. N. (2012, December). Cloud implementation security challenges. In *2012 International Conference on Cloud Computing Technologies, Applications and Management (ICCCTAM)* (pp. 174–178). IEEE.
2. Mushtaq, M. F., Akram, U., Khan, I., Khan, S. N., Shahzad, A., & Ullah, A. (2017). Cloud computing environment and security challenges: A review. *International Journal of Advanced Computer Science and Applications*, *8*(10), 183–195).
3. Ertaul, L., Singhal, S., & Saldamli, G. (2010, July). Security Challenges in Cloud Computing. In *Security and Management* (pp. 36–42).
4. Padhy, R. P., Patra, M. R., & Satapathy, S. C. (2011). Cloud computing: security issues and research challenges. *International Journal of Computer Science and Information Technology & Security (IJCSITS)*, *1*(2), 136–146.
5. Ali, M., Khan, S. U., & Vasilakos, A. V. (2015). Security in cloud computing: Opportunities and challenges. *Information Sciences*, *305*, 357–383.
6. Subramanian, N., & Jeyaraj, A. (2018). Recent security challenges in cloud computing. *Computers & Electrical Engineering*, *71*, 28–42.
7. Yang, P., Xiong, N., & Ren, J. (2020). Data security and privacy protection for cloud storage: A survey. *IEEE Access*, *8*, 131723–131740.
8. Indu, I., Anand, P. R., & Bhaskar, V. (2018). Identity and access management in cloud environment: Mechanisms and challenges. *Engineering Science and Technology, An International Journal*, *21*(4), 574–588.
9. Yimam, D., & Fernandez, E. B. (2016). A survey of compliance issues in cloud computing. *Journal of Internet Services and Applications*, *7*, 1–12.
10. Hashmi, A., Ranjan, A., & Anand, A. (2018). Security and compliance management in cloud computing. *International Journal of Advanced Studies in Computers, Science and Engineering*, *7*(1), 47–54.
11. Bhisikar, P., & Sahu, A. (2013). Security in data storage and transmission in cloud computing. *International Journal of Advanced Research in Computer Science and Software Engineering*, *3*(3), 410–415).
12. Kim, S., & Na, W. (2016). Safe data transmission architecture based on cloud for Internet of Things. *Wireless Personal Communications*, *86*, 287–300.
13. Lombardi, F., & Di Pietro, R. (2011). Secure virtualization for cloud computing. *Journal of Network and Computer Applications*, *34*(4), 1113–1122.
14. Ahmed, A., & Zakariae, T. (2018). IaaS cloud model security issues on behalf cloud provider and user security behaviors. *Procedia Computer Science*, *134*, 328–333.
15. Dang, H., Purwanto, E., & Chang, E. C. (2017, April). Proofs of data residency: Checking whether your cloud files have been relocated. In *Proceedings of the 2017 ACM on Asia Conference on Computer and Communications Security* (pp. 408–422).
16. Rao, K. R., & Nayak, A. (2019). Data residency as a service: a secure mechanism for storing data in the cloud. *International Journal of Embedded Systems*, *11*(4), 397–418.
17. Gharote, M., Mondal, S., Roy, S., Sahu, P., & Ramamurthy, A. (2022). Decision support framework for data residency compliance in cloud. *CSI Transactions on ICT*, *10*(1), 61–69.
18. Raju, B. K., & Geethakumari, G. (2014, October). A novel approach for incident response in cloud using forensics. In *Proceedings of the 7th ACM India Computing Conference* (pp. 1–6).
19. Urias, V. E., Stout, W. M., Loverro, C., & Young, J. W. (2016, December). Hypervisor assisted forensics and incident response in the cloud. In *2016 IEEE International Conference on Computer and Information Technology (CIT)* (pp. 768–775). IEEE.

20. Thuraisingham, B. (2020, October). Cloud governance. In *2020 IEEE 13th International Conference on Cloud Computing (CLOUD)* (pp. 86–90). IEEE.
21. Opara-Martins, J., Sahandi, R., & Tian, F. (2014, November). Critical review of vendor lock-in and its impact on adoption of cloud computing. In *International Conference on Information Society (i-Society 2014)* (pp. 92–97). IEEE.
22. Yang, P., Xiong, N., & Ren, J. (2020). Data security and privacy protection for cloud storage: A survey. *IEEE Access*, *8*, 131723–131740.
23. Habiba, M., Islam, M. R., & Ali, A. S. (2013, July). Access control management for cloud. In *2013 12th IEEE International Conference on Trust, Security and Privacy in Computing and Communications* (pp. 485–492). IEEE.
24. Massonet, P., Naqvi, S., Ponsard, C., Latanicki, J., Rochwerger, B., & Villari, M. (2011, May). A monitoring and audit logging architecture for data location compliance in federated cloud infrastructures. In *2011 IEEE international symposium on parallel and distributed processing workshops and PhD forum* (pp. 1510–1517). IEEE.
25. Banyal, R. K., Jain, P., & Jain, V. K. (2013, September). Multi-factor authentication framework for cloud computing. In *2013 Fifth International Conference on Computational Intelligence, Modelling and Simulation* (pp. 105–110). IEEE.
26. Barona, R., & Anita, E. M. (2017, April). A survey on data breach challenges in cloud computing security: Issues and threats. In *2017 International Conference on Circuit, Power and Computing Technologies (ICCPCT)* (pp. 1–8). IEEE.
27. Nabi, M., Toeroe, M., & Khendek, F. (2016). Availability in the cloud: State of the art. *Journal of Network and Computer Applications*, *60*, 54–67.
28. Opara-Martins, J., Sahandi, R., & Tian, F. (2016). Critical analysis of vendor lock-in and its impact on cloud computing migration: a business perspective. *Journal of Cloud Computing*, *5*, 1–18.
29. Quint, P. C., & Kratzke, N. (2016). Overcome vendor lock-in by integrating already available container technologies towards transferability in cloud computing for SMEs. *Cloud Computing*, *50*.
30. Silva, G. C., Rose, L. M., & Calinescu, R. (2013, December). A systematic review of cloud lock-in solutions. In *2013 IEEE 5th International Conference on Cloud Computing Technology and Science* (Vol. 2, pp. 363–368). IEEE.
31. Bachlechner, D., Thalmann, S., & Maier, R. (2014). Security and compliance challenges in complex IT outsourcing arrangements: A multi-stakeholder perspective. *Computers & Security*, *40*, 38–59.
32. Pauley, W. (2010). Cloud provider transparency: An empirical evaluation. *IEEE Security & Privacy*, *8*(6), 32–39.
33. Flittner, M., Balaban, S., & Bless, R. (2016, April). Cloudinspector: A transparency-as-a-service solution for legal issues in cloud computing. In *2016 IEEE International Conference on Cloud Engineering Workshop (IC2EW)* (pp. 94–99). IEEE.
34. Ismail, U. M., Islam, S., Ouedraogo, M., & Weippl, E. (2016). A framework for security transparency in cloud computing. *Future Internet*, *8*(1), 5.
35. Ismail, U. M., & Islam, S. (2020). A unified framework for cloud security transparency and audit. *Journal of Information Security and Applications*, *54*, 102594.

7 Extension to Cloud Computing

7.1 INTRODUCTION

Cloud computing technology has undergone significant evolution, with several key extensions shaping its landscape. Serverless computing has revolutionized application development by abstracting away infrastructure management, allowing developers to focus solely on code. Edge computing has decentralized data processing, reducing latency and enhancing performance for real-time applications and IoT devices. Multi-cloud and hybrid cloud strategies have gained prominence, enabling organizations to optimize costs, increase redundancy, and leverage specialized services from different providers. Emerging technologies such as machine learning services, blockchain integration, and quantum computing offer advanced capabilities in analytics, security, and computational power. These extensions collectively enhance flexibility, scalability, and innovation in cloud computing, driving efficiencies across industries and paving the way for future advancements.

7.2 SERVERLESS COMPUTING

Serverless computing is a cloud computing execution model where the cloud provider dynamically manages the allocation and provisioning of servers. In traditional cloud computing, developers need to provision and manage servers to run applications. In contrast, serverless computing abstracts away the infrastructure, allowing developers to focus on writing code without worrying about the underlying hardware [1]. Some of the common pros/cons of serverless computing are listed in Figure 7.1.

7.2.1 Key Characteristics

Key characteristics of serverless computing include [1,2]:

1. **No Server Management**: Developers do not have to deal with provisioning, scaling, or managing servers. The cloud provider handles all infrastructure management, including server maintenance, capacity provisioning, and scaling.

DOI: 10.1201/9781003510772-7

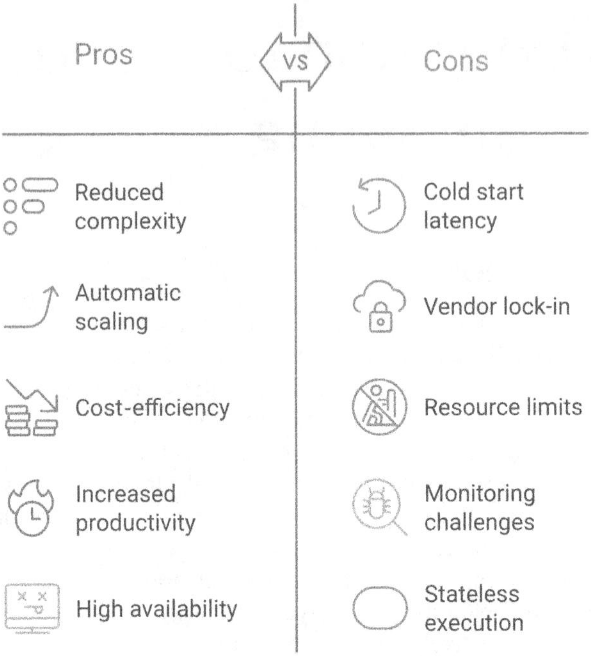

Pros
VS
Cons
Reduced complexity
Automatic scaling
Cost-efficiency
Increased productivity
High availability
Cold start latency
Vendor lock-in
Resource limits
Monitoring challenges
Stateless execution

FIGURE 7.1 General pros/cons of serverless computing.

2. **Event-Driven**: Serverless applications are typically triggered by events. Functions (often called serverless functions or just functions) are executed in response to events such as HTTP requests, database changes, file uploads, etc.
3. **Automatic Scaling**: Serverless platforms automatically scale the number of instances of a function based on the number of incoming requests. Functions are scaled out to accommodate incoming traffic and scaled down to zero when not in use, which can lead to cost savings.
4. **Pay-Per-Use Billing**: Users are charged based on the actual execution time and resources consumed by their functions, rather than paying for a predetermined amount of capacity or instances.
5. **Stateless Execution**: Functions are designed to be stateless and ephemeral. They are invoked, perform their task, and then terminate. Any state that needs to persist between invocations is typically stored externally, such as in a database or object storage.

Serverless computing is suitable for various use cases, including web applications, real-time file processing, Internet of Things (IoT) applications, data processing tasks, and more. It offers benefits such as reduced operational complexity, improved scalability, and cost efficiency, but it also comes with considerations around vendor lock-in, cold start latency, and architectural complexity in some scenarios.

7.2.2 Benefits

Serverless computing offers several benefits that make it attractive for modern application development and deployment [3]:

1. **Reduced Operational Complexity**: With serverless computing, developers can focus solely on writing code to implement business logic, without the need to manage servers, operating systems, or infrastructure scaling. This reduces the operational overhead and allows teams to iterate and deploy applications more quickly.
2. **Auto-Scaling and High Availability**: Serverless platforms automatically scale functions to handle incoming traffic and scale down to zero when functions are not in use. This auto-scaling capability ensures that applications can handle varying workloads without manual intervention. Additionally, serverless architectures often leverage high availability features provided by cloud providers, enhancing the reliability of applications.
3. **Cost Efficiency**: Serverless computing follows a pay-per-use pricing model, where you are billed only for the actual resources consumed during function execution (e.g., compute time, memory usage). This can lead to cost savings compared to traditional cloud computing models, where you may be paying for provisioned capacity even if it's not fully utilized.
4. **Increased Developer Productivity**: By abstracting away infrastructure management, serverless allows developers to focus more on writing code and delivering business value. This can accelerate development cycles and reduce time-to-market for new features and applications.
5. **Event-Driven Architecture**: Serverless functions are typically triggered by events such as HTTP requests, database changes, or file uploads. This event-driven architecture promotes loose coupling between components and enables a more modular and scalable application design.
6. **Scalability and Performance**: Serverless platforms can handle sudden spikes in traffic by automatically scaling out function instances. This elasticity ensures that applications remain responsive under varying load conditions, without requiring manual intervention or capacity planning.
7. **Vendor Management of Maintenance**: Cloud providers handle server maintenance tasks such as patching, hardware updates, and security configurations. This offloads these responsibilities from development teams, allowing them to focus on building and improving application functionality.
8. **Easier Integration with Third-Party Services**: Serverless platforms often provide integrations with various third-party services (such as databases, messaging queues, authentication services) through APIs or SDKs. This simplifies the integration of external services into applications, facilitating the adoption of microservices architectures.

Overall, serverless computing enables organizations to build and deploy applications more efficiently, with reduced overhead, improved scalability, and cost-effective resource utilization. However, it is important to evaluate specific use cases and consider factors such as cold start latency, vendor lock-in, and operational monitoring when adopting serverless architectures.

7.2.3 Challenges and Issues

While serverless computing offers many benefits, there are also challenges and issues that organizations need to consider [4]:

1. **Cold Start Latency**: Serverless functions may experience latency when they are invoked for the first time or after being idle for a while. This delay, known as cold start latency, occurs because the cloud provider needs to initialize the execution environment for the function. Depending on the platform and the programming language used, cold starts can range from milliseconds to several seconds, which can impact application responsiveness, especially for real-time or interactive applications.
2. **Vendor Lock-in**: Adopting serverless platforms often involves using proprietary services and APIs provided by a specific cloud provider. This can create vendor lock-in, where migrating applications to another provider or back to on-premises infrastructure becomes challenging. Organizations need to carefully evaluate the long-term implications of vendor lock-in and consider strategies to mitigate risks, such as using multi-cloud architectures or abstraction layers.
3. **Limits on Execution Time and Resource Allocation**: Serverless platforms impose limits on the maximum execution time and resource allocation (such as memory and CPU) for individual functions. Long-running tasks or functions requiring large amounts of memory may not be suitable for serverless architectures. Developers need to carefully design functions to adhere to these limits and consider alternative architectures for tasks that exceed them.
4. **Monitoring and Debugging**: Serverless architectures can introduce complexity in monitoring and debugging applications. Traditional monitoring tools may not provide visibility into serverless function execution, including performance metrics, logs, and error tracing. Cloud providers offer monitoring and debugging tools tailored for serverless environments, but integrating these tools effectively and gaining actionable insights can require additional effort.
5. **State Management**: Serverless functions are designed to be stateless, meaning they do not maintain state between invocations. Any data that needs to persist between function calls must be stored externally, such as in databases, object storage, or external caching services. Managing stateful workflows in a serverless environment can introduce complexity and require careful consideration of data consistency and synchronization.
6. **Security and Compliance**: Serverless applications may introduce new security challenges, such as managing access controls, securing function endpoints, and handling sensitive data within functions. Cloud providers typically offer security features and compliance certifications, but organizations

are responsible for implementing secure coding practices and configuring appropriate security measures for their applications.

7. **Cost Management**: While serverless computing can be cost-effective for applications with variable or unpredictable workloads, it's essential to monitor and manage costs effectively. Functions that scale frequently or handle high volumes of requests can incur unexpected costs if not optimized. Organizations should implement cost monitoring, budgeting, and optimization strategies to avoid bill shock and ensure cost efficiency.
8. **Operational Complexity for Large-scale Applications**: While serverless simplifies infrastructure management for individual functions, managing and orchestrating complex applications composed of multiple interconnected functions can become challenging. Organizations need to adopt best practices for deployment, versioning, monitoring, and managing dependencies to maintain reliability and scalability in large-scale serverless applications.

Addressing these challenges requires careful planning, architecture design, and operational practices tailored to the specific requirements and constraints of serverless computing environments. As the technology evolves, cloud providers and the developer community continue to innovate and address these challenges through improved tooling, best practices, and architectural patterns.

7.2.4 Future Research Directions

Future research in serverless computing is focused on addressing existing challenges and exploring new capabilities to further enhance the adoption and effectiveness of serverless architectures [4]. Some key research directions include:

1. **Reducing Cold Start Latency**: Significant effort is being invested in minimizing cold start latency, which can impact the responsiveness of serverless applications. Research explores techniques such as pre-warming function instances, optimizing runtime environments, and improving resource allocation strategies to reduce cold start times.
2. **Improving Resource Efficiency**: Research aims to optimize resource allocation and utilization in serverless platforms. This includes dynamic resource provisioning based on workload characteristics, efficient memory management, and exploring alternative execution models to reduce overhead and improve cost-effectiveness.
3. **Enhancing Function Composition and Orchestration**: As serverless applications become more complex, there is a need to improve support for function composition, workflow orchestration, and managing dependencies between functions. Research focuses on developing robust frameworks and tools for composing and orchestrating serverless functions effectively.
4. **State Management and Data Consistency**: Addressing challenges related to managing stateful applications in serverless environments remains a key area of research. Future work includes developing efficient mechanisms for

state management, ensuring data consistency across distributed function executions, and exploring serverless-compatible database solutions.

5. **Security and Privacy**: Research continues to focus on enhancing security measures and privacy protections in serverless computing. This includes developing secure coding practices, improving isolation between functions, implementing fine-grained access controls, and addressing potential vulnerabilities associated with serverless architectures.
6. **Multi-cloud and Hybrid Deployments**: Enabling seamless deployment and management of serverless applications across multiple cloud providers (multi-cloud) or integrating serverless with traditional on-premises environments (hybrid cloud) is an emerging research area. Future work aims to develop interoperability standards, migration strategies, and tools for managing hybrid serverless deployments.
7. **Performance Optimization**: Research aims to optimize the performance of serverless applications, including reducing overheads introduced by serverless platforms (e.g., invocation overheads, networking latency) and improving the overall efficiency of function execution and resource utilization.
8. **Serverless for Edge Computing**: Exploring the integration of serverless computing with edge computing architectures presents opportunities for research. This includes optimizing function deployment and execution at the network edge to reduce latency and enhance the responsiveness of edge applications.
9. **Serverless for AI and Machine Learning**: Research is exploring the application of serverless computing for AI and machine learning workloads. This includes developing frameworks and optimizations for deploying and scaling machine learning models as serverless functions, enabling efficient inference and training in distributed environments.
10. **Economic and Business Models**: Understanding the economic implications of serverless computing and developing new business models that leverage its benefits are important research directions. This includes studying cost models, pricing strategies, and economic incentives for adopting serverless architectures in various domains.

Overall, future research in serverless computing is focused on advancing the capabilities, efficiency, security, and scalability of serverless architectures to address diverse application requirements and deployment scenarios. As the technology matures, interdisciplinary research efforts will continue to shape the evolution of serverless computing and its broader impact on cloud computing and application development paradigms.

Analysis of the key aspects of serverless computing is provided in Table 7.1. The table summarizes the major aspects of serverless computing based on the key points, examples, and implications.

TABLE 7.1
Comprehensive Analysis of Serverless Computing

Category	Key Points	Examples	Implications
Key Characteristics	No Server Management: Cloud handles infrastructure.	AWS Lambda, Azure Functions.	Developers focus on code, reducing operational complexity.
	Event-Driven: Functions triggered by events like HTTP requests.	File uploads, database updates.	Supports modular and scalable app designs.
	Automatic Scaling: Scales functions based on demand.	Real-time data processing, web apps.	Ensures apps handle varying traffic without manual intervention.
	Pay-Per-Use Billing: Charges based on function execution time.	API services, image processing.	Cost-effective for variable workloads, no idle server costs.
	Stateless Execution: Functions do not maintain state between runs.	Data processing jobs, notification services.	External storage needed for persistent data.
Benefits	Reduced Operational Complexity: No infrastructure management.	Web apps, microservices.	Faster development cycles, easier deployments.
	Auto-Scaling and High Availability: Scales automatically as needed.	E-commerce platforms, IoT.	Ensures reliability and performance under load.
	Cost Efficiency: Only pay for actual resource use.	Mobile backends, event-driven systems.	Reduces cost compared to paying for reserved resources.
	Increased Developer Productivity: Focus on code, not infrastructure.	SaaS applications, API backends.	Faster delivery of business features, reduced time-to-market.
Challenges	Cold Start Latency: Delay when functions start after idle.	Serverless APIs, webhooks.	Impacts performance for real-time apps, requires optimization.
	Vendor Lock-In: Dependency on specific cloud services.	AWS, Google Cloud.	Difficult to migrate to other providers or on-prem solutions.
	Limits on Execution Time and Resources: Constraints on function size and duration.	Long-running tasks, heavy computation.	Not suitable for tasks needing extended runtime or large resources.
	Monitoring and Debugging: Hard to track and debug functions.	Event-driven services, batch jobs.	Requires specialized tools for visibility and troubleshooting.
Future Research	Cold Start Reduction: Minimizing latency in serverless environments.	Real-time systems, mobile apps.	Improves responsiveness for time-sensitive applications.

TABLE 7.1
(Continued)

Category	Key Points	Examples	Implications
	Multi-cloud and Hybrid Deployments: Support for diverse environments.	Large-scale enterprise systems.	Facilitates flexibility and reduces vendor lock-in.
	Security Enhancements: Addressing new security challenges.	Financial apps, health data processing.	Ensures secure, compliant handling of sensitive data.
	Serverless for AI/ML: Integrating serverless with AI workflows.	AI inference, model training.	Allows scalable AI applications without infrastructure concerns.

7.3 EDGE COMPUTING

Edge computing refers to the paradigm of processing data closer to where it is generated rather than relying on a centralized data-processing warehouse or cloud. This approach aims to reduce latency and bandwidth usage by performing computation and data storage closer to the source of data generation. Some of the common pros/cons of edge computing are listed in Figure 7.2.

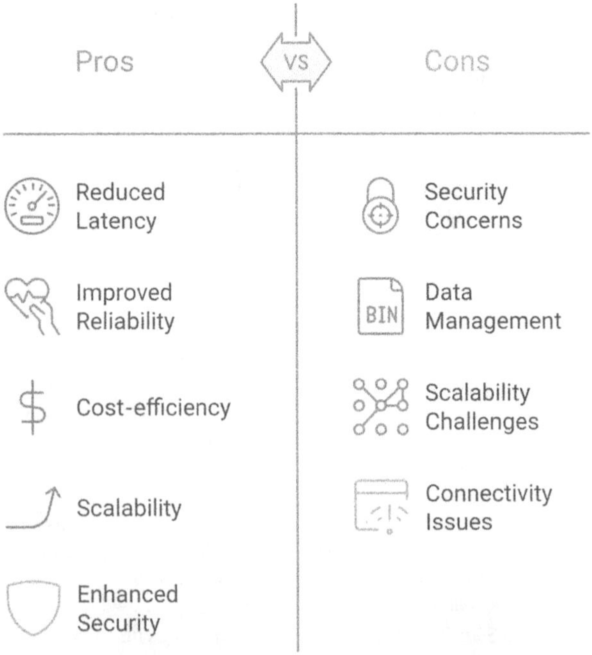

FIGURE 7.2 General pros/cons of edge computing.

7.3.1 Key Characteristics

Edge computing is characterized by several key features that distinguish it from traditional centralized computing models [5]:

1. **Proximity to Data Source**: Edge computing places computational resources close to where data is generated, whether it's within a factory floor, a vehicle, a smart city sensor, or a retail store. This proximity minimizes latency and reduces the time it takes for data to travel between the source and the processing unit.
2. **Decentralization**: Unlike centralized cloud computing, which relies on a few data centers for processing and storage, edge computing distributes these functions across a network of edge devices. This decentralization improves reliability and ensures that applications can continue to operate even if connectivity to the cloud is disrupted.
3. **Real-Time Processing**: Edge computing enables real-time data processing and analytics at the edge devices themselves. This capability is crucial for applications that require immediate decision-making and response, such as autonomous vehicles, remote monitoring, and industrial automation.
4. **Bandwidth Efficiency**: By processing data locally, edge computing reduces the amount of data that needs to be transmitted over the network to centralized data centers or the cloud. This optimization minimizes bandwidth usage and helps in managing network congestion.
5. **Scalability**: Edge computing supports scalable deployments across distributed locations. It allows organizations to easily add new edge devices or scale existing infrastructure to accommodate growing data volumes and processing needs.
6. **Security and Privacy**: Edge computing enhances data security and privacy by processing sensitive information locally rather than transmitting it across potentially insecure networks to centralized data centers. This approach reduces the risk of data breaches and ensures compliance with privacy regulations.
7. **Flexibility**: Edge computing offers flexibility in deploying applications across diverse environments, from industrial settings to remote locations and mobile devices. This flexibility enables organizations to tailor their computing infrastructure to meet specific operational requirements and regulatory constraints.
8. **Support for Offline Operations**: Edge computing allows devices to operate autonomously and continue processing data even when disconnected from the central cloud infrastructure. This capability is particularly beneficial in environments with intermittent or unreliable connectivity.
9. **Cost Efficiency**: Edge computing can lead to cost savings by reducing the need for extensive data transfer and minimizing cloud usage. It also lowers operational costs associated with network bandwidth, storage, and infrastructure maintenance.

In summary, edge computing revolutionizes the way data is processed, stored, and managed by bringing computational capabilities closer to the data source. This paradigm shift enables faster, more reliable, and secure operations, making it a compelling choice for various industries and applications.

7.3.2 Benefits

Edge computing offers several compelling benefits across various industries and applications [6]:

1. **Reduced Latency**: By processing data closer to where it is generated, edge computing significantly reduces the time it takes for data to travel, resulting in lower latency. This is critical for applications requiring real-time responsiveness, such as autonomous vehicles, industrial automation, and augmented reality.
2. **Improved Reliability**: Edge computing enhances system reliability by decentralizing processing capabilities. Devices at the edge can continue to operate independently even if there are issues with connectivity to centralized data centers or the cloud. This resilience is crucial for applications where uptime is essential.
3. **Bandwidth Optimization**: Edge computing minimizes the amount of data that needs to be transmitted to centralized data centers or the cloud. This optimization reduces bandwidth usage and associated costs, making it more feasible to deploy applications in bandwidth-constrained environments.
4. **Enhanced Privacy and Security**: Processing sensitive data locally at the edge reduces the risk of data exposure during transit to centralized locations. This approach enhances data privacy and security compliance, which is particularly important in industries such as healthcare, finance, and government.
5. **Scalability**: Edge computing supports scalable deployments across distributed locations. This scalability is beneficial for applications involving a large number of devices or sensors spread over wide geographical areas, such as smart cities and industrial IoT.
6. **Real-Time Insights**: Edge computing enables real-time data processing and analytics at the point of origin. This capability allows organizations to derive actionable insights faster, leading to more informed decision-making and operational efficiencies.
7. **Support for Offline Operations**: Edge computing enables devices to continue functioning and processing data even when disconnected from the central cloud infrastructure. This is advantageous in remote or mobile environments where consistent connectivity may not be guaranteed.
8. **Cost Efficiency**: By reducing the need for extensive data transfer and minimizing cloud usage, edge computing can lead to cost savings in terms of network bandwidth, storage, and infrastructure maintenance.

Overall, edge computing offers a versatile solution to the challenges posed by centralized data processing models, providing businesses and organizations with the agility, speed, and reliability needed to thrive in today's digital landscape.

7.3.3 Challenges and Issues

While edge computing offers numerous advantages, it also presents several challenges and issues that organizations need to address [7]:

1. **Security Concerns**: Distributing computational resources across numerous edge devices increases the attack surface, making them potentially vulnerable to cyber threats. Securing edge devices against unauthorized access, data breaches, and malware attacks is critical but can be challenging due to diverse device types and locations.
2. **Data Management**: Edge computing generates vast amounts of data that need to be managed effectively. Ensuring data integrity, consistency, and compliance with regulations while processing and storing data at the edge poses significant challenges. Data synchronization between edge devices and central systems also needs careful management.
3. **Scalability**: Managing a large number of distributed edge devices and scaling infrastructure to meet growing demands can be complex. Organizations must plan for scalability in terms of hardware, software, and network capacity to accommodate increasing data volumes and processing requirements.
4. **Interoperability**: Edge computing environments often consist of heterogeneous devices and platforms from different vendors. Achieving seamless interoperability and integration across these devices and systems can be challenging, requiring standardized protocols and interfaces.
5. **Network Connectivity and Latency**: Edge computing relies heavily on network connectivity between edge devices and central data centers or the cloud. Inconsistent or unreliable network connections can impact performance, latency, and the ability to synchronize data between edge and centralized systems.
6. **Deployment and Management Complexity**: Deploying and managing edge computing infrastructure across diverse geographical locations and environments can be complex. It requires specialized skills and tools for monitoring, updating, and maintaining edge devices, especially in remote or harsh environments.
7. **Cost Considerations**: While edge computing can reduce bandwidth costs by processing data locally, the initial investment in edge infrastructure and ongoing maintenance costs can be significant. Organizations need to carefully evaluate the cost-benefit ratio and ROI of deploying edge computing solutions.
8. **Regulatory Compliance**: Ensuring compliance with data protection regulations and privacy laws, especially when processing sensitive data at the edge, presents challenges. Organizations must implement robust data governance practices and security measures to mitigate risks and comply with legal requirements.
9. **Integration with Existing IT Systems**: Integrating edge computing solutions with existing IT systems, applications, and workflows can be complex. Ensuring seamless data flow and interoperability between edge devices and centralized systems is essential for achieving operational efficiency and maximizing the value of edge computing investments.

Addressing these challenges requires careful planning, robust cybersecurity measures, scalable architecture designs, and effective management strategies. Despite these challenges, the potential benefits of edge computing make it a compelling option for organizations seeking to improve agility, performance, and reliability in their digital operations.

7.3.4 Future Research Directions

Future research in edge computing is poised to address several key areas to enhance its capabilities and address emerging challenges [8–10]:

1. **Security and Privacy**: Research will focus on developing robust security mechanisms tailored for edge computing environments. This includes solutions for secure data storage, transmission, access control, and authentication methods suitable for distributed edge devices. Privacy-preserving techniques, such as differential privacy and encrypted processing, will also be explored to protect sensitive data processed at the edge.
2. **Edge AI and Machine Learning**: Advancements in edge AI will enable more sophisticated and autonomous decision-making at the edge. Research will focus on optimizing AI algorithms for edge devices with limited computational resources and energy constraints. Techniques for federated learning and distributed machine learning will be explored to train models collaboratively across edge devices while preserving data privacy.
3. **Edge-to-Cloud Integration**: Future research will aim to optimize the interaction between edge computing nodes and centralized cloud resources. This includes developing efficient data synchronization, workload offloading strategies, and dynamic resource management techniques to seamlessly integrate edge and cloud computing infrastructures.
4. **Autonomous Edge Management**: Research will explore autonomous management and orchestration frameworks for edge computing environments. This includes self-configuration, self-healing, and self-optimization mechanisms to dynamically adapt to changing network conditions, workload demands, and device failures without human intervention.
5. **Edge Computing Architecture and Standards**: Standardization efforts will focus on defining common architectures, protocols, and interfaces for edge computing deployments. This includes developing interoperable solutions that facilitate seamless integration and communication between heterogeneous edge devices and centralized systems.
6. **Edge Computing for IoT and Industry 4.0**: Research will continue to explore the application of edge computing in IoT and Industry 4.0 scenarios. This includes developing edge-enabled solutions for real-time monitoring, predictive maintenance, and optimizing resource utilization in smart factories, smart cities, and connected vehicles.
7. **Edge Computing for Edge-to-Edge and Multi-Access Edge Computing (MEC)**: Research will explore extending edge computing capabilities to support edge-to-edge communication and Multi-Access Edge Computing (MEC). This includes developing frameworks for collaboration and data

sharing between adjacent edge nodes to enhance scalability, fault tolerance, and service continuity.

8. **Energy Efficiency and Sustainability**: Research efforts will focus on optimizing energy consumption in edge computing infrastructures. This includes developing energy-efficient algorithms, hardware architectures, and power management techniques to prolong battery life and reduce carbon footprint in edge deployments.
9. **Edge Computing in Healthcare and Smart Grids**: Research will explore specialized applications of edge computing in sectors such as healthcare and smart grids. This includes developing secure and privacy-preserving healthcare monitoring systems and edge-enabled solutions for real-time energy management and optimization in smart grid infrastructures.
10. **Edge Computing Testbeds and Experimental Platforms**: Future research will emphasize the development of comprehensive testbeds and experimental platforms for evaluating edge computing solutions in real-world scenarios. This includes creating simulation environments and validation frameworks to assess performance, scalability, reliability, and security aspects of edge deployments.

Overall, future research in edge computing will focus on advancing technology capabilities, addressing scalability and security challenges, fostering interoperability, and exploring new application domains to unlock the full potential of decentralized computing at the edge of the network.

A comprehensive analysis of edge computing is provided in Table 7.2. The table combines all key characteristics, benefits, challenges, and future research directions of edge computing into one concise format.

TABLE 7.2
Comprehensive Analysis of Edge Computing

Category	Key Points	Examples	Implications
Key Characteristics	Proximity to Data: Processes data closer to its source.	Smart cities, factories	Reduced latency, faster decision-making.
	Decentralization: Distributed processing across devices.	Industrial IoT, smart homes	Increased reliability, continuous operation.
	Real-Time Processing: Enables immediate data analysis at the edge.	Autonomous vehicles, robotics	Immediate responses, essential for safety and efficiency.
	Bandwidth Efficiency: Local processing reduces data transfer needs.	Video streaming, retail IoT	Reduced bandwidth usage, lower costs.
	Security and Privacy: Local processing enhances data security.	Healthcare apps, financial systems	Improved data security, better privacy compliance.
	Support for Offline Operations: Devices function without constant cloud access.	Remote monitoring, fleet management	Continuous operation even in areas with no connectivity.

TABLE 7.2
(Continued)

Category	Key Points	Examples	Implications
Benefits	Reduced Latency: Local data processing speeds up response time.	Autonomous vehicles, AR	Essential for real-time applications.
	Improved Reliability: Devices continue working even with cloud outages.	Industrial IoT, remote monitoring	Ensures uninterrupted service.
	Cost Efficiency: Reduces cloud storage and data transfer costs.	Retail analytics, IoT devices	Lowers operational costs.
	Scalability: Supports large-scale, distributed systems.	Smart cities, global IoT networks	Easy to scale operations as needed.
Challenges	Security Concerns: More edge devices increase attack surface.	Smart homes, industrial IoT	Requires robust security measures.
	Data Management: Managing large amounts of data from multiple sources.	IoT devices, environmental sensors	Complex data synchronization and integrity issues.
	Scalability: Managing growth in distributed devices can be challenging.	Smart city infrastructure, large sensor networks	Complex scaling, requires careful planning.
	Connectivity Issues: Reliant on stable networks for synchronization.	Remote monitoring, fleet management	Network issues can impact performance and reliability.
Future Directions	Security and Privacy: Developing secure solutions for edge environments.	Healthcare, finance	Focus on privacy and secure data processing.
	Edge AI: Advancing AI for limited resource devices.	Federated learning, real-time decision-making	Enables autonomous decision-making at the edge.
	Edge-to-Cloud Integration: Optimizing hybrid systems.	Smart cities, connected vehicles	Enhances cloud-edge coordination.
	Energy Efficiency: Researching energy-efficient edge systems.	Smart grids, IoT devices	Focus on sustainable, energy-efficient solutions.

7.4 FOG COMPUTING

Fog computing is a decentralized computing infrastructure that extends cloud computing to the edge of the network, bringing data, compute, storage, and applications closer to where data is created and acted upon. This approach is designed to handle the increasing volume of data generated by IoT devices and other edge devices, reducing latency and improving efficiency. Fog computing nodes, often referred to as fog

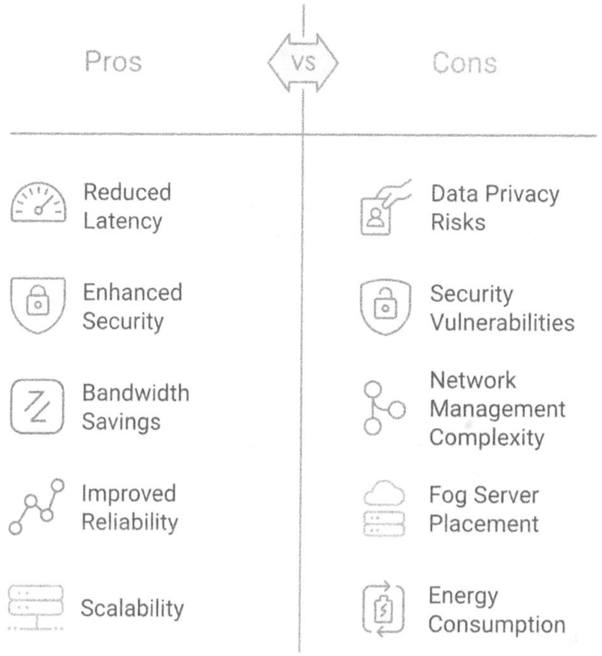

FIGURE 7.3 General pros/cons of fog computing.

devices, perform local processing and analysis, minimizing the need to send raw data to the cloud for processing. This strategy not only conserves bandwidth but also enhances security and privacy by keeping sensitive data closer to its source. Applications of fog computing include real-time monitoring and analysis in industries such as healthcare, transportation, and energy management, where low latency and local processing are crucial. Some of the common pros/cons of fog computing are listed in Figure 7.3.

7.4.1 Key Characteristics

The key characteristics of fog computing are [11]:

1. **Geographical Distribution**: Fog computing nodes are distributed geographically, unlike the centralized nature of cloud computing.
2. **Decentralization**: Fog computing is a decentralized architecture, with data processing and storage happening closer to the edge devices rather than in centralized cloud data centers.
3. **Heterogeneity**: Fog computing integrates a variety of devices and technologies, including sensors, gateways, routers, and other edge devices.
4. **Real-Time Interaction**: Fog computing enables real-time data processing and response, as opposed to the batch processing common in cloud computing.
5. **Low Latency**: By processing data closer to the edge, fog computing can reduce latency compared to sending all data to the cloud.

6. **Mobility**: Fog computing can support mobile devices and applications through techniques such as the Locator/ID Separation Protocol (LISP).
7. **Scalability and Agility**: Fog computing clusters can adapt to network variations, compute elasticity, and changes in data load.

In summary, the key characteristics of fog computing are its distributed, decentralized, and heterogeneous nature, which enables real-time interaction, low latency, and mobility, making it well-suited for applications that require fast response times and localized data processing.

7.4.2 Benefits

Here are the key benefits of fog computing [12]:

1. **Reduced Latency**: Fog computing reduces latency by processing data closer to the source, rather than sending it all the way to the cloud. This is critical for time-sensitive applications such as self-driving cars, where sensor data needs to be analyzed and acted upon instantly.
2. **Enhanced Security**: Fog nodes can be secured using the same techniques as in an IT environment. Data is evaluated locally rather than sent to the cloud, providing better privacy protection. Fog computing's decentralized nature also makes it more challenging to hack or disrupt.
3. **Bandwidth Savings**: By processing selected data locally instead of sending it all to the cloud, fog computing can significantly reduce network bandwidth usage. This leads to lower operational costs.
4. **Improved Reliability**: Fog nodes are mobile and can withstand harsh environments, allowing them to be deployed in remote locations. They can continue operating even if the connection to the cloud is lost.
5. **Scalability**: Fog computing allows services to be provided over a large geographical area to many devices. New fog nodes can easily join the network as needed.
6. **Flexibility**: Fog computing provides a flexible platform that can integrate various hardware and software components. It can interface with both other fog nodes and cloud solutions.

In summary, fog computing brings the benefits of the cloud closer to the edge of the network, reducing latency, improving security and reliability, and enabling new applications that require real-time analytics. However, it also introduces challenges around data consistency, scheduling, and power consumption.

7.4.3 Challenges and Issues

The key research challenges and issues in fog computing include [13]:

1. **Data Privacy**: As fog computing involves deploying fog nodes at the edge of the Internet, more end users have access to sensitive data collected by these nodes. This increases the risk of data breaches and makes fog computing a target for cyberattacks.

2. **Security**: One of the critical security risks in fog computing is the potential for malicious users to access data stored in fog nodes by using fake IP addresses, as fog computing requires authentication of devices at different gateways. This necessitates the use of intrusion detection systems at every layer of the platform.
3. **Network Management**: Without software-defined networking (SDN) and network function virtualization (NFV) techniques, managing the fog nodes, network, and connections between nodes is a complex task, as fog computing involves heterogeneous devices.
4. **Positioning of Fog Servers**: Optimizing the placement of fog servers requires analyzing the workload of each node to ensure efficient service delivery and lower maintenance costs.
5. **Energy Consumption**: Fog computing environments with a large number of fog nodes tend to have high energy consumption, which is a significant challenge.
6. **Latency, Location Awareness, Geo-distribution, and Security**: These are some of the key issues that led to the introduction of fog computing as an extension to cloud computing.
7. **Resource Management, Security, Latency, Energy Usage, and Traffic Modeling**: Developing fog computing applications and implementing fog services in these areas have become more popular in recent years.

In summary, the main research challenges in fog computing revolve around data privacy, security, network management, server placement, and energy efficiency, as well as addressing issues such as latency, location awareness, and geo-distribution.

7.4.4 Future Research Directions

The key future research directions in fog computing based on the provided search results are [14,15]:

1. **Addressing Technical Challenges**: The search results highlight several technical challenges that need to be addressed to enable widespread adoption of fog computing, including developing robust fog computing frameworks, simulators, and resource management strategies.
2. **Addressing Non-Technical Challenges**: The search results also identify non-technical challenges that hinder fog computing adoption, such as establishing clear business cases and economic models for fog computing.
3. **Emerging Trends and Technologies**: The search results suggest exploring the integration of fog computing with emerging technologies such as federated learning to enable distributed learning at the edge.
4. **Realizing Real-Time IoT Applications**: A key future direction is to enable the deployment of large-scale, real-world fog computing networks that can support latency-sensitive and privacy-preserving IoT applications, moving beyond just pilot studies and small-scale testbeds.

In summary, the future research in fog computing should focus on addressing the technical, non-technical, and economic challenges, as well as exploring the integration of fog computing with emerging technologies to enable the widespread deployment of fog-powered IoT applications.

Table 7.3 encapsulates the key points, examples, and implications of fog computing across various categories including characteristics, benefits, challenges, and future research directions.

TABLE 7.3
Comprehensive Analysis of Fog Computing

Category	Key Points	Examples	Implications
Key Characteristics	Geographical Distribution: Fog nodes are distributed geographically.	Smart cities, transportation systems	Better performance in distributed networks.
	Decentralization: Data processing happens closer to edge devices, not centralized.	IoT, industrial monitoring	Reduces reliance on cloud, improves resilience.
	Heterogeneity: Fog integrates multiple devices (sensors, routers, etc.).	Smart homes, automated factories	Wide application support with diverse tech.
	Real-Time Interaction: Enables real-time processing.	Autonomous vehicles, real-time healthcare monitoring	Essential for time-sensitive operations.
	Low Latency: Local processing reduces data travel time.	Self-driving cars, remote patient monitoring	Crucial for fast decision-making and safety.
	Mobility: Supports mobile devices with techniques like LISP.	Mobile applications, smart transport	Enables mobility support in fog infrastructure.
	Scalability and Agility: Fog can scale across large areas and adapt to changes.	Global IoT networks, smart cities	Supports growing systems with dynamic demands.
Benefits	Reduced Latency: Local data processing reduces time delays.	Self-driving cars, industrial robots	Critical for applications requiring immediate responses.
	Enhanced Security: Data is processed locally, reducing risk of breaches.	Healthcare, finance	Strengthens privacy and reduces attack surface.
	Bandwidth Savings: Reduces the need for constant cloud communication.	Smart homes, retail analytics	Cuts costs and optimizes network traffic.

TABLE 7.3
(Continued)

Category	Key Points	Examples	Implications
	Improved Reliability: Fog nodes can operate independently, even during cloud outages.	Remote mining, agriculture	Increases system reliability, especially in harsh environments.
	Scalability: Easily scale the number of nodes across regions.	Large IoT networks, city-wide sensors	Facilitates widespread, scalable IoT deployment.
	Flexibility: Integrates different hardware and software components.	Industrial automation, smart cities	Adapts to diverse environments and needs.
Challenges	Data Privacy: Increased access to sensitive data raises security risks.	Healthcare, surveillance systems	Demands robust security protocols to prevent breaches.
	Security: Vulnerability to attacks due to multiple distributed nodes.	Edge devices, IoT networks	Requires advanced security measures across all layers.
	Network Management: Managing complex network of heterogeneous devices can be difficult.	Multi-device IoT systems, smart homes	Challenges in maintaining a consistent, secure network.
	Fog Server Placement: Optimizing where to place servers to balance workload.	Data centers, urban network distribution	Critical for cost-effective and efficient service delivery.
	Energy Consumption: High number of nodes increases energy usage.	Smart grid, industrial applications	Needs strategies for power-efficient operation.
Future Research	Technical Challenges: Development of robust frameworks, simulators, and resource management strategies.	Smart transportation, smart cities	Key to supporting large-scale, real-world fog systems.
	Non-Technical Challenges: Establishing clear business models for fog computing.	Business analytics, IoT integrations	Important for economic feasibility and adoption.
	Emerging Technologies: Integration with federated learning and real-time IoT applications.	Edge AI, privacy-preserving IoT applications	Advances in IoT and AI depend on fog computing.
	Real-Time IoT Applications: Support for large-scale, real-world fog IoT deployments.	Healthcare monitoring, industrial automation	Vital for making fog computing suitable for large-scale IoT.

7.5 MULTI-CLOUD AND HYBRID CLOUD

Multi-cloud and hybrid cloud are two distinct cloud computing strategies, although they share some similarities. A multi-cloud approach involves using multiple public cloud services from different providers, such as AWS, Azure, and Google Cloud, for various applications and workloads. This allows organizations to leverage the unique strengths of each cloud platform and avoid vendor lock-in. In contrast, a hybrid cloud combines a private cloud (either on-premises or hosted by a third party) with at least one public cloud service. Hybrid cloud provides the control and security of a private cloud with the flexibility and scalability of public cloud resources. While a multi-cloud deployment can also include a private cloud, making it a hybrid multi-cloud, the key difference is that a hybrid cloud always includes a private cloud component, whereas a multi-cloud consists solely of public cloud services from multiple providers.

7.5.1 Key Characteristics

The key characteristics of multi-cloud and hybrid cloud include [16]:

Multi-cloud:

1. Uses multiple public cloud services (e.g., AWS, Azure, Google Cloud) without connecting them
2. Allows organizations to pick the best cloud services for specific workloads and applications
3. Provides flexibility, redundancy, and avoids vendor lock-in
4. Requires managing multiple cloud providers and tools, which can increase complexity
5. Does not involve a private cloud component

Hybrid Cloud:

1. Combines a private cloud (on-premises or hosted) with one or more public cloud services
2. Allows organizations to leverage the benefits of both private and public clouds
3. Provides more control and security over sensitive data in the private cloud, while benefiting from the scalability and flexibility of public clouds
4. Requires integrating and orchestrating the private and public cloud components, which can be technically challenging
5. Typically more expensive than a pure public cloud approach due to the need to maintain private cloud infrastructure
6. Provides a more unified and interconnected cloud environment compared to multi-cloud

In summary, multi-cloud focuses on using multiple public cloud providers, while hybrid cloud combines private and public cloud resources. Both approaches offer benefits but have different architectural and operational characteristics.

7.5.2 Benefits

Both multi-cloud and hybrid cloud strategies offer distinct benefits to organizations, each addressing different needs and challenges in cloud computing [17, 18].

Benefits of Multi-cloud

1. **Flexibility and Choice**: Organizations can choose from multiple cloud providers, allowing them to select the best service for each workload based on factors such as speed, performance, reliability, geographical location, and security and compliance requirements.
2. **Avoiding Vendor Lock-In**: By not relying on a single provider, multi-cloud reduces the risk of being locked into a specific vendor's ecosystem, enabling businesses to deploy the latest best-of-breed solutions and avoid vendor-specific limitations.
3. **Cost Efficiency**: Public cloud services offer less overhead and the ability to scale up or down according to needs, potentially lowering the total cost of ownership (TCO) while taking advantage of the best combination of pricing and performance across different providers.
4. **Innovative Technology**: Multi-cloud enables organizations to leverage new technologies as they emerge, improving their own offerings without being limited to the choices offered by a single-cloud provider.
5. **Advanced Security and Regulatory Compliance**: It allows for the deployment and scaling of workloads while implementing security policies and compliance technologies consistently across all workloads, regardless of service, vendor, or environment.
6. **Increased Reliability and Redundancy**: Multi-cloud reduces the risk of a single point of failure, ensuring that an outage in one cloud does not impact services in other clouds. This also provides better failover options and enhanced disaster recovery.
7. **Better Latency and Global Reach**: By extending networks to multiple cloud providers, organizations can develop connections that improve response time and user experience, especially for global organizations.
8. **Meeting Compliance Requirements**: It enables organizations to deliver specific data storage requirements without having to build and manage their own on-premises data centers.

Benefits of Hybrid Cloud

1. **Flexibility and Scalability**: Hybrid clouds combine the scalability and flexibility of cloud computing with the control and security of on-premises infrastructure, allowing for a balance between the benefits of cloud computing and the need to maintain control over certain aspects of infrastructure.
2. **Improved Security**: By keeping sensitive data on-premises, hybrid clouds provide greater control and security over sensitive data, which is especially important for organizations handling sensitive information.
3. **Reduced Complexity**: Hybrid clouds often use common virtualization layers, such as VMware, to simplify workload migration and enable the use

of common tools across both private and public cloud platforms, reducing complexity and the need for multiple management tools.

4. **Enhanced Disaster Recovery**: Hybrid clouds can provide better disaster recovery options by allowing for the replication of data and applications between on-premises and cloud environments, ensuring business continuity in case of outages.
5. **Cost Efficiency**: Hybrid clouds can help organizations reduce costs by leveraging the public cloud for scalable and flexible services while keeping critical workloads on-premises for better control and security.

Summary

- Multi-cloud: Offers flexibility, choice, cost efficiency, and improved reliability by leveraging multiple cloud providers. It is ideal for organizations looking to avoid vendor lock-in and take advantage of the best features of different cloud services.
- Hybrid Cloud: Combines the scalability and flexibility of cloud computing with the control and security of on-premises infrastructure. It is suitable for organizations needing to maintain control over sensitive data and ensuring business continuity through disaster recovery.

Both strategies have their own strengths and can be used in different scenarios depending on the organization's specific needs and goals.

7.5.3 Challenges and Issues

The key challenges and issues in managing multi-cloud and hybrid cloud environments are discussed below [16–18]:

Architectural Complexity

- Migrating to multi-cloud requires substantial changes to existing architecture, often needing to redesign applications to run in the new cloud environment.
- Increased complexity usually requires additional time and expenses to implement correctly, spanning areas such as networking, automation, data services, recoverability, and security.

Cloud Sprawl and Costs

- Multi-cloud can lead to cloud sprawl with resources and tools spread across multiple providers.
- Costs can increase due to retaining individuals with specific knowledge about each cloud provider.

Data Protection and Compliance

- Regulations such as GDPR hold organizations responsible for data governance across multiple cloud providers.
- Compliance and preparing for audits are major challenges, with 76% of organizations finding it moderately to maximally challenging.

Visibility and Monitoring

- 39% of organizations are concerned about visibility into resources across multi-cloud environments.
- Manually monitoring disparate tools can lead to more frustrations than resolutions.

Networking and Integration

- Network integration is a key challenge, with companies often addressing tricky issues involving technology, protocols, and standards after the hybrid cloud is already running.
- Integrating the public cloud with current on-premises infrastructure is a concern for 50% of organizations.

Lack of Expertise

- 73% of cloud users cite lack of expertise as a challenge for security management.
- 32% report lack of expertise and 25% lack of staff to manage their cloud environments.

In summary, the key challenges revolve around the increased complexity, cost, security, and operational overhead of managing data, applications and infrastructure across multiple cloud providers and on-premises systems. Overcoming these challenges requires a comprehensive strategy, the right tools, and dedicated cloud expertise.

7.5.4 Future Research Directions

Multi-cloud and hybrid cloud architectures represent the future of cloud computing, offering unparalleled flexibility, scalability, and resilience for businesses of all sizes. As organizations continue to embrace these cloud strategies, several key research directions are emerging [19–20]:

1. **Machine Learning and Multi-cloud Computing**: The study then explores the nuances of hybrid cloud architectures and future directions for machine learning and multi-cloud computing research. Integrating machine learning capabilities into multi-cloud environments can enable intelligent workload placement, automated scaling, and optimization of resource utilization across multiple cloud providers.
2. **Hybrid Cloud Security and Compliance**: Ensuring the security and privacy of data in hybrid cloud environments is crucial to maintain trust with customers and meet regulatory requirements. Future research should focus on developing comprehensive strategies encompassing regulatory compliance, emerging technologies, and best practices for securing hybrid cloud environments. This includes leveraging encryption, access controls, and monitoring tools to protect sensitive data.
3. **Serverless Computing in Multi-cloud**: Serverless computing, which abstracts infrastructure management from developers, presents numerous advantages for modern business requirements. Exploring the integration of

serverless architectures with multi-cloud strategies can enable organizations to take full advantage of the flexibility and cost-efficiency offered by both approaches. Future research should investigate the challenges and best practices for deploying serverless functions across multiple cloud providers.

4. **Containerization and Orchestration in Hybrid Cloud**: When looking at the future of cloud computing, containerization and orchestration technologies play a key role in enabling seamless deployment and management of applications across hybrid cloud environments. Future research should focus on developing advanced container orchestration platforms that can manage and optimize workloads across on-premises infrastructure and multiple public clouds.
5. **Data Governance and Privacy in Multi-cloud**: With the increasing adoption of multi-cloud strategies, concerns regarding data governance and privacy have become critically important. Future research should explore innovative approaches to ensure the security and privacy of data in multi-cloud environments, including the use of emerging technologies such as blockchain and homomorphic encryption to protect data at rest and in transit across multiple cloud providers.

By addressing these research directions, the scientific community can help organizations fully harness the potential of multi-cloud and hybrid cloud architectures to drive innovation, improve efficiency, and enhance their competitive advantage in the rapidly evolving cloud computing landscape.

Table 7.4 covers the key characteristics, benefits, challenges, and future research directions of multi-cloud and hybrid cloud computing strategies.

TABLE 7.4
Comprehensive Analysis of Fog Computing

Category	Key Points	Examples	Implications
Key Characteristics	Multi-cloud: Uses multiple public cloud providers without connecting them.	AWS, Azure, Google Cloud	Flexibility, avoids vendor lock-in, and offers redundancy.
	Hybrid Cloud: Combines private cloud with at least one public cloud.	Private cloud + AWS or Azure	Balances control and security with flexibility and scalability.
	Multi-cloud Flexibility: Allows selecting the best services for specific workloads.	Selecting AWS for storage, Azure for analytics	Tailor services based on performance, cost, and geographical needs.
	Hybrid Cloud Control: Provides control over sensitive data via private cloud.	Sensitive data in on-premises private cloud	More secure data management, especially for compliance.
	Integration Complexity: Hybrid cloud requires integrating and orchestrating both public and private clouds.	Connecting on-prem systems with cloud platforms	Integration is technically complex but creates a unified environment.

TABLE 7.4
(Continued)

Category	Key Points	Examples	Implications
Multi-cloud Benefits	Flexibility and Choice: Choose the best provider for each workload.	Choosing best-fit services from multiple clouds	Avoids vendor lock-in, improves performance and cost efficiency.
	Avoiding Vendor Lock-In: Reduces reliance on a single-cloud provider.	Using AWS for computing, Azure for data storage	Freedom to adapt to changing technologies and offerings.
	Cost Efficiency: Public cloud scalability allows cost savings based on demand.	Scaling services on AWS or Google Cloud	Lowers Total Cost of Ownership (TCO) while optimizing resources.
	Advanced Security: Enables consistent security policies across multiple clouds.	Applying uniform security across AWS and Azure	Ensures compliance across multiple platforms.
	Increased Reliability: Multi-cloud offers redundancy and disaster recovery options.	Using both AWS and Azure to handle outages	Avoids single point of failure, improves service continuity.
	Better Latency and Global Reach: Global networks of cloud providers improve response time.	Global access to apps via multiple cloud providers	Enhances global reach and user experience.
	Meeting Compliance Requirements: Allows specific data storage requirements.	Storing data in compliant regions across providers	Ensures regulatory compliance without the need for on-premises data centers.
Hybrid Cloud Benefits	Flexibility and Scalability: Balances cloud scalability with on-premises control.	Scaling operations with AWS while keeping data private	Provides a hybrid approach to scalability and control.
	Improved Security: Keeps sensitive data within the private cloud for higher control.	Healthcare, financial data in private cloud	Enhances security and reduces risk for sensitive data.
	Reduced Complexity: Simplifies migration with common virtualization tools.	VMware for hybrid deployment	Eases management and migration across platforms.
	Enhanced Disaster Recovery: Replicates data between on-premises and cloud environments for better recovery.	Replicating critical data between private cloud and AWS	Ensures business continuity in case of disruptions.
	Cost Efficiency: Leverages public cloud for flexibility while keeping critical workloads on-premises.	Storing large files in the cloud, keeping sensitive on-prem	Balances cost savings and control.

TABLE 7.4
(Continued)

Category	Key Points	Examples	Implications
Challenges	Architectural Complexity: Migrating or integrating multi-cloud and hybrid cloud requires substantial changes.	Redesigning applications for multi-cloud environments	Increases migration complexity and operational overhead.
	Cloud Sprawl and Costs: Resources spread across multiple clouds can lead to inefficiencies and high costs.	Managing services across AWS, Azure, and Google Cloud	Requires careful management to avoid inefficiencies.
	Data Protection and Compliance: Ensuring data governance across multiple clouds can be challenging.	GDPR compliance across multiple cloud platforms	Regulatory requirements add complexity to multi-cloud environments.
	Visibility and Monitoring: Difficulty in monitoring resources across multiple cloud environments.	Tracking assets across AWS, Google Cloud, and Azure	Demands advanced monitoring and reporting systems.
	Networking and Integration: Integration of on-prem infrastructure with public clouds is technically difficult.	Migrating legacy systems to the cloud	Requires expertise in cloud networking and protocol handling.
	Lack of Expertise: Many organizations face a lack of cloud-specific expertise.	Lack of staff for multi-cloud management	Increases need for skilled personnel for cloud management.
Future Research	Machine Learning and Multi-cloud: Research into optimizing resource allocation and scaling across clouds.	Automated workload placement, optimization algorithms	Improves performance and cost-efficiency using ML techniques.
	Hybrid Cloud Security and Compliance: Future work on securing hybrid environments with advanced technologies.	Using encryption, access controls, and monitoring tools	Ensures that hybrid environments are secure and comply with regulations.
	Serverless Computing in Multi-cloud: Investigating serverless functions across multiple cloud providers.	Deploying serverless functions in AWS and Azure	Makes use of both multi-cloud flexibility and serverless efficiency.
	Containerization and Orchestration in Hybrid Cloud: Enhancing management of containerized apps across hybrid clouds.	Kubernetes on-prem and in the cloud	Simplifies hybrid cloud deployment with container orchestration.
	Data Governance and Privacy in Multi-cloud: Ensuring data protection with emerging technologies.	Blockchain for secure data across clouds	Protects data across multiple providers with next-gen privacy tech.

7.6 CONTAINERS AND KUBERNETES

Kubernetes is an open-source container orchestration platform that automates the deployment, scaling, and management of containerized applications [21]. It provides a way to manage and scale containers across multiple hosts, ensuring high availability and fault tolerance. Kubernetes containers are lightweight, portable, and can share the same operating system, making them more efficient than traditional virtual machines. Each Kubernetes container runs in a pod, which is the smallest deployable unit in the Kubernetes ecosystem. Pods can contain one or more containers that share the same network and storage resources. Kubernetes manages the lifecycle of these pods, automatically scaling them up or down based on demand and ensuring that the desired state of the application is maintained. By using Kubernetes, developers can focus on building and deploying their applications, while the platform handles the complexities of container orchestration.

7.6.1 Key Characteristics

The key characteristics of containers and Kubernetes are as follows:

Containers

1. Containers package an application with all the necessary dependencies, libraries, and configuration files it needs to run.
2. Containers are designed to be stateless and immutable – you should not change the code of a container that is already running.
3. Containers decouple applications from the underlying host infrastructure, making deployment easier in different cloud or OS environments.
4. Each container is repeatable and standardized, with dependencies included to ensure the same behavior wherever it runs.

Kubernetes

1. Kubernetes is an open-source platform for automating deployment, scaling, and management of containerized applications.
2. It groups containers that make up an application into logical units for easy management and discovery.
3. Kubernetes provides features such as service discovery, load balancing, storage orchestration, automated rollouts and rollbacks, self-healing, and secret management.
4. It automatically places containers based on their resource requirements and constraints to optimize utilization.
5. Kubernetes is designed for extensibility, allowing you to add features to the cluster without changing upstream source code.
6. It provides high availability and fault tolerance through automated failover, multi-zone/region deployment, and a rich ecosystem of tools and extensions.
7. Kubernetes has comprehensive security features such as RBAC, network policies, and container image scanning.

In summary, containers package applications with dependencies for portability, while Kubernetes orchestrates and manages containers at scale with advanced features for automation, scaling, resilience, and security.

7.6.2 Benefits

The key benefits of using Kubernetes for container orchestration are illustrated below [22]:

1. **Scalability and Elasticity**: Kubernetes provides automatic scaling of containers based on resource utilization, allowing applications to handle increased traffic and demand without manual intervention. It can automatically scale containers up and down to match the workload.
2. **High Availability and Self-Healing**: Kubernetes monitors the health of containers and automatically restarts or replaces failed containers, ensuring high availability of applications. It has built-in self-healing capabilities to maintain the desired state.
3. **Portability and Flexibility**: Kubernetes is a vendor-neutral platform that allows running containerized applications across different cloud providers, on-premises, or in hybrid environments, avoiding vendor lock-in.
4. **Simplified Deployment and Updates**: Kubernetes makes it easy to deploy, update, and roll back applications through declarative configuration files, reducing manual effort and errors.
5. **Cost Optimization**: Kubernetes can help optimize costs by efficiently utilizing infrastructure resources and automatically scaling resources based on demand, avoiding over-provisioning.
6. **Increased DevOps Efficiency**: Kubernetes integrates well with DevOps practices, enabling teams to build, test, and deploy microservices-based applications more efficiently.
7. **Robust Ecosystem and Community**: Kubernetes has a large and active community, providing a wealth of resources, tools, and integrations to extend its functionality.

In summary, Kubernetes provides a powerful and flexible container orchestration platform that enables organizations to deploy and manage containerized applications at scale, with benefits around scalability, availability, portability, deployment, cost optimization, and DevOps efficiency.

7.6.3 Challenges and Issues

The key challenges and issues with containers and Kubernetes include [23]:

1. **Complexity**: Kubernetes environments are highly complex, multi-layered, and dynamic, creating limitations and blind spots for observability and troubleshooting. Comprehensive monitoring and observability solutions are needed to provide full-stack visibility.

2. **Networking**: Large-scale, multi-cloud Kubernetes deployments can introduce challenges with network visibility and interoperability. Traditional network management approaches do not work well in dynamic Kubernetes environments. Solutions such as Container Network Interface (CNI) and service meshes are needed to manage networking.
3. **Observability**: While there are many monitoring tools available, most are narrow in scope. A full-stack observability platform that provides access to logs, traces, and metrics in context is required to effectively identify and resolve issues in Kubernetes.
4. **Cluster Stability**: The ephemeral and dynamic nature of Kubernetes containers creates challenges in maintaining cluster stability. Robust logging, tracing, and monitoring mechanisms are necessary to ensure cluster reliability and prevent failures.
5. **Security**: Securing Kubernetes is complex due to the large attack surface and vulnerabilities introduced by the many APIs and components. Careful configuration and security best practices are critical to protect Kubernetes environments.
6. **Resource Management**: Efficiently managing resources such as CPU and memory across the many containers and workloads in a Kubernetes cluster can be challenging. AI-driven forecasting and capacity planning are needed to optimize resource utilization.
7. **Interoperability**: Enabling interoperability between cloud-native apps running on Kubernetes can be tricky, especially when migrating from development/testing to production environments. Using common APIs, interfaces, and collaborative projects can help address interoperability challenges.
8. **Storage**: Managing storage, especially for on-premises Kubernetes deployments, can be problematic. Leveraging cloud-based persistent storage or solutions like ephemeral and persistent volumes can help overcome storage challenges.

In summary, the complexity, networking, observability, stability, security, resource management, interoperability, and storage challenges of Kubernetes require comprehensive solutions and best practices to effectively deploy and manage containerized applications at scale.

7.6.4 Future Research Directions

According to the bibliometric analysis, some of the key emerging trends and frontiers for future Kubernetes research include [24]:

1. **Automation**: Improving automation capabilities for container deployment, scaling, and management on Kubernetes.
2. **5G**: Exploring the integration of Kubernetes with 5G networks and edge computing.
3. Scalability: Enhancing the scalability of Kubernetes to handle large-scale, distributed container deployments.

4. **Resource Scheduling**: Advancing resource scheduling algorithms and techniques for optimizing container placement and utilization on Kubernetes.
5. **Serverless**: Integrating Kubernetes with serverless computing frameworks and technologies.
6. **Service Mesh**: Investigating the role of service mesh architectures in Kubernetes-based applications.
7. **Blockchain**: Exploring the use of blockchain technologies in conjunction with Kubernetes for improved security and decentralization.

Overall, the future of Kubernetes appears promising, with the platform expected to continue evolving and expanding to meet the growing demands of container-based applications and distributed computing environments. Researchers and practitioners should focus on addressing the emerging trends and frontiers identified in the search results to drive further advancements in the Kubernetes ecosystem.

Table 7.5 summarizes the key characteristics, benefits, challenges, and future research directions related to Kubernetes and Container orchestration.

TABLE 7.5
Comprehensive Analysis of Kubernetes and Container

Category	Key Points	Examples	Implications
Key Characteristics	Containers: Package applications with dependencies to ensure portability across different environments.	Docker containers, Kubernetes pods	Easier deployment and consistency across diverse environments.
	Containers are Stateless and Immutable: Once running, containers should not change.	Immutable Docker containers	Ensures consistency, reduces issues from manual changes.
	Kubernetes: Open-source platform that automates deployment, scaling, and management of containerized apps.	Kubernetes clusters managing containers at scale	Streamlines orchestration and scaling of containerized applications.
	Pod Management: Containers are grouped into pods, which are the smallest deployable units in Kubernetes.	Pods containing multiple containers	Simplifies the management and scaling of containers.
	Extensibility: Kubernetes is designed to be extensible, allowing feature additions without altering the core.	Adding tools like Helm or custom controllers	Supports customization and evolution of Kubernetes clusters.
	High Availability and Fault Tolerance: Automated failover and multi-zone deployments ensure application uptime.	Multi-zone/region Kubernetes clusters	Increases reliability and resilience.

TABLE 7.5
(Continued)

Category	Key Points	Examples	Implications
Benefits	Scalability and Elasticity: Kubernetes can scale containers automatically based on workload demands.	Auto-scaling of container workloads	Handles increased demand efficiently without manual intervention.
	High Availability and Self-Healing: Kubernetes monitors container health and automatically replaces failed ones.	Restarting failed containers, scaling based on demand	Ensures consistent availability and application reliability.
	Portability and Flexibility: Kubernetes runs containers across any cloud or on-premises setup, avoiding vendor lock-in.	Deploying Kubernetes on AWS, Azure, or on-prem	Increases flexibility and vendor independence.
	Simplified Deployment and Updates: Declarative configuration simplifies deploying and updating applications.	Using YAML configuration files to deploy apps	Reduces errors, improves consistency, and simplifies deployment.
	Cost Optimization: Kubernetes optimizes resource usage and scaling, preventing over-provisioning of resources.	Scaling apps up and down based on load	Helps optimize infrastructure costs.
	DevOps Efficiency: Kubernetes integrates well with DevOps practices to improve development speed and reliability.	Automating microservice deployment pipelines	Enhances collaboration between development and operations teams.
	Robust Ecosystem: Kubernetes has a thriving community and rich ecosystem for extended functionality.	Tools like Helm, Prometheus, and Istio	Provides vast resources for additional tools and support.
Challenges	Complexity: Kubernetes environments are dynamic and multi-layered, creating complexities in observability.	Difficulty in troubleshooting in large Kubernetes setups	Requires advanced monitoring solutions for full-stack visibility.
	Networking: Multi-cloud deployments face network visibility and interoperability challenges.	Container Network Interface (CNI), service meshes	Solutions needed for effective network management in dynamic environments.
	Observability: Most monitoring tools are narrow, and comprehensive observability is essential for resolving issues.	Using monitoring tools like Prometheus and Grafana	Increases the need for a full-stack observability platform.

TABLE 7.5
(Continued)

Category	Key Points	Examples	Implications
	Cluster Stability: The ephemeral nature of containers can challenge the stability of clusters.	Containers starting and stopping frequently	Requires strong logging, tracing, and monitoring mechanisms.
	Security: Kubernetes has a large attack surface with many components and APIs, making it vulnerable to threats.	Role-Based Access Control (RBAC), Network Policies	Requires robust configuration and adherence to security best practices.
	Resource Management: Managing CPU and memory across many containers can be difficult without proper planning.	Resource allocation for CPU and memory within clusters	Efficient resource utilization requires AI-driven tools and forecasting.
	Interoperability: Moving apps from testing to production can be challenging in Kubernetes.	Deployment across different Kubernetes environments	Requires common APIs and standardized tools for smooth operations.
	Storage: On-prem Kubernetes deployments face challenges in managing persistent storage.	Cloud storage solutions, persistent volumes in Kubernetes	Overcome by cloud-native persistent storage or specialized tools.
Future Research	Automation: Further improving automation for deployment, scaling, and management of containers.	Auto-scaling of applications in Kubernetes	Will enhance Kubernetes' ease of use and efficiency.
	5G Integration: Investigating Kubernetes' integration with 5G and edge computing for low-latency applications.	Kubernetes managing edge computing and IoT devices	Opens up new use cases for Kubernetes in 5G environments.
	Scalability: Enhancing Kubernetes' ability to handle large-scale, distributed container deployments.	Large-scale multi-cluster Kubernetes environments	Improves Kubernetes performance in complex distributed systems.
	Resource Scheduling: Advancing scheduling algorithms for optimized resource utilization.	AI-driven resource management algorithms	Optimizes performance and cost-effectiveness in large clusters.
	Serverless Computing: Investigating integration of serverless frameworks with Kubernetes.	Serverless frameworks running on Kubernetes	Extends Kubernetes' ability to manage serverless applications.

TABLE 7.5
(Continued)

Category	Key Points	Examples	Implications
	Service Mesh: Exploring the role of service meshes in Kubernetes applications.	Istio for microservice management	Enhances communication, security, and monitoring within Kubernetes.
	Blockchain Integration: Researching Kubernetes' use with blockchain for improved security and decentralization.	Blockchain for decentralized application management	Enhances trust and security in Kubernetes ecosystems.
	Kubernetes Evolution: Kubernetes will evolve to handle emerging technologies like multi-cloud, ML, and security.	Adapting to next-gen technologies and environments	Kubernetes will remain a dominant platform in the containerized ecosystem.

7.7 SUMMARY

This chapter explores the emerging extensions to cloud computing. Serverless computing, edge computing, fog computing, multi-cloud, hybrid cloud, containers, and Kubernetes are all extensions and advancements of cloud computing that have emerged in recent years. Serverless computing allows developers to build and run applications without managing servers, paying only for the resources used. Edge computing brings computation and data storage closer to the devices that generate it, reducing latency. Fog computing extends cloud computing to the edge of the network, enabling new applications and services. Multi-cloud and Hybrid cloud strategies allow organizations to leverage multiple cloud providers and on-premises infrastructure. Containers package software into standardized units for development, shipment, and deployment. Kubernetes is an open-source system for automating deployment, scaling, and management of containerized applications. The comprehensive analysis of each of these extensions is also provided in this chapter.

7.8 PRACTICE QUESTIONS/SOLUTIONS

MULTIPLE OBJECTIVE QUESTIONS

1 **What is the primary advantage of serverless computing?**
A) Reduced operational costs
B) Complete control over infrastructure
C) High performance for all applications
D) Easier hardware provisioning

Answer: A) Reduced operational costs

2 Which cloud service model does serverless computing fall under?
A) Infrastructure as a Service (IaaS)
B) Platform as a Service (PaaS)
C) Software as a Service (SaaS)
D) Function as a Service (FaaS)

Answer: D) Function as a Service (FaaS)

3 In serverless computing, who is responsible for provisioning, scaling, and managing the underlying infrastructure?
A) End users
B) Cloud service provider
C) Dedicated IT operations team
D) Third-party vendors

Answer: B) Cloud service provider

4 What is a characteristic feature of serverless architecture regarding scalability?
A) Fixed scaling limits
B) Automatic scaling
C) Manual scaling
D) Linear scaling

Answer: B) Automatic scaling

5 What is a key benefit of edge computing for IoT (Internet of Things) applications?
A) Reduced device connectivity
B) Lower device cost
C) Decreased data security
D) Improved real-time processing

Answer: D) Improved real-time processing

6 Which technology is closely related to edge computing for delivering content faster to end users?
A) Blockchain
B) Content Delivery Network (CDN)
C) Virtual Private Network (VPN)
D) Peer-to-Peer (P2P) network

Answer: B) Content Delivery Network (CDN)

7 What role does edge computing play in enhancing data privacy and security?

A) Centralizing sensitive data storage
B) Reducing encryption overhead
C) Securing data at the source
D) Increasing network exposure

Answer: C) Securing data at the source

8 Which factor is critical in determining the success of edge computing deployments?

A) Availability of high-speed Internet
B) Centralized data storage
C) Proximity to urban areas
D) Edge device reliability

Answer: A) Availability of high-speed Internet

9 How does fog computing contribute to efficient data management in IoT networks?

A) By centralizing data storage
B) By reducing encryption overhead
C) By enabling real-time data processing
D) By increasing network exposure

Answer: C) By enabling real-time data processing

10 What role does edge computing play in the context of fog computing architecture?

A) Acting as a data center
B) Providing global connectivity
C) Enhancing cloud storage
D) Serving as a gateway for local data processing

Answer: D) Serving as a gateway for local data processing

11 In fog computing, what are fog nodes responsible for?

A) Processing data in the cloud
B) Storing large datasets
C) Executing computations locally
D) Managing network protocols

Answer: C) Executing computations locally

12 What is the primary characteristic of a multi-cloud architecture?

A) Utilizing multiple cloud services from different providers
B) Running applications exclusively on private clouds
C) Integrating cloud services with on-premises infrastructure
D) Using a single-cloud provider for all services

Answer: A) Utilizing multiple cloud services from different providers

13 In a hybrid cloud setup, what is typically managed by the organization's IT team?

A) Public cloud services
B) Private cloud infrastructure
C) Data centers
D) Virtual machine instances

Answer: B) Private cloud infrastructure

14 How does a multi-cloud strategy contribute to business continuity?

A) By reducing application latency
B) By eliminating data silos
C) By spreading risk across providers
D) By optimizing resource allocation

Answer: C) By spreading risk across providers

15 What is a common use case for hybrid cloud computing in enterprise environments?

A) Hosting development environments
B) Disaster recovery solutions
C) Social media analytics
D) Video streaming services

Answer: B) Disaster recovery solutions

16 Which factor is crucial when selecting cloud providers for a multi-cloud strategy?

A) Geographical location
B) CPU architecture
C) Network bandwidth
D) Data encryption standards

Answer: A) Geographical location

17 What is the purpose of a container image in the context of Docker or similar platforms?

A) To store data securely
B) To execute code on the host OS
C) To define the runtime environment
D) To manage network traffic

Answer: C) To define the runtime environment

18 How does Kubernetes manage containerized applications across multiple nodes?

A) By automatically scaling applications
B) By distributing workloads
C) By optimizing disk space
D) By managing hardware resources

Answer: B) By distributing workloads

19 What does a Kubernetes pod represent?

A) A group of interconnected containers
B) A single container instance
C) A virtual machine
D) A network bridge

Answer: A) A group of interconnected containers

20 What is the purpose of a Kubernetes Deployment object?

A) To provision storage volumes
B) To manage container lifecycles
C) To define network policies
D) To handle DNS resolution

Answer: B) To manage container lifecycles

DESCRIPTIVE QUESTIONS

1 What is serverless computing, and how does it differ from traditional cloud computing?

Answer: Serverless computing is a cloud computing execution model where the cloud provider dynamically manages the allocation and provisioning of servers. In serverless computing, developers focus on writing code (functions) that responds to events or triggers, without the need to manage the infrastructure. Unlike traditional cloud computing where virtual machines or containers are managed explicitly by users, serverless abstracts away infrastructure management, offering scalability and reduced operational overhead.

2 Describe the architecture of a typical serverless application.

Answer: A typical serverless application consists of functions, events, and triggers. Functions are individual pieces of code that are executed in response to events or triggers such as HTTP requests, database changes, file uploads, etc. Events or triggers initiate the execution of these functions. Serverless applications often utilize managed services (such as databases, storage, authentication) provided by cloud providers to handle persistent state or external dependencies.

3 Explain the concept of "cold start" in serverless computing. How can it be mitigated?

Answer: A cold start refers to the initial delay experienced when a serverless function is invoked for the first time or after a period of inactivity. During a cold start, the cloud provider provisions the necessary resources and initializes the function environment. Cold starts can impact latency-sensitive applications. Mitigation strategies include:

- **Pre-warming**: Triggering functions periodically to keep them warm.
- **Optimizing Code**: Optimizing function code and reducing dependencies.
- **Choosing Appropriate Memory Allocation**: Higher memory allocation can reduce cold start times.

4 How does serverless computing enhance the development of microservices architectures?

Answer: Serverless computing enables microservices by allowing developers to deploy small, independent functions that perform specific tasks. Each function can be independently scaled and managed, aligning with the principles of microservices architecture. Serverless also simplifies the deployment and operation of microservices by abstracting away infrastructure management concerns.

5 What are the challenges associated with implementing edge computing solutions?

Answer: Challenges of edge computing include:

- **Management Complexity**: Deploying and managing a distributed network of edge devices and servers can be complex and require specialized expertise.

- **Security Concerns**: Edge devices may lack robust security measures, making them vulnerable to attacks. Securing distributed infrastructure and data at the edge is critical.
- **Standardization**: Lack of standardized protocols and frameworks for edge computing interoperability may hinder seamless integration and scalability.
- **Resource Constraints**: Edge devices often have limited processing power, memory, and storage capacity, requiring efficient resource allocation and optimization.
- **Data Governance**: Ensuring consistent data governance policies across distributed edge nodes while adhering to regulatory compliance can be challenging.

6 Explain how edge computing supports autonomous vehicles and smart cities.

Answer: Edge computing enhances autonomous vehicles and smart cities by:

- **Real-time Decision-Making**: Edge nodes process sensor data locally to make split-second decisions, such as collision avoidance in autonomous vehicles or traffic management in smart cities.
- **Reduced Latency**: Local processing reduces communication delays, ensuring immediate responses to changing environmental conditions.
- **Data Privacy**: Personal and sensitive data collected by autonomous vehicles or smart city sensors can be processed locally at the edge, enhancing privacy and compliance with data protection regulations.
- **Scalability**: Edge infrastructure supports the scalability of autonomous vehicle fleets and smart city deployments by distributing computational resources closer to where data is generated and action is required.

7 How does edge computing contribute to improving the efficiency of industrial IoT (IIoT) applications?

Answer: Edge computing improves IIoT efficiency by:

- **Real-time Data Analysis**: Edge devices analyze sensor data locally, enabling immediate detection of anomalies or equipment failures in industrial processes.
- **Predictive Maintenance**: Edge analytics enable predictive maintenance by processing historical and real-time data to forecast equipment failures, optimizing maintenance schedules and reducing downtime.
- **Operational Efficiency**: Local processing reduces latency and optimizes bandwidth usage, ensuring timely control and monitoring of industrial operations without reliance on centralized cloud servers.
- **Safety and Compliance**: Edge computing enhances safety and regulatory compliance by processing sensitive industrial data locally, minimizing exposure to cybersecurity threats and ensuring data integrity.

8 Describe the relationship between edge computing and cloud computing.

Answer: Edge computing and cloud computing complement each other in hybrid architectures:

- **Edge-to-Cloud Integration**: Edge devices preprocess data locally and send relevant insights to centralized cloud servers for storage, further analysis, or long-term archival.
- **Cloud-to-Edge Services**: Cloud platforms provide management tools, updates, and AI/ML services that can be deployed at the edge to enhance local processing capabilities.
- **Hybrid Deployment**: Organizations deploy hybrid cloud-edge architectures to leverage the scalability, flexibility, and data processing capabilities of both edge and cloud environments based on workload requirements.

9 What is fog computing, and how does it differ from edge and cloud computing?

Answer: Fog computing extends the principles of edge computing by bringing computational resources closer to the data source, often at the edge of the network. Unlike edge computing, which focuses on processing data at the edge devices themselves, fog computing introduces intermediary computing nodes (fog nodes) between edge devices and centralized cloud servers. This approach enables more complex processing tasks and enhances real-time data analysis capabilities while reducing latency compared to traditional cloud computing, which processes data in remote data centers.

10 Describe the architecture of a typical fog computing environment.

Answer: A typical fog computing architecture includes:

- **Edge Devices**: Sensors, IoT devices, and endpoints that generate data.
- **Fog Nodes**: Intermediate computing nodes located closer to the edge devices, capable of processing data locally.
- **Cloud Servers**: Centralized data centers that store and process aggregated data from fog nodes.
- **Network Infrastructure**: Provides connectivity between edge devices, fog nodes, and cloud servers.

Fog nodes aggregate, filter, and preprocess data from edge devices before transmitting relevant information to the cloud for further analysis or storage. This architecture enhances data processing efficiency, reduces latency, and supports real-time applications.

11 What are the key advantages of deploying fog computing solutions?

Answer: Fog computing offers several advantages:

- **Low Latency**: Processing data closer to the edge reduces communication delays and improves response times for time-sensitive applications.
- **Scalability**: Fog nodes can scale horizontally to accommodate increasing data volumes and computing demands at the network edge.
- **Bandwidth Optimization**: Local data processing reduces the amount of data transmitted to centralized cloud servers, optimizing bandwidth usage.
- **Enhanced Privacy and Security**: Data can be processed and filtered locally at fog nodes, minimizing exposure to security risks and ensuring compliance with data privacy regulations.
- **Resilience**: Fog computing enhances resilience by distributing computational tasks across multiple fog nodes, reducing dependency on centralized resources and improving system reliability.

12 How does fog computing contribute to the development of smart cities and autonomous vehicles?

Answer: Fog computing supports smart cities and autonomous vehicles by:

- **Real-time Decision-Making**: Fog nodes process data locally, enabling real-time decision-making for traffic management, environmental monitoring, and emergency response in smart cities.
- **Reduced Latency**: Local data processing at the edge reduces communication delays, ensuring timely responses and enhancing safety for autonomous vehicles.
- **Scalability**: Fog computing scales to support large-scale deployments of IoT devices, sensors, and connected infrastructure in smart cities and autonomous vehicle fleets.
- **Data Privacy**: Fog nodes facilitate local data processing and analysis, enhancing data privacy compliance and minimizing exposure to cybersecurity risks in smart city applications and autonomous vehicle operations.

13 How does multi-cloud differ from hybrid cloud?

Answer: Multi-cloud involves using services from multiple cloud providers independently, while hybrid cloud integrates services from multiple clouds (public or private) into a single architecture. Hybrid cloud typically involves connecting on-premises infrastructure with public cloud resources.

14 What are the benefits of a multi-cloud strategy?

Answer: A multi-cloud strategy offers flexibility, redundancy, and cost optimization. It allows organizations to choose the best services from different providers, enhance resilience against failures, and negotiate better pricing.

15 What challenges does multi-cloud adoption present?

Answer: Multi-cloud adoption can introduce complexities in management, integration, and security. Organizations must deal with different APIs, data consistency across clouds, and ensuring compliance with various regulatory requirements.

16 Why would an organization choose a hybrid cloud approach?

Answer: An organization might choose a hybrid cloud approach to maintain control over sensitive data or legacy systems while leveraging the scalability and flexibility of public cloud services. It can also help in meeting specific compliance or regulatory requirements.

17 What are containers and how do they differ from virtual machines (VMs)?

Answer: Containers are lightweight, portable, and isolated environments for running applications. Unlike VMs, which virtualize hardware, containers virtualize the operating system, allowing for faster startup times and greater efficiency in resource utilization.

18 What is Kubernetes and why is it popular for container orchestration?

Answer: Kubernetes is an open-source container orchestration platform that automates the deployment, scaling, and management of containerized applications. It simplifies the process of managing containerized workloads across clusters of machines.

19 How does Kubernetes facilitate scalability and resilience of applications?

Answer: Kubernetes uses a declarative approach to manage application containers. It automatically scales applications based on resource usage metrics and ensures high availability by restarting containers that fail or become unresponsive.

20 What are the key components of Kubernetes architecture?

Answer: Kubernetes architecture includes the Master node (which manages the cluster), Worker nodes (where containers run), etcd (for cluster state management), kubelet (agent on each node), and kube-proxy (for network proxying).

REFERENCES

1. Hassan, H. B., Barakat, S. A., & Sarhan, Q. I. (2021). Survey on serverless computing. *Journal of Cloud Computing*, *10*, 1–29.
2. McGrath, G., & Brenner, P. R. (2017, June). Serverless computing: Design, implementation, and performance. In *2017 IEEE 37th International Conference on Distributed Computing Systems Workshops (ICDCSW)* (pp. 405–410). IEEE.
3. Li, Y., Lin, Y., Wang, Y., Ye, K., & Xu, C. (2022). Serverless computing: state-of-the-art, challenges and opportunities. *IEEE Transactions on Services Computing*, *16*(2), 1522–1539.
4. Shafiei, H., Khonsari, A., & Mousavi, P. (2022). Serverless computing: a survey of opportunities, challenges, and applications. *ACM Computing Surveys*, *54*(11s), 1–32.
5. Cao, K., Liu, Y., Meng, G., & Sun, Q. (2020). An overview on edge computing research. *IEEE Access*, *8*, 85714–85728.
6. Khan, W. Z., Ahmed, E., Hakak, S., Yaqoob, I., & Ahmed, A. (2019). Edge computing: A survey. *Future Generation Computer Systems*, *97*, 219–235.
7. Shi, W., Cao, J., Zhang, Q., Li, Y., & Xu, L. (2016). Edge computing: Vision and challenges. *IEEE Internet of Things Journal*, *3*(5), 637–646.
8. Yu, W., Liang, F., He, X., Hatcher, W. G., Lu, C., Lin, J., & Yang, X. (2017). A survey on the edge computing for the Internet of Things. *IEEE Access*, *6*, 6900–6919.
9. Satyanarayanan, M. (2017). The emergence of edge computing. *Computer*, *50*(1), 30–39.
10. Chen, J., & Ran, X. (2019). Deep learning with edge computing: A review. *Proceedings of the IEEE*, *107*(8), 1655–1674.
11. Dastjerdi, A. V., Gupta, H., Calheiros, R. N., Ghosh, S. K., & Buyya, R. (2016). Fog computing: Principles, architectures, and applications. In *Internet of Things* (pp. 61–75). Morgan Kaufmann.
12. Vaquero, L. M., & Rodero-Merino, L. (2014). Finding your way in the fog: Towards a comprehensive definition of fog computing. *ACM SIGCOMM Computer Communication Review*, *44*(5), 27–32.
13. Stojmenovic, I., Wen, S., Huang, X., & Luan, H. (2016). An overview of fog computing and its security issues. *Concurrency and Computation: Practice and Experience*, *28*(10), 2991–3005.
14. Mahmud, R., Kotagiri, R., & Buyya, R. (2018). Fog computing: A taxonomy, survey and future directions. *Internet of Everything: Algorithms, Methodologies, Technologies and Perspectives*, 103–130.
15. Bermbach, D., Pallas, F., Pérez, D. G., Plebani, P., Anderson, M., Kat, R., & Tai, S. (2018). A research perspective on fog computing. In *Service-Oriented Computing–ICSoC 2017 Workshops: ASOCA, ISyCC, WESOACS, and Satellite Events*, Malaga, Spain, November 13–16, 2017, Revised Selected Papers (pp. 198–210). Springer International Publishing.
16. Hong, J., Dreibholz, T., Schenkel, J. A., & Hu, J. A. (2019). An overview of multi-cloud computing. In Web, Artificial Intelligence and Network Applications: *Proceedings of the Workshops of the 33rd International Conference on Advanced Information Networking and Applications (WAINA-2019)* 33 (pp. 1055–1068). Springer International Publishing.
17. Gundu, S. R., Panem, C. A., & Thimmapuram, A. (2020). Hybrid IT and multi cloud an emerging trend and improved performance in cloud computing. *SN Computer Science*, *1*(5), 256.
18. Georgios, C., Evangelia, F., Christos, M., & Maria, N. (2021). Exploring cost-efficient bundling in a multi-cloud environment. *Simulation Modelling Practice and Theory*, *111*, 102338.

19. Celesti, A., Galletta, A., Fazio, M., & Villari, M. (2019). Towards hybrid multi-cloud storage systems: Understanding how to perform data transfer. *Big Data Research, 16*, 1–17.
20. Khan, M. A. (2020). Optimized hybrid service brokering for multi-cloud architectures. *The Journal of Supercomputing*, *76*(1), 666–687.
21. Bernstein, D. (2014). Containers and cloud: From LXC to docker to Kubernetes. *IEEE Cloud Computing*, *1*(3), 81–84.
22. Rossi, F., Cardellini, V., Presti, F. L., & Nardelli, M. (2020). Geo-distributed efficient deployment of containers with Kubernetes. *Computer Communications*, *159*, 161–174.
23. Carrión, C. (2022). Kubernetes scheduling: Taxonomy, ongoing issues and challenges. *ACM Computing Surveys*, *55*(7), 1–37.
24. Netto, H. V., Luiz, A. F., Correia, M., de Oliveira Rech, L., & Oliveira, C. P. (2018, June). Koordinator: A service approach for replicating docker containers in Kubernetes. In *2018 IEEE Symposium on Computers and Communications (ISCC)* (pp. 00058–00063). IEEE.

8 Cloud Technologies

8.1 CLOUD SIMILAR TECHNOLOGIES

Many related or comparable technologies exist that are similar to cloud computing. A general overview of some common technologies is given in Figure 8.1. Additionally, a summary showcasing cloud similar technologies is shown in Table 8.1.

The table provides a brief description of each technology that is similar to cloud computing. Each technology has its own distinct characteristics and applications within the context of computing and industry.

The general challenges in adopting the cloud-similar technologies are listed in Figure 8.2. Furthermore, a multi-attribute table showcasing cloud-related technologies is provided in Table 8.2.

The table provides a concise overview of the key benefits, challenges, and primary use cases of each technology. The technologies listed in the table are all closely related to or share similarities with cloud computing. They often rely on cloud infrastructure for data storage, processing, and scalability, with some, approaches such as Mobile Edge Computing, extending cloud capabilities to the edge to enhance

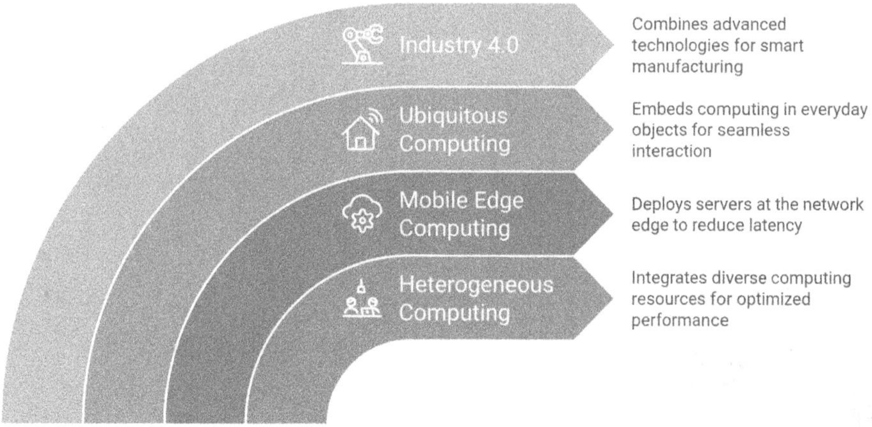

FIGURE 8.1 General overview of cloud similar technologies.

DOI: 10.1201/9781003510772-8

TABLE 8.1
The Cloud-Similar Technologies

Technology	Description
Heterogeneous Computing [1]	Involves the integration and use of different types of computing resources, such as CPUs, GPUs, FPGAs, and specialized hardware, to optimize performance for diverse tasks. It enables parallel processing, reduces bottlenecks, and enhances efficiency in complex applications such as AI, machine learning, and big data analytics.
Mobile Edge Computing [2]	Brings cloud computing resources closer to end-users by deploying servers at the edge of mobile networks. This reduces latency, improves data processing speeds, and supports real-time applications such as autonomous vehicles, IoT, and AR/VR by reducing reliance on distant cloud data centers.
Ubiquitous Computing [3]	Envisions a world where computing devices are seamlessly embedded in everyday objects, environments, and systems. The goal is to create a network of interconnected devices that are always on, smart, and capable of interacting with each other, enhancing convenience and automation without user intervention.
Industry 4.0 [4]	Marks the fourth industrial revolution, which integrates advanced technologies such as IoT (Internet of Things), AI (Artificial Intelligence), machine learning, robotics, cloud computing, and big data into manufacturing processes. This creates smart factories that are more efficient, automated, and responsive to changes.

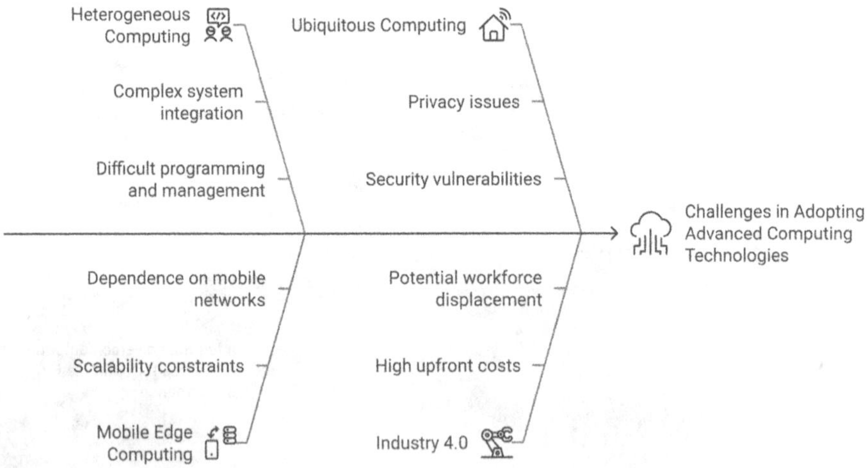

FIGURE 8.2 General challenges in cloud-similar technologies' adoption.

performance. While not purely cloud technologies, these innovations complement cloud computing and enhance its applications in fields such as AI, IoT, automation, and smart environments.

These technologies could share features or offer comparable advantages. The discussion of each of these technologies is provided below.

TABLE 8.2
Comparative Analysis of Cloud-Similar Technologies

Technology	Key Benefits	Challenges	Primary Use Cases
Heterogeneous Computing	Enhanced performance, optimized for specialized tasks	Complex system integration, difficult programming and management	High-performance computing (HPC), AI, data analytics
Mobile Edge Computing	Low-latency, better user experience, reduced network load	Scalability constraints, dependence on mobile networks	IoT, real-time data processing, smart cities, AR/VR
Ubiquitous Computing	Seamless integration into daily life, intuitive user experiences	Privacy issues, security vulnerabilities	Smart homes, wearables, connected environments
Industry 4.0	Automation, efficiency improvements, data-driven decisions	High upfront costs, potential workforce displacement	Smart manufacturing, robotics, supply chain optimization

8.1.1 Heterogeneous Computing

The usage of many types of processing units or architectural designs inside a single computer system is known as heterogeneous computing. Different types of processors, including Central Processing Unit (CPU), Graphics Processing Unit (GPU), Field-Programmable Gate Array (FPGA), or specialized accelerators, collaborate to carry out particular tasks or enhance overall computational performance in a heterogeneous computing environment. The idea of heterogeneous computing emerged from the realization that various processor architectures excel at certain task architectures. For instance, GPUs are very effective at parallel processing and are frequently utilized for activities such as performing scientific computations and producing images. FPGAs are appropriate for activities that call for low latency and high throughput because they offer programmable hardware that can be tailored for certain applications. The common features of heterogeneous computing are listed in Figure 8.3.

Heterogeneous computing tries to maximize the benefits of each architecture by integrating many processor types into a single system in order to gain better performance, increased energy efficiency, or specialized functionality. Depending on their distinct capabilities, the processors may be employed independently for various tasks or they may cooperate to handle different facets of the job. In many different fields, such as scientific research, data analytics, machine learning, computer vision, and high-performance computing, heterogeneous computing architectures are often used. They provide benefits like:

- ***Performance Optimization*:** Heterogeneous computing may considerably improve overall system performance by offloading certain processes to processors that are optimized for those activities. For instance, sophisticated simulations or data processing jobs can be accelerated by employing GPUs for parallelizable operations.
- ***Energy Efficiency*:** The power consumption characteristics of various CPUs differ. By distributing workload among processors, heterogeneous

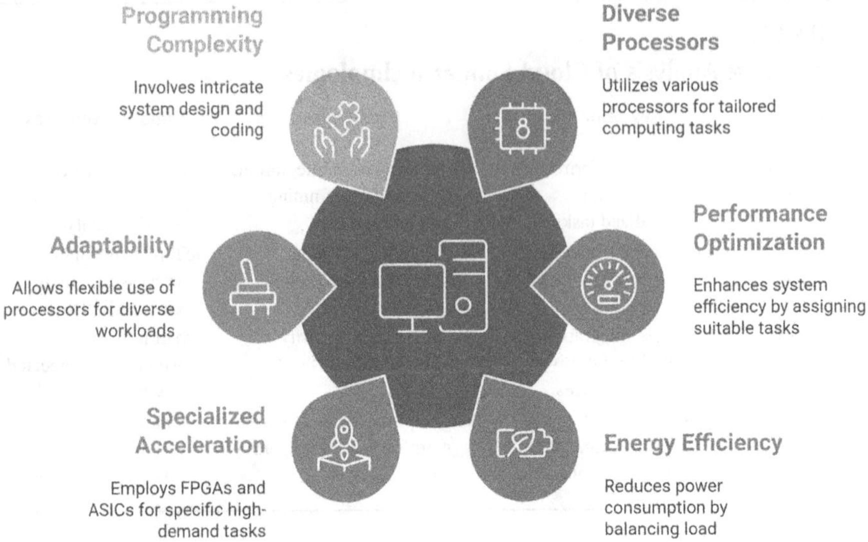

FIGURE 8.3 Common features of heterogeneous computing.

computing enables the adoption of more power-efficient architectures for jobs that do not necessitate a high-power CPU's full capabilities.

- ***Specialized Acceleration*:** Certain processors, such FPGAs or Application-Specific Integrated Circuits (ASICs), may be tailored or programmed for certain algorithms or functions, giving highly optimized and effective acceleration for those jobs.
- ***Adaptability and Flexibility*:** Heterogeneous computing enables adaptability in selecting the best processor for various tasks. It makes it possible to use the hardware that is most suited for each unique activity, enhancing performance and efficiency.

But heterogeneous computing also has many drawbacks, including the complexity of programming, the necessity for efficient data synchronization and transfer, and the requirement for specialized software tools and frameworks. To maximize performance improvements, researchers and developers working with heterogeneous systems must carefully optimize their code and control data flows across CPUs. Overall, heterogeneous computing offers a strong method for combining the various capabilities of many processors into a single system, providing enhanced performance, increased energy economy, and specialized acceleration for a variety of computational workloads and applications.

Heterogeneous computing leverages the unique strengths of different types of processors to achieve superior performance, energy efficiency, and specialized acceleration for a variety of computational tasks. By utilizing CPUs, GPUs, FPGAs, and ASICs, it enables tasks to be handled by the most appropriate hardware, offering clear advantages in fields such as machine learning, data analytics, and scientific computing. However, these benefits come with challenges in programming complexity, data synchronization, and system management, which require specialized tools and careful system design to optimize performance across the different components. Table 8.3 offers an overview of Heterogeneous Computing.

TABLE 8.3
Overview of Heterogeneous Computing

Aspect	Description	Advantages	Challenges	Key Examples/ Applications
Overview	The use of multiple types of processing units (CPUs, GPUs, FPGAs, ASICs) within a single computer system to improve performance and efficiency.	Combines strengths of different processors, improving overall system performance, energy efficiency, and specialized functionality.	Requires coordination between different processor types, which can complicate the design and programming of the system.	Data analytics, Machine learning, High-performance computing (HPC), Scientific computing, Computer vision.
Types of Processors	Includes CPUs (general-purpose), GPUs (parallel computation), FPGAs (programmable hardware), and specialized accelerators (ASICs).	Allows for tailored use of different processors based on specific workload needs.	Managing the diversity in processors (e.g., programming different architectures, synchronization) can be complex.	CPUs – general-purpose tasks, GPUs – parallel processing, FPGAs – low-latency tasks, ASICs – specialized acceleration tasks.
Performance Optimization	Uses the most suitable processor for specific tasks to enhance overall system performance.	Offloads computation to processors best suited for the task (e.g., GPUs for parallelizable tasks). Leads to performance gains in scientific simulations, image processing, etc.	Optimizing code for various processors can be difficult and requires a deep understanding of each processor's strengths and weaknesses.	Simulation, Data processing, Image rendering.
Energy Efficiency	Distributes computational tasks to processors based on their energy consumption profiles, improving energy usage.	Enables energy-efficient processors (e.g., low-power FPGAs) to be used for less computationally intensive tasks. Reduces overall power consumption compared to using a single high-power processor.	Managing power consumption across different processors, while ensuring task balance and energy optimization, can be difficult.	Mobile computing, IoT devices, Edge computing.
Specialized Acceleration	Utilizes FPGAs and ASICs for highly optimized, specific tasks that require high throughput or low latency.	Enables accelerators to be programmed for specific workloads, providing significant performance improvements (e.g., deep learning inference).	Development of custom accelerators requires specialized knowledge and time. Hardware reprogramming (in the case of FPGAs) can be resource-intensive.	Deep learning, Cryptocurrency mining, Signal processing, Networking.

(Continued)

TABLE 8.3 (Continued)

Aspect	Description	Advantages	Challenges	Key Examples/ Applications
Adaptability and Flexibility	Allows the use of various processors for different workloads within a system, improving performance and resource allocation.	Flexibility to choose the best processor for each task leads to better resource allocation and efficiency.	Requires sophisticated scheduling and workload management systems to ensure tasks are assigned to the most appropriate processor.	Machine learning workloads, Scientific research (for simulations and data processing), Robotics, Real-time data analytics.
Programming Complexity	Involves designing systems where multiple processors work together, often requiring specialized tools and frameworks.	Enhances system capabilities by enabling the use of multiple processor types.	Programming heterogeneous systems requires knowledge of each processor's architecture, specialized tools (CUDA for GPUs, OpenCL for general heterogeneous systems, etc.), and intricate data synchronization.	OpenCL, CUDA, TensorFlow, PyTorch, FPGA programming languages.
Data Synchronization and Transfer	Requires efficient management of data exchange between processors to prevent bottlenecks and ensure smooth execution.	Allows more efficient data transfer between processors by utilizing dedicated communication frameworks, improving overall system throughput.	Data movement between different processors (e.g., CPU to GPU or FPGA) can be a bottleneck. Efficient data synchronization is required to prevent delays.	Big Data applications, Cloud computing, Data centers, Multi-node supercomputing systems.
Scalability	The ability to scale performance by adding more processing units or increasing processor diversity as computational needs grow.	Heterogeneous systems can be scaled horizontally (adding more units) or vertically (adding more powerful units), improving computational power as needed.	Managing the increasing complexity of large-scale heterogeneous systems and ensuring that workload distribution remains optimal at scale.	Large-scale machine learning models, Distributed scientific simulations, High-performance data analysis.
Use Cases	Heterogeneous computing is applied in areas where performance, speed, and specialization are critical.	Improved performance and functionality for a range of complex tasks.	Requires balancing trade-offs in system complexity, software compatibility, and hardware requirements.	Artificial Intelligence (AI), Computer Vision, Data Analytics, Scientific Research, Cloud gaming, Healthcare imaging.

8.1.2 Mobile Edge Computing

A distributed computing paradigm called mobile edge computing (MEC), often referred to as multi-access edge computing, puts cloud computing capabilities and services closer to the network edge. It is made to deal with the problems that emerge while processing data in centralized cloud data centers, such as latency, capacity restrictions, and network congestion. MEC relocates the computing assets and services closer to the end-users' mobile devices and the edge of the network. According to the conventional cloud computing concept, mobile device data is sent to a distant data center for processing and analysis. Due to the round-trip time between the device and the distant server, this method, however, causes delays. By locating computational resources, such as servers and storage, near base stations or access points at the network's edge, MEC hopes to get around these restrictions. The common features of MEC are listed in Figure 8.4.

MEC provides the following advantages and opportunities:

- ***Lower Latency*:** MEC speeds up data transmission between a device and the cloud by processing data and running applications at the network edge. Reduced latency makes it possible for real-time and low-latency applications, including gaming, augmented reality (AR), and virtual reality (VR).
- ***Greater Bandwidth Efficiency*:** MEC allows for the local processing of data-intensive operations close to the edge, lowering the amount of data that must be sent to distant cloud servers. This lessens network congestion and increases bandwidth efficiency.
- ***Localized Processing and Analysis*:** Localized processing and analysis of data produced by mobile devices are possible. Faster reaction times are made possible, privacy is improved by keeping private information on-site, and there is less need to send vast volumes of data to distant computers for processing.

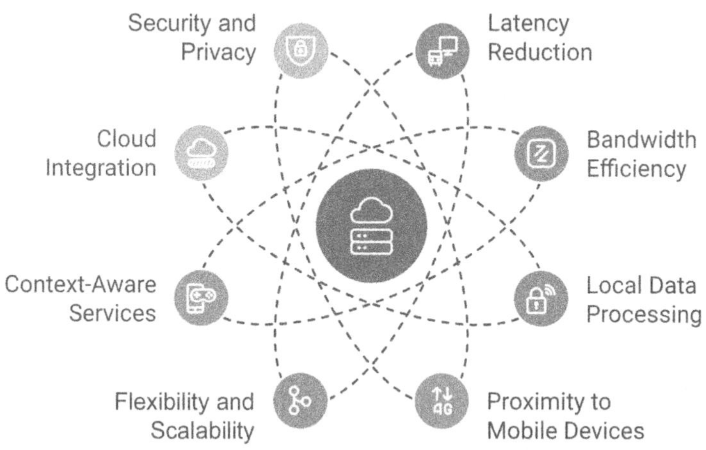

FIGURE 8.4 Common features of MEC.

- ***Proximity to Mobile Devices*:** By placing computing resources adjacent to mobile devices, it is possible to communicate with them directly and effectively. This makes it easier to implement applications that call for real-time communication, quick answers, or location-based services.
- ***Flexibility and Scalability*:** MEC offers a distributed computing architecture with the capacity to scale up or down depending on demand. It provides for the flexible and scalable deployment of services and applications, supporting shifting workloads and user needs.
- ***Context-Aware Services*:** MEC is able to provide individualized and context-aware services by utilizing the contextual data that is accessible at the edge, such as device location, network circumstances, and user preferences. This makes it possible to create cutting-edge applications that benefit from local context and improve user experience.

MEC is particularly pertinent in situations where real-time processing, increased user experiences, and reduced latency are essential, such as in Internet of Things (IoT) deployments, smart cities, industrial automation, healthcare, and immersive multimedia applications. It is crucial to keep in mind that MEC is a concept that complements cloud computing, allowing some applications and services to be transferred to the cloud for resource-intensive processing or long-term storage while using the advantages of edge computing for time-sensitive and latency-critical applications. MEC is becoming more popular and is becoming standardized by several business associations and organizations. In the era of more connected and data-driven mobile settings, it offers a viable strategy to allow new and enhanced applications and services that need real-time responsiveness, decreased latency, and effective use of network resources. A comprehensive analysis of MEC, highlighting its key characteristics, advantages, potential use cases, etc., is presented in Table 8.4.

8.1.3 Ubiquitous Computing

The idea of effortlessly incorporating computing technology into the environment and common things, making it omnipresent and invisible in our daily lives, is known as ubiquitous computing, sometimes known as pervasive computing or ambient intelligence. In an environment where computing systems and gadgets are pervasive, always accessible, and capable of communicating with people and one another without the users' conscious involvement. A world where computers are integrated into everyday things, infrastructure, and the physical environment is what ubiquitous computing envisions. In order to assist numerous jobs and activities, it attempts to build a ubiquitous network of networked gadgets and sensors that work together to offer intelligent services. The common features of ubiquitous computing are listed in Figure 8.5.

The following are some essential attributes and concepts of ubiquitous computing:

- ***Accessibility and Presence*:** Computing devices are incorporated into a wide range of things, contexts, and locations. They function transparently in the background and are effortlessly incorporated into our regular activities.

TABLE 8.4
Comprehensive Overview of Mobile Edge Computing

Aspect	Description	Advantages	Challenges	Key Examples/ Applications
Overview	MEC moves cloud computing resources to the network edge, closer to mobile devices, reducing latency and improving bandwidth efficiency.	Reduces latency, enhances real-time processing, and supports mobile applications that require low latency and fast response times.	Requires integration of edge computing with existing cloud infrastructure. Managing decentralized resources can also be complex.	Mobile gaming, Augmented Reality (AR), Virtual Reality (VR), IoT, Smart Cities, Healthcare.
Latency Reduction	By processing data closer to the edge (near mobile devices), MEC minimizes the round-trip time to distant data centers, reducing delays.	Real-time processing of data enhances user experiences, enabling low-latency applications such as gaming, AR, VR, and autonomous vehicles.	Edge resources must be sufficient to handle local processing; otherwise, the benefit of low latency may be compromised.	Real-time gaming, Autonomous driving, VR/AR applications.
Bandwidth Efficiency	MEC reduces data traffic by processing data locally at the edge, reducing the amount of data sent to centralized cloud servers.	Helps alleviate network congestion and optimizes bandwidth by reducing the need to transfer large data volumes to central servers.	Managing bandwidth between edge and central servers and ensuring seamless transition of workloads can be complex.	IoT networks, Smart homes, Wearable devices, Data-intensive mobile applications.
Local Data Processing	MEC allows for localized processing and analysis of data generated by mobile devices, keeping data closer to the source.	Improved privacy by keeping sensitive data on-site, reduced reliance on centralized data centers, and quicker processing for real-time applications.	Securing local data processing and maintaining privacy across decentralized systems is challenging.	Mobile health apps, Smart grids, Personalized services.
Proximity to Mobile Devices	Places computational resources near mobile devices, reducing the physical and network distance for communication and data processing.	Enables more efficient, direct, and faster communication with mobile devices. Critical for applications requiring location-based services and real-time interactions.	Ensuring consistent quality of service (QoS) across various edge locations can be difficult, especially when mobile devices move across different coverage areas.	Location-based services, Interactive gaming, Real-time navigation systems.

(Continued)

TABLE 8.4
(Continued)

Aspect	Description	Advantages	Challenges	Key Examples/ Applications
Flexibility and Scalability	Offers a distributed architecture that can scale up or down based on user demands and network conditions.	Easily adaptable to varying workloads, capable of scaling depending on demand and network requirements.	Handling dynamic and fluctuating workloads, ensuring resource allocation is optimized at all times.	E-commerce platforms, Edge AI applications, Dynamic content delivery.
Context-Aware Services	Uses contextual data (e.g., location, device status, network conditions) at the edge to deliver personalized and context-aware services.	Enables the development of intelligent, context-sensitive applications that can tailor content and services based on the immediate environment and user preferences.	Ensuring privacy and security of contextual data, as well as managing context-aware services across diverse devices, poses challenges.	Smart cities, Retail applications, Autonomous drones, Smart healthcare.
Cloud Integration	MEC complements traditional cloud computing by offloading time-sensitive tasks to the edge while leaving resource-intensive tasks to the cloud.	Seamlessly combines the advantages of cloud computing (powerful computing, storage) with the low-latency benefits of edge computing. Allows for optimal resource usage by segmenting tasks based on processing needs.	Proper task segmentation between edge and cloud can be challenging, especially for applications with hybrid demands (real-time + resource-heavy tasks).	Hybrid cloud-edge computing models, Big data processing, Machine learning.
Security and Privacy	Localized data processing helps to keep sensitive data closer to its origin, enhancing security and privacy.	Reduced data transmission to central cloud servers minimizes the risk of interception during transmission.	Securing decentralized systems, especially with data distributed across numerous edge nodes, presents significant challenges.	Healthcare applications, Personalized ads, Banking services.
Use Cases	MEC is essential in scenarios that require real-time processing, fast responses, and efficient use of network resources.	Provides faster, more efficient solutions for latency-sensitive applications. Offers scalability for a wide range of use cases, improving the performance of mobile devices and other connected technologies.	Coordination of various edge devices, ensuring effective resource management, and guaranteeing uninterrupted service during network changes (e.g., device mobility) are significant hurdles.	Autonomous vehicles, Smart homes, Healthcare (real-time diagnostics), Interactive entertainment.

FIGURE 8.5 Common features of ubiquitous computing.

- ***Context-Awareness*:** Systems with ubiquitous computing are conscious of their operating environment. They compile data from sensors and other sources to comprehend the location, preferences, actions, and environmental factors of the user, providing personalized and adaptable experiences.
- ***Connectivity*:** In a ubiquitous computing environment, devices and systems are connected and interact with one another to exchange information, plan actions, and offer improved functions. This makes it possible for smooth device interoperability and cooperation.
- ***Adaptability*:** Ubiquitous computing systems are made to change to meet user needs and changing environmental circumstances. Based on user requirements and environmental variables, they may dynamically reconfigure themselves, modify their behavior, and customize services.
- ***Intelligence*:** To make sense of the data gathered from the environment, devices, and human interactions, ubiquitous computing systems use artificial intelligence and machine learning techniques. In order to offer intelligent services, make predictions, and aid in decision-making, they may process and analyze information.
- ***User-Centric Design*:** Ubiquitous computing places a strong emphasis on creating systems that put the user experience first. To effortlessly integrate into users' daily activities, technology must be intuitive, user-friendly, and allow natural interaction modalities including speech, gestures, and touch.

Numerous industries, including smart homes, wearable technology, smart cities, healthcare, transportation, retail, and entertainment, use ubiquitous computing. The following are some instances of ubiquitous computing in action:

- Smart houses with linked gadgets, where lighting, thermostats, appliances, and security systems may be remotely or automatically controlled based on human preferences and environmental factors.

- Wearable technology, such as fitness trackers and smartwatches that track physical activity and health metrics and offer individualized feedback and suggestions.
- Intelligent transportation systems that enable linked cars, improve traffic flow, and employ sensors, GPS, and communication technology.
- Smart cities that make use of pervasive computing to improve public services, maximize energy use, keep an eye on the environment, and raise citizen quality of life.
- Interactive retail environments that provide individualized offers, location-based suggestions, and seamless shopping experiences using beacons, sensors, and mobile devices.

Although the idea of ubiquitous computing has many advantages, such as more comfort, greater effectiveness, and superior experiences, it also raises questions about privacy, security, data ownership, and ethical implications. To guarantee the proper deployment and usage of ubiquitous computing technology, several factors must be balanced. The concept of ubiquitous computing involves the seamless integration of computing devices into everyday environments and objects. This integration aims to make computing omnipresent and invisible in our daily lives, while enhancing user experiences across various applications and industries. A comprehensive analysis in Table 8.5 highlights the essential attributes, examples, and challenges associated with ubiquitous computing.

8.1.4 Industry 4.0

The integration of cutting-edge digital technology and automation into the manufacturing and industrial sectors is referred to as Industry 4.0 or the fourth industrial revolution. It signifies a shift in the way things are made, allowing for a more connected, effective, and intelligent manufacturing strategy. Germany was the birthplace of the phrase "Industry 4.0" as part of a strategy plan to update the nation's industrial sector. Since then, it has grown in popularity and is now frequently used to describe how industrial processes are being continually digitalized and automated. The common features of Industry 4.0 are listed in Figure 8.6.

Industry 4.0's primary elements and technologies include:

- ***Internet of Things (IoT) and Industrial Internet of Things (IIoT)***: The IoT refers to the process of linking physical objects, such as machines, sensors, and gadgets, to the Internet so they may gather and share data. This is known as the IIoT in an industrial setting, where networked machines and industrial equipment enable real-time data monitoring, analysis, and control.
- ***Big Data and Analytics***: Industry 4.0 makes use of the enormous amounts of data that sensors, machines, and systems create in order to obtain knowledge and make data-driven choices. When analyzing data for process optimization, predictive maintenance, and quality control, advanced analytics techniques such as machine learning and artificial intelligence are used.

TABLE 8.5
Comprehensive Analysis of Ubiquitous Computing

Aspect	Description	Advantages	Challenges	Key Examples/Applications
Overview	Ubiquitous computing involves embedding computing technology into everyday objects and environments, making it pervasive and seamless in daily life.	Enhances user experiences by making computing invisible and accessible in all aspects of life. Creates a network of devices working together without explicit user involvement.	Integration of various devices into everyday objects can be complex, and ensuring smooth interoperability and communication between them is a challenge.	Smart homes, Wearable devices, Smart cities, Interactive retail, Healthcare monitoring systems.
Accessibility and Presence	Computing devices are embedded into daily environments and objects, ensuring they are always accessible and operational, often without user intervention.	Provides continuous, effortless access to technology and services. Users can interact naturally with the environment without needing to consciously operate devices.	Managing constant accessibility of devices can raise concerns about over-reliance on technology and the potential for tech overload.	Smart home devices (thermostats, security cameras), Wearables (smartwatches, fitness trackers).
Context-Awareness	Systems sense and understand environmental conditions, user preferences, and activities, adjusting services accordingly for personalized experiences.	Delivers highly personalized and adaptive services by responding to real-time context such as location, mood, or environmental changes.	Privacy concerns arise from the constant collection of data from users and their environments, including sensitive personal information.	Smart homes (temperature control, lighting), Location-based services (restaurants, offers), Personalized healthcare (medical alerts, reminders).
Connectivity	Devices and systems are interconnected, sharing information and collaborating to enhance functions and services.	Enables seamless communication between devices and systems, creating a cohesive and efficient environment for the user. Promotes interoperability across a wide range of technologies.	Maintaining reliable connectivity across devices and networks, ensuring uninterrupted service and data integrity, especially in large-scale systems.	IoT networks, Smart cities (public services integration), Automated transportation systems (connected vehicles, traffic management).
Adaptability	Ubiquitous computing systems are designed to adapt to changing user needs, environmental factors, and context.	Offers highly flexible and dynamic services, capable of adjusting to evolving user needs, preferences, and environmental changes.	Ensuring seamless reconfiguration without disrupting user experience or requiring manual intervention. There's a risk that systems could adapt in unexpected or undesired ways.	Smart home systems (energy-efficient adjustments), Adaptive learning platforms (tailored educational experiences), Healthcare monitoring (real-time adjustments).

(Continued)

TABLE 8.5
(Continued)

Aspect	Description	Advantages	Challenges	Key Examples/Applications
Intelligence	Ubiquitous computing systems utilize AI and machine learning to analyze data and make decisions to offer intelligent services.	Enables systems to process data intelligently, make predictions, and automate decisions, improving the efficiency and responsiveness of services.	Ensuring the accuracy and reliability of AI-driven decisions and preventing incorrect or biased outcomes. The systems also need continuous learning to stay relevant.	Personalized shopping experiences, Healthcare diagnosis, Predictive traffic systems (reducing congestion).
User-Centric Design	Emphasis on intuitive interfaces and seamless interactions that integrate naturally into users' daily routines.	Technology is easy to use and aligns with natural human behavior (e.g., voice commands, gestures, touch), improving the overall user experience.	Striking the right balance between ease of use and system complexity. Ensuring accessibility for users with varied needs and abilities.	Voice-activated assistants (Siri, Alexa), Gesture-controlled devices, Interactive displays in retail (touchscreens, smart mirrors).
Privacy and Security	Continuous monitoring and data collection raise concerns about the security of personal data and how it's used or shared across connected devices.	Ubiquitous computing provides potential for higher levels of convenience and personalization, which could increase security (e.g., biometrics for authentication).	Maintaining user privacy and data security while enabling continuous data collection and system access. Ethical concerns related to constant monitoring and surveillance.	Healthcare monitoring systems, Banking apps (biometrics), Location tracking apps (privacy concerns).
Scalability	Ubiquitous computing systems are designed to scale to accommodate large numbers of connected devices and users.	Can support a growing number of devices and applications, allowing for the expansion of smart environments and services across large-scale infrastructures.	Managing system scalability while maintaining efficiency and minimizing latency. Ensuring infrastructure is capable of supporting widespread device deployment without performance degradation.	Smart cities, Automated transport systems, Retail networks (scalable smart product displays, kiosks).
Ethical and Social Implications	Ubiquitous computing brings both positive societal impacts and ethical concerns, particularly regarding autonomy, control, and consent.	Enhances convenience and quality of life, contributing to sustainability (e.g., smart grids, energy-efficient buildings). Promotes equitable access to technology and services for diverse groups.	Raises questions about data ownership, user autonomy, informed consent, and the potential for surveillance. Ethical use of AI and the balance of technological benefits with personal rights are major considerations.	AI-powered decision-making, Public surveillance, Smart healthcare (data sharing and usage consent).

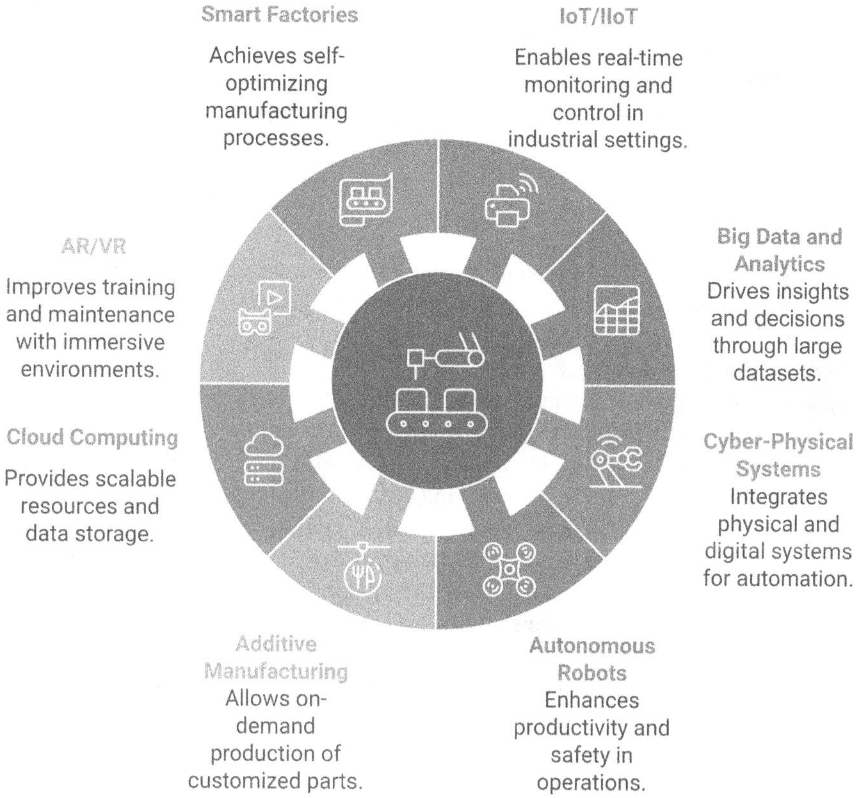

FIGURE 8.6 Common Features of Industry 4.0.

- ***Cyber-Physical Systems (CPS)*:** The integration of physical systems with computer-based control and monitoring systems is referred to as CPS. It includes the interaction of physical elements – such as machines or robots – with computer systems that direct and plan their operations. CPS makes it possible to monitor, coordinate, and improve industrial processes in real time.
- ***Autonomous Robots and Systems*:** A key component of Industry 4.0 is the employment of autonomous robots and systems, which may work alone or in tandem with people in a manufacturing setting. These robots have sensors, computer vision, and AI capabilities that allow them to interact and carry out difficult jobs.
- ***Additive Manufacturing (3D Printing)*:** A key component of Industry 4.0 is additive manufacturing technology. Due to the on-demand creation of specialized parts or goods made possible by 3D printing, lead times are shortened, conventional assembly lines are not required, and decentralized manufacturing is made possible.
- ***Cloud Computing*:** By offering scalable and on-demand computing resources, storage, and software applications, cloud computing plays a crucial role in Industry 4.0. It makes it possible to store and analyze massive

volumes of data, as well as to share information and work together with many stakeholders.

- ***Augmented Reality (AR) and Virtual Reality (VR) Technologies***: These technologies are employed in Industry 4.0 to improve training, maintenance, and visualization of complicated processes. They enhance efficiency, productivity, and safety by allowing employees to access real-time data, instructions, and virtual simulations.

Industry 4.0 aims to increase manufacturing processes' productivity, efficiency, and adaptability while also enabling mass customization, cutting costs, and speeding up innovation. Industry 4.0 aspires to develop "smart factories" that are networked, adaptable, and capable of making decisions on their own by merging digital technology, automation, and intelligent systems. Industry 4.0 has several advantages, including greater productivity and competitiveness, but it also presents difficulties in terms of cybersecurity, data privacy, labor skills, and possible job effects. For the Industry 4.0 vision to be successfully adopted and realized, it is essential to address these issues and ensure responsible implementation. While these technologies and cloud computing are similar, each has unique characteristics, advantages, and applications. Based on their unique needs and objectives, organizations may assess and mix various technologies to optimize their IT infrastructure, boost performance, and achieve desired results. A comprehensive analysis of the key technologies and elements of Industry 4.0, outlining their characteristics, advantages, challenges, and applications, is presented in Table 8.6.

8.2 CLOUD-BASED TECHNOLOGIES

Utilizing computer resources, services, and applications that are made available via the Internet using cloud computing models is referred to as cloud-based technology. Cloud-based solutions rely on remote servers stored in data centers to give on-demand access to computing resources rather than executing software or storing data on local devices or servers. Table 8.7 showcases various cloud-based technologies, providing a brief description of each cloud-based technology. Each technology has its own unique characteristics and applications within the context of cloud computing and network connectivity.

Table 8.8 showcases cloud-based technologies with additional attributes. The table includes additional attributes for each cloud-based technology, providing a more comprehensive overview of their characteristics and use cases.

8.2.1 Cloud-LAN

A concept known as cloud-LAN, often referred to as cloud local area network, combines the advantages of cloud computing and conventional local area network (LAN) technology. By fusing on-premises LAN infrastructure and cloud-based networking services, it seeks to give businesses a scalable, adaptable, and effective networking solution. In a conventional LAN, network components such as switches, routers, and servers are placed inside the walls of the company and are in charge of managing

TABLE 8.6
Comprehensive Analysis of Industry 4.0

Element	Description	Advantages	Challenges	Applications
Internet of Things (IoT) / Industrial IoT (IIoT)	IoT involves connecting physical objects (machines, sensors, devices) to the internet for data collection and exchange. In industry, IIoT refers to networked industrial equipment for real-time data monitoring.	• Real-time monitoring and control • Improved operational efficiency • Predictive maintenance	• Security risks (cyberattacks) • Data overload • Integration complexity	• Real-time data collection • Predictive maintenance • Smart inventory management
Big Data and Analytics	Utilizes large datasets generated by sensors and machines to drive insights and decisions, often leveraging AI and machine learning.	• Data-driven decision-making • Improved quality control • Predictive analytics for maintenance	• Data storage and processing challenges • Data privacy concerns	• Process optimization • Predictive maintenance • Quality control • Supply chain optimization
Cyber-Physical Systems (CPS)	Integration of physical systems with computer-based monitoring and control. Involves real-time interaction between physical elements (e.g., robots) and computational systems.	• Real-time monitoring and control • Improved automation • Enhanced efficiency	• Complex system integration • Maintenance complexity • High initial cost	• Automated production lines • Robotics coordination • Industrial monitoring and coordination
Autonomous Robots and Systems	Robots that can perform tasks independently or in collaboration with humans, leveraging sensors, AI, and computer vision.	• Enhanced productivity • Precision and consistency • Increased safety	• High cost of implementation • Workforce displacement • Training requirements	• Automated assembly lines • Inspection and maintenance • Hazardous environment operations
Additive Manufacturing (3D Printing)	Technology that creates objects layer by layer based on digital models, enabling on-demand production of customized parts.	• Rapid prototyping • Customization • Reduced waste and material costs	• Limited material selection • Slow production speed for large volumes • High upfront cost	• Rapid prototyping • On-demand manufacturing • Customized spare parts production

(*Continued*)

TABLE 8.6
(Continued)

Element	Description	Advantages	Challenges	Applications
Cloud Computing	Cloud services provide scalable resources, data storage, and software applications, enabling data analysis and sharing among multiple stakeholders.	• Scalability and flexibility • Lower IT infrastructure costs • Easy data sharing and collaboration	• Data security and privacy concerns • Downtime risks • Vendor lock-in	• Data storage and processing • Collaborative project management • Data analysis and visualization
Augmented Reality (AR) / Virtual Reality (VR)	Technologies that provide interactive, immersive environments for training, maintenance, and process visualization. AR overlays digital information in the real world, while VR creates fully simulated environments.	• Enhanced training capabilities • Improved maintenance procedures • Better design and process visualization	• High setup costs • Need for specialized hardware • Training and adaptation challenges	• Employee training • Remote maintenance assistance • Product design and simulation • Complex process visualization
Smart Factories	Factories that leverage digital technologies (IoT, robotics, AI, etc.) to enable self-optimizing, adaptive manufacturing processes.	• Increased automation and efficiency • Adaptable production systems • Improved decision-making	• High initial investment • Integration of diverse technologies • Cybersecurity risks	• Fully automated manufacturing systems • Flexible production systems • Real-time process optimization

TABLE 8.7
Different Cloud-based Technologies

Technology	Description
Cloud-LAN	Extends traditional Local Area Network (LAN) functionality to the cloud, allowing businesses to manage secure, scalable, and geographically distributed networks as if they were on-premises. Enables seamless connectivity and centralized management.
Cloud-WAN	Uses cloud infrastructure to deliver Wide Area Network (WAN) capabilities, connecting multiple sites over large distances. Optimizes performance, scalability, and security with reduced hardware dependencies, making it easier to manage remote offices or branches.
Cloud-MAN	Leverages cloud computing to establish a Metropolitan Area Network (MAN) that connects organizations and services within a specific region or city. Facilitates high-bandwidth, low-latency data transfer and improves access to cloud resources for urban-centric businesses.
Cloud-SDN	Merges cloud computing with Software-Defined Networking (SDN) to centralize the control of network traffic and infrastructure. This enables dynamic, programmable management of network resources, improving flexibility, security, and automation within cloud-based environments.
Cloud-IoT	Integrates cloud infrastructure with the Internet of Things (IoT) to enable scalable data storage, processing, and real-time analytics of sensor and device-generated data. Cloud-IoT solutions improve decision-making, automation, and operational efficiency across industries such as manufacturing, healthcare, and smart cities.

network resources, directing traffic, and connecting local devices. But as cloud computing has grown in popularity, businesses have begun to use cloud-based services for different parts of their IT architecture.

A cloud-LAN expands a company's LAN capabilities outside of its physical location and into the cloud. In order to enable organizations to centrally manage and control their network resources, rules, and security across both on-premises and cloud environments, it entails integrating cloud networking services with the already-existing LAN infrastructure.

A few crucial elements of Cloud-LAN are given below:

- ***Centralized Network Management***: Cloud-LAN offers a framework for centrally controlling and managing the LAN infrastructure. Regardless of where they are physically located, network administrators may set up, monitor, and administer network devices, rules, and services using a cloud-based interface.
- ***Virtual Networking***: Using Cloud-LAN, it is possible to build virtual networks in the cloud and connect them to on-premises LANs. In order to provide seamless connectivity and communication between on-premises devices and cloud-based services, virtual networks that span numerous locations can be created.
- ***Scalability and Flexibility***: Cloud-LAN provides scalability by making it simple for businesses to add new network equipment as their requirements change. It allows for the dynamic addition and deletion of network resources without the need for substantial hardware expenditures or complicated settings.

TABLE 8.8
Comparative Analysis of Cloud-based Technologies

Technology	Description	Use Cases	Benefits	Comparison
Cloud-LAN	Extends the concept of a local area network (LAN) to the cloud, enabling secure and scalable networking capabilities.	• Enterprise networking across offices or branches • Secure remote work setup • Connecting hybrid cloud environments	• Simplified network management • Scalable infrastructure • Enhanced security through cloud-based controls	• Traditional LANs are limited to physical locations; Cloud-LAN leverages cloud scalability and security.
Cloud-WAN	Leverages cloud infrastructure to provide wide area network (WAN) capabilities, connecting geographically dispersed locations.	• Connecting remote offices or branches • Optimizing traffic flow across long distances • Enabling cloud-based SD-WAN solutions	• Improved network performance with optimized routing • Cost-effective compared to traditional WAN • Flexible and scalable	• Unlike MPLS or traditional WAN, Cloud-WAN uses cloud resources for dynamic and efficient connectivity.
Cloud-MAN	Utilizes cloud computing resources to establish metropolitan area network (MAN) connectivity, enabling efficient data transfer within a city or region.	• Regional connectivity between data centers • High-speed connectivity for regional businesses • Citywide smart infrastructure	• High-speed data transfer within large geographical areas • Cost savings on infrastructure • Scalable and adaptive to growing cities	• - MANs typically cover a city or large campus, whereas Cloud-MAN offers cloud-based management and scalability.
Cloud-SDN	Combines cloud computing and software-defined networking (SDN) to provide centralized control and management of network infrastructure.	• Dynamic network configuration for cloud services • Efficient management of hybrid or multi-cloud environments • Enhancing security with real-time policy updates	• Centralized network control • Real-time traffic management • Cost reduction in hardware and maintenance	• Unlike traditional networking, Cloud-SDN decouples network control from hardware, providing flexibility and automation.
Cloud-IoT	Integrates cloud computing with the Internet of Things (IoT), enabling storage, processing, and analysis of IoT-generated data in the cloud.	• Smart home devices • Industrial IoT (IIoT) for predictive maintenance • Health monitoring systems • Smart cities for data-driven infrastructure	• Scalable storage and processing power • Real-time analytics • Cost-efficient management of IoT data	• Traditional IoT solutions might lack the storage or computational power of cloud-integrated systems, limiting scalability. Cloud-IoT offers more flexibility and real-time capabilities.

- ***Hybrid Networking***: A hybrid network environment is created by integrating on-premises infrastructure with cloud-based services via Cloud-LAN. As a result, businesses may take use of the LAN's local data processing and storage capabilities as well as the scalability and accessibility of cloud services.
- ***Security and Compliance***: To secure data and network resources, cloud-LAN systems include security measures. These could include monitoring tools, access limits, network segmentation, and encryption. Enforcing uniform security rules across LAN and cloud settings is another way to meet compliance requirements.
- ***Cloud-LAN Integration***: The integration of Cloud-LAN with other cloud-based services, such as cloud storage, virtual machines, or container platforms, is possible. Through this connection, on-premises equipment and cloud-based services may communicate and exchange data without any interruptions.

Cloud-LAN offers organizations better flexibility, scalability, and centralized control of their network infrastructure by fusing the characteristics of LAN and cloud networking. While retaining control over the local network environment, it enables effective resource utilization, streamlines network management, and encourages the use of cloud services. A comprehensive analysis of Cloud-LAN, which integrates the benefits of traditional LAN infrastructure with cloud-based networking services, is presented in Table 8.9.

The concept of Cloud-LAN blends cloud computing with traditional LAN technologies to provide a more flexible, scalable, and centrally managed networking solution. Table 8.10 offers a comparative analysis that highlights the differences and advantages of Cloud-LAN versus Traditional LAN.

8.2.2 Cloud-WAN

The combination of cloud computing with Wide Area Network (WAN) technology is referred to as cloud-WAN. To optimize and improve the connection and performance of a globally dispersed network infrastructure, cloud-based networking services are used. WANs are used to connect several remote sites over vast distances, including branch offices and data centers. To establish communication between sites, they often rely on dedicated private network connections or open Internet connections. However, organizations are increasingly turning to cloud-based solutions to enhance their WAN connectivity as a result of the emergence of cloud computing and the requirement for effective and scalable network infrastructures.

To improve the functionality and performance of a typical WAN, cloud-based networking services and technology are introduced as cloud-WAN. Some of the crucial Cloud-WAN features are illustrated below:

- Cloud-WAN's core element is software-defined wide area networking (SD-WAN). Through software-defined policies, it enables organizations to centrally manage and regulate their WAN infrastructure. In order to enable real-time monitoring, control, and optimization of network traffic across different sites, SD-WAN systems frequently make use of cloud-based management tools.

TABLE 8.9
Overview of Cloud-LAN

Feature	Description	Benefits
Centralized Network Management	A cloud-LAN framework allows businesses to centrally manage LAN infrastructure through a cloud interface. Network administrators can configure, monitor, and control devices, rules, and services remotely.	• Streamlined network administration • Simplified monitoring • Reduced need for on-site IT resources
Virtual Networking	Virtual networks are created in the cloud and connected to on-premises LANs, enabling seamless communication between local devices and cloud-based services across multiple locations.	• Seamless integration between cloud and on-premises environments • Flexibility in network expansion
Scalability and Flexibility	Cloud-LAN allows businesses to scale network resources up or down according to needs, without requiring major hardware changes or complex configurations.	• Easy addition/removal of network resources • No need for significant hardware investments
Hybrid Networking	Cloud-LAN integrates on-premises LAN infrastructure with cloud-based services, combining the benefits of local data processing and cloud scalability.	• Leverages local storage and processing power • Harnesses the scalability and flexibility of cloud services
Security and Compliance	Security tools such as encryption, monitoring, network segmentation, and access controls are integrated into the Cloud-LAN system. Ensures that security policies are enforced across LAN and cloud environments.	• Strengthened data protection • Easier compliance with industry regulations • Improved threat detection
Integration with Cloud Services	Cloud-LAN enables integration with other cloud-based services such as cloud storage, virtual machines, and container platforms. This facilitates uninterrupted data exchange between on-premises and cloud systems.	• Streamlined data exchange between local and cloud services • Reduced data silos and operational friction
Cost Efficiency	The dynamic nature of Cloud-LAN allows businesses to avoid upfront capital expenditures for hardware, reducing the need for large on-premises infrastructure.	• Lower operational costs • Avoidance of over-investment in infrastructure • Pay-as-you-grow model
Network Flexibility	Cloud-LAN's ability to create virtual networks that span multiple locations offers enhanced flexibility, enabling businesses to connect remote offices, devices, and services easily.	• Seamless inter-office connectivity • Remote work enablement • Adaptive to business expansion
Performance Optimization	Cloud-LAN can optimize network performance by routing traffic based on network conditions, balancing loads, and ensuring high availability across both cloud and on-premises systems.	• Improved network reliability • Reduced latency • Optimized resource allocation
Disaster Recovery and Continuity	By leveraging cloud services for network backup, data replication, and recovery, Cloud-LAN helps ensure business continuity in the event of hardware failures or disasters.	• Better disaster recovery capabilities • Reduced downtime • Improved business continuity

TABLE 8.10
Cloud-LAN vs. Traditional LAN

Feature	Traditional LAN	Cloud-LAN
Network Infrastructure	On-premises hardware (e.g., switches, routers, servers).	Combines on-premises hardware with cloud-based services.
Network Management	Typically managed locally by IT staff via on-site tools.	Centralized management via cloud interface, accessible remotely.
Scalability	Limited scalability; requires physical hardware upgrades.	Highly scalable with the ability to add resources dynamically via the cloud.
Flexibility	Less flexible; hardware and software are typically fixed to physical locations.	Highly flexible; resources can be provisioned, modified, or decommissioned as needed in the cloud.
Geographical Coverage	Restricted to a single physical location or site.	Network resources can span multiple locations, including remote or global sites.
Connectivity	Devices communicate within a fixed local network perimeter.	Seamless connectivity between on-premises and cloud-based resources.
Virtualization	Limited to physical or virtual machines within the LAN.	Supports full virtual networking; creates virtual networks spanning LAN and cloud environments.
Network Security	Security is managed on-site, often relying on perimeter defenses.	Security is centrally controlled, with cloud-based monitoring, encryption, and access controls integrated into the network.
Cost	High initial cost for physical infrastructure; ongoing maintenance expenses.	Pay-as-you-go model with reduced capital expenditures; operational cost depends on usage.
Management Complexity	Requires local IT staff for on-site management, troubleshooting, and upgrades.	Simplifies management via centralized cloud interface, reducing local IT workload.
Performance	High performance for local traffic, but limited by physical hardware capabilities.	Can provide high performance, especially with cloud-based infrastructure optimized for scalability and load balancing.
Resilience and Redundancy	Resilience depends on physical infrastructure and backup systems.	Built-in redundancy and failover mechanisms through cloud resources, enhancing reliability.
Hybrid Capabilities	Difficult to integrate with cloud services without additional tools or third-party solutions.	Seamless hybrid integration with cloud services such as storage, virtual machines, and containers.
Compliance	Compliance is often managed through on-premises tools and systems.	Easier to enforce compliance with unified security and data management policies across both LAN and cloud.
Resource Utilization	Often underutilized due to over-provisioning for peak loads.	Optimized resource usage, scaling automatically with demand.

TABLE 8.10
(Continued)

Feature	Traditional LAN	Cloud-LAN
Network Upgrade Cycle	Physical upgrades are time-consuming and costly.	Cloud infrastructure upgrades are handled by the cloud provider, ensuring up-to-date technology.
Disaster Recovery	Requires manual setup of disaster recovery mechanisms.	Built-in disaster recovery through cloud redundancy and distributed resources.
Cloud Integration	Limited cloud integration; usually requires third-party networking tools.	Native integration with cloud services for seamless interaction between on-premises and cloud-based resources.
Security and Compliance Management	Security policies are applied locally, which may be less consistent.	Security policies can be consistently enforced across both LAN and cloud environments, aiding compliance.

- Virtual Private Networks (VPNs): To provide safe and secure connections between remote locations and the cloud, Cloud-WAN makes use of VPN technology. When sending private information across open networks, such as the Internet, VPNs protect data privacy and confidentiality.
- Dynamic Path Selection: To intelligently route traffic across the best network pathways, Cloud-WAN systems use dynamic path selection algorithms. To guarantee effective utilization of available bandwidth and to prioritize traffic depending on particular requirements, this involves utilizing numerous Internet connections, such as MPLS, broadband, or 4G/5G.
- Bandwidth Optimization: To maximize the use of available bandwidth, Cloud-WAN makes use of methods including data compression, deduplication, and traffic prioritization. This ensures effective utilization of the available network resources, enhances application performance, and lessens network congestion.
- Seamless Integration with Cloud Services: To offer direct and secure connection to cloud-based services, Cloud-WAN integrates with cloud service providers. By doing away with traffic backhauling to the company's data center, this connection offers quicker access to cloud apps, enhancing user experience and productivity.
- Centralized Management and Control: Cloud-WAN solutions offer a management and control layer that is centralized, making it simple for network administrators to set up, watch over, and administer the WAN infrastructure. With this centralized method, network administration is made easier, operational complexity is decreased, and network upgrades and modifications can be deployed quickly.
- Scalability and Flexibility: Cloud-WAN provides scalability by making it simple for businesses to add or remove network resources and change bandwidth capacity as necessary. It offers the adaptability needed to meet shifting business needs and effectively supports the expansion of the network infrastructure.

Improved network speed, increased security, easier management, and cost optimization are just a few advantages of cloud-WAN. In order to improve WAN connection, lessen dependency on specialized hardware, and expand their network architecture to suit changing business demands, it enables organizations to use cloud-based networking services. A comprehensive analysis of Cloud-WAN, which integrates cloud-based networking services with traditional WAN technology to enhance connectivity and performance for globally distributed networks, is given in Table 8.11.

Cloud-WAN is an evolution of traditional WANs, leveraging cloud computing to optimize connectivity, improve performance, and enhance network management. Table 8.12 offers a comparative analysis highlighting the key differences and advantages of Cloud-WAN versus Traditional WAN.

TABLE 8.11
Overview of Cloud-WAN

Feature	Description	Benefits
Software-Defined WAN (SD-WAN)	Cloud-WAN's core component, SD-WAN, enables centralized management and policy control over WAN infrastructure. This allows for real-time monitoring and optimization of traffic across remote sites.	• Centralized control and management • Simplified traffic optimization • Increased agility in network management
Virtual Private Networks (VPNs)	Cloud-WAN uses VPN technology to secure communication between remote locations and the cloud, ensuring privacy and confidentiality when sending data across open networks like the Internet.	• Enhanced data privacy and security • Safe transmission of sensitive information • Secure remote access
Dynamic Path Selection	Cloud-WAN utilizes algorithms for dynamic path selection, intelligently routing traffic across the most efficient network paths based on real-time conditions.	• Optimized traffic routing • Better bandwidth utilization • Prioritization of critical traffic
Bandwidth Optimization	Cloud-WAN employs techniques such as data compression, deduplication, and traffic prioritization to make better use of available bandwidth, reduce congestion, and enhance performance.	• Improved application performance • Reduced network congestion • More efficient use of network resources
Seamless Integration with Cloud Services	Cloud-WAN directly integrates with cloud services, eliminating the need for traffic backhauling to a central data center. This provides faster, more direct access to cloud applications.	• Faster access to cloud services • Enhanced user experience • Reduced latency for cloud-based applications
Centralized Management and Control	Cloud-WAN offers centralized management, simplifying network setup, monitoring, and administration. This reduces operational complexity and facilitates quick network adjustments.	• Simplified network administration • Reduced operational complexity • Quicker deployment of network changes

TABLE 8.11 (Continued)

Feature	Description	Benefits
Scalability and Flexibility	Cloud-WAN allows businesses to easily scale their network by adding or removing resources and adjusting bandwidth capacity as needed. It supports growth and changing business needs.	• Scalable network infrastructure • Flexibility to adapt to changing requirements • Supports network expansion
Cost Optimization	By leveraging cloud-based services, Cloud-WAN reduces reliance on expensive dedicated hardware and improves the efficiency of bandwidth utilization, resulting in lower operational costs.	• Reduced hardware costs • Optimized bandwidth utilization • Cost-effective scalability
Improved Performance and Speed	Cloud-WAN enhances network speed by using cloud-based management tools to prioritize traffic, balance loads, and select optimal paths, which reduces latency and improves user experience.	• Reduced latency • Improved application performance • Faster and more reliable network connectivity
Global Network Connectivity	Cloud-WAN provides improved connectivity between global remote sites, branch offices, and data centers by optimizing routing and utilizing cloud-based network resources.	• Enhanced global connectivity • More reliable inter-office communication • Support for remote offices and distributed teams

TABLE 8.12
Cloud-WAN vs. Traditional WAN

Feature	Traditional WAN	Cloud-WAN
Infrastructure	Relies on physical hardware (e.g., leased lines, MPLS, private circuits).	Uses cloud-based networking services combined with SD-WAN for optimized traffic management.
Network Management	Managed on-site, with local control over each remote site.	Centrally managed through cloud-based software, allowing for real-time monitoring and optimization.
Scalability	Scaling requires adding physical network resources (e.g., additional circuits, devices).	Highly scalable; resources can be dynamically added or removed with cloud integration, often without physical hardware changes.
Flexibility	Less flexible due to dependence on physical connections and dedicated hardware.	Very flexible; can use multiple connections (MPLS, broadband, 4G/5G) and adapt quickly to changing traffic needs.

TABLE 8.12
(Continued)

Feature	Traditional WAN	Cloud-WAN
Cost Structure	High upfront costs for dedicated circuits and equipment; ongoing maintenance fees.	Opex (Operational expenditure) model; pay-as-you-go or subscription-based pricing with reduced capital expenditures.
Performance Optimization	Typically uses fixed routing protocols and static bandwidth allocations, which can lead to inefficiencies.	Uses SD-WAN technology to dynamically select optimal paths based on real-time traffic conditions, improving overall performance.
Traffic Routing	Relies on static routing or manual traffic engineering, often resulting in less efficient traffic management.	Dynamic path selection algorithms optimize traffic routes based on available bandwidth and application needs.
Security	Security primarily relies on traditional VPNs, firewalls, and encryption over leased lines or internet connections.	Uses VPNs along with centralized security policies and advanced encryption to protect data in transit across various network paths.
Bandwidth Utilization	Bandwidth is typically fixed and may lead to under-utilization or congestion.	Optimizes bandwidth through techniques such as data compression, deduplication, and traffic prioritization.
Integration with Cloud Services	Requires backhauling traffic through data centers, adding latency and reducing performance for cloud-based apps.	Direct, secure connection to cloud services, removing the need for backhauling, improving cloud app performance and user experience.
Management Complexity	Requires local IT staff at each site to manage and configure network equipment.	Centralized, cloud-based management simplifies setup, monitoring, troubleshooting, and updates.
Disaster Recovery and Redundancy	Requires manual setup of redundant paths, and disaster recovery may be localized.	Built-in cloud redundancy and failover, enhancing network resilience and disaster recovery capabilities.
Deployment Speed	Physical installation and configuration of network devices can be time-consuming.	Quick deployment and provisioning through cloud-based services, reducing time to scale or make changes.
Global Connectivity	Typically limited by the physical network infrastructure and may incur high costs for international connections.	Cloud-WAN provides seamless, cost-effective global connectivity by leveraging Internet links and cloud infrastructure.
Compliance and Policy Enforcement	Security and compliance policies are managed locally, which can lead to inconsistency across sites.	Centralized policy enforcement across all sites, ensuring uniform security and compliance measures.
Cost of Network Upgrades	Upgrades involve significant capital investment in hardware and dedicated circuits.	Cloud-WAN upgrades are handled by the cloud provider, with no need for physical hardware investment, reducing overall costs.
Vendor Dependency	Often dependent on traditional telecommunication providers and hardware vendors.	Less vendor lock-in as cloud-based services are more flexible and can support multiple service providers.

8.2.3 Cloud-MAN

The term "Cloud-MAN," which stands for Cloud Metropolitan Area Network, refers to a networking idea that blends cloud computing functionality with MAN architecture. A MAN is a network that covers a metropolitan area, usually a city or a sizable piece of land. The advantages of cloud computing are expanded by Cloud-MAN to the local network infrastructure. To improve the scalability, flexibility, and administration of a MAN, it entails the integration of cloud-based networking services, virtualization, and software-defined networking (SDN) technologies.

The main features of Cloud-MAN are given below:

- ***Cloud-Based Networking Services*:** To offer network functionalities within the MAN, Cloud-MAN makes use of cloud-based networking services, such as virtual routers, switches, firewalls, and load balancers. Physical network appliances are not required at any site because these services are delivered and controlled in the cloud.
- ***Software-Defined Networking (SDN)*:** By separating the network control plane from the underlying hardware architecture, SDN is essential to Cloud-MAN. It makes it simpler to set up and deploy network services throughout the MAN by enabling centralized administration and control of network resources. Network optimizations, policy enforcement, and dynamic traffic routing are all made possible by SDN.
- ***Virtualization*:** Cloud-MAN makes use of network virtualization methods to build logical networks separate from the actual network infrastructure. The segmentation of the MAN into virtual network domains made possible by virtualization allows for better resource allocation, security, and isolation.
- ***Scalability and Flexibility*:** By utilizing cloud resources to increase network capacity as needed, Cloud-MAN offers scalability and flexibility. Without the need to replace their physical infrastructure, businesses may quickly add or remove network resources and change bandwidth to meet changing demands.
- ***Centralized Network Administration*:** Within the metropolitan region, Cloud-MAN provides centralized administration and control of the complete network infrastructure. From a centralized management platform, network administrators may set up, monitor, and manage network services, rules, and security, giving them improved visibility and control over the network.
- ***Resource Optimization*:** By dynamically distributing bandwidth in accordance with demand, Cloud-MAN maximizes the use of network resources. It ensures effective use of the available network capacity, improving performance and lowering costs.
- ***High Availability and Resilience*:** By utilizing cloud-based redundancy and failover techniques, Cloud-MAN improves the network's availability and resilience. Traffic can be automatically diverted through other pathways inside the cloud architecture in the case of a network breakdown or disruption.

Improved scalability, flexibility, and management of the network infrastructure within a metropolitan region are only a few advantages provided by cloud-MAN. It allows businesses to take use of cloud-based networking services to maximize resource usage, simplify network maintenance, and adjust to shifting business needs. A basis for installing cutting-edge technologies such as IoT, edge computing, and real-time analytics within the metropolitan area network is also provided by cloud-MAN.

A comprehensive tabular analysis of Cloud-MAN, which integrates cloud computing technologies with MAN architecture to enhance scalability, flexibility, and network management, is provided in Table 8.13.

TABLE 8.13
Overview of Cloud-MAN

Feature	Description	Benefits
Cloud-Based Networking Services	Cloud-MAN uses cloud-based services such as virtual routers, switches, firewalls, and load balancers to provide network functionalities, eliminating the need for physical appliances at each site.	• No need for on-site physical hardware • Simplified network management • Reduced hardware maintenance costs
Software-Defined Networking (SDN)	SDN enables centralized control of the network, separating the control plane from hardware. It allows dynamic traffic routing, policy enforcement, and optimized network resource management.	• Centralized control and automation • Easier network configuration and deployment • Efficient resource management
Virtualization	Cloud-MAN utilizes network virtualization to create logical networks distinct from the physical infrastructure, enabling better network segmentation, isolation, and resource allocation.	• Improved network isolation and security • Better resource allocation and management • Enhanced scalability
Scalability and Flexibility	Cloud-MAN can scale its network capacity by leveraging cloud resources. Businesses can easily add or remove network resources or adjust bandwidth as needed without upgrading physical infrastructure.	• Quick scaling to meet growing demand • Adaptability to business changes • No need for costly infrastructure upgrades
Centralized Network Administration	Centralized management allows network administrators to monitor, configure, and control the entire network from a single platform, giving them full visibility and control.	• Simplified network management • Enhanced visibility and control • Faster issue identification and resolution
Resource Optimization	Cloud-MAN dynamically allocates bandwidth based on real-time demand, ensuring efficient utilization of available resources and improved network performance.	• Better performance with optimized resource use • Reduced network congestion • Cost savings by using resources efficiently

TABLE 8.13 (Continued)

Feature	Description	Benefits
High Availability and Resilience	Cloud-MAN increases network availability by using cloud-based redundancy and failover mechanisms. Traffic can be automatically rerouted if there is a network failure or disruption.	• Increased network uptime and reliability • Reduced impact of network disruptions • Improved business continuity
Support for Advanced Technologies	Cloud-MAN facilitates the deployment of cutting-edge technologies such as IoT, edge computing, and real-time analytics within the metropolitan area network.	• Enables deployment of advanced technologies • Supports smart city applications • Serves as a better support for real-time data processing
Cost Efficiency	By eliminating the need for physical network hardware and offering pay-as-you-go cloud resources, Cloud-MAN reduces capital expenditures and operational costs for businesses.	• Reduced capital and operational costs • No need for expensive physical infrastructure • Flexible pricing models based on demand
Improved Network Performance	Cloud-MAN improves network performance by utilizing cloud-based resources and optimizations, ensuring efficient routing and low-latency connections across the metropolitan network.	• Optimized network traffic routing • Lower latency for critical applications • Enhanced user experience

Cloud-MAN represents a modern approach to metropolitan area networking by integrating cloud computing, SDN, and virtualization. Cloud-MAN offers significant advantages for businesses by providing a flexible, scalable, and cost-efficient network infrastructure within a metropolitan region. By integrating cloud computing with MAN architecture, it simplifies network maintenance, improves performance, and enables the deployment of next-generation technologies such as IoT, edge computing, and real-time analytics. Table 8.14 offers a tabular comparative analysis of Cloud-MAN and Traditional MAN to highlight the differences and advantages of each approach.

8.2.4 Cloud-SDN

Cloud-SDN, also known as cloud software-defined networking, is the combination of cloud computing with SDN concepts. In order to create a flexible, scalable, and programmable network architecture, it combines the advantages of cloud-based infrastructure with software-defined network control.

Similar to how virtual computers or containers are deployed in a cloud environment, Cloud-SDN virtualizes and abstracts the network infrastructure from the underlying physical hardware. The data plane, which manages real data forwarding,

TABLE 8.14
Cloud-MAN vs. Traditional MAN

Feature	Traditional MAN	Cloud-MAN
Infrastructure	Relies on physical network appliances such as routers, switches, and firewalls deployed in various locations within the metropolitan area.	Utilizes cloud-based services such as virtual routers, switches, firewalls, and load balancers, minimizing the need for on-site hardware.
Network Control	Typically controlled and managed through a centralized local infrastructure, requiring manual configuration and updates.	Uses Software-Defined Networking (SDN) to separate the control plane from the physical hardware, enabling centralized, dynamic management via a cloud platform.
Scalability	Scaling up requires adding physical devices or upgrading existing network equipment, which is often slow and costly.	Cloud-MAN offers on-demand scalability using cloud resources, allowing businesses to easily adjust capacity without changing physical infrastructure.
Flexibility	Limited flexibility due to reliance on fixed, physical infrastructure.	Highly flexible as resources, bandwidth, and network configurations can be adjusted in real-time based on demand and changing requirements.
Cost Structure	High upfront capital expenses for purchasing and maintaining physical hardware (e.g., routers, switches, fiber lines).	Reduced capital expenditure with pay-as-you-go cloud services, lowering both upfront and operational costs.
Network Management	Network management is often decentralized with local administrators managing individual sites or segments.	Centralized network management allows network administrators to oversee and control the entire metropolitan area network through a single-cloud platform.
Resource Optimization	Less efficient use of available resources, with fixed bandwidth allocations and static network paths.	Dynamic resource allocation and bandwidth optimization, adjusting in real-time to traffic patterns and demand, maximizing efficiency.
Virtualization	Limited or no use of network virtualization; physical infrastructure dictates the network's configuration and topology.	Network virtualization is central to Cloud-MAN, creating logical, isolated networks within the same physical infrastructure to improve resource usage, security, and management.
Traffic Routing	Static routing based on pre-configured rules or static bandwidth allocations.	Dynamic traffic routing enabled by SDN, intelligently selecting the best network paths based on current traffic, congestion, and availability.
Network Resilience	Relies on physical redundancy, which can be costly and complex to maintain.	Built-in resilience through cloud-based redundancy, with automatic failover and traffic rerouting in case of network disruptions or failures.

TABLE 8.14
(Continued)

Feature	Traditional MAN	Cloud-MAN
Security	Security is often managed via on-site firewalls and physical network segmentation, potentially creating gaps in uniform policy enforcement.	Centralized security policies can be enforced across the entire network, with encryption, traffic monitoring, and automated policy enforcement through SDN and cloud services.
Cloud Integration	Limited cloud integration; cloud services often require backhauling traffic through centralized data centers, which can add latency.	Seamless integration with cloud-based services, enabling direct, low-latency connections to cloud platforms, improving the performance of cloud applications.
Deployment Speed	Deployment of new services or infrastructure is slow, requiring physical installation of equipment and connectivity.	Rapid deployment and provisioning of network resources, services, and bandwidth adjustments through cloud-based infrastructure.
Vendor Lock-in	Dependent on specific telecom or hardware vendors, leading to potential vendor lock-in.	More flexibility in vendor choice, as Cloud-MAN can leverage a variety of cloud providers and networking technologies, reducing dependence on any one vendor.
Compliance and Policy Enforcement	Compliance management is often decentralized and dependent on manual configuration at each network node.	Centralized control allows for consistent policy enforcement, ensuring compliance with industry standards across all locations in the metropolitan area.
Cost of Maintenance	Ongoing maintenance costs for physical equipment, including upgrades, replacements, and management of network devices.	Lower maintenance costs due to reliance on cloud providers who handle infrastructure upkeep, upgrades, and security.
Adaptability for Emerging Technologies	Limited support for modern technologies such as IoT, edge computing, or real-time analytics, which often require substantial physical infrastructure.	Ideal for emerging technologies, with Cloud-MAN enabling support for IoT devices, edge computing nodes, and real-time data analytics, all easily integrated into the cloud infrastructure.

is decoupled from the control plane, which is in charge of network administration and setup. Because of this division, network resources can be managed and orchestrated centrally and throughout the whole cloud architecture.

Following are some crucial Cloud-SDN features:

- ***Centralized Network Control*:** Cloud-SDN centralizes the control plane, which is a cloud-based controller where network policies and settings are controlled. In order to manage and configure network resources effectively, this controller serves as a single point of control and offers a global view of the network.

- ***Virtualized Network Functions***: Cloud-SDN virtualized network functions and services using Network Function Virtualization (NFV). In the cloud context, network services such as load balancing, routing, switching, and firewalls are implemented as virtual instances that can be dynamically created, scaled, and controlled.
- ***Automation and Programmability***: Through open APIs (Application Programming Interfaces) and standards such as OpenFlow, Cloud-SDN makes networks programmable. This boosts operational effectiveness and speeds up service rollout by enabling network administrators and developers to automate network setup, provisioning, and administration processes.
- ***Dynamic Network Resource Allocation***: Cloud-SDN allows for the dynamic allocation and reallocation of network resources in response to application demand. This flexibility enables on-demand scaling to accommodate shifting traffic patterns and needs while enabling effective network capacity utilization.
- ***Service-Level Agreement (SLA) Enforcement***: By dynamically implementing network policies and quality of service (QoS) parameters, Cloud-SDN enables ways to enforce Service-Level Agreements (SLAs). This assures the network speed, capacity, and security requirements for cloud-based applications and services.
- ***Support for Multi-Tenancy***: With the help of Cloud-SDN, many businesses or clients may safely share a single-cloud infrastructure while retaining logical seclusion. With independent control and data plane instances for each tenant, each virtual network may provide privacy and security.
- ***Cloud-SDN Integration***: The integration of cloud-SDN with cloud computing infrastructure, including virtualized servers, storage, and orchestration platforms. This connection enables seamless network resource provisioning and management with other cloud services, facilitating effective resource management and improved application performance.

Among the many advantages of cloud-SDN are increased network flexibility, scalability, and agility. It gives businesses the ability to manage and optimize network resources on a dynamic basis in accordance with application requirements, improving performance, lowering operating costs, and accelerating service delivery. Cloud-SDN offers a strong foundation for creating and operating contemporary, software-defined networks within cloud settings by fusing the strengths of cloud computing with SDN. A comprehensive analysis of Cloud-SDN, which virtualizes and abstracts network infrastructure in cloud environments, providing centralized control and enhanced network management capabilities, is provided in Table 8.15.

Cloud-SDN integrates the flexibility and scalability of cloud computing with the capabilities of SDN. By virtualizing and abstracting the network infrastructure, Cloud-SDN offers a more dynamic, centralized approach to network management. Table 8.16 offers a comparative analysis of Cloud-SDN versus Traditional SDN, outlining key features and differences between the two approaches.

TABLE 8.15
Overview of Cloud-SDN

Feature	Description	Benefits
Centralized Network Control	Cloud-SDN centralizes the control plane in a cloud-based controller, which manages network policies and settings. It offers a global view of the network and simplifies management.	• Single point of control for network policies • Enhanced network visibility • Simplified network configuration
Virtualized Network Functions	Network functions such as load balancing, routing, switching, and firewalls are virtualized using Network Function Virtualization (NFV), enabling dynamic creation, scaling, and control of network services.	• On-demand network service provisioning • Dynamic scaling of services • Reduced dependency on physical hardware
Automation and Programmability	Cloud-SDN enables network programmability using open APIs like OpenFlow. This allows for automation of network setup, provisioning, and administration, increasing operational efficiency.	• Faster service rollout • Streamlined network management • Reduced manual intervention and errors
Dynamic Network Resource Allocation	Cloud-SDN allows for dynamic allocation and reallocation of network resources based on real-time application demand, optimizing network performance and capacity utilization.	• On-demand network resource allocation • Improved capacity utilization • Adaptive network to traffic demands
Service-Level Agreement (SLA) Enforcement	Cloud-SDN enforces SLAs by implementing network policies and quality of service (QoS) parameters, ensuring that network speed, capacity, and security requirements are met.	• Ensures consistent performance for cloud applications • Guarantees network reliability • Optimized QoS management
Support for Multi-Tenancy	Cloud-SDN allows multiple businesses or clients to securely share the same cloud infrastructure while maintaining logical isolation, ensuring privacy and security for each tenant.	• Safe multi-tenant environment • Logical separation of tenants • Secure sharing of cloud resources
Integration with Cloud Infrastructure	Cloud-SDN integrates seamlessly with other cloud-based resources, such as virtualized servers, storage, and orchestration platforms, enabling effective network resource provisioning.	• Seamless integration with cloud services • Improved resource management • Enhanced application performance
Network Flexibility and Agility	Cloud-SDN enhances network flexibility and agility by decoupling the control plane from the data plane, allowing for rapid adjustments and changes based on business requirements.	• Agile network architecture • Faster response to changes in traffic and application demands • Enhanced adaptability
Cost Efficiency	By virtualizing network functions and leveraging cloud resources, Cloud-SDN reduces the need for dedicated physical infrastructure, leading to significant cost savings.	• Lower capital and operational costs • Reduced need for physical hardware • Pay-as-you-grow scalability

TABLE 8.15
(Continued)

Feature	Description	Benefits
Enhanced Network Performance	Cloud-SDN optimizes network performance by dynamically allocating resources, optimizing traffic flow, and ensuring effective capacity utilization across the cloud environment.	• Improved application performance • Reduced latency • Better traffic management across the network

TABLE 8.16
Cloud-SDN vs. Traditional SDN

Feature	Traditional SDN	Cloud-SDN
Control Plane	Control plane is typically decentralized or localized, often managed by physical SDN controllers or switches in the data center.	Centralized control plane located in the cloud, allowing for a unified and global view of the network, with centralized policy management.
Network Virtualization	Focuses on virtualizing network functions within the data center or specific locations, but still often relies on physical hardware for network traffic management.	Fully virtualized network functions (e.g., routing, switching, load balancing, firewalling) in the cloud using Network Function Virtualization (NFV).
Resource Allocation	Static resource allocation, often requiring manual configuration and provisioning of physical network devices or virtual appliances.	Dynamic, on-demand resource allocation based on real-time traffic demand, with flexible scaling in the cloud environment.
Network Automation	Limited to specific programmable configurations for devices and network services; automation depends on available SDN controllers and scripts.	Full automation through open APIs (e.g., OpenFlow), allowing for end-to-end network provisioning, configuration, and management at scale.
Management and Orchestration	Managed within a single physical or virtual environment, requiring manual updates and patches to SDN controllers and network devices.	Cloud-SDN supports automated orchestration across large, distributed environments, allowing for real-time monitoring, updates, and configurations from a single platform.
Scalability	Scalability is often constrained by the physical hardware limitations of the SDN controller and underlying infrastructure.	Highly scalable with the cloud's elastic resource allocation, allowing seamless scaling without hardware constraints.
Multi-Tenancy Support	SDN can support multi-tenancy in isolated, predefined environments, often requiring additional hardware or software configurations for each tenant.	Built-in support for multi-tenancy through logical isolation in the cloud, with each tenant having their own virtualized network resources while maintaining data privacy and security.

TABLE 8.16 (Continued)

Feature	Traditional SDN	Cloud-SDN
Quality of Service (QoS) and SLA	Typically, SDN enforces policies based on predefined traffic patterns or rules; SLA enforcement requires manual configuration.	Dynamic SLA enforcement, with real-time QoS adjustments based on cloud-based application performance, ensuring consistent service levels across varying traffic demands.
Deployment Flexibility	Deployment often requires hardware installation and setup of SDN controllers, which can be limited by existing infrastructure.	Cloud-SDN offers flexible deployment and integration, allowing networks to be deployed as a service and rapidly scaled across multiple cloud platforms.
Cost Structure	Involves higher upfront costs for physical hardware, SDN controllers, and network infrastructure. Ongoing operational costs depend on the size and complexity of the SDN environment.	Subscription-based or pay-as-you-go pricing models for cloud resources, reducing capital expenditures and offering flexible, operational cost management.
Security	Security relies on local SDN controllers and network policies, which are manually managed and configured for each network segment.	Enhanced security through centralized control and the ability to dynamically enforce security policies, encryption, and access controls across the entire cloud-based network.
Integration with Cloud Services	Integrates with cloud services but often requires additional configurations for hybrid cloud environments, especially across multiple vendors.	Seamless integration with cloud computing platforms (virtualized servers, storage, orchestration), allowing for unified management of cloud resources and applications.
Latency	Latency depends on the physical distance between SDN controllers and network devices, and the complexity of managing traffic within physical boundaries.	Reduced latency due to cloud proximity to network resources, offering faster response times for traffic management and policy enforcement in distributed environments.
Network Visibility	Provides visibility into the network only within specific locations or environments, requiring multiple tools for full network monitoring across different sites.	Centralized, cloud-based visibility across the entire network, providing real-time insights into performance, security, and traffic from a unified platform.
Disaster Recovery and Resilience	Relies on physical redundancy, which may require separate infrastructure for failover and disaster recovery.	Built-in cloud resilience with automatic failover, redundancy, and traffic rerouting, ensuring high availability and continuous operation even in case of network failures.
Support for Emerging Technologies	SDN can support modern technologies such as IoT, but integration and management can be complex and require additional infrastructure.	Seamless support for IoT, edge computing, and real-time analytics through cloud-native integrations, providing an efficient foundation for these emerging technologies.

8.2.5 Cloud-IoT

The combination of cloud computing with the Internet of Things (IoT) ecosystem is known as cloud-IoT. It enables scalable, secure, and effective IoT deployments by fusing the capabilities of cloud platforms and services with those of IoT devices, networks, and applications. IoT devices, sensors, and actuators gather and produce data in a Cloud-IoT architecture, which is then sent to the cloud for archival, processing, and analysis. The infrastructure and services required to manage and value-extract from the enormous volumes of IoT data are provided by cloud platforms.

Some crucial features of Cloud-IoT are discussed below:

- ***Data Processing and Storage*:** Cloud-IoT makes use of the processing and storage resources of the cloud to manage the enormous amounts of data produced by IoT devices. Data is safely transported to the cloud, where it may be archived, catalogued, and organized for further research and understanding.
- ***Scalability and Elasticity*:** Cloud systems provide the scalability and elasticity needed to handle the data streams and IoT devices that are constantly increasing in number. The cloud architecture can dynamically scale resources up or down to meet demand as the IoT deployment grows, enabling seamless operations and effective resource utilization.
- ***Real-time Analytics and Insights*:** By using cloud-based analytics services, Cloud-IoT makes real-time data analytics and insights possible. Organizations may get valuable insights from IoT data in almost real-time by utilizing machine learning algorithms, complicated event processing, and predictive analytics, enabling proactive decision-making and useful knowledge.
- ***Device Provisioning and Management*:** Cloud-IoT offers centralized capabilities for device provisioning and management. In order to ensure effective device onboarding, software upgrades, and security patching, IoT devices may be remotely setup, monitored, and controlled via the cloud.
- ***Integration and Connectivity*:** Cloud-IoT enables easy integration and connectivity of various IoT devices and protocols. Diverse IoT communication protocols, including MQTT or HTTP, are supported by cloud platforms, enabling data sharing and communication between devices from diverse suppliers in the IoT ecosystem.
- ***Security and Privacy*:** To safeguard IoT data, devices, and communications, Cloud-IoT integrates strong security mechanisms. To protect IoT deployments from cyber threats and unauthorized access, cloud platforms include authentication, encryption, access control, and security monitoring features.
- ***Application Enablement*:** By offering application enablement services, cloud-based IoT platforms allow developers create IoT applications more quickly. These services, which make it easier to create and deploy IoT applications, may comprise APIs, development frameworks, software development kits (SDKs), and pre-built components.

Scalability, flexibility, cost-effectiveness, and a quicker time to market for IoT solutions are just a few advantages of cloud-IoT. It enables businesses to take advantage of cloud computing's capabilities to manage and get insights from IoT data, improving operational effectiveness, enhancing customer experiences, and creating cutting-edge IoT applications and services. A comprehensive analysis of Cloud-IoT, which combines cloud computing with the IoT ecosystem to enable scalable, secure, and effective IoT deployments, is provided in Table 8.17.

TABLE 8.17
Overview of Cloud-IoT

Feature	Description	Benefits
Data Processing and Storage	Cloud-IoT utilizes cloud resources for processing and storing large volumes of data generated by IoT devices. Data is securely transmitted to the cloud for archival, organization, and further analysis.	• Efficient storage and management of IoT data • Scalable data processing capacity • Enhanced data accessibility
Scalability and Elasticity	Cloud-IoT leverages the inherent scalability and elasticity of cloud platforms to handle the increasing number of IoT devices and data streams. Resources can be scaled dynamically based on demand.	• Seamless expansion as IoT deployments grow • Cost-effective resource utilization • Flexibility to meet growing needs
Real-time Analytics and Insights	Cloud-IoT uses cloud-based analytics services to perform real-time analytics on IoT data, applying machine learning and predictive analytics for proactive decision-making.	• Timely insights and informed decision-making • Predictive maintenance and anomaly detection • Real-time operational visibility
Device Provisioning and Management	Cloud-IoT provides centralized control for provisioning, managing, and monitoring IoT devices. Remote onboarding, software upgrades, and security patching can be done via the cloud.	• Streamlined device setup and management • Remote updates and security maintenance • Enhanced device lifecycle management
Integration and Connectivity	Cloud-IoT ensures easy integration and communication between diverse IoT devices and protocols. It supports various IoT communication protocols (e.g., MQTT, HTTP) for seamless data exchange.	• Interoperability between different devices and ecosystems • Simplified data sharing • Enhanced device connectivity
Security and Privacy	Cloud-IoT incorporates robust security features such as encryption, authentication, access control, and security monitoring to protect IoT data and devices from cyber threats and unauthorized access.	• Enhanced protection against cyber threats • Secure data transmission • Privacy controls to safeguard user information

TABLE 8.17
(Continued)

Feature	Description	Benefits
Application Enablement	Cloud-IoT platforms provide application enablement services that assist developers in creating, deploying, and managing IoT applications quickly. This includes APIs, SDKs, and pre-built components.	• Accelerated IoT application development • Simplified application deployment • Pre-built components for faster innovation
Cost Efficiency	Cloud-IoT offers a pay-as-you-go model, eliminating the need for businesses to invest in expensive on-premises infrastructure. Cloud resources can be utilized effectively as per IoT needs.	• Reduced capital expenditure • Flexible cost structure based on usage • Efficient resource allocation to meet demand
Operational Efficiency	By integrating cloud computing with IoT, businesses can optimize their operations, improve automation, and increase productivity with data-driven insights and cloud-based services.	• Improved operational workflows • Automation of routine tasks • Greater operational efficiency and decision support
Faster Time to Market	Cloud-IoT helps businesses quickly scale their IoT deployments and get products and services to market faster by leveraging cloud-based tools and resources.	• Accelerated IoT product development • Rapid deployment of IoT solutions • Reduced time for prototyping and testing

Cloud-IoT combines cloud computing's scalability and flexibility with the capabilities of the IoT ecosystem. This integration significantly enhances the management, analysis, and processing of IoT data, enabling organizations to deploy scalable and secure IoT solutions. Table 8.18 offers a comparative analysis between Cloud-IoT and Traditional IoT Architecture to highlight key differences and benefits.

TABLE 8.18
Cloud-IoT vs. Traditional IoT Architecture

Feature	Traditional IoT Architecture	Cloud-IoT
Data Processing and Storage	Typically relies on edge devices, local servers, or on-premises systems to process and store IoT data. This can lead to storage limitations and higher processing delays.	Utilizes cloud platforms for scalable data storage and processing, enabling efficient management of vast IoT data volumes with fast processing capabilities.

TABLE 8.18 (Continued)

Feature	Traditional IoT Architecture	Cloud-IoT
Scalability	Scalability is limited by the capacity of local infrastructure (e.g., on-premises servers, gateways). Scaling often involves significant investment in hardware and system upgrades.	Cloud-IoT provides on-demand scalability, automatically adjusting resources to meet the growing number of devices and data streams. This allows seamless expansion without major infrastructure changes.
Real-Time Analytics and Insights	Real-time analytics are often limited or require on-premises solutions like edge computing, which may not be as powerful as cloud-based analytics.	Cloud-IoT enables real-time data analytics and machine learning (ML) for immediate insights and predictions, helping organizations make data-driven decisions quickly.
Device Provisioning and Management	Device management is usually handled locally, with manual configuration or software updates, which can be cumbersome for large IoT deployments.	Cloud-IoT offers centralized device provisioning and management, enabling remote configuration, monitoring, software updates, and security patching, streamlining operations.
Integration and Connectivity	IoT devices may use proprietary or non-standard communication protocols, making integration between different IoT systems or vendors more complex.	Cloud-IoT supports multiple communication protocols (e.g., MQTT, HTTP), allowing seamless integration of a wide range of IoT devices and vendors, promoting interoperability.
Security and Privacy	Security measures are typically implemented locally and may involve complex configurations for each device and gateway, often lacking centralized monitoring.	Cloud-IoT integrates strong cloud-based security features such as encryption, authentication, access control, and continuous monitoring, offering a unified and proactive security approach.
Application Enablement	Developing IoT applications may require significant in-house infrastructure, tools, and expertise to handle data storage, processing, and device management.	Cloud-IoT platforms provide development tools, APIs, and pre-built components that accelerate the creation and deployment of IoT applications, reducing time to market.
Cost Efficiency	High initial costs for infrastructure, maintenance, and scaling (e.g., adding more servers or storage). Costs can increase as IoT deployments grow.	Cloud-IoT uses a pay-as-you-go model, reducing upfront capital investment and operational costs. It allows businesses to scale and pay for only the resources they use, making it cost-effective as deployments expand.
Edge Computing vs. Cloud Processing	Edge computing is often required to handle data processing closer to the IoT devices to reduce latency and bandwidth use, especially in real-time applications.	Cloud-IoT allows both cloud and edge computing, enabling a hybrid approach that provides the flexibility to process critical data at the edge and less time-sensitive data in the cloud.

TABLE 8.18
(Continued)

Feature	Traditional IoT Architecture	Cloud-IoT
Operational Complexity	Managing an IoT network is more complex and resource-intensive with on-premises infrastructure, especially as the number of devices increases.	Cloud-IoT simplifies management with centralized, cloud-based platforms that provide easy-to-use dashboards, monitoring, and automated management features.
Data Sharing and Collaboration	Data sharing across different systems or departments may be slower and more difficult, especially if they rely on different local infrastructures or platforms.	Cloud-IoT enables easy sharing of IoT data across teams, organizations, and stakeholders in real-time, fostering collaboration and improving decision-making.
Reliability and Redundancy	Traditional IoT systems may lack built-in redundancy or rely on dedicated hardware for failover, which increases cost and complexity.	Cloud-IoT benefits from cloud-based redundancy, failover mechanisms, and distributed infrastructure, offering higher availability and reliability with minimal manual intervention.
Latency	Higher latency in traditional IoT setups due to reliance on local networks, servers, and edge computing. Latency issues can affect real-time applications.	Cloud-IoT minimizes latency with optimized cloud infrastructure and hybrid cloud-edge models that ensure timely data processing, even in real-time IoT applications.
Maintenance and Upgrades	Maintenance and upgrades are often manual, requiring downtime and physical interventions to update or replace devices and servers.	Cloud-IoT simplifies maintenance by allowing software upgrades, patches, and device updates to be done remotely and automatically, reducing downtime and maintenance costs.
Environment Monitoring and Control	On-premises IoT solutions may require manual intervention for system monitoring and adjustments based on local conditions.	Cloud-IoT platforms provide continuous monitoring, automatic system adjustments, and remote control from a single interface, improving the efficiency of IoT management.

8.3 SUMMARY

In this chapter, cloud-similar and cloud-based technologies are discussed in detail. Several cloud-similar technologies such as heterogeneous computing, mobile-edge computing, ubiquitous computing, and Industry 4.0 are explored. Furthermore, in cloud-based technologies, Cloud-LAN, Cloud-WAN, Cloud-MAN, Cloud-SDN, and Cloud-IoT are discussed. The comprehensive comparative analysis of each technology is also provided. Scalability, flexibility, affordability, simplicity of deployment, and accessibility are just a few advantages of cloud-based technology. They make it possible for organizations and people to take advantage of sophisticated computing resources and services without having to make an initial investment in hardware or infrastructure. When implementing and utilizing cloud-based technology, however, organizations need to take into account elements such as data security, vendor lock-in, and regulatory compliance.

8.4 PRACTICE QUESTIONS/SOLUTIONS

MULTIPLE OBJECTIVE QUESTIONS

1 **What does heterogeneous computing refer to?**
A) Using multiple types of processors in a single system
B) Using a single type of processor for all tasks
C) Using only CPUs for computing tasks
D) Using GPUs exclusively for graphics rendering

Answer: A) Using multiple types of processors in a single system

2 **Which of the following is a key advantage of heterogeneous computing?**
A) Reduced power consumption
B) Limited scalability
C) Increased software complexity
D) Single-threaded performance improvement

Answer: A) Reduced power consumption

3 **What is Mobile Edge Computing (MEC) primarily designed to improve?**
A) Battery life of mobile devices
B) Network latency for mobile applications
C) Mobile device screen resolution
D) Mobile device security

Answer: B) Network latency for mobile applications

4 **What role does the edge server play in Mobile Edge Computing (MEC)?**
A) Storing large amounts of data
B) Providing computing resources closer to end-users
C) Managing network infrastructure
D) Performing heavy computations offline

Answer: B) Providing computing resources closer to end-users

5 **What is the main challenge associated with ubiquitous computing environments?**
A) Limited availability of computing resources
B) High cost of implementation
C) Security and privacy concerns
D) Lack of skilled workforce

Answer: C) Security and privacy concerns

6 Which technology concept is closely related to the vision of ubiquitous computing?

A) Internet of Things (IoT)
B) Augmented Reality (AR)
C) Quantum Computing
D) Virtual Reality (VR)

Answer: C) Security and privacy concerns

7 Which technology enables machines and systems to communicate and cooperate with each other in Industry 4.0?

A) LAN (Local Area Network)
B) Blockchain
C) Internet of Things (IoT)
D) Vacuum tubes

Answer: C) Internet of Things (IoT)

8 What role does Big Data analytics play in Industry 4.0?

A) Decreasing data storage capabilities
B) Increasing cybersecurity risks
C) Analyzing large volumes of data for insights and decision-making
D) Reducing the need for automation

Answer: C) Analyzing large volumes of data for insights and decision-making

9 What security measure is crucial for protecting data in Cloud-LAN environments?

A) Port forwarding
B) VPN encryption
C) DHCP configuration
D) MAC address filtering

Answer: B) VPN encryption

10 Which network protocol is commonly used for Cloud-LAN connectivity?

A) FTP (File Transfer Protocol)
B) HTTP (Hypertext Transfer Protocol)
C) TCP/IP (Transmission Control Protocol/Internet Protocol)
D) SMTP (Simple Mail Transfer Protocol)

Answer: C) TCP/IP (Transmission Control Protocol/Internet Protocol)

11 What is a potential challenge of implementing Cloud-WAN?

A) Limited scalability
B) Higher network latency
C) Reduced data security
D) Incompatibility with legacy systems

Answer: B) Higher network latency

12 How does Cloud-WAN support remote workforce and distributed teams?
A) By limiting access to corporate resources
B) By centralizing data storage in on-premises servers
C) By providing secure and seamless access to WAN resources via the cloud
D) By increasing reliance on physical office spaces

Answer: C) By providing secure and seamless access to WAN resources via the cloud

13 Which technology enables Cloud-MAN connectivity within a metropolitan area?
A) Fiber optics
B) Bluetooth
C) 4G LTE
D) Dial-up modem

Answer: A) Fiber optics

14 What is a primary benefit of implementing Cloud-MAN over traditional MAN setups?
A) Lower bandwidth capacity
B) Limited scalability
C) Improved reliability and performance
D) Decreased security measures

Answer: C) Improved reliability and performance

15 How does Cloud-SDN contribute to efficient network management?
A) By increasing manual configuration tasks
B) By reducing visibility into network performance
C) By enabling centralized control and orchestration of network resources
D) By limiting scalability options

Answer: C) By enabling centralized control and orchestration of network resources

16 What security measure is crucial for protecting data in Cloud-SDN environments?
A) Port forwarding
B) VPN encryption
C) DHCP configuration
D) MAC address filtering

Answer: B) VPN encryption

17 Which network protocol is commonly used for Cloud-SDN connectivity?

A) FTP (File Transfer Protocol)
B) HTTP (Hypertext Transfer Protocol)
C) TCP/IP (Transmission Control Protocol/Internet Protocol)
D) SNMP (Simple Network Management Protocol)

Answer: C) TCP/IP (Transmission Control Protocol/Internet Protocol)

18 What security measure is crucial for protecting data in Cloud-WAN environments?

A) Port forwarding
B) VPN encryption
C) DHCP configuration
D) MAC address filtering

Answer: B) VPN encryption

19 How does Cloud-MAN contribute to disaster recovery and business continuity?

A) By increasing data vulnerability
B) By decentralizing data storage
C) By relying solely on local backups
D) By enabling data replication and redundancy across cloud servers

Answer: D) By enabling data replication and redundancy across cloud servers

20 How does Cloud-SDN support businesses and organizations in cloud environments?

A) By limiting access to corporate resources
B) By centralizing data storage in on-premises servers
C) By providing dynamic and programmable network capabilities via the cloud
D) By increasing reliance on physical office spaces

Answer: C) By providing dynamic and programmable network capabilities via the cloud

DESCRIPTIVE QUESTIONS

1 What is heterogeneous computing, and how does it differ from homogeneous computing architectures?

Answer: Heterogeneous computing refers to systems that use more than one kind of processor or core, typically combining CPUs with GPUs, DSPs, or other specialized processors. Unlike homogeneous architectures where identical processors execute tasks, heterogeneous systems leverage diverse processors to optimize performance and energy efficiency for specific workloads.

2 Explain the advantages of heterogeneous computing over homogeneous computing architectures.

Answer: Heterogeneous computing offers several advantages:

- Enhanced performance: Tasks suited for specialized processors can execute faster compared to general-purpose CPUs alone.
- Energy efficiency: Specialized processors consume less power for specific tasks, reducing overall energy consumption.
- Scalability: Allows scaling performance by adding more specialized processors without increasing the CPU count.
- Cost-effectiveness: Optimizes hardware resources by using processors tailored to specific tasks, reducing overall system costs.

3 Provide examples of applications that benefit from homogeneous computing.

Answer: Examples include:

- Traditional data processing: Tasks such as database management, file serving, and web hosting benefit from consistent computing resources.
- Enterprise applications: CRM systems, ERP software, and financial applications that require stable and predictable performance.
- Scientific simulations: Simulating physical phenomena, climate modeling, and computational chemistry using consistent computing resources.
- Gaming: Rendering graphics, physics simulations, and AI algorithms in gaming consoles and PCs.

4 How does MEC support the deployment of 5G networks?

Answer: MEC complements 5G networks by hosting applications, services, and content at the edge of the network. This proximity reduces latency for data-intensive applications such as augmented reality (AR), virtual reality (VR), autonomous vehicles, and IoT devices. MEC also offloads traffic from the core network, optimizing bandwidth usage and improving overall network efficiency.

5 What are the key benefits of deploying MEC in IoT environments?

Answer: MEC provides several benefits for IoT:

- **Low latency**: Enables real-time data processing and decision-making, critical for IoT applications such as industrial automation and smart grids.

- **Scalability**: Distributes computational tasks closer to IoT devices, reducing strain on centralized cloud resources and supporting a larger number of connected devices.
- **Improved reliability**: Redundant edge servers enhance reliability and resilience in IoT deployments, ensuring continuous operation even in network disruptions.

6 Explain the concept of context-aware computing in Ubiquitous Computing.

Answer: Context-aware computing involves understanding and responding to the situational context in which computing devices operate, including user location, preferences, activities, and environmental conditions. By leveraging sensors, data analytics, and machine learning algorithms, context-aware systems adapt their behavior and provide personalized services and information tailored to the user's current context, enhancing usability and relevance.

7 How does Ubiquitous Computing contribute to improving efficiency in industrial and manufacturing environments?

Answer: Ubiquitous Computing in industrial settings:

- **Predictive maintenance**: Monitoring equipment performance and detecting potential failures before they occur, minimizing downtime and optimizing asset utilization.
- **Automation and robotics**: Integrating smart sensors and actuators to automate production processes, improve precision, and enhance operational efficiency.
- **Supply chain management**: Tracking inventory, shipments, and logistics in real-time using IoT devices and RFID technology to streamline operations and reduce costs.

8 What is Industry 4.0, and how does it differ from previous industrial revolutions?

Answer: Industry 4.0 refers to the fourth industrial revolution characterized by the integration of digital technologies, automation, and data exchange in manufacturing and industrial processes. Unlike previous revolutions that introduced mechanization (1st), mass production (2nd), and automation (3rd), Industry 4.0 leverages cyber-physical systems, IoT, cloud computing, and AI to create smart factories and interconnected systems that optimize production, improve efficiency, and enable real-time decision-making.

9 What are the key technologies driving Industry 4.0 transformation?

Answer: Key technologies include:

- **IoT (Internet of Things)**: Connecting machines, devices, and sensors to gather real-time data for monitoring and control.
- **Big Data and Analytics**: Analyzing large volumes of data to derive insights, predict outcomes, and optimize processes.
- **Artificial Intelligence (AI) and Machine Learning**: Automating decision-making, predictive maintenance, and quality control.
- **Cyber-Physical Systems (CPS)**: Integrating physical systems with digital capabilities to monitor and manage production processes.
- **Cloud Computing**: Providing scalable storage, computing power, and access to software applications for data processing and collaboration.

10 How does Cloud-LAN enhance network scalability and flexibility?

Answer: Cloud-LAN enhances scalability and flexibility by:

- **Elasticity**: Scaling network resources up or down dynamically based on demand without the need for physical hardware upgrades.
- **Virtualization**: Creating virtual LAN segments and networks that can span multiple geographical locations, accommodating distributed workforces and branch offices.
- **Resource pooling**: Consolidating network resources in the cloud, allowing efficient allocation and utilization across multiple users and applications.

11 What are the key components of a Cloud-LAN architecture?

Answer: Key components include:

- **Virtual Private Cloud (VPC)**: Virtual network environment in the cloud that provides isolation and security for cloud-based LAN services.
- **Software-Defined Networking (SDN)**: Network management approach that separates control and data planes, enabling programmable and agile network configurations.
- **Cloud-based Gateways**: Connect on-premises networks to the cloud, facilitating secure and seamless data transmission.
- **Network Function Virtualization (NFV)**: Virtualizing network functions such as routing, firewalling, and load balancing to optimize network performance and management.

12 How does Cloud-WAN facilitate disaster recovery and business continuity planning?

Answer: Cloud-WAN facilitates disaster recovery and business continuity by:

- **Redundant connectivity**: Providing redundant links and failover mechanisms to maintain connectivity and ensure seamless operations during network disruptions.
- **Data replication**: Replicating critical data and applications across geographically diverse locations or cloud regions, minimizing data loss and downtime.
- **Automated failover**: Automatically rerouting traffic and resources to backup sites or cloud environments in case of primary site failures, reducing recovery time objectives (RTO) and improving resilience.

13 Discuss the challenges of managing performance and latency in Cloud-WAN environments.

Answer: Challenges include:

- **Network latency**: Ensuring low latency for real-time applications and services that require immediate data processing and response times.
- **Bandwidth constraints**: Managing bandwidth availability and congestion to maintain consistent performance across distributed locations and cloud services.
- **Quality of Service (QoS)**: Balancing competing demands and priorities for network resources to meet SLAs and performance expectations for diverse applications and users.

14 How does Cloud-MAN contribute to digital transformation and smart city initiatives?

Answer: Cloud-MAN contributes to digital transformation and smart city initiatives by:

- **IoT connectivity**: Connecting IoT devices, sensors, and smart infrastructure across metropolitan areas to collect and analyze real-time data for urban management and services.
- **Smart grid management**: Monitoring and optimizing energy distribution, consumption, and sustainability through cloud-enabled smart grid solutions.

- **Public safety and security**: Enhancing surveillance, emergency response, and disaster management capabilities with cloud-based video analytics and data-driven insights.
- **Smart transportation**: Improving traffic management, public transit systems, and logistics through real-time data sharing and intelligent routing algorithms.

15 Discuss the security considerations and measures in Cloud-MAN deployments.

Answer: Security considerations include:

- **Data encryption**: Implementing strong encryption protocols (e.g., AES-256) to protect data confidentiality and integrity during transmission and storage.
- **Access controls**: Enforcing role-based access controls (RBAC) and authentication mechanisms to regulate user permissions and prevent unauthorized access to Cloud-MAN resources.
- **Network segmentation**: Segmenting network traffic and implementing firewalls to isolate critical applications and sensitive data from potential cyber threats and attacks.
- **Compliance**: Adhering to industry regulations and standards (e.g., GDPR, NIST) for data protection, privacy, and regulatory compliance in Cloud-MAN environments.

16 How does Cloud-SDN enhance network agility and scalability?

Answer: Cloud-SDN enhances network agility and scalability by:

- **Centralized management**: Allowing administrators to manage and configure network policies, traffic flows, and security rules from a centralized cloud-based controller.
- **Dynamic provisioning**: Dynamically allocating and scaling network resources (such as bandwidth and virtual networks) based on application demand and workload requirements.
- **Automation**: Automating network provisioning, configuration changes, and policy enforcement through programmable interfaces and APIs, reducing manual overhead and improving operational efficiency.

17 How does Cloud-SDN optimize network performance and resource utilization?

Answer: Cloud-SDN optimizes network performance and resource utilization by:

- **Traffic engineering**: Directing network traffic along optimal paths and routes to minimize latency, packet loss, and congestion.

- **Quality of Service (QoS)**: Prioritizing and guaranteeing bandwidth, latency, and packet delivery for critical applications and services through granular QoS controls.
- **Load balancing**: Distributing network traffic evenly across multiple paths and links to maximize throughput, resilience, and availability.
- **Elastic scaling**: Scaling network resources up or down dynamically based on workload fluctuations and demand spikes to ensure efficient resource utilization and cost savings.

18 What is Cloud-IoT, and how does it integrate with Internet of Things (IoT) devices?

Answer: Cloud-IoT refers to the integration of cloud computing technologies with Internet of Things devices, enabling data storage, processing, and analysis in the cloud. It allows IoT devices to connect, communicate, and transmit data to cloud-based platforms for real-time analytics, remote monitoring, and control.

19 How does Cloud-IoT enhance scalability and flexibility in IoT deployments?

Answer: Cloud-IoT enhances scalability and flexibility by:

- **Scalable storage**: Storing vast amounts of IoT data in cloud databases and object storage solutions, enabling seamless scaling based on data growth and business needs.
- **Flexible analytics**: Performing complex data analytics and machine learning algorithms on cloud platforms to derive insights and actionable intelligence from IoT data.
- **Global reach**: Supporting IoT deployments across geographical locations with cloud-based services and resources accessible from anywhere, enhancing operational efficiency and reach.

20 What are the key components of a Cloud-IoT architecture?

Answer: Key components include:

- **IoT Devices**: Sensors, actuators, and connected devices that collect and transmit data over the Internet.
- **Edge Computing**: Processing data near the source (at the edge) to reduce latency and bandwidth usage before sending relevant data to the cloud.
- **Cloud Infrastructure**: Virtualized compute, storage, and networking resources provided by cloud service providers (e.g., AWS IoT, Azure IoT) to manage and analyze IoT data.
- **Analytics and Machine Learning**: Tools and services for processing, analyzing, and deriving insights from IoT data to drive informed decision-making and predictive maintenance.

REFERENCES

1. Khokhar, A. A., Prasanna, V. K., Shaaban, M. E., & Wang, C. L. (1993). Heterogeneous computing: Challenges and opportunities. *Computer*, *26*(6), 18–27.
2. Mao, Y., You, C., Zhang, J., Huang, K., & Letaief, K. B. (2017). A survey on mobile edge computing: The communication perspective. *IEEE Communications Surveys & Tutorials*, *19*(4), 2322–2358.
3. Lyytinen, K., & Yoo, Y. (2002). Ubiquitous computing. *Communications of the ACM*, *45*(12), 63–96.
4. Lasi, H., Fettke, P., Kemper, H. G., Feld, T., & Hoffmann, M. (2014). Industry 4.0. *Business & Information Systems Engineering*, *6*, 239–242.

9 Case Studies

9.1 INTRODUCTION

Cloud computing platforms have revolutionized the way businesses operate by providing scalable, cost-effective, and flexible solutions for managing IT infrastructure. Several case studies highlight the successful adoption of cloud services by enterprises across various industries. One case study showcases how Siemens Gas and Power leveraged cloud computing to reduce and prioritize alerts from their monitoring systems. By using cloud-based analytics, they were able to analyze 500 alerts per day, allowing their teams to focus on the most critical issues and prevent potential breakdowns or regulatory actions. Another case study features how Deloitte partnered with IBM to develop the Medicaid Enterprise Solution (MES) HealthInteractive Platform, running on IBM Cloud technology. This solution helps state Medicaid programs keep their IT systems up to date with less effort and expense while aligning with federal guidance [1]. UBank, a financial institution, utilized cloud computing to shrink its time to market by building a loan app virtual assistant on the IBM Cloud platform. Similarly, Allianz created an AI-powered virtual assistant using IBM Cloud and IBM Watson Assistant to handle 80% of its most frequent customer requests [1]. These case studies demonstrate how cloud computing platforms enable enterprises to unlock innovation, catalyze business growth, and deliver enhanced customer experiences. By leveraging cloud services, companies can access scalable resources, reduce IT infrastructure costs, and focus on achieving their business goals [2–4].

Cloud computing offers numerous benefits for businesses, transforming the way they operate and enhancing their efficiency and security. Some key benefits include:

- **Cost Savings**: Cloud computing allows businesses to reduce upfront capital expenses and ongoing maintenance costs by eliminating the need to invest in hardware and infrastructure. Additionally, the ability to scale computing resources up or down as needed helps in cost reduction.
- **Flexibility**: Businesses can benefit from the flexibility of cloud computing, enabling easy access to computing resources from anywhere via the Internet. This is particularly advantageous for remote teams and businesses with employees in different locations.

DOI: 10.1201/9781003510772-9

- **Improved Efficiency**: Cloud computing enables businesses to access and use computing resources on demand, enhancing their ability to respond quickly to changing business needs and opportunities, thus improving overall efficiency.
- **Enhanced Security**: Cloud computing providers implement advanced security measures to protect computing resources, reducing the risk of data breaches and enhancing the overall security of business operations.
- **Increased Collaboration**: Cloud computing facilitates collaboration by allowing multiple users to access and use the same computing resources. This fosters easier information sharing and project collaboration among teams, regardless of their location.

By leveraging cloud computing, businesses can enjoy these benefits and more, enabling them to streamline operations, enhance productivity, and stay competitive in today's digital landscape [5,6].

To ensure cloud migration success, companies should:

- Get Organizational Buy-in: Ensure all stakeholders are aware of their roles and responsibilities.
- Define Cloud Roles and Ownership: Determine who is responsible for managing various aspects of the cloud workload.
- Pick the Right Cloud Services: Choose the most suitable cloud services for the workload, avoiding unnecessary costs and complexity.
- Understand Security Risks: Establish security policies and perform comprehensive security testing to identify potential vulnerabilities.
- Calculate Cloud Costs: Monitor and manage cloud costs to avoid unexpected expenses.
- Devise a Long-term Cloud Roadmap: Plan for future cloud migrations and deployments, considering different deployment options and criteria.

By following these stages, types, and best practices, companies can successfully migrate to cloud computing platforms, unlocking the benefits of cloud computing and enhancing their business operations [7–9].

9.2 AMAZON WEB SERVICES

Amazon Web Services (AWS) has been instrumental in revolutionizing cloud computing, attracting a vast customer base including major companies such as Dropbox, Netflix, and NASA [10,11]. It highlights the strategic decisions made by AWS, such as its variable pricing model and operational diversification, amidst competition from tech giants such as Google and Microsoft. The case study also emphasizes AWS's role in enabling startups to access computing resources easily and affordably, transforming the tech landscape. A comprehensive overview of AWS cloud services and benefits is provided in Figure 9.1.

AWS's success is underscored by its pivotal role in the tech industry, providing essential services to a wide array of companies across various sectors, from healthcare to entertainment. The case study showcases how AWS has become a profit

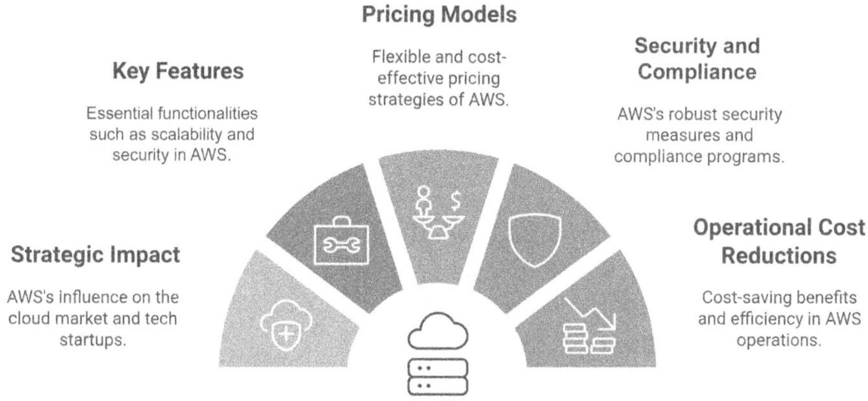

FIGURE 9.1 General overview of AWS cloud services and benefits.

engine for Amazon, contributing significantly to its operating profit and maintaining a dominant position in the cloud computing market. Moreover, AWS's innovative services, such as AI and machine learning, have positioned it as a leader in cloud technology, driving advancements in areas such as 5G, edge computing, and serverless architecture [12]. In essence, the case study on Amazon Web Services portrays a compelling narrative of how a side project within Amazon evolved into a powerhouse in cloud computing, reshaping the industry and setting new standards for innovation and service delivery [12].

9.2.1 Key Features

The key features of Amazon Web Services (AWS) encompass a range of functionalities that have contributed to its popularity and success in the cloud computing industry. These features are highlighted across various sources [13]:

1. *Mobile Friendly Access*: AWS Mobile Hub and AWS Mobile SDK provide mobile-friendly access to AWS services, supporting both Android and iOS platforms.
2. *Serverless Cloud Functions*: AWS offers serverless cloud functions through Amazon API Gateway, allowing users to run and scale their code without managing servers, focusing solely on building applications.
3. *Databases*: AWS provides managed databases tailored to specific requirements, offering services like Relational Databases for transactional purposes.
4. *Physical Security*: AWS ensures physical security by operating large-scale data centers globally, incorporating physical security measures to prevent unauthorized access.
5. *Secure Services*: Each service within AWS cloud is designed to be secure, ensuring data privacy and encryption for personal and business data.
6. *Cost-Effective Scalability*: AWS offers a cost-effective pricing model, allowing users to pay only for the services they use without long-term commitments, making it affordable and scalable based on demand.

7. *Flexibility and Elasticity*: AWS services are highly flexible and elastic, enabling users to scale computing resources up or down based on business needs, ensuring optimal performance and resource utilization.
8. *Security and Compliance*: AWS prioritizes security and compliance, providing maximum security for data and offering features that allow clients to control and monitor their services securely.

These features collectively contribute to AWS's reputation as a leading cloud computing platform, offering a robust and secure environment for businesses to build and deploy their applications efficiently and cost-effectively.

9.2.2 Pricing Options

Amazon Web Services (AWS) offers several pricing options to provide flexibility and cost savings for customers. The main pricing models are [14]:

1. *Pay-as-you-go*: Pay only for the services you use, without long-term contracts or upfront commitments.
2. *Savings Plans*: Offer discounted prices on EC2, Lambda, and Fargate services in exchange for a commitment to a consistent amount of usage (measured in $/hour) for a one or three-year term.
3. *Reserved Instances*: Provide significant discounts, ranging from 30% to 72%, on EC2 instances by reserving compute capacity for a one- or three-year term.
4. *Spot Instances*: Allow customers to bid on unused EC2 capacity, offering discounts of up to 90% compared to On-Demand pricing.
5. *Free Tier*: Offers a limited set of services for free for the first 12 months or with certain usage limits.

AWS also provides volume-based discounts, where the price per unit decreases as usage increases for certain services like Amazon S3. The AWS Pricing Calculator is a useful tool that allows customers to estimate costs for individual services or entire solutions based on their specific usage requirements.

9.2.3 Security and Compliance

Amazon Web Services (AWS) ensures security and compliance through a combination of robust measures and shared responsibility with customers [15,16]. The key ways AWS ensures security and compliance based on the provided sources are listed below:

1. *Shared Responsibility Model*: AWS operates under a shared responsibility model where AWS manages security.
2. *Comprehensive Compliance Programs*: AWS complies with a wide range of assurance programs and standards such as SOC 1/ISAE 3402, SOC 2, SOC 3, FISMA, DIACAP, FedRAMP, PCI DSS Level 1, ISO 9001, ISO 27001,

ISO 27017, and ISO 27018, among others, ensuring adherence to stringent security and compliance requirements.
3. *Security Best Practices*: AWS implements best practices in policies, architecture, and operational processes to meet the security needs of its most sensitive customers, providing customers with the flexibility and agility needed in security controls.
4. *Guidance and Expertise*: AWS offers guidance, expertise, advisories, and access to hundreds of security-specific tools and features to help customers meet their security objectives and address security issues effectively.
5. *Continuous Auditing and Certifications*: AWS environments undergo continuous auditing and hold certifications from accreditation bodies across various geographies and industries, ensuring adherence to security standards and best practices.
6. *Automated Tools and Reporting*: AWS provides automated tools for asset inventory, privileged access reporting, and compliance reporting through services like AWS Artifact, simplifying compliance management and reporting for customers.
7. *Data Privacy and Control*: AWS gives customers ownership and control over their data content, offering tools to determine where data is stored, secure data in transit or at rest, and manage access to AWS services and resources, ensuring data privacy and security.

By implementing these measures and fostering a shared responsibility model, AWS ensures a secure and compliant environment for its customers, enabling them to leverage cloud services with confidence while meeting their security and compliance requirements effectively.

9.2.4 Operational Costs for Businesses

AWS helps reduce operational costs for businesses in several key ways:

1. *Eliminating upfront infrastructure costs*: AWS allows businesses to avoid the high upfront costs of purchasing, configuring, and maintaining their own on-premises infrastructure. With AWS, companies only pay for the compute power, storage, and services they actually use.
2. *Reducing IT management overhead*: By outsourcing infrastructure management to AWS, businesses can significantly reduce the time and resources spent on tasks such as provisioning servers, applying patches, and managing backups. This allows IT teams to focus on higher-value activities.
3. *Enabling rapid scaling*: AWS allows businesses to quickly scale computing resources up or down based on demand. This helps avoid over-provisioning resources during peak periods or under-provisioning during growth, both of which can lead to inefficient spending.
4. *Leveraging AWS's economies of scale*: As a massive cloud provider, AWS can achieve significant economies of scale that it passes on to customers

through low prices. AWS can negotiate better rates with suppliers and spread fixed costs across a large customer base.

5. *Optimizing costs with pricing models*: AWS offers several pricing models like On-Demand, Reserved Instances, and Spot Instances that allow businesses to optimize costs based on their specific needs. Reserved Instances provide discounts of up to 75% compared to On-Demand for steady-state workloads.
6. *Providing cost management tools*: AWS offers tools like Cost Explorer, Budgets, and Cost & Usage Reports that help businesses monitor, analyze, and optimize their cloud spending. These tools provide visibility into costs by account, service, and resource.
7. *Rightsizing instances*: AWS provides recommendations to help businesses "rightsize" their EC2 instances to the optimal configuration based on utilization data. This ensures they are not over-provisioning and paying for unused resources.

In summary, by eliminating upfront costs, reducing management overhead, enabling rapid scaling, leveraging economies of scale, offering flexible pricing models, providing cost management tools, and rightsizing instances, AWS helps businesses significantly reduce their operational costs compared to on-premises infrastructure. A comprehensive tabular analysis of AWS is provided in Table 9.1.

TABLE 9.1
Analysis of Key AWS Aspects

Aspect	Details	Key Benefits
Strategic Impact	AWS revolutionized cloud computing, attracting major clients such as Dropbox, Netflix, and NASA. It enabled startups to access affordable computing resources.	• Dominant position in cloud market • Key enabler for tech startups • Significant revenue contribution to Amazon
Key Features	Mobile access, serverless functions, databases, physical security, secure services, cost-effective scalability, flexibility, and compliance.	• Scalable, secure cloud services • Ease of application deployment • Cost-effective and flexible infrastructure
Pricing Models	Pay-as-you-go, Savings Plans, Reserved Instances, Spot Instances, Free Tier, volume-based discounts. AWS also offers a Pricing Calculator.	• Flexible pricing options • Discounts for committed usage • Cost optimization tools
Security and Compliance	Shared responsibility model, comprehensive compliance programs (e.g., ISO 27001, SOC 2), continuous auditing, automated tools, and data privacy controls.	• Robust security and compliance • Data privacy and access control • Continuous monitoring and reporting
Operational Cost Reductions	Eliminates upfront infrastructure costs, reduces IT management overhead, enables rapid scaling, leverages economies of scale, and offers cost management tools.	• Avoids capital expenditure • Reduces IT management burden • Optimizes cloud spending with smart scaling

9.3 MICROSOFT AZURE

Microsoft Azure is a cloud computing platform and infrastructure created by Microsoft for building, deploying, and managing applications and services through a global network of Microsoft-managed data centers [17]. It provides software as a service (SaaS), platform as a service (PaaS), and infrastructure as a service (IaaS) and supports many different programming languages, tools, and frameworks, including both Microsoft-specific and third-party software and systems. The key benefits and services of Azure are depicted in Figure 9.2.

Microsoft Azure is a private and public cloud platform that helps developers and IT professionals to build, deploy, and manage applications. It uses the technology known as virtualization, which separates the tight coupling between the hardware and the operating system using an abstraction layer called a hypervisor. This allows for the emulation of all the functions of a computer in the virtual machine, enabling the running of multiple virtual machines at the same time, each capable of running

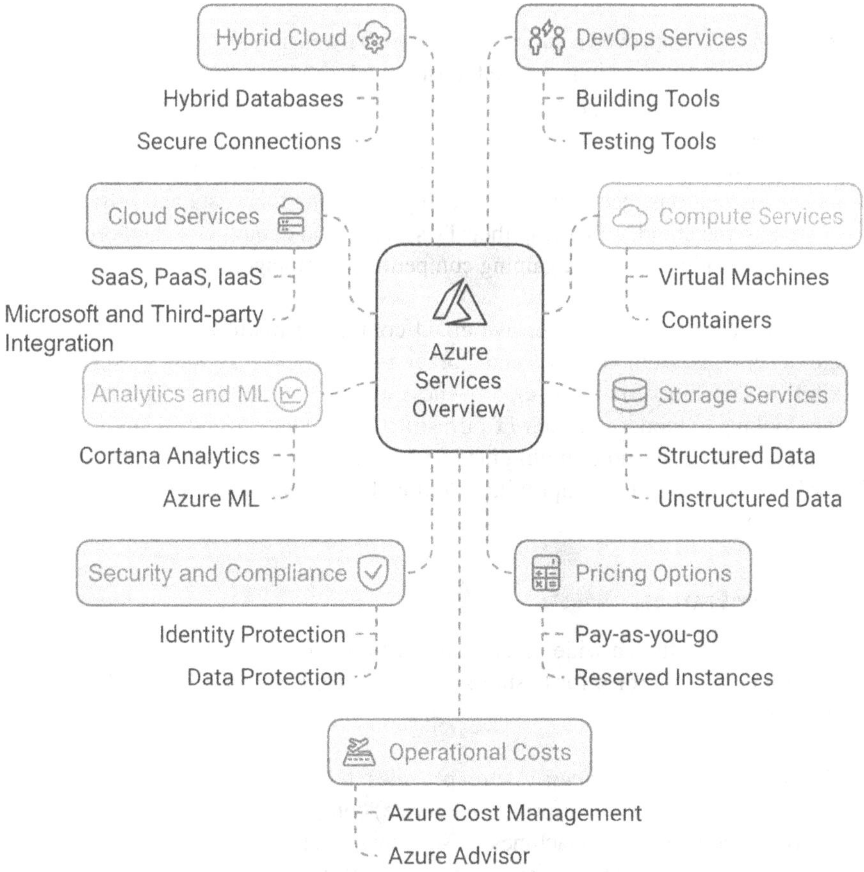

FIGURE 9.2 Key benefits and services of Microsoft Azure.

any operating system such as Windows or Linux. Azure offers a wide variety of services, including:

- *Compute Services*: Enables the deployment and management of virtual machines, containers, and batch jobs, as well as support for remote application access.
- *Analytics*: Provides services for data analysis and insights.
- *Storage*: Offers four core services for persistent and durable data storage in the cloud, including Azure Table Service, which provides a table-structured storage mechanism.
- *Networking*: Provides connectivity to all servers within the data center.
- *Cognitive Services*: Offers services for artificial intelligence, machine learning, and IoT.
- *Databases*: Supports a wide range of databases, including SQL Azure.

Several case studies have demonstrated the effectiveness of Microsoft Azure in various industries:

- *Connance*: Improved solution delivery with a transition to Azure cloud from RackSpace, achieving reduced turnaround time, on-demand scalability, decreased licensing and upfront costs, improved security, and centralized manageability.
- *Five Organizations*: Innovated and adapted to rapid change by adopting cloud solutions, becoming AI-ready by migrating their data and infrastructure to the cloud, enhancing their IT security and compliance, and optimizing migration costs and gaining competitive advantage.

Microsoft Azure is a comprehensive cloud computing platform that offers a wide range of services, from compute and storage to analytics and cognitive services. Its flexibility, scalability, and cost-effectiveness make it an attractive option for businesses looking to modernize their IT infrastructure and leverage the benefits of cloud computing. The case studies highlighted demonstrate the real-world impact of adopting Microsoft Azure, from improving solution delivery to enhancing IT security and compliance [18].

9.3.1 Key Features

Microsoft Azure offers a wide range of powerful features that make it a compelling cloud computing platform for businesses of all sizes. Here are some of the key features of Azure:

1. *Computational Services*: Azure provides both IaaS (Infrastructure as a Service) and PaaS (Platform as a Service) computational services. It allows you to launch virtual machines on Windows and Linux platforms, and offers pre-configured machine images for many software packages. The PaaS features enable developers to easily publish and manage websites and apps.

2. Storage Services: Azure offers scalable cloud storage for structured and unstructured data, supporting big data projects, persistent storage, and archival storage. It provides a file service that allows data storage and access on the cloud using REST APIs and SMB protocols. Azure Queue Services enable programs to communicate in an asynchronous fashion using queues.
3. *Analytics and Machine Learning*: Azure has strong built-in support for data analytics and machine learning. It offers features such as Cortana Analytics, Stream Analytics, Machine Learning, and SQL services that help businesses gain insights, discover opportunities, enhance customer service, and make informed decisions. Azure Machine Learning is part of the Cortana Intelligence Suite and provides predictive analytics and natural language processing capabilities.
4. *DevOps*: Azure provides DevOps services that help break down barriers between development and IT operations teams, enabling them to create higher-quality products faster and at lower cost. It offers tools for building, testing, deploying and managing applications through a global network of data centers.
5. *Hybrid Cloud Integration*: Azure integrates seamlessly with existing on-premises IT environments through hybrid databases, storage solutions, and secure private connections. It allows businesses to extend their data centers into the cloud, providing flexibility and cost-effectiveness.
6. *Scalability and Flexibility*: Azure offers a pay-as-you-go model and can be quickly scaled up or down based on business needs. It provides the flexibility to use any level of functionality required, supporting the same technologies that developers already depend on.

These features, combined with Azure's global reach, strong security, and broad partner ecosystem, make it a compelling choice for businesses looking to leverage the power of cloud computing.

9.3.2 Pricing Options

The key pricing options for Microsoft Azure are [19]:

1. *Pay-as-you-go*: This model allows businesses to pay only for the resources they consume, without any upfront commitments or termination fees. Pricing is based on hourly usage rates for each service.
2. *Reserved Instances*: This model allows businesses to commit to using a specific amount of resources for a one- or three-year term, in exchange for discounted rates.
3. *Hybrid Benefit*: This model allows businesses to use their existing Windows Server or SQL Server licenses to reduce the cost of Azure services.
4. *Spot Instances*: This model allows businesses to bid on unused Azure capacity at significantly discounted rates, though availability is not guaranteed.
5. *Azure Dev/Test*: This model provides discounted rates for virtual machines and other services used specifically for development and testing purposes.

6. *Azure Savings Plan*: This model allows businesses to save up to 65% on select compute services by committing to a fixed hourly spend for one or three years.
7. *Azure Reservations*: This model allows businesses to receive discounts on Azure services by purchasing a one- or three-year reservation agreement.

The pricing for specific Azure services like App Service and Cloud Services is detailed in the search results. Businesses can also take advantage of price matching against AWS, as well as free enterprise-grade cost management tools to optimize their Azure spending.

9.3.3 Security and Compliance

Microsoft Azure provides a highly secure and compliant cloud platform to help organizations meet their security and compliance requirements. Here are the key aspects of Azure's security [20] and compliance [21] offerings:

Security

- Azure is built on a secure foundation with multi-layered security across physical data centers, infrastructure, and operations.
- It provides built-in security controls and services for identity, data, networking, and applications.
- Azure uses unique intelligence from the Microsoft Intelligent Security Graph to detect threats early by analyzing data from various Microsoft services.

Compliance

- Azure leads the industry with over 100 compliance offerings, including 50+ specific to global regions and countries, and 35+ for key industries.
- It provides tools and guidance to help develop compliant solutions faster, such as built-in compliance controls, configuration management tools, and third-party audit reports.
- Azure adheres to some of the most rigorous security and compliance standards in the world, verified by independent audit reports for ISO, SOC, FedRAMP, HITRUST, and more.

Shared Responsibility

- Azure follows a shared responsibility model for data protection, with Microsoft assuming responsibility depending on the cloud service used.
- Microsoft provides various tools to help customers manage their part of the shared responsibility, such as encryption options, Azure Active Directory, Azure Key Vault, and Azure Security Center.

By leveraging Azure's security and compliance capabilities, organizations can reduce costs and complexity while strengthening their security posture in the cloud. Azure's comprehensive approach helps customers meet their domestic and international regulatory needs more effectively.

9.3.4 Operational Costs for Businesses

A concise summary of the key points about operational costs for businesses using Microsoft Azure is given below:

Estimating operational costs is crucial for creating an accurate cost model when using Azure. Key considerations include:

- Ongoing expenses for monitoring, testing, and maintenance of the infrastructure. This includes monitoring tools and services, regular testing activities, and routine maintenance tasks such as applying patches and updates.
- Costs for monitoring the performance and health of the infrastructure to track system metrics, detect issues, and ensure availability.
- Resources and tools required for testing the system's resilience, scalability, and security.

Microsoft provides several tools and resources to help businesses optimize and control their Azure costs:

- Microsoft Cost Management – Provides visibility into cloud spending, allows setting budgets and allocating costs to teams, and offers insights to make informed decisions.
- Azure Advisor – Provides recommendations for cost savings, such as shutting down unused resources, right-sizing underused resources, and choosing the right Azure compute service.
- Azure offers and licensing terms – Options such as Azure Hybrid Benefit, Azure Reservations, Azure Spot VMs, and Azure dev/test pricing can lead to significant savings.

Microsoft has implemented cost optimization internally by adopting data-driven techniques, investing in central governance, and driving modernization efforts. Key lessons include:

- Implementing central governance with local accountability
- Using a data-driven approach with accurate metrics and monitoring
- Being proactive in implementing cost-saving recommendations
- Adopting modern engineering practices aligned with the Azure Well-Architected Framework

By carefully estimating and optimizing operational costs using Azure's tools and best practices, businesses can significantly reduce their total cost of ownership and increase the efficiency of their cloud investments. An analysis of different Microsoft Azure aspects is provided in Table 9.2.

TABLE 9.2
Analysis of Key Azure Aspects

Aspect	Details	Key Benefits
Cloud Services	Provides SaaS, PaaS, and IaaS for applications and services, supporting both Microsoft and third-party technologies.	Flexibility to choose the right solution for various needs; seamless integration of Microsoft and third-party tools.
Compute Services	Offers virtual machines, containers, and batch jobs; supports remote application access and hybrid cloud.	Scalability, on-demand resource availability, and cost savings by leveraging cloud resources.
Storage Services	Includes scalable solutions for structured/unstructured data, with Azure Table Service and Queue Services.	Reliable, durable data storage and fast access to cloud data.
Analytics and ML	Built-in support for data analytics and machine learning (e.g., Cortana Analytics, Azure ML).	Enhanced decision-making, customer insights, and predictive analytics capabilities.
Security and Compliance	Multi-layered security, tools for identity, networking, and data protection; over 100 compliance offerings.	Robust security framework with regulatory compliance, reducing risks.
Pricing Options	Models include Pay-as-you-go, Reserved Instances, Hybrid Benefit, and Spot Instances.	Cost flexibility, potential discounts, and optimization of cloud expenditure.
Hybrid Cloud	Seamlessly integrates on-premises IT with cloud services via hybrid databases, storage, and secure connections.	Flexibility to extend existing data centers into the cloud, optimizing cost and resource usage.
DevOps Services	Supports collaboration between development and IT ops teams, offering tools for building, testing, deploying, and managing applications.	Faster development cycles, improved collaboration, and efficient deployment.
Operational Costs	Businesses can optimize costs using tools such as Azure Cost Management, Azure Advisor, and Azure Reservations.	Cost control, accurate spending predictions, and efficient resource management.
Global Reach	Azure offers a global network of Microsoft-managed data centers for high availability and low latency services.	Global scalability, performance optimization, and reliable service delivery across regions.

9.4 GOOGLE CLOUD PLATFORM

Google Cloud Platform (GCP) [22] provides a powerful infrastructure, data analytics, and machine learning capabilities that allow organizations to build sophisticated applications without the overhead of managing their own infrastructure. Many large companies such as Coca-Cola, Spotify, and King are already running mission-critical applications on GCP. Multiple universities collaborated with GCP to customize the platform to meet the unique needs of higher education, including security, scalability, identity management integration, and reduced data egress fees. This has enabled universities to more easily adopt GCP to support research and teaching. Figure 9.3 highlights that unlocking business potential with Google Cloud Platform's comprehensive solutions drives innovation, efficiency, and growth.

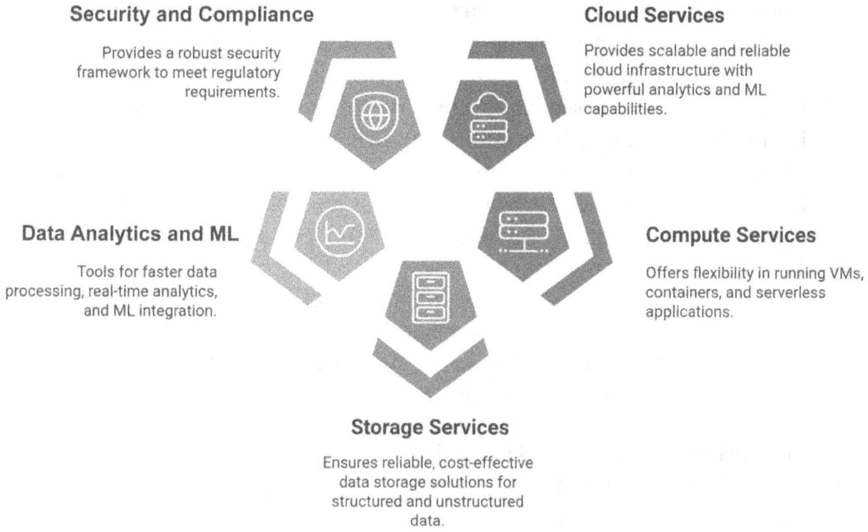
Security and Compliance
Provides a robust security framework to meet regulatory requirements.
Cloud Services
Provides scalable and reliable cloud infrastructure with powerful analytics and ML capabilities.
Data Analytics and ML
Tools for faster data processing, real-time analytics, and ML integration.
Compute Services
Offers flexibility in running VMs, containers, and serverless applications.
Storage Services
Ensures reliable, cost-effective data storage solutions for structured and unstructured data.

FIGURE 9.3 The comprehensive solutions and benefits of GCP.

Recently, a financial technology company moved to GCP, resulting in a sevenfold sustainable increase in its user base and elimination of system downtime. GCP's managed services for containers and databases enabled a 400% improvement in time-to-market for new features and an 80% reduction in error resolution times. Similarly, King, a gaming company, built a scalable data warehousing and analytics platform on GCP using BigQuery. This enabled King's data scientists to be more efficient and agile by unifying data in one place and allowing teams to solve problems with fewer dependencies.

In summary, these case studies demonstrate how GCP's powerful yet flexible services allow organizations across industries to build reliable, scalable applications that meet their unique requirements, while reducing infrastructure management overhead and enabling teams to focus on innovation [23,24].

9.4.1 Key Features

The key features of Google Cloud Platform (GCP) are summarized as follows:

1. *Cloud Storage*: GCP offers cost-effective storage solutions allowing users to store data securely, with the capacity to store up to 10TB in the cloud.
2. *Cloud Dataproc*: A highly scalable, fully managed cluster computing system for configuring and managing Hadoop or other types of clusters with ease.
3. *Cloud Pub/Sub*: A messaging service facilitating communication between user-facing APIs and other applications, enabling message publishing and subscription.
4. *Cloud SQL*: A fully featured relational database providing quick and easy access to data using SQL, offering MySQL instances on Google's infrastructure.
5. *Google App Engine*: Allows the development and hosting of web applications on scalable systems, similar to those powering Google applications.

6. *Compute Engine*: A fully managed cloud computing service for virtual machines, storage, networking, and load balancing, enabling rapid deployment of virtual machines.
7. *BigQuery*: A SQL-based data warehouse for running ad hoc queries, analyzing data, and exporting results for further analysis.
8. *Cloud Spanner*: The world's largest fully distributed transactional database, offering partitioning and transactions across multiple storage groups.
9. *Google Cloud Datalab*: An interactive tool for analyzing databases on Cloud SQL instances.
10. *Google Container Engine*: Allows running Docker containers on managed infrastructure for DevOps and container management.
11. *Cloud Bigtable*: A high-performance, fully managed NoSQL cluster database service for efficient data storage and retrieval.

These features collectively make Google Cloud Platform a robust and versatile cloud computing solution, catering to a wide range of computing needs for businesses and developers.

9.4.2 Pricing Options

Google Cloud Platform offers several pricing options to suit different needs [25]:

1. *Pay-as-you-go*
   - Flexible, on-demand pricing where you only pay for the services you use
   - No upfront costs or termination fees
   - Most expensive option per hour
2. *Long-term commitments*
   - Committed Use Discounts for one-year or three-year terms
   - Upfront commitment in exchange for significant savings, up to 70% on Compute Engine
3. *Free tier*
   - $300 free credit for new customers to try out services
   - 20+ products available for free within monthly usage limits
   - Suitable for low-usage requirements or trying out services
4. *Spot VMs*
   - Discounts of up to 91% compared to on-demand pricing
   - Excess compute capacity available at steep discounts

9.4.3 SECURITY AND COMPLIANCE

GCP offers robust security and compliance features to protect your data and applications:

1. *Shared Responsibility Model*: Google follows a shared responsibility model for security. Google is responsible for the security of the cloud infrastructure, while customers are responsible for security in the cloud, including data, applications, and configurations.
2. *Compliance Offerings*: Google Cloud regularly undergoes independent verification to achieve certifications against global standards, including ISO,

SOC, PCI DSS, HIPAA, FedRAMP, and many others. This helps customers demonstrate compliance with various regulations.
3. *Data Center Security*: Google's data centers are built with custom-designed servers running a custom hardened operating system. Google employs over 500 security engineers to monitor threats and quickly respond to vulnerabilities.
4. *Encryption*: Google encrypts data in transit between Google and customers, between data centers, and at rest in Cloud Platform services. In 2013, Google doubled the length of RSA encryption keys to 2048 bits to protect against cryptanalytic advances.
5. *Access Control*: Proper configuration of access controls is crucial. Google recommends using strong passwords, securing the project firewall, and monitoring project usage closely for any abnormal behavior.
6. *Monitoring and Logging*: Google Cloud offers advanced monitoring and logging capabilities through Stackdriver Logging and Monitoring. This allows customers to collect logs, create metrics, and monitor for unusual activity.

By following Google's security best practices and leveraging the built-in security features, customers can build secure and compliant applications on Google Cloud Platform.

9.4.4 Operational Costs for Businesses

A concise summary of the key points about Google Cloud Platform (GCP) operational costs for businesses is provided below:

1. Pricing Models: GCP offers several pricing models to suit different needs:
   - Pay-as-you-go – Flexible model with no upfront costs, but highest hourly rates
   - Committed Use (one- to three-year contracts) - Up to 70% discounts compared to pay-as-you-go
   - Preemptible VMs (Spot VMs) – 60–91% discounts on machine types and GPUs
   - Free tier – Access to 24 products with monthly usage limits, plus $300 free credit for new customers
2. Cost Components: GCP costs are based on usage of the following resources:
   - Compute – Virtual machines, containers, serverless functions
   - Storage – Different classes with varying costs based on data volume, access type, and region
   - Networking – Virtual networks, load balancing, VPN, data transfer
3. Cost Management Tools: GCP provides several free tools to help control and optimize costs:
   - Budgets and alerts – Set spending limits and get notifications when exceeded
   - Billing export – Export detailed usage data to BigQuery for custom analysis
   - Recommendations – AI-powered suggestions to optimize usage and save money
   - Quotas – Set limits to prevent unexpected spikes in usage

4. Best Practices: Key strategies to minimize GCP costs include:
    - Choosing the right pricing model based on your usage patterns
    - Rightsizing compute resources to avoid over-provisioning
    - Using preemptible VMs for batch jobs and fault-tolerant workloads
    - Leveraging storage classes optimized for access patterns
    - Monitoring usage and costs with budgets, alerts, and custom dashboards
    - Automating cost-saving actions based on budget thresholds

By understanding the pricing models, cost components, and management tools, businesses can effectively control and optimize their Google Cloud costs. An analysis of GCP, highlighting key aspects, details, and benefits, is provided in Table 9.3.

TABLE 9.3
Analysis of Key GCP Aspects

Aspect	Details	Key Benefits
Cloud Services	Provides infrastructure, data analytics, and machine learning services. Includes Cloud Storage, Compute Engine, BigQuery, Cloud Pub/Sub, etc.	Scalable, reliable cloud services with powerful analytics and ML capabilities, reducing infrastructure management.
Compute Services	Offers managed services such as Compute Engine (VMs), Google App Engine (web apps), and Google Kubernetes Engine (containers).	Flexibility in running VMs, containers, and serverless applications with high scalability and low management overhead.
Storage Services	Includes Cloud Storage (secure, scalable data storage), Cloud SQL, and Cloud Bigtable (NoSQL database service).	Reliable, cost-effective data storage solutions for both structured and unstructured data.
Data Analytics and ML	Tools such as BigQuery (data warehousing), Cloud Dataproc (cluster management), and Google Cloud Datalab (interactive analysis) for data-driven insights.	Faster data processing, real-time analytics, and machine learning integration to drive business intelligence.
Security and Compliance	Multi-layered security including encryption, access control, and compliance with standards such as ISO, SOC, HIPAA, and FedRAMP.	Robust security framework to meet regulatory requirements and protect sensitive data.
Pricing Options	Offers Pay-as-you-go, Committed Use Discounts, Spot VMs, Free tier with $300 credit, and Preemptible VMs.	Cost flexibility with discounts, free credits, and the ability to scale resources as needed.
Operational Costs	Costs based on compute, storage, and networking. Includes tools for managing budgets, usage, and recommendations for optimization.	Better cost control and optimization with built-in cost management tools, reducing unnecessary spending.
DevOps Services	Integration with tools for continuous integration/continuous deployment (CI/CD), container management, and development environments.	Increased development agility and faster time-to-market for applications.
Global Reach	GCP has a global network of data centers, ensuring high availability and low-latency access to services.	Global scalability and performance, ensuring reliable service delivery across multiple regions.

9.5 SALESFORCE

Salesforce, Inc. is an American cloud-based software company headquartered in San Francisco, California. It provides customer relationship management (CRM) software and applications focused on sales, customer service, marketing automation, e-commerce, analytics, and application development [26].

Founded by former Oracle executive Marc Benioff in 1999, Salesforce grew quickly, making its initial public offering in 2004. As of September 2022, Salesforce is the 61st largest company in the world by market cap with a value of nearly US$153 billion. A general overview of the features and services of Salesforce is provided in Figure 9.4.

Salesforce's main services include [27]:

- Sales Cloud: Close more deals and speed up growth with the #1 CRM
- Service Cloud: Make customers happy faster and build loyalty
- Marketing Cloud: Build customer relationships for life with data-first digital marketing
- Commerce Cloud: Personalize every experience along the customer journey

The company also offers a platform called Salesforce Platform (formerly Force.com) that allows developers to build custom applications [26].

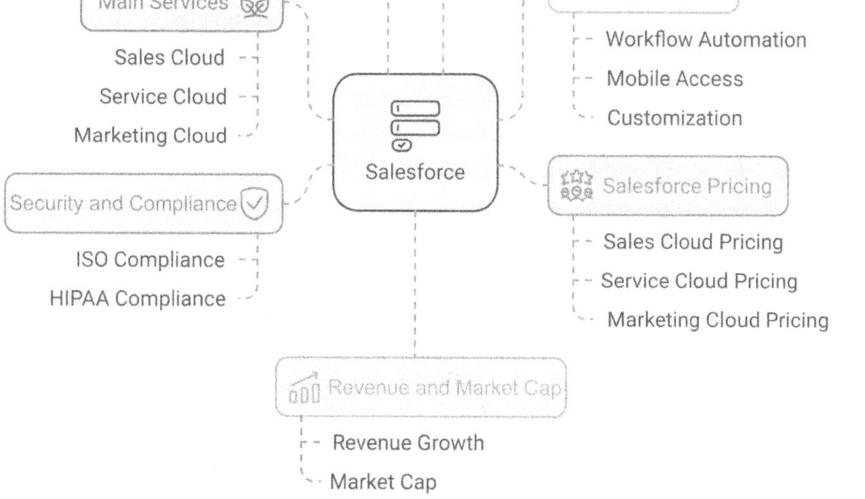

FIGURE 9.4 General overview of Salesforce services and benefits.

For the fiscal year 2022, Salesforce reported a revenue of US$26.49 billion, an increase of 25% year-over-year [26]. Salesforce stock closed at $252.49 on July 10, 2024.

9.5.1 Key Features

A concise summary of the key features of Salesforce is given below:

1. *Customer Relationship Management (CRM)*: Salesforce provides a comprehensive CRM platform to help businesses manage customer data, streamline sales processes, and deliver personalized experiences. It includes features such as account and contact management, opportunity management, and lead management.
2. *Sales Cloud*: The Sales Cloud is a core part of Salesforce that empowers sales teams to manage the entire sales cycle, from lead generation to deal closure. It offers features such as sales collaboration, sales performance management, and sales forecasting.
3. *Service Cloud*: The Service Cloud enables businesses to deliver personalized customer service at scale. It includes features such as customer service AI, data-driven service, field service, and self-service portals.
4. *Analytics and Reporting*: Salesforce provides robust analytics and reporting capabilities, including real-time dashboards, custom reports, and predictive analytics powered by Einstein AI.
5. *Workflow and Approvals*: Salesforce allows businesses to automate their sales and business processes with visual workflow tools and flexible approval processes.
6. *Mobile and Collaboration*: The Salesforce mobile app and Chatter collaboration features enable teams to access customer data, share insights, and work together from anywhere.
7. *Integration and Customization*: Salesforce can be easily integrated with other business applications and customized to fit the unique needs of each organization.

9.5.2 Pricing Options

Here is a summary of the key Salesforce pricing options [28]:

1. Salesforce CRM Pricing: Salesforce offers several pricing plans for its sales CRM software:
   - Starter: $25 per user per month, up to ten users
   - Professional: $80 per user per month, unlimited users
   - Enterprise: $165 per user per month, unlimited users
   - Unlimited: $330 per user per month, unlimited users
   - Einstein 1 Service: $500 per user per month, unlimited users

   The plans scale up in features and functionality as the price increases. Key features include the Salesforce mobile app, email integration, and workflow automation.

2. Salesforce Service Pricing: Salesforce also offers pricing plans for its service software:
   - Starter: $25 per user per month
   - Professional: $80 per user per month
   - Enterprise: $165 per user per month
   - Unlimited: $330 per user per month
   - Einstein 1 Service: $500 per user per month

   This software simplifies case management and includes a knowledge base.

3. Salesforce Marketing – Pardot Pricing: Pardot, Salesforce's marketing automation tool, has the following pricing plans:
   - Growth: $1,250 per month, up to 10,000 contacts
   - Plus: $2,750 per month, up to 10,000 contacts
   - Advanced: $4,400 per month, up to 10,000 contacts
   - Premium: $15,000 per month, up to 75,000 contacts

   Pardot provides marketing automation and advanced analytics for the customer journey.

4. Other Salesforce Add-On Pricing: Salesforce also offers a range of additional products and add-ons with their own pricing, including:
   - Salesforce Maps: Starting at $105 per user per month
   - Einstein Relationship Insights: $70–$210 per user per month
   - Quip Advanced: $140 per user per month
   - CPQ (Configure, Price, Quote): $105–$210 per user per month

   These add-ons enhance the core CRM functionality for sales, service, and marketing.

9.5.3 Security and Compliance

Salesforce emphasizes security and compliance as critical aspects of its platform to ensure the trust and protection of customer data. Here are some key points regarding security and compliance in Salesforce [29–32]:

1. Compliance Certifications: Salesforce maintains a comprehensive set of compliance certifications and attestations to validate its commitment to trust and security. These certifications include:
   - APEC Certification for Processors and Controllers: Ensures compliance with the Asia-Pacific Economic Cooperation (APEC) privacy framework.
   - ISAE 3000: Compliance with the Cloud Computing Compliance Controls Catalogue (C5).
   - CSA STAR: Registry of security and privacy controls for cloud computing offerings.
   - CyberGRX: Dynamic and comprehensive third-party risk assessment.
   - DoD IL2, IL4, and IL5: Compliance with U.S. Department of Defense security requirements.
   - EU Cloud Code of Conduct: Adherence to EU standards.

- FedRAMP High and Moderate: U.S. government security and authorization programs.
- HIPAA: Compliance with U.S. privacy requirements for personal health information.
- HITRUST: Comprehensive approach to regulatory compliance and risk management.
- ISO 27001, 27017, and 27018: Compliance with international information security standards.
- NEN 7510: Protecting health information for organizations in the Netherlands.
- NIST SP 800-171: U.S. security requirements for protecting Controlled Unclassified Information.
- PCI DSS: Validation of controls around cardholder data.
- PrivacyMark: Privacy-centric certification for organizations in Japan.
- SOC 1, 2, and 3: Reports covering internal controls over financial reporting systems.
- TISAX: European information security assessment for the automotive industry.
- TX-RAMP: Texas Risk and Authorization Management Program.
- UK Cyber Essentials Plus: UK government information security assurance scheme.
- U.S. Data Privacy Framework (DPF): Framework for complying with EU, UK, and Swiss privacy requirements.
- WCAG 2.1 AA: Accessibility standards for web content.

2. Security Best Practices: To enhance security and ensure compliance, Salesforce recommends several best practices:
   - Utilize Strong Authentication Methods: Implement complex passwords and multi-factor authentication (MFA) to secure access.
   - Define and Enforce User Permissions: Grant users only the necessary access to data and functions, following the principle of least privilege.
   - Use Data Encryption: Encrypt sensitive data both at rest and in transit to protect against unauthorized access.
   - Leverage Audit Trails: Monitor user activities and detect irregular patterns or unauthorized access attempts.
   - Implement Field-Level Security: Restrict access to specific fields to maintain data privacy and compliance with regulations such as GDPR and HIPAA.
   - Regularly Update and Patch: Keep Salesforce and integrated applications up to date to minimize security vulnerabilities.
   - Educate and Train Users: Regular training sessions on security best practices can significantly reduce the risk of human error.
   - Use Salesforce Health Check: Evaluate security settings against Salesforce-recommended best practices to identify areas for improvement.
   - Backup Your Data: Regularly back up Salesforce data to ensure data integrity and availability.

   - Monitor Third-Party Apps and Integrations: Vet third-party solutions thoroughly before integration and monitor them regularly for security updates or alerts.
3. Trust and Compliance Documentation: Salesforce provides detailed documentation for each service, including:
   - Security, Privacy, and Architecture (SPARC): Describes the architecture, security, and privacy audits and certifications.
   - Notices and License Information (NLI): Details features, restrictions, and notices associated with services.
   - Infrastructure & Sub-processors (I&S): Lists the infrastructure environment, sub-processors, and countries where data is stored.
   - Product Terms Directory (PTD): Sets forth terms associated with services purchased on Order Forms.
4. Email Security Compliance: Salesforce offers features to enable compliance with standard email security mechanisms, ensuring secure email communication.

By adhering to these security and compliance measures, Salesforce aims to provide a robust and trustworthy platform for its customers.

9.5.4 Operational Costs for Businesses

Salesforce operational costs for businesses can vary significantly depending on the specific products and services used. Here are some key points [33]:

1. Salesforce Pricing:
   - Sales Cloud: Pricing starts at $25 per user per month for the Essentials Edition, going up to $330 per user per month for the Unlimited Edition. The Enterprise Edition costs $165 per user per month, and the Einstein 1 Sales Edition costs $500 per user per month.
   - Service Cloud: Pricing starts at $25 per user per month for the Essentials Edition, going up to $330 per user per month for the Unlimited Edition. The Enterprise Edition costs $165 per user per month, and the Einstein 1 Service Edition costs $500 per user per month.
   - Marketing Cloud Account Engagement: Pricing starts at $1,250 per month for up to 10,000 contacts.
2. Implementation and Customization Costs:
   - Training: For a mid-sized company, training can cost up to $15,000.
   - Customization: Costs range from $10,000 to $85,000, depending on the complexity of the modifications required.
   - Integration: Costs typically range from $10,000 to $50,000, but can vary based on the specific integration needs.
3. Operational Expenses:
   - Salesforce's annual operating expenses for 2024 were $29.846 billion, a 1.57% decline from 2023. Quarterly operating expenses for the quarter ending April 30, 2024, were $7.424 billion, a 5.25% decline year-over-year.

These costs are subject to change and can vary based on the specific needs and size of the business. It is recommended to consult with a Salesforce representative for detailed pricing information and to discuss the best options for your business. A concise tabular analysis of Salesforce is provided in Table 9.4. This table summarizes Salesforce's features, business operational insights, etc., illustrating how it can cater to businesses of all sizes while ensuring robust security and regulatory compliance.

TABLE 9.4
Analysis of Key Salesforce Aspects

Aspect	Details	Key Benefits
Company Overview	Cloud-based software company providing CRM, sales, marketing, customer service, and analytics solutions. Founded in 1999.	Leading CRM solution, enabling businesses to manage customer relationships and improve sales and service outcomes.
Main Services	Sales Cloud, Service Cloud, Marketing Cloud, Commerce Cloud, Salesforce Platform (app development)	Comprehensive suite for managing sales, customer service, marketing, and e-commerce.
Key Features	• CRM platform for managing data and sales processes • Sales Cloud, Service Cloud, Marketing Cloud for specific functions • Workflow automation, mobile access, customization, and integration	Increased efficiency in sales, marketing, and customer service with automation, real-time analytics, and scalability.
Salesforce Pricing	• Sales Cloud: $25–$330/user/month- Service Cloud: $25–$330/user/month- Marketing Cloud: $1,250–$15,000/month- Add-ons: Prices vary (e.g., $70-$210/user/month for Einstein insights)	Flexible pricing based on features, making it accessible for small businesses while providing advanced tools for larger enterprises.
Security and Compliance	• Compliance with ISO, HIPAA, FedRAMP, SOC, GDPR, etc. • Strong authentication, encryption, audit trails, and field-level security	Ensures robust data protection, regulatory compliance, and customer trust.
Operational Costs	• Pricing based on subscriptions for Sales, Service, and Marketing Clouds • Implementation and customization costs (e.g., $10K-$85K) • Training and integration can add significant costs	Operational expenses depend on services used, with flexibility to scale and adapt to business needs.
Customization and Integration Costs	• Customization: $10K-$85K • Integration: $10K-$50K • Training: Up to $15K	Flexible, scalable solutions that cater to diverse business needs but require investment for customization and integration.
Revenue and Market Cap	• FY2022 Revenue: $26.49B (25% YoY growth) • Market Cap: ~$153B (as of Sep 2022)	Strong financial growth, highlighting Salesforce's market dominance and scalability.

9.6 DROPBOX

Dropbox is a file hosting service that was founded in 2007 by MIT students Drew Houston and Arash Ferdowsi. Some key points about the history of Dropbox [34]:

- Dropbox was initially funded by seed accelerator Y Combinator when it was founded as a startup company in 2007.
- Dropbox was officially launched in September 2008 and has since grown to become one of the most popular cloud storage and file synchronization services.
- In March 2013, Dropbox acquired the popular email app Mailbox, and in April 2014, the company introduced Dropbox Carousel, a photo and video gallery app. Both Mailbox and Carousel were later shut down in December 2015, with key features incorporated into the main Dropbox service.
- In October 2015, Dropbox announced the launch of Dropbox Paper, its collaborative document editing tool.
- Over time, Dropbox has moved away from relying on Amazon's S3 storage system and has built its own proprietary storage infrastructure referred to as "Magic Pocket".
- In June 2017, Dropbox announced a major global network expansion to increase synchronization speeds and reduce costs.
- Dropbox has faced some criticism and controversy over the years, including security breaches and privacy concerns.

The short comprehensive insights of Dropbox are highlighted in Figure 9.5.

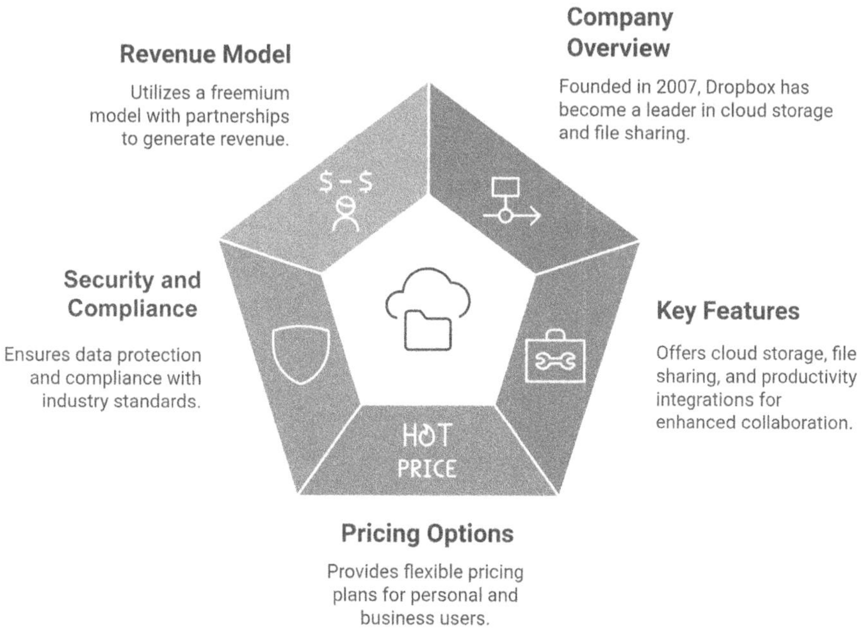
Company Overview
Founded in 2007, Dropbox has become a leader in cloud storage and file sharing.
Revenue Model
Utilizes a freemium model with partnerships to generate revenue.
$-$
Security and Compliance
Ensures data protection and compliance with industry standards.
Key Features
Offers cloud storage, file sharing, and productivity integrations for enhanced collaboration.
HOT PRICE
Pricing Options
Provides flexible pricing plans for personal and business users.

FIGURE 9.5 General Insights about Dropbox services and features.

In summary, Dropbox has evolved from a startup founded by MIT students in 2007 to become one of the leading cloud storage and file sharing platforms, with a history of acquisitions, product launches, and infrastructure improvements over the past 15+ years.

9.6.1 Key Features

Dropbox is a popular cloud storage and file-sharing platform that offers several key features:

1. File Storage and Sync: Dropbox allows you to store and access your files from anywhere, across your computer, phone, and tablet. Any changes you make to files in your Dropbox will automatically sync across your devices [35].
2. File Sharing and Collaboration: You can easily share files and folders with others, and collaborate on documents in real time. Dropbox offers features such as password protection, expiring links, and granular sharing permissions to control access.
3. Productivity Tools: Dropbox integrates with various productivity apps such as Microsoft Office, Slack, and Zoom, allowing you to work on and share content directly within the Dropbox ecosystem.
4. Data Protection: Dropbox provides advanced data protection features such as version history, file recovery, and remote wipe to safeguard your files. It also offers enterprise-grade security with 256-bit AES encryption [36].
5. Team Management: For businesses, Dropbox offers team folders, admin controls, and an insights dashboard to help manage and monitor team activity and file sharing.
6. Mobile Access: The Dropbox mobile app allows you to access your files, share content, and automatically back up photos and videos from your mobile devices.

In summary, Dropbox's key features revolve around secure cloud storage, seamless file sharing and collaboration, productivity enhancement, and robust data protection – making it a popular choice for both individuals and teams.

9.6.2 Pricing Options

Dropbox offers several pricing plans for personal, professional, and team use [37–40]:

Personal Plans

- Basic (Free): 2 GB of storage, one user, connect up to three devices.
- Plus ($9.99/month): 2 TB of storage, one user, transfer files up to 50 GB, 30 days to restore deleted files
- Essentials ($16.58/month): 3 TB of storage, one user, transfer files up to 100 GB, 180 days to restore deleted files, track file engagement, unlimited signature requests, PDF editing, record/review/edit video

Family Plans

- Family ($16.99/month): 2 TB of storage, up to six users, transfer files up to 50 GB, 30 days to restore deleted files, family folder for photos/files, secure/share passwords

Business Plans

- Essentials ($16.58/month): 3 TB of storage, one user, transfer files up to 100 GB, 180 days to restore deleted files, track file engagement, unlimited signature requests, PDF editing, record/review/edit video
- Business ($15/user/month): Start at 9 TB for the team, transfer files up to 100 GB, 180 days to restore deleted files, track file engagement, unlimited signature requests, PDF editing, record/review/edit video, set up admins, and know what content is shared
- Business Plus ($24/user/month): Start at 15 TB for the team, transfer files up to 250 GB, 1 year to restore deleted files, track file engagement, unlimited signature requests, PDF editing, record/review/edit video, set up tiered admin roles, suspicious activity alerts, compliance tracking
- Enterprise: Customizable plans for large organizations, with enterprise-grade security, integrations, and live support

9.6.3 Security and Compliance

Dropbox emphasizes security, compliance, and privacy as fundamental aspects of its operations [41–44]. Here are the key points regarding Dropbox's security and compliance:

Security Measures

- Data Encryption: Dropbox uses multiple layers of protection, including secure file data transfer and encryption, to keep data secure.
- Application-Level Controls: Dropbox employs application-level controls to enhance security across its scalable and secure infrastructure.
- Privacy by Design: Dropbox embeds privacy considerations into its products and features, ensuring that personal data is protected at all times.

Compliance Standards

- ISO Certifications: Dropbox has certified its data centers, systems, applications, people, and processes through ISO 27001, ISO 27017, and ISO 27018, which focus on information security management, cloud security, and cloud privacy and data protection, respectively.
- SOC Reports: Dropbox complies with SOC 1, 2, and 3 reports, which provide assurance on the controls at service organizations relevant to financial reporting and internal control over financial reporting.
- HIPAA/HITECH: Dropbox meets the standards for HIPAA/HITECH compliance, ensuring that protected health information is handled securely.

- EU-U.S. Data Privacy Frameworks: Dropbox adheres to the EU-U.S. Data Privacy Framework, the UK Extension to the EU-U.S. Data Privacy Framework, and the Swiss-U.S. Data Privacy Framework.
- FDA 21 CFR Part 11: Dropbox supports compliance with FDA 21 CFR Part 11, which sets criteria for electronic records and signatures.
- PCI DSS: Dropbox is a Payment Card Industry Data Security Standard (PCI DSS) compliant merchant.

Additional Compliance Measures

- Independent Audits: Dropbox undergoes independent third-party ethics and compliance audits to ensure its systems and controls meet the most widely accepted security standards.
- Compliance Risk Assessment: Dropbox combines accepted standards with compliance risk assessment measures tailored to the specific needs of its customers.
- Continuous Improvement: Dropbox demonstrates continued improvement in its security practices through regular audits and compliance reviews.

Trust Center

Dropbox provides a Trust Center where users can learn about its security posture and request access to security, compliance, and privacy documentation. This center includes details on various security measures, compliance frameworks, and regulatory certifications.

By adhering to these stringent standards and practices, Dropbox aims to provide a secure and reliable platform for its users.

9.6.4 Operational Costs for Businesses

The key points about Dropbox's operating expenses for businesses are as follows [45–47]:

Dropbox Operating Expenses Overview

- Dropbox's operating expenses for the 12 months ending March 31, 2024 were $1.924B, a 12.47% decline year-over-year.
- In Q2 2023, Dropbox's operating expenses were $445.9M, up from $384.0M in Q2 2022.

Dropbox Business Plan Pricing

- Dropbox Business Standard costs 12 euros per license per month in Germany, plus 19% tax for a total of 14.28 euros.
- However, some users have reported seeing prices in dollars instead of euros, even when the billing country is set to Germany.

Dropbox Business Plan Features

- Dropbox Business plans start at 9 TB for teams of 3+ users.
- Features include 180 days to restore deleted files, file engagement tracking, unlimited signature requests, PDF editing, and video recording/editing.

- Enterprise plans allow customizing the number of users and storage, with enterprise-grade security and integrations with security solutions.

In summary, while Dropbox's overall operating expenses have declined year-over-year, the company's business plans offer a range of features at competitive prices, though some users have reported inconsistencies in the displayed pricing. Businesses should check the current pricing for their location and plan needs.

Dropbox optimized its operational costs in several key ways:

1. Migrating from AWS to its own custom storage infrastructure called Magic Pocket. This allowed Dropbox to reduce its operating expenses by $75 million per year, a 90% reduction in storage costs. The migration took over two years to complete but resulted in significant cost savings.
2. Designing a storage system tailored to its specific needs. Magic Pocket is a distributed storage system optimized for Dropbox's use cases and performance goals. By building its own system, Dropbox could leverage economies of scale and hardware innovations to reduce costs.
3. Improving storage efficiency by 25%. Dropbox was able to store more data with less hardware, further reducing costs. The custom system also improved performance by 40%.
4. Offering freemium subscription plans. Dropbox generates revenue by charging for premium features and additional storage space. Plans such as Dropbox Plus, Family, and Business provide varying levels of storage and functionality at different price points.
5. Monetizing through partnerships and integrations. Dropbox earns revenue by licensing its services to other companies and platforms. For example, integrations with Microsoft Office and Google Workspace allow users to access Dropbox files within those applications.
6. Migrating its metadata store to Amazon DynamoDB and S3. When Dropbox's on-premises metadata storage reached capacity, it migrated to AWS in less than two weeks. This saved millions in expansion costs and allowed ingesting data at 4,000–6,000 queries per second.

By optimizing its storage infrastructure, offering tiered subscription plans, leveraging partnerships, and selectively using cloud services, Dropbox was able to significantly reduce its operational costs while continuing to scale its business. A tabular analysis of Dropbox, summarizing key features, security and compliance, operational costs, etc., is provided in Table 9.5.

This table highlights Dropbox's evolution, focusing on its cost-efficient infrastructure, security practices, and flexible pricing plans, making it an attractive choice for both individuals and enterprises.

TABLE 9.5
Analysis of Key Dropbox Aspects

Aspect	Details	Key Benefits
Company Overview	Founded in 2007 by Drew Houston and Arash Ferdowsi, Dropbox is a cloud storage and file-sharing service. It has grown into one of the leading platforms for file synchronization and collaboration.	Pioneered the cloud storage market with easy file sharing and collaboration tools, continuously expanding its offerings.
Key Features	• Cloud storage and syncing across devices • File sharing with password protection and expiring links • Productivity integrations (Office, Slack, Zoom) • Version history, remote wipe	Enhanced collaboration, file security, and integration with popular productivity tools for businesses and individuals.
Pricing Options	• Personal Plans: Free (2GB), Plus ($9.99/month for 2TB), Essentials ($16.58/month for 3TB) • Business Plans: Essentials ($16.58/user/month), Business ($15/user/month), Enterprise (custom pricing)	Flexible pricing for personal users to large enterprises, with features tailored to specific needs such as advanced file sharing and security.
Security and Compliance	• Uses AES 256-bit encryption for data protection • Compliance with ISO 27001, SOC 1-3, HIPAA, PCI DSS, and other frameworks • Regular independent audits and security reviews	Ensures high levels of security and privacy for users, meeting regulatory requirements for industries such as healthcare and finance.
Operational Costs	• Operating expenses (FY 2024): $1.924B (12.47% decline YoY) • Significant cost savings from migrating to own infrastructure, Magic Pocket • Reduction in storage costs by 90%	Cost-efficient due to optimized infrastructure, offering scalable solutions for businesses without compromising performance.
Custom Infrastructure	Dropbox migrated from AWS to its proprietary storage system, Magic Pocket, cutting storage costs by $75 million annually.	Significant savings on cloud storage, enhanced performance, and improved scalability for the growing user base.
Revenue Model	Freemium subscription model; premium features (increased storage, advanced collaboration tools) and partnerships (e.g., Microsoft, Google) help generate revenue.	Flexible plans allow Dropbox to cater to both personal users and large enterprises, while partnerships expand its reach.
Additional Business Features	Business and Enterprise plans include admin controls, file engagement tracking, and compliance tracking.	Tailored for businesses needing advanced collaboration tools, enhanced security, and control over user activity.

9.7 SUMMARY

Cloud computing platforms provide on-demand access to computing resources such as data storage and processing power without requiring direct management by the user. This chapter provides a brief summary of the major cloud computing platforms. AWS offers a wide range of cloud services including virtual compute (EC2), storage (S3), networking, databases, and more. EC2 provides customizable virtual hardware that can be used as infrastructure for deploying computing systems. S3 offers scalable object storage for storing and retrieving data. Azure is a cloud operating system that provides a scalable runtime for web and distributed applications. Applications are organized into roles which express the application logic. Azure provides additional services such as storage, networking, caching, content delivery, and more. GCP provides a scalable runtime environment for executing web applications. It offers services such as in-memory caching, scalable data storage, job queues, messaging, and cron tasks to simplify building scalable web apps. Supported languages include Python, Java, and Go. Salesforce Platform (Force.com) is a cloud platform for developing social enterprise applications. It provides a set of ready-to-use components covering various enterprise activities from data modeling to defining business rules and UI. The entire platform is cloud-hosted and accessible via web services.

Cloud computing platforms offer benefits such as reduced costs, increased scalability, better performance, improved security, and easier deployment of applications. They allow users to quickly provision resources on-demand without the need for managing underlying infrastructure. Dropbox is a popular cloud storage and file hosting service that allows users to store, access, and share digital files from a centralized location across multiple devices. It offers features such as file synchronization, collaboration tools, and version history to help users stay organized and work efficiently. Dropbox uses a freemium business model, providing a free basic account with limited storage, while offering paid subscriptions with more capacity and additional features. The service is designed to be user-friendly and secure, with multiple layers of protection for users' data.

9.8 PRACTICE QUESTIONS/SOLUTIONS

MULTIPLE OBJECTIVE QUESTIONS

1 **What is the primary function of Amazon S3 in AWS?**

A) Virtual Private Cloud (VPC) management
B) Database administration
C) Object storage
D) Serverless computing

Answer: C) Object storage

2 **Which AWS service is used to distribute incoming application traffic across multiple targets, such as EC2 instances?**

A) Amazon Route 53
B) AWS Lambda

C) Amazon SQS
D) Elastic Load Balancing (ELB)

Answer: D) Elastic Load Balancing (ELB)

3 **Which AWS service is used to set up and manage a relational database?**
A) Amazon RDS
B) Amazon S3
C) Amazon DynamoDB
D) Amazon EC2

Answer: A) Amazon RDS

4 **What AWS service is used to create and manage a data warehouse for analytics?**
A) Amazon Redshift
B) Amazon Athena
C) AWS Glue
D) Amazon Aurora

Answer: A) Amazon Redshift

5 **What Azure service provides a globally distributed, multi-model database for any scale?**
A) Azure Cosmos DB
B) Azure SQL Database
C) Azure Blob Storage
D) Azure Data Lake Storage

Answer: A) Azure Cosmos DB

6 **What Azure service is used for building, testing, and deploying containerized applications?**
A) Azure Kubernetes Service (AKS)
B) Azure Functions
C) Azure Container Instances
D) Azure App Service

Answer: A) Azure Kubernetes Service (AKS)

7 **Which Azure service provides a fully managed analytics service for real-time insights using big data?**
A) Azure Stream Analytics
B) Azure Data Factory
C) Azure HDInsight
D) Azure Data Lake Analytics

Answer: C) Azure HDInsight

8 What Azure service is used for creating and managing a data warehouse for analytics?

A) Azure SQL Data Warehouse
B) Azure Data Lake Storage
C) Azure Data Factory
D) Azure Blob Storage

Answer: A) Azure SQL Data Warehouse

9 Which Google Cloud service is used for managing and deploying containerized applications using Kubernetes?

A) Google Compute Engine
B) Google Cloud Functions
C) Google Kubernetes Engine (GKE)
D) Google Cloud Pub/Sub

Answer: C) Google Kubernetes Engine (GKE)

10 Which Google Cloud service provides a managed platform for building and deploying applications without managing the underlying infrastructure?

A) Google Cloud Functions
B) Google App Engine
C) Google Compute Engine
D) Google Cloud SQL

Answer: B) Google App Engine

11 What Google Cloud service is used for real-time messaging and event ingestion?

A) Google Cloud Pub/Sub
B) Google Cloud Dataflow
C) Google Cloud Spanner
D) Google Cloud Storage

Answer: A) Google Cloud Pub/Sub

12 Which Google Cloud service is a fully managed relational database service that supports MySQL, PostgreSQL, and SQL Server?

A) Google Cloud SQL
B) Google Cloud Bigtable
C) Google Cloud Firestore
D) Google Cloud Datastore

Answer: A) Google Cloud SQL

13 What is Salesforce primarily known for in the realm of cloud computing?

A) Customer Relationship Management (CRM)
B) Enterprise Resource Planning (ERP)
C) Project Management
D) Business Intelligence

Answer: A) Customer Relationship Management (CRM)

14 Which Salesforce product allows businesses to track customer interactions and manage customer data?

A) Salesforce Marketing Cloud
B) Salesforce Commerce Cloud
C) Salesforce Service Cloud
D) Salesforce Sales Cloud

Answer: D) Salesforce Sales Cloud

15 What Salesforce product is designed for creating personalized customer journeys across various channels?

A) Salesforce Sales Cloud
B) Salesforce Service Cloud
C) Salesforce Marketing Cloud
D) Salesforce Community Cloud

Answer: C) Salesforce Marketing Cloud

16 Which Salesforce product provides tools for managing customer support and service interactions?

A) Salesforce Pardot
B) Salesforce Commerce Cloud
C) Salesforce Service Cloud
D) Salesforce Einstein Analytics

Answer: C) Salesforce Service Cloud

17 Which feature of Dropbox allows users to synchronize files across devices?

A) Dropbox Paper
B) Dropbox Showcase
C) Dropbox Spaces
D) Dropbox Sync

Answer: D) Dropbox Sync

18 What is the maximum file size limit for uploads through Dropbox Basic (free) accounts?

A) 2 GB
B) 5 GB

C) 10 GB
D) 15 GB

Answer: A) 2 GB

19 Which Dropbox plan provides users with 3 TB of storage per user and is designed for small to medium-sized businesses?
A) Dropbox Plus
B) Dropbox Business Standard
C) Dropbox Business Advanced
D) Dropbox Professional

Answer: B) Dropbox Business Standard

20 What feature of Dropbox allows users to create and collaborate on documents in real time?
A) Dropbox Showcase
B) Dropbox Paper
C) Dropbox Spaces
D) Dropbox Vault

Answer: B) Dropbox Paper

DESCRIPTIVE QUESTIONS

1 Explain the concept of Elastic Load Balancing (ELB) in AWS.

Answer: Elastic Load Balancing (ELB) is a service provided by AWS that automatically distributes incoming application traffic across multiple targets, such as EC2 instances, containers, and IP addresses, in multiple Availability Zones within a region. ELB helps improve the availability and fault tolerance of your applications by ensuring that no single resource becomes a bottleneck. It automatically scales its request handling capacity in response to incoming traffic, thereby facilitating seamless scaling of your application horizontally.

2 Describe the key features and benefits of Amazon S3 (Simple Storage Service).

Answer: Amazon S3 is an object storage service offered by AWS that provides scalability, data availability, security, and performance. Key features include:

- **Scalability**: Virtually unlimited storage capacity with automatic scaling.
- **Data Availability**: Designed for 99.999999999% (11 nines) durability, ensuring data is highly available.

- **Security**: Various encryption options for data at rest and in transit, access controls, and compliance certifications.
- **Performance**: Low-latency access to data, support for large objects (up to 5 TB), and multi-part upload for efficient data transfer.
- **Cost-effective**: Pay-as-you-go pricing model based on storage usage, with tiered pricing for different storage classes (e.g., S3 Standard, S3 Intelligent-Tiering, S3 Glacier).

3 Explain the difference between Amazon EC2 and AWS Lambda.

Answer:

- **Amazon EC2 (Elastic Compute Cloud)**: EC2 provides resizable compute capacity in the cloud, allowing users to launch virtual servers (instances) tailored to specific needs. It offers full control over the operating system, applications, and configuration, making it suitable for a wide range of applications from simple to complex.
- **AWS Lambda**: AWS Lambda is a serverless compute service that runs code in response to events and automatically manages the underlying compute resources. It supports multiple programming languages and allows developers to execute code without provisioning or managing servers. Lambda scales automatically based on the incoming traffic and charges only for the compute time consumed.

4 How does Amazon RDS (Relational Database Service) simplify database management in AWS?

Answer: Amazon RDS is a managed database service that simplifies database setup, operation, and scaling in the cloud. Key benefits include:

- **Automated backups**: RDS automatically backs up databases and enables point-in-time recovery.
- **Scalability**: Allows scaling compute and storage resources vertically and horizontally as per demand.
- **Managed patches and updates**: Handles routine maintenance tasks, including database software patching.
- **High availability**: Offers Multi-AZ deployments for automatic failover to a standby database instance in case of a failure.

5 Explain the purpose and advantages of Amazon VPC (Virtual Private Cloud).

Answer: Amazon VPC allows you to provision a logically isolated section of AWS cloud where you can launch AWS resources in a virtual network that you define. Advantages include:

- **Controlled network environment**: Define your IP address range, subnets, route tables, and gateways.
- **Secure connectivity**: Establish secure communication with other AWS resources, on-premises data centers, or remote networks using VPN or AWS Direct Connect.
- **Scalability**: Scale your VPC as needed, including adding or removing subnets, route tables, and network gateways.
- **Customization**: Configure network settings such as DNS resolution, DHCP options, and network ACLs (Access Control Lists) for fine-grained control over traffic flow.

6 Describe Azure Active Directory (Azure AD) and its role in identity and access management (IAM) in Azure.

Answer: Azure Active Directory (Azure AD) is Microsoft's cloud-based identity and access management service that helps users sign in and access resources securely. Key aspects include:

- **Single sign-on (SSO)**: Provides seamless access to thousands of cloud applications with a single identity.
- **Identity protection**: Detects suspicious activities and potential vulnerabilities using advanced analytics and adaptive machine learning algorithms.
- **Integration**: Integrates with Microsoft 365, Azure services, and thousands of third-party SaaS applications for unified access management.
- **Security**: Implements multi-factor authentication (MFA), conditional access policies, and privileged identity management (PIM) for enhanced security controls.

7 Explain the purpose of Azure Kubernetes Service (AKS) and its benefits for container orchestration.

Answer: Azure Kubernetes Service (AKS) is a managed Kubernetes container orchestration service provided by Microsoft Azure, designed to simplify deploying, managing, and scaling containerized applications using Kubernetes. Benefits include:

- **Managed service**: Automates Kubernetes cluster management tasks such as upgrades, scaling, and monitoring.
- **Flexibility**: Supports both Linux and Windows containers and integrates seamlessly with Azure DevOps and other CI/CD tools.
- **Scalability**: Automatically scales the cluster nodes based on workload demands and integrates with Azure Monitor for performance monitoring.
- **Security**: Integrates with Azure Active Directory for identity and access management, and provides network security policies for container traffic.

8 Describe Azure Functions and their role in serverless computing.

Answer: Azure Functions is a serverless compute service provided by Microsoft Azure that allows developers to run event-triggered code without provisioning or managing servers. Key features include:

- **Event-driven**: Executes code in response to events from various Azure services (e.g., HTTP triggers, Azure Blob Storage events, timer triggers).
- **Scalability**: Scales automatically based on the number of incoming events or workload demands.
- **Integration**: Integrates with other Azure services and third-party services, enabling seamless development of microservices and event-driven applications.
- **Cost-effective**: Pay-per-use pricing model based on the number of executions and resource consumption, with free tiers for experimentation and testing.

9 Discuss the role of Azure DevOps in continuous integration and continuous delivery (CI/CD) pipelines.

Answer: Azure DevOps is a set of cloud services provided by Microsoft Azure for managing the entire software development lifecycle, including planning, development, testing, delivery, and monitoring. Key capabilities include:

- **Version control**: Provides Git repositories for source code management and collaboration.
- **CI/CD pipelines**: Automates build, test, and deployment processes with Azure Pipelines, integrating with GitHub, Bitbucket, and other repositories.
- **Agile planning**: Supports Agile methodologies with tools for backlog management, sprint planning, and task tracking.
- **Monitoring and feedback**: Integrates with Azure Monitor and Application Insights for monitoring application performance and collecting user feedback.

10 Explain the concept of Azure Cosmos DB and its benefits for globally distributed applications.

Answer: Azure Cosmos DB is a globally distributed, multi-model database service provided by Microsoft Azure, designed to provide low-latency access to data at global scale. Benefits include:

- **Global distribution**: Replicates data across multiple Azure regions worldwide for low-latency access and high availability.

- **Multi-model support**: Supports multiple data models (e.g., SQL, MongoDB, Cassandra, Gremlin) with automatic indexing and query capabilities.
- **Scalability**: Scales throughput and storage independently based on application demands, with guaranteed low latency and high availability.
- **Consistency**: Offers five well-defined consistency levels to choose from, balancing between consistency, availability, and performance based on application requirements.

11 Describe the concept of Google Cloud Platform (GCP) and its key services.

Answer: Google Cloud Platform (GCP) is a suite of cloud computing services provided by Google, offering infrastructure, platform, and software-as-a-service (IaaS, PaaS, and SaaS) solutions. Key services include:

- **Compute**: Google Compute Engine for virtual machines (VMs), Google Kubernetes Engine (GKE) for container orchestration, and Google App Engine for serverless applications.
- **Storage**: Google Cloud Storage for object storage, Cloud SQL for managed SQL databases, and BigQuery for serverless data warehousing and analytics.
- **Networking**: Virtual Private Cloud (VPC) for networking isolation, Cloud Load Balancing for global load balancing, and Cloud CDN for content delivery.
- **Big Data**: BigQuery for real-time analytics, Dataflow for stream and batch processing, and Dataproc for managed Apache Spark and Hadoop clusters.
- **Machine Learning and AI**: TensorFlow and AI Platform for machine learning, Vision API and Natural Language API for AI-powered services, and AutoML for custom model training.

12 Explain the architecture and benefits of Google Kubernetes Engine (GKE) for container orchestration.

Answer: Google Kubernetes Engine (GKE) is a managed Kubernetes service provided by Google Cloud Platform. Its architecture includes:

- **Cluster management**: Automates the deployment, scaling, and operation of Kubernetes clusters.
- **Node pools**: Groups of compute instances within a cluster, each running Kubernetes processes like kubelet and Kube-proxy.
- **Master node**: Manages the Kubernetes control plane components like API server, scheduler, and controller manager.
- **Worker nodes**: Run containerized applications orchestrated by Kubernetes.

- **Benefits**: GKE simplifies container management, ensures high availability with automated scaling, integrates with CI/CD pipelines, and supports hybrid and multi-cloud deployments.

13 Describe the purpose and advantages of Google Cloud Storage for cloud-based data storage.

Answer: Google Cloud Storage is an object storage service designed to store and retrieve large, unstructured datasets. Advantages include:

- **Scalability**: Scales seamlessly to petabytes of data with high availability and durability.
- **Multi-regional and regional storage**: Options for storing data across multiple regions for redundancy and low-latency access.
- **Security**: Encryption at rest and in transit, IAM policies for access control, and integration with Google Cloud Identity-Aware Proxy (IAP).
- **Cost-effectiveness**: Pay-as-you-go pricing model based on storage usage, with different storage classes (e.g., Standard, Nearline, Coldline) optimized for various access patterns.

14 Explain the use case and benefits of Google BigQuery for data analytics and business intelligence.

Answer: Google BigQuery is a serverless, highly scalable, and cost-effective data warehouse designed for real-time analytics. Use cases and benefits include:

- **Real-time analytics**: Analyzes terabytes to petabytes of data with SQL-like queries.
- **Serverless architecture**: Automatically scales compute and storage resources based on workload demands.
- **Integration**: Integrates with Google Cloud Storage, Cloud Dataflow, and other GCP services for data ingestion and processing.
- **Machine learning integration**: Allows running ML models directly on BigQuery data using BigQuery ML for predictive analytics.

15 Explain the benefits of Google Cloud Platform for hybrid and multi-cloud environments.

Answer: Google Cloud Platform supports hybrid and multi-cloud deployments, offering benefits such as:

- **Flexibility**: Integrates with Anthos for managing Kubernetes clusters across on-premises and cloud environments.
- **Portability**: Allows workload migration between GCP and other cloud providers using Google Cloud Interconnect and third-party tools.

- **Consistency**: Provides a consistent development and operational experience across hybrid and multi-cloud environments.
- **Scalability**: Scales applications and services seamlessly across GCP regions and availability zones.

16 Describe the key features of Dropbox Business and their benefits for organizational use.

Answer: Dropbox Business is designed for teams and organizations, offering features such as:

- **Team folders**: Centralized storage for team collaboration and file sharing.
- **Admin controls**: Tools for managing users, permissions, and security settings.
- **Integration**: Integrates with productivity tools like Microsoft Office 365, Google Workspace, and Slack.
- **Advanced collaboration**: Real-time co-editing, commenting, and version history for seamless teamwork.

17 Explain the role of Dropbox Paper in enhancing collaborative work within teams.

Answer: Dropbox Paper is a collaborative workspace within Dropbox that allows teams to create, edit, and share documents in real-time. Key features include:

- **Rich content creation**: Supports text, images, videos, and embedded files for creating multimedia documents.
- **Commenting and task assignment**: Enables team members to comment on documents and assign tasks.
- **Version history**: Tracks changes and revisions, making it easy to revert to previous versions.
- **Integration**: Integrates with Dropbox files and external applications for streamlined workflow management.

18 Describe the security measures implemented by Dropbox to protect user data in the cloud.

Answer: Dropbox employs several security measures to protect user data, including:

- **Encryption**: Uses AES 256-bit encryption for data at rest and SSL/TLS for data in transit.
- **Two-factor authentication (2FA)**: Adds an extra layer of security by requiring a verification code in addition to a password.

- **File recovery and version history**: Allows users to restore deleted files and access previous versions of files.
- **Permissions and access controls**: Provides granular control over sharing permissions and access levels.

18 Explain how Dropbox handles data synchronization across multiple devices and platforms.

Answer: Dropbox uses synchronization technology to ensure that files are up-to-date and accessible across devices and platforms. Key aspects include:

- **Automatic syncing**: Syncs changes made to files in the Dropbox folder across connected devices in real time.
- **Selective sync**: Allows users to choose which folders and files to sync to each device, optimizing storage usage.
- **Offline access**: Provides offline access to synchronized files, enabling users to work without an Internet connection.
- **Bandwidth management**: Adjusts synchronization speed based on available bandwidth to optimize performance.

19 Describe the benefits of Dropbox for Business Continuity and Disaster Recovery (BCDR) planning.

Answer: Dropbox supports Business Continuity and Disaster Recovery (BCDR) by:

- **Cloud storage**: Storing files in the cloud ensures data availability even in the event of local hardware failure or disasters.
- **Version history**: Maintaining a history of file versions allows for recovery of previous versions in case of accidental deletion or corruption.
- **Remote access**: Enabling users to access files from any location with Internet access supports remote work and business continuity efforts.
- **Data redundancy**: Replicating data across multiple data centers enhances data durability and resilience against data loss.

REFERENCES

1. https://www.ibm.com/cloud/case-studies
2. https://www.clearscale.com/case-studies
3. https://www2.deloitte.com/us/en/pages/consulting/articles/cloud-computing-case-studies.html
4. https://cyfuture.cloud/blog/case-studies-of-successful-cloud-service-adoption-by-enterprises/
5. https://www.bespokesoftwaredevelopment.com/blog/benefits-cloud-computing-businesses/

6. https://www.redswitches.com/blog/benefits-of-cloud-computing-for-your-business/
7. https://azure.microsoft.com/en-in/resources/cloud-computing-dictionary/what-is-cloud-migration
8. https://www.accenture.com/in-en/insights/cloud-migration-index
9. https://www.techtarget.com/searchcloudcomputing/definition/cloud-migration
10. https://infoscience.epfl.ch/record/181192?ln=en&v=pdf
11. https://www.hbs.edu/faculty/Pages/item.aspx?num=36511
12. https://fortune.com/longform/amazon-web-services-ceo-adam-selipsky-cloud-computing/
13. https://www.geeksforgeeks.org/features-of-aws/
14. https://aws.amazon.com/pricing/
15. https://docs.aws.amazon.com/whitepapers/latest/aws-overview/security-and-compliance.html
16. https://aws.amazon.com/compliance/
17. https://azure.microsoft.com/en-in
18. https://info.microsoft.com/ww-landing-case-studies-in-cloud-modernization.html
19. https://azure.microsoft.com/en-in/pricing/
20. https://azure.microsoft.com/en-in/explore/security
21. https://azure.microsoft.com/en-in/explore/trusted-cloud/compliance
22. https://cloud.google.com
23. https://cloud.google.com/customers/current
24. https://cloud.google.com/customers/king
25. https://cloud.google.com/pricing
26. https://www.wikiwand.com/en/Salesforce
27. https://www.salesforce.com/in/
28. https://www.salesforce.com/in/sales/pricing/
29. https://help.salesforce.com/s/articleView?id=000382043&type=1
30. https://www.salesforce.com/company/legal/trust-and-compliance-documentation/
31. https://security.salesforce.com/
32. https://www.capstorm.com/salesforce-compliance/
33. https://www.salesforce.com/in/small-business/pricing/
34. https://www.wikiwand.com/en/Dropbox
35. https://www.dropbox.com/features
36. https://www.dropbox.com/business/tour
37. https://www.dropbox.com/plans
38. https://www.dropbox.com/individual
39. https://www.dropbox.com/buy
40. https://www.dropbox.com/business/plans-comparison
41. https://www.dropbox.com/business/trust
42. https://www.dropbox.com/business/trust/compliance/certifications-compliance
43. https://help.dropbox.com/security/standards-regulations
44. https://www.dropbox.com/business/trust/compliance
45. https://www.dropbox.com/business/plans-comparison
46. https://www.dropboxforum.com/t5/Plans-and-Subscriptions/Why-is-the-price-different-for-Dropbox-Business-Standard/td-p/724553
47. https://www.macrotrends.net/stocks/charts/DBX/dropbox/operating-expenses

10 Practical Hands-on Platforms

10.1 INTRODUCTION

There are several practical hands-on platforms for cloud computing that one can use to gain experience and expertise in this field. Some popular cloud computing platforms are illustrated below:

- One of the most well-known cloud platforms is Amazon Web Services (AWS), which offers a variety of cloud computing services, including computation, storage, and databases, among others. The AWS Free Tier offers cost-free experimentation and learning opportunities.
- Google Cloud Platform (GCP): GCP offers various cloud computing services, such as networking, storage, and computation. The GCP Free Tier is available for experimentation and learning.
- Microsoft Azure is another well-known cloud computing platform that offers services including virtual machines, storage, and app services. To get started with Azure and test out the services, utilize the Azure Free Account.
- DigitalOcean: This cloud platform specializes in offering straightforward and reasonably priced infrastructure for developers. Launching databases, containers, and virtual machines are all possible with DigitalOcean.
- Heroku is a cloud computing platform that focuses on hosting web applications. Heroku makes it simple to deploy and scale your applications.
- IBM Cloud: This company offers a variety of cloud computing services, such as computation, storage, and networking. The IBM Cloud Free Tier may be used for testing new ideas and education.
- Oracle Cloud Infrastructure (OCI) is a cloud platform that offers networking, storage, and computing services. The OCI Free Tier is available for experimentation and learning.

These platforms offer various tutorials, documentation, and community support to help you get started with cloud computing. Choose the one that best suits your needs and start exploring the world of cloud computing.

DOI: 10.1201/9781003510772-10

10.2 AMAZON WEB SERVICES (AWS)

Amazon Web Services (AWS) [1] is a comprehensive and widely adopted cloud computing platform that offers a broad array of services aimed at both businesses and individuals. These services facilitate the development, deployment, and scaling of a wide range of applications, allowing users to access and utilize computing resources on demand. AWS is known for its scalability, flexibility, and global reach, making it a top choice for organizations looking to leverage cloud infrastructure. Below is a detailed expansion of several key features and services that AWS provides for cloud computing. An in-detail view of AWS cloud services is provided in Figure 10.1.

10.2.1 Amazon Elastic Compute Cloud (EC2)

Amazon EC2 is a scalable computing service that allows users to run virtual servers, known as instances, on-demand. This service is designed to cater to a variety

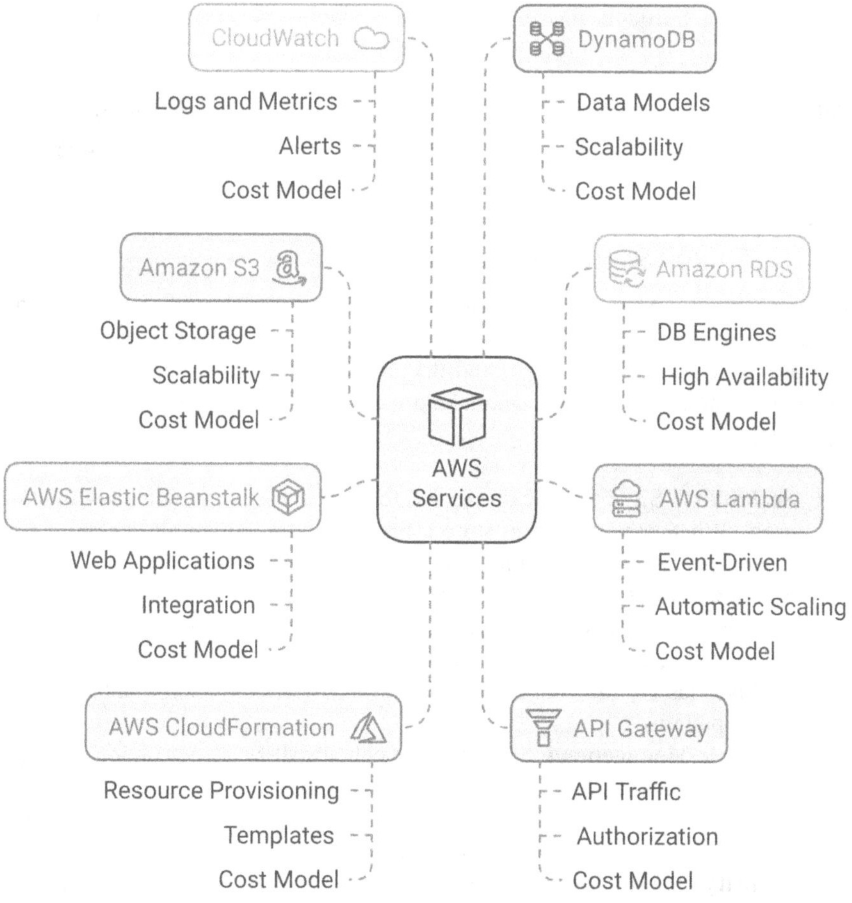

FIGURE 10.1 Detailed view of AWS cloud services.

of computational needs, from hosting simple web applications to running complex batch processing tasks or machine learning models. EC2 instances can be easily scaled up or down depending on the workload requirements, offering flexibility and cost efficiency.

- **Instance Types**: EC2 offers a wide range of instance types that are optimized for different use cases. These include compute-optimized, memory-optimized, storage-optimized, and GPU instances. This allows businesses to select the right resources tailored to their specific application requirements.
- **Operating Systems**: Users can choose from a variety of operating systems, including various versions of Linux, Microsoft Windows, and even specialized systems like Ubuntu or Red Hat.
- **Auto-scaling**: EC2's Auto-scaling feature allows applications to automatically adjust their instance count based on traffic fluctuations, helping businesses manage unpredictable workloads efficiently while minimizing costs.
- **Elastic Load Balancing (ELB)**: Combined with EC2, ELB ensures that incoming traffic is distributed across multiple instances, ensuring high availability and reliability for web applications.

With EC2, users can host anything from simple websites to complex enterprise applications, leveraging its flexible compute capacity and cost-effective pay-as-you-go pricing model.

10.2.2 Amazon Simple Storage Service (S3)

Amazon S3 is an object storage service that provides scalable and secure data storage accessible over the Internet. It is commonly used for storing and retrieving data such as images, videos, backups, and documents. S3 is known for its durability, availability, and high performance, making it a foundational service for many cloud applications.

- **Scalability**: S3 automatically scales to meet the storage demands of its users. Whether you need to store a few gigabytes of data or several petabytes, S3 can handle it without requiring manual intervention.
- **Storage Classes**: S3 offers a variety of storage classes, each designed to meet different performance, availability, and cost requirements. These include the Standard, Intelligent-Tiering, One Zone-IA, Glacier, and Glacier Deep Archive classes, allowing users to choose a cost-effective solution based on access patterns.
- **Lifecycle Management**: S3's lifecycle policies allow users to automate the process of moving data between storage classes or deleting it after a certain period. This can significantly reduce costs by automatically transitioning infrequently accessed data to lower-cost storage.
- **Security**: S3 provides robust security features, including encryption (at rest and in transit), access control policies, and identity and access management (IAM) for fine-grained access control.

S3 is used by millions of customers worldwide for diverse purposes, from serving static website content to storing large-scale data backups and machine learning datasets.

10.2.3 Amazon Relational Database Service (RDS)

Amazon RDS is a fully managed relational database service that simplifies the process of setting up, operating, and scaling relational databases in the cloud. It supports several widely used database engines, such as MySQL, PostgreSQL, MariaDB, Oracle, and SQL Server.

- **Database Engines**: With RDS, users can deploy databases on a wide variety of platforms without needing to manually handle administrative tasks such as patching, backups, and scaling. Users can choose the engine that best fits their needs based on existing familiarity or specific feature requirements.
- **High Availability**: RDS offers Multi-AZ (Availability Zone) deployments for high availability and failover support. This ensures that in case of a failure in one data center, the database continues to function without downtime.
- **Automated Backups**: RDS provides automated backups and snapshot capabilities, ensuring that data is always backed up and recoverable.
- **Scalability**: RDS allows users to scale their databases vertically by choosing larger instance types, or horizontally by adding read replicas to distribute read traffic and improve performance.
- **Performance Optimization**: With integrated performance monitoring through Amazon CloudWatch, users can fine-tune database performance to meet the demands of their application.

This service is ideal for use cases that require a traditional relational database but want to offload much of the maintenance to AWS's managed service.

10.2.4 AWS Lambda

AWS Lambda is a serverless computing service that enables users to run code in response to events without the need to manage servers or infrastructure. Lambda automatically provisions the compute resources required to run the code and scales the execution environment depending on the number of requests.

- **Event-Driven Execution**: Lambda functions are triggered by specific events, such as HTTP requests through API Gateway, changes in data in S3, or messages from an SNS topic. This makes it ideal for creating event-driven applications.
- **Automatic Scaling**: Lambda automatically scales to handle any volume of incoming requests, from a few executions per day to thousands per second. This makes it a great option for fluctuating workloads.
- **Cost Efficiency**: Lambda follows a pay-per-use pricing model, where users only pay for the time their code runs, making it an extremely cost-efficient option for many applications.

- **Language Support**: Lambda supports a variety of programming languages, including Node.js, Python, Java, C#, Go, and Ruby, providing developers flexibility in their development process.

Lambda is used for tasks such as building APIs, automating workflows, real-time file processing, and integrating with other AWS services in a seamless, serverless manner.

10.2.5 AWS Elastic Beanstalk

AWS Elastic Beanstalk is a fully managed service that makes it easy to deploy and scale web applications and services. Users can simply upload their code, and Elastic Beanstalk handles the deployment, capacity provisioning, load balancing, and scaling automatically.

- **Supported Platforms**: Elastic Beanstalk supports a variety of programming languages and frameworks, including Node.js, Ruby, Python, PHP, Java, and .NET. It also supports Docker containers and custom application environments.
- **Managed Deployment**: With Elastic Beanstalk, users do not need to worry about managing the underlying infrastructure. It handles the entire deployment lifecycle, including provisioning instances, balancing load, and scaling to meet demand.
- **Environment Customization**: While Beanstalk provides managed services, users can still customize the environment and configuration, allowing them to tailor the deployment to their application's specific needs.

Elastic Beanstalk simplifies the process of deploying web applications, making it a good choice for developers who want to focus on building their applications rather than managing infrastructure.

10.2.6 AWS CloudFormation

AWS CloudFormation is an Infrastructure as Code (IaC) service that allows users to model and provision AWS resources using templates written in JSON or YAML. CloudFormation helps users automate the deployment of complex infrastructure setups.

- **Infrastructure as Code**: CloudFormation allows users to define their entire AWS infrastructure in code, making it reproducible and consistent. This eliminates manual configuration errors and ensures that the infrastructure can be easily replicated or modified.
- **Stacks and Templates**: CloudFormation uses templates to define infrastructure in a declarative way. These templates can be shared and reused across multiple accounts or environments.
- **Change Sets**: Before applying changes to your infrastructure, CloudFormation generates change sets that preview the updates, ensuring that you can review the impact before making changes live.

CloudFormation is an essential tool for automating the creation and management of AWS resources, particularly for large-scale or complex deployments.

10.2.7 Additional AWS Services

While EC2, S3, RDS, Lambda, Elastic Beanstalk, and CloudFormation are among the most commonly used services, AWS offers a wide range of additional services that are critical for various use cases:

- **API Gateway**: A fully managed service that allows developers to create and manage APIs at any scale, ensuring high availability and security.
- **CloudWatch**: Provides monitoring and observability across AWS services, helping users to keep track of their applications' health and performance.
- **DynamoDB**: A fully managed NoSQL database service designed for low-latency and high-throughput applications, ideal for use cases such as mobile apps, IoT devices, and gaming.

AWS's diverse suite of services enables developers and businesses to design and operate applications of any scale, making it a powerful and flexible platform for cloud computing. A tabular analysis summarizing the key features and characteristics of the AWS services is presented in Table 10.1

10.3 MICROSOFT AZURE

Microsoft Azure is a robust and comprehensive cloud computing platform that provides a vast array of services aimed at businesses and individuals. Known for its seamless integration with Microsoft's software suite and strong enterprise support, Azure has become one of the leading cloud platforms globally. It offers a broad range of cloud services, including computing, analytics, storage, and networking, which allow users to build, deploy, and manage applications through Microsoft's global data centers. Figure 10.2 highlights the detailed expansion of key services available on Azure for cloud computing.

10.3.1 Azure Virtual Machines (VMs)

Azure Virtual Machines (VMs) [2] are scalable, on-demand compute resources that allow users to run virtualized instances of operating systems in the cloud. These virtual machines can be customized to suit a wide range of applications, from simple websites to complex enterprise systems.

- **Customizable Sizes and Operating Systems**: Azure offers a variety of VM sizes and configurations, allowing users to select the optimal instance type based on their workload requirements. Whether it's a lightweight VM for development purposes or a compute-intensive machine for high-performance computing, Azure provides ample options. Users can choose

TABLE 10.1
Key Features and Characteristics of the AWS Services

Service	Key Features	Use Cases	Scalability	Security	Cost Model
Amazon S3	• Object storage for a wide range of data types (images, videos, backups, etc.) • Multiple storage classes (Standard, Intelligent-Tiering, Glacier, etc.) • Lifecycle management • Encryption at rest and in transit	• Data backup and recovery • Static website hosting • Machine learning data storage • Archival storage	• Automatically scales to meet storage demand (from GBs to PBs) • Can handle varying storage needs	• Encryption options (both at rest and in transit) • IAM for fine-grained access control	• Pay-as-you-go based on storage usage • Cost-effective for varying access patterns (e.g., frequent or infrequent access)
Amazon RDS	• Fully managed relational database service • Supports multiple DB engines (MySQL, PostgreSQL, MariaDB, Oracle, SQL Server) • Automated backups • Multi-AZ deployments for high availability	• Traditional relational database applications • Data warehousing • CRM and ERP systems	• Vertical scaling with larger instance types • Horizontal scaling with read replicas for read-heavy workloads	• Encryption at rest and in transit • Automated backups and point-in-time recovery • IAM for access control	• Pay-per-use based on instance size and storage • Costs for backup storage and data transfer
AWS Lambda	• Serverless compute service • Event-driven execution (e.g., HTTP requests, data changes in S3) • Automatic scaling • Pay-per-use pricing	• Event-driven applications • APIs and microservices • Real-time data processing (e.g., file uploads)	• Automatically scales to handle variable workloads • No server management required	• Data encryption in transit and at rest • Fine-grained access control with IAM • VPC integration for enhanced security	• Pay-per-use based on execution time and resources consumed during the execution (no cost for idle time)
AWS Elastic Beanstalk	• Fully managed platform for deploying and scaling web applications • Supports multiple languages (Node.js, Java, .NET, etc.) • Integrated with AWS services like RDS and S3 • Environment management	• Web application deployment • API backends • Microservices architecture	• Automatically scales based on demand Load balancing and instance management handled automatically	• IAM roles for access control • Security groups and encryption support • Can deploy in a VPC for network isolation	• Pay-as-you-go for the underlying resources used (EC2, RDS, etc.) • No additional charge for Beanstalk itself

AWS CloudFormation	• Infrastructure as Code (IaC) • Automates resource provisioning and management • Uses JSON or YAML templates • Change sets to preview updates	• Infrastructure automation • Large-scale cloud deployments • Version-controlled infrastructure templates	• Easily replicable and scalable infrastructure setups • Supports multi-region and multi-account configurations	• IAM for resource-level access control • Can be used with CloudTrail for auditing changes	• No additional cost for CloudFormation itself • Costs for underlying resources (e.g., EC2, S3) apply
API Gateway	• Fully managed API creation and management • Handles API traffic routing, authorization, and monitoring • Scales automatically with demand	• Building and managing RESTful APIs • Mobile and web application backends	• Automatically scales to accommodate high API traffic	• Built-in authorization (e.g., Cognito, IAM) • Encryption at rest and in transit • Request validation	• Pay-per-request pricing • Charges for data transfer and optional features (e.g., caching)
CloudWatch	• Monitoring and observability service • Provides logs, metrics, and alarms • Integrated with most AWS services • Can trigger actions based on metrics	• Real-time monitoring of application health • Proactive alerting for resource utilization and performance	• Scales with your AWS infrastructure • Monitors resources across regions and accounts	• IAM for access control • Integration with CloudTrail for audit logging • Data encryption	• Pay-as-you-go for metrics, logs, and alarms • Optional charges for custom metrics or longer data retention
DynamoDB	• Managed NoSQL database service • Supports key-value and document data models • Automatically scales to handle high throughput and low latency	• High-throughput, low-latency applications (e.g., gaming, IoT) • Real-time analytics • Mobile and web apps	• Automatically scales to meet workload demands • Handles large-scale, high-velocity data	• Built-in encryption at rest • IAM for fine-grained access control • Global tables for multi-region replication	• Pay-per-use based on throughput and storage • Option for on-demand or provisioned c

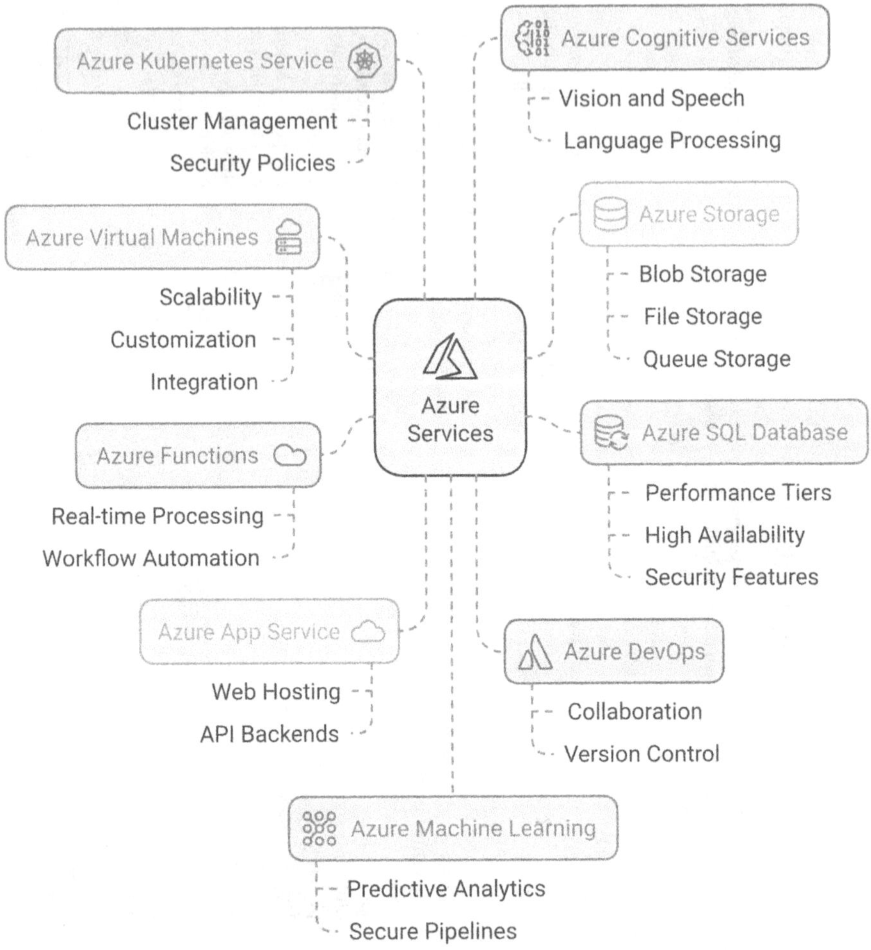

FIGURE 10.2 Detailed view of Azure cloud services.

from Windows or Linux operating systems and even deploy custom images based on their needs.

- **Scaling**: Azure VMs can be scaled up or down based on the workload, making it easy to handle varying demand. With features such as **Azure Scale Sets**, users can create and manage a group of load-balanced VMs that automatically scale based on demand, ensuring high availability and performance.
- **Automation**: Azure provides automation capabilities to manage the lifecycle of virtual machines, including automatic provisioning, deallocation, and scaling. This reduces manual intervention and helps ensure that resources are efficiently utilized.
- **Integration with Azure Services**: Azure VMs integrate seamlessly with other Azure services, such as Azure Storage, Azure Networking, and Azure Load Balancer, which ensures a complete and scalable infrastructure solution.

Azure Virtual Machines are ideal for a wide range of use cases, including hosting applications, running batch jobs, and providing high-performance computing resources.

10.3.2 Azure Storage

Azure offers several storage solutions designed to handle various types of data, from structured to unstructured, and across different storage tiers. The key storage options in Azure include Blob Storage, File Storage, and Queue Storage.

- **Blob Storage**: **Azure Blob Storage** is an object storage solution optimized for storing large amounts of unstructured data, such as text, images, videos, and backups. With its high availability, security, and scalability, Blob Storage is ideal for cloud-based applications that require easy access to large datasets.
  - **Hot, Cool, and Archive Tiers**: Blob Storage offers different access tiers (Hot, Cool, and Archive) to manage costs based on data access patterns. The Hot tier is for frequently accessed data, while the Cool tier is for infrequently accessed data, and the Archive tier is designed for long-term storage at the lowest cost.
  - **Security**: Blob Storage ensures high levels of data security with features such as encryption at rest and in transit, as well as fine-grained access controls through **Azure Active Directory (AAD)** and **Shared Access Signatures (SAS)**.
- **File Storage**: **Azure File Storage** provides managed file shares in the cloud, accessible via SMB (Server Message Block) protocol. This makes it simple to store and share files between different VMs in the Azure environment, enabling organizations to move legacy applications to the cloud without re-engineering their file systems.
  - **SMB Access**: Azure File Storage supports SMB 3.0, allowing applications running on on-premises servers or in Azure to access shared files.
  - **Backup and Recovery**: Azure File Storage integrates with **Azure Backup** and **Azure Site Recovery**, providing data redundancy and disaster recovery options.
- **Queue Storage**: **Azure Queue Storage** enables reliable, asynchronous messaging between components of an application. It allows different parts of a system to communicate with each other by placing messages in queues, ensuring that they are processed independently and at scale.
  - **Scalability and Reliability**: Queue Storage can handle millions of messages per day and provides durability and reliability even in the event of system failures.

These storage solutions are essential for building scalable, distributed applications that need to handle large volumes of data or ensure seamless communication across services.

10.3.3 Azure SQL Database

Azure SQL Database is a fully managed relational database-as-a-service (DBaaS) offering that allows users to deploy, scale, and manage SQL-based databases in the cloud. It is built on Microsoft SQL Server technology, ensuring compatibility with applications that rely on SQL-based data storage.

- **Fully Managed**: With Azure SQL Database, users can offload database management tasks, such as patching, backups, and failover to Microsoft, freeing up resources for development. This fully managed service reduces operational overhead and ensures a high level of performance and reliability.
- **Scalability**: Azure SQL Database provides options to scale both vertically and horizontally. Users can choose from various performance tiers, including General Purpose, Business Critical, and Hyperscale, depending on their workload and budget requirements.
- **Built-in High Availability**: Azure SQL Database includes built-in high availability and disaster recovery features, including Geo-Replication and Automatic Failover, ensuring that data is always accessible, even in the event of regional outages.
- **Advanced Security**: Features such as Transparent Data Encryption (TDE), Advanced Threat Protection, and SQL Injection Detection enhance security by protecting data both at rest and in transit.

Azure SQL Database is well-suited for running mission-critical applications, online transaction processing (OLTP), business intelligence, and analytics workloads.

10.3.4 Azure Functions

Azure Functions is a serverless compute service that allows users to run event-driven code without worrying about the underlying infrastructure. With Azure Functions, users can focus on writing code to respond to events, and Azure automatically handles scaling, execution, and resource management.

- **Event-Driven**: Azure Functions can be triggered by a variety of events, such as HTTP requests, changes in storage, or messages in a queue. This allows developers to build event-driven applications with minimal effort.
- **Automatic Scaling**: Azure Functions automatically scales to handle varying loads. Whether you have a few requests per day or thousands per second, Azure Functions will scale the required compute resources to meet the demand, only charging for the actual execution time.
- **Multiple Programming Languages**: Azure Functions supports several programming languages, including C#, Java, JavaScript, Python, and PowerShell, providing developers with the flexibility to choose their preferred language.
- **Integrations**: Azure Functions integrates with a wide variety of other Azure services, such as Azure Event Grid, Azure Logic Apps, and Azure Service Bus, making it easy to build complex, automated workflows and microservices architectures.

Azure Functions is ideal for use cases such as automating workflows, real-time data processing, and integrating various systems within the Azure ecosystem.

10.3.5 Azure App Service

Azure App Service is a fully managed platform for building, deploying, and scaling web apps, APIs, and mobile backends. It abstracts away the underlying infrastructure, enabling developers to focus on coding and deploying their applications without worrying about managing servers.

- **Multiple Frameworks**: Azure App Service supports a variety of web application frameworks, including Node.js, .NET, PHP, Python, Ruby, and Java, allowing developers to deploy applications in their preferred environment.
- **Built-in Scaling**: App Service offers automatic scaling capabilities, ensuring that applications can handle varying levels of traffic. Users can configure auto-scaling rules based on CPU usage, memory usage, or request count.
- **DevOps Integration**: Azure App Service integrates with Azure DevOps, GitHub, and Bitbucket for continuous integration and continuous deployment (CI/CD) pipelines, simplifying the process of deploying and updating applications.
- **Security and Monitoring**: App Service offers built-in security features such as Azure Active Directory (AAD) authentication, SSL/TLS support, and Web Application Firewall (WAF). It also integrates with Azure Monitor and Azure Application Insights to provide deep insights into application performance.

Azure App Service is perfect for businesses that need to deploy web applications quickly and manage them at scale, without having to manually handle infrastructure.

10.3.6 Azure DevOps

Azure DevOps is a suite of tools that provides a complete DevOps solution for planning, developing, testing, and deploying applications. It includes tools for managing the entire lifecycle of an application, from source code management to deployment.

- **Azure Boards**: Azure Boards provides agile project management tools, including Kanban boards, Scrum boards, and work item tracking, allowing teams to manage and track progress on tasks and features.
- **Azure Repos**: Azure Repos offers Git repositories for source code management, with features such as pull requests, branching, and version control, ensuring smooth collaboration among development teams.
- **Azure Pipelines**: Azure Pipelines automates the building, testing, and deployment of applications, integrating seamlessly with other Azure services. It supports both continuous integration (CI) and continuous deployment (CD) workflows.
- **Azure Artifacts**: Azure Artifacts is a package management service that allows teams to store and share code packages (such as NuGet, npm, and Maven) securely and efficiently.

Azure DevOps is designed to streamline development processes and improve collaboration among teams, ensuring faster and more reliable software delivery.

10.3.7 Additional Azure Services

While Azure Virtual Machines, SQL Database, Functions, App Service, and DevOps are some of the core offerings, Microsoft Azure also provides a wide range of additional services:

- **Azure Kubernetes Service (AKS)**: A fully managed Kubernetes container orchestration service that simplifies the deployment and management of containerized applications.
- **Azure Cognitive Services**: A collection of pre-built APIs for adding artificial intelligence (AI) capabilities to applications, such as computer vision, language processing, and speech recognition.
- **Azure Machine Learning**: A cloud-based service for building, training, and deploying machine learning models.

Azure's diverse suite of services enables businesses and developers to build and scale applications in a flexible, cost-effective, and secure manner, making it a top choice for enterprise cloud computing. A detailed tabular analysis summarizing the key features and characteristics of the key services offered by Microsoft Azure is presented in Table 10.2.

10.4 GOOGLE CLOUD PLATFORM (GCP)

Google Cloud Platform (GCP) [3] is a comprehensive cloud computing suite of services that offers powerful tools for businesses and individuals to build, deploy, and scale applications. Known for its high-performance infrastructure and advanced machine learning capabilities, GCP is a favorite among developers, data scientists, and enterprises looking to harness Google's global reach and innovation. Figure 10.3 offers an expanded look at some of the key services provided by GCP for cloud computing.

10.4.1 Google Compute Engine

Google Compute Engine (GCE) is a flexible and scalable Infrastructure-as-a-Service (IaaS) platform that allows users to create and manage virtual machines (VMs) in Google's cloud. This service provides powerful and customizable compute instances to run a wide range of workloads, from web applications to large-scale batch processing tasks.

- **Customizable Virtual Machines**: Compute Engine provides a variety of VM sizes and types, including Preemptible VMs for cost savings and GPU-enabled VMs for high-performance applications such as machine learning.

TABLE 10.2
Key Features and Characteristics of the Microsoft Azure Services

Service	Key Features	Use Cases	Scalability	Security	Cost Model
Azure Virtual Machines (VMs)	• Scalable, on-demand compute resources • Customizable VM sizes and configurations (Windows, Linux, or custom images) • Integration with Azure services like Storage and Networking • Automation for provisioning and scaling	• Hosting applications • High-performance computing (HPC) • Batch processing jobs • Development and testing environments	• VM scaling via Azure Scale Sets • Horizontal and vertical scaling based on demand and workload requirements	• Encryption at rest and in transit • Integration with Azure Active Directory (AAD) for access control • Secure network configurations	• Pay-as-you-go pricing based on VM size and usage • Charges for storage, networking, and additional features (e.g., public IP addresses)
Azure Storage	• Blob Storage (object storage for large data) • File Storage (managed SMB file shares) • Queue Storage (asynchronous messaging) • Hot, Cool, and Archive tiers for cost optimization	• Data storage for cloud apps • Backup and disaster recovery • Communication between microservices • File sharing for applications	• Scalability based on data size and access frequency • Handles millions of messages and large unstructured data	• Data encryption at rest and in transit • Fine-grained access control (e.g., SAS, Azure AD) • Backup and disaster recovery integration	• Pay-per-use based on storage tier, data access, and transaction counts • Lower costs for Archive and Cool tiers
Azure SQL Database	• Fully managed relational database-as-a-service (DBaaS) • Built on Microsoft SQL Server technology • Performance tiers (General Purpose, Business Critical, Hyperscale) • Automated backups and failover	• Mission-critical applications • Online transaction processing (OLTP) • Data analytics and business intelligence	• Horizontal and vertical scaling with elastic pools and Geo-Replication • High availability with automatic failover	• Transparent Data Encryption (TDE) • Advanced Threat Protection • Automatic patching and backups • Managed firewall	• Pay-as-you-go based on performance tiers and storage usage • Charges for backup storage and additional features

(Continued)

TABLE 10.2 (Continued)

Service	Key Features	Use Cases	Scalability	Security	Cost Model
Azure Functions	• Serverless compute for event-driven applications • Supports multiple languages (C#, Java, JavaScript, Python, PowerShell) • Event triggers (HTTP, storage changes, message queues) • Integrates with other Azure services	• Real-time data processing • Workflow automation • Microservices and APIs • Event-driven backends	• Automatically scales with demand • Pay-per-use model based on execution time and resources consumed	• Built-in authentication and authorization • Integration with Azure AD • Data encryption at rest and in transit	• Pay-per-use based on execution time (in 100ms increments) • No charge for idle time, only active execution
Azure App Service	• Fully managed platform for web apps, APIs, and mobile backends • Supports various frameworks (Node.js, .NET, PHP, Python, Ruby, Java) • Automatic scaling and load balancing • Continuous integration/deployment (CI/CD)	• Web and mobile app hosting • API backends • Enterprise applications • Microservices architecture	• Auto-scaling based on traffic or custom rules • Load balancing across multiple instances	• Built-in SSL/TLS support • Integration with Azure Active Directory (AAD) • Web Application Firewall (WAF)	• Pay-as-you-go for resource usage (compute, storage, and data transfer) • Pricing based on tier and instance size
Azure DevOps	• Full DevOps toolset (Boards, Repos, Pipelines, Artifacts) • Continuous integration and deployment (CI/CD) • Git repositories and Agile tools • Collaboration and version control	• DevOps workflows • Continuous delivery pipelines • Collaboration and project management • Automated testing	• Scalable with customizable pipelines and repositories • Integrates with other Azure services for CI/CD	• Role-based access control (RBAC) • Integration with Azure Active Directory • Secure artifact management	• Pay-as-you-go for build and release pipeline usage • Free tier with additional costs for larger teams or advanced features

Azure Kubernetes Service (AKS)	• Fully managed Kubernetes service for containerized applications • Integrated with Azure Active Directory • Automatic scaling and updates • Easy cluster management	• Containerized application management • Microservices architecture • CI/CD for containerized apps	• Automatically scales with workload • Handles large numbers of containerized applications and microservices	• Managed identity integration for access control • Network security policies • Encryption for sensitive data	• Pay-as-you-go for compute and storage usage • No charge for the Kubernetes master nodes, charges apply to worker nodes and storage
Azure Cognitive Services	• Pre-built APIs for AI capabilities (Computer Vision, Speech, Language, etc.) • Customizable AI models • Integrates with other Azure services for end-to-end AI solutions	• Image and speech recognition • Natural language processing • Chatbots and virtual assistants • Predictive analytics	• Scales as needed based on API usage • Flexible pricing based on service consumption	• Built-in security (OAuth, API keys) • Encryption for data at rest and in transit • Access control via Azure AD	• Pay-per-use based on API calls and processing time • Pricing varies based on specific cognitive service used
Azure Machine Learning	• Cloud-based service for building, training, and deploying machine learning models • Automated ML capabilities • Integrates with Azure Databricks and other services	• Predictive analytics • AI model training and deployment • Business intelligence and data insights	• Scalable compute resources for model training and inference • Auto-scaling based on workload	• Secure model and data storage • Role-based access control (RBAC) • Secure data pipelines	• Pay-as-you-go based on compute usage, storage, and model deployment time • Free tier available with limited resources

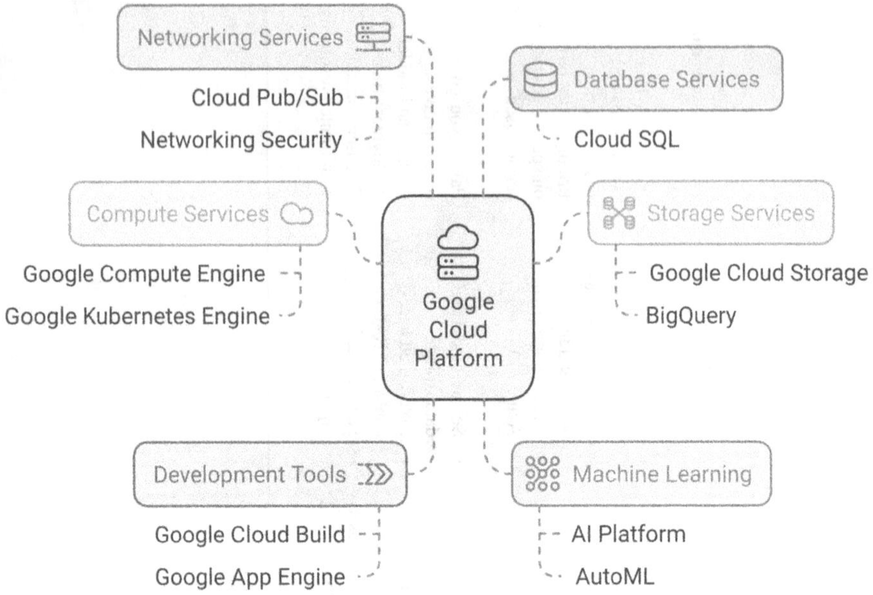

FIGURE 10.3 Detailed view of GCP cloud services.

Users can select from a wide range of operating systems, including Linux, Windows, and custom images.

- **Auto-scaling**: Compute Engine supports automatic scaling, where the number of VM instances increases or decreases in response to changes in traffic or workload. This ensures high availability and optimal resource utilization without manual intervention.
- **Global Network**: Leveraging Google's global private network infrastructure, Compute Engine offers low-latency and high-performance access to cloud resources, making it ideal for running geographically distributed applications.
- **Integration with Google Services**: Google Compute Engine integrates seamlessly with other Google Cloud services, such as Google Cloud Storage, Google Cloud Networking, and Google Cloud Monitoring, to provide a comprehensive and efficient cloud infrastructure.

Google Compute Engine is perfect for hosting applications, processing large datasets, and running enterprise workloads that require custom configurations and scaling capabilities.

10.4.2 Google Cloud Storage

Google Cloud Storage is a suite of storage options designed to store and manage large amounts of data with high durability, availability, and scalability. It provides various storage classes to meet the needs of different types of data and access patterns.

- **Object Storage**: Google Cloud Storage offers scalable object storage for storing unstructured data, such as images, videos, backups, and archives. The service is designed for high throughput and low latency, ensuring fast data access.
  - **Storage Classes**: Cloud Storage provides multiple storage classes to optimize cost and performance based on how frequently data is accessed:
    - **Standard**: For frequently accessed data.
    - **Nearline**: For data that is accessed less than once a month.
    - **Coldline**: Ideal for long-term storage with infrequent access.
    - **Archive**: For long-term archival storage with very low access frequency, offering the lowest cost.
- **Security and Durability**: Google Cloud Storage ensures the security of data through encryption at rest and in transit, as well as access control policies using Identity and Access Management (IAM) roles. Additionally, the service offers high availability and durability with multi-region replication, ensuring that data is always accessible and protected.
- **Data Transfer**: Google Cloud Storage supports a variety of data transfer methods, including Cloud Storage Transfer Service and Storage Transfer Appliance, allowing businesses to efficiently move large volumes of data from on-premises systems to the cloud.

Cloud Storage is ideal for applications that require scalable, durable, and secure storage for various types of unstructured data, including media, logs, and backups.

10.4.3 Cloud SQL

Google Cloud SQL is a fully managed relational database service that allows users to set up, maintain, and scale SQL-based databases in the cloud. Cloud SQL supports popular relational database management systems (RDBMS) such as MySQL, PostgreSQL, and SQL Server.

- **Fully Managed**: Cloud SQL eliminates the need for database administration tasks such as patching, backups, and failover management, making it easier for users to focus on application development. Google handles maintenance, updates, and replication, ensuring high availability and disaster recovery.
- **Scalability**: Cloud SQL allows users to easily scale database instances vertically (increasing compute resources) or horizontally (sharding databases across multiple instances) based on demand. Users can also configure automatic scaling for read replicas to distribute traffic.
- **Integrated with GCP**: Cloud SQL integrates with other GCP services such as Google Cloud Functions, Google Kubernetes Engine (GKE), and Google App Engine, ensuring that applications can use SQL databases as part of their cloud infrastructure seamlessly.
- **Security**: Cloud SQL ensures secure database operations with built-in encryption, both at rest and in transit. Users can also configure IAM roles to restrict access to databases and enable auditing.

Cloud SQL is perfect for developers who need a managed relational database service with minimal maintenance overhead and scalability for applications and analytics.

10.4.4 Google Cloud Functions

Google Cloud Functions is a serverless compute platform that allows users to run code in response to events without the need to manage servers or infrastructure. It simplifies the development of event-driven applications by automatically scaling based on the volume of events.

- **Event-Driven Architecture**: Cloud Functions can be triggered by a variety of events, including changes in **Cloud Storage**, HTTP requests, messages from Cloud Pub/Sub, and database changes. This makes it ideal for building microservices and automating workflows.
- **Scalability**: Cloud Functions automatically scale based on incoming event volume, ensuring that the system can handle both small and large workloads without requiring manual intervention or configuration.
- **Simplified Development**: Developers can write their functions in multiple programming languages, including Node.js, Python, Go, and Java, and deploy them directly from the console or command line.
- **Cost Efficiency**: Cloud Functions only charge for the actual execution time, with no fixed costs or idle charges, making it a cost-effective solution for handling sporadic or burst workloads.

Cloud Functions is ideal for creating lightweight, event-driven applications that need to scale automatically and respond to various triggers without complex infrastructure setup.

10.4.5 Google App Engine

Google App Engine (GAE) is a fully managed platform-as-a-service (PaaS) that allows developers to build, deploy, and scale web applications without worrying about infrastructure management. App Engine supports multiple programming languages and frameworks, including Python, Java, Go, and Node.js.

- **Managed Environment**: With App Engine, developers can focus on writing code while Google automatically handles tasks such as load balancing, scaling, and provisioning infrastructure. This makes it ideal for developers who want to avoid managing servers and infrastructure.
- **Automatic Scaling**: App Engine automatically scales applications based on traffic, ensuring that web apps can handle varying loads without manual configuration. It supports both standard and flexible environments, providing flexibility in terms of custom configurations and programming language choices.
- **Integration with Google Services**: App Engine integrates with a wide range of other Google Cloud services, including Cloud SQL, Cloud Firestore,

Cloud Pub/Sub, and Cloud Monitoring, enabling seamless development and operation of cloud-native applications.

- **Security and Compliance**: App Engine provides built-in security features such as IAM access control, SSL/TLS encryption, and the ability to authenticate users via Google Sign-In.

Google App Engine is suitable for developers who want to build and deploy scalable web applications without dealing with the complexities of managing infrastructure.

10.4.6 Google Cloud Build

Google Cloud Build is a fully managed service that automates the process of building, testing, and deploying applications. It is designed for continuous integration (CI) and continuous delivery (CD) workflows, supporting a variety of deployment environments such as Kubernetes, App Engine, and Cloud Run.

- **Automated Pipelines**: Cloud Build allows users to define automated pipelines for building, testing, and deploying applications, making it easier to release software in an agile and controlled manner. Cloud Build supports integration with GitHub, GitLab, and Bitbucket for version control.
- **Containerization Support**: Cloud Build integrates with Google Kubernetes Engine (GKE), allowing users to build and deploy containerized applications directly to Kubernetes clusters. It supports building **Docker images** and deploying them seamlessly to various environments.
- **Fast and Scalable**: Cloud Build can handle large-scale builds and parallel executions, ensuring that even complex applications can be built and tested quickly. It scales automatically to meet demand, allowing users to focus on development rather than managing build infrastructure.
- **Security**: Cloud Build ensures secure operations with features such as integration with Cloud IAM, allowing developers to control access to resources, and secret management to protect sensitive information such as API keys and credentials.

Google Cloud Build is ideal for teams looking to automate their DevOps workflows, ensure continuous integration, and accelerate software delivery.

10.4.7 Additional GCP Services

While Google Compute Engine, Cloud Storage, Cloud SQL, Cloud Functions, App Engine, and Cloud Build are some of the core offerings, GCP also provides a rich set of other services:

- **Google Kubernetes Engine (GKE)**: A fully managed Kubernetes service that simplifies container orchestration, allowing users to deploy and manage containerized applications.

- **BigQuery**: A fully managed data warehouse solution that enables real-time analytics on large datasets using SQL-like queries. BigQuery is highly scalable and optimized for big data workloads.
- **Google AI and Machine Learning**: GCP offers various AI and machine learning tools, including the AI Platform, AutoML, and TensorFlow, providing developers with the tools to build, train, and deploy advanced machine learning models.

GCP's extensive suite of services provides everything needed for building and deploying applications in the cloud, from compute and storage to advanced analytics and machine learning, making it a versatile choice for cloud computing. A detailed tabular analysis summarizing the key features and characteristics of the core services offered by GCP is offered in Table 10.3.

10.5 DIGITALOCEAN

DigitalOcean [4] is a cloud computing platform known for its simplicity, affordability, and ease of use. It targets developers, startups, and small- to medium-sized businesses by providing essential cloud infrastructure services without overwhelming complexity. DigitalOcean's platform enables users to quickly deploy, manage, and scale applications with minimal overhead. A detailed illustration of some of DigitalOcean's key services for cloud computing is given in Figure. 10.4.

10.5.1 Droplets (Virtual Machines)

Droplets are the cornerstone of DigitalOcean's compute offering. These are virtual machines (VMs) that allow users to deploy cloud-based servers with ease.

- **Scalability and Flexibility**: Droplets come in a variety of configurations, allowing you to choose the appropriate combination of CPU, RAM, and storage based on your workload's requirements. You can scale up or down as necessary, enabling you to match your infrastructure to current needs while optimizing costs.
- **Simple Deployment**: With DigitalOcean's intuitive interface, you can launch a Droplet in just a few clicks. The platform provides one-click application installation, enabling you to quickly deploy popular software stacks such as LAMP (Linux, Apache, MySQL, PHP), WordPress, Docker, and more.
- **Custom Images**: You can also create custom images for your Droplets, making it easy to replicate server environments for consistency across multiple instances. This is ideal for use cases that require identical server setups, such as web application clusters.
- **Global Data Centers**: DigitalOcean offers data centers in various geographical locations, providing users the flexibility to deploy applications closer to their target audience, improving performance and reducing latency.
- **Managed Scaling**: Droplets support features such as auto-scaling, which dynamically adjusts the number of VMs based on traffic demands, making it easier to handle fluctuating workloads without manual intervention.

TABLE 10.3
Key Features and Characteristics of the GCP Services

Service	Key Features	Use Cases	Scalability	Security	Cost Model
Google Compute Engine (GCE)	• Customizable VM instances (Linux, Windows, Custom OS images) • Preemptible VMs for cost savings • GPU-enabled VMs for high-performance tasks • Auto-scaling based on workload • Global network with low-latency access	• Hosting web apps • High-performance computing (HPC) • Data processing and analytics • Batch jobs and workloads	• Automatic scaling of VMs • Horizontal and vertical scaling based on demand • Global distribution of workloads	• Encryption at rest and in transit • Integration with Identity and Access Management (IAM) for access control	• Pay-as-you-go pricing based on VM type, usage, and storage • Discounts for sustained usage and preemptible VMs
Google Cloud Storage	• Scalable object storage for unstructured data (images, videos, backups) • Multiple storage classes (Standard, Nearline, Coldline, Archive) • Multi-region replication for high durability • Fast data access and transfer	• Storing media files and backups • Archival data storage • Disaster recovery solutions • Log management	• Scales with data size and access frequency • Supports high-throughput, low-latency access	• Data encryption at rest and in transit • IAM roles for access control • Fine-grained security and audit logging	• Pay-as-you-go based on storage class, volume, and data transfer • Lower costs for Coldline and Archive tiers
Cloud SQL	• Fully managed relational database service • Supports MySQL, PostgreSQL, and SQL Server • Automatic backups and failover • Integration with other GCP services	• Web and enterprise applications • Data analytics and reporting • OLTP applications and business systems	• Horizontal and vertical scaling of database instances • Auto-scaling read replicas for increased traffic	• Encryption at rest and in transit • IAM-based access control • Automated security patches and auditing	• Pay-as-you-go based on database instance size, storage, and backups • Optional charges for additional features

(*Continued*)

TABLE 10.3
(Continued)

Service	Key Features	Use Cases	Scalability	Security	Cost Model
Google Cloud Functions	• Serverless compute for event-driven code execution • Supports multiple languages (Node.js, Python, Go, Java) • Automatic scaling based on events • Event triggers from Cloud Storage, HTTP, Pub/Sub, etc.	• Event-driven microservices • Real-time data processing • Workflow automation • API backends and webhooks	• Automatically scales based on event volume • No need for manual resource management or configuration	• Built-in authentication with IAM and Google Sign-In • Encryption for data at rest and in transit	• Pay-as-you-go based on execution time and resources used • No cost for idle time, only active execution time
Google App Engine (GAE)	• Fully managed PaaS for building web applications • Supports multiple languages (Python, Java, Go, Node.js) • Automatic scaling based on traffic • No infrastructure management	• Building and deploying web apps and APIs • Scalable mobile backends • Cloud-native application deployment	• Automatic scaling based on traffic • Scalable from small to enterprise-level applications	• SSL/TLS encryption for secure traffic • Integration with IAM for access control • User authentication via Google Sign-In	• Pay-as-you-go pricing for resources (compute, storage) • Discounts for sustained traffic and flexible environments
Google Cloud Build	• Fully managed CI/CD service • Automates building, testing, and deploying code • Integrates with GitHub, GitLab, and Bitbucket • Containerization support with Kubernetes and Docker	• Continuous Integration and Continuous Delivery (CI/CD) • Automated testing and deployment • Building containerized applications	• Automatically scales to handle large builds and parallel executions • Optimized for large and complex codebases	• Secure build environment with IAM integration • Secret management for API keys, passwords, etc. • Access control for repositories	• Pay-as-you-go based on usage for build time and resources • Free tier with additional charges for higher usage

Google Kubernetes Engine (GKE)	• Fully managed Kubernetes service • Simplifies container orchestration and management • Automatic scaling and self-healing clusters • Integrated with GCP services like Cloud Storage, IAM	• Containerized application deployment • Microservices management • Scalable web applications and APIs	• Auto-scaling of clusters and containers based on resource demands • Supports large-scale applications	• Role-based access control (RBAC) • Integration with IAM for access management • Network security policies	• Pay-as-you-go based on node usage (compute and storage) • Charges for Kubernetes clusters and networking resources
BigQuery	• Fully managed, serverless data warehouse • Real-time analytics on large datasets • SQL-like query interface • Scalable for petabyte-scale data	• Big data analytics • Business intelligence and reporting • Real-time data insights and data mining	• Scales effortlessly to handle petabytes of data • Parallel processing for high performance	• Data encryption at rest and in transit • IAM integration for access control • Secure data sharing and auditing	• Pay-per-query pricing based on data processed • Storage costs based on data volume • Separate costs for streaming and queries
Google AI and Machine Learning	• AI Platform for building and deploying models • AutoML for customized model training • TensorFlow support for deep learning • Pre-built models for NLP, vision, and speech tasks	• Machine learning model training and deployment • AI-powered applications • Image and speech recognition	• Scalable compute resources for model training • Auto-scaling based on workload and model complexity	• Built-in encryption for sensitive data • Identity management for access control • Secure model deployment	• Pay-as-you-go based on compute and storage usage • Additional costs for model training, deployment, and API calls
Cloud Pub/Sub	• Real-time messaging and event-driven system • Decoupled messaging for microservices • High-throughput, low-latency messaging • Global scalability	• Event-driven applications • Real-time data streaming • Message queues for microservices and decoupled systems	• Auto-scaling based on message volume • Handles high-frequency messages without delays	• Data encryption at rest and in transit • IAM access control for topic and subscription management	• Pay-as-you-go based on message volume and throughput • No charge for idle periods, only active message processing

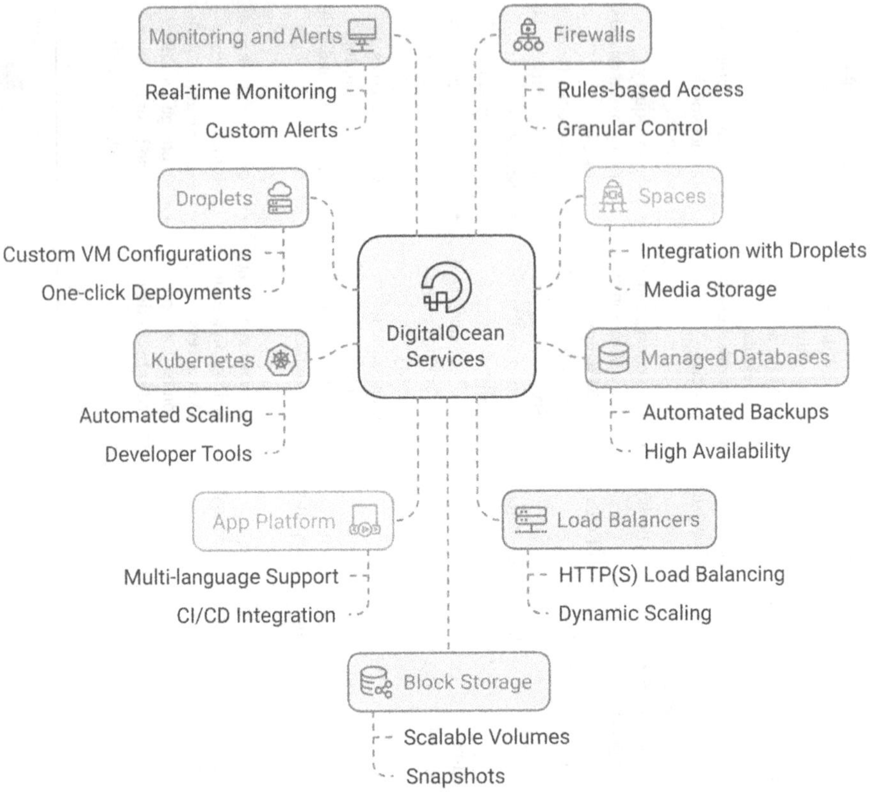

FIGURE 10.4 Detailed overview of DigitalOcean cloud services.

Droplets are perfect for a wide range of applications, from hosting web apps to running microservices or processing large datasets.

10.5.2 Spaces (Object Storage)

Spaces is DigitalOcean's object storage service that provides scalable, secure storage for unstructured data such as images, videos, backups, and other large files.

- **Scalable Storage**: Spaces allows you to store an unlimited amount of data and access it from anywhere in the world. It's optimized for high performance, enabling rapid upload and retrieval of large files.
- **Seamless Integration**: Spaces integrates well with DigitalOcean's Droplets, enabling you to easily store and serve static content such as images and videos for your web applications. You can configure access controls to ensure that only authorized users or applications can access your data.
- **Content Delivery**: Spaces includes built-in support for CDN (Content Delivery Network) integration, allowing you to distribute static content like media files to users across the globe with low latency. This is particularly

useful for websites and applications that need to serve static assets such as images, video streams, or downloadable files.
- **Security**: Spaces ensure that your data is protected with encryption both at rest and in transit. You can also configure Access Control Lists (ACLs) and bucket policies to manage permissions for different users and applications.

Spaces is ideal for applications that require large-scale storage of unstructured data, such as media libraries, backups, or content hosting for web apps.

10.5.3 Managed Databases

Managed Databases is a fully managed database service offered by DigitalOcean, enabling users to set up, manage, and scale databases in the cloud with minimal maintenance and effort.

- **Supported Database Engines**: DigitalOcean provides managed services for popular relational databases such as PostgreSQL, MySQL, and Redis. These managed instances come with automatic backups, performance monitoring, and security patches, reducing the administrative burden on users.
- **High Availability**: Managed Databases offer automated failover mechanisms, ensuring high availability and minimal downtime. In case of failure, traffic is automatically redirected to a standby node, allowing applications to continue running without interruption.
- **Scalability**: You can scale your database instances vertically (by increasing CPU and RAM) or horizontally (by adding read replicas for improved read performance). Managed Databases support automatic scaling to accommodate growing data volumes and traffic demands.
- **Automated Backups and Monitoring**: DigitalOcean's managed database service includes automated backups that allow you to restore your database to any point within the last seven days. The platform also provides real-time monitoring tools that track database performance, helping you identify and resolve issues quickly.
- **Security and Compliance**: Managed Databases are protected with built-in encryption, both at rest and in transit. Additionally, users can configure firewall rules and VPC (Virtual Private Cloud) peering to restrict access to database instances.

Managed Databases are perfect for developers who need to deploy production-ready, highly available databases without the hassle of manual configuration, maintenance, and scaling.

10.5.4 Kubernetes

DigitalOcean Kubernetes (DOKS) is a fully managed Kubernetes service that simplifies the deployment, management, and scaling of containerized applications.

- **Simplified Kubernetes Management**: DigitalOcean provides an easy-to-use interface for creating, scaling, and managing Kubernetes clusters. It handles the complexities of Kubernetes administration, including version updates, patches, and node management.
- **Automated Scaling**: Kubernetes clusters in DigitalOcean automatically scale to meet demand, ensuring that your containerized applications are highly available and can handle fluctuating workloads. You can add or remove worker nodes with just a few clicks.
- **Integration with Other Services**: Kubernetes integrates well with other DigitalOcean services, such as Spaces for object storage, Managed Databases for database services, and Load Balancers for distributing traffic to containerized applications. This makes it easier to deploy complex, microservices-based applications in the cloud.
- **Cost-Effective**: DigitalOcean's Kubernetes service is designed to be cost-efficient, with no additional charges for control plane management. Users only pay for the resources they use, such as compute and storage, making it a budget-friendly option for developers and businesses.
- **Developer-Friendly**: DigitalOcean Kubernetes offers out-of-the-box integration with tools like Helm for package management and Kubernetes Dashboard for monitoring, enabling developers to quickly deploy and manage containerized applications.

Kubernetes is ideal for teams building microservices-based applications or those looking to adopt containerized infrastructure in a simplified and cost-effective manner.

10.5.5 App Platform

DigitalOcean App Platform is a fully managed platform-as-a-service (PaaS) solution that simplifies the deployment, management, and scaling of web applications.

- **One-Click Deployment**: The App Platform allows developers to deploy applications with a few clicks, eliminating the need to configure servers and load balancers manually. You can deploy code directly from GitHub, GitLab, or Bitbucket repositories.
- **Support for Multiple Frameworks**: App Platform supports a wide range of web application frameworks, including Node.js, Python, Ruby, Go, PHP, and Java. It also supports static sites and containerized applications, providing flexibility for different types of applications.
- **Automatic Scaling**: The platform automatically scales your application based on incoming traffic, ensuring optimal performance without requiring manual intervention. It can scale vertically by adjusting compute resources or horizontally by adding more application instances.
- **Integrated CI/CD Pipelines**: App Platform includes built-in continuous integration and continuous deployment (CI/CD) pipelines, enabling you to automatically test and deploy your code changes. This streamlines development and accelerates time-to-market.

- **Managed Infrastructure**: With App Platform, you don't need to manage the underlying infrastructure. DigitalOcean handles provisioning, load balancing, SSL certificates, and scaling, freeing developers to focus on building and improving applications.

App Platform is ideal for developers looking to deploy and manage web applications with minimal infrastructure management and configuration, allowing them to focus on coding rather than server maintenance.

10.5.6 Additional DigitalOcean Services

In addition to Droplets, Spaces, Managed Databases, Kubernetes, and App Platform, DigitalOcean offers a variety of other services to enhance cloud infrastructure and application management:

- **Load Balancers**: DigitalOcean offers managed load balancers that distribute traffic across multiple Droplets, ensuring high availability and efficient resource utilization for applications.
- **Monitoring**: DigitalOcean provides built-in monitoring and alerting tools that allow users to track the performance of their infrastructure, set up alerts for unusual activity, and identify potential bottlenecks.
- **Firewalls**: DigitalOcean provides firewall management, allowing users to set rules for controlling network access to their Droplets and other cloud resources, enhancing security.

DigitalOcean is an excellent choice for developers and small-to-medium-sized businesses that need a straightforward, cost-effective cloud platform to build and scale applications. With services such as Droplets for compute, Spaces for storage, Managed Databases for scalable databases, Kubernetes for container orchestration, and the App Platform for web application deployment, DigitalOcean offers a comprehensive set of tools to support cloud-based application development, all with a focus on simplicity and ease of use. A detailed comparative summary of DigitalOcean's key cloud services and their features, ideal use cases, scalability, security, etc., is presented in Table 10.4.

10.6 HEROKU

Heroku [5] is a cloud-based platform-as-a-service (PaaS) that simplifies the process of building, deploying, and scaling applications. Heroku is particularly known for its ease of use, developer-friendly features, and its focus on streamlining the cloud infrastructure management process. It abstracts away much of the complexity involved in handling cloud services, allowing developers to focus on writing code rather than managing servers and infrastructure. An in-detail view of Heroku services is provided in Figure 10.5.

TABLE 10.4
Key Features and Characteristics of the DigitalOcean Services

Service	Key Features	Use Cases	Scalability	Security	Cost Model
Droplets (Virtual Machines)	• Customizable VM configurations (CPU, RAM, storage) • One-click application deployment (LAMP, WordPress, Docker, etc.) • Custom images for replication • Global data center locations • Managed scaling and auto-scaling	• Hosting web applications • Running microservices • Data processing and batch jobs • Custom server environments	• Vertical and horizontal scaling based on traffic and resource demand • Global scaling with multiple data center locations	• Encryption for data in transit and at rest • Firewalls for network security • Automated backups	• Pay-as-you-go for resources (compute, storage) • Monthly and hourly billing options based on Droplet specs
Spaces (Object Storage)	• Scalable object storage for unstructured data (images, videos, backups) • Integration with Droplets and CDN for media delivery • Encryption at rest and in transit • Simple API for access and management	• Media storage (images, videos) • Backups and archiving • Static content delivery (web apps, streaming media)	• Scalable storage with automatic growth • Optimized for high throughput and low-latency access	• Encryption at rest and in transit • Access Control Lists (ACLs) and bucket policies for granular permissions	• Pay-as-you-go based on storage volume and data transfer • Lower costs for lower access frequency (cold data)
Managed Databases	• Managed PostgreSQL, MySQL, and Redis instances • Automated backups and failover • High availability with automatic failover • Real-time monitoring and scaling	• Web and enterprise applications • Data analytics and reporting • Distributed systems with high uptime requirements	• Vertical and horizontal scaling of database instances • Automated scaling with read replicas for high demand	• Encryption at rest and in transit • VPC peering for private network access • Firewall rules for access control	• Pay-as-you-go based on instance type, storage, and backup frequency • Additional charges for extra resources
Kubernetes (DOKS)	• Fully managed Kubernetes clusters • Automated node management, scaling, and updates • Integration with other DigitalOcean services (Spaces, Managed Databases, Load Balancers) • Developer-friendly tools (Helm, Dashboard)	• Containerized application deployment • Microservices-based architecture • DevOps and CI/CD workflows	• Automated scaling based on resource demand • Cluster and node scaling with ease	• Role-based access control (RBAC) • Integration with VPC for private networking • Automated security patches	• Pay-as-you-go for compute and storage resources • No additional charges for control plane management

App Platform	• Managed PaaS solution • One-click deployment from GitHub, GitLab, Bitbucket • Supports multiple languages and frameworks (Node.js, Python, Ruby, Go, PHP, Java) • Auto-scaling for traffic spikes • Integrated CI/CD pipelines	• Web application hosting • API backends and microservices • Static sites and containerized apps	• Automatic vertical and horizontal scaling based on traffic demand • No manual configuration required	• SSL/TLS certificates for secure communication • Automated scaling with load balancing • AM integration	• Pay-as-you-go based on resource consumption (compute, storage) • Monthly and hourly pricing for application instances
Load Balancers	• Managed load balancing across Droplets or Kubernetes clusters • Supports HTTP(S), TCP, and UDP load balancing • Automatic scaling with traffic changes	• Distributing traffic for high-availability applications • Enhancing fault tolerance and scalability	• Dynamic scaling based on traffic volume • Configurable rules for load distribution	• Built-in SSL termination • Integration with firewalls and VPC for access control • Secure session management	• Pay-as-you-go based on the number of load balancers and throughput • Additional charges for SSL termination
Monitoring & Alerts	• Real-time monitoring of Droplets, databases, and Kubernetes clusters • Customizable alerting for performance metrics • Integration with other DigitalOcean services	• Infrastructure monitoring • Performance optimization • Proactive issue detection and resolution	• Scales with the infrastructure being monitored • Custom alerts based on thresholds	• Secure access to monitoring data • Integration with IAM for role-based access control	• Free tier for basic monitoring • Additional costs for advanced features and higher resource usage
Firewalls	• Managed firewalls for controlling network access to Droplets and other cloud resources • Support for both IPv4 and IPv6 • Rules-based access control	• Protecting cloud resources from unauthorized access • Defining granular access rules for applications	• Easy scaling by adding or removing firewall rules • Supports complex network architectures	• Granular access control with custom rules • Integration with IAM for managing firewall access	• Free tier available • No additional cost for basic firewall setup • Charges may apply for advanced configurations
Block Storage	• Scalable and high-performance block storage volumes • Easily attachable to Droplets or other resources • Snapshots for backups and replication	• Expanding Droplet storage • Persistent storage for databases or file systems • Backups and data recovery	• Scalable storage with easy attachment to Droplets or instances • Snapshot-based scaling and replication	• Data encryption at rest and in transit • Customizable access control with IAM and VPC	• Pay-as-you-go based on storage volume and I/O performance • Lower cost for cold or infrequent access storage

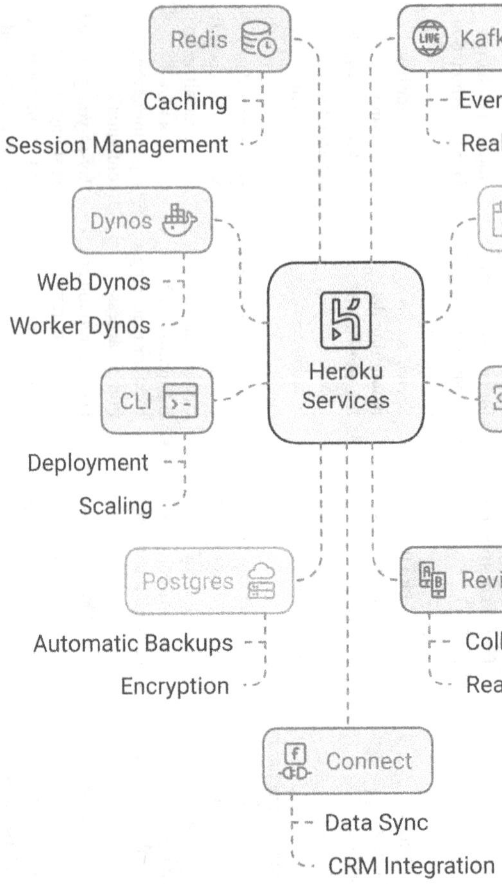

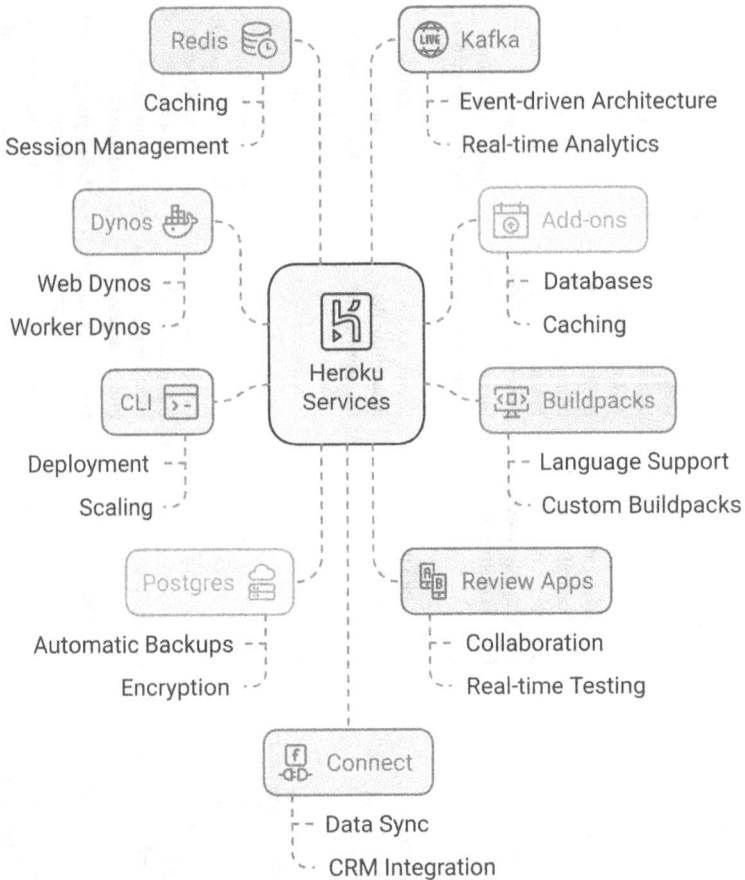

FIGURE 10.5 Detailed view of Heroku cloud services.

10.6.1 Heroku Dynos

Heroku Dynos are lightweight, virtualized containers that run applications and background jobs.

- **Instant Scaling**: Dynos provide a simple and powerful way to scale applications. You can easily scale your app up or down by adjusting the number of Dynos running for a particular service, making it easy to accommodate changes in demand or handle traffic spikes.
- **Types of Dynos**: Heroku provides several types of Dynos, including web Dynos, which handle HTTP requests for web applications, and worker Dynos, which are used to run background tasks, such as processing jobs from a queue, sending emails, or handling data processing.
- **Zero Maintenance**: Developers do not have to manage the underlying infrastructure of the Dynos. Heroku handles infrastructure management tasks such as server provisioning, resource allocation, and fault tolerance.

- **Ephemeral File System**: Dynos have an ephemeral file system, meaning any data stored on a Dyno is lost when the Dyno is restarted or re-deployed. For persistent storage, developers typically use managed services such as Heroku Postgres or Heroku Redis.

Dynos allow developers to focus on building applications without worrying about the complexities of managing servers and hardware resources. Scaling and resource allocation are simplified through Heroku's management interface.

10.6.2 Heroku Add-ons

Heroku makes it easy to enhance the functionality of applications with Heroku Add-ons, which are third-party services that integrate seamlessly into the Heroku ecosystem.

- **Third-Party Integrations**: Add-ons cover a wide range of categories, such as databases, caching, monitoring, logging, email delivery, and error tracking. These add-ons enable developers to quickly add complex services without needing to worry about configuration or management.
- **Examples of Popular Add-ons**: Heroku offers a variety of Add-ons for services such as SendGrid (for email delivery), Papertrail (for log management), New Relic (for performance monitoring), Redis (for caching), and PostgreSQL (for database management).
- **Automated Integration**: Add-ons are integrated directly into the Heroku platform, meaning developers can manage them easily through the Heroku Dashboard or CLI. Adding an Add-on is as simple as running a single command in the Heroku CLI or clicking through the web interface.
- **Managed Services**: Add-ons provided by Heroku come fully managed, meaning that Heroku handles maintenance, updates, and scaling, ensuring that these services are always up and running without requiring intervention from developers.

Add-ons help developers quickly enhance the functionality of their applications by leveraging third-party services, saving time and reducing the complexity of integrating new features.

10.6.3 Heroku Buildpacks

Heroku Buildpacks are scripts used to compile and prepare an application for deployment on the platform.

- **Automatic Environment Setup**: Buildpacks automatically detect the type of application being deployed (e.g., Ruby, Node.js, Python, Java) and configure the appropriate runtime environment. This makes deployment easy as developers don't need to worry about setting up the runtime or dependencies manually.

- **Custom Buildpacks**: While Heroku provides a variety of official buildpacks for common languages and frameworks, developers can also create and use custom buildpacks for specialized use cases or less common programming languages.
- **Multi-Language Support**: Buildpacks are designed to support a wide range of programming languages, including Ruby, Node.js, Python, Java, Go, PHP, Scala, and more. This flexibility allows Heroku to support various types of web and backend applications.
- **Efficiency and Speed**: Buildpacks streamline the process of preparing an application for deployment, ensuring that apps are compiled, dependencies are installed, and configuration is correctly set up in a standardized and efficient manner.

Heroku Buildpacks help simplify and automate the process of setting up an application's environment, making the deployment process faster and more consistent.

10.6.4 Heroku CLI

The Heroku Command Line Interface (CLI) is a powerful tool that allows developers to manage and deploy their Heroku applications directly from the command line.

- **Deployment and Management**: Through the CLI, developers can deploy code, check application logs, scale Dynos, manage add-ons, and perform administrative tasks all from a terminal. The CLI is particularly useful for automating workflows or managing applications on the go.
- **Automated Tasks**: Developers can use the Heroku CLI to automate routine tasks by writing scripts. For example, you can write scripts for deploying applications, managing databases, or rolling back changes. The CLI makes it easy to manage applications in a consistent and repeatable way.
- **Local Development**: The CLI also supports local application development, allowing you to run a local version of your Heroku app on your own machine for testing purposes. You can use the Heroku Local command to simulate the Heroku environment locally.
- **Interfacing with Git**: The Heroku CLI integrates well with Git, enabling you to deploy directly from your Git repository. You can deploy code changes using a simple *"git push heroku master"* command, making it easy to integrate with your existing version control practices.

The Heroku CLI is a developer-centric tool that streamlines the process of managing and deploying applications, while also enabling easy automation of repetitive tasks.

10.6.5 Heroku Postgres

Heroku Postgres is a fully managed, scalable, and secure relational database service for PostgreSQL offered by Heroku.

- **Fully Managed**: Heroku Postgres removes the complexity of database management by handling routine maintenance tasks such as patching, backups, and scaling. This allows developers to focus on building applications rather than managing databases.
- **Scalable and Flexible**: You can easily scale your Heroku Postgres database to meet the needs of your application. Heroku Postgres offers various pricing tiers with different performance and storage levels, making it flexible for apps of any size.
- **High Availability**: Heroku Postgres offers high availability through features such as automated failover and replication, ensuring that your database remains up and running even during maintenance or hardware failures.
- **Automated Backups**: The service provides automatic daily backups, ensuring that your data is safe and can be restored in case of failure or loss. Backups are stored for up to 30 days, and you can restore to any point within this window.
- **Security**: Heroku Postgres includes built-in encryption both at rest and in transit, as well as automated security patches to ensure that your database remains secure against potential vulnerabilities.

Heroku Postgres simplifies database management for developers by offering a fully managed, secure, and scalable PostgreSQL service integrated directly into the Heroku platform.

10.6.6 Heroku Review Apps

Heroku Review Apps is a feature that enables developers to automatically create temporary environments for testing changes before they are merged into the main codebase.

- **Pre-Production Testing**: Review Apps allow developers to preview and test code changes in an isolated environment before they go live. This ensures that any new changes or features are thoroughly tested in a real-world environment, helping to catch potential issues early.
- **Automated Setup**: When a pull request is created, Heroku automatically spins up a temporary application environment where the proposed changes can be reviewed. This allows teams to collaborate on modifications and test new features without affecting the main production environment.
- **Easy Collaboration**: Review Apps make it easier for team members to collaborate by providing a working preview of the application with the latest code changes. Team members can review, test, and provide feedback in real time, improving the overall quality of the software.

Heroku Review Apps provide a seamless and efficient way to handle pre-production testing and collaboration, making it easier to catch bugs and issues before they reach production.

10.6.7 Additional Heroku Services

Beyond the core services mentioned above, Heroku also offers a variety of other useful tools and integrations to enhance application development:

- **Heroku Redis**: A fully managed in-memory data store based on Redis, ideal for caching, session management, and real-time data processing.
- **Heroku Kafka**: A fully managed streaming platform for building real-time event-driven applications.
- **Heroku Connect**: A service that enables seamless integration between Heroku and Salesforce, allowing applications to easily access Salesforce data.

Heroku is a powerful platform-as-a-service (PaaS) offering that allows developers to easily deploy, manage, and scale applications. With features such as Dynos for simple and scalable compute, Heroku Add-ons for quick integrations with third-party services, Heroku Postgres for fully managed relational databases, and Review Apps for testing new code, Heroku streamlines the entire development lifecycle. It's particularly suited for developers who want to focus on writing code and building features without worrying about infrastructure management. A comprehensive summary of Heroku's key cloud services, highlighting their features, ideal use cases, scalability, security, etc., is presented in Table 10.5.

10.7 IBM CLOUD

IBM Cloud [6] is a comprehensive cloud computing platform that provides a wide range of services, including infrastructure as a service (IaaS), platform as a service (PaaS), and software as a service (SaaS), tailored for businesses and individual developers. It is designed to help users build, deploy, and scale applications efficiently using a mix of powerful tools, artificial intelligence, and advanced analytics. Figure 10.6 highlights the detailed expansion of key services available on IBM for cloud computing.

10.7.1 IBM Cloud Virtual Servers

IBM Cloud Virtual Servers are scalable virtual machines that provide on-demand computing power for applications.

- **Scalable and Flexible**: Virtual Servers allow you to scale up or down based on your needs. Whether you're hosting a small web app or running large data processing tasks, you can select from various configurations, including different CPU sizes, RAM amounts, and storage capacities.
- **Customization**: You can choose between different operating systems, including various distributions of Linux and Windows, to run your applications. This flexibility enables the deployment of diverse applications with different system requirements.

TABLE 10.5
Key Features and Characteristics of the Heroku Services

Service	Key Features	Use Cases	Scalability	Security	Cost Model
Heroku Dynos	• Lightweight, virtualized containers • Types include web Dynos (HTTP requests) and worker Dynos (background tasks) • Ephemeral file system • Zero maintenance, Heroku manages infrastructure	• Web application hosting • Background task processing (e.g., emails, data processing) • Scalable applications	• Scale vertically or horizontally by adjusting the number of Dynos • Flexible scaling to accommodate demand changes	• Ephemeral file system for short-lived data • SSL support for secure communication • Automatic resource allocation	• Pay-as-you-go based on Dyno type and number • Free tier available for testing and small applications
Heroku Add-ons	• Integration of third-party services for databases, caching, logging, performance monitoring, etc. • Easy to add via CLI or Dashboard • Managed services with no maintenance required	• Integrating services like databases, caching, email, performance monitoring • Quickly enhancing app functionality	• Most add-ons are scalable based on usage and are fully managed • Add-ons can be upgraded or scaled with the app	• Add-ons typically offer encryption and security features like SSL, automated updates, and maintenance handling	• Pricing depends on the add-on service (e.g., SendGrid, Papertrail) • Pay-as-you-go based on resource consumption
Heroku Buildpacks	• Scripts to compile and prepare applications for deployment • Automatic environment setup based on app language • Support for multiple languages and frameworks	• Automating application setup and deployment • Multi-language applications • Framework-specific environments	• Multiple buildpacks can be used to suit different languages or tech stacks • Custom buildpacks available	• Buildpacks standardize environment setup but do not handle application-level security • Secure code compilation	• No additional cost for using standard buildpacks • Custom buildpacks may involve extra development costs
Heroku CLI	• Command-line interface for app deployment, scaling, logging, and management • Automates workflows with scripts • Local development with Heroku Local	• Managing apps from terminal • Deploying code from Git • Automating workflows • Local development testing	• Supports scalable workflows with easy integration into CI/CD pipelines • Local testing environment setup	• CLI requires secure access control (e.g., using SSH keys) • Integrates with Git securely for deployments	• Free to use • Costs associated with usage are based on app services rather than the CLI itself

(*Continued*)

TABLE 10.5 (Continued)

Service	Key Features	Use Cases	Scalability	Security	Cost Model
Heroku Postgres	• Fully managed PostgreSQL service • Scalable, high-availability database with replication • Automatic backups • Built-in security features like encryption	• Web and enterprise applications • Real-time data processing • Data analytics and reporting systems	• Easily scale with multiple performance tiers (horizontal and vertical) • Automatic failover and replication	• Data encryption at rest and in transit • Automatic security patches • Built-in backup and recovery options	• Pay-as-you-go based on instance type, storage, and backup frequency • Free tier for small projects
Heroku Review Apps	• Automatic creation of temporary environments for code testing • Isolated pre-production environment • Easy collaboration and feedback sharing	• Pre-production code testing • Collaboration on new features • Real-time testing and bug identification	• Temporary environments are automatically created and destroyed • Scaling within review apps as required	• Secure access control and preview URLs • Typically secure app testing environments	• Free for temporary environments • Costs for scaling or persistent services if needed
Heroku Redis	• Fully managed in-memory key-value data store • Ideal for caching, session management, and real-time data • High-speed data access and low latency	• Caching for web apps • Session storage • Real-time data processing • Leaderboards, counters	• Scalable based on app's caching needs and data volume • Memory-based scaling	• Encryption in transit • Managed service with security patches and updates • Access control and ACLs	• Pay-as-you-go based on storage size and access frequency • Free tier available for small-scale applications
Heroku Kafka	• Managed streaming platform for real-time event-driven applications • High-throughput data streaming • Integrates easily with other Heroku services	• Event-driven architecture • Real-time analytics • Building streaming data pipelines	• Scales horizontally with partitioning • Handles high-throughput events in real-time	• Secure connections with SSL • Managed service with encryption and access control	• Pay-as-you-go based on resource usage (data throughput, storage) • Free tier for testing and small use cases
Heroku Connect	• Seamless integration between Heroku and Salesforce • Access Salesforce data directly within Heroku apps • Easy to sync data between Heroku and Salesforce	• Syncing data between Salesforce and Heroku apps • Building CRM-integrated applications	• Scalable based on data sync needs • Automatically handles large data loads and sync intervals	• Secure data exchange between Heroku and Salesforce • Access control based on user permissions	• Pay-as-you-go based on data sync volume and API usage • Pricing tier based on data volume

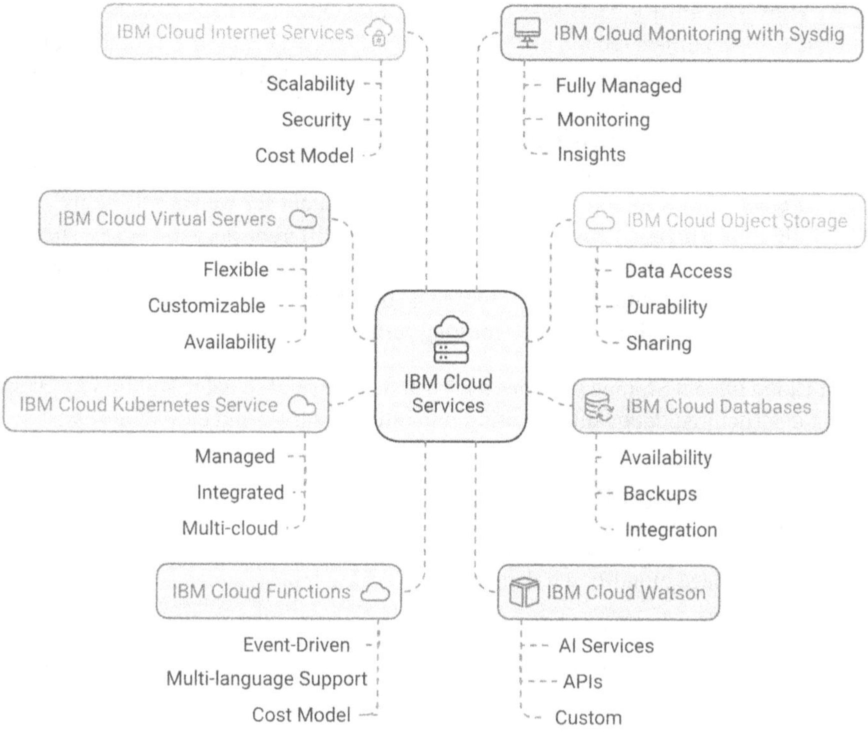

FIGURE 10.6 Detailed view of IBM cloud services.

- **Deployment Made Easy**: Virtual Servers are ideal for deploying web applications, running batch processing tasks, managing databases, or hosting other cloud workloads. IBM Cloud's dashboard and API make it easy to launch, manage, and monitor virtual servers at scale.
- **High Availability**: IBM Cloud Virtual Servers come with built-in redundancy, ensuring that applications remain operational even in the event of hardware failure. Users can also configure their Virtual Servers for high availability and fault tolerance.

IBM Cloud Virtual Servers offer scalable and reliable computing resources, enabling developers and businesses to deploy applications and services quickly with customizable configurations.

10.7.2 IBM Cloud Object Storage

IBM Cloud Object Storage is a fully managed, scalable storage service that allows businesses to store unstructured data, such as images, videos, and documents.

- **Scalable Storage**: IBM Cloud Object Storage can scale to accommodate large amounts of unstructured data. It supports multiple use cases, from content delivery networks to backup and archiving.

- **High Durability**: Data stored in IBM Cloud Object Storage is highly durable, with built-in redundancy and automatic data replication across multiple data centers. This ensures that your data is protected and available even in the event of hardware or regional failures.
- **Data Access and Sharing**: You can store and access files from anywhere on the Internet, and easily share data across multiple Virtual Servers, making it a convenient solution for distributing static content for web applications.
- **Flexible Storage Classes**: IBM Cloud offers different storage classes, such as Standard, Vault, and Cold Vault, to cater to different data access patterns and cost requirements. Vault storage is ideal for infrequently accessed data, while Cold Vault is designed for long-term data archiving.

IBM Cloud Object Storage provides a robust, flexible, and scalable solution for managing unstructured data while ensuring reliability, security, and ease of access.

10.7.3 IBM Cloud Databases

IBM Cloud Databases is a fully managed service that allows businesses to set up, scale, and manage cloud-based databases.

- **Fully Managed**: IBM Cloud Databases support several database engines, including PostgreSQL, MySQL, Redis, Elasticsearch, and MongoDB. These databases are fully managed, meaning IBM handles tasks such as patching, backups, scaling, and monitoring.
- **Scalable**: Just like other IBM Cloud services, Cloud Databases are scalable. You can scale up or down based on your application's needs, adjusting CPU, memory, and storage as required.
- **High Availability and Fault Tolerance**: IBM Cloud Databases offer automated backups, failover, and replication, ensuring high availability and data redundancy. This ensures your applications run smoothly even during failures or hardware issues.
- **Integrated Analytics**: IBM Cloud Databases can easily integrate with other IBM services, such as IBM Cloud Functions and IBM Watson, to add intelligence and analytics to your applications.

With IBM Cloud Databases, businesses can leverage reliable, scalable, and fully managed database solutions to power their cloud-based applications.

10.7.4 IBM Cloud Kubernetes Service

IBM Cloud Kubernetes Service is a fully managed platform for deploying, managing, and scaling containerized applications using Kubernetes.

- **Managed Kubernetes**: IBM Cloud takes care of the Kubernetes infrastructure, including patching, scaling, and monitoring, so you don't need to worry about managing your own Kubernetes cluster.

- **Integrated with IBM Cloud Services**: The Kubernetes Service integrates seamlessly with other IBM Cloud services, such as IBM Cloud Object Storage, IBM Cloud Databases, and IBM Cloud Functions, making it easy to automate the deployment, scaling, and management of containerized applications.
- **Auto-Scaling**: Kubernetes can automatically scale containers based on application demand, ensuring that the right resources are available as needed without manual intervention.
- **Multi-Cloud Support**: IBM Cloud Kubernetes Service also offers multi-cloud and hybrid cloud capabilities, allowing you to deploy applications across multiple clouds or on-premise systems for greater flexibility and reliability.

IBM Cloud Kubernetes Service provides a powerful and flexible solution for containerized application management, making it easier to deploy and scale apps in the cloud.

10.7.5 IBM Cloud Functions

IBM Cloud Functions is a serverless computing service that allows developers to run code in response to events without provisioning or managing servers.

- **Event-Driven Architecture**: With IBM Cloud Functions, you can create applications that respond to events, such as HTTP requests, changes in data, or updates to cloud resources. Functions are triggered automatically when certain events occur, enabling fast, event-driven processing.
- **Scalability and Cost Efficiency**: IBM Cloud Functions automatically scale based on demand, so you only pay for the compute power you use. This makes it a cost-effective solution for processing events and running background tasks.
- **No Infrastructure Management**: Cloud Functions eliminates the need to manage servers, enabling developers to focus solely on writing the logic for their applications. The infrastructure is fully managed by IBM Cloud, providing simplicity and ease of use.
- **Support for Multiple Languages**: IBM Cloud Functions supports various programming languages, such as JavaScript, Python, Java, and Go, enabling developers to use the language they are most comfortable with.

IBM Cloud Functions offers a simple and cost-efficient way to build event-driven applications without the need to manage server infrastructure.

10.7.6 IBM Cloud Watson

IBM Watson is a suite of AI and machine learning services that developers can use to integrate artificial intelligence capabilities into their applications.

- **AI Services**: IBM Cloud Watson includes services for Natural Language Processing (NLP), Speech Recognition, Text-to-Speech, Visual Recognition, and more. These services allow you to add advanced AI capabilities to your apps without needing to create complex algorithms.
- **Pre-Trained Models**: Watson provides access to pre-trained models for common use cases such as chatbots, sentiment analysis, image recognition, and language translation. These pre-built models can be easily integrated into applications via APIs.
- **Customizable Models**: Watson also enables users to build and train custom models for specific use cases, allowing businesses to tailor AI capabilities to their unique needs.
- **Scalability**: IBM Watson's AI services are fully scalable and can handle increasing amounts of data and user requests as your application grows.

IBM Cloud Watson makes it easy to infuse artificial intelligence into applications, empowering developers to create smarter, more intelligent software without deep expertise in machine learning.

10.7.7 Additional IBM Cloud Services

IBM Cloud offers an extensive set of other services to complement its cloud computing offerings, including:

- **IBM Cloud Internet Services (CIS)**: A suite of security, performance, and traffic management solutions designed to protect applications and improve their performance.
- **IBM Cloud Monitoring with Sysdig**: A fully managed service for real-time monitoring and management of cloud resources and applications. It provides insights into your system's performance, resource utilization, and application health.
- **IBM Cloud Object Storage Flex**: A flexible version of IBM Cloud Object Storage that provides additional features such as flexible file management and enhanced performance for large datasets.

IBM Cloud provides a comprehensive suite of cloud services that help businesses and developers build, deploy, and scale applications with ease. With tools like IBM Cloud Virtual Servers for scalable computing, IBM Cloud Databases for fully managed databases, IBM Cloud Functions for serverless computing, and IBM Watson for AI capabilities, IBM Cloud makes it easy to leverage the full potential of cloud technologies. The platform's robust security features, high availability, and seamless integrations with a wide range of cloud services make it an excellent choice for businesses looking to scale their applications and integrate advanced capabilities into their workflows. A comparative analysis table summarizing IBM Cloud's core services and their features, use cases, scalability, security, etc., is provided in Table 10.6.

TABLE 10.6
Key Features and Characteristics of the IBM Cloud

Service	Key Features	Use Cases	Scalability	Security	Cost Model
IBM Cloud Virtual Servers	• Scalable and customizable virtual machines • Supports both Linux and Windows OS • High availability with redundancy • Easy deployment via dashboard or API	• Hosting web applications • Running batch jobs • Managing databases • Virtualized compute workloads	• Scale up or down as needed • Choose CPU, RAM, storage based on needs • Horizontal and vertical scaling options	• Built-in redundancy and failover • Data encryption in transit and at rest • Network isolation options	• Pay-as-you-go based on VM configuration (CPU, memory, storage) • Monthly or hourly billing
IBM Cloud Object Storage	• Fully managed, scalable storage for unstructured data • Supports multiple storage classes (Standard, Vault, Cold Vault) • Built-in redundancy and replication	• Storing and serving images, videos, documents • Backup and archiving • Content delivery networks	• Highly scalable for large amounts of data • Auto-tiering between storage classes based on access patterns	• Data redundancy across multiple data centers • Built-in encryption at rest and in transit • Access controls	• Pay-as-you-go based on storage volume, retrieval frequency, and access class • Pricing tiers based on data type
IBM Cloud Databases	• Fully managed databases (PostgreSQL, MySQL, MongoDB, Redis, Elasticsearch) • Automated backups, scaling, and monitoring • Integrated analytics	• Web and mobile app databases • Real-time analytics • Business intelligence solutions	• Easily scale resources (CPU, memory, storage) • Auto-scaling and high availability • Geo-replication	• Automated backups and encryption at rest and in transit • Access control and monitoring tools	• Pay-as-you-go based on database instance size and storage volume • Free tiers available for basic usage
IBM Cloud Kubernetes Service	• Fully managed Kubernetes platform • Auto-scaling of containers • Multi-cloud and hybrid cloud support • Integrates with other IBM Cloud services	• Deploying containerized applications • Running microservices • Hybrid or multi-cloud container orchestration	• Automatically scales based on app demand • Horizontal scaling of containers with automated load balancing	• Built-in security with Kubernetes RBAC (role-based access control) • SSL/TLS encryption • Multi-cloud security	• Pay-as-you-go based on cluster resources (CPU, memory, storage) • Pricing also based on instance types

(Continued)

TABLE 10.6 (Continued)

Service	Key Features	Use Cases	Scalability	Security	Cost Model
IBM Cloud Functions	• Serverless, event-driven platform • Automatically scales based on events • Supports JavaScript, Python, Java, Go • No server management needed	• Real-time event processing • Trigger-based workflows (e.g., HTTP requests, cloud events, data changes)	• Fully auto-scaling based on events • Pay only for the execution time • Easily handles high throughput	• Secure event-driven environment with automatic resource scaling • Role-based access control (RBAC)	• Pay-as-you-go based on the number of invocations and execution time • Free tier available
IBM Cloud Watson	• AI and machine learning services (NLP, Speech Recognition, Visual Recognition, etc.) • Pre-trained and customizable models • Integrated with other IBM Cloud services	• Adding AI capabilities (chatbots, sentiment analysis, translation) • Integrating AI into apps for automation	• Scales with demand for AI services • Handles large data processing for AI tasks • Flexible resource allocation	• Data encryption and compliance with industry standards (e.g., GDPR, HIPAA) • Pre-built models with security features	• Pay-as-you-go for API calls based on usage • Pricing based on number of API requests and data processed
IBM Cloud Internet Services (CIS)	• Security, performance, and traffic management solutions • DDoS protection, content delivery optimization, traffic routing • Global edge locations	• Securing web apps • Improving app performance • Protecting against DDoS attacks and traffic spikes	• Global scalability with edge servers and CDN • Automatic traffic rerouting and load balancing based on demand	• Comprehensive security features (DDoS, WAF, SSL/TLS encryption) • Real-time traffic monitoring	• Pay-as-you-go based on the services used (e.g., security, routing, CDN) • Pricing based on traffic volume
IBM Cloud Monitoring with Sysdig	• Real-time cloud resource and app monitoring • Provides insights into system health, performance, and resource usage • Alerts and notifications	• Monitoring cloud infrastructure • Real-time performance tracking • Troubleshooting and resource management	• Scales with your infrastructure • Provides insights at both the container and infrastructure level	• Secure data transmission and storage • Alerts for potential security breaches • Granular access controls	• Pay-as-you-go based on monitoring data usage and alert configurations • Free tiers available

10.8 ORACLE CLOUD INFRASTRUCTURE (OCI)

Oracle Cloud Infrastructure (OCI) [7] is a comprehensive and scalable cloud computing platform offering a broad range of cloud services, including computing, storage, networking, databases, and more. It is designed for businesses and developers to build, deploy, and scale applications with high availability, security, and flexibility. Figure 10.7 offers an expanded look at some of the key services provided by OCI for cloud computing.

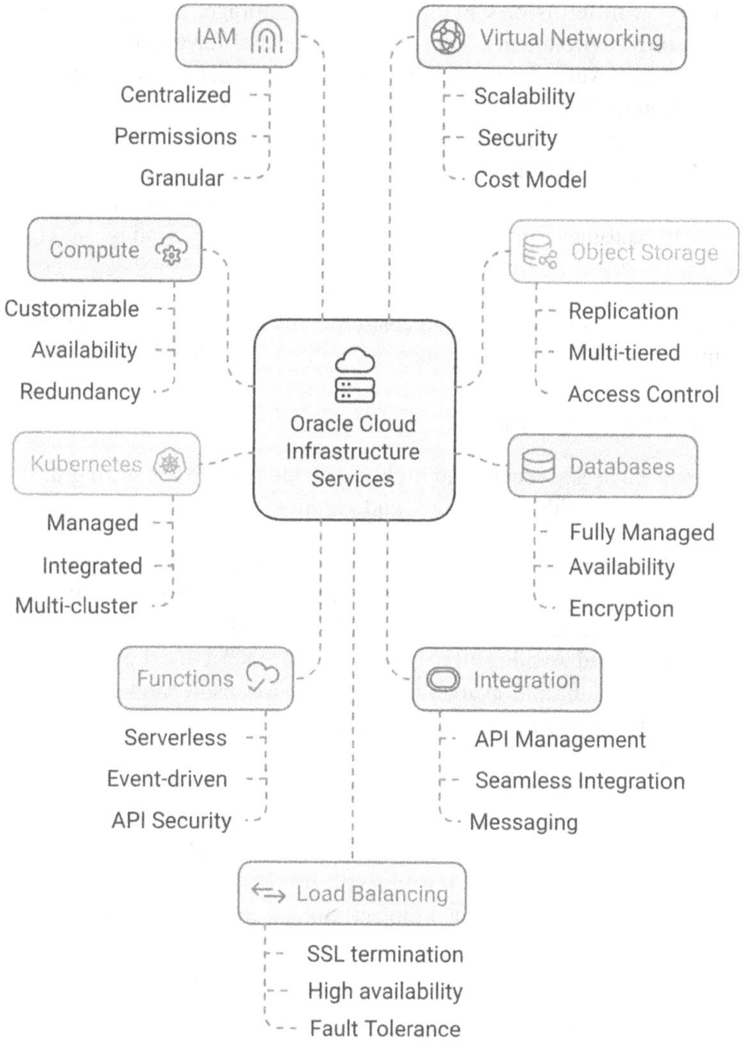

FIGURE 10.7 Detailed view of OCI cloud services.

10.8.1 OCI Compute

OCI Compute provides scalable virtual machines (VMs) for deploying cloud-based servers.

- **Scalable and Flexible**: With OCI Compute, you can choose from a variety of virtual machine sizes and configurations, scaling up or down based on the needs of your application. This allows you to optimize your infrastructure for different workloads, from simple web applications to resource-intensive data processing tasks.
- **Customizable Resources**: You can select from a wide range of VM configurations in terms of CPU, memory, and storage, allowing for tailored computing environments. This flexibility is ideal for a range of use cases, from hosting web apps to running batch jobs or scientific simulations.
- **High Availability**: OCI Compute offers options to deploy VMs in multiple availability domains, ensuring that applications remain online and resilient to hardware or network failures.
- **Automation**: You can use OCI's API and command-line interface (CLI) tools to automate provisioning, management, and scaling of compute instances, streamlining deployment processes.

OCI Compute provides an elastic and cost-efficient solution for running cloud-based servers, making it easier to deploy, manage, and scale applications.

10.8.2 OCI Object Storage

OCI Object Storage is a secure and highly scalable service for storing unstructured data, such as images, videos, backups, and log files.

- **Scalable Storage**: OCI Object Storage can handle vast amounts of data, and it automatically scales as your storage needs grow. This makes it a reliable option for large-scale data storage in cloud-based applications.
- **Durability and Availability**: Data stored in OCI Object Storage is replicated across multiple availability domains to ensure high durability and availability, providing peace of mind that your data is protected from hardware failure.
- **Easy Access and Sharing**: You can easily store and retrieve data from OCI Object Storage via APIs or a simple web interface, and share data across multiple virtual machines (VMs) and applications. It's an ideal solution for distributing static content for web applications.
- **Lifecycle Management**: OCI Object Storage offers lifecycle management policies, enabling you to automate the movement of data between different storage classes, such as standard or archive storage, based on its age or access frequency.

OCI Object Storage provides a robust and secure way to manage unstructured data with automatic scaling, ensuring easy access and long-term durability.

10.8.3 OCI Databases

OCI Database is a fully managed database service that allows you to deploy, scale, and manage databases in the cloud.

- **Fully Managed**: OCI Database eliminates the need for users to manage database infrastructure. Oracle handles the maintenance, patching, backup, and high availability aspects, allowing you to focus on your applications rather than database administration.
- **Multiple Database Engines**: You can choose from a variety of database options, including Oracle Autonomous Database, Oracle MySQL Database, and Oracle NoSQL Database, giving you flexibility in selecting the right database engine for your needs.
- **Scalable and Secure**: OCI Database offers scalability options, so you can adjust the size and capacity of your databases as required. Security features, including encryption at rest and in transit, help protect sensitive data from unauthorized access.
- **Performance Optimization**: OCI's Autonomous Database offers self-tuning capabilities that automatically optimize performance without manual intervention. This ensures that your applications run smoothly, even under heavy workloads.

OCI Databases provide a reliable, scalable, and managed environment for hosting various types of databases, whether for transactional systems, web apps, or large-scale analytics.

10.8.4 OCI Kubernetes

OCI Kubernetes is a fully managed service for deploying, scaling, and managing containerized applications using Kubernetes.

- **Fully Managed Kubernetes**: OCI Kubernetes simplifies the management of Kubernetes clusters by taking care of the infrastructure, including updates, scaling, and maintenance. This allows you to focus on deploying and managing containerized applications without worrying about the underlying infrastructure.
- **Seamless Integration**: OCI Kubernetes integrates smoothly with other Oracle Cloud services such as Object Storage, Databases, and Compute, enabling you to build and scale applications in a cohesive cloud ecosystem.
- **Auto-Scaling**: Kubernetes automatically adjusts the number of containers based on application demand, ensuring that you have the right resources available during peak times and saving costs during low-demand periods.
- **Multi-Cluster and Multi-Cloud**: OCI Kubernetes supports multi-cluster and hybrid cloud environments, allowing you to deploy and manage containerized applications across on-premises and cloud infrastructures.

OCI Kubernetes provides a powerful and flexible solution for managing containerized applications in the cloud, enabling automated scaling, load balancing, and resource optimization.

10.8.5 OCI Functions

OCI Functions is a serverless computing service that enables you to run code in response to events without managing servers.

- **Event-Driven Architecture**: OCI Functions allows you to create applications that respond to events such as changes in data or HTTP requests. Your functions automatically scale based on demand, making it easy to handle spikes in usage without manual intervention.
- **Cost Efficiency**: With OCI Functions, you only pay for the compute resources consumed during execution, which helps reduce operational costs. Since no infrastructure needs to be provisioned or maintained, it's a cost-effective way to run small code snippets or handle specific tasks.
- **Scalable and Flexible**: OCI Functions can automatically scale in response to changes in load, ensuring that your code executes efficiently, whether it's handling a small request or a large number of events.
- **Multiple Languages Supported**: You can write functions in several programming languages, including Java, Python, Go, and Node.js, making it easier to use OCI Functions with your existing application stack.

OCI Functions provides a scalable, serverless environment for running code in response to events, offering a high degree of flexibility and reducing operational overhead.

10.8.6 OCI Integration

OCI Integration provides a suite of services to help you connect applications, data, and systems across cloud and on-premises environments.

- **APIs**: OCI offers an API Gateway and API Management service, which allows you to create, secure, and manage APIs that connect your applications with other services and platforms.
- **Event-Driven Architecture**: With OCI Integration, you can set up event-driven workflows that automatically trigger actions across your applications and services based on predefined conditions. This ensures a seamless flow of data between systems.
- **Messaging and Queuing**: OCI supports messaging services, such as Oracle Cloud Messaging and Oracle Event Hub, enabling reliable and asynchronous communication between different components of your application architecture.

- **Seamless Integration**: OCI Integration enables quick integration between Oracle Cloud services and third-party applications, as well as connecting on-premises systems with cloud-based workloads. This helps streamline workflows and enhance operational efficiency.

OCI Integration provides powerful tools for connecting and automating workflows between cloud and on-premises systems, making it easier to integrate applications and data across different platforms.

10.8.7 Additional OCI Services

In addition to the core services mentioned, Oracle Cloud Infrastructure offers a wide range of additional features to enhance your cloud-based applications:

- **Identity and Access Management (IAM)**: OCI provides robust security features for managing user access and permissions to cloud resources, ensuring secure and compliant access controls.
- **Virtual Networking**: With OCI's Virtual Cloud Network (VCN), you can design, configure, and manage private network environments for your cloud resources, ensuring secure communication between services.
- **Load Balancing**: OCI's Load Balancer service distributes incoming traffic across multiple instances to ensure high availability and reliability for your applications.
- **Cloud Monitoring and Logging**: Oracle offers integrated monitoring and logging tools to track the performance, availability, and security of your cloud resources, helping you identify and troubleshoot issues quickly.

Oracle Cloud Infrastructure (OCI) provides a wide range of powerful and flexible services for businesses and developers looking to build, deploy, and scale applications in the cloud. With services like OCI Compute for scalable virtual machines, OCI Object Storage for managing unstructured data, OCI Databases for fully managed database solutions, and OCI Kubernetes for container management, OCI offers a comprehensive suite of tools to support modern cloud-based applications. Whether you're running web apps, processing big data, or developing machine learning models, OCI provides the resources and services you need to achieve your cloud computing goals. A detailed comparative summary of OCI and its core services, focusing on features, use cases, scalability, security, etc., is provided in Table 10.7.

TABLE 10.7
Key Features and Characteristics of Oracle Cloud Infrastructure Services

Service	Key Features	Use Cases	Scalability	Security	Cost Model
OCI Compute	• Scalable virtual machines (VMs) for cloud-based servers • Customizable resources (CPU, memory, storage) • High availability with multi-availability domains	• Hosting web applications • Running batch processing tasks • Scientific simulations • Data processing jobs	• Easily scalable (up/down) based on needs • Supports a wide range of VM sizes • Auto-scaling through APIs	• Built-in redundancy and failover • Network security features • Data encryption at rest and in transit	• Pay-as-you-go based on VM size (CPU, memory, storage) • Option for reserved instances with long-term commitments
OCI Object Storage	• Highly scalable storage for unstructured data (e.g., images, videos, backups) • Automatic replication across availability domains • Lifecycle management	• Data storage for web apps • Backup and archival • Content distribution and media hosting	• Scalable to handle vast amounts of data • Supports multi-tiered storage classes (standard, archive, etc.)	• Data replication for high durability • Encryption at rest and in transit • Fine-grained access control	• Pay-as-you-go based on storage volume • Charges for data access and retrieval, with cost based on storage class
OCI Databases	• Fully managed databases (Oracle Autonomous Database, Oracle MySQL, Oracle NoSQL) • Automated patching, backup, and scaling • Performance tuning capabilities	• Hosting transactional databases • Web and mobile app databases • Large-scale analytics and reporting	• Auto-scaling for both storage and compute • Supports high availability and load balancing across multiple instances	• End-to-end encryption (at rest, in transit) • Automated backups • Granular access control and audit logging	• Pay-as-you-go based on instance size, storage, and I/O requests • Reserved pricing for long-term usage
OCI Kubernetes	• Managed Kubernetes service for deploying, scaling, and managing containerized applications • Integration with OCI services like Object Storage and Compute	• Managing containerized applications • Running microservices architectures • Hybrid cloud app deployments	• Auto-scaling of clusters and containers based on demand • Multi-cluster support • Horizontal scaling of pods	• Kubernetes RBAC for access control • Network policies for security • Encryption of containerized data	• Pay-as-you-go based on cluster resources (compute, storage) • Free tier for basic usage

Service	Key Features	Use Cases	Scalability	Security	Cost Model
OCI Functions	• Serverless computing with event-driven architecture • Auto-scaling based on events (e.g., HTTP requests, data changes) • Supports multiple programming languages	• Event-driven tasks and automation • Handling spikes in traffic • Running small, isolated functions in response to events	• Automatically scales based on events • Pay-per-use with no need to manage infrastructure	• Secure execution environment • Integration with IAM for access control • Fine-grained API security	• Pay-as-you-go based on function execution time and resources consumed • Free tier available
OCI Integration	• API management, event-driven workflows, and messaging services • Seamless integration with Oracle Cloud and third-party services • Real-time data orchestration	• API management and security • Event-driven data workflows • Messaging and queuing for cloud-to-cloud communication	• Scales with demand for event handling and data processing • Handles hybrid and multi-cloud integrations	• Secure data communication (SSL/TLS) • IAM-based access control • Real-time monitoring and auditing	• Pay-as-you-go based on API calls, data transfer, and messaging volume • Pricing based on usage and integration complexity
OCI Identity and Access Management (IAM)	• Centralized user management and access control • Fine-grained permissions with policy management • Multi-factor authentication (MFA)	• Secure access to cloud resources • Managing user roles and permissions • Compliance and audit management	• Scalable user management • Can manage multiple roles and policies across large organizations	• Strong security with MFA, identity federation, and granular policy enforcement • Audit logs for compliance	• Typically included with other OCI services • Cost applies to enterprise-wide IAM use and policy configurations
OCI Virtual Networking (VCN)	• Private networking for OCI resources • Fully customizable subnets, routing tables, and firewalls • Integration with other OCI services for secure communication	• Creating isolated network environments for applications • Connecting on-premises resources to cloud infrastructure	• Scales with the number of resources (VMs, containers, etc.) deployed in the VCN • Flexible network expansion	• Virtual firewalls, private IPs, and security lists • Encryption of network traffic • Access control lists (ACLs)	• Pay-as-you-go based on data transfer, public IPs, and other network resources • Free tier available for basic use

(Continued)

TABLE 8.7
(Continued)

Service	Key Features	Use Cases	Scalability	Security	Cost Model
OCI Load Balancing	• Distributes traffic across multiple instances for high availability and reliability • Global and regional load balancing options • SSL termination support	• High availability for web applications • Ensuring fault tolerance during traffic spikes • Redundancy in traffic management	• Scales dynamically with incoming traffic • Handles traffic distribution for large-scale apps	• Built-in DDoS protection • SSL encryption for secure communication • Health checks and automatic failover	• Pay-as-you-go based on traffic volume and number of load balancers • Free tier for low-traffic scenarios
OCI Monitoring and Logging	• Integrated monitoring and log management tools • Real-time performance insights and metrics • Set alerts and automated responses	• Cloud resource performance monitoring • Debugging and troubleshooting applications • Compliance tracking	• Scales with cloud resource usage • Monitors all types of OCI services (Compute, Storage, Networking, etc.)	• Security logging, alerting, and audit capabilities • Data encryption • Access control through IAM policies	• Pay-as-you-go based on the number of logs and metrics collected • Free tier available for basic use

10.9 PRACTICE QUESTIONS/SOLUTIONS

MULTIPLE CHOICE QUESTIONS

1 **Which of the following cloud platforms is primarily used for infrastructure-as-a-service (IaaS)?**
A) Google Firebase
B) Microsoft Azure
C) AWS Lambda
D) Google App Engine

Answer: B) Microsoft Azure

2 **Which cloud platform is known for its serverless computing service, allowing users to run code without provisioning servers?**
A) Google Cloud Functions
B) Amazon EC2
C) IBM Cloud
D) Microsoft Azure Storage

Answer: A) Google Cloud Functions

3 **Which of the following is a popular platform for hands-on experience with cloud computing, offering free tier resources to learn and experiment?**
A) AWS Free Tier
B) Oracle Cloud Academy
C) Red Hat OpenShift
D) VMware Cloud

Answer: A) AWS Free Tier

4 **In the context of practical cloud computing, which platform provides container orchestration services using Kubernetes?**
A) AWS Elastic Beanstalk
B) Google Kubernetes Engine (GKE)
C) Microsoft Power BI
D) IBM Watson Studio

Answer: B) Google Kubernetes Engine (GKE)

5 **Which cloud platform is used for creating virtual machines, managing storage, and networking as part of infrastructure as a service (IaaS)?**
A) AWS EC2
B) AWS Lambda
C) Azure DevOps
D) Google Cloud Pub/Sub

Answer: A) AWS EC2

6 **Which platform allows developers to create, deploy, and scale web applications with minimal management effort and is a key service for platform-as-a-service (PaaS)?**
A) Google App Engine
B) AWS EC2
C) IBM Cloud Functions
D) Docker

Answer: A) Google App Engine

7 **What is the primary benefit of using AWS Elastic Beanstalk for deploying cloud applications?**
A) It allows automatic management of cloud infrastructure.
B) It requires manual server setup and maintenance.
C) It is only useful for hosting static websites.
D) It is limited to AWS-specific services only.

Answer: A) It allows automatic management of cloud infrastructure.

8 **Which of the following is a hands-on platform that offers cloud simulation labs for practicing cloud skills?**
A) Cloud Academy
B) GitHub
C) Oracle Cloud Free Tier
D) Docker Hub

Answer: A) Cloud Academy

9 **Which feature of Microsoft Azure allows users to manage their cloud resources through a command-line interface (CLI)?**
A) Azure Cloud Shell
B) Azure Cognitive Services
C) Azure Functions
D) Azure DevOps

Answer: A) Azure Cloud Shell

10 **What is the primary purpose of using Google Cloud's Firebase platform in cloud computing?**
A) To run containerized applications at scale
B) To provide cloud-based storage and real-time databases
C) To manage virtual machines and networking
D) To deploy serverless microservices

Answer: B) To provide cloud-based storage and real-time databases

11 **Which of the following is a platform used for deploying and managing machine learning models at scale on cloud infrastructure?**
A) Amazon SageMaker
B) Google Cloud Pub/Sub
C) Microsoft Power BI
D) AWS Lambda

Answer: A) Amazon SageMaker

12 **Which of the following platforms offers a fully managed Kubernetes service for container orchestration?**
A) Amazon ECS
B) Google Kubernetes Engine (GKE)
C) Microsoft Azure App Services
D) AWS Lambda

Answer: B) Google Kubernetes Engine (GKE)

13 **Which cloud platform provides the service "CloudFormation" to automate the provisioning of infrastructure using code?**
A) Microsoft Azure
B) Google Cloud Platform
C) Amazon Web Services (AWS)
D) IBM Cloud

Answer: C) Amazon Web Services (AWS)

14 **Which of the following cloud services offers scalable object storage for unstructured data?**
A) Amazon S3
B) Google Cloud BigQuery
C) Microsoft Azure SQL Database
D) IBM Cloud Foundry

Answer: A) Amazon S3

15 **Which cloud computing platform is known for its integrated development environment (IDE) that supports containerized applications?**
A) Google Cloud Shell
B) Microsoft Visual Studio
C) IBM Cloud Code Engine
D) Amazon Lightsail

Answer: C) IBM Cloud Code Engine

16 **Which of the following is a primary use case for the AWS Elastic Load Balancer (ELB)?**
A) Data storage
B) Serverless computing
C) Traffic distribution across multiple servers
D) Machine learning model deployment

Answer: C) Traffic distribution across multiple servers

17 **Which cloud platform provides a service called "Cloud Functions" that allows you to run event-driven functions without managing servers?**
A) AWS Lambda
B) Google Cloud Functions
C) Azure App Service
D) IBM Cloud Functions

Answer: B) Google Cloud Functions

18 **What is the main purpose of Azure DevOps in cloud computing?**
A) To provide database-as-a-service
B) To enable version control and automate CI/CD pipelines
C) To manage virtual machine instances
D) To host serverless applications

Answer: B) To enable version control and automate CI/CD pipelines

19 **Which of the following tools would you use for hands-on learning of Google Cloud services and infrastructure?**
A) Cloud Academy
B) Google Cloud Skills Boost
C) Microsoft Learn
D) AWS Educate

Answer: B) Google Cloud Skills Boost

20 **What is the main advantage of using a cloud platform like Microsoft Azure or AWS for hosting web applications over traditional on-premise solutions?**
A) Cloud platforms offer better control over physical hardware
B) Cloud platforms provide more affordable licensing for software
C) Cloud platforms offer scalability and flexibility based on demand
D) Cloud platforms have no security concerns

Answer: C) Cloud platforms offer scalability and flexibility based on demand

DESCRIPTIVE QUESTIONS

1 **What is IaaS, and how is it implemented using AWS EC2?**

Answer: IaaS (Infrastructure-as-a-Service) provides virtual resources like servers and storage over the Internet. AWS EC2 allows users launch virtual servers (called instances) on the cloud, allowing flexible hosting for applications without managing physical hardware.

2 **What is serverless computing, and how do AWS Lambda and Google Cloud Functions help in building applications?**

Answer: Serverless computing allows developers to run code without managing servers. AWS Lambda and Google Cloud Functions automatically handle scaling and execution based on demand, making it easier and more cost-effective to run event-driven applications.

3 **How does Google Kubernetes Engine (GKE) assist in managing containerized applications?**

Answer: Google Kubernetes Engine (GKE) helps manage containerized applications by automating tasks like scaling, load balancing, and recovery. It simplifies the process of running and managing containers in the cloud.

4 **What is the difference between Google App Engine and AWS Elastic Beanstalk?**

Answer: Both are Platform-as-a-Service (PaaS) platforms. Google App Engine automatically handles infrastructure and scaling, while AWS Elastic Beanstalk offers more customization and supports multiple languages and frameworks. Both help simplify app deployment.

5 **How does AWS Free Tier help beginners with cloud computing?**

Answer: AWS Free Tier gives free access to a limited set of AWS services, allowing beginners to explore and learn cloud computing without any charges. It includes services such as EC2, S3, and Lambda for testing and experimenting.

6 **What is the role of Azure DevOps in cloud computing?**

Answer: Azure DevOps helps developers automate the software development process, including tasks such as coding, testing, and deployment. It integrates with Microsoft Azure for easy management of cloud applications.

7 **What is the function of Amazon S3 in cloud computing?**

Answer: Amazon S3 is a storage service that lets users store and retrieve large amounts of data. It's commonly used for backups, archiving, and hosting static content like images or websites.

8 **What is Terraform, and how is it used in cloud computing?**

Answer: Terraform is a tool used to manage cloud infrastructure using code. It allows developers to define and provision cloud resources (like servers, networks, and storage) in a repeatable and automated way.

9 **What is AWS Elastic Beanstalk, and how does it simplify app deployment?**

Answer: AWS Elastic Beanstalk is a Platform-as-a-Service (PaaS) that makes it easy to deploy, manage, and scale web applications. You just upload your code, and Elastic Beanstalk handles the rest, including server setup, load balancing, and scaling.

10 **What is the primary purpose of Google Cloud Functions in cloud computing?**

Answer: Google Cloud Functions is a serverless platform that allows you run small pieces of code in response to events, like a file upload or an HTTP request, without managing servers. It's ideal for event-driven apps.

11 **How does Microsoft Azure Cloud Shell help developers?**

Answer: Azure Cloud Shell is an online command-line interface that allows developers manage Azure resources directly from their browser. It comes pre-configured with tools and a storage account, making it easier to manage cloud resources without installing anything locally.

12 **What is the advantage of using a cloud platform for managing databases instead of on-premises solutions?**

Answer: Cloud platforms such as AWS RDS, Google Cloud SQL, and Azure SQL Database offer scalable, managed databases that automatically handle tasks such as backups, patching, and scaling. This reduces the need for manual management and makes databases more reliable and cost-effective.

13 **What is the purpose of the Google Cloud Console, and how do you use it for managing cloud resources?**

Answer: The Google Cloud Console is a web interface for managing Google Cloud services. It allows you create and configure resources such as virtual machines, databases, and storage. You can monitor usage, configure permissions, and set up billing.

14 **How does Docker integrate with cloud platforms for application deployment?**

Answer: Docker allows developers package applications and their dependencies into containers, which can be easily deployed across different cloud platforms such as AWS, Google Cloud, or Azure. Containers ensure that the application runs consistently in any environment.

15 **What is the role of a cloud load balancer, and how does it improve application performance?**

Answer: A cloud load balancer distributes incoming traffic across multiple servers to ensure no single server gets overwhelmed. This improves the performance and availability of applications, especially during high traffic periods.

16 **What are the main benefits of using cloud platforms such as AWS, Google Cloud, and Azure for businesses?**

Answer: Cloud platforms offer benefits such as scalability (resources grow with demand), cost efficiency (pay only for what you use), flexibility (access services globally), and high availability (services run across multiple data centers).

17 **How does Google Firebase help developers build mobile and web applications?**

Answer: Google Firebase provides a suite of backend services, including real-time databases, authentication, and file storage. It simplifies building apps by handling server-side infrastructure, allowing developers to focus on coding the app itself.

18 **What is the significance of using Infrastructure-as-Code (IaC) tools like Terraform in cloud computing?**

Answer: IaC tools like Terraform allow developers to define cloud infrastructure using code, making it easier to automate the creation, configuration, and management of resources. This ensures consistency, reduces errors, and speeds up deployment.

19 **What is the purpose of Azure Functions, and when would you use it in cloud-based applications?**

Answer: Azure Functions is a serverless computing service that lets you run code in response to events without managing the underlying server. It's useful for tasks like automating workflows, processing data, or handling HTTP requests.

20 **What is the difference between object storage and block storage in cloud computing?**

Answer: Object storage (like AWS S3) stores data as objects (files) with metadata, making it ideal for unstructured data such as images and videos. Block storage (like AWS EBS) stores data in fixed-size blocks, suitable for structured data and applications that require fast read/write operations.

REFERENCES

1. https://www.aws.training/
2. https://www.microsoft.com/handsonlabs
3. https://cloud.google.com/training/free-labs
4. https://www.digitalocean.com/
5. https://www.heroku.com/training-and-education
6. https://www.ibm.com/training/cloud
7. https://www.oracle.com/in/education/training/oracle.cloud-infrastructure/

11 Major Research Fields

11.1 INTRODUCTION

A crucial topic of research in cloud computing is cloud security. Major cloud security-based research areas include:

- The field of cloud access control is focused on the development of access control techniques for cloud computing systems, including the management of user identities, authentication, authorization, and access restrictions.
- The field of cloud data protection focuses on developing technology for data encryption, backup and recovery, and secure data deletion in cloud computing environments.
- The major focus of the "cloud threat detection" topic is the development of techniques to identify security threats in cloud computing environments, such as malware detection, intrusion detection, and threat intelligence.
- The major focus of the field of cloud network security is the development of secure network architectures for cloud computing environments, including network segmentation, firewalls, and intrusion prevention systems.
- Cloud compliance and auditing is concerned with ensuring that cloud computing environments comply with industry standards and laws, such as HIPAA and PCI DSS compliance frameworks, as well as data privacy laws and policies.
- The focus of the area of cloud incident response is on developing incident response techniques and processes to handle security challenges in cloud computing systems, including incident detection, containment, eradication, and recovery.

These are only a few illustrations of the main cloud computing security-based study areas. New study topics are expected to appear as the field develops and new security risks appear.

11.2 ARCHITECTURAL-LEVEL SECURITY

Architectural-level security in cloud computing is crucial due to the shared responsibility model between cloud providers and customers. How architectural-level security applies specifically in the context of cloud computing is illustrated below [1–3]:

DOI: 10.1201/9781003510772-11

1. **Shared Responsibility**: Cloud providers (such as AWS, Azure, Google Cloud) are responsible for securing the infrastructure that runs the cloud services, while customers are responsible for securing their data, applications, and identities within the cloud.
2. **Identity and Access Management (IAM)**: Implementing robust IAM policies to manage user identities, roles, and permissions within the cloud environment. This includes principles of least privilege and ensuring only authorized entities have access to resources.
3. **Network Security**: Designing secure network architectures using Virtual Private Clouds (VPCs), network access control lists (ACLs), and security groups to control traffic and isolate resources. Implementing encryption (both in transit and at rest) to protect data moving within and outside the cloud.
4. **Data Protection**: Applying encryption and tokenization techniques to protect sensitive data stored in the cloud. Implementing data loss prevention (DLP) policies to prevent unauthorized access and leakage of sensitive information.
5. **Application Security**: Integrating security into the application architecture by following secure coding practices, conducting regular security testing (such as static and dynamic code analysis, penetration testing), and leveraging web application firewalls (WAFs) to protect against common attacks.
6. **Resilience and Disaster Recovery**: Architecting for resilience by leveraging redundancy, failover mechanisms, and backup strategies. Implementing disaster recovery plans to ensure business continuity in case of disruptions or security incidents.
7. **Logging and Monitoring**: Implementing logging and monitoring mechanisms to track and analyze activities within the cloud environment. Utilizing Security Information and Event Management (SIEM) tools to detect and respond to security incidents in real time.
8. **Compliance and Auditing**: Ensuring compliance with regulatory requirements and industry standards (such as GDPR, PCI-DSS) through proper configuration and auditing of cloud resources. Conducting regular security assessments and audits to validate adherence to security policies.
9. **Incident Response**: Establishing incident response processes and procedures to promptly respond to and mitigate security breaches or incidents. This includes defining roles and responsibilities, communication channels, and recovery steps.
10. **Cloud Security Best Practices**: Staying updated with cloud security best practices, guidelines, and frameworks provided by cloud service providers and industry experts. Continuously evaluating and improving security posture based on evolving threats and vulnerabilities.

Figure 11.1 highlights these concepts and their roles very well, and urges to ensure the right orchestration.

Architectural-level security in cloud computing involves a holistic approach to designing and implementing security measures across various layers of the cloud infrastructure and applications. It ensures that cloud deployments are resilient, compliant, and secure against a wide range of cyber threats and risks.

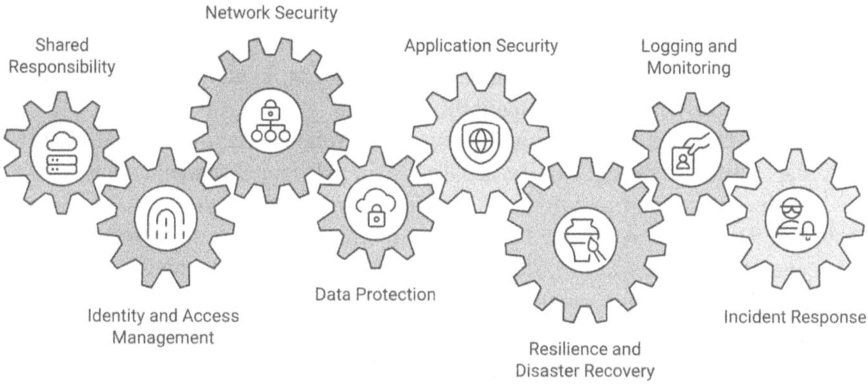

FIGURE 11.1 Achieving architectural-level cloud security.

11.2.1 Research Challenges and Issues

Research challenges and issues at the architecture level in cloud computing encompass a wide range of topics that researchers and practitioners are actively exploring. These challenges often arise due to the dynamic and complex nature of cloud environments, the need for scalability, reliability, and security. Major key research challenges and issues are given below:

1. **Scalability and Elasticity**: Designing architectures that can efficiently scale resources based on demand while maintaining performance and cost-effectiveness. This includes research into auto-scaling algorithms, resource allocation strategies, and load balancing techniques.
2. **Multi-tenancy and Isolation**: Ensuring secure isolation between tenants sharing the same physical infrastructure to prevent unauthorized access and leakage of data. Research focuses on virtualization techniques, containerization, and isolation mechanisms at the hypervisor and network levels.
3. **Performance Optimization**: Optimizing architecture to minimize latency and maximize throughput for applications running in the cloud. This involves research in distributed systems, data locality, caching strategies, and efficient data processing techniques.
4. **Security and Privacy**: Addressing security challenges such as data breaches, insider threats, and compliance with regulatory requirements (e.g., GDPR, HIPAA). Research areas include encryption mechanisms, access control models, secure communication protocols, and identity management.
5. **Reliability and Availability**: Ensuring high availability and fault tolerance in cloud architectures to minimize downtime and service disruptions. Research focuses on fault tolerance mechanisms, redundancy strategies, and disaster recovery solutions.
6. **Cost Management**: Optimizing cost in cloud architectures by balancing resource provisioning with actual usage, identifying cost-effective deployment strategies, and researching pricing models offered by cloud providers.

7. **Interoperability and Portability**: Facilitating seamless integration and migration of applications and data across different cloud platforms and providers. Research includes standardization efforts, container orchestration (e.g., Kubernetes), and compatibility testing.
8. **Edge and Fog Computing**: Investigating architectures that extend cloud capabilities to the edge of the network (e.g., IoT devices, mobile edge computing) to support real-time and latency-sensitive applications.
9. **Big Data and Analytics**: Designing architectures that support scalable and efficient processing, storage, and analysis of large volumes of data in the cloud. Research includes distributed data processing frameworks (e.g., Hadoop, Spark), data streaming, and real-time analytics.
10. **Ethical and Legal Issues**: Exploring the ethical implications of cloud computing, such as data sovereignty, vendor lock-in, and the impact on jobs and economies. Research also addresses legal aspects related to data protection laws, intellectual property rights, and liability.

Addressing these research challenges requires collaboration between academia, industry, and policymakers to develop innovative solutions that enhance the scalability, security, performance, and reliability of cloud computing architectures while ensuring compliance with regulatory requirements and ethical considerations.

11.2.2 Future Research Directions

Future research directions in architectural-level cloud security are crucial as cloud computing continues to evolve and face new challenges. Several promising areas for future research are illustrated below:

1. **Zero Trust Architectures**: Developing and refining architectural frameworks that implement zero trust principles across cloud environments. This includes continuous verification of identities, strict access controls, and segmentation of network traffic to mitigate insider threats and lateral movement.
2. **AI and Machine Learning for Security**: Exploring the application of artificial intelligence (AI) and machine learning (ML) techniques to enhance cloud security architectures. This includes anomaly detection, predictive analytics for threat intelligence, and automated response to security incidents.
3. **Secure Cloud-Native Architectures**: Researching architectural patterns and best practices for designing secure cloud-native applications and microservices. This involves integrating security into DevOps processes, leveraging containerization (e.g., Docker, Kubernetes) securely, and implementing service mesh technologies.
4. **Homomorphic Encryption and Privacy-Preserving Techniques**: Advancing research in homomorphic encryption and other privacy-preserving techniques that allow computations on encrypted data without decrypting it.

This supports secure data processing and analytics in cloud environments while protecting sensitive information.

5. **Blockchain and Distributed Ledger Technologies**: Investigating the use of blockchain and distributed ledger technologies to enhance the security, transparency, and auditability of cloud architectures. Research includes secure decentralized storage, identity management, and smart contract security.
6. **Quantum-Safe Cryptography**: Developing quantum-resistant cryptographic algorithms and protocols to protect cloud data and communications from future quantum computing threats.
7. **Threat Intelligence and Automated Response**: Enhancing architectural designs with real-time threat intelligence feeds and automated response mechanisms. This includes integrating threat detection systems with cloud orchestration platforms to enable proactive security measures.
8. **Resilient Cloud Architectures**: Researching resilient cloud architectures that can withstand sophisticated cyberattacks, natural disasters, and other disruptions. This involves designing for continuous operation, rapid recovery, and adaptive security controls.
9. **Regulatory Compliance and Assurance**: Addressing architectural challenges related to regulatory compliance (e.g., GDPR, PCI-DSS) and assurance frameworks. Research focuses on automated compliance auditing, secure data handling practices, and accountability in multi-cloud environments.
10. **Human Factors and Usability**: Investigating the impact of human factors, usability, and cognitive biases on the effectiveness of cloud security architectures. This includes designing intuitive security interfaces, user-centric access controls, and security awareness training programs.
11. **Integration of Security into DevOps**: Researching methodologies and tools to seamlessly integrate security practices (DevSecOps) into the entire software development lifecycle (SDLC) of cloud applications. This includes automated security testing, continuous security monitoring, and secure configuration management.
12. **Economic and Business Aspects**: Exploring the economic implications of cloud security architectures, such as cost-effectiveness of security investments, risk management strategies, and business continuity planning.

Future research in these areas will contribute to advancing the state-of-the-art in architectural-level cloud security, ensuring that cloud computing remains a secure and trusted platform for hosting critical applications and services.

11.3 DATA-LEVEL SECURITY

Data-level security in cloud computing refers to the measures and practices implemented to protect data stored, processed, and transmitted within cloud environments. Figure 11.2 highlights different cloud data security measures and their roles in achieving the overall data-level security [4–6].

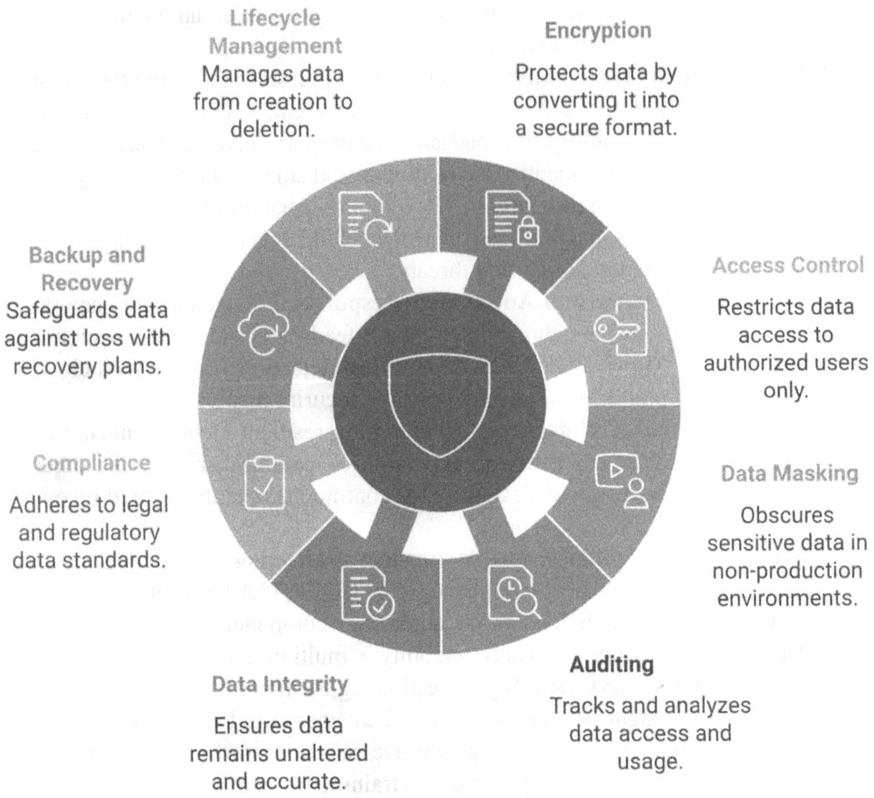
Lifecycle Management
Manages data from creation to deletion.
Encryption
Protects data by converting it into a secure format.
Backup and Recovery
Safeguards data against loss with recovery plans.
Access Control
Restricts data access to authorized users only.
Compliance
Adheres to legal and regulatory data standards.
Data Masking
Obscures sensitive data in non-production environments.
Auditing
Tracks and analyzes data access and usage.
Data Integrity
Ensures data remains unaltered and accurate.

FIGURE 11.2 Different cloud data security measures.

Given the shared responsibility model between cloud providers and customers, ensuring robust data security involves addressing various aspects throughout the data lifecycle:

1. **Encryption**: Encrypting data both at rest (stored data) and in transit (data being transmitted) is fundamental to protecting sensitive information from unauthorized access. Cloud providers typically offer encryption mechanisms and key management services to secure data storage and communication channels.
2. **Access Control**: Implementing granular access control policies to ensure that only authorized users and applications have access to specific data. This involves using identity and access management (IAM) tools to manage user permissions, roles, and privileges.
3. **Data Masking and Tokenization**: Employing techniques such as data masking to obfuscate sensitive data in non-production environments and tokenization to replace sensitive data with non-sensitive equivalents (tokens) while maintaining referential integrity.
4. **Auditing and Monitoring**: Establishing robust logging and monitoring mechanisms to track access to sensitive data and detect suspicious activities

or unauthorized attempts to access data. Security information and event management (SIEM) tools are often used for real-time monitoring and analysis.

5. **Data Integrity**: Ensuring the integrity of data by implementing measures to detect and prevent unauthorized modifications or tampering. Techniques such as checksums and digital signatures can be used to verify data integrity.
6. **Data Residency and Compliance**: Addressing legal and regulatory requirements regarding data residency and compliance (e.g., GDPR, HIPAA). Cloud providers may offer capabilities to specify where data is stored geographically and provide compliance certifications to meet regulatory standards.
7. **Backup and Recovery**: Implementing robust backup and disaster recovery strategies to protect against data loss due to accidental deletion, hardware failures, or cyberattacks. This includes regular backups, data replication across multiple geographical regions, and testing of recovery procedures.
8. **Data Lifecycle Management**: Managing the entire lifecycle of data from creation to deletion, including secure archival and deletion practices. This involves defining retention policies, data classification based on sensitivity, and secure disposal of data no longer needed.
9. **Third-Party Services and APIs**: Ensuring that data shared with third-party services or accessed via APIs is protected according to the same security standards applied within the cloud environment. This includes verifying the security practices and certifications of third-party providers.
10. **Employee Training and Awareness**: Educating employees about data security best practices, the importance of protecting sensitive information, and recognizing potential security threats such as phishing attacks or social engineering attempts.

Data-level security in cloud computing requires a gradual approach, combining technical controls, security policies, and ongoing monitoring to safeguard sensitive data against evolving threats and vulnerabilities. It is essential for organizations to collaborate closely with cloud providers, implement robust security practices, and stay informed about emerging security trends and technologies.

11.3.1 Research Challenges and Issues

Research challenges and issues at the data level in cloud computing encompass a variety of complex topics that researchers are actively exploring to enhance security, privacy, and reliability of data stored and processed in cloud environments. Some key challenges and issues are as follows:

1. **Data Privacy and Confidentiality**: Ensuring that sensitive data is protected against unauthorized access, disclosure, and leakage. Challenges include effective encryption techniques, secure key management, and policies for data anonymization or pseudonymization.
2. **Data Access Control**: Managing access permissions to data stored in the cloud to prevent unauthorized users or applications from accessing sensitive

information. Challenges include fine-grained access control policies, identity and access management (IAM) integration, and enforcing access controls across multi-cloud environments.

3. **Data Integrity and Trustworthiness**: Ensuring that data remains accurate, consistent, and reliable throughout its lifecycle in the cloud. Challenges include detecting and preventing data tampering, maintaining data integrity during transfer and storage, and verifying data authenticity.
4. **Data Residency and Compliance**: Addressing legal and regulatory requirements regarding where data can be stored geographically (data residency) and ensuring compliance with industry-specific regulations (e.g., GDPR, HIPAA). Challenges include navigating international data protection laws, data sovereignty concerns, and ensuring cloud providers meet compliance standards.
5. **Data Portability and Interoperability**: Facilitating seamless movement of data between different cloud providers or between on-premises and cloud environments. Challenges include data format compatibility, API standardization, and minimizing vendor lock-in while maintaining data security and integrity.
6. **Big Data Security**: Securing large volumes of diverse data (structured and unstructured) used in big data analytics within cloud environments. Challenges include protecting data during processing, ensuring secure data sharing among multiple users or applications, and addressing privacy concerns in data analytics.
7. **Data Governance and Lifecycle Management**: Establishing policies and procedures for managing data throughout its lifecycle, from creation and storage to archiving and deletion. Challenges include defining data retention policies, managing data versioning, and ensuring secure data disposal practices.
8. **Data Recovery and Disaster Resilience**: Ensuring timely recovery of data in the event of data loss, accidental deletion, or service disruptions. Challenges include implementing reliable backup strategies, data replication across geographical regions, and testing disaster recovery plans in cloud environments.
9. **Security in Data Sharing and Collaboration**: Enabling secure data sharing and collaboration among multiple users, organizations, or applications in cloud environments. Challenges include secure data sharing protocols, ensuring data confidentiality and integrity during sharing, and managing access permissions dynamically.
10. **Emerging Technologies and Risks**: Addressing security implications of emerging technologies such as Internet of Things (IoT), edge computing, and AI/ML-driven data analytics in cloud environments. Challenges include securing IoT data streams, protecting AI models and training data, and mitigating risks associated with new attack vectors.
11. **Ethical Considerations**: Exploring ethical implications of data usage, such as ensuring fairness and transparency in data-driven decision-making, respecting user privacy preferences, and addressing biases in data analytics algorithms.

12. **Quantum-Safe Cryptography**: Developing and deploying cryptographic algorithms and protocols that are resistant to quantum computing threats, ensuring long-term security of data stored and transmitted in cloud environments.

Addressing these research challenges requires interdisciplinary collaboration between computer scientists, cybersecurity experts, legal scholars, and policymakers. Research efforts aim to develop innovative solutions, best practices, and standards to strengthen data security, privacy, and governance in cloud computing, thereby fostering trust and reliability in cloud-based services.

11.3.2 Future Research Directions

Future research directions in cloud data-level security are critical as organizations increasingly rely on cloud services to store, process, and analyze vast amounts of data. Several promising research directions are discussed below:

1. **Enhanced Encryption Techniques**: Developing more efficient and robust encryption techniques to protect data both at rest and in transit. Future research may focus on advancing homomorphic encryption, searchable encryption, and quantum-resistant cryptography to address evolving threats.
2. **Secure Multi-tenancy**: Investigating techniques to strengthen isolation and security between tenants sharing the same cloud infrastructure. Research may explore new approaches to virtualization, containerization, and network segmentation to mitigate risks of cross-tenant attacks.
3. **Privacy-Preserving Data Analytics**: Advancing techniques for performing data analytics while preserving the privacy of sensitive information. Research may focus on differential privacy, secure multiparty computation (MPC), and federated learning approaches to enable collaborative data analysis without compromising privacy.
4. **Dynamic Access Control**: Developing adaptive access control mechanisms that can dynamically adjust permissions based on contextual factors such as user behavior, location, and device status. Future research may explore machine learning and AI-driven approaches for context-aware access control.
5. **Data Integrity Assurance**: Enhancing methods for ensuring data integrity throughout its lifecycle in the cloud. Research directions may include blockchain-based solutions for distributed data integrity verification, proactive detection of data tampering, and secure logging mechanisms.
6. **Secure Data Sharing**: Developing secure protocols and frameworks for sharing data between different organizations or across cloud environments. Future research may focus on attribute-based encryption (ABE), secure data exchange formats, and policy-driven data sharing mechanisms.
7. **Resilient Data Storage and Backup**: Researching techniques for improving resilience and reliability of data storage and backup in cloud environments. This may include fault-tolerant storage architectures, geo-redundant data replication strategies, and automated recovery mechanisms.

8. **Behavioral Analytics and Threat Detection**: Advancing research in behavioral analytics and anomaly detection techniques to identify suspicious activities and potential data breaches in real time. Future directions may involve leveraging AI/ML models trained on large-scale datasets to detect complex attack patterns.
9. **Compliance and Governance**: Addressing challenges related to regulatory compliance and governance in cloud data security. Future research may explore automated compliance auditing, secure data provenance tracking, and transparency mechanisms to demonstrate adherence to data protection laws.
10. **Human Factors and Usability**: Investigating the impact of human factors on cloud data security, such as user awareness, training effectiveness, and the usability of security controls. Research may focus on designing intuitive security interfaces, enhancing user-centric security policies, and understanding user behaviors that influence data security.
11. **Quantum-Safe Security**: Developing post-quantum cryptography solutions to protect cloud data against future quantum computing threats. Future research may explore algorithms resistant to quantum attacks and transition strategies for deploying quantum-safe encryption in cloud environments.
12. **Ethical and Societal Implications**: Exploring the ethical considerations and societal impacts of cloud data security, such as data ownership, transparency in data processing, and fairness in algorithmic decision-making. Future research may address biases in AI models, promote ethical data governance frameworks, and engage stakeholders in discussions on responsible data use.

These research directions aim to address current challenges and anticipate future trends in cloud data security, ensuring that organizations can securely leverage cloud computing while maintaining the confidentiality, integrity, and availability of their data assets.

11.4 APPLICATION-LEVEL SECURITY

Application-level security in cloud computing focuses on securing the software applications deployed in cloud environments to protect against various threats and vulnerabilities. The detailed key aspects and considerations for application-level security in the cloud are as follows:

1. **Secure Development Practices**: Promoting secure coding practices throughout the software development lifecycle (SDLC) to mitigate common vulnerabilities such as injection flaws (SQL injection, XSS), insecure deserialization, and improper authentication.
2. **Authentication and Authorization**: Implementing robust authentication mechanisms (e.g., multi-factor authentication) to verify the identity of users and applications accessing cloud services. Ensuring fine-grained authorization controls to enforce least privilege access based on roles and permissions.

3. **Data Input Validation**: Validating and sanitizing all inputs received by applications to prevent injection attacks and ensure that only expected data formats and values are processed.
4. **Session Management**: Implementing secure session management practices to protect session tokens, prevent session hijacking, and enforce session expiration policies.
5. **Secure APIs and Interfaces**: Securing APIs and web interfaces used by applications to interact with other components or external services. This includes implementing strong authentication, input validation, rate limiting, and encryption of sensitive data in transit.
6. **Encryption**: Utilizing encryption techniques (both in transit and at rest) to protect sensitive data handled by applications. This includes data encryption within the application code and leveraging cloud provider encryption services for data storage.
7. **Logging and Monitoring**: Implementing logging mechanisms to record application activities and security events. Monitoring these logs in real time to detect anomalies, suspicious activities, or potential security incidents.
8. **Vulnerability Management**: Regularly scanning applications for vulnerabilities using automated tools and conducting manual penetration testing to identify and remediate security weaknesses.
9. **Container Security**: Securing containerized applications (e.g., Docker containers) by implementing best practices such as image signing, runtime protection, and isolation mechanisms provided by container orchestration platforms like Kubernetes.
10. **Secure Deployment Practices**: Implementing secure deployment pipelines (DevSecOps) to automate security checks and ensure that applications are deployed securely without introducing vulnerabilities.
11. **Patch Management**: Maintaining up-to-date patches and security updates for application dependencies and libraries to address known vulnerabilities and reduce the attack surface.
12. **Incident Response and Forensics**: Developing and testing incident response plans to quickly detect, respond to, and recover from security breaches or incidents affecting cloud-hosted applications. Conducting forensic analysis to understand the root cause and prevent future occurrences.
13. **Compliance and Audit**: Ensuring that applications adhere to regulatory requirements (e.g., GDPR, PCI-DSS) and industry standards. Conducting regular security audits and assessments to validate compliance and identify areas for improvement.

Figure 11.3 highlights some common cloud application-level measures to strengthen the cloud security through comprehensive application protection.

Application-level security in cloud computing requires a comprehensive approach that integrates security into every aspect of application development, deployment, and operations. By implementing these practices and staying informed about emerging threats and best practices, organizations can enhance the security posture of their cloud-hosted applications and protect sensitive data from unauthorized access and exploitation.

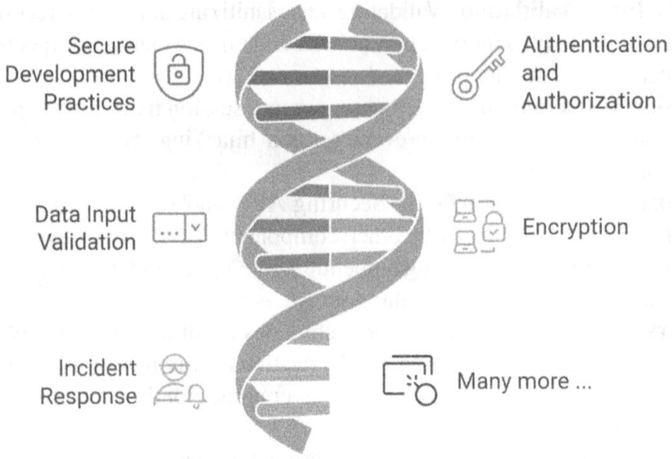

FIGURE 11.3 General cloud application security measures.

11.4.1 Research Challenges and Issues

Research challenges and issues in application-level security in cloud computing involve addressing complex threats and vulnerabilities specific to software applications deployed in cloud environments. The major key research challenges and issues are as follows:

1. **Securing Microservices and Serverless Architectures**: As organizations adopt microservices and serverless architectures in the cloud, ensuring the security of individual services and function endpoints becomes critical. Challenges include securing communication between microservices, managing authentication and authorization in a decentralized environment, and ensuring isolation and resource protection in serverless computing.
2. **API Security**: Securing APIs used by cloud applications to interact with other services and applications. Challenges include protecting against API abuse (e.g., API spoofing, parameter manipulation), implementing strong authentication and authorization mechanisms for API endpoints, and ensuring API availability and reliability.
3. **Container Security**: Securing containerized applications (e.g., Docker containers) and container orchestration platforms (e.g., Kubernetes). Challenges include securing container images, implementing runtime security controls (e.g., container isolation, network segmentation), and ensuring secure configuration of container orchestration frameworks.
4. **Authentication and Authorization Challenges**: Researching advanced authentication mechanisms (e.g., biometrics, adaptive authentication) that are resilient to cloud-specific threats such as distributed denial-of-service (DDoS) attacks, credential stuffing, and identity theft. Addressing challenges in implementing fine-grained authorization policies across distributed and dynamic cloud environments.

5. **Data Protection**: Researching techniques to ensure data confidentiality, integrity, and availability within cloud applications. Challenges include securing data at rest and in transit, implementing data masking and tokenization, and addressing data leakage risks through APIs or application vulnerabilities.
6. **DevSecOps Integration**: Integrating security practices into DevOps processes to enable continuous security testing, vulnerability assessment, and secure deployment of cloud applications. Challenges include automating security checks in CI/CD pipelines, integrating security tools with cloud-native development platforms, and promoting security awareness and collaboration among development, operations, and security teams.
7. **Threat Detection and Response**: Researching proactive and reactive approaches to detect and respond to security incidents in cloud applications. Challenges include developing machine learning and AI-driven techniques for anomaly detection, real-time monitoring of application behaviors, and integrating threat intelligence feeds into cloud security operations.
8. **Compliance and Governance**: Researching strategies and technologies to ensure cloud applications comply with regulatory requirements (e.g., GDPR, PCI-DSS) and industry standards. Challenges include automating compliance auditing, managing data sovereignty concerns in multi-cloud environments, and addressing legal implications of cloud-based application security breaches.
9. **Secure Software Development Lifecycle (SDLC)**: Researching secure SDLC practices tailored for cloud environments. Challenges include educating developers on secure coding practices specific to cloud services, integrating security testing tools into cloud development platforms, and ensuring traceability of security requirements throughout the SDLC phases.
10. **Resilience and Business Continuity**: Researching strategies to enhance resilience and ensure business continuity of cloud applications in the face of cyberattacks, natural disasters, and operational failures. Challenges include implementing disaster recovery plans for cloud services, testing failover mechanisms, and minimizing downtime during incident response and recovery processes.

Addressing these research challenges requires collaboration between academia, industry practitioners, and cloud service providers to develop innovative solutions, frameworks, and best practices for securing cloud-based applications effectively. By focusing on these areas, researchers can contribute to advancing the state-of-the-art in application-level security and enhancing the overall security posture of cloud computing environments.

11.4.2 Future Research Directions

Future research directions in cloud application-level security will focus on advancing capabilities to protect software applications deployed in cloud environments against emerging threats and evolving attack vectors. Several promising directions for future research are provided below:

1. **Security of Serverless Architectures**: Serverless computing has gained popularity for its scalability and cost-effectiveness, but it introduces new security challenges. Future research will focus on securing serverless functions, ensuring isolation between functions, managing permissions and access controls effectively, and detecting and mitigating serverless-specific vulnerabilities.
2. **Advanced Authentication Mechanisms**: Research will continue to explore and develop advanced authentication mechanisms beyond traditional username/password authentication. This includes biometric authentication, adaptive authentication that adjusts based on user behavior and context, and continuous authentication methods to continuously verify user identities.
3. **API Security**: Given the critical role of APIs in cloud applications, future research will focus on securing APIs against a wide range of threats such as API abuse, injection attacks, and improper input validation. Techniques will include API encryption, rate limiting, API gateway security, and monitoring API traffic for anomalies.
4. **Securing Microservices**: With the rise of microservices architectures, research will explore security challenges such as securing communication between microservices, managing authentication and authorization across distributed services, and ensuring resilience against microservices-specific attacks such as service mesh vulnerabilities.
5. **Machine Learning for Security**: Advancing the use of machine learning and AI techniques to enhance cloud application security. This includes developing ML models for anomaly detection in application behavior, predicting and mitigating security threats, and automating incident response and remediation.
6. **Secure DevOps (DevSecOps)**: Further integrating security into the DevOps pipeline to enable continuous security testing, vulnerability assessment, and secure deployment practices. Future research will focus on automating security checks, integrating security tools with CI/CD pipelines, and fostering collaboration between development, operations, and security teams.
7. **Data-Centric Security**: Research will continue to advance techniques for protecting data within cloud applications. This includes enhancing data encryption methods (e.g., homomorphic encryption, attribute-based encryption), improving data access controls and auditing mechanisms, and addressing data privacy challenges in distributed cloud environments.
8. **Blockchain for Application Security**: Exploring the potential of blockchain technology to enhance application security in the cloud. Research directions include using blockchain for secure identity management, ensuring data integrity and provenance, and developing decentralized security mechanisms for cloud applications.
9. **Threat Intelligence and Response**: Research will focus on leveraging threat intelligence feeds and security analytics to enhance cloud application security. This includes real-time monitoring of application logs and behaviors, proactive threat hunting, and developing automated response mechanisms to mitigate security incidents swiftly.

10. **Ethical and Legal Implications**: Addressing ethical considerations and legal implications of cloud application security, such as ensuring fairness and transparency in AI-driven security solutions, respecting user privacy rights, and complying with data protection regulations (e.g., GDPR, CCPA).
11. **Quantum-Safe Security**: Developing and deploying quantum-resistant cryptographic algorithms and protocols to protect cloud applications against future quantum computing threats.
12. **Resilience and Business Continuity**: Researching strategies to enhance resilience and ensure business continuity of cloud applications in the face of cyberattacks, natural disasters, and operational failures. This includes developing adaptive resilience frameworks, testing disaster recovery plans, and minimizing downtime during incident response and recovery processes.

By focusing on these research directions, academia, industry, and cloud service providers can collaboratively advance the state-of-the-art in cloud application-level security, mitigate emerging threats, and build more secure and resilient cloud computing ecosystems.

11.5 AUDIT-LEVEL SECURITY

Audit-level security in cloud computing refers to the practices and mechanisms used to ensure that cloud environments are continuously monitored, evaluated, and audited for compliance with security policies, regulatory requirements, and best practices. Figure 11.4 highlights some general audit-level measures to improvise the cloud Security.

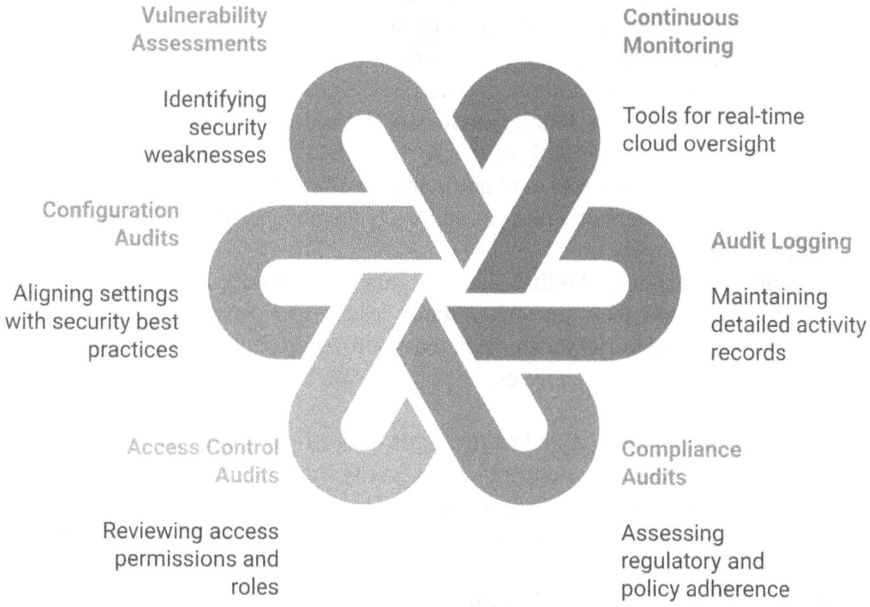

FIGURE 11.4 General cloud security audit measures.

Numerous key aspects of audit-level security in cloud computing are illustrated below [7–10]:

1. **Continuous Monitoring**: Implementing tools and processes to monitor cloud infrastructure, services, and applications in real time. This includes monitoring network traffic, access logs, configuration changes, and system events to detect anomalies and potential security incidents.
2. **Audit Logging**: Generating and maintaining comprehensive audit logs that capture detailed information about activities and events within the cloud environment. Audit logs provide a record of user actions, access attempts, data modifications, and system operations, which are essential for forensic analysis and compliance audits.
3. **Compliance Audits**: Conducting regular audits to assess compliance with regulatory requirements (e.g., GDPR, HIPAA), industry standards (e.g., PCI-DSS), and organizational security policies. Audits may involve reviewing security controls, assessing risk management practices, and verifying adherence to audit trails and documentation requirements.
4. **Access Control Audits**: Reviewing and auditing access control mechanisms to ensure that access permissions are appropriately configured and enforced. This includes auditing user accounts, roles, privileges, and access rights across cloud services and resources.
5. **Configuration Audits**: Auditing cloud configuration settings and parameters to ensure they align with security best practices and organizational policies. This includes auditing cloud provider configurations, network security settings, encryption settings, and resource provisioning.
6. **Vulnerability Assessments**: Conducting regular vulnerability assessments and audits to identify security weaknesses and potential exposures in cloud infrastructure, applications, and services. Audits may involve vulnerability scanning, penetration testing, and risk assessment exercises.
7. **Identity and Access Management (IAM) Audits**: Reviewing IAM policies, practices, and controls to ensure they are effectively managing identities, authenticating users, and enforcing least privilege access. IAM audits help identify unauthorized access attempts, inactive accounts, and configuration errors.
8. **Incident Response Audits**: Auditing incident response plans and procedures to ensure they are well-defined, tested, and capable of effectively responding to security incidents in the cloud. Audits may involve reviewing incident detection capabilities, response times, containment measures, and recovery processes.
9. **Third-Party Audits**: Conducting audits of third-party vendors and service providers to verify their adherence to security standards, contractual obligations, and data protection requirements. Third-party audits ensure that outsourced services and data handling practices meet organizational security expectations.
10. **Audit Trail Integrity**: Ensuring the integrity and reliability of audit trails to prevent tampering or unauthorized modifications. This includes

implementing secure logging mechanisms, storing audit logs in tamper-evident formats, and restricting access to audit trail repositories.
11. **Automated Auditing and Reporting**: Implementing automated auditing tools and systems that continuously monitor and analyze cloud environments. Automated auditing facilitates real-time alerting, trend analysis, and generation of audit reports for stakeholders and regulatory authorities.
12. **Training and Awareness**: Providing training and raising awareness among cloud administrators, users, and stakeholders about audit-level security practices, responsibilities, and the importance of maintaining security controls.

Audit-level security in cloud computing is essential for maintaining transparency, accountability, and trust in cloud services. By implementing rigorous auditing practices and continuously improving security controls, organizations can effectively mitigate risks, comply with regulatory requirements, and protect sensitive data and resources in the cloud.

11.5.1 Research Challenges and Issues

Research challenges and issues in audit-level security in cloud computing encompass a range of complexities and considerations that researchers and practitioners need to address to ensure effective auditing and compliance in cloud environments. Here are some key challenges and issues:

1. **Audit Trail Integrity and Trustworthiness**: Ensuring the integrity and reliability of audit logs and trails in cloud environments is challenging due to potential risks such as tampering, deletion, or unauthorized access. Research is needed to develop secure logging mechanisms, tamper-evident storage solutions, and cryptographic techniques to protect audit trail integrity.
2. **Scalability and Granularity**: Cloud environments are highly dynamic and scalable, making it challenging to capture and analyze audit logs at scale. Research is needed to develop scalable auditing solutions that can handle large volumes of data generated by diverse cloud services and resources. Additionally, ensuring granularity in audit logs to capture detailed information without overwhelming storage and processing capabilities is crucial.
3. **Complexity of Multi-Cloud and Hybrid Cloud Environments**: Organizations increasingly adopt multi-cloud and hybrid cloud architectures, which involve integrating services from multiple providers and on-premises infrastructure. Auditing across these heterogeneous environments poses challenges in maintaining consistency, interoperability of audit mechanisms, and ensuring comprehensive coverage of security controls.
4. **Privacy-Preserving Auditing**: Balancing the need for comprehensive auditing with privacy requirements, especially in regulated industries (e.g., healthcare, finance), where sensitive data must be protected. Research is needed on techniques such as differential privacy, secure multi-party computation (MPC), and anonymization methods to enable effective auditing without compromising data privacy.

5. **Real-Time Monitoring and Alerting**: Traditional audit practices often rely on periodic audits, which may not be sufficient to detect and respond to security incidents in real time. Research is needed to develop real-time monitoring and alerting systems that can analyze audit logs continuously, detect anomalies, and trigger timely responses to potential threats and breaches.
6. **Auditing Cloud Service Providers**: Verifying the security practices and compliance of cloud service providers (CSPs) poses challenges due to limited transparency and control over CSP infrastructure and operations. Research is needed on auditing methodologies, tools, and standards for assessing CSP security posture, data handling practices, and adherence to contractual agreements.
7. **Audit Automation and Orchestration**: Automating audit processes to reduce manual effort and improve efficiency is crucial. However, integrating audit automation with cloud orchestration platforms and DevOps pipelines requires addressing challenges such as compatibility with diverse cloud APIs, ensuring audit tool scalability, and maintaining audit trail consistency across automated processes.
8. **Audit Standardization and Interoperability**: Lack of standardized audit frameworks and interoperability between auditing tools and cloud environments complicates compliance management and auditing practices. Research is needed to establish common audit standards, protocols, and APIs that facilitate interoperability between cloud providers and auditing solutions.
9. **Response and Remediation**: Integrating audit findings with incident response and remediation processes is critical for effective security management. Research is needed on automated response mechanisms, orchestration of remediation actions based on audit findings, and ensuring timely resolution of identified security issues.
10. **User and Administrator Accountability**: Ensuring accountability of users and administrators for their actions in cloud environments poses challenges due to shared responsibilities and complex access control policies. Research is needed on identity management, authentication mechanisms, and auditing techniques that enforce accountability without hindering operational agility.

Addressing these research challenges requires collaborative efforts from academia, industry, and regulatory bodies to advance audit-level security practices in cloud computing. By developing innovative solutions, standards, and best practices, researchers can enhance the transparency, reliability, and effectiveness of auditing processes in cloud environments, thereby strengthening overall cloud security posture.

11.5.2 Future Research Directions

Future research directions in audit-level security in cloud computing will focus on addressing emerging challenges and advancing capabilities to ensure robust auditing, compliance, and security management in dynamic cloud environments. Here are several promising research directions:

1. **Automated and Continuous Auditing**: Research will focus on advancing automated auditing techniques that can continuously monitor and analyze cloud environments in real time. This includes developing machine learning and AI-driven approaches for anomaly detection, pattern recognition in audit logs, and automated response to security incidents based on audit findings.
2. **Scalable Audit Log Management**: Developing scalable solutions for managing audit logs generated from diverse cloud services and resources. Research will explore distributed storage solutions, efficient indexing and querying mechanisms, and techniques for reducing storage overhead while maintaining audit log integrity and accessibility.
3. **Privacy-Preserving Auditing**: Research will continue to explore privacy-preserving auditing techniques that enable comprehensive auditing without compromising sensitive data. This includes investigating differential privacy, secure aggregation methods, and anonymization techniques to protect user and organizational data during auditing processes.
4. **Blockchain for Audit Trails**: Exploring the use of blockchain technology to enhance the integrity and transparency of audit trails in cloud environments. Research directions include developing blockchain-based solutions for immutable audit log storage, secure timestamping of audit events, and decentralized audit trail verification mechanisms.
5. **Auditing Multi-Cloud and Hybrid Cloud Environments**: Addressing challenges in auditing across multi-cloud and hybrid cloud architectures. Research will focus on developing unified audit frameworks, interoperable audit tools, and standardized auditing methodologies that can provide consistent visibility and compliance management across diverse cloud environments.
6. **Behavioral and Contextual Auditing**: Researching behavioral analytics and contextual auditing techniques to enhance the accuracy and relevance of audit findings. This includes integrating user behavior analytics (UBA), context-aware access controls, and risk-based auditing approaches that consider environmental factors and user activities.
7. **Audit Trail Analysis and Visualization**: Developing advanced analytics and visualization tools for audit trails to facilitate meaningful insights and decision-making. Research will explore techniques for correlation analysis, anomaly visualization, and interactive audit trail exploration to improve incident detection, forensic analysis, and compliance reporting.
8. **Compliance Automation and Assurance**: Researching automation techniques for compliance management and assurance in cloud environments. This includes developing automated compliance auditing frameworks, policy enforcement mechanisms, and regulatory mapping tools that streamline audit preparation, validation, and reporting processes.
9. **Audit Resilience and Continuity**: Enhancing resilience and continuity of audit processes during disruptions and cyber incidents. Research will focus on developing resilient audit trail storage solutions, disaster recovery mechanisms for audit logs, and continuity planning strategies that ensure audit operations remain effective and available.

10. **Trustworthiness and Transparency**: Research will explore mechanisms to enhance the trustworthiness and transparency of audit processes in cloud computing. This includes developing audit certifications, audit assurance frameworks, and transparency mechanisms that enhance stakeholder confidence in cloud service providers' security practices.

By focusing on these future research directions, academia, industry, and regulatory bodies can collaborate to advance audit-level security practices in cloud computing. These efforts will contribute to enhancing the reliability, compliance, and security of cloud-based services, ultimately fostering trust and resilience in cloud environments.

11.6 VIRTUALIZATION-LEVEL SECURITY

Virtualization-level security refers to the security measures and best practices implemented to protect virtualized environments, such as virtual machines (VMs) and containers, from various threats and vulnerabilities. Virtualization technology allows multiple virtual instances of operating systems and applications to run on a single physical server, which introduces specific security considerations. Figure 11.5 highlights some common virtualization-level measures to design a comprehensive virtualization security framework [11–15].

The key aspects of virtualization-level security are as follows:

1. **Hypervisor Security**: The hypervisor, or virtual machine monitor (VMM), is a critical component that manages and allocates resources among virtual machines. Securing the hypervisor is essential to prevent unauthorized access, isolation breaches between VMs, and exploitation of hypervisor vulnerabilities. Techniques include applying hypervisor patches and updates, configuring secure boot options, and implementing access controls to restrict hypervisor management interfaces.

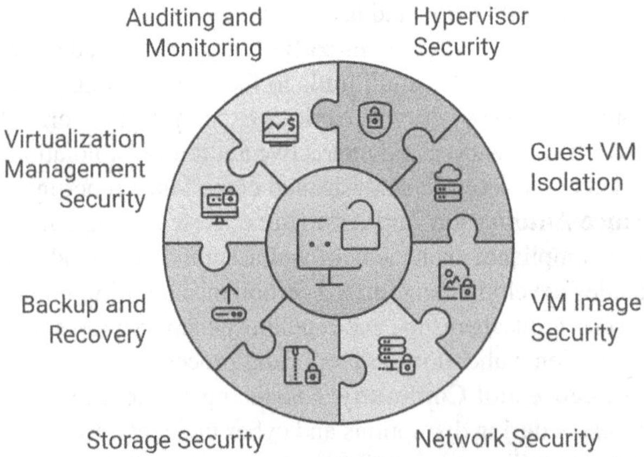

FIGURE 11.5 Common measures of a comprehensive virtualization security framework.

2. **Guest VM Isolation**: Ensuring strong isolation between guest VMs running on the same physical server to prevent one compromised VM from affecting others. This includes configuring virtual network segmentation, implementing firewall rules between VMs, and leveraging hypervisor-enforced memory and CPU isolation mechanisms.
3. **VM Image Security**: Securing VM images and templates to prevent unauthorized access, tampering, or injection of malicious code. Best practices include using trusted sources for VM images, regularly updating and patching VM images, and applying encryption to protect sensitive data within VM images.
4. **Network Security**: Implementing network security controls within virtualized environments to protect against network-based attacks. This includes configuring virtual switches and network interfaces securely, implementing VLANs and network segmentation, and using virtualized firewalls and intrusion detection/prevention systems (IDS/IPS).
5. **Storage Security**: Securing virtualized storage resources to protect data integrity and confidentiality. Best practices include encrypting data at rest and in transit, implementing access controls to storage volumes and snapshots, and auditing storage configurations for compliance with security policies.
6. **Backup and Recovery**: Implementing secure backup and recovery procedures for virtualized environments to ensure data availability and resilience against data loss or corruption. This includes encrypting backup data, regularly testing backup and recovery processes, and implementing access controls to backup repositories.
7. **Virtualization Management Security**: Securing management interfaces and tools used to administer virtualized environments (e.g., management consoles, APIs). Best practices include using strong authentication and authorization mechanisms, monitoring administrative activities, and restricting access based on the principle of least privilege.
8. **Auditing and Monitoring**: Implementing robust auditing and monitoring mechanisms to detect unauthorized activities, configuration changes, and potential security incidents within virtualized environments. This includes monitoring VM performance metrics, network traffic patterns, and audit logs generated by hypervisors and virtualization management platforms.
9. **Compliance and Governance**: Ensuring virtualized environments comply with regulatory requirements (e.g., GDPR, PCI-DSS) and industry standards for data protection and security. This includes conducting regular security assessments, audits, and vulnerability scans to verify compliance and address security gaps.
10. **Integration with Cloud Security**: Addressing security considerations when virtualized environments are deployed in cloud infrastructure (e.g., public cloud, hybrid cloud). This includes understanding shared responsibility models, integrating virtualization security controls with cloud security frameworks, and leveraging cloud-native security services for enhanced protection.

Virtualization-level security is critical for ensuring the confidentiality, integrity, and availability of applications and data running in virtualized environments. By implementing these security measures and best practices, organizations can mitigate risks associated with virtualization technology and maintain a secure computing environment.

11.6.1 Research Challenges and Issues

Research challenges and issues in cloud virtualization-level security encompass a range of complex considerations that need to be addressed to ensure the secure deployment and management of virtualized environments. The key challenges and issues in this domain are illustrated below:

1. **Hypervisor Vulnerabilities**: Hypervisors are critical components in virtualized environments, and vulnerabilities in hypervisor software pose significant security risks. Research is needed to identify and mitigate vulnerabilities such as privilege escalation, denial-of-service (DoS) attacks, and VM escape techniques that could compromise the entire virtualization infrastructure.
2. **VM Isolation and Escape**: Ensuring strong isolation between virtual machines (VMs) running on the same physical server is essential to prevent VM escape attacks. Research challenges include exploring new isolation mechanisms, improving memory and CPU scheduling techniques, and addressing covert channel attacks that exploit shared resources.
3. **Multi-Tenancy Security**: Addressing security challenges in multi-tenant virtualized environments where multiple customers share the same physical infrastructure. Research is needed on enhancing tenant isolation, managing resource contention, and ensuring compliance with data segregation requirements across different tenants.
4. **VM Image and Template Security**: Securing VM images and templates to prevent tampering, injection of malicious code, and unauthorized access. Challenges include developing trusted image repositories, ensuring integrity during image distribution and deployment, and automating security checks for VM images.
5. **Network Security in Virtualized Environments**: Securing virtual networks and communications between VMs and between VMs and external networks. Research challenges include protecting against network-based attacks (e.g., man-in-the-middle attacks, VLAN hopping), implementing effective segmentation and isolation controls, and ensuring secure communication channels within virtualized environments.
6. **Performance Overhead**: Balancing security measures with performance considerations in virtualized environments. Research is needed to optimize security controls such as encryption, isolation mechanisms, and monitoring without significantly impacting VM performance and resource utilization.
7. **Virtualization Management Security**: Securing management interfaces, APIs, and tools used to administer virtualized environments. Challenges

include preventing unauthorized access to management consoles, protecting against API vulnerabilities (e.g., injection attacks), and ensuring secure configuration and monitoring of management activities.

8. **Data Protection and Privacy**: Addressing challenges related to data confidentiality, integrity, and privacy within virtualized environments. Research is needed on encryption techniques for data at rest and in transit, secure key management solutions, and compliance with data protection regulations (e.g., GDPR, CCPA) in virtualized deployments.
9. **Dynamic Provisioning and Orchestration**: Securing dynamic provisioning and orchestration processes in cloud environments where VMs and containers are automatically deployed, scaled, and managed. Challenges include ensuring security during automated deployments, validating configurations, and maintaining consistency across dynamically provisioned instances.
10. **Auditing and Compliance**: Developing effective auditing mechanisms and tools to monitor and enforce compliance with security policies, regulatory requirements, and industry standards in virtualized environments. Research challenges include auditing across heterogeneous virtualization platforms, ensuring integrity of audit trails, and automating compliance checks and reporting.
11. **Resilience and Disaster Recovery**: Researching resilience strategies and disaster recovery mechanisms specific to virtualized environments. Challenges include ensuring data availability and continuity during VM migration, failover, and recovery processes, and minimizing downtime in the event of security incidents or infrastructure failures.
12. **Integration with Cloud Security**: Addressing security considerations when virtualized environments are integrated with cloud services and infrastructure. Research is needed on aligning virtualization security controls with cloud security frameworks, understanding shared responsibility models, and leveraging cloud-native security services for enhanced protection.

Addressing these research challenges requires interdisciplinary collaboration between researchers, practitioners, and industry stakeholders. By advancing knowledge and developing innovative solutions, researchers can contribute to enhancing the security, resilience, and trustworthiness of virtualized environments in cloud computing.

11.6.2 Future Research Directions

Future research directions in cloud virtualization-level security will focus on advancing capabilities to address emerging threats, improve security posture, and enhance the resilience of virtualized environments. Several promising research directions are given below:

1. **Hypervisor Security Enhancements**: Research will focus on developing more secure hypervisor architectures and mechanisms to mitigate vulnerabilities such as VM escape attacks, privilege escalation, and memory isolation flaws. Future directions include exploring novel isolation techniques,

hardware-assisted security features (e.g., Intel SGX), and formal verification methods for hypervisor security.

2. **Container Security**: With the widespread adoption of containers in cloud environments, research will continue to enhance container security mechanisms. This includes developing secure container runtimes, improving container isolation techniques (e.g., using lightweight virtualization), and addressing challenges such as container image security, orchestration security (e.g., Kubernetes), and runtime protection.
3. **Multi-Tenancy Security**: Research will focus on improving security isolation between tenants in multi-tenant virtualized environments. Future directions include developing fine-grained access controls, enhancing resource allocation policies, and implementing secure multi-tenancy architectures that ensure data segregation and isolation while optimizing resource utilization.
4. **Zero Trust Security Models**: Future research will explore zero trust security principles and their application in virtualized environments. This includes implementing identity-centric security, least privilege access controls, and continuous authentication mechanisms to verify and enforce security posture at every access attempt within virtualized infrastructures.
5. **Security Automation and Orchestration**: Research will focus on automating security operations and orchestration in virtualized environments. Future directions include integrating security into DevOps pipelines (DevSecOps), automating vulnerability assessment and remediation, and leveraging AI/ML for real-time threat detection and response.
6. **Secure DevOps (DevSecOps)**: Future research will advance the integration of security into the software development lifecycle (SDLC) for virtualized environments. This includes promoting secure coding practices, automating security testing in CI/CD pipelines, and enhancing collaboration between development, operations, and security teams to proactively address security issues.
7. **Privacy-Preserving Virtualization**: Research will explore techniques to enhance data privacy and confidentiality in virtualized environments. Future directions include developing privacy-preserving computing models (e.g., homomorphic encryption, secure multiparty computation) that protect sensitive data while allowing computation and analysis within virtualized infrastructures.
8. **Resilience and Disaster Recovery**: Future research will focus on enhancing resilience and disaster recovery capabilities in virtualized environments. This includes developing fault-tolerant architectures, optimizing VM migration and failover processes, and integrating automated recovery mechanisms to minimize downtime and data loss during security incidents or infrastructure failures.
9. **Trustworthy Computing and Assurance**: Research will explore methodologies and frameworks to enhance trustworthiness and assurance in virtualized environments. This includes developing certification and assurance models for secure virtualization platforms, conducting rigorous security assessments and audits, and enhancing transparency and accountability in virtualization security practices.

10. **Securing Emerging Virtualization Technologies**: Future research will address security challenges in emerging virtualization technologies and paradigms, such as serverless computing, edge computing, and virtualized network functions (VNFs). This includes adapting security controls and best practices to unique characteristics and requirements of these technologies, ensuring robust protection against evolving threats.
11. **Governance, Risk Management, and Compliance (GRC)**: Future directions will focus on integrating GRC practices into virtualized environments. This includes developing frameworks for risk assessment, establishing governance structures for security policies and controls, and automating compliance monitoring and reporting to meet regulatory requirements and industry standards.

By pursuing these research directions, academia, industry, and practitioners can collaboratively advance the state-of-the-art in cloud virtualization-level security. These efforts will contribute to building more resilient, secure, and trustworthy virtualized infrastructures that can effectively mitigate risks and support the evolving demands of cloud computing.

11.7 SUMMARY

Security in cloud computing spans multiple levels, each presenting distinct challenges and considerations. At the architectural level, securing data centers against physical threats is crucial. Network security involves protecting data during transmission and defending against network-based attacks. Perimeter security focuses on safeguarding access to cloud resources from external threats. Data security includes encryption, access control, and compliance with data protection regulations. Identity and access management ensures secure user authentication and authorization. Application security addresses vulnerabilities in cloud-hosted applications and APIs. Virtualization security protects hypervisors, VMs, and containers from exploitation. Compliance and legal issues involve meeting regulatory requirements and contractual obligations. Incident response and governance are essential for detecting and responding to security incidents and managing risks effectively across cloud environments.

11.8 PRACTICE QUESTIONS/SOLUTIONS

MULTIPLE CHOICE QUESTIONS

1 **Which of the following is a primary focus of research in secure cloud computing?**
A) Network speed optimization
B) Data confidentiality and encryption
C) User interface design
D) Cloud server cooling techniques

Answer: B) Data confidentiality and encryption

2 What is the primary concern addressed by "access control" in secure cloud computing?

A) Ensuring that data is not corrupted
B) Protecting data from unauthorized access
C) Optimizing cloud resource allocation
D) Minimizing the operational costs of cloud services

Answer: B) Protecting data from unauthorized access

3 Which research area focuses on ensuring that cloud services can continue to operate even during a cyberattack or hardware failure?

A) Cloud scalability
B) Cloud resilience and fault tolerance
C) Cloud pricing models
D) Cloud user experience

Answer: B) Cloud resilience and fault tolerance

4 Which cloud computing concept is crucial for ensuring the privacy of sensitive data when outsourcing storage to a third-party provider?

A) Cloud data replication
B) Data encryption and cryptographic techniques
C) Virtualization
D) Multi-cloud architecture

Answer: B) Data encryption and cryptographic techniques

5 What does "secure multi-party computation" (SMPC) in cloud computing primarily aim to achieve?

A) Increasing cloud service uptime
B) Enabling secure computations on private data without revealing it to others
C) Optimizing the cost of cloud resources
D) Improving network bandwidth efficiency

Answer: B) Enabling secure computations on private data without revealing it to others

6 Which of the following research topics is important for maintaining data integrity in cloud computing?

A) Cloud resource management
B) Blockchain and distributed ledgers
C) Cloud pricing models
D) Virtual machine optimization

Answer: B) Blockchain and distributed ledgers

7 What is the focus of "secure cloud auditing" in cloud computing?

A) Ensuring faster data access
B) Verifying the correctness and security of data in the cloud
C) Reducing data storage costs
D) Optimizing cloud resource allocation

Answer: B) Verifying the correctness and security of data in the cloud

8 What does "homomorphic encryption" allow in cloud computing?

A) Compression of cloud data
B) Encrypted data to be processed without decryption
C) Faster cloud server performance
D) Direct access to data without security restrictions

Answer: B) Encrypted data to be processed without decryption

9 Which of the following is a challenge in ensuring "secure data sharing" in cloud environments?

A) Data encryption
B) Efficient bandwidth usage
C) Avoiding unauthorized data access
D) Reducing cloud resource costs

Answer: C) Avoiding unauthorized data access

10 Which research field in secure cloud computing aims to protect against malicious insiders accessing sensitive cloud data?

A) Insider threat mitigation
B) Cloud pricing strategies
C) Resource scheduling
D) Multi-tenancy optimization

Answer: A) Insider threat mitigation

11 Which of the following is a technique used in secure cloud computing to ensure that only authorized users can access data stored in the cloud?

A) Data replication
B) Authentication and authorization mechanisms
C) Data compression
D) Cloud load balancing

Answer: B) Authentication and authorization mechanisms

12 What is "cloud data provenance" concerned with in secure cloud computing?

A) The process of encrypting data before storage
B) Tracking the origins and changes of data to ensure its integrity
C) Reducing the cost of cloud storage
D) Improving cloud server performance

Answer: B) Tracking the origins and changes of data to ensure its integrity

13 Which concept in secure cloud computing helps to ensure data is available even in the event of a server failure or attack?

A) Data replication
B) Data encryption
C) Multi-factor authentication
D) Cloud load balancing

Answer: A) Data replication

14 In the context of cloud security, what does "data masking" help to achieve?

A) Data availability
B) Data confidentiality by obscuring sensitive data
C) Faster data retrieval
D) Minimizing cloud service costs

Answer: B) Data confidentiality by obscuring sensitive data

15 Which of the following is a key research challenge in "cloud computing trust management"?

A) Efficient data compression
B) Ensuring the reliability of cloud service providers
C) Reducing latency in cloud services
D) Managing cloud resource allocation

Answer: B) Ensuring the reliability of cloud service providers

16 Which research area focuses on preventing unauthorized modification of cloud data by external attackers or malicious insiders?

A) Cloud data integrity
B) Cloud resource management
C) Cloud scalability
D) Virtualization security

Answer: A) Cloud data integrity

17 What is the main goal of "secure virtualization" in cloud computing?

A) Optimizing cloud resource allocation
B) Protecting virtual machines from attacks and isolation breaches
C) Increasing the speed of data transfer between users
D) Reducing cloud server costs

Answer: B) Protecting virtual machines from attacks and isolation breaches

18 What does "cloud encryption key management" primarily address?

A) Ensuring that data is processed efficiently
B) Managing and safeguarding the encryption keys used for protecting cloud data
C) Distributing cloud resources among users
D) Increasing the speed of cloud servers

Answer: B) Managing and safeguarding the encryption keys used for protecting cloud data

19 Which technology is used in secure cloud computing to ensure data confidentiality while performing computations on encrypted data?

A) Homomorphic encryption
B) Public key infrastructure (PKI)
C) Data replication
D) Load balancing algorithms

Answer: A) Homomorphic encryption

20 Which of the following research fields in cloud security aims to protect against the risks associated with sharing data across multiple cloud platforms?

A) Multi-cloud security
B) Cloud resource management
C) Cloud virtualization
D) Data compression techniques

Answer: A) Multi-cloud security

21 What is the focus of "cloud service provider auditing" in secure cloud computing?

A) Verifying the security practices and compliance of cloud service providers
B) Managing cloud storage costs
C) Optimizing server performance
D) Increasing the speed of cloud applications

Answer: A) Verifying the security practices and compliance of cloud service providers

22 What does "attribute-based encryption" (ABE) help achieve in cloud computing?

A) Allowing data encryption based on user attributes to improve access control
B) Improving cloud service provider uptime
C) Optimizing cloud resource utilization
D) Reducing data access latency

Answer: A) Allowing data encryption based on user attributes to improve access control

23 Which technique in cloud security ensures that only certain users can access specific pieces of data, based on their roles or attributes?

A) Role-based access control (RBAC)
B) Cloud load balancing
C) Data replication
D) Multi-tenancy

Answer: A) Role-based access control (RBAC)

24 Which research challenge in secure cloud computing involves ensuring that users' data is protected against both accidental and malicious deletion?

A) Data availability
B) Data encryption
C) Data backup and recovery
D) Data compression

Answer: C) Data backup and recovery

25 In the context of secure cloud computing, what is the purpose of "secure APIs"?

A) To provide a fast interface for data sharing
B) To allow encrypted communication between cloud services and clients
C) To increase cloud storage capacity
D) To improve the user interface of cloud applications

Answer: B) To allow encrypted communication between cloud services and clients

DESCRIPTIVE QUESTIONS

1 What is the importance of data confidentiality in cloud computing?

Answer: Data confidentiality ensures that sensitive data stored in the cloud is protected from unauthorized access. Encryption and access control mechanisms are commonly used to achieve confidentiality.

2 What is the role of access control in cloud security?

Answer: Access control ensures that only authorized users can access cloud resources. It involves techniques such as authentication, authorization, and role-based access control (RBAC) to manage user permissions.

3 What is cloud data provenance?

Answer: Cloud data provenance tracks the origins, changes, and movement of data within the cloud to ensure data integrity and transparency. It helps verify the authenticity and history of the data.

4 Why is fault tolerance important in cloud computing?

Answer: Fault tolerance ensures cloud services remain available and functional even during hardware failures or cyberattacks. Techniques such as data replication and failover systems are used to achieve fault tolerance.

5 What is secure multi-party computation (SMPC) in cloud computing?

Answer: SMPC enables multiple parties to jointly compute a function over their data without revealing their private inputs. This allows secure computations on sensitive data in the cloud.

6 What is secure virtualization in cloud computing?

Answer: Secure virtualization involves techniques to protect virtual machines (VMs) from attacks and ensure isolation between VMs to prevent unauthorized access or data leakage.

7 What is cloud encryption key management?

Answer: Cloud encryption key management refers to the processes and tools used to generate, store, and manage encryption keys to protect data in the cloud, ensuring that only authorized users can decrypt the data.

8 What is homomorphic encryption in cloud computing?

Answer: Homomorphic encryption allows computations to be performed on encrypted data without decrypting it. This ensures the privacy of data while still allowing for analysis or processing.

9 What are the challenges of secure data sharing in cloud computing?

Answer: Challenges include ensuring data privacy, preventing unauthorized access, and managing data integrity when data is shared across different cloud services or users.

10 What is attribute-based encryption (ABE)?

Answer: ABE is an encryption technique that allows data to be encrypted based on specific attributes (e.g., role or user group). Only users with the correct attributes can decrypt the data, enhancing access control.

11 What is the role of cloud service provider auditing in cloud security?

Answer: Cloud service provider auditing involves evaluating and verifying the security practices of cloud providers to ensure they comply with standards and regulations, helping customers trust the cloud environment.

12 What is the concept of multi-cloud security?

Answer: Multi-cloud security involves protecting data and applications distributed across multiple cloud platforms. It addresses challenges such as data sharing, access control, and ensuring consistent security policies across different providers.

13 What is the purpose of data replication in cloud computing?

Answer: Data replication ensures that copies of data are stored across multiple locations to improve data availability, fault tolerance, and disaster recovery, ensuring that data remains accessible even in the event of a failure.

14 What are the benefits of using encryption in cloud computing?

Answer: Encryption protects sensitive data from unauthorized access, ensuring confidentiality and integrity. It also helps organizations comply with regulatory requirements and secures data during storage and transmission.

15 What is the significance of blockchain in secure cloud computing?

Answer: Blockchain technology provides a decentralized and transparent way to track data transactions, ensuring data integrity, transparency, and tamper-proof records, which is useful for securing cloud-based data exchanges.

16 How does role-based access control (RBAC) enhance cloud security?

Answer: RBAC assigns specific roles to users and grants permissions based on these roles. This ensures that users can only access the data and resources necessary for their tasks, reducing the risk of unauthorized access.

17 What is the role of identity and access management (IAM) in cloud computing?

Answer: IAM systems manage and control user identities and access privileges in cloud environments, ensuring that only authorized individuals can access specific resources and services, enhancing security and compliance.

18 What is the concept of secure cloud computing?

Answer: Secure cloud computing involves implementing security measures to protect data, applications, and services hosted in the cloud from unauthorized access, cyberattacks, data breaches, and other threats.

19 What is the difference between public and private cloud security?

Answer: Public cloud security refers to protecting data and applications in cloud environments shared by multiple customers, while private cloud security focuses on securing resources within a single organization's private infrastructure.

20 How does data masking contribute to cloud security?

Answer: Data masking involves replacing sensitive data with fictitious values to protect it from unauthorized access. It helps maintain data confidentiality while allowing organizations to use realistic data for testing and analysis purposes.

REFERENCES

1. Khaldi, A., Karoui, K., Tanabène, N., & Ghzala, H. B. (2014, April). A secure cloud computing architecture design. In *2014 2nd IEEE International Conference on Mobile Cloud Computing, Services, and Engineering* (pp. 289–294). IEEE.
2. Khari, M., Gupta, S., & Kumar, M. (2016, March). Security outlook for cloud computing: A proposed architectural-based security classification for cloud computing. In *2016 3rd International Conference on Computing for Sustainable Global Development (INDIACom)* (pp. 2153–2158). IEEE.
3. Odun-Ayo, I., Ananya, M., Agono, F., & Goddy-Worlu, R. (2018, July). Cloud computing architecture: A critical analysis. In *2018 18th international conference on computational science and applications (ICCSA)* (pp. 1–7). IEEE.
4. Sood, S. K. (2012). A combined approach to ensure data security in cloud computing. *Journal of Network and Computer Applications*, *35*(6), 1831–1838.
5. Chang, V., & Ramachandran, M. (2015). Towards achieving data security with the cloud computing adoption framework. *IEEE Transactions on Services Computing*, *9*(1), 138–151.
6. Kaufman, L. M. (2009). Data security in the world of cloud computing. *IEEE Security & Privacy*, *7*(4), 61–64.

7. Majumdar, S., Madi, T., Wang, Y., Jarraya, Y., Pourzandi, M., Wang, L., & Debbabi, M. (2017). User-level runtime security auditing for the cloud. *IEEE Transactions on Information Forensics and Security*, *13*(5), 1185–1199.
8. Ryoo, J., Rizvi, S., Aiken, W., & Kissell, J. (2013). Cloud security auditing: challenges and emerging approaches. *IEEE Security & Privacy*, *12*(6), 68–74.
9. Majumdar, S., Madi, T., Jarraya, Y., Pourzandi, M., Wang, L., & Debbabi, M. (2019). Cloud security auditing: Major approaches and existing challenges. In Foundations and Practice of Security: *11th International Symposium, FPS 2018*, Montreal, QC, Canada, November 13–15, 2018, Revised Selected Papers 11 (pp. 61–77). Springer International Publishing.
10. Rizvi, S., Ryoo, J., Kissell, J., Aiken, W., & Liu, Y. (2018). A security evaluation framework for cloud security auditing. *The Journal of Supercomputing*, *74*, 5774–5796.
11. Luo, S., Lin, Z., Chen, X., Yang, Z., & Chen, J. (2011, December). Virtualization security for cloud computing service. In *2011 International Conference on Cloud and Service Computing* (pp. 174–179). IEEE.
12. Li, J., Li, B., Wo, T., Hu, C., Huai, J., Liu, L., & Lam, K. P. (2012). CyberGuarder: A virtualization security assurance architecture for green cloud computing. *Future Generation Computer Systems*, *28*(2), 379–390.
13. Kazim, M., Masood, R., Shibli, M. A., & Abbasi, A. G. (2013). Security aspects of virtualization in cloud computing. In *Computer Information Systems and Industrial Management: 12th IFIP TC8 International Conference, CISIM 2013*, Krakow, Poland, September 25–27, 2013. *Proceedings* (pp. 229–240). Springer Berlin Heidelberg.
14. Kumar, V., & Rathore, R. S. (2018, October). Security issues with virtualization in cloud computing. In *2018 International Conference on Advances in Computing, Communication Control and Networking (ICACCCN)* (pp. 487–491). IEEE.
15. Sabahi, F. (2011, May). Virtualization-level security in cloud computing. In *2011 IEEE 3rd International Conference on Communication Software and Networks* (pp. 250–254). IEEE.

12 Hands-on Projects for Practice

12.1 SECURE DATA TRANSMISSION WITH TLS/SSL

In this project, you will learn how to configure Transport Layer Security (TLS) or Secure Sockets Layer (SSL) to secure data transmission between a client and a server. Securing data in transit is a critical practice in ensuring privacy and integrity, particularly when handling sensitive information over the Internet.

Tools and Services Required:

- **OpenSSL**: A software library for implementing cryptographic protocols and functions.
- **Apache or Nginx Web Server**: Popular web server software that supports SSL/TLS configurations.
- **Valid SSL/TLS Certificate**: You will need a certificate to enable HTTPS. You can obtain a free certificate from Let's Encrypt.

Steps:

1. **Install and Configure Web Server**:
   - Begin by setting up an Apache or Nginx web server on a cloud-based Linux instance. Ensure the server is running correctly and is accessible.
2. **Generate Private Key and CSR with OpenSSL**:
   - Use OpenSSL to create a private key for your server, which will be used to encrypt and decrypt data during secure communications.
   - Next, generate a Certificate Signing Request (CSR). This CSR contains information about your organization and the server, which you will submit to a Certificate Authority (CA) to request a legitimate SSL/TLS certificate.
3. **Obtain and Install SSL/TLS Certificate**:
   - Submit the CSR to a trusted Certificate Authority (CA) like Let's Encrypt to get a legitimate SSL/TLS certificate.
   - Once you have the certificate, install it on your web server, ensuring it is placed in the appropriate directory and properly configured.

DOI: 10.1201/9781003510772-12

4. **Configure HTTP to HTTPS Redirect**:
   - Update your web server settings to ensure that all HTTP traffic is automatically redirected to HTTPS. This step is critical in forcing secure connections.
   - Modify the configuration files of Apache or Nginx to enable HTTPS and require secure connections for all users.
5. **Test HTTPS Connection**:
   - Using a web browser, visit your web server over HTTPS. You should see a secure padlock symbol in the browser's address bar, indicating that the connection is encrypted.
   - Verify that the SSL/TLS certificate is valid by inspecting the certificate details, ensuring it matches your domain and is issued by a trusted CA.
6. **Validate Certificate and Secure Connection**:
   - Examine the SSL/TLS certificate to confirm that it is legitimate and correctly issued for your domain. The certificate should be signed by a trusted CA and must not be expired.
   - You can use online tools like SSL Labs' SSL Test to validate your server's configuration and the strength of the encryption used.
7. **Secure Other Services**:
   - Explore securing additional services, such as email (e.g., using SMTP over SSL/TLS) or file transfer services (e.g., FTPS), to ensure that all data exchanged over the network is encrypted.
   - Apply SSL/TLS to these services to further enhance your system's security posture.
8. **Monitor and Analyze Network Traffic**:
   - To ensure your data is securely transmitted, use tools like Wireshark to capture and analyze network traffic. This will help you verify that sensitive data is encrypted and not transmitted in plain text.
   - Inspect packets to confirm that all HTTP traffic is redirected to HTTPS and that SSL/TLS handshakes are occurring correctly.

By completing this project, you will gain hands-on experience in configuring and securing data transmission with SSL/TLS. This is a crucial skill in protecting data privacy and integrity, particularly in cloud environments where sensitive data is often exchanged over potentially insecure networks.

12.2 PRIVACY PROTECTION WITH DATA ENCRYPTION

In this project, you will practice encrypting data to ensure its privacy both in transit and at rest. Encrypting sensitive data is an essential aspect of protecting privacy in modern cloud environments, where data is often stored or transmitted over potentially unsecured networks.

Tools and Services Required:

- **OpenSSL**: A toolkit for implementing cryptography functions, including key generation and data encryption.

- **AWS Key Management Service (KMS)**: A fully managed service for creating and controlling encryption keys used to encrypt data.

Steps:

1. **Install OpenSSL on a Cloud-Based Linux Instance**:
   - Start by installing OpenSSL on your cloud-based Linux instance. OpenSSL will allow you to create keys and encrypt data, providing the cryptographic tools necessary for the project.
2. **Generate a Private and Public Key Pair**:
   - Using OpenSSL, generate a pair of cryptographic keys: a private key and a public key. The public key will be used to encrypt data, while the private key will be used to decrypt it.
   - Store the private key securely and use the public key to protect sensitive information.
3. **Encrypt Data with the Public Key**:
   - Utilize the public key generated earlier to encrypt sensitive data. This ensures that only someone with the corresponding private key can decrypt and access the original data.
   - OpenSSL provides commands for encrypting files or data with the public key, offering a simple method of protecting information before transmission or storage.
4. **Post the Encrypted Data to Cloud Storage**:
   - Once the data is encrypted, upload it to a cloud storage platform like Amazon S3. S3 allows for the storage of encrypted data while ensuring that access control policies are applied to manage who can retrieve the encrypted content.
   - Ensure that only authorized users or services with the correct decryption key can access the sensitive data stored in S3.
5. **Decrypt the Data using the Private Key**:
   - Use the private key to decrypt the data that was previously encrypted with the public key. This step demonstrates the process of accessing protected information securely.
   - Ensure that the private key is stored safely and is not exposed, as it is crucial for accessing the original data.
6. **Experiment with SSL/TLS Data Encryption**:
   - As detailed in the **Secure Data Transmission** project, apply SSL/TLS encryption to protect data in transit. This encryption protects data as it moves between the client and server, ensuring it cannot be intercepted or tampered with during communication.
   - This practice reinforces the concept of encryption not only for stored data (at rest) but also for data in transit, making the entire data lifecycle secure.
7. **Encrypt Data on Amazon EBS using AWS KMS**:
   - AWS Key Management Service (KMS) provides a managed service for creating and managing encryption keys. Use AWS KMS to encrypt sensitive data stored on Amazon Elastic Block Store (EBS) volumes.

- Set up encryption policies in AWS KMS to ensure that your data is automatically encrypted when stored on EBS and that only authorized users can access the decryption keys.

8. **Regularly Rotate AWS KMS Encryption Keys**:
   - For enhanced security, regularly rotate the encryption keys managed by AWS KMS. Key rotation ensures that your data is shielded by the most current and secure encryption keys.
   - Implement a process to rotate keys periodically, mitigating risks associated with key compromise.
9. **Track Access to Encrypted Data using AWS CloudTrail and CloudWatch**:
   - Use **AWS CloudTrail** to monitor and log API calls related to your encrypted data. CloudTrail helps track who accessed the data, when, and what actions were taken.
   - Integrate **AWS CloudWatch** to set up alerts and monitoring for suspicious access patterns, enabling you to quickly identify unauthorized access to encrypted data.
   - These tools are crucial in maintaining security and ensuring that your encryption policies are followed.

By completing this project, you will gain valuable hands-on experience in encrypting data to protect its privacy in a cloud environment. This skill is essential for ensuring that sensitive data remains secure, whether it is being transmitted over the Internet or stored on cloud infrastructure. You will also become familiar with best practices for key management, encryption, and access monitoring, which are critical components of modern cloud security.

12.3 SMART CYBER-PHYSICAL SYSTEM FOR MONITORING AND CONTROLLING DEVICES

In this project, you will build a smart cyber-physical system (CPS) that monitors and controls devices within a cloud environment. CPS combines physical systems with computational elements, allowing for real-time monitoring, data collection, and device control through the cloud. You will work with various AWS tools to create, manage, and secure IoT devices.

Tools and Services Required:

- **AWS IoT Core**: A cloud service for connecting Internet of Things (IoT) devices to the AWS Cloud.
- **AWS Lambda**: A compute service that allows you to run code without provisioning or managing servers.
- **AWS IoT Device SDK for Python**: A software development kit for connecting IoT devices to AWS IoT Core using Python.
- **Raspberry Pi or Similar IoT Device**: A small, affordable computer used for building IoT projects, equipped with sensors or actuators.

Steps:

1. **Set Up AWS IoT Core**:
   - Begin by setting up an AWS IoT Core environment to manage your IoT devices. AWS IoT Core allows devices to securely connect to the cloud and interact with other AWS services. Follow the setup process to create things, policies, and certificates for your IoT devices.
2. **Connect Raspberry Pi or IoT Device to AWS IoT Core**:
   - Using the AWS IoT Device SDK for Python, establish a connection between your Raspberry Pi or another IoT device and AWS IoT Core. This SDK provides the necessary libraries and functions to facilitate communication between your physical device and the cloud.
3. **Read Sensor Data and Upload to AWS IoT Core**:
   - Develop a Python script to collect sensor data from your IoT device (e.g., temperature, humidity, or motion data). Use this script to upload the collected data to AWS IoT Core, enabling you to monitor the sensor information remotely via the cloud.
4. **Create an AWS Lambda Function**:
   - Create an AWS Lambda function that will process the sensor data received from your IoT devices. Depending on the data, the function can trigger actions, such as sending an alarm if a threshold is reached, controlling an actuator to adjust the environment, or logging the data for analysis.
5. **Simulate Sensor Data and Monitor Lambda Responses**:
   - Simulate sensor data to test how your Lambda function responds. For example, simulate a temperature sensor reading and check if the Lambda function triggers the desired action, such as activating a fan or sending a notification.
   - Monitor the output and response of your Lambda function to ensure that it performs as expected in real-world scenarios.
6. **Secure IoT Connections with Authentication and Permissions**:
   - To ensure the security of your IoT devices and the data they transmit, enable authentication and define permissions within AWS IoT Core. Use X.509 certificates to authenticate devices and apply AWS IoT policies to control access to the IoT services and resources based on roles.
7. **Monitor and Analyze Data with AWS IoT Analytics and AWS CloudWatch**:
   - Use **AWS IoT Analytics** to process, analyze, and visualize the sensor data collected from your IoT devices. Set up data pipelines and queries to extract meaningful insights from the data in real time.
   - Use **AWS CloudWatch** to monitor your Lambda functions and IoT devices. Set up alerts and dashboards to track the performance, status, and errors of your smart CPS.
8. **Implement Auto-scaling of IoT Devices**:
   - To scale your smart CPS, configure AWS IoT Core to automatically add more IoT devices as the system grows. You can manage device registration and onboarding in bulk and automatically handle increased device traffic and data processing.

By completing this project, you will gain practical experience in building, managing, and securing smart cyber-physical systems in a cloud environment. This is an essential skill for developing and deploying IoT devices, ensuring secure data transmission, and managing large-scale IoT deployments using cloud services. You will also be prepared to use AWS tools such as Lambda, IoT Core, and CloudWatch to create scalable and secure IoT solutions.

12.4 IMPLEMENTING MULTI-FACTOR AUTHENTICATION SYSTEM

In this project, you will implement a multi-factor authentication (MFA) system to enhance the security of your cloud environment. MFA adds an additional layer of protection beyond just passwords by requiring users to authenticate using multiple methods, such as a one-time code sent via SMS.

Tools and Services Required:

- **AWS IAM (Identity and Access Management)**: Manages user access to AWS services and resources.
- **AWS Lambda**: A serverless compute service to run code in response to events.
- **Amazon Cognito**: A service to handle user authentication and authorization.
- **Twilio (or another SMS service)**: A platform for sending SMS messages, which will be used for MFA.

Steps:

1. **Create a User Pool in Amazon Cognito**:
   - Begin by setting up a user pool in **Amazon Cognito**. The user pool will manage your users and handle the authentication process, such as user registration, sign-in, and password management. The user pool can be configured to handle different authentication factors, such as passwords and MFA.
2. **Set Up Amazon Cognito as an External Identity Provider in AWS IAM**:
   - Configure **AWS Identity and Access Management (IAM)** to use the Amazon Cognito user pool as an external identity provider. This setup will allow you to integrate MFA into your IAM roles and policies, providing additional security when users interact with your AWS resources.
3. **Create an AWS Lambda Function for MFA**:
   - Develop an **AWS Lambda function** that facilitates MFA by generating and sending one-time passcodes (OTP) to users. This function will use an SMS service like **Twilio** (or any other SMS provider) to deliver the passcodes to users' mobile phones.
   - The Lambda function will listen for authentication events and trigger the sending of an OTP after the user enters their username and password.
4. **Configure Twilio (or Another SMS Provider) for One-Time Code Delivery**:
   - Set up **Twilio** (or another SMS provider) in your Lambda function to send the one-time passcode via text message to the user's registered mobile phone number. Ensure the delivery method is configured securely

and that the OTP expires after a short period (e.g., 5 minutes) for security purposes.

5. **Update IAM Policies to Require MFA for Sensitive Actions**:
   - Modify your **IAM policies** to enforce MFA for specific actions, such as:
     - Changing a user's password
     - Accessing critical resources or data
     - Performing administrative functions
   - By requiring MFA for these actions, you enhance the security of your environment by ensuring that even if an attacker knows the password, they cannot gain access without the second authentication factor.
6. **Test the MFA System**:
   - Log in using a user account that requires MFA. After entering the password, the system should prompt for the one-time passcode sent via SMS. Enter the code to verify that the MFA system is functioning correctly.
   - Test the entire authentication flow to ensure the user experience is seamless and secure.
7. **Implement Rate Limiting and Other Security Measures**:
   - To protect your MFA system from brute-force attacks, implement **rate limiting** on the number of failed attempts to enter the OTP. Configure additional security measures, such as account lockouts after a certain number of failed attempts.
   - Use AWS tools such as **AWS WAF** (Web Application Firewall) and **AWS Shield** for additional protection against malicious attacks.
8. **Monitor and Analyze Data using AWS CloudWatch and AWS Config**:
   - Use **AWS CloudWatch** to monitor and log events related to MFA authentication attempts. Set up alarms for unusual login activity or failed MFA attempts, which could indicate a security breach.
   - Use **AWS Config** to track configuration changes and ensure that MFA is being enforced according to your security policies.

By completing this project, you will gain hands-on experience in implementing a multi-factor authentication system, which is a key practice in securing cloud environments. With MFA, you add an extra layer of protection to your resources, making it much harder for unauthorized users to gain access. You'll also become familiar with integrating services such as Amazon Cognito, AWS IAM, AWS Lambda, and Twilio to build secure authentication workflows and monitor their performance effectively.

12.5 IMPLEMENTING ROLE-BASED ACCESS CONTROL (RBAC) IN AWS

In this project, you will implement a **role-based access control (RBAC)** system within AWS to enhance the security of your cloud environment. RBAC allows you to manage user permissions based on their roles, ensuring that each user or service has only the necessary access to perform their tasks, thereby minimizing the risk of unauthorized access.

Tools and Services Required:

- **AWS IAM (Identity and Access Management)**: To create and manage roles, policies, and permissions for users and services.
- **AWS Lambda**: For running serverless functions that can automate the management of RBAC data.
- **Amazon S3**: For storing RBAC data, such as role definitions and associated policies.

Steps:

1. **Define User Roles for RBAC System**:
   - Start by identifying the roles that users and applications will have in your system. Common roles may include:
     - **Admin**: Full access to all AWS resources and the ability to manage IAM roles and policies.
     - **Developer**: Limited access to deploy and manage specific resources, such as EC2 instances or S3 buckets.
     - **Guest**: Restricted access, typically only for reading public resources.
   - Define these roles clearly and decide the level of access each role should have.
2. **Create IAM Policies for Each Role**:
   - Develop **IAM policies** for each role that specify the exact permissions associated with that role. Policies define what actions a user or service can perform on AWS resources. For example:
     - An **Admin** role would have full access to EC2, S3, Lambda, and IAM.
     - A **Developer** role may have access to EC2 instances but not to modify IAM policies.
     - A **Guest** role may have read-only access to specific S3 buckets but cannot modify them.
   - Use **JSON** syntax to write these policies, specifying actions (e.g., s3:ListBucket, ec2:DescribeInstances) and resources.
3. **Create IAM Roles and Assign Policies**:
   - Create **IAM roles** for each of the defined user roles. Attach the corresponding IAM policies to these roles to enforce the permissions that you've set up.
   - Ensure that each IAM role has the appropriate permissions for users or services to perform the required tasks. For example, assign the "Developer" role with the limited EC2 permissions and the "Admin" role with full access.
4. **Create an AWS Lambda Function for RBAC Data Management**:
   - Develop an **AWS Lambda function** that will handle the RBAC data, such as role definitions and the associated policies. This function can store RBAC data in **Amazon S3** as a file storage system, allowing you to manage the roles and permissions centrally.
   - The Lambda function can be triggered to update or change RBAC data as needed, automating the process of managing permissions and roles.

5. **Apply RBAC Rules to Authorization Requests**:
   - Configure your **Lambda function** to take updates to RBAC data (e.g., adding new roles, updating policies) and automatically apply the rules when a user requests access to resources.
   - Ensure that when a user or application makes an authorization request, the Lambda function checks the relevant role and policy before allowing access.
6. **Test Your RBAC System**:
   - Sign in with various user identities that correspond to the roles you've defined (Admin, Developer, Guest). Test whether the users can only access the resources and perform the actions that their roles permit.
   - For example, a "Guest" should only have read access to public S3 buckets, while an "Admin" should have the ability to modify those buckets.
7. **Implement Monitoring and Security Measures**:
   - To ensure the integrity and security of your RBAC system, use **AWS CloudWatch** to monitor actions and events related to role access. Set up alarms for any unauthorized access attempts or other suspicious activities.
   - Use **AWS Config** to track changes to IAM roles and policies, ensuring that any modifications are logged and compliant with your security requirements.
   - You may also want to integrate AWS **CloudTrail** to log all API requests related to IAM and ensure accountability.
8. **Ensure Protection against Unauthorized Access**:
   - Protect your RBAC system from potential misuse or unauthorized access by implementing additional security measures such as:
     - Multi-factor authentication (MFA) for sensitive roles like Admin.
     - Regularly reviewing and auditing IAM policies to ensure they follow the principle of least privilege.
     - Enforcing least privilege access for IAM roles by ensuring users have only the permissions they absolutely need to perform their tasks.

By completing this project, you will gain practical experience in implementing and managing an RBAC system in AWS, a critical security practice for managing access to cloud resources. You'll also learn how to use AWS tools such as IAM, Lambda, S3, CloudWatch, and CloudTrail to build, monitor, and secure your cloud environment. This system is essential for protecting sensitive resources and ensuring that only authorized users can perform specific tasks within the AWS infrastructure.

12.6 IMPLEMENTING NETWORK SECURITY GROUPS IN AZURE

In this project, you will implement a **Network Security Group (NSG)** in Microsoft Azure to secure your virtual infrastructure. NSGs are used to control inbound and outbound traffic to Azure resources, such as Virtual Machines (VMs), ensuring only authorized connections are allowed.

Tools and Services Required:

- **Azure Portal**: The web-based interface for managing Azure resources.
- **Azure Virtual Network**: A service that enables you to create isolated networks within Azure.
- **Azure Network Security Group (NSG)**: A network security feature that controls traffic to and from Azure resources.

Steps:

1. **Configure an Azure Virtual Network**:
   - Begin by setting up an **Azure Virtual Network (VNet)**, which will act as the foundation for your cloud infrastructure. The VNet enables communication between your Azure resources, such as VMs, databases, and other services. You'll need to define the address space and subnets for your network.
2. **Create a Network Security Group (NSG)**:
   - In the **Azure Portal**, create a **Network Security Group (NSG)**. An NSG contains a set of security rules that define allowed or denied inbound and outbound traffic to network interfaces (NICs), VMs, or subnets within your Virtual Network.
   - The NSG will help you filter traffic based on source/destination IP addresses, ports, and protocols, enhancing the security of your network.
3. **Create Rules for Your NSG**:
   - Develop inbound and outbound rules for your NSG based on your specific security requirements. Common rules might include:
     - **Allow specific IP addresses**: Permit traffic only from certain trusted IP addresses (e.g., office IPs or trusted partner systems).
     - **Deny traffic to specific ports**: Block access to ports that aren't needed for communication, such as remote desktop protocol (RDP) or SSH for all but authorized users.
     - **Allow traffic from specific services**: Ensure that only required services, such as HTTP (port 80) and HTTPS (port 443), are allowed for web servers.
   - You can define rules based on source and destination IPs, ports, and protocols (TCP/UDP).
4. **Apply the NSG to Your Virtual Network**:
   - Once the NSG and its rules are configured, apply the NSG to your Virtual Network or directly to the individual network interfaces (NICs) of the Virtual Machines.
   - Applying the NSG to your VNet ensures that all traffic flowing in and out of the VMs in that network is filtered based on the defined security rules.
5. **Test Your NSG**:
   - Test your NSG configuration by attempting to connect to your VMs from different external networks or IP addresses. Ensure that only authorized traffic can access the VMs based on the rules you've set.
   - For example, try to access a VM via RDP or SSH if the corresponding port is blocked, or attempt a connection from an unauthorized IP address to confirm the deny rules are working properly.

6. **Implement Additional Security Measures**:
   - In addition to NSGs, implement other security measures to strengthen the protection of your infrastructure:
     - **Access Control Policies**: Use Azure Active Directory (Azure AD) to manage user access and roles for your virtual network and other resources.
     - **Virtual Machine Encryption**: Encrypt sensitive data on your VMs to prevent unauthorized access, even if someone bypasses network security controls.
     - **Azure Bastion**: Consider using **Azure Bastion** to securely access VMs via RDP or SSH without exposing them directly to the Internet.
7. **Monitor and Analyze Traffic with Azure Monitor and Azure Security Center**:
   - Use **Azure Monitor** to track the performance and health of your network infrastructure, including the NSG rules and the traffic flowing through your VNet. Set up alerts for unusual traffic patterns or potential security threats.
   - Leverage **Azure Security Center** to gain insights into potential vulnerabilities in your network configuration and to receive recommendations on how to improve your NSG and overall security posture.
8. **Automate NSG Management with Infrastructure-as-Code**:
   - Use **Azure Resource Manager (ARM) templates** or other infrastructure-as-code (IaC) solutions like **Terraform** to automate the deployment and management of your NSGs. By using templates, you can ensure consistent configurations across multiple environments and streamline the process of managing network security.
   - Create reusable templates that define your NSG rules and policies, allowing you to deploy them easily whenever needed.

By completing this project, you will gain practical experience in using **Azure Network Security Groups** to manage and secure network traffic within your cloud infrastructure. You'll learn how to configure and apply security rules to safeguard virtual machines, ensuring that only legitimate traffic is allowed while preventing unauthorized access. Additionally, you'll become familiar with Azure services such as **Azure Monitor** and **Azure Security Center** to monitor and improve the security of your virtual network, and how to use infrastructure-as-code to automate the deployment of NSGs, making it easier to manage large-scale cloud environments.

12.7 IMPLEMENTING DEEP PACKET INSPECTION (DPI) IN OPENWRT

In this project, you will implement Deep Packet Inspection (DPI) in OpenWrt to classify network traffic effectively and enhance network security. DPI allows you to inspect the contents of network packets and categorize them according to the protocols they use, enabling more granular control over traffic and improving overall network performance and security.

Tools and Services Required:

- OpenWrt Router: A router running OpenWrt, a Linux-based router firmware, which provides a flexible platform for network management and traffic control.
- DPI Module: A Deep Packet Inspection module such as nDPI, which can identify and classify traffic based on application protocols.
- Wireshark: A network protocol analyzer that helps you monitor and inspect network traffic in real time.

Steps:

1. **Install OpenWrt on Your Router**:
   - Begin by installing OpenWrt on your router. OpenWrt provides a customizable, open-source platform for managing network traffic, making it an ideal choice for implementing DPI.
   - Follow the installation guide provided by OpenWrt to set up the firmware on your router and configure the basic network settings.
2. **Install a DPI Module (e.g., nDPI)**:
   - After setting up OpenWrt, install a DPI module such as nDPI. This module will enable your router to analyze network traffic in detail and classify it based on specific application protocols.
   - Install nDPI or other compatible DPI modules via the OpenWrt package manager. This will allow the router to examine packet headers and payloads to identify traffic patterns associated with protocols such as HTTP, FTP, or peer-to-peer (P2P) traffic.
3. **Configure the DPI Module**:
   - Once the DPI module is installed, configure it to recognize and classify different types of network traffic. Set up rules or pattern matching techniques to identify and categorize traffic such as:
     - HTTP traffic: Web browsing activity.
     - FTP traffic: File transfers.
     - P2P traffic: Peer-to-peer file sharing.
   - You may need to tweak the module's settings to ensure it is correctly classifying traffic based on the application layer protocols.
4. **Analyze Network Traffic with Wireshark**:
   - Use Wireshark to capture and analyze network packets. Wireshark will help you monitor the traffic flowing through your OpenWrt router and validate the DPI module's classification.
   - Look for the packet details to verify that the DPI module is correctly identifying and categorizing traffic as expected. Wireshark will also help you identify any anomalies or traffic that needs further classification or special handling.
5. **Enhance Network Security and Performance**:
   - Based on the classification of network traffic by the DPI system, you can apply additional security measures or optimize network performance:

- Firewall Rules: Use the OpenWrt firewall to block or allow traffic based on the DPI classification, such as blocking unwanted P2P traffic or restricting access to certain HTTP services.
- Bandwidth Limiting: Apply bandwidth restrictions to specific traffic types (e.g., limiting P2P traffic to ensure it does not impact critical services).

- You can use DPI to enforce more precise traffic management policies that enhance both security and network performance.

6. **Optimize DPI Performance**:
   - Fine-tune the DPI system by adjusting classification rules and policies. This can include:
     - Modifying the criteria used to identify traffic (e.g., adjusting the sensitivity of protocol detection).
     - Adding or removing specific traffic categories as your network evolves.
     - Implementing additional DPI modules if needed to improve traffic classification capabilities.
   - Monitor the performance of the DPI system, ensuring that it does not degrade the overall performance of your network.
7. **Monitor and Analyze Data from the DPI System**:
   - Use OpenWrt's logging tools to monitor the DPI system's performance and detect any issues. Review the logs to ensure traffic is being categorized correctly and check for any potential security risks or performance bottlenecks.
   - Leverage other network management tools provided by OpenWrt to analyze DPI logs and statistics, which can offer insights into your network's health and security posture.
8. **Automate DPI Deployment and Management**:
   - For easier maintenance and scalability, automate the deployment and management of your DPI system using OpenWrt scripts or other automation tools.
   - Write custom scripts to apply configuration changes, update DPI rules, or restart services when necessary. Automation ensures that your DPI system can scale with network growth and handle traffic dynamically.

By completing this project, you will gain practical experience in implementing Deep Packet Inspection (DPI) in OpenWrt, enabling you to classify and manage network traffic more efficiently. You will learn how to:

- Install and configure DPI modules like nDPI.
- Use tools like Wireshark to analyze and verify traffic classification.
- Apply security measures such as firewall rules and bandwidth limiting based on DPI results.
- Optimize and automate DPI for improved performance and scalability.

This is an essential skill for improving network security and performance, as DPI allows you to gain deep insights into network traffic, providing fine-grained control over your network infrastructure.

12.8 PRACTICE QUESTIONS/SOLUTIONS

MULTIPLE CHOICE QUESTIONS

1 **Which of the following is a key objective when implementing secure cloud computing in hands-on projects?**

A) Maximizing the number of virtual machines
B) Ensuring data privacy, integrity, and availability
C) Reducing the cost of cloud services
D) Increasing the bandwidth for cloud storage

Answer: B) Ensuring data privacy, integrity, and availability

2 **When setting up a secure cloud environment for practice, which of the following is an essential security practice to follow?**

A) Using the default security settings for cloud services
B) Implementing strong identity and access management (IAM) controls
C) Avoiding encryption for sensitive data
D) Disabling multi-factor authentication

Answer: B) Implementing strong identity and access management (IAM) controls

3 **In the context of a hands-on project in secure cloud computing, what is the primary benefit of using multi-factor authentication (MFA)?**

A) To ensure quick provisioning of cloud resources
B) To add an extra layer of security by requiring multiple forms of identification
C) To reduce the complexity of cloud storage configurations
D) To lower the overall cost of cloud services

Answer: B) To add an extra layer of security by requiring multiple forms of identification

4 **Which of the following is the most common way to secure data in transit while working on cloud computing projects?**

A) Data masking
B) Encryption using SSL/TLS
C) Local backups
D) Virtual private cloud (VPC) peering

Answer: B) Encryption using SSL/TLS

5 When deploying a cloud-based web application, which security principle is crucial for minimizing exposure to attacks?

A) Keeping the application open to all inbound traffic
B) Restricting access to sensitive systems through network segmentation
C) Using a single authentication method for all users
D) Disabling logging to avoid data leaks

Answer: B) Restricting access to sensitive systems through network segmentation

6 Which tool would be most useful for monitoring security and performance issues in a cloud environment during a hands-on project?

A) AWS CloudFormation
B) Google Cloud Armor
C) Azure Security Center
D) AWS Lambda

Answer: C) Azure Security Center

7 What is the main advantage of using a "zero trust" model in secure cloud computing projects?

A) It allows unrestricted access to resources for trusted users
B) It assumes no user or device is trustworthy by default, enforcing strict access controls
C) It reduces the need for encryption
D) It eliminates the need for identity and access management

Answer: B) It assumes no user or device is trustworthy by default, enforcing strict access controls

8 In a cloud security practice project, which of the following would help to ensure compliance with data protection regulations such as GDPR?

A) Disabling encryption to reduce overhead
B) Using public cloud services without any access restrictions
C) Implementing data encryption and implementing data residency controls
D) Not monitoring data access patterns

Answer: C) Implementing data encryption and implementing data residency controls

9 During a hands-on project to build a secure cloud infrastructure, which type of cloud service model provides the highest level of control over security configurations?

A) Software as a Service (SaaS)
B) Platform as a Service (PaaS)
C) Infrastructure as a Service (IaaS)
D) Network as a Service (NaaS)

Answer: C) Infrastructure as a Service (IaaS)

10 In the context of secure cloud computing, what is the purpose of a Virtual Private Network (VPN)?

A) To create a secure, encrypted connection between the user and the cloud environment
B) To reduce the cost of cloud computing resources
C) To automatically back up all cloud data
D) To allow public access to the cloud network

Answer: A) To create a secure, encrypted connection between the user and the cloud environment

11 Which of the following is an effective method for securing sensitive data stored in the cloud?

A) Using public cloud storage without encryption
B) Storing sensitive data in an unencrypted format
C) Encrypting data both at rest and in transit
D) Relying on cloud providers for data security

Answer: C) Encrypting data both at rest and in transit

12 What is the primary function of a cloud access security broker (CASB)?

A) To monitor network traffic for performance optimization
B) To enforce security policies and control access to cloud services
C) To increase cloud service reliability
D) To provide cloud cost management tools

Answer: B) To enforce security policies and control access to cloud services

13 When implementing a cloud-based disaster recovery plan, which of the following is a key consideration?

A) Only backing up data on-premises
B) Storing backups in multiple geographical regions
C) Using a single-cloud provider for all disaster recovery needs
D) Ignoring the costs associated with disaster recovery solutions

Answer: B) Storing backups in multiple geographical regions

14 Which cloud deployment model provides the highest level of control over security for an organization?

A) Public Cloud
B) Private Cloud
C) Hybrid Cloud
D) Community Cloud

Answer: B) Private Cloud

15 In secure cloud computing, which of the following would be the best approach to mitigate the risk of unauthorized access to cloud-based resources?

A) Enabling root access for all users
B) Using role-based access control (RBAC) to restrict permissions
C) Disabling password expiration policies
D) Allowing users to share authentication credentials

Answer: B) Using role-based access control (RBAC) to restrict permissions

16 What is the role of an Intrusion Detection System (IDS) in a secure cloud environment?

A) To increase the speed of cloud service delivery
B) To detect and respond to potential security breaches or attacks
C) To provide data backups
D) To automatically provision cloud resources

Answer: B) To detect and respond to potential security breaches or attacks

17 Which of the following tools or services is commonly used to implement automated security testing in a cloud environment?

A) AWS CloudTrail
B) Google Cloud Security Command Center
C) Jenkins for continuous integration
D) AWS CodeDeploy

Answer: B) Google Cloud Security Command Center

18 Which of the following is a best practice when securing APIs used in cloud applications?

A) Disabling rate limiting to improve performance
B) Enforcing authentication and authorization for all API calls
C) Sharing API keys publicly for ease of access
D) Avoiding the use of encryption to reduce latency

Answer: B) Enforcing authentication and authorization for all API calls

19 What is the purpose of a security information and event management (SIEM) system in a secure cloud infrastructure?

A) To track user activity and network performance
B) To analyze and correlate security data for threat detection and compliance monitoring
C) To reduce the cost of cloud services
D) To increase the speed of cloud application deployment

Answer: B) To analyze and correlate security data for threat detection and compliance monitoring

20 Which cloud security practice helps to ensure that a cloud provider is meeting the necessary security and compliance standards for your organization?

A) Allowing the provider to manage all security settings
B) Conducting regular third-party audits and assessments of the provider's security practices
C) Relying solely on the provider's default security configurations
D) Storing all data in a single location to simplify management

Answer: B) Conducting regular third-party audits and assessments of the provider's security practices

21 Which type of cloud service model provides a ready-made environment for developers to build and deploy applications, but leaves the responsibility for security to the user?

A) Software as a Service (SaaS)
B) Platform as a Service (PaaS)
C) Infrastructure as a Service (IaaS)
D) Network as a Service (NaaS)

Answer: B) Platform as a Service (PaaS)

22 What is the primary function of data loss prevention (DLP) tools in cloud computing environments?

A) To monitor network performance
B) To prevent sensitive data from being accessed, shared, or leaked
C) To manage cloud billing
D) To provision resources in the cloud

Answer: B) To prevent sensitive data from being accessed, shared, or leaked

23 In a cloud security context, what does the principle of least privilege mean?

A) Granting users the minimum level of access necessary to perform their job functions
B) Allowing unrestricted access to all cloud resources
C) Providing admin-level privileges to all users for convenience
D) Limiting access to public cloud services only

Answer: A) Granting users the minimum level of access necessary to perform their job functions

24 What is the key benefit of using a managed security service provider (MSSP) in a cloud computing environment?

A) Lowering cloud service costs
B) Providing additional layers of security expertise and monitoring

C) Eliminating the need for internal security teams
D) Reducing the need for encryption

Answer: B) Providing additional layers of security expertise and monitoring

25 In secure cloud computing, what is the purpose of segmentation and micro-segmentation in network design?
A) To enhance data accessibility for all users
B) To separate different parts of the network and limit the spread of security breaches
C) To ensure cloud applications are always available
D) To prevent all traffic from being encrypted

Answer: B) To separate different parts of the network and limit the spread of security breaches

26 When securing cloud infrastructure, why is it important to regularly update and patch virtual machines (VMs)?
A) To enhance the speed of the VMs
B) To fix vulnerabilities and reduce the risk of exploitation by attackers
C) To reduce the cost of cloud services
D) To improve the scalability of the VMs

Answer: B) To fix vulnerabilities and reduce the risk of exploitation by attackers

27 Which of the following is a key component of a secure cloud architecture in a multi-cloud environment?
A) Using the same cloud provider for all services
B) Ensuring consistent security policies and tools across different cloud platforms
C) Disabling firewalls to improve performance
D) Allowing unrestricted access between cloud environments

Answer: B) Ensuring consistent security policies and tools across different cloud platforms

28 What is the main purpose of a cloud firewall?
A) To increase cloud service performance
B) To monitor and control incoming and outgoing network traffic to ensure security
C) To automatically provision cloud services
D) To enable unlimited access to cloud resources

Answer: B) To monitor and control incoming and outgoing network traffic to ensure security

29 What is an important consideration when configuring identity and access management (IAM) in a secure cloud environment?

A) Granting all users administrator access for convenience
B) Defining roles and permissions according to the principle of least privilege
C) Allowing users to manage their own security settings
D) Disabling logging to reduce overhead

Answer: B) Defining roles and permissions according to the principle of least privilege

30 What is a common vulnerability associated with cloud-based applications that can be mitigated through proper secure coding practices?

A) Insufficient scalability
B) Cross-site scripting (XSS)
C) High operational costs
D) Lack of automation

Answer: B) Cross-site scripting (XSS)

DESCRIPTIVE QUESTIONS

1 What is the primary goal of securing cloud computing environments in hands-on projects?

Answer: The primary goal is to ensure the confidentiality, integrity, and availability of data and services, while protecting against unauthorized access, data breaches, and cyber threats.

2 Why is multi-factor authentication (MFA) important in cloud security projects?

Answer: MFA adds an extra layer of security by requiring users to provide multiple forms of verification before granting access, which helps prevent unauthorized access even if credentials are compromised.

3 What is the significance of encryption in secure cloud computing projects?

Answer: Encryption ensures that sensitive data is protected both at rest (stored data) and in transit (data being transferred), making it unreadable to unauthorized parties and helping to maintain data confidentiality.

4 In a cloud security project, why is it essential to implement Identity and Access Management (IAM)?

Answer: IAM allows administrators to define and control access policies, ensuring that only authorized users have access to specific cloud resources based on roles and responsibilities, reducing the risk of unauthorized access.

5 **How can network segmentation help secure a cloud environment in practice projects?**

Answer: Network segmentation divides a cloud network into isolated zones, restricting access between them to minimize the spread of security breaches and limit the exposure of sensitive data and systems.

6 **What role does a Virtual Private Network (VPN) play in securing cloud resources during practice projects?**

Answer: A VPN establishes a secure, encrypted connection between users and cloud resources, ensuring that data in transit is protected from interception or tampering by unauthorized entities.

7 **How do cloud firewalls contribute to the security of cloud-based applications?**

Answer: Cloud firewalls monitor and control incoming and outgoing network traffic based on predefined security rules, helping to block malicious traffic and prevent unauthorized access to cloud applications and services.

8 **Why is regular patching and updating of cloud infrastructure critical for security in hands-on projects?**

Answer: Regular patching and updates help close security vulnerabilities in software, reducing the risk of exploitation by attackers and ensuring that the cloud infrastructure remains resilient to emerging threats.

9 **What is a Cloud Access Security Broker (CASB), and why is it used in secure cloud computing projects?**

Answer: A CASB acts as a security policy enforcement point between users and cloud service providers, allowing organizations to monitor and control the use of cloud services, ensure compliance, and protect data from threats.

10 **What are the benefits of using a "Zero Trust" security model in cloud computing practice projects?**

Answer: The "Zero Trust" model assumes that no user or device is inherently trusted, enforcing strict authentication and authorization for every access request to minimize the risk of internal and external security breaches.

11 How can automated security testing tools be useful in a secure cloud computing project?

Answer: Automated security testing tools can help identify vulnerabilities and misconfigurations in cloud environments quickly, enabling faster remediation and ensuring that cloud applications meet security best practices.

12 What is the role of monitoring and logging in securing cloud resources during hands-on projects?

Answer: Continuous monitoring and logging allow for real-time detection of security incidents, auditing user activity, and analyzing potential threats or vulnerabilities, aiding in the prevention and response to security breaches.

13 Why is data backup and disaster recovery planning critical in cloud security practice projects?

Answer: Data backup and disaster recovery plans ensure that critical data and systems can be quickly restored in case of an outage, attack, or data loss, ensuring business continuity and minimizing the impact of security incidents.

14 What is the significance of compliance in cloud security practice projects?

Answer: Compliance ensures that cloud environments meet legal and regulatory requirements (e.g., GDPR, HIPAA), which is crucial for protecting sensitive data and avoiding legal consequences for non-compliance.

15 How can role-based access control (RBAC) enhance security in a cloud project?

Answer: RBAC ensures that users are granted access only to the resources they need based on their roles within the organization, reducing the risk of unauthorized access and limiting the damage from compromised accounts.

16 Why is using private cloud infrastructure more secure than public cloud in certain practice projects?

Answer: Private cloud environments offer more control over security settings, access policies, and data handling, which can be beneficial for organizations with specific security and compliance requirements.

17 What is the function of an Intrusion Detection System (IDS) in a secure cloud project?

Answer: An IDS monitors network traffic for suspicious activity and potential security threats, alerting administrators to possible intrusions or attacks on cloud-based systems.

18 How does using cloud-native security tools enhance security in a hands-on cloud computing project?

Answer: Cloud-native security tools are specifically designed to integrate with cloud platforms, providing more effective and scalable security solutions, such as threat detection, encryption, and access control, within the cloud environment.

19 What is the purpose of security groups and network access control lists (NACLs) in cloud security?

Answer: Security groups and NACLs define inbound and outbound traffic rules for cloud resources, controlling access based on IP addresses and port ranges, thus protecting cloud resources from unauthorized access.

20 What are some key challenges in securing cloud environments during hands-on projects?

Answer: Key challenges include managing complex access control policies, ensuring data privacy and compliance, securing APIs, handling third-party integrations securely, and mitigating the risks of misconfigurations and human error.

21 What is the role of a Security Information and Event Management (SIEM) system in a cloud environment?

Answer: A SIEM system collects and analyzes security data from cloud environments to detect potential security incidents, provide real-time alerts, and help with compliance reporting.

22 Why is it important to use cloud encryption keys management in secure cloud computing?

Answer: Encryption key management ensures that encryption keys are securely stored, rotated, and accessed only by authorized users, preventing unauthorized decryption and protecting sensitive data.

23 What does the "shared responsibility model" mean in cloud security?

Answer: The shared responsibility model outlines the division of security responsibilities between the cloud service provider and the customer. The provider is responsible for the security of the cloud infrastructure, while the customer is responsible for securing data, applications, and user access.

24 How does a Web Application Firewall (WAF) protect cloud applications?

Answer: A WAF filters and monitors HTTP traffic to and from a web application, blocking malicious requests such as SQL injection and cross-site scripting (XSS), protecting the application from common web-based attacks.

25 What are the benefits of using a multi-cloud strategy in secure cloud computing projects?

Answer: A multi-cloud strategy reduces the risk of vendor lock-in, improves redundancy and availability, and enhances security by diversifying risk across multiple cloud providers.

26 What is the purpose of performing a vulnerability assessment in a cloud environment?

Answer: A vulnerability assessment helps identify security weaknesses in the cloud infrastructure, applications, and configurations, enabling proactive remediation before an attacker can exploit them.

27 Why is it essential to secure APIs in cloud-based applications?

Answer: Securing APIs prevents unauthorized access to sensitive data and cloud resources by ensuring proper authentication, encryption, and input validation, protecting applications from common API attacks such as injection and data leaks.

28 What is the purpose of using a cloud security posture management (CSPM) tool in practice projects?

Answer: CSPM tools automatically monitor and assess cloud configurations for compliance with security best practices, helping identify and mitigate misconfigurations, which could otherwise lead to security vulnerabilities.

29 How can using an automated deployment pipeline enhance cloud security?

Answer: An automated deployment pipeline helps ensure that security best practices, such as vulnerability scanning, configuration validation, and security testing, are consistently applied during the development and deployment phases.

30 What is the importance of creating a cloud-specific disaster recovery plan in a security project?

Answer: A cloud-specific disaster recovery plan ensures that critical data and applications can be quickly restored in case of an attack or system failure, minimizing downtime and ensuring business continuity.

31 What is a common security risk associated with misconfigured cloud storage settings?

Answer: Misconfigured cloud storage settings can lead to unauthorized access to sensitive data, potentially exposing it to the public or unauthorized users, creating a serious data breach risk.

32 What is the role of a Virtual Private Cloud (VPC) in secure cloud computing?

Answer: A VPC isolates resources within a private network in the cloud, allowing for fine-grained control over security settings, such as access controls, subnets, and routing, to enhance the security of cloud-based applications and data.

33 Why should organizations implement logging and monitoring in their cloud security strategy?

Answer: Logging and monitoring provide visibility into user activities and system performance, enabling the detection of suspicious behavior, tracking incidents, and maintaining compliance with security policies and regulations.

34 How does implementing secure network architecture improve cloud security?

Answer: Secure network architecture, including segmentation, firewalls, and access controls, reduces the attack surface, limits lateral movement in case of a breach, and enhances the protection of critical resources in the cloud.

35 What are cloud-native security tools, and why are they important?

Answer: Cloud-native security tools are built specifically for cloud environments and provide security functionalities such as automated threat detection, compliance checks, and identity management, offering better integration and scalability for securing cloud resources.

36 What is the advantage of using a centralized identity provider (IdP) in a cloud-based environment?

Answer: A centralized IdP simplifies user authentication and management, enabling Single Sign-On (SSO), reducing the risk of password fatigue, and allowing for centralized security controls across multiple cloud applications.

37 Why is "least privilege" access control crucial for securing cloud environments?

Answer: The least privilege principle ensures users only have access to the resources necessary for their role, minimizing the potential damage from compromised accounts or accidental misuse of cloud resources.

38 What is the function of "auto-scaling" in securing cloud infrastructure?

Answer: Auto-scaling automatically adjusts the number of cloud resources based on demand, ensuring sufficient resources are available during high traffic or load, preventing service disruptions, and reducing the risk of security vulnerabilities associated with overloaded systems.

39 Why is it important to secure cloud storage buckets?

Answer: Securing cloud storage buckets prevents unauthorized access to stored data, ensuring that only authorized users can read, modify, or delete sensitive information, thus protecting against data breaches.

40 How can organizations ensure compliance with data protection regulations in cloud computing projects?

Answer: Organizations can implement encryption, access controls, regular audits, and secure data storage practices, along with selecting compliant cloud providers, to meet data protection regulations such as GDPR, HIPAA, or CCPA.

Index

Pages in *italics* refer to figures and pages in **bold** refer to tables.

F

G

H

I

J

K

L

M

N

O

P

V

W

X

Y

Z

For Product Safety Concerns and Information please contact our EU
representative GPSR@taylorandfrancis.com
Taylor & Francis Verlag GmbH, Kaufingerstraße 24, 80331 München, Germany

www.ingramcontent.com/pod-product-compliance
Lightning Source LLC
Chambersburg PA
CBHW060742220326
41598CB00022B/2305
* 9 7 8 1 0 3 2 8 4 0 0 9 3 *